THE OXFORD HANDBOOK OF

ENVIRONMENTAL ETHICS

THE OXFORD HANDBOOK OF

ENVIRONMENTAL ETHICS

Edited by

STEPHEN M. GARDINER

and

ALLEN THOMPSON

OXFORD
UNIVERSITY PRESS

OXFORD

UNIVERSITY PRESS

Oxford University Press is a department of the University of Oxford. It furthers
the University's objective of excellence in research, scholarship, and education
by publishing worldwide. Oxford is a registered trade mark of Oxford University
Press in the UK and certain other countries.

Published in the United States of America by Oxford University Press
198 Madison Avenue, New York, NY 10016, United States of America.

Library of Congress Cataloging-in-Publication Data
Names: Gardiner, Stephen Mark, editor.
Title: The Oxford handbook of environmental ethics / edited by Stephen M. Gardiner and
Allen Thompson.
Other titles: Handbook of environmental ethics
Description: New York, NY : Oxford University Press, 2017. |
Series: Oxford handbooks
Identifiers: LCCN 2016014553 | ISBN 9780199941339 (hardcover : alk. paper)
Subjects: LCSH: Environmental ethics. | Environmental protection—Moral and
ethical aspects. | Nature—Effect of human beings on—Moral and ethical aspects.
Classification: LCC GE42 .O84 2017 | DDC 179/.1—dc23
LC record available at https://lccn.loc.gov/2016014553

3 5 7 9 8 6 4

Printed by Sheridan Books, Inc., United States of America

Contents

The Contributors   xi

1. Introduction
   Introducing Contemporary Environmental Ethics   1
   ALLEN THOMPSON AND STEPHEN M. GARDINER

PART I CONTEXT
Broad Social Conditions in Which We Find Ourselves

2. History
   A History of Environmental Ethics   13
   JASON KAWALL

3. Science
   Environmental Science: Empirical Claims in
   Environmental Ethics   27
   WENDY S. PARKER

4. Economics
   Markets, Ethics, and Environment   40
   JOHN O'NEILL

5. Governance
   Law, Governance, and the Ecological Ethos   51
   DANIEL BUTT

6. Anthropocene
   The Anthropocene!: Beyond the Natural?   62
   HOLMES ROLSTON, III

PART II SUBJECTS OF VALUE
What Ought to Count Morally and How

7. Humanity
   Anthropocentrism: Humanity as Peril and Promise   77
   ALLEN THOMPSON

8. Conscious Animals
   Conscious Animals and the Value of Experience   91
   LORI GRUEN

9. Living Indiviudals
   Living Individuals: Biocentrism in Environmental Ethics   101
   CLARE PALMER

10. Ecological Collectives
    How Ecological Collectives are Morally Considerable   113
    J. BAIRD CALLICOTT

11. Wild Nature
    Valuing Wild Nature   125
    PHILIP CAFARO

PART III NATURE OF VALUE
The Meaning of Value and Normative Claims

12. Truth and Goodness
    Truth and Goodness: Metaethics in Environmental Ethics   139
    KATIE MCSHANE

13. Practical Reasons
    Practical Reasons and Environmental Commitment   151
    ALAN HOLLAND

14. Hermeneutics
    Environmental Hermeneutics and the Meaning of Nature   162
    MARTIN DRENTHEN

15. Phenomenology
    Phenomenology and Environmental Ethics   174
    TED TOADVINE

16. Aesthetics
    Aesthetic Value, Nature, and Environment   186
    EMILY BRADY

PART IV HOW THINGS MATTER
Theoretical Perspectives on the Way We Ought to Act

17. States of Affairs
     Consequentialism in Environmental Ethics   199
     AVRAM HILLER

18. Duty & Obligation
     Rights, Rules, and Respect for Nature   211
     BENJAMIN HALE

19. Character
     Environmental Virtue Ethics: Value, Normativity,
     and Right Action   223
     RONALD SANDLER

20. Caring Relations
     Ethics of Caring in Environmental Ethics: Indigenous
     and Feminist Philosophies   234
     KYLE POWYS WHYTE AND CHRIS J. CUOMO

21. The Sacred
     The Sacred, Reverence for Life, and Environmental Ethics
     in America   248
     BRON TAYLOR

PART V KEY CONCEPTS
Tools for Framing and Addressing Problems

22. Responsibility
     Individual and Contributory Responsibility for
     Environmental Harm   265
     KENNETH SHOCKLEY

23. Justice
     Justice on One Planet   276
     DEREK BELL

24. Gender
     Sexual Politics in Environmental Ethics: Impacts,
     Causes, Alternatives   288
     CHRIS J. CUOMO

25. Rights
    Human Rights and the Environment   301
    STEVE VANDERHEIDEN

26. Ecological Space
    Ecological Space: The Concept and Its Ethical Significance   311
    TIM HAYWARD

27. Risk & Precaution
    Risk and Precaution in Decision Making about Nature   321
    JONATHAN ALDRED

28. Citizenship
    Citizenship and (Un)Sustainability: A Green Republican
    Perspective   333
    JOHN BARRY

29. Future Generations
    Future Generations in Environmental Ethics   344
    JOHN NOLT

30. Sustainability
    Sustainability as the Multigenerational Public Interest   355
    BRYAN G. NORTON

PART VI CENTRAL ISSUES
Specific Areas of Environmental Concern

31. Pollution
    The Ethics of Environmental Pollution   369
    KEVIN C. ELLIOTT

32. Population
    Population and Environment : The Impossible,
    the Impermissible, and the Imperative   380
    ELIZABETH CRIPPS

33. Energy
    Ethical Energy Choices   391
    KRISTIN SHRADER-FRECHETTE

34. Food
   Narratives of Food, Agriculture, and the Environment   404
   DAVID M. KAPLAN

35. Water
   Water Ethics: Toward Ecological Cooperation   416
   ANGELA KALLHOFF

36. Mass Extinction
   Anthropogenic Mass Extinction: The Science, the Ethics,
   and the Civics   427
   JEREMY DAVID BENDIK-KEYMER AND CHRIS HAUFE

37. Technology
   Philosophy of Technology and the Environment   438
   PAUL B. THOMPSON

38. Ecosystem Managment
   The Ethics of Ecosystem Management   449
   MARION HOURDEQUIN

PART VII CLIMATE CHANGE
The Defining Environmental Problem of Our Time

39. Mitigation
   Mitigation: First Imperative of Environmental Ethics   465
   HENRY SHUE

40. Adaptation
   Ethics and Climate Adaptation   474
   CLARE HEYWARD

41. Diplomacy
   Climate Diplomacy   487
   ANDREW LIGHT

42. Geoengineering
   Geoengineering: Ethical Questions for Deliberate
   Climate Manipulators   501
   STEPHEN M. GARDINER

PART VIII SOCIAL CHANGE
Doing What We Ought to Do

43. Conflict
    Environmental Conflict   517
    DAVID SCHMIDTZ

44. Pragmatism
    Environmental Ethics, Sustainability Science, and the Recovery
    of Pragmatism   528
    BEN A. MINTEER

45. Sacrifice
    Sacrifice and the Possibilities for Environmental Action   541
    JOHN M. MEYER

46. Action
    From Environmental Ethics to Environmental Action   552
    AVNER DE SHALIT

Index   563

THE CONTRIBUTORS

Jonathan Aldred is Fellow and Director of Studies in Economics at Emmanuel College and Affiliated Lecturer in the Department of Land Economy, University of Cambridge, UK. He is interested in the ethical foundations of orthodox economics and the economic policy derived from it, with a particular focus on environmental policy. He has published on ethical issues arising in the cost-benefit analysis of climate change, the precautionary principle, and carbon trading. More general publications include *The Skeptical Economist* (Earthscan/Routledge, 2009), which explores the ethical assumptions behind popular economic arguments.

John Barry is Professor of Green Political Economy at Queens University Belfast. He is the author of *The Politics of Actually Existing Unsustainability* (Oxford, 2012) and co-editor of *Global Ecological Politics* (Emerald, 2011) and *Environmental Philosophy: The Art of Living in a World of Limits* (Emerald, 2013). His research focuses on the political economy of un/sustainability, low carbon energy transitions, and civic republicanism.

Derek Bell is Professor of Environmental Political Theory at Newcastle University, UK. He is the co-editor of *Environmental Citizenship* (MIT Press, 2006) and *Justice and Fairness in the City* (Policy Press, 2016). His work on environmental justice and climate justice has been published in leading journals, including *The Monist, Political Studies, Environmental Ethics,* and *Environmental Politics.*

Jeremy David Bendik-Keymer is the Beamer-Schneider Professor in Ethics and Associate Professor of Philosophy at Case Western Reserve University. He is the author of *The Ecological Life: Discovering Citizenship and a Sense of Humanity* (Rowman & Littlefield, 2006) and the mixed-genre, *Solar Calendar, and Other Ways of Marking Time* (Punctum, 2016). He co-edited *Ethical Adaptation to Climate Change: Human Virtues of the Future* (MIT, 2012) with Allen Thompson. His research is on anthroponomy (the goal of planetary, environmental civics), relational reason (interpersonal phenomenology), and *askesis* (philosophy as a way of life).

Emily Brady is Professor of Environment and Philosophy at the University of Edinburgh. She is the author of *The Sublime in Modern Philosophy: Aesthetics, Ethics, and Nature* (Cambridge, 2013) and *Aesthetics of the Natural Environment* (Edinburgh, 2003), and is co-editor of *Human-Environment Relations: Transformative Values in Theory and Practice* (Springer, 2012) and *Aesthetic Concepts: Essays After Sibley* (Oxford, 2001). She has research interests in aesthetics and philosophy of art, environmental ethics, eighteenth-century philosophy, and animal studies.

Daniel Butt is Associate Professor in Political Theory at the University of Oxford and Fellow and Tutor in Politics at Balliol College, Oxford. He is the Director of the Centre for the Study of Social Justice and the author of *Rectifying International Injustice: Principles of Compensation and Restitution Between Nations* (Oxford, 2009). He has written on a range of topics relating to global justice, historical wrongdoing, and environmental ethics.

Philip Cafaro is Professor of Philosophy at Colorado State University and an affiliated faculty member of CSU's School of Global Environmental Sustainability. He is the author of *Thoreau's Living Ethics: Walden and the Pursuit of Virtue* (Georgia, 2004) and *How Many Is Too Many? The Progressive Argument for Reducing Immigration into the United States* (Chicago, 2015) and is co-editor of *Life on the Brink: Environmentalists Confront Overpopulation* (Georgia, 2012). His research centers on virtue ethics, environmental ethics, population and consumption issues, and the preservation of wild nature. Cafaro is immediate past president of the International Society for Environmental Ethics.

J. Baird Callicott retired as University Distinguished Research Professor and Regents Professor of Philosophy at the University of North Texas. He is the author of *Thinking Like a Planet* (Oxford, 2013) and the author or editor of a score of other books and author of dozens of journal articles, encyclopedia articles, and book chapters. His research concerns theoretical environmental ethics; comparative environmental ethics and philosophy; the philosophy of ecology and conservation policy; and biocomplexity in the environment, coupled natural and human systems. He taught the world's first course in environmental ethics in 1971 at the University of Wisconsin-Stevens Point.

Elizabeth Cripps is a Senior Lecturer in Political Theory at the University of Edinburgh and former British Academy Postdoctoral Fellow. Her publications include *Climate Change and the Moral Agent: Individual Duties in an Interdependent World* (Oxford, 2013). Her research focuses on climate change justice and ethics, particularly collective responsibility, individual climate duties, population and justice, and parents' climate duties.

Chris J. Cuomo is Professor of Philosophy and Women's Studies at the University of Georgia. She is the author of *Feminism and Ecological Communities: An Ethic of Flourishing* (Routledge, 1998) and *The Philosopher Queen: Feminist Essays on War, Love, and Knowledge* (Rowman & Littlefield, 2002) and is co-editor of *The Feminist Philosophy Reader* (McGraw-Hill, 2007).

Martin Drenthen is Associate Professor of Philosophy at Radboud University (Nijmegen, The Netherlands). He is co-editor of *New Visions of Nature: Complexity and Authenticity* (Springer, 2009), *Interpreting Nature. The Emerging Field of Environmental Hermeneutics* (Fordham University Press, 2013), *Environmental Aesthetics: Crossing Divides and Breaking Ground* (Fordham University Press, 2014), and *Old World and New World Perspectives in Environmental Philosophy: Transatlantic Conversations.* (Springer, 2014). Currently, he leads a research project on a hermeneutic landscape ethics, which focuses on the relation between ecological restoration and rewilding landscapes, cultures of place, and moral identity.

Kevin C. Elliott is Associate Professor of Philosophy in Lyman Briggs College, the Department of Fisheries & Wildlife, and the Department of Philosophy at Michigan State University. He is the author of *Is a Little Pollution Good for You? Incorporating Societal Values in Environmental Research* (Oxford, 2011), as well as a number of journal articles and book chapters on issues at the intersection of the philosophy of science and practical ethics. His research focuses on the role of values in science, financial conflicts of interest in research, and ethical issues related to environmental pollution and emerging technologies.

Stephen M. Gardiner is Professor of Philosophy and Ben Rabinowitz Endowed Professor of the Human Dimensions of the Environment at the University of Washington, Seattle. He is the author of *A Perfect Moral Storm* (Oxford, 2011), co-author of *Debating Climate Ethics* (Oxford, 2016), editor of *Virtue Ethics, Old and New* (Cornell, 2005), and co-editor of *Climate Ethics: Essential Readings* (Oxford, 2010). His research focuses on global environmental problems, future generations, and virtue ethics.

Lori Gruen is the William Griffin Professor of Philosophy at Wesleyan University. She is also a professor of Feminist, Gender, and Sexuality Studies and coordinator of Wesleyan Animal Studies. She is the author and editor of nine books, including *Ethics and Animals: An Introduction* (Cambridge, 2011), *Reflecting on Nature: Readings in Environmental Philosophy and Ethics* (Oxford, 2012), *Ethics of Captivity* (Oxford, 2014), and *Entangled Empathy* (Lantern, 2015). Her work in practical ethics focuses on issues that impact those often overlooked in traditional ethical investigations; for example, women, people of color, non-human animals.

Benjamin Hale is Associate Professor in the Philosophy Department and the Environmental Studies Program at the University of Colorado, Boulder. He is co-editor of *Ethics, Policy & Environment* and president of the International Society for Environmental Ethics. At Boulder, he served as director of the Center for Values and Social Policy and is co-coordinator of the annual Rocky Mountain Ethics Congress. He has published in *The Monist, Metaphilosophy, Public Affairs Quarterly, Environmental Ethics, Environmental Values, Science, Technology, and Human Values*, and popular essays in *The New York Times* and *Slate*. His work has focused emerging technologies, conservation, and the Anthropocene.

Chris Haufe is Assistant professor in the Department of Philosophy at Case Western Reserve University, where he works on problems in the history and philosophy of science. He is currently completing two books, one on the concept of fruitfulness, and one on the evolutionary nature of scientific progress.

Tim Hayward is Professor of Environmental Political Theory at the University of Edinburgh. He is the author of *Constitutional Environmental Rights* (Oxford, 2005), *Political Theory and Ecological Values* (Polity, 1998), and *Ecological Thought: An Introduction* (Polity, 1995). He is currently writing on global justice versus global finance, ecological debt, and human rights in relation to natural resources.

Clare Heyward is currently a Leverhulme Early Career Fellow at the University of Warwick. She is interested in issues of global distributive justice and intergenerational justice, especially those connected to climate change. Clare's current project is about the issues of "geoengineering" technologies and global climate justice. Before joining the University of Warwick, she was James Martin Research Fellow on the Oxford Geoengineering Programme and before that, a doctoral student at Oxford University.

Avram Hiller is Associate Professor of Philosophy at Portland State University. He co-edited *Consequentialism and Environmental Ethics* (Routledge, 2014) and has research interests in environmental ethics as well as in epistemology, metaphysics, and philosophy of language. His work has appeared in journals including *Economics and Philosophy; Environmental Values; Public Affairs Quarterly; Essays in Philosophy; Ethics, Policy, & Environment; The Monist;* and *Synthese*.

Alan Holland is Emeritus Professor of Applied Philosophy at Lancaster University, UK. After an early focus on epistemology and philosophical logic, his more recent work focuses on topics in environmental philosophy, environmental decision-making, ecological theory and bioethics. He is a former editor of the journal *Environmental Values* and co-author with Andrew Light and John O'Neill of a monograph, *Environmental Values* (Routledge, 2008). He also served for eight years on the UK government's Animal Procedures Committee.

Marion Hourdequin is Associate Professor and Chair of the Philosophy Department at Colorado College. Her recent work focuses on the ethics of climate change and climate engineering, and on the social and ethical dimensions of ecological restoration. She is the author of *Environmental Ethics: From Theory to Practice* (Bloomsbury, 2015) and editor, with David Havlick, of *Restoring Layered Landscapes* (Oxford, 2015).

Angela Kallhoff is Professor of Ethics with special emphasis on Applied Ethics at the University of Vienna, Austria. She is the author of *Prinzipien der Pflanzenethik* (Campus, 2002), *Ethischer Naturalismus nach Aristoteles* (Mentis, 2010), *Why Democracy Needs Public Goods* (Lexington, 2011), and *Politische Philosophie des Bürgers* (Böhlau, 2013) and is editor of *Klimaethik und Klimagerechtigkeit* (De Gruyter, 2015). Her research focuses on environmental ethics, ethical naturalism, and political philosophy.

David M. Kaplan is Associate Professor, Department of Philosophy and Religion, University of North Texas. His research focuses on three sets of issues: hermeneutics, food, and technology. He is the editor of *Readings in the Philosophy of Technology*, second edition (Rowman and Littlefield, 2009); *Philosophy of Food* (University of California Press, 2012); *Reading Ricoeur* (SUNY Press, 2008); and co-editor with Paul B. Thompson of *The Encyclopedia of Food and Agricultural Ethics* (Springer, 2014). Kaplan runs the Philosophy of Food Project at the University of North Texas: www.food.unt.edu

Jason Kawall is Associate Professor of Philosophy and Environmental Studies and Director of the Lampert Institute for Civic and Global Affairs at Colgate University. His research focuses on virtue ethics and epistemology, with a particular emphasis on their application to environmental issues. He has published many articles in these and related areas, with his work appearing in such journals as *American Philosophical Quarterly; Canadian Journal of Philosophy; Environmental Ethics; Ethics, Policy &Environment;* and *Philosophical Studies* and in a number of edited volumes, including the forthcoming *Oxford Handbook of Virtue*.

Andrew Light is University Professor and Director of the Institute for Philosophy and Public Policy at George Mason University and Distinguished Senior Fellow in the Climate Program at the World Resources Institute. From 2013 to 2016 he served as Senior Adviser and India Counselor to the Special Envoy on Climate Change, and Staff Climate Adviser in the Secretary's Office of Policy Planning, in the US Department of State. He has authored, co-authored, and edited 19 books, including *Environmental Values* (Routledge, 2008), *Moral and Political Reasoning in Environmental Practice* (MIT, 2003), *Environmental Pragmatism*

(Routledge, 1996), and the forthcoming *Ethics in the Anthropocene* (MIT). In recognition of his role in creating the 2015 Paris Agreement on climate change, he received the inaugural Alain Locke Award for Public Philosophy from the Society for the Advancement of American Philosophy.

Katie McShane is Associate Professor of Philosophy at Colorado State University specializing in environmental ethics and ethical theory. She has written articles on ecosystem health, the place of environmental concerns in theories of value, and the moral significance of our emotional engagements with nature. Her work has been published in journals such as *Philosophical Studies, Environmental Ethics, Environmental Values,* and *Ethics and the Environment.*

John M. Meyer is a Professor in the Department of Politics and in the programs on Environmental Studies and Environment and Community at Humboldt State University, Arcata, California. He is the author of *Engaging the Everyday: Environmental Social Criticism and the Resonance Dilemma* (MIT, 2015), co-editor of *The Oxford Handbook of Environmental Political Theory* (Oxford, 2016), and co-editor of *The Greening of Everyday Life: Challenging Practices, Imagining Possibilities* (Oxford, 2016).

Ben A. Minteer holds the Arizona Zoological Society Endowed Chair at Arizona State University, where he is also Professor of Environmental Ethics and Conservation in ASU's School of Life Sciences. His work explores our responsibility toward species and wildlands in a rapidly changing environment, as well as the intellectual history of conservation and environmentalism. He is author or editor of a number of books, including most recently *After Preservation: Saving American Nature in the Age of Humans* (Chicago, 2015).

John Nolt is a Professor in the Philosophy Department of the University of Tennessee and a Research Fellow in the Energy and Environment Program of the Howard H. Baker, Jr. Center for Public Policy. He works in environmental ethics, intergenerational ethics, climate ethics, formal value theory, and philosophical logic. His publications include seven books—most recently *Environmental Ethics for the Long Term* (Routledge, 2015).

Bryan G. Norton is Distinguished Professor Emeritus in Philosophy and Policy at the Georgia Institute of Technology. He is the author of *Sustainable Values, Sustainable Change: A Guide to Environmental Decision Making* (Chicago, 2015), *Why Preserve Natural Variety?* (Princeton, 1987), *Toward Unity Among Environmentalists* (Oxford, 1991), *Searching for Sustainability* (Cambridge, 2003), and *Sustainability: A Philosophy of Adaptive Ecosystem Management* (Chicago, 2005). Norton has contributed to journals in several fields, served as a member of the US EPA Science Advisory Board, the Governing Board of the Society for Conservation Biology, and the Board of Directors of Defenders of Wildlife.

John O'Neill is Hallsworth Professor of Political Economy at Manchester University and Director of the Political Economy Institute. He has written widely on philosophy, political economy, and environmental policy. His books include *Markets, Deliberation, and Environment* (Routledge, 2007), *The Market: Ethics, Knowledge, and Politics* (Routledge, 1998), and *Ecology, Policy, and Politics: Human Well-Being and the Natural World* (Routledge, 1993). He is co-author of *Environmental Values* (Routledge, 2008) with Alan Holland and Andrew Light.

Clare Palmer is Professor of Philosophy and Cornerstone Fellow in the Liberal Arts at Texas A&M University. She works in environmental ethics, animal ethics, and climate ethics. She is the author of several books including *Animal Ethics in Context* (Columbia University Press, 2010) and she co-authored *Companion Animal Ethics* with Peter Sandoe and Sandra Corr (Wiley Blackwell, 2015). She has edited or co-edited a number of volumes in environmental and animal ethics, including *Animal Rights* (Ashgate, 2008) and, with J. Baird Callicott, the fifth-volume set *Environmental Philosophy* (Routledge, 2005).

Wendy S. Parker is Reader in Philosophy and Associate Director of the Centre for Humanities Engaging Science and Society (CHESS) at Durham University. Her research focuses on the methodology and epistemology of contemporary science, with special attention to climate science. She is particularly interested in questions about scientific evidence, computer simulation, measurement, explanation, and values in science.

Holmes Rolston, III, is University Distinguished Professor and Professor of Philosophy at Colorado State University. He has written seven books, most recently *A New Environmental Ethics: The Next Millennium for Life on Earth*. He gave the Gifford Lectures, University of Edinburgh, 1997–1998, and won the Templeton Prize in Religion in 2003. Rolston has spoken as distinguished lecturer on all seven continents. He is featured in Joy A. Palmer, ed., *Fifty Key Thinkers on the Environment* (Routledge, 2001). He is past and founding president of the International Society for Environmental Ethics. He is a founding editor of the journal *Environmental Ethics*.

Ronald Sandler is Professor of Philosophy and Director of the Ethics Institute at Northeastern University. His primary areas of research are environmental ethics, ethics and technology, and ethical theory. He is author of *Food Ethics: The Basics* (Routledge, 2015), *The Ethics of Species* (Cambridge, 2012), and *Character and Environment* (Columbia, 2007), as well as editor of *Ethics and Emerging Technologies* (Palgrave, 2014) and co-editor of *Environmental Justice and Environmentalism* (MIT, 2007) and *Environmental Virtue Ethics* (Rowman & Littlefield, 2005).

David Schmidtz is Kendrick Professor at the University of Arizona and editor-in-chief of *Social Philosophy and Policy*. His fourteen former doctoral students all hold faculty positions and have published articles in *Journal of Philosophy* and *Ethics*. Oxford, Cambridge, and Princeton University Presses have published their books.

Avner de Shalit is the Max Kampelman Professor of Democracy and Human Rights at the Hebrew University of Jerusalem. He is the author of *Why Posterity Matters* (Routledge, 1995), *The Environment: Between Theory and Practice* (Oxford, 2000), *Power to the People* (Lexington, 2004), *Disadvantage* (with Jonathan Wolff, Oxford, 2011), and *The Spirit of Cities* (with Daniel Bell, Princeton 2011). He is co-editor (with Shlomo Avineri) of *Communitarianism and Individualism* (Oxford, 1993) and (with Andrew Light) of *Moral and Political Reasoning in Environmental Practice* (MIT, 2003). His research and teaching focuses on environmental political theory, urban politics, democracy, and inequality.

Kenneth Shockley is Associate Professor at Colorado State University where he holds the Rolston Chair in Environmental Ethics and Philosophy. He has published widely in climate ethics, environmental ethics, and ethical theory. He is coeditor of *Ethics and the Anthropocene* (forthcoming, MIT), and has coedited several special journal issues on the ethical dimensions of climate change and climate policy. His current research focuses on the expression of environmental values in public policy, the ethical dimensions of climate policy, ecological restoration, and several problems in philosophical ethics. He taught previously at the University at Buffalo, Barnard College, and the University of Malawi.

Kristin Shrader-Frechette, O'Neill Professor, University of Notre Dame, in both Philosophy and Biological Sciences, has NSF-funded post-docs in biology, economics, and hydrogeology and 28 years of NSF-research funding. Her work has been translated into 13 languages. Author of 16 books and 400 articles appearing in journals such as *Science*, Shrader-Frechette has served on many US National Academy of Sciences, EPA, WHO, and international boards/committees. Named one of 12 "Heroes for the US and the World" for her pro-bono scientific/ethics work to protect poor/minority communities from environmental injustice, she is only the third American to win the World Technology Association's Ethics Prize.

Henry Shue is Senior Research Fellow at the Centre for International Studies, Department of Politics and International Relations, University of Oxford; and Senior Research Fellow Emeritus, Merton College, Oxford. He is the author of *Basic Rights* (Princeton, 1980; 2nd ed., 1996); *Climate Justice: Vulnerability and Protection* (Oxford, 2014); and *Fighting Hurt: Rule and Exception in Torture and War* (Oxford, 2016). He co-edited *Preemption* (Oxford, 2007); *Just and Unjust Warriors* (Oxford, 2008); and *Climate Ethics* (Oxford, 2010). His most recent article is "Uncertainty as the Reason for Action: Last Opportunity and Future Climate Disaster," *Global Justice: Theory Practice Rhetoric* (2016).

Bron Taylor is Professor of Religion and Environmental Ethics at the University of Florida and a Fellow of the Rachel Carson Center for Environment and Society at Ludwig-Maximilians-Universität, Munich, Germany. His books include *Dark Green Religion: Nature Spirituality and the Planetary Future* (UC Press, 2010) and he is editor of the award-winning *Encyclopedia of Religion and Nature* (Bloomsbury, 2008), *Avatar and Nature Spirituality* (Wilfrid Laurier, 2013), and *Ecological Resistance Movements* (SUNY, 1995). In 2006 he founded the International Society for the Study of Religion, Nature, and Culture and the *Journal for the Study of Religion, Nature, and Culture*, which he edits. See also www.brontaylor.com.

Allen Thompson is Associate Professor of Ethics and Environmental Philosophy at Oregon State University and a Fellow with the Rachel Carson Center for Environment and Society at Ludwig Maximilian University. His research concerns broadening our conception of environmental virtue and moral responsibility as part of understanding human excellence in adapting to new ecological conditions of the Anthropocene. He is co-editor of *Ethical Adaptation to Climate Change: Human Virtues of the Future* (MIT, 2012) and serves as an officer for the International Society for Environmental Ethics (Treasurer 2013–2015, Vice-President 2016–2018, and President 2019–2021).

Paul B. Thompson holds the W. K. Kellogg Chair in Agricultural, Food, and Community Ethics at Michigan State University. He has published extensively on the environmental ethics of emerging technologies, including nuclear power, GMOs, nanotechnology, and synthetic biology. Thompson's work on agriculture has appeared in scientific journals such as *Poultry Science, Plant Physiology,* and *The Journal of Animal Science*. His book *From Field to Fork: Food Ethics for Everyone* was published by Oxford University Press in 2015.

Ted Toadvine, incoming Director of the Rock Ethics Institute at the Pennsylvania State University, is currently Professor of Philosophy and Environmental Studies at the University of Oregon. He is author of *Merleau-Ponty's Philosophy of Nature* (Northwestern, 2009); editor of *Merleau-Ponty: Critical Assessments* (Routledge, 2006); and co-editor of *Nature's Edge* (SUNY, 2007), *The Merleau-Ponty Reader* (Northwestern, 2007), *Eco-Phenomenology* (SUNY, 2003), and *Merleau-Ponty's Reading of Husserl* (Kluwer, 2002). Toadvine directs the Series in Continental Thought at Ohio University Press, is Editor-in-Chief of the journal *Environmental Philosophy*, and is a co-editor of *Chiasmi International*. His current research addresses environmental apocalypticism, deep time, and geomateriality.

Steve Vanderheiden is Associate Professor of Political Science and Environmental Studies at the University of Colorado at Boulder, and Professorial Fellow with the Centre for Applied Philosophy and Public Ethics (CAPPE) at Charles Sturt University in Australia. He is the author of *Atmospheric Justice: A Political Theory of Climate Change* (Oxford, 2008) and editor of *Political Theory and Global Climate Change* (MIT, 2008). His work focuses upon justice and responsibility issues in global environmental governance.

Kyle Powys Whyte holds the Timnick Chair in the Humanities at Michigan State University. He is Associate Professor of Philosophy and Community Sustainability, a faculty member of the Environmental Philosophy & Ethics graduate concentration, and a faculty affiliate of the American Indian Studies and Environmental Science & Policy programs. His primary research addresses moral and political issues concerning climate policy and Indigenous peoples and the ethics of cooperative relationships between Indigenous peoples and climate science organizations. He is an enrolled member of the Citizen Potawatomi Nation.

CHAPTER 1

INTRODUCING CONTEMPORARY ENVIRONMENTAL ETHICS

ALLEN THOMPSON AND STEPHEN M. GARDINER

1 PERSPECTIVE ON THE ANTHROPOCENE

HUMANS are relative newcomers. The Earth is around 4.6 billion years old, and multicellular life evolved 2.1 billion years ago, yet the oldest fossil remains of anatomically modern *Homo sapiens sapiens* date back a mere 195,000 years, or 0.004% of the planet's history. For the vast majority of humanity's existence so far, its influence on the terrestrial environment and biotic communities was the result of activities of small bands of hunter-gatherers. Consequently, human impacts were likely to have been relatively limited, being local in scope and modest in magnitude, or at least comparable to many other species.

At some point, humans began to have much more exceptional effects. One plausible example occurs about 12,000 years ago, on the cusp between the Pleistocene and Holocene geological epochs. The Late Pleistocene Extinction Event was a worldwide phenomenon of megafauna extinctions, especially pronounced in North America. Paleontologists have hypothesized three possible causal drivers: natural climate change (as the ice sheets retreated), human predation (the "prehistoric overkill hypothesis"), and significant trophic cascades following the (anthropogenic) demise of woolly mammoths (Sandom et al., 2014). Here, for the first time, human activity is put forward as potentially a *major cause of global and systematic environmental change*.

A more familiar example is associated with the First Agricultural (or Neolithic) Revolution, which originated around 10,000 BC in Mesopotamia and then spread across the Middle East into Europe, Asia, parts of Africa and eventually into the Americas. With new techniques of food cultivation, including agriculture and the domestication of animals, human beings engaged in the *wholesale alteration of landscapes and ecosystems to suit human purposes* (see Lyons et al., 2015). Similar increases in human impact are associated with the Age of Enlightenment and "scientific revolution" of the 17th and 18th centuries (see Merchant, 1980) and the shift from agrarian to industrial societies in the 19th and early 20th centuries.

Still, perhaps the most striking shift is much more recent. In the "Great Acceleration" after World War II, the human "population doubled in just 50 years, to over 6 billion by the end of the 20th century [and] the global economy increased by more than 15-fold" (Steffen et al., 2007: 617. See also Steffen et al., 2004). This radical human expansion has had dramatic effects, from the emerging threat of dangerous climate change (see Section 7) to the onset of the Earth's sixth great extinction event.[1]

Consider, for example, the "Planetary Boundaries" analysis, which sets out the limits of a "safe operating space for humanity" and suggests that several of the planet's major biosystems are currently at risk or in decline (Rockström et al. (2009). Rockström and his colleagues identify nine sectors of Earth system operation relevant to human well-being and propose quantification for seven: climate change, ocean acidification, stratospheric ozone, biochemical nitrogen cycle and phosphorus cycle, global freshwater use, land system use, and biodiversity loss. Within the quantified sectors, they claim that we have already crossed boundaries pertaining to climate change, the rate of interference with the nitrogen cycle, and the rate of biodiversity loss.[2] The remaining four quantified boundaries (global freshwater use, land system change, ocean acidification, and stratospheric ozone depletion) remain areas of great uncertainty, largely because we lack scientific knowledge about the nature of biophysical thresholds at the planetary scale. This, of course, is hardly comforting, since we may already be outside the "safe operating space."

The sheer scale of human impact has become so great that some have proposed defining a new unit within the geological time scale: the Anthropocene, the age of "human dominance of biological, chemical and geological processes on Earth" (Crutzen & Schwägerl, 2011). The idea and the language of the Anthropocene are now widely employed. Indeed, this term is currently being taken so seriously that an official decision on its usage from the geologists is expected from the International Commission on Stratigraphy in 2016. Still, the proposal continues to generate significant controversy. Some consider it grossly hubristic to name a geologic period after one's own kind and morally repugnant, if not dangerous (Vucetich et al., 2015; Hamilton, 2014). By contrast, some seem to enthusiastically embrace an open future of "new nature" designed by us and for us, exhibiting our human ingenuity (Ellis, 2011; Seielstad, 2012; Pearce, 2015). Others still have taken the idea of the Anthropocene to be purely descriptive but representing something morally significant—human responsibility for the state of the planet—thus they find the idea heuristically useful for advancing a more traditional environmental ethos of Earth stewardship (Purdy, 2015; Marris, 2011).[3]

As editors, we do not need to take a stance on controversies surrounding "the Anthropocene." Nevertheless, we do believe that the proposal that we are entering, or have recently entered, a new geological period is no accident. Today human activity effects environmental change globally, systematically, and at a fundamental level. Moreover, its scale has increased dramatically in just a few generations, a very small portion of human history. Human activities now threaten basic planetary systems, yet we continue to accelerate rapidly into an uncertain environmental future.

2 ORGANIZATION OF THE VOLUME

In such a context, the field of environmental ethics provides much needed analysis of values, norms, and concepts relevant to responding well to the radical anthropogenic environmental change that the 21st century promises. Established as a professional subfield of academic philosophy only in the early 1970s, the field is changing to confront new environmental, social, technical, and political realities.

In this collection, we hope to provide guidance for those interested in exploring this relatively new territory. Our strategy is as follows. Each chapter reviews the role of a key topic, idea, concept, problem, or approach in the field and briefly reflects on its future. It provides an informed entry-point into the area that helps situate the reader in the relevant literature. Although the chapters do not aspire to represent consensus opinion, the authors do aim to provide a solid grounding in the relevant concepts and basic positions, as well as an informed opinion about possible future developments in the subject area. Consequently, each chapter can be seen as an authoritative "first step" on some topic to get you started, rather than the "last word." Think of the collection as a set of maps, compasses, and other tools that one might take along when setting out on an evolving journey whose destination is yet to be decided.

Our selection has been influenced by our own sense of where the field stands, what is exciting about it, and what is needed.[4] One decision we made was to emphasize an increasing *politicization* of environmental ethics, in the positive sense of the increasing attention being paid to justice and other political values. A related decision was to expand the range of authors represented to include not just traditional, theoretical moral philosophers, but also philosophers of science, political philosophers, applied ethicists, political theorists, and philosophers of law.

A third choice was to set aside areas already well-covered elsewhere. For example, we did not commission a section on traditional, cultural attitudes, such as those of classical China, India, or Greece. Nor are there chapters representing diverse religious perspectives on the environment, such as Buddhism, Judaism, Christianity, or Islam (see Jamieson, 2001).[5] Similarly, we did not commission chapters on the history of the environment in political thought (see Gabrielson et al., 2016), nor those representing the global plurality of diverse worldviews, such as Polynesian paganism, South American eco-eroticism, African biocommunitarianism, and Australian Dreamtime (see Callicott, 1997).

In general, we have tried to be guided in our commissions by an emphasis on the importance of confronting radical environmental change and the special challenges facing humanity in this vital period of its history. In our view, if this volume plays even a small part in preparing the next generation of scholars to contribute to this work, then it will have achieved something of real importance.

3 DESCRIPTION OF CHAPTERS

The Handbook is organized into eight sections. In the remainder of this introduction, we explain the theme unifying each section and provide a very brief description of each chapter.[6]

Section 1 sets out a variety of *social* contexts for contemporary environmental ethics. In chapter 2, Jason Kawall provides a clear and detailed history of the field of environmental ethics, providing an account of key movements and theories shaping the field, including anthropocentrism, biocentrism, eco-holism, deep ecology, ecofeminism, pragmatism, and virtue theory. In chapter 3, Wendy Parker illuminates the practice of environmental science through contemporary philosophy of science, covering issues such as the nature of scientific evidence, the use and evaluation of scientific models, and questions of values and objectivity in scientific practice. In chapter 4, John O'Neill examines the role of economic values by considering two alternative and competing sets of answers to the question: Is there a relation between the increasing extension of markets and market norms to previously non-market goods and the growth of environmental problems? His exploration sheds light on the role of cost-benefit analysis in environmental policy formation and the development of new markets for goods such as emission rights and biodiversity offsets. In chapter 5, Daniel Butt's focus is on the limitations of command-and-control and market-based legal mechanisms in the pursuit of environmental justice. He argues for a need to supplement existing instruments of environmental governance with an "ecological ethos" shared among a wide range of cooperative non-state actors. Holmes Rolston wraps up the opening section in chapter 6 by reflecting on the controversial proposal that we have entered the Anthropocene, the age of human domination, by considering three distinct sets of responses to the provocative idea that we are now moving "beyond the natural."

Against these background social conditions, the chapters in Section 2 present a version of the influential "expanding circle of moral considerability" framework for setting out distinct accounts of who or what direct moral duties are owed to my moral agents In chapter 7, Allen Thompson considers the widely accepted thesis that anthropocentrism—the view that all and only human beings have an intrinsic moral value—is the ideological root of our "environmental crisis." Thompson distinguishes three types of anthropocentrism and, following others, suggests how one form may be simply unavoidable. He argues that, nonetheless, an appropriate focus on our very humanity remains a promising way forward in environmental ethics. In chapter 8, Lori Gruen set outs one form of non-anthropocentrism, sometimes called sentiocentrism, the view that locates human beings in a wider class of animals capable of conscious experience who thus have morally relevant interests in the content of their experiences. She argues that empathy and respect leads us to focus on what counts as the well-being of conscious others from their own perspective. In chapter 9, Clare Palmer considers ideas associated with biocentrism, the perspective that life itself is deserving of moral respect and perhaps bears an intrinsic value or inherent worth. Palmer distinguishes among egalitarian, inegalitarian, monistic, and pluralistic versions of biocentrism and whether they are grounded in a virtue, consequentialist, or deontological ethical theory. In chapter 10, J. Baird Callicott considers the view that collections of entities, such as species, ecosystems, landscapes, and biomes, may be the loci of intrinsic moral value, the objects of direct moral duties, and deserving of due moral consideration. Callicott describes how developments in the study of the human microbiome support a surprising conclusion that even "individual" human beings are themselves actually ecological collectives. In chapter 11, Philip Cafaro moves one step beyond customary accounts of who or what counts as a subject of value in nature to offer a spirited defense of wildness as a value-conferring property. Cafaro argues that although preserving the wild has long been a central value in "new world" conservation and preservation philosophies, we are quickly losing wild nature, due primarily to human overpopulation and overconsumption.

Section 3 considers diverse theoretical accounts of the *nature* of environmental value (rather than the *subjects* or bearers of that value, as in Section 2). In chapter 12 Katie McShane argues against the popular claim that metaethics is irrelevant for environmental ethics. Instead, she claims that contemporary views in analytical metaethics are able to address concerns in environmental ethics from several different theoretical perspectives. In chapter 13,

Alan Holland discusses how reasons for doing something vis-à-vis the environment are connected with our motivational repertoire and quest for meaning. He distinguishes three types of practical reasons and concludes that a Leopoldian position of having regard for the land community is superior to other perspectives well represented in the field, including traditional appeals to intrinsic value, relational accounts of caring, or perfectionist views about the well-lived human life. In chapter 14, Martin Drenthen develops a hermeneutic account of how we find meaning in nature through normatively potent acts of interpretation, directed at landscapes and other environments, and the connection of such meaning with the development of an environmental identity. In chapter 15, Ted Toadvine explores how the tradition of phenomenology contributes to environmental thought by emphasizing the primacy of experience and providing a critique of the metaphysical naturalism and instrumentalist framing characteristic of technocratic, economic, and managerial approaches to nature. Finally, in chapter 16 Emily Brady explores key issues about aesthetic experience and valuing natural objects, processes, and phenomenon. She parses the debate as being between two central views, "scientific cognitivism" and "non-cognitivism"; stresses the values of a pluralistic approach; and closes with concern for developing further accounts of interactions between aesthetic and ethical values.

As the last section with an explicit focus in ethical theory, Section 4 contains chapters canvasing different theoretical perspectives on how we ought to think about the normative basis of environmentalism, including consequentialist, deontic, virtue, care, and spiritual grounds. In chapter 17, Avram Hiller discusses consequentialist environmental ethics; distinguishes classical utilitarian, biocentric, and ecocentric forms; and contrasts the consequentialist approach to environmentalism with deontological, virtue theoretic, and pragmatic approaches. The deontological approach is taken up and defended in chapter 18 by Ben Hale, who develops a theory of right action based on Habermasian discourse ethics and an account of interpersonal justifications. In chapter 19, Ronald Sandler sets out an alternative non-consequentialist normative theory, based in the virtues of personal character. He describes virtue ethics as a distinctive approach to normative theory, attempting to demonstrate how virtue ethics can accommodate whatever the correct account of value in nature is, how its pluralism is indispensable to environmental ethics, and how it offers a plausible principle of right action for use in decision making. In chapter 20, Kyle Powys Whyte and Chris Cuomo relate two alternatives to mainstream normative ethics, each based in the notion of care. Indigenous approaches to environmental ethics highlight caring relations within interdependent human and non-human communities, whereas feminist environmental care ethics bring out the importance of empowering communities to care for themselves, along with the social and ecological communities with which they are integrated. Bron Taylor in chapter 21 closes this section with a historical tour of the important role that perceptions of environmental systems and places as sacred have in grounding environmental ethics—both in the past and the present. Taylor contrasts this perception of the sacred in nature with the transcendent focus more characteristic of the major world religions, on one hand, and the scientific materialist worldview that underlies most contemporary environmental ethics, on the other.

Section 5 tackles a variety of key concepts that are useful for framing and addressing problems in environmental ethics. The topic of chapter 22 is moral responsibility. Ken Shockley investigates the difficulties encountered when trying to give an account of our individual contributions to collective harms, emphasizing the influence individuals can have through connections with institutions and practices. Justice is taken up in chapter 23 by Derek Bell, who presents three kinds of challenges to traditional liberal conceptions of justice and argues that an ecologically aware theory of justice is likely to exhibit some striking differences. In chapter 24, Chris Cuomo details the significance that norms of gender, sexual inequalities, and the often-overlooked perspective of women have for environmental ethics. Gender norms and roles, she explains, are often promoted as "natural" rather than socially constructed and connect the oppression of women with the domination of nature. Steve Vanderheiden, in chapter 25, evaluates human rights as an ethical construct and a political mechanism for developing protections against environmental harms that threaten human well-being. In chapter 26, Tim Hayward develops the concept of "ecological space" and its connection to a minimally decent human life. Hayward then distinguishes between *using, occupying*, and *commanding* ecological space, which enables him to address distributional inequities though a variety of distinct deontic categories. Chapter 27 presents Jonathan Aldred's treatment of risk and precaution, in which the appropriate place of cost-benefit analysis and its relation to a precautionary principle in decision making are carefully examined. Chapter 28, by John Barry, proposes an account of "green republican citizenship" after exploring connections between the decline in active citizenship with the development of consumer identities and a transactional mode of democratic politics. Chapter 29 concerns intergenerational ethics. John Nolt argues that responsibilities owed to future individuals—human or not—demand that we reduce the human population and must keep most fossil fuels in the ground. In chapter 30, Bryan Norton presents a communitarian, public-interest conception of sustainability as offering a path to favor protecting ecophysical features of the environment, rather than a mere transfer of wealth or utility, across generations.

Section 6 focuses on specific areas of concern for the application of environmental ethics. Classic issues of environmental pollution are explored in chapter 31 by Kevin Elliott, who identifies pollution as a significant threat to disadvantaged, low-income countries and non-human organisms, calling for greater attention to be given to ethical issues in the scientific research needed to identify harmful pollutants and policy issues concerning their regulation. Chapter 32 concerns human population growth, identified as morally urgent by Elizabeth Cripps, who urges us to approach policy formation with both environmental ethics and global justice in mind. In chapter 33, Kristin Schrader-Frechette describes the environmental harms caused by energy produced from fossil fuels and nuclear power and critically analyzes excuses for society not switching to clean, renewable energy. David Kaplan's work in chapter 34 examines the role of narratives in a practical approach to understanding the relationships among food, agriculture, and environmental ethics. Angela Kalloff's contribution, chapter 35, sets out four distinct normative approaches to an ethics of water: human rights, ecocentric non-instrumentalism, water justice, and water cooperation. She concludes that a co-operative approach is the most promising, in part because it already incorporates dimensions of the rights-based and ecocentric perspectives. In chapter 36, Jeremy Bendik-Keymer and Chris Haufe begin the development of an ethical position on anthropogenic mass extinction, opening with insights about the banality of evil and built with appeals to environmental justice, loss of value, and the failure of autonomy. Paul Thompson examines the fascinating place of technology in chapter 37, discussing not only its role mediating human environmental impacts but also its place in shaping our perceptions of and orientation toward the world. Much of the work in philosophy of technology crosses interdisciplinary boundaries as it bears on the connections between science and technology. Section 6 closes with chapter 38, in which Marion Hourdequin confronts the practices of ecosystem management and identifies both conceptual and ethical challenges for the practice introduced as an improved alternative to other strategies aimed simply at maximizing yields of single-species resources.

There is little argument that anthropogenic global climate change is the defining environmental problem of our time. Whereas many chapters in the collection consider it as illustrating their respective subjects, the chapters in Section 7 focus exclusively on key dimensions the problem. In chapter 39, Henry Shue offers a compelling case for climate mitigation based on elimination of carbon dioxide emissions by the rapid global transition to an energy regime based on clean sources of affordable power. Cooperation in this transition, he argues, cannot be expected from poorer countries without needed assistance with adaptation. In chapter 40, Clare Heyward contends that justice in adaptation should register not only protection of the basic material interest of individuals but also include efforts directed at securing the conditions necessary to maintain one's cultural identity. In chapter 41, Andrew Light discusses important issues of international climate diplomacy, drawing on his experience working to direct strategies for the US State Department at international meetings under the United Nations Framework Convention on Climate Change. Finally in chapter 42, Steve Gardiner addresses geoengineering (roughly, "grand technological interventions into basic planetary systems at a global scale"). Focusing on climate engineering, he argues that early policy framings often marginalize salient ethical concerns, avoiding both important questions of justification and vital contextual issues.

The concluding Section 8 contains essays dedicated to issues raised in our attempts to realize the requisite social change. David Schmidtz explains how principles of justice are complemented and importantly matched by principles of conflict resolution in chapter 43. Then, in chapter 44, Ben Minteer presents a pragmatic conception of environmental ethics for the purpose of integrating it with the rapidly growing normative enterprise of sustainability science and its goal of moving society toward a durable socio-ecological relationship. In chapter 45, John Meyer offers a strategy for circumventing the barrier to protective environmental policy, most pronounced in wealthy societies, affected by a perceived dichotomy between self-interest and sacrifice. He draws attention to the ubiquity of notions of sacrifice in everyday life and attempts to reduce its ability to short-circuit ambitious calls to action. In chapter 46, Avner de Shalit encourages the move from articulating an environmental ethic to undertaking environmental action by distinguishing two ways a particular problem may be framed, either as a problem of environmental awareness or a problem of political consciousness. He closes by arguing how democracy remains a viable avenue for achieving radical changes.

4 CONCLUSION

As at the beginning of the Holocene, today humanity faces radical global climate change, mass species extinctions, and unprecedented transformations to both terrestrial and aquatic ecosystems across the globe. Yet this time there is no doubt that human activity is the primary driver, the scale of human affect is much greater, and the rate of global ecological change is unprecedented. The future of the basic conditions for all life on the planet—indeed all known life in the universe—is in our hands. So, what shall we do? The forty-six chapters assembled here represent some of the best and most contemporary thinking in environmental ethics, the field expressly concerned with understanding normative and evaluative dimensions of the many and diverse environmental problems that confront us. Hopefully, taking the issues and concerns they highlight seriously is a good first step.

NOTES

1. On climate change, see Section 7 of the *Oxford Hanbook of Environmental Ethics*; on mass extinction, see Bendik-Keymer and Haufe, chapter 36 (all subsequent chapter references herein are to chapters in the Handbook).
2. The proposed "boundaries" are human-set values keeping us a safe distance from systemic thresholds, which are defined "non-linear transitions in the functioning of coupled human-environmental systems." Thus, crossing the boundaries puts humanity at significant risk of radical and unpredictable changes to the global environmental conditions.
3. On the idea that we have entered the Anthropocene, see Holmes Rolston, chapter 6.
4. For various reasons we were unable to include chapters on all the subjects that are important and merit attention.
5. See, however, Bron Taylor's contribution on reverence for the sacred, in chapter 21.
6. The method employed in the table of contents is meant to quickly reveal the structure of the collection. Each section title is followed by a short description, and each chapter is labeled with a descriptive subject term, followed by the proper title given by author.

REFERENCES

Callicott, J. B. (1997). *Earth's Insights: A Multicultural Survey of Ecological Ethics from the Mediterranean Basin to the Australian Outback*. Berkeley: University of California Press.
Crutzen, P., and Schwägerl, C. (2011). "Living in the Anthropocene: Toward a New Global Ethos." *Yale Environment* 360. http://e360.yale.edu/feature/living_in_the_anthropocene_toward_a_new_global_ethos/2363/
Ellis, E. (2011). "The Planet of No Return." *Breakthrough Journal*, 2 (Fall). http://breakthrough-journal.org/content/authors/erle-ellis/the-planet-of-no-return.shtml
Gabrielson, T., Hall, C., Meyer, J. M., and Schlosberg, D. eds. (2016). *The Oxford Handbook of Environmental Political Theory*. New York: Oxford University Press.
Hamilton, C. (2014). "The New Environmentalism Will Lead Us to Disaster." *Scientific American*. http://www.scientificamerican.com/article/the-new-environmentalism-will-lead-us-to-disaster/
Jamieson, D., ed. (2001). *A Companion to Environmental Philosophy*. Malden, MA: Wiley-Blackwell Publishers.
Lyons, S. K., Amatangelo, K. L., Behrensmeyer, A. K., Bercovici, A., Blois, J. L., Davis, M., Gotelli, J. L. (2015). "Holocene Shifts in the Assembly of Plant and Animal Communities Implicate Human Impacts." *Nature* (2015) doi: 10.1038/nature16447
Marris, E. (2011). *Rambunctious Garden: Saving Nature in a Post Wild World*. New York: Bloomsbury.

Merchant, C. (1980). *The Death of Nature: Women, Ecology and the Scientific Revolution.* New York: Harper and Row.

Pearce, F. (2015). *"The New Wild: Why Invasive Species Will Be Nature's Salvation."* Boston, MA: Beacon Press.

Purdy, J. (2015). *After Nature: A Politics for the Anthropocene.* Cambridge, MA: Harvard University Press.

Rockström, J., Steffen, W., Noone, K., Persson, Å., Chapin, F. S. III, Lambin, E., Foley, J. (2009). "Planetary Boundaries: Exploring the Safe Operating Space For Humanity." *Ecology and Society* 14(2): 32. http://www.ecologyandsociety.org/vol14/iss2/art32/

Sandom, C., Faurby, S., Sandel, B., Svenning, J. C. (2014). "Global Late Quaternary Megafauna Extinctions Linked to Humans, Not Climate Change." *Proceedings of the Royal Society* 281 (1787). http://rspb.royalsocietypublishing.org/content/281/1787.toc (accessed Sept. 3, 2015).

Seielstad, G. A. (2012). *Dawn of the Anthropocene: Humanity's Defining Moment.* Alexandria, VA: American Geosciences Institute. (A digital book).

Steffen. W., Crutzen, P., McNeill, J. (2007). "The Anthropocene: Are Humans Now the Overwhelming Force of Nature?" *Ambio* 36: 614–621.

Steffen, W., Sanderson, A., Tyson, P. D., Jäger, J., Matson, P. A., Moore, B. III, Wasson, R. J. (2004). *Global Change and the Earth System: A Planet Under Pressure.* Berlin Heidelberg New York: Springer-Verlag.

Vucetich, J., Nelson, M., and Batavia, C. (2015). "The Anthropocene: Disturbing Name, Limited Insight." In *After Preservation,* edited by Minteer and Pyne. Chicago: University of Chicago Press.

PART I

CONTEXT

Broad Social Conditions in which We Find Ourselves

CHAPTER 2

··

A HISTORY OF
ENVIRONMENTAL ETHICS

··

JASON KAWALL

THIS chapter presents a history of environmental ethics as a distinct field of philosophy, and attempts to characterize its most prominent and influential movements.[1] While myriad factors contributed to the emergence of environmental ethics, three influential works published in the 1960s can be seen, with some justification, as especially important catalysts. Rachel Carson's classic *Silent Spring* (1962) drew attention to the effects of synthetic pesticides such as DDT on our food, the environment, and upon birds in particular. The book was very widely read, and it is credited with playing a key role in drawing both public and academic attention to environmental issues.

Lynn White, Jr.'s article, "The Historical Roots of Our Ecological Crisis" (1967) also received much attention, particularly within the academic world. White argued that widely accepted strands of Christian theology have played a key role in justifying a deeply exploitative attitude toward the natural world. Judeo-Christian claims that God has given mankind dominion over nature, and that mankind is made in God's image, have created and justified a problematic dualism between humanity and the rest of the natural world. Given this worldview, our ongoing technological advances have been aimed at subduing and exerting control over nature; these manipulations have in turn led to ecological crisis.

White's article provoked dozens of responses, particularly from theologians who held that a properly understood Christianity would encourage caring stewardship of the natural world because, they argued, God sees the world as good, and humanity's dominion gives us the role of steward, rather than conqueror. White himself pointed to St. Francis of Assisi and the Eastern Orthodox traditions as presenting more humble, non-dominating forms of Christianity (for early responses, see Cobb, 1972 and Barbour, 1973). White's piece brought to the fore questions about the values and worldviews that would lead to environmental degradation—and how to change or overcome them.

Finally, Garrett Hardin's "The Tragedy of the Commons" (1968) raised important questions about human population growth, resource use, and collective action. Hardin argued that individuals will use more resources, have more children, and so on, so long as the benefits they gain from these goods outweigh the costs they incur, regardless of the broader impacts on society or future generations. Humanity risks resource shortages and environmental collapse as we grow beyond the Earth's carrying capacity (see also Ehrlich, 1968). We might hope for restraint in such circumstances, but unless an individual has reason to expect others to restrain themselves, her sacrifice is likely to have little or no beneficial impact while costing her dearly; such sacrifice seems irrational. We are thus faced with a collective action problem, where a set of individually rational actions will ultimately lead to a worse outcome for everyone involved than if they were able to cooperate in restraint. Hardin's paper led to extensive consideration of such collective action problems while also drawing attention to the impacts of human consumption and population.

1 The Emergence of Environmental Ethics in the 1970s

Philosophical responses to the questions raised by Carson, White, and Hardin began to appear by the early 1970s, and during this decade came crucial works that established a number of distinct traditions within environmental ethics.

Among the first roots was a conference organized by William T. Blackstone at the University of Georgia, in 1971; the papers were later published in 1974 as *Philosophy and Environmental Crisis*. This conference, which featured both theologians and philosophers, is widely regarded as the first conference on environmental ethics with significant participation by philosophers.

Early work in the field was often concerned with the question of whether the environmental crisis faced by humanity required new approaches to ethics. Richard Routley (later Sylvan) presented "Is There a Need for a New, an Ecological Ethic?" at the 15th World Congress of Philosophy in 1973. In it, Routley presented his famous "last man" argument: following a catastrophe, would there be anything wrong with last surviving human, in his final days, destroying all remaining life? After all, once he passes away there would be no further human interests or needs at stake. Routley believed that such actions would strike us as wrong but argued that traditional ethical theories, which typically treat the rest of nature simply in terms of human interests, cannot capture this fundamental intuition, thus pointing to the need to develop a new ecological ethic.

Christopher Stone, a legal scholar, wrote "Should Trees Have Standing?" (1972) in response to plans by Walt Disney Enterprises to build a ski resort in the Mineral King valley of Sequoia National Forest, California. In the article, which soon after he expanded and published as a book (Stone, 1974), Stone argued for the legal rights of trees, forests, oceans, and other "natural objects" in the environment. He proposed that the interests of such entities could be represented in the courts by guardians or trustees—this was already done for human infants and others, and would be similar to the protections afforded to corporations, municipalities, and other such inanimate rights-holders.

Holmes Rolston III published his "Is There an Ecological Ethic?" in the journal *Ethics* in 1975; in it he sketches proposals, including the attribution of intrinsic value to species, that he would later develop in great depth. Rolston's paper is perhaps most significant as it appeared in one of the most widely read and respected journals in the analytic philosophical tradition. This was something of a coup, and it would serve to introduce the wider philosophical community to the emerging field and its questions.

The issues raised in these early articles brought to the fore a distinction between non-anthropocentric and anthropocentric approaches to the field. Anthropocentric theories treat environmental issues solely in terms of human preferences or interests. Such theories would point to such things as the needs of future generations for clean water, the recreational and aesthetic values of wilderness areas, and the broad range of services provided by various ecosystems. But in every case, the value is to be understood in terms of the interests of humans—past, present, or future.

Early anthropocentrists include John Passmore and Eugene Hargrove. Passmore's *Man's Responsibility for Nature* (1974) rigorously defended moral obligations toward the environment, but in terms in of human interests. Passmore was skeptical of attributing rights to other animals (who cannot communicate or recognize mutual obligations), and especially skeptical of attributing rights to such entities as rivers and mountains (largely because he was skeptical of their having interests at all).

Hargrove, the founding editor of the journal *Environmental Ethics* in 1979, developed his views in a series of articles through the 1970s and 1980s, culminating in his *Foundations of Environmental Ethics* (1989). Broadly, Hargrove emphasized the aesthetic value of the natural world as central to our obligations, where aesthetic value is to be understood in terms of human preferences and sensibilities, but allowing that we can value entities with aesthetic value for their own sake, as ends in themselves. Hargrove further argued that excessive interventions in the processes of the natural world can undermine the authenticity and beauty of various environments.

Non-anthropocentric theories hold that there can be values and reasons for action that do not reduce to human interests; non-human entities are seen as having some form of value or moral status independently of human needs.[2] Within the broad category of non-anthropocentric views, distinctions can be drawn. The most basic is between those views that hold that only individual living things can possess any sort of moral status and those that attribute some form of value or moral status to collective entities or wholes. The individualistic theories vary in the exact range of individuals that are treated as having moral status, and whether all individuals have such status equally. Holistic theories vary in the wholes that they treat as valuable (such as species, biomes, or ecosystems), the kind of value(s) attributed to such wholes, and whether these wholes possess these values equally.

2 INDIVIDUALISTIC ENVIRONMENTAL ETHICS

Individualistic, extensionist ethics were among the most prominent as the field of environmental ethics began to emerge in the early 1970s, and they remain influential to this day. Individualistic theories extend the moral concern traditionally given only to humans to include other beings. Most commonly, this is a matter of extending moral status to other sentient beings.

Peter Singer's *Animal Liberation* (1975) is considered a seminal work in animal and environmental ethics; Singer himself noted the importance of two prior works in developing his views: Rosalind Godlovitch's 1971 paper "Animals and Morals," and Ruth Harrison's *Animal Machines* (1964), an early and important exposé of intensive farming.

Singer embraced a consequentialist approach to animal welfare, holding that we are to give equal consideration to the interests of all sentient beings, regardless of species. To treat the suffering of a living thing as counting for less—or not at all—simply on the basis of species membership amounts to a speciesism akin to racism or sexism. Of course different individuals will have different interests—we need not treat an average adult human in the very same way we would treat a juvenile dog. But what is not permissible is to ignore the interests of a dog on the basis of its species membership.

Over time Singer refined his approach, later drawing a distinction between replaceable and irreplaceable individuals. Individuals who are self-conscious have desires and plans concerning the future and themselves that other creatures lack. Singer argued that while it would be acceptable to painlessly kill a non-self-conscious creature like a chicken (after a healthy, flourishing life) and replace it with another chicken raised under similar conditions, it would not be acceptable to similarly replace self-conscious humans (or others) because their self-conscious, future-focused interests would be thwarted (see Singer, 1979).

Tom Regan is perhaps the best-known proponent of a deontological, animal rights position, a view developed with great precision in his book *The Case for Animal Rights* (1983). Regan argued that utilitarian positions like Singer's effectively treat even self-conscious sentient beings as mere containers for pleasure and thus allow individuals to be sacrificed too easily for the sake of creating the greatest good. Regan instead held that all subjects of a life (sentient beings with feelings, beliefs, and desires) have an equal inherent value, regardless of intelligence, species, etc. In turn, this inherent value grounds a set of equal moral rights. Against those who would claim that non-human subjects of a life have no inherent value, or less value than humans, Regan argued that any plausible criterion that could serve to justify such claims (such as a lack of reason or moral autonomy) would also exclude many humans, including infants and those with significant mental disabilities. But these humans have equal inherent value to other humans, thus the proposed criterion is flawed; we have no sound basis for denying equal inherent value to all subjects of a life.

Other philosophers have held that restricting moral status to sentient beings does not go far enough. It seems, for example, that we can harm plants and other non-sentient organisms, even if we cannot cause them pain. However, we can also contribute to a plant's well-being and health by making sure it has appropriate light to grow and flourish, by providing it adequate water and so on.

Paul Taylor is prominent among these biocentric individualists who argue that moral status ought to be extended to all living things (Taylor, 1986; see also Johnson, 1991, Varner, 1998, and Agar, 2001). Taylor defended a strictly egalitarian position whereby all individual living beings have equal inherent value. While humans might be tempted to judge intelligent, rational beings as superior to other creatures, Taylor argued that these are biased criteria: although intelligence is very important to humans, what justifies using it as a criterion for evaluating beings who have no need for it? Plants lack our intelligence but can engage in photosynthesis; why not evaluate creatures on this ability instead? More broadly, Taylor takes a deontological approach to ethics and defends a set of moral principles to guide us in interactions with other creatures, particularly in cases in which conflicts of interest occur.

Still, not all philosophers who would attribute moral status to all living things would embrace Taylor's strict biocentric equality (Schmidtz, 1998). Instead, many treat moral status as a matter of degree, with those creatures possessing various traits deemed morally relevant (such as an ability to suffer, self-awareness, rationality) having greater status than those with fewer or less developed capacities (Attfield, 1987).

During the 1980s there was significant dispute as to whether individualistic theories, particularly when restricted to sentient beings, were viable as environmental ethics (Callicott, 1980; Sagoff, 1984). Many worried that individualist positions were ecologically naïve and could not allow for the possibility of culling overpopulated sentient species or for the removal of invasive sentient species, and they would seem to have absurd consequences— for example, that we ought to prevent predation because this involves the death of a valuable sentient being, whether killed by a lion or by a human. Of course, this latter point struck many as an effective *reductio ad absurdum* of individualism.

Individualists in turn pointed to significant problems with many holistic theories, while arguing that individualism could address the worries raised for their views. For example, they stressed the need for functioning ecosystems to allow for the flourishing of sentient creatures (thus justifying the removal of invasive species in a wide range of cases) and recognizing the difference between (1) the taking of sentient life by humans who are moral agents and (2) the predation of non-humans who lack moral understanding and agency; one could oppose the former while accepting the latter.[3]

3 HOLISTIC ENVIRONMENTAL ETHICS

3.1 Leopold and Callicott

In the 1970s Aldo Leopold's *A Sand County Almanac* (1949) was rediscovered some twenty years after its first publication after a long period of relative neglect. While gaining attention primarily among ecologists and biologists, interest soon spread to other academics and to the public more broadly. Leopold argued that we can—and must—extend our sense of moral community to include the land (where this includes soils, waters, non-human animals, and so on). Once within our community, moral concern is extended to the land; we should not value it merely in terms of simple instrumental or economic values. The summary statement of Leopold's land ethic is now well-known: "A thing is right when it tends to promote the integrity, stability, and beauty of the land community. It is wrong when it tends otherwise" (Leopold, 1949).

Philosophers soon recognized the importance and potential of Leopold's work. Perhaps the most influential philosophical proponent of Leopold's views is J. Baird Callicott, who has refined and developed an ethic firmly grounded in Leopold's work since the late 1970s. In early work (1979, 1980), Callicott emphasized the holism of Leopold's land ethic: what was of fundamental importance, ethically, was the integrity and stability of the land community. Individual living things were of comparatively little importance; if culling a population or removing an invasive species would promote the health of the land community, then such actions would be justified.

Critics argued that so-understood, the land ethic gave far too little significance to individual creatures; indeed it would seem to justify a widespread culling of humans to promote the integrity and stability of the land community (the charge of "eco-fascism"; see, for example, Regan, 1983). In response, Callicott stressed that we belong to a range of communities, each with their own sets of duties. While the land ethic (taken in isolation) might call for culling humans, we are members of additional, closer communities that prohibit such actions; with this more refined view, Callicott hoped to overcome worries of eco-fascism (see Callicott, 2001 for a recent statement of his interpretation of the land ethic).

Many other philosophers have also drawn upon Leopold (for example, Rolston, 1975, Norton, 1988), and not all have agreed with Callicott's influential interpretation. For example, Norton (1988) argued that Leopold's land ethic can be read in a much less radical fashion—that Leopold is not deeply committed to non-anthropocentrism and could readily accept a far-sighted anthropocentrism (i.e., we are wise to manage the land in accordance with the land ethic, but this can be justified ultimately in terms of human interests).

3.2 Holmes Rolston

Holmes Rolston developed a rich, thorough-going environmental ethic in a series of articles and books, beginning with his 1975 contribution to *Ethics*. Most fundamentally, Rolston argued that there are objective values inherent in nature that exist prior to and independently of any human (or other) valuing agents—contrary to much anti-realist theorizing in the field. This robust realism has attracted many to Rolston's views—but of course it also led to some criticism.

Rolston attributed intrinsic value to individual living things, but also to species—he argued that species can be seen as "superorganisms" that exhibit many of the same fundamental traits of individual living things (they adapt, reproduce themselves, and so on). Beyond attributing intrinsic value to species, Rolston attributed what he referred to as "systemic" value to ecosystems—the value such systems have as both generators and preservers of life: we cannot have individual living things, nor can we have species, without environments in which they interact, feed, find shelter, and so forth. Ecosystems thus have a distinctive value as the complex systems that are the source and sustainer of all life (see Rolston, 1986, 1994; see Johnson, 1991 for another influential holistic approach).

3.3 Deep Ecology

The deep ecological movement arose in Norway during the 1960s and 1970s. The term "deep ecology" itself was coined in Arne Naess's 1973 paper, "The Shallow and the Deep, Long-Range Ecology Movement. A Summary." Naess contrasted "shallow ecology," which he characterized as a movement concerned with pollution and resource management for the sake of short-term human economic interests, with deep ecology, which emphasizes the interrelatedness of living (and non-living) things, and posits an equality across all living things.

The biocentric equality embraced by Naess can be seen as resulting from his understanding of the self. Naess suggested that our self is not restricted to our bodies; rather, our self expands as we identify with other individuals, taking on and treating their interests as our own. Ultimately, we can identify with all living things, but also with mountains, rivers, whole species, and so on. As parts of a greater overall Self, all living individuals share equally in the inherent value we attribute to individual human selves; we arrive at biocentric equality. Naess argued that with an expanded sense of self, we would not feel alienated from other beings, and thus would not feel burdened or constrained by morality to take their interests into account. Instead, through identification, in acting on their interests we would also be willingly acting in our own (expanded) self-interest (Naess, 1989).

Alongside the more metaphysical strands of deep ecology there has evolved a platform of practical principles; while these principles would be justified by the metaphysics proposed by Naess, deep ecologists accept that there might be alternative metaphysics that would equally support the platform. Naess proposed an initial set of principles in his 1973 paper, but these were refined and revised by Naess and George Sessions in 1984 (Devall and Sessions, 1985). The resulting set of eight principles is now commonly treated as the fundamental platform linking all deep ecologists. Broadly, the principles attribute intrinsic value to all living things, and from this starting point emerge principles calling for reduced human population and resource use in order to allow other beings to flourish; this calls for significant changes in how humans understand well-being, politics, the goals of an economy, and so on. The most fundamental change comes in recognizing that human flourishing does not require vast material consumption, but rather such things as friendships, the development of talents, and ties to a local environment.[4]

4 ENVIRONMENTAL PRAGMATISM AND ANTHROPOCENTRISM REVISITED

Environmental pragmatism can be understood as emerging in the 1980s, with Anthony Weston's "Beyond Intrinsic Value: Pragmatism in Environmental Ethics" (1985) serving as an influential early paper. Weston argued that much work in environmental ethics is misguided in trying to show that sentient beings or ecosystems have intrinsic value; he drew attention to a range of metaphysical and epistemological problems in attempting to understand the very notion of intrinsic value and in arguing that any given entity possesses such value. Instead, Weston proposed that we understand environmental values holistically. Compare: we might value hiking in part as it contributes to our physical health, allows us to experience beauty, and so on. But equally we might value our health in part as it allows us to hike—the values can cohere and provide mutual support. Similarly, we need not try to secure environmental values as foundational and intrinsic; rather, we can articulate a wide range of values and justify each through their relationship to the others.

More broadly, environmental pragmatists have tended to embrace a plurality of values and principles and often a willingness to utilize different moral theories for different cases or contexts. If there were good ecofeminist, aesthetic, and deep ecological reasons to endorse a particular policy proposal, pragmatists would typically be happy to embrace all of them; each of the standpoints might capture something worthwhile while appealing to different actors and stakeholders. Relatedly, environmental pragmatists worry that too often mainstream environmental ethics treats some form of nonanthropocentric holism as a necessary condition for any genuine environmental ethic. Instead, ecopragmatists are committed to environmental ethics becoming more effective in shaping public policy and attitudes—they tend to be open to a range of theoretical perspectives, including anthropocentric ones, in developing policy proposals (see Katz, 1987; Light and Katz, 1996; Light, 2002).

This openness to anthropocentric perspectives can be seen in influential work by Bryan Norton. His 1984 "Environmental Ethics and Weak Anthropocentrism" suggested that a weak anthropocentricism (where value is determined by the considered, informed preferences of humans) would arrive at policy outcomes similar to nonanthropocentric, holistic environmental ethics while avoiding some of the more difficult metaphysical and moral assumptions of these nonanthropocentric theories; this has become known as the "convergence hypothesis." This was a pragmatic approach that allowed for the possibility of a plurality of relevant theories and reasons, but focused on those reasons that Norton believed would be most compelling and effective in actually motivating policy. He has developed his pragmatically inspired weak anthropocentrism in a variety of influential papers and books (see, for example, Norton, 1991, 2003).

The environmental pragmatist approach remains vibrant with continuing work from Weston, Norton, Light, and others (e.g., Minteer, 2011). More broadly, there has been an ongoing and increasing concern with real-world issues among environmental ethicists, going beyond the development of general theories and axiologies.

For example, there has been significant discussion of the ethics (and aesthetics) of ecological restoration—efforts to restore degraded or damaged ecosystems through direct human intervention. In "Faking Nature" (1982), Robert Elliot (1990) argued that restored environments typically have less value than the originals because the causal origins and histories of the originals are lost; a restored environment is akin to a forged painting.[5] More recently philosophers have considered further aspects of restoration, including the implications of climate change for restoration: for example, should we modify efforts at restoration to allow for new climatic conditions? (See Sandler 2012).

Global climate change itself has received significant attention, particularly the collective action aspects of the problem. For example, Stephen Gardiner has drawn attention to the important complications that arise out of the intergenerational aspect of climate change (see Gardiner, 2001, 2011). Baylor Johnson (2003) argued that our responsibility as individuals is to work toward collective agreements to address climate change, rather than engaging in individual acts of restraint that cannot adequately address the problem. Marion Hourdequin (2011) has argued in response that individual actions of restraint can have a communicative value that encourages trust in others, thus making collective problems easier to solve (see also Schmidtz, 2000; Jamieson, 2007; Hourdequin, 2010). More generally, there has been increasing discussion of issues related to climate change, including the ethics of geoengineering and the nature and extent of our obligations to future generations.

5 Ecological Feminism

The origins of ecological feminism can be traced back to the mid-1970s, with the term "ecofeminism" being coined in 1975 by Françoise d'Eaubonne in her *Le Feminisme ou la Mort* ("Feminism or Death"). This book, along with Rosemary Radford Ruether's *New Woman / New Earth* (1975), can plausibly be seen as initial roots for this rich and wide-ranging movement. Still, ecofeminism fully came into its own during the mid to late 1980s with the publication of several articles, books, and special editions of journals.

Karen J. Warren characterizes ecofeminist philosophy as embracing "the view that there are important connections between the domination of women (and other human subordinates) and the domination of nature *and* that a failure to recognize these connections results in inadequate feminisms, environmentalism, and environmental philosophy" (Warren, 1996). A central focus of much ecofeminist philosophical thought has thus been to discover and elaborate these connections and to consider their implications.[6]

Ecofeminists have argued that Western societies have tended to embrace a series of related, problematic dualisms such as human/animal, male/female, reason/emotion; in each case the latter is considered inferior and peripheral to the former (see Ruether, 1975; Plumwood, 1986, 1993). Karen Warren has argued that these value dualisms are then added to a "logic of domination" whereby (supposed) superiority is taken to justify subordination. Thus, according to such a patriarchal conceptual framework, women, animals, and nature ought to be controlled and dominated (Warren, 1990). This, of course, harkens back to White's early paper (1967) and the Christian theological tradition where nature, animals, and women are seen as rightfully subject to the dominion of men.

Another important connection concerns the differing impacts of environmental degradation upon men and women. Ecofeminists have argued that women and children often bear the worst impacts of environmental harms—in the effects of pollution, in having to work harder to maintain a subsistence livelihood, and so on. Furthermore, Western development policies have often adversely affected those in developing nations, again particularly women and children (see Shiva, 1989 for a classic statement). Some ecofeminists have also argued that women, due to their life experiences and circumstances, may be more in tune with the natural world than men and thus both feel and understand the health or degradation of the land more keenly than men (Salleh, 1984). Victoria Davion (1994) carefully critiqued some less plausible versions of this latter claim.

6   ENVIRONMENTAL VIRTUE ETHICS

A recent approach to environmental ethics, environmental virtue ethics (EVE), has followed upon the revival of virtue ethics more broadly and has become one of the most active areas of both environmental and applied virtue ethics. Thomas Hill's "Ideals of Human Excellence and Preserving Natural Environments" (1983) is considered to be the first essay explicitly articulating a virtue ethics approach to environmental ethics. Hill argued that those who would view the natural world solely in terms of costs and benefits, or who would not bat an eye at chopping down trees or destroying environments, would possess important character flaws—for example, a lack of humility, gratitude, and other related virtues—regardless of whatever other values or concerns might be at stake.

Geoffrey Frasz's "Environmental Virtue Ethics: A New Direction for Environmental Ethics" (1993) and Louke van Wensveen's *Dirty Virtues: The Emergence of Ecological Virtue Ethics* (2000) are crucial works in the development of EVE. Frasz carefully articulated key elements of virtue ethics and their potential importance to environmental ethics, while also reexamining Hill's discussion of humility in light of the broader virtue ethical tradition. Van Wensveen's book, the first devoted to EVE, explored how the language of virtue and vice has been embedded in much environmental discourse and how a virtue ethics approach could integrate and refine important strands of environmental ethical thinking.

Since 2000 there has been tremendous interest in EVE, with scores of articles being published, along with a number of edited collections and special journal issues (Sandler and Cafaro, 2005; Sandler, 2007; and Thompson and Bendik-Keymer, 2012). In part this simply reflects the ongoing and increasing interest in virtue ethics in philosophy more generally. But virtue ethics has several features that may make it particularly attractive as an approach to environmental ethics.

For example, it captures an intuition that human character—including our goals, values, dispositions, and habits—is crucial to arriving at environmentally and ethically viable ways of living. We cannot isolate environmental concerns from our more general ways of being in the world (Frasz, 1993; Jamieson, 2007). Second, prominent versions of EVE treat the virtues as those traits required for human (and in some cases non-human) flourishing; in turn, there is a recognition that our flourishing depends fundamentally upon the flourishing of the environments in which we live (Sandler, 2007; van Wensveen, 2000). Finally, EVE stresses the importance of looking to exemplars as guides to appropriate actions and ways of life. Looking to exemplars—from Thoreau to Carson—can provide us with a way of understanding broader values, character, and ways of life that we can use in modeling our own lives (Frasz, 1993; Cafaro, 2004).

7 LOOKING AHEAD

One of the most promising trends in environmental ethics lies in the attention being paid to work in psychology, economics, and other social sciences. These fields can provide valuable tools in translating moral reflection into effective action and policy, while also informing and influencing this reflection. As we come to understand human character, its possibilities and limits, we may be better able to shape society and its norms in ways that encourage us to become more virtuous—or at least to act in better ways. Learning about the arguments and other factors that motivate the public and policymakers can help us in addressing collective action issues, while empirical studies of happiness and well-being can help us see new ways of flourishing. Such empirically grounded approaches to environmental ethics—going beyond ecology and biology—could well have a transformative impact on the field.

NOTES

1. For a more general history of environmental ethics that delves back to the 19th century, see Nash (1989).
2. We should distinguish between anthropocentric ethics, and certain subjectivist, non-realist meta-ethical positions. For example, one could hold (meta-ethically) that values are grounded in or constituted by certain human attitudes. Species could have intrinsic value in such a view, in the sense that they are valued for their own sake, even if what this means, meta-ethically, is that certain humans under certain conditions would have some sort of

positive response to species. In other words, even if values are constituted by human attitudes, this does not necessarily result in an anthropocentric ethics that only values entities
insofar as they contribute to human interests and well-being. Thus, Hargrove's position,
while described by himself as a form of anthropocentrism, could instead be understood
as a non-anthropocentric ethics with a subjectivist/anthropocentric meta-ethics, where
intrinsic aesthetic value is determined by human responses.

3. See Jamieson (1998) for an overview of individualistic responses; see Callicott (1989) for a
more conciliatory response to individualistic approaches.

4. Beyond the foundational work of Naess, and Devall and Sessions, deep ecological thought
has been revised and refined by a number of thinkers; see, for example Fox (1990), Devall
& Sessions (1985), Katz, Light, and Rothenberg (2000).

5. For further discussion of restoration, and responses to Elliot, see the papers in Throop
(2000) and Hourdequin and Havlick (2013).

6. Ecofeminists have also made significant contributions to discussions of deep ecology, the
moral status of animals, and other important issues; see, for example, Sallah (1984) and
Plumwood (1993) on deep ecology, and Adams (1994), Gruen (1993), Kheel (1985), and
Warren (2000) on the moral status of animals.

REFERENCES

Adams, C. J. (1994). *Neither Man nor Beast: Feminism and the Defense of Animals.*
New York: Continuum International.

Agar, N. (2001). *Life's Intrinsic Value: Science, Ethics, and Nature.* New York: Columbia
University Press.

Attfield, Robin (1987). *A Theory of Value and Obligation.* London: Croom Helm.

Barbour, I. G., ed. (1973). *Western Man and Environmental Ethics.* Reading, MA: Addison-Wesley.

Blackstone, W. T., ed. (1974). *Philosophy and Environmental Crisis.* Athens, GA: University of
Georgia Press.

Cafaro, P. (2004). *Thoreau's Living Ethics: Walden and the Pursuit of Virtue.* Athens,
GA: University of Georgia Press.

Callicott, J. B. (1979). "Elements of an Environmental Ethic: Moral Considerability and the
Biotic Community." *Environmental Ethics* 1 (1): 71–81.

Callicott, J. B. (1980). "Animal Liberation: A Triangular Affair." *Environmental Ethics* 2
(4): 311–338.

Callicott, J. B. (1989). *In Defense of the Land Ethic.* Albany: SUNY Press.

Callicott, J. B. (2001). "The Land Ethic." In *A Companion to Environmental Philosophy*, edited
by D. Jamieson, 204–217. Malden, MA: Blackwell.

Carson, R. (1962). *Silent Spring.* New York: Houghton Mifflin.

Cobb, J. B. Jr. (1972). *Is It Too Late? A Theology of Ecology.* Beverley Hills: Bruce.

Davion, V. (1994). "Is Ecofeminism Feminist?" In *Ecological Feminism*, edited by K. J. Warren,
8–28. London: Routledge.

d'Eaubonne, F. (1974). *Le Feminisme ou la Mort.* Paris: Pierre Horay.

Devall, B., and Sessions, G. (1985). *Deep Ecology: Living as If Nature Mattered.* Layton,
UT: Gibbs Smith.

Ehrlich, P. (1968). *The Population Bomb.* New York: Sierra Club-Ballantine.

Elliot, R. (1982). "Faking Nature." *Inquiry* 25 (1): 81–93.

Fox, W. (1990). *Toward a Transpersonal Ecology: Developing New Foundations for Environmentalism*. Boston: Shambhala.

Frasz, G. (1993). "Environmental Virtue Ethics: A New Direction for Environmental Ethics." *Environmental Ethics* 15 (3): 259–274.

Gardiner, S. M. (2001). "The Real Tragedy of the Commons." *Philosophy & Public Affairs* 30 (4): 387–416.

Gardiner, S. M. (2011). *A Perfect Moral Storm: The Ethical Tragedy of Climate Change*. New York: Oxford University Press.

Godlovitch, R. (1971). Animals and Morals. *Philosophy* 46 (175): 23–33.

Gruen, L. (1993). "Dismantling Oppression: An Analysis of the Connection between Women and Animals." In *Ecofeminism: Women, Animals. Nature*, edited by G. Gaard, 60–90. Philadelphia: Temple University Press.

Hardin, G. (1968). "The Tragedy of the Commons." *Science* 162: 1243–1248.

Hargrove, E. (1989). *Foundations of Environmental Ethics*. Englewood Cliffs, NJ: Prentice-Hall.

Harrison, R. (1964). *Animal Machines*. London: Vincent Stuart.

Hill, T. E. (1983). "Ideals of Human Excellence and Preserving Natural Environments." *Environmental Ethics* 5 (3): 211–224.

Hourdequin, M. (2010). "Climate, Collective Action and Individual Ethical Obligations." *Environmental Values* 19 (4): 443–464.

Hourdequin, M. (2011). "Climate Change and Individual Responsibility: A Reply to Johnson." *Environmental Values* 20 (2): 157–162.

Hourdequin, M., and Havlick, D. G. (2013). "Restoration and Authenticity Revisited." *Environmental Ethics* 35 (1): 79–93.

Jamieson, D. (1998). "Animal Liberation is an Environmental Ethic." *Environmental Values* 7 (1): 41–57.

Jamieson, D. (2007). "When Utilitarians Should Be Virtue Ethicists." *Utilitas* 19 (2): 160–183.

Johnson, B. L. (2003). "Ethical Obligations in a Tragedy of the Commons." *Environmental Values* 12 (3): 271–287.

Johnson, L. E. (1991). *A Morally Deep World: An Essay on Moral Significance and Environmental Ethics*. New York: Cambridge University Press.

Katz, E. (1987). "Searching for Intrinsic Value: Pragmatism and Despair in Environmental Ethics." *Environmental Ethics* 9 (3): 231–241.

Katz, E., Light, A., and Rothenberg, D., eds. (2000). *Beneath the Surface: Critical Essays in the Philosophy of Deep Ecology*. Cambridge, MA: The MIT Press.

Kheel, M. (1985). "The Liberation of Nature: A Circular Affair." *Environmental Ethics* 7 (2): 135–149.

Leopold, A. (1949). *A Sand County Almanac: And Sketches Here and There*. New York: Oxford University Press.

Light, A. (2002). "Contemporary Environmental Ethics: From Metaethics to Public Philosophy." *Metaphilosophy* 33 (4): 426–449.

Light, A. and Katz, E., eds. (1996). *Environmental Pragmatism*. New York: Routledge.

Minteer, B. (2011). *Refounding Environmental Ethics: Pragmatism, Principle, and Practice*. Philadelphia: Temple University Press.

Naess, A. (1973). "The Shallow and the Deep: Long-Range Ecology Movements." *Inquiry* 16: 95–100.

Naess, A. (1989). *Ecology, Community, and Lifestyle: Outline of an Ecosophy*. Trans. David Rothenberg. New York: Cambridge University Press.

Nash, R. (1989). *The Rights of Nature: A History of Environmental Ethics*. Madison: University of Wisconsin Press.

Norton, B., ed. (1984). "Environmental Ethics and Weak Anthropocentrism." *Environmental Ethics* 6 (2): 131–148.

Norton, B. (1988). "The Constancy of Leopold's Land Ethic." *Conservation Biology* 2 (1): 93–102.

Norton, B. (1991). *Toward Unity among Environmentalists*. New York: Oxford University Press.

Norton, B. (2003). *Searching for Sustainability: Interdisciplinary Essays in the Philosophy of Conservation Biology*. New York: Cambridge University Press.

Passmore, J. (1974). *Man's Responsibility to Nature: Ecological Problems and Western Traditions*. New York: Charles Scribner's Sons.

Plumwood, V. (1986). "Ecofeminism: An Overview and Discussion of Positions and Arguments." *Australasian Journal of Philosophy* 64 (Supplemental): 120–138.

Plumwood, V. (1993). *Feminism and the Mastery of Nature*. London: Routledge.

Regan, T. (1983). *The Case for Animal Rights*. Berkeley: University of California Press.

Rolston, H. (1975). "Is there an Ecological Ethic?" *Ethics* 85: 93–109.

Rolston, H. (1986). *Philosophy Gone Wild: Environmental Ethics*. Amherst, NY: Prometheus Press.

Rolston, H. (1994). *Conserving Natural Value*. New York: Columbia University Press.

Ruether, R. R. (1975). *New Woman, New Earth: Sexist Ideologies and Human Liberation*. New York: Seabury Publishers.

Sagoff, M. (1984). "Animal Liberation and Environmental Ethics: Bad Marriage, Quick Divorce." *Osgoode Hall Law Journal* 22: 297–307.

Salleh, A. (1984). "Deeper than Deep Ecology: The Eco-Feminist Connection." *Environmental Ethics* 6 (4): 339–345.

Sandler, R. (2007). *Character and Environment: A Virtue-Oriented Approach to Environmental Ethics*. New York: Columbia University Press.

Sandler, R. (2012). "Global Warming and the Virtues of Ecological Restoration." In *Ethical Adaptation to Climate Change: Human Virtues of the Future*, edited by A. Thompson and J. Bendik-Keymer, 63–79. Cambridge, MA: The MIT Press.

Sandler, R., and Cafaro, P., eds. (2005). *Environmental Virtue Ethics*. Lanham, MD: Rowman & Littlefield.

Schmidtz, D. (1998). "Are All Species Equal?" *Journal of Applied Philosophy* 15 (1): 57–67.

Schmidtz, D. (2000). "Natural Enemies: An Anatomy of Environmental Conflict." *Environmental Ethics* 22 (4): 397–408.

Shiva, V. (1989). *Staying Alive: Women, Ecology, and Development*. London: Zed Books.

Singer, P. (1975). *Animal Liberation*. New York: New York Review / Random House.

Singer, P. (1979). *Practical Ethics*. New York: Cambridge University Press.

Stone, C. (1972). "Should Trees Have Standing? Toward Legal Rights for Natural Objects." *Southern California Law Review* 45: 450–501.

Stone, C. (1974). *Should Trees Have Standing? Toward Legal Rights for Natural Objects*. Los Altos, CA: William Kaufmann Inc.

Taylor, P. (1986). *Respect for Nature*. Princeton: Princeton University Press.

Thompson, A., and Bendik-Keymer, J., eds (2012). *Ethical Adaptation to Climate Change: Human Virtues of the Future*. Cambridge, MA: The MIT Press.

Throop, W., ed. (2000). *Environmental Restoration: Ethics, Theory, and Practice*. Amerherst, NY: Humanity Books.

Van Wensveen, L. (2000). *Dirty Virtues: The Emergence of Ecological Virtue Ethics*. Amherst, NY: Humanity Books (Prometheus Press).

Varner, G. E. (1998). *In Nature's Interests? Interests, Animal Rights, and Environmental Ethics*. New York: Oxford University Press.

Warren, K. J. (1990). "The Power and Promise of Ecological Feminism." *Environmental Ethics* 12 (2): 125–146.

Warren, K. J. ed. (1996). *Ecological Feminist Philosophies*. Bloomington: Indiana University Press (A Hypatia Book).

Warren, K. J. (1996). "Ecological Feminist Philosophies: An Overview of the Issues." In *Ecological Feminist Philosophies*, edited by K. J. Warren, ix–xxvi. Bloomington: Indiana University Press (A Hypatia Book).

Warren, K. J. (2000). *Ecofeminist Philosophy: A Western Perspective on What It Is and Why It Matters*. Lanham, MD: Rowman & Littlefield.

Weston, A. (1985). "Beyond Intrinsic Value: Pragmatism in Environmental Ethics." *Environmental Ethics* 7 (4): 321–339.

White, L. Jr. (1967). "The Historical Roots of Our Ecological Crisis." *Science* 155: 1203–1207.

CHAPTER 3

....

ENVIRONMENTAL SCIENCE
Empirical Claims in Environmental Ethics

....

WENDY S. PARKER

ARGUMENTS in environmental ethics often depend on scientific information. Why should we establish habitat corridors? Because they will help maintain biodiversity, and biodiversity is both intrinsically and instrumentally valuable. Why should we reduce air pollution in our locale? Because current levels are causing cardiovascular problems and increased rates of cancer, and we should prevent such harms to human health when we can. Why should industrialized nations provide funding for climate change adaptation in developing nations? Because it is required as a matter of justice: harmful future climate change, due to past greenhouse gas emissions from industrialized nations, is virtually unavoidable and will disproportionately impact populations in developing countries. Arguments like these appeal not only to ethical principles and values, but also to information provided by environmental science.

Environmental science encompasses a wide range of investigative activities that aim to advance understanding of environmental systems and, in some cases, to identify and solve environmental problems. Many environmental systems are complex, incorporating a range of interacting physical, chemical, biological, and social processes. Consequently, doing environmental science often requires integrating knowledge and expertise from several disciplines. For example, at the extreme, the study of earth's climate system relies upon knowledge and expertise from physics, chemistry, meteorology, oceanography, geography, ecology, biology, statistics, and a number of other fields.

The complexity of environmental systems can make it challenging to understand their behavior and to predict how they will respond to interventions. These difficulties are exacerbated by the fact that direct experimental tests of hypotheses in environmental science often are out of reach, whether for in-principle, practical, or ethical reasons. For example, since there is only one earth, we cannot directly test hypotheses about how earth's climate would change over the next century under several different greenhouse gas emission scenarios. In many cases, evidence in environmental science instead comes in the form of limited observational data collected in non-ideal circumstances, and conclusions are informed by results from *scientific models*, including computer models.

In part because environmental science has these features, its findings often are contested, especially when they bear directly on environmental policy decisions. Debates often center on whether scientific investigation has provided sufficient *evidence* that a serious environmental problem exists, that its causes have been correctly identified, and so on. In the context of such debates, concerns about *objectivity* frequently are expressed, with each side accusing the other of biased assessment or even deliberate misrepresentation of the available evidence. These accusations sometimes are leveled not just at policymakers, but at environmental scientists as well.

Contemporary work in philosophy of science can shed light on the practice of environmental science as well as some of the challenges it faces. This chapter surveys some of this work. The first section discusses philosophical conceptions of scientific evidence and the closely related issues of uncertainty and consensus. The second section outlines a view of scientific models, argues that blanket dismissals of results from scientific models are unjustified, and explains why multiple models are sometimes used together when conducting research in environmental science. The third section examines different views on the roles of social and political values in science, especially science that bears on public policy. As will become apparent, the topics of the different sections are connected in a number of ways.

1 Evidence, Uncertainty, and Consensus

Not infrequently, it is claimed that scientists have not "proven" that an environmental problem exists or that it is caused in a particular way. It might be said, for instance, that scientists have not proven that a particular pollutant is the primary cause of declining populations of fish in a local stream. Talk of "proof" in science is misleading, however, insofar as it carries connotations of absolute certainty (see also Oreskes, 2004). No empirical hypothesis is ever established with absolute (logical) certainty. It would be better to say that there is not yet strong *evidence* for a hypothesis, or that we cannot yet be *confident* that the hypothesis is true.

What is scientific evidence? A piece of scientific evidence is an empirical finding that, in combination with background information, is relevant to the evaluation of a hypothesis of interest—either supporting the hypothesis or speaking against it. Though various philosophical accounts of evidence have been developed, for present purposes accounts that gauge the strength of available evidence, or that indicate how confident we should be in a hypothesis in light of available information, are of greatest interest.

A standard version of Bayesian confirmation theory is one example (Howson and Urbach, 1993). It assumes that any hypothesis, H, can be assigned a probability, $p(H)$, which represents the degree of belief or confidence that an epistemic agent currently has in the hypothesis. Bayes' Theorem indicates how the probability assigned to H should be updated in light of new data, e.[1] The new data *confirm* (*disconfirm*) hypothesis H if and only if the updated probability for H is greater than (less than) the probability assigned to H before encountering e. The Bayesian picture is thus a dynamic one: as new evidence becomes available, the probability that an agent assigns to H is increased or decreased. Learning that an animal ingested large amounts of a toxic chemical, for example, might lower substantially the probability that a scientist assigns to the hypothesis that the animal's illness was caused primarily by a genetic mutation present from birth. Different scientists may assign different probabilities to a hypothesis at a given time but, in many cases, their probabilities will converge as more and more information becomes available.[2]

A rival account is the error-statistical account of evidence (Mayo, 1996), which denies that most scientific hypotheses should be assigned probabilities at all. It focuses instead on properties of the procedures by which hypotheses are tested. On this view, data *e* from a test or set of tests constitute *good evidence for* a hypothesis just to the extent that it is very unlikely that the test procedure would deliver data that fit the hypothesis as well as *e* do if the hypothesis were false (Mayo, 1996: 178–181). In this case, the hypothesis is said to have *passed a severe test* with *e*. Severely testing a hypothesis often involves a battery of "lower-level" tests that are designed to check for various canonical sources of error—confounding factors, failure to meet experimental design assumptions, mistakes, and so forth—and to thereby rule out alternatives to the hypothesis of interest. Returning to the earlier example, the error-statistician would not assign any probability to the hypothesis that the animal's illness was genetic in origin; she would focus instead on formulating tests that have a good chance of revealing that hypothesis to be false if in fact it is false.

While these philosophical accounts provide general theories of scientific evidence, in practice they are sometimes difficult to apply. For instance, when there is quite limited understanding of an environmental system or problem, the probabilities required for Bayesian updating may be poorly constrained, or it may be unclear how to perform a severe test of the hypothesis of interest. How to reach conclusions in situations like these, especially when there is conflicting information to be aggregated and weighed, is a topic of ongoing discussion both in philosophy of science and among practitioners (see e.g. van der Sluijs et al., 2008; Douglas, 2012; Stegenga, 2013).

Rather than appealing to general philosophical theories of evidence, groups and agencies charged with assessing evidence to help inform environmental policy decisions sometimes develop subject-specific guidance and/or informal tools for evidence assessment. For example, the US Environmental Protection Agency provides detailed guidance for assessing evidence regarding the carcinogenicity of chemicals (US EPA, 2005). Among other things, the guidance specifies what sorts of study findings should typically be had before a chemical is classified as "carcinogenic to humans" or "likely to be carcinogenic to humans." Likewise, guidance provided by the Intergovernmental Panel on Climate Change (IPCC) encourages its experts to consider both the "type, amount, quality and consistency" of available evidence and the extent to which there is "agreement" in the scientific community on what the evidence indicates (Mastrandrea et al., 2010). Depending on what this evaluation reveals, the group of experts can express a qualitative level of confidence in a hypothesis or finding (e.g., "medium" or "high"), assign a rough probability to the hypothesis, or report their conclusion in some other way (Mastrandrea et al., 2010).

By reporting conclusions in these different ways, the IPCC aims to communicate the extent of current *uncertainty* about hypotheses of interest. (Another way of saying that empirical hypotheses are never established with absolute certainty is to say that there is always some uncertainty about their truth or falsity.) Sometimes, of course, the uncertainty associated with hypotheses is negligible: it is virtually certain that the sun will rise tomorrow and that the earth is not flat. When it comes to hypotheses in environmental science, however, there is often non-negligible uncertainty. Sometimes this uncertainty can be accurately expressed using relatively precise probabilities; the meteorologist, for example, might report that there is roughly a 75% chance of rain tomorrow. Other times, it is clear that the available information is insufficient to warrant such probabilities; this is known as a situation of *deep uncertainty* (Kandlikar et al., 2005). In these situations, uncertainty will be more accurately represented with probability intervals (e.g., our confidence in *H* is roughly 70–90%) or in qualitative terms (e.g., *H* is plausible).³ It is important to recognize that accurately gauging and representing uncertainty is not just an epistemic matter; it can be important from a practical point of view as well, since inaccurate expressions of uncertainty—for example, reporting precise probabilities when in reality uncertainty is deeper than this—may mislead decision makers in ways that result in poor decisions.

Decision makers and members of the public often rely on what scientists report about the state of current knowledge because they are not in a position to survey and evaluate the available scientific information themselves. *Consensus* among experts can serve as a kind of second-order evidence for a scientific hypothesis—an indication that the available evidence favors or even strongly supports the hypothesis—but only if the consensus is "produced in the right manner" (Odenbaugh, 2012). When is consensus produced in the right manner? Here it is instructive to return to the philosophical accounts of evidence discussed previously (see also Oreskes, 2007). The error-statistician, for example, might argue that the consensus must emerge from a process that is very unlikely to produce such a consensus if the scientific evidence does not actually favor the agreed-upon hypothesis. A process that gives free rein to shared bias or vested interest or groupthink (Ranalli, 2012), or that does not require that those surveyed have relevant expertise, presumably would not qualify. On the other hand, perhaps a "hard won" consensus—one that emerges despite the reluctance of independent-minded and critical parties, after "vigorous debate and a thorough examination of the range of alternative explanations" (Ranalli, 2012: 187)—would constitute such evidence (see also the discussion of "deliberative acceptance" in Beatty and Moore, 2010). This is not to say that a consensus counts as indirect evidence for a scientific hypothesis only if it is hard won; when individually reliable and relatively independent sources agree that a hypothesis is true, this also can also warrant increased confidence in the hypothesis (relative to the case in which only one source is available; see also Odenbaugh, 2010, 2012). But it is important to keep in mind that the evidential significance of a consensus depends on how it was produced.

2 SCIENTIFIC MODELING

If chemists want to know whether one catalyst is more effective than another in facilitating a particular chemical reaction, they might try out both in the laboratory. This kind of direct experimentation often is not an option in environmental science. Investigation frequently proceeds in a less direct way, with the help of *scientific models*. A scientific model is a representational tool: it is a representation of some real or imagined system (the *target system*), and it is used for particular epistemic or practical purposes (see Giere, 2004, Morgan and Morrison, 1999; Weisberg, 2013). Often these purposes are predictive or explanatory—the aim is to predict aspects of the behavior of the target system or to inform explanations of its already-known behaviors. More generally, the goal is to correctly answer questions about the target system by studying the model.

Scientific models, including those used in environmental science, come in various forms. Typically they are concrete, mathematical, or computational (Weisberg, 2013). Non-human animals often serve as concrete models of human beings in laboratory experiments that investigate whether chemicals are carcinogenic. The Lotka-Volterra equations might be employed as a mathematical model of predator-prey interactions in a simple, imagined ecosystem. Most climate models are computational models—computer-implemented algorithms for solving equations of a mathematical model; typically the algorithm is designed to solve dynamical equations repeatedly, to produce a *simulation* of the evolution of target system properties through time.

Scientific models of real-world target systems differ from—and thus typically misrepresent—those target systems to some extent. A mouse is not identical to a human. The equations of a climate model describe the actual relations among climate system properties only in a simplified and idealized way. But an imperfect model can still be *adequate* for one or more purposes of interest (Caswell, 1976; Beck, 2002; Odenbaugh, 2005; NRC, 2007; Parker, 2011a). The biology of a mouse may be similar enough, in relevant respects, to the biology of a human that we can learn something of interest about the carcinogenicity of a particular chemical in humans by studying its carcinogenicity in mice (see e.g. Giere, 2004; Steel, 2007). A climate model might represent key physical processes accurately enough that we can use the model to roughly quantify the contribution of anthropogenic greenhouse gas emissions to late 20th century global warming. The same climate model, however, might be inadequate for accurately predicting how winter snowfall in a particular locale will change in coming decades, because that change is very sensitive to physical processes that are represented crudely in the model. Indeed, it might be well known that the model represents those processes too crudely to make the desired predictions.

In debates surrounding environmental issues, it is not uncommon to hear sweeping dismissals of results from scientific models: it is "only a model" that predicts that a leak at a proposed nuclear waste disposal site could take as little as fifty years to contaminate the water supply of nearby towns. Such dismissals are unfair. Scientists can have good reason to think that their models are informative in particular ways and thus are adequate for particular purposes. Weather forecasting models, for example, have a track record of reliability when it comes to predicting next-day high temperatures. In other cases, a model might have no such track record, but scientists understand the target system well enough to argue that the model represents the relevant target system processes with sufficient accuracy for the purpose at hand. Equally, of course, there can be reason to believe that a model is not a trustworthy source of particular information about a target, as in the winter snowfall prediction example. The point is that scientific models should be evaluated on a case by case basis with respect to their adequacy for particular purposes; the question is not whether a model is true or "valid" in some general way (see also Oreskes et al., 1994) but whether it is a good enough model for our purposes.

In practice, it is often unclear whether a model is adequate for a purpose of interest. When this happens for a demanding purpose, such as predicting very accurately the future values of environmental variable X, there may be good reason to think that the model is adequate for a less demanding purpose. For example, there might be good reason to think that the model can indicate values of X to within 50%, or that it can indicate values of X that are real possibilities, that is, values cannot be ruled out, given current understanding (Betz, 2010, Katzav, 2014). This can be valuable information in its own right, especially when these real possibilities include catastrophic outcomes whose risk of occurrence could be greatly reduced by implementing relatively low-cost policies or actions (see Chapter 27).

When there is uncertainty about how to build a model that is adequate for a purpose of interest, one strategy is to build multiple models that reflect different, but still reasonable, choices in model construction and then see what each model indicates about the target system. Thus, in climate science, an "ensemble" of different computer models is used to project future climate change; rather than a single prediction from a single model, predictions are obtained from multiple models for each greenhouse gas emission scenario. If each model's prediction of X can be considered a real possibility, then the set of predictions produced by the ensemble indicates a lower bound on current uncertainty about X (see e.g. Stainforth et al., 2007; for a critical perspective, see Betz, 2015). The extent to which uncertainty about X can be further quantified on the basis of a set of modeling results depends on details of the case at hand and, in the climate context, remains a topic of debate (see Parker, 2013). In practice, various methodologies and approaches are employed. In the most recent IPCC report (AR5), for instance, projections of global temperature change from an ensemble of state-of-the-art climate models provided a starting point for quantifying uncertainty about that change, but expert judgment concerning the limitations of those models was also important in shaping the conclusions reached (see Collins et al., 2013).

Sometimes, the majority of models used to investigate an environmental system agree in supporting a hypothesis. In this situation, it is tempting to assume that significantly increased confidence in that hypothesis is warranted (compared to the situation in which only one model is available). But this is not necessarily so. Just as in the case of consensus among experts, the significance of consensus among scientific modeling results depends on whether the consensus is produced in the right way. Indeed, the two cases are closely analogous. If the construction of the models is heavily influenced by groupthink or shared biases among modelers, then there may be little reason to have extra confidence in the agreed-upon hypothesis. On the other hand, if the models are known to be rather reliable individually and to give results independently, then consensus among models can warrant significantly increased confidence in the agreed-upon hypothesis (see also Pirtle et al., 2010; Parker, 2011b).

Agreement among results from multiple models can also be of interest when models are used for purposes other than prediction. For instance, suppose we are interested in learning about the mechanisms at work in an environmental system. When multiple models that share a set of core assumptions but differ in some auxiliary assumptions nevertheless all behave in a similar fashion, this may suggest that there is a robust underlying mechanism producing that behavior (see e.g. Levins, 1966; Weisberg, 2006; Lloyd, 2010).

3 VALUES AND OBJECTIVITY

A long-standing issue in philosophy of science concerns the appropriate roles of values in science—in particular, the roles of social, political, and ethical values. These sometimes are referred to as non-epistemic or *contextual* values (Longino, 1990). While it is widely agreed that it is appropriate for contextual values to influence both the selection of research priorities as well as decisions about which technological applications of scientific knowledge to pursue, there is less agreement over the appropriate place of these values in the assessment of scientific hypotheses. A traditional view is that the influence of contextual values here ought to be minimized (e.g., Jeffrey, 1956; Lacey, 1999); this is a central commitment of what is known as the *value-free ideal* for science.

Recent philosophical discussion of the value-free ideal often begins from Rudner's (1953) argument that contextual value judgments are routinely involved in the assessment of scientific hypotheses: evidence never establishes a scientific hypothesis with absolute certainty; the fact that stronger evidence is demanded before accepting some hypotheses than others reflects the value judgment that the consequences of error in those cases are judged to be particularly bad. For example, stronger evidence is demanded before accepting that a new drug is an effective treatment for malaria than before accepting that the average life span of ferrets is more than seven and a half years, because the consequences of erroneously accepting the former can be expected to be worse than the consequences of erroneously accepting the latter.[4] Thus, the argument goes, contextual values often play a role when deciding whether to accept or reject hypotheses in the face of some risk of error, known as *inductive risk* (Hempel, 1965; Douglas, 2000).

Various methodological choices in science can affect the balance of inductive risk. As Rudner's analysis suggests, requiring a higher statistical significance level before accepting a hypothesis (e.g., 99% rather than 90%) increases the risk of erroneously rejecting a true hypothesis, while requiring a lower significance level increases the risk of erroneously accepting a false one. Choices made in the course of collecting and analyzing data can also influence the balance of inductive risk (see also Shrader-Frechette and McCoy, 1993). An example offered by Douglas (2000) is instructive: suppose a scientist encounters ambiguous tissue specimens in a study investigating whether a chemical is carcinogenic; classifying these ambiguous cases as cancerous will increase the risk that the chemical is erroneously considered carcinogenic, while classifying them as benign will increase the risk that the chemical is erroneously considered safe.

Douglas (2009) argues that when facing uncertain methodological choices like these, which affect the balance of inductive risk, scientists' decisions *ought* to be informed by their judgments of how bad the consequences of each type of error would be. Their obligation to do so stems from the general moral responsibilities that agents have to consider the consequences of their actions (Douglas, 2009, ch. 4). The scientist in the example might decide to classify the ambiguous tissue specimens as carcinogenic, because he judges that it would be worse to erroneously classify the chemical as safe than to erroneously classify it as carcinogenic.[5] Of course, that such value-laden methodological choices were made should be reported by the scientist along with the conclusions reached (Douglas, 2009, ch. 8; see also Kloprogge et al., 2011; Elliott and Resnik, 2014). Moreover, the influence of contextual values should be limited to situations of genuine methodological uncertainty; values should not be invoked as direct reasons for accepting hypotheses. But the value-free ideal should be rejected, according to Douglas, insofar as it overlooks some of the moral responsibilities of scientists.

A standard line of reply to arguments from inductive risk begins with Jeffrey (1956). Taking a Bayesian point of view, he denies that scientists must accept or reject hypotheses; their job is to assign probabilities in light of the available information, and this does not require contextual value judgments. (It simply requires the application of Bayes' Theorem.) It is then up to policymakers and other decision-makers to decide, in light of their social, political, and ethical values, whether the probabilities are sufficient to warrant various courses of action. In other words, from a classic decision-theoretic perspective, scientists provide the probabilities and decision-makers provide the utilities.

A more recent response in a somewhat similar vein is offered by Betz (2013). He argues that rather than appealing to contextual values to make a choice in the face of methodological uncertainty, scientists can acknowledge that the choice is uncertain and attempt to determine the implications of this for the matter under investigation. For instance, different methodological options can be explored. In the example above, this might mean calculating relative cancer risk first under the assumption that ambiguous cases are benign and then under the assumption that they are cancerous, thus arriving at a range of relative risk values bounded by the two results. The ensemble modeling studies of future climate change mentioned previously aim to explore the implications of methodological uncertainty in a similar way: the different climate models used to project future temperature change are intended to reflect different reasonable choices in model construction. Betz argues that, in light of what is found by exploring different methodological choices in this way, scientists can offer hedged conclusions to decision-makers. These conclusions might be probabilistic, as Jeffrey assumed, or, if uncertainty is deeper, they might take other appropriate forms (e.g., outcome X is plausible). Betz thus concludes that contextual value judgments *can* be avoided in the assessment of hypotheses.[6]

Challengers of the value-free ideal find this sort of response insufficient. They contend that, even if scientists report uncertainties using probabilities or in some other way, those uncertainty estimates will themselves be somewhat uncertain, and so contextual value considerations will need to resurface as scientists consider the consequences of error or inaccuracy in their uncertainty estimates (Douglas, 2009; see also Rudner, 1953). This second-order uncertainty arises in part because the range of reasonable methodological choices is itself somewhat uncertain: it is not perfectly clear where to draw the line between ambiguous and unambiguous tissue specimens, nor between reasonable and unreasonable assumptions that might be included in climate models.[7] In addition, practical realities, such as limited computing power, sometimes limit the extent to which scientists can explore the implications of whatever set of reasonable methodological options is identified.

Betz in turn counters that scientists can simply weaken their conclusions until they are, for all practical purposes, beyond any reasonable doubt—that is, until there is negligible inductive risk (2013: 218). For example, climate scientists may be quite unsure whether a global temperature increase of more than 2°C should be considered "likely" (i.e., ≥0.66 likelihood) or merely "more likely than not" (i.e., ≥0.50 likelihood) under a particular emission scenario, but they might judge it beyond any reasonable doubt that such a temperature increase cannot yet be ruled out. By simply reporting the latter conclusion, they can avoid any significant inductive risk. But while Betz is correct that weak claims of this sort are sometimes of interest to policymakers, in many cases they may want something more. For instance, they might ask scientists to give them a best estimate (plus 95% confidence interval) of the number of deaths per year that result from a given air pollutant. Or they might require scientists to express their confidence in a hypothesis in one of a limited set of ways—for example, "high," "medium," "low" (see also Steele, 2012). In these cases, significant second-order uncertainty, and thus inductive risk, can remain. The defender of the value-free ideal presumably will advise that scientists probe and report this second-order uncertainty as well. Is this then sufficient? The debate surrounding inductive risk is still unfolding.

The inductive risk debate is just one thread in a wide-ranging discourse concerning the influence of contextual values in science (see e.g. Intemann, 2005; Douglas, 2011; Elliott, 2011; Brown, 2013). Other important threads focus on the ways contextual value judgments are encoded in the very terms used in science, for example, in ecosystem "health" or ecosystem "services" (see also Dupré, 2007), and on other subtle ways in which contextual values influence scientific reasoning, even when this is not intended. For instance, Longino (1990) argues that contextual values sometimes shape scientists' background assumptions, which in turn influence the range of hypotheses that they consider plausible and the extent to which they understand data to provide evidence for a hypothesis (see also Sarewitz, 2004). In this way, the conclusions reached by a scientist may be subtly biased by his or her values. For example, suppose that a scientist values helping people and, in part as a consequence of this, has as an implicit background assumption that most social ills can be mitigated substantially with interventions to the social environment; when analyzing a particular social problem, this scientist may not even consider the hypothesis that a genetic or other non-social cause may be a significant factor.

Longino thus recommends that objectivity be understood as a community-level feature of science: the practices of a scientific community are *objective* to the extent that they not only allow for criticism of background assumptions, data, and methods from a range of perspectives but also are responsive to such criticism (1990: 76–80; Longino, 2002: 128–135).[8] This is not to suggest that individual scientists should not make an honest effort to find out what the world is like (see also Douglas, 2009, ch. 6). The point, rather, is that critical dialogue with others—whether in the published literature or in more informal venues—brings additional opportunities for uncovering and transcending biases at the individual level.

This is a salutary reminder in the face of entrenched, opposing views on environmental issues. Of course, sometimes uncertainty and controversy are manufactured deliberately, with the aim of forestalling undesirable policy action.[9] Likewise, sometimes evidence is deliberately presented in a selective way in order to give a misleading impression of what scientific investigation has uncovered. But other times entrenched disagreement may reflect an unwillingness to question preferred background assumptions or to seriously engage with individuals who, despite some shared standards, nevertheless interpret the available data differently. When this unwillingness is a persistent feature of a community, it too can be understood as a failure of objectivity.

4 Concluding Remarks

Arguments in environmental ethics often appeal not only to ethical principles and values but also to conclusions from environmental science. These conclusions are never established with absolute (logical) certainty, but typically they are conclusions for which there is substantial evidence. Philosophical accounts of evidence, such as Bayesian and error-statistical accounts, can aid discussion of what it means to have good or strong evidence. Further work is needed, however, to better understand how evidence evaluation should proceed when frameworks like these are not readily applied. In practice, some groups and agencies charged with assessing evidence to inform environmental policy have developed subject-specific guidance and informal tools to aid assessment.

For many questions in environmental science, evidence cannot be obtained by experimenting directly on the environmental system of interest. Instead, scientific models of the environmental system are constructed, and they are studied in place of the system itself.

General scepticism about results obtained from models is unwarranted; though a model may differ from its target in salient ways, it may still be adequate for the purposes for which it is used. Indeed, there can be good reason to believe that a model is adequate for a particular purpose, even when some of its results fail to match observations of the target system. When there is uncertainty about how to build an adequate model, investigative strategies involving multiple models can be useful, but interpreting results can be tricky. For instance, just as consensus among scientists takes on special epistemic significance only under certain circumstances, so does agreement among modeling results.

Debate continues over the appropriate roles of social, political, and ethical values in science. Arguments from inductive risk see an actual and/or desirable role for these values when faced with uncertain methodological choices. Opponents contend that appeal to values here can and/or should be avoided. More broadly, it has been argued that contextual values shape background assumptions in subtle ways that influence the way evidence is evaluated. This has led to the proposal that objectivity be understood as a community-level feature of science, which is achieved to the extent that a community allows and is responsive to criticism of background assumptions, data, and methods from a range of perspectives.

Notes

1. According to Bayes' Theorem: $p(H \mid e) = p(H) \times p(e \mid H) / p(e)$, where p(H|e) is the probability that the agent should assign to H if e is obtained, i.e. the updated probability for H; p(H) is the probability that the agent assigns to H before obtaining e; p(e|H) is the probability of obtaining e if H is true; and p(e) is the probability of obtaining e whether H is true or false, i.e. the expectedness of e. This simple formulation of Bayes' Theorem leaves implicit the role of background information, b; including it results in a slightly different formulation: $p(H \mid e \& b) = p(H \mid b) \times p(e \mid H \& b) / p(e \mid b)$.

2. Such convergence is not guaranteed. For instance, if scientists often disagree on whether $p(e \mid H) > p(e)$ for new pieces of evidence, their probabilities might not converge.

3. Situations in which probabilities cannot be assigned to hypotheses are also known as situations of *Knightian uncertainty* (see Knight, 1921).

4. Brysse et al. (2012) suggest that in fact the scientific community has a tendency to "err on the side of least drama"—to "demand greater levels of evidence in support of surprising, dramatic, or alarming conclusions than in support of conclusions that are less surprising, less alarming, or more consistent with the scientific status quo" (pp. 327–328).

5. It is interesting that the EPA guidelines for carcinogen risk assessment (2005), mentioned earlier, provide a number of 'default options' that can be employed in situations of methodological uncertainty; these options are said to be "consistent with EPA's mission to protect human health while adhering to the tenets of sound science" (pp. 1–7).

6. Note that Betz does not argue that the value-free ideal *should* be adopted; he simply argues that contextual value judgments *can* be avoided in the face of methodological uncertainty.

7. Biddle and Winsberg (2010) argue that contextual values also influence which climate model variables are prioritized for accurate simulation and that the effects of this prioritization cannot be removed from probabilistic estimates of uncertainty about future climate change (see also Winsberg, 2012; Parker, 2014).

8. Note that in such a community, consensus on policy-relevant scientific questions may indeed be "hard won" (see under Evidence, Uncertainty, and Consensus).

9. For examples in public health (e.g., tobacco, asbestos) and climate change, see Michaels, 2006; Edwards, 2010, ch. 15; Oreskes and Conway, 2011.

REFERENCES

Beatty, J., and Moore, A. (2010). "Should We Aim for Consensus?" *Episteme* 7(3): 198–214.

Beck, M. B. (2002). "Model Evaluation and Performance." In *Encyclopedia of Environmetrics,* edited by A. H. El-Shaarawi and W. W. Piegorsch, 1275–1279. Chichester: Wiley.

Betz, G. (2010). "What's the Worst Case? The Methodology of Possibilistic Prediction." *Analyse und Kritik* 31(1): 87–106.

Betz, G. (2013). "In Defense of the Value-Free Ideal." *European Journal for Philosophy of Science* 3(2): 207–220.

Betz, G. (2015). "Are Climate Models Credible Worlds? Prospects and Limitations of Possibilistic Climate Prediction." *European Journal for Philosophy of Science* 5(2): 191–215. doi: 0.1007/s13194-015-0108-y.

Biddle, J. and Winsberg, E. (2010). "Value Judgments and the Estimation of Uncertainty in Climate Modeling." In *New Waves in the Philosophy of Science,* edited by P. D. Magnus and J. Busch, 172–197. New York: Palgrave MacMillan.

Brown, M. (2013). "Values in Science beyond Underdetermination and Inductive Risk." *Philosophy of Science* 80(5): 829–839.

Brysse, K., Oreskes, N., O'Reilly, J., and Oppenheimer, M. (2012). "Climate Change Prediction: Erring on the Side of Least Drama?" *Global Environmental Change* 23(1): 327–337.

Caswell, H. (1976). "The Validation Problem" In *Systems Analysis and Simulation in Ecology,* vol. 4, edited by B. C. Patter, 313–325. New York: Academic Press.

Collins, M., et al. (2013). "Long-Term Climate Change: Projections, Commitments and Irreversibility." In *Climate Change 2013: The Physical Science Basis. Contribution of Working Group I to the Fifth Assessment Report of the Intergovernmental Panel on Climate Change,* edited by T. F. Stocker. New York: Cambridge University Press.

Douglas, H. (2000). "Inductive Risk and Values in Science." *Philosophy of Science* 67: 559–579.

Douglas, H. (2009). *Science, Policy, and the Value-Free Ideal.* Pittsburgh: Pittsburgh University Press.

Douglas, H. (2011). "Facts, Values, and Objectivity." In *The SAGE Handbook of Philosophy of Social Science,* edited by I. Jarvie and J. Zamora-Bonilla, 513–529. London: SAGE Publications.

Douglas, H. (2012). "Weighing Complex Evidence in a Democratic Society." *Kennedy Institute of Ethics Journal* 22(2): 139–162.

Dupré, J. (2007). "Fact and Value." In *Value-Free Science? Ideals and Illusions,* edited by H. Kincaid, J. Dupré, and A. Wylie, 27–41. New York: Oxford University Press.

Edwards, P. (2010). *A Vast Machine: Computer Models, Climate Data and Politics of Global Warming.* Boston: MIT Press.

Elliott, K. C. (2011). *Is a Little Pollution Good for You? Incorporating Societal Values in Environmental Research.* New York: Oxford University Press.

Elliott, K. C. and Resnik, D. B. (2014). "Science, Policy and the Transparency of Values." *Environmental Health Perspectives,* http://dx.doi.org/10.1289/ehp.1408107.

Giere, R. (2004). "How Models Are Used to Represent Reality." *Philosophy of Science* 71: 742–752.

Hempel, C. G. (1965). "Science and Human Values." In *Aspects of Scientific Explanation and other Essays in the Philosophy of Science,* edited by C. G. Hempel, 81–96. New York: The Free Press.

Howson, C., and Urbach, P. (1993). *Scientific Reasoning: The Bayesian Approach,* 2nd ed. Chicago: Open Court.

Intemann, K. (2005). "Feminism, Underdetermination, and Values in Science." *Philosophy of Science* 72(5): 1001–1012.

Jeffrey, R. (1956). "Valuation and Acceptance of Scientific Hypotheses." *Philosophy of Science* 22: 237–246.

Kandlikar, M., Risbey, J., and Dessai, S. (2005). "Representing and Communicating Deep Uncertainty in Climate-Change Assessments." *Comptes Rendus Geoscience* 337: 443–455.

Katzav, J. (2014). "The Epistemology of Climate Models and Some of Its Implications for Climate Science and the Philosophy of Science." *Studies in History and Philosophy of Modern Physics* 46: 228–238.

Kloprogge, P., van der Sluijs, J. P., and Petersen, A. C. (2011). "A Method for the Analysis of Assumptions in Model-Based Environmental Assessments." *Environmental Modelling and Software* 26(3): 289–301.

Knight, F. (1921). *Risk, Uncertainty and Profit.* Boston: Houghton Mifflin.

Lacey, H. (1999). *Is Science Value Free? Values and Scientific Understanding.* New York: Routledge.

Levins, R. (1966). "The Strategy of Model Building in Population Biology." *American Scientist* 54(4): 421–431.

Lloyd, E. (2010). "Confirmation and Robustness of Climate Models." *Philosophy of Science* 77: 971–984.

Longino, H. (1990). *Science as Social Knowledge.* Princeton: Princeton University Press.

Longino, H. (2002). *The Fate of Knowledge* (Princeton: Princeton University Press).

Mastrandrea, M. D., et al. (2010). *Guidance Note for Lead Authors of the IPCC Fifth Assessment Report on Consistent Treatment of Uncertainties.* Intergovernmental Panel on Climate Change (IPCC). Available at <http://www.ipcc.ch>.

Mayo, D. (1996). *Error and the Growth of Experimental Knowledge.* Chicago: University of Chicago Press.

Michaels, D. (2006). "Manufactured Uncertainty." *Annals of the New York Academy of Sciences* 1076: 149–162.

Morgan, M. S., and Morrison, M. (1999). *Models as Mediators: Perspectives on Natural and Social Science.* New York: Cambridge University Press.

National Research Council (NRC) (2007). *Models in Environmental Regulatory Decision Making.* Washington, DC: The National Academies Press.

Odenbaugh, J. (2005). "Idealized, Inaccurate but Successful: A Pragmatic Approach to Evaluating Models in Theoretical Biology." *Biology and Philosophy* 20: 231–255.

Odenbaugh, J. (2010). "Philosophy of the Environmental Sciences." In *New Waves in Philosophy of Science,* edited by P. D. Magnus and J. Busch, 155–171. New York: Palgrave MacMillan.

Odenbaugh, J. (2012). "Consensus, Climate, and Contrarians." In *The Environment: Philosophy, Science, and Ethics,* edited by W. P. Kabasenche, M. O'Rourke, and M. H. Slater, 137–150. Boston: MIT Press.

Oreskes, N., Belitz, K., and Shrader-Frechette, K. (1994). "Verification, Validation and Confirmation of Numerical Models in the Earth Sciences." *Science* 263(5147): 641–646.

Oreskes, N. (2004). "Science and Public Policy: What's Proof Got to Do with It?" *Environmental Science and Policy* 7: 369–383.

Oreskes, N. (2007). "The Scientific Consensus on Climate Change: How Do We Know We're Not Wrong?" In *Climate Change: What It Means for Us, Our Children, and Our Grandchildren*, edited by J. F. C. DiMento and P. Doughman, 65–99. Boston: MIT Press.

Oreskes, N. and Conway, E. (2011). *Merchants of Doubt: How a Handful of Scientists Obscured the Truth on Issues from Tobacco Smoke to Global Warming*. New York: Bloomsbury Press.

Parker, W. S. (2011a). "Scientific Models and Adequacy-for-Purpose." *Modern Schoolman: A Quarterly Journal of Philosophy* 87(3, 4), 285–293.

Parker, W. S. (2011b). "When Climate Models Agree: The Significance of Robust Model Predictions." *Philosophy of Science* 78(4): 579–600.

Parker, W. S. (2013). "Ensemble Modeling, Uncertainty and Robust Predictions." *Wiley Interdisciplinary Reviews (WIREs) Climate Change* 4: 213–223.

Parker, W. S. (2014). "Values and Uncertainties in Climate Prediction, Revisited." *Studies in History and Philosophy of Science* 46: 24–30.

Pirtle, Z., Meyer, R., and Hamilton, A. (2010). "What Does It Mean when Climate Models Agree? A Case for Assessing Independence among General Circulation Models." *Environmental Science and Policy* 13: 351–361.

Ranalli, B. (2012). "'Climate Science, Character and the 'Hard Won' Consensus." *Kennedy Institute of Ethics Journal* 22(2): 183–210.

Rudner, R. (1953). "The Scientist qua Scientist Makes Value Judgments." *Philosophy of Science* 20: 1–6.

Sarewitz, D. (2004). "How Science Makes Environmental Controversies Worse." *Environmental Science and Policy* 7: 385–403.

Shrader-Frechette, K. S., and McCoy, E. D. (1993). *Method in Ecology: Strategies for Conservation*. Cambridge: Cambridge University Press.

Stainforth, D. A. et al. (2007). "Confidence, Uncertainty and Decision-Support Relevance in Climate Predictions." *Philosophical Transactions of the Royal Society* A 365: 2145–2161.

Steel, D. (2007). *Across the Boundaries: Extrapolation in Biology and Social Science*. New York: Oxford University Press.

Steele, K. (2012). "The Scientist qua Policy Advisor Makes Value Judgments." *Philosophy of Science* 79: 893–904.

Stegenga, J. (2013). "An Impossibility Theorem for Amalgamating Evidence." *Synthese* 190(12): 2391–2411.

US EPA (2005). "Guidelines for Carcinogen Risk Assessment." Washington, DC: US Environmental Protection Agency, EPA/630/P-03/001F.

van der Sluijs, J. et al. (2008). "Exploring the Quality of Evidence for Complex and Contested Policy Decisions." *Environmental Research Letters* 3: 024008 doi:10.1088/1748-9326/3/2/024008.

Weisberg, M. (2006). "Robustness Analysis." *Philosophy of Science* 73(5): 730–742.

Weisberg, M. (2013). *Simulation and Similarity: Using Models to Understand the World*. New York: Oxford University Press.

Winsberg, E. (2012). "Values and Uncertainties in the Predictions of Global Climate Models." *Kennedy Institute of Ethics Journal* 22(2): 111–137.

CHAPTER 4

··

MARKETS, ETHICS, AND ENVIRONMENT

··

JOHN O'NEILL

1 ECONOMIC SYSTEMS AND VALUATION

WE live in market economies in which previously non-market goods and services are increasingly becoming either the direct objects of market exchange or treated according to market norms and forms of evaluation. We live in a social and economic world with increasing environmental problems—climate change, biodiversity loss, ocean acidification, resource depletion, and so on. What relation, if any, holds between these two features of modern economic life? In the academic literature, policy debates, and civil society deliberations it is possible to discern two very different perspectives on the relationship between the market economy and environmental problems, what we may call market-endorsing and market-skeptical.

On the one hand there are market-endorsing positions that argue that the extension of markets or market modes of valuation to environmental goods offers the best way of protecting them.

1. An influential version of the claim is that the very absence of markets is the source of environmental problems. Preferences for environmental goods are not captured in market exchange (Arrow, 1984: 155). Correspondingly the solution requires the extension of market prices to environmental goods to ensure that they are so captured. The extension can take one of two broad forms. First, property rights might be defined over environmental goods or services so that they can be traded directly in market. Second, public authorities can use market-mimicking procedures. Shadow prices over environmental goods can be constructed by ascertaining what individuals would be willing to pay at the margin for such goods, were there a market for them. The construction of shadow prices can proceed through "revealed preference methods" which infer a monetary value for unpriced environmental goods from the actual behavior of people in markets, for example from differential house prices in so far as they reflect the value of environmental amenities. Alternatively, it can proceed through "stated preference methods", such as contingent valuation, which ask people

how much they would be willing to pay for a good or accept in compensation for its loss in a hypothetical market. Shadow prices can then enter a cost-benefit analysis that aims to capture the full range of benefits and losses associated with some projected change. This position assumes that a monetary metric can be extended to capture the value of environmental goods.

2. A distinct line of defense of markets as an institutional form for protecting environmental goods is one that, while it might concede that not all values can be captured by monetary metrics, holds that market modes of governance provide the most efficient and effective mechanism for achieving environmental goals (Caney, 2010: 206). Cap and trade schemes such as emissions trading are sometimes defended on these grounds. By allowing polluters to trade rights set within a total cap, the schemes are taken to provide a mechanism for abatements in pollution to occur where they are cheapest while keeping total levels of pollution under a certain total. The market is merely the means through which emissions are kept within a total cap that might be set by political and scientific criteria without the use of any monetary metric.

3. A third position, associated with libertarian and Austrian traditions in economics, are critical of both shadow pricing and politically set cap-and-trade schemes. Market prices are not measures of value, but rather the means through which different actors with their local, particular, and practical knowledge are able to coordinate their actions. According to this view, the solution to environmental problems lies in the definition of property rights over and market exchange in environmental goods such that actors can coordinate their behavior in ways consistent with environmental ends (Sagoff, 2008).

On the other hand, there are a variety of positions that are market-skeptical. One can distinguish the following positions.

1. Market measures of value cannot be expanded to include environmental values. One of the founding figures in ecological economics, Kapp, writes, "environmental values are social use values for which markets provide neither a direct measure nor an adequate indirect indicator" (Kapp, 1974: 38). This claim conflicts with the position that environmental protection requires the extension of monetary measures to environmental goods.

2. Markets provide neither an effective nor ethically defensible means to protect the environment. This claim conflicts with the more minimal position that markets offer an effective and ethical means of realizing environmental goals.

3. Markets and the spread of market norms are a source of environmental problems. Two influential forms of this claims are (a) that market economies involve the removal of customary or ethical constraints on the unsustainable exploitation of environmental goods (Polanyi, 1957: 73) and (b) market economies require or foster the constant material growth of the economy (Marx, 1970: ch.4) and this growth is unsustainable and the source of many of our increasing environmental problems.

Within the tradition of political ecology, market-skeptical positions can take stronger or weaker forms. Stronger forms argue for decision-making procedures that employ not monetary measures but direct physical, environmental and social measures of welfare; some aim ultimately at replacing markets with non-market economic institutions (Neurath, 1920; O'Neill, 2004). Weaker forms are critical not of markets but the disembedding of markets from the constraints of social and environmental norms (Polanyi, 1957; O'Neill, 2007: ch.1.). Both traditions have been sources of continuing skepticism of market-based modes of environmental governance. Their influence is to be found, for example, in arguments for the use of multicriteria and deliberative approaches to environmental decision making that do not require the capture of environmental benefits and losses in a single monetary unit (Martinez-Alier et al., 1998).

Beyond these specific traditions in political ecology and ecological economics, the question of how far markets and markets norms should play a role in the governance of environmental goods has a wider role in debates about the boundaries of markets (Anderson, 1993; Satz, 2010; Sandel, 2013; Walzer, 1983). There is a long-standing argument about what classes of goods are such that they could not or should not be treated as commodities that can be bought or sold. Typical examples include persons, votes, bodily parts, sexual services, reproductive services, blood, indulgences, knowledge, educational service, many cultural goods, parks, and environmental goods. A variety of different arguments are presented for such ethical limits: Kantian-based arguments that certain beings have a dignity that demands respect should not be treated merely as a means, and hence should not be treated as fungible goods to be bought and sold; common-property arguments that there exist a variety of goods that are common property and should not be privatized; arguments that the nature of social relationships and goods that sustain social relations are constituted by a refusal to treat them as commodities with a price on them; solidarity-based arguments concerning the ways that market relations corrode forms of social solidarity and moral commitment; distributional arguments that the allocation of goods through markets exchange issues in outcomes that are unjust; consequentialist arguments that market exchanges fail as an institutional means to realizing valuable ends such as social welfare; democratic arguments that it is a constitutive condition of democratic political procedures that votes, political office and political influence should not be objects of market-exchange. As will be evident, a number of these arguments have been invoked to advance the claim that certain environmental goods are not the proper objects of market exchange. The following sections examine some of the central arguments between market-endorsing and market-skeptical positions in more detail.

2 EXTENDING MONETARY VALUES— INCOMMENSURABILITY, INEQUALITY, AND REASON

A standard argument within the neoclassical tradition is that the source of environmental problems lies in the absence of markets in environmental goods and their solution in the extension of market prices to include those preferences for environmental goods, either directly through the definition of property rights allowing the goods can be traded in markets or indirectly though the construction of shadow prices. There are three central criticisms of this position.

The first concerns the distributional consequences of willingness-to pay-measures of environmental goods: since the marginal value of a dollar or euro for a poor person is much higher than it is for a richer person, willingness-to pay-measures put a lower value on the preferences of the less wealthy. Hence, the use of willingness-to-pay measures entails that environmental benefits will be valued higher for the rich, and environmental harms lower for the poor. There are various possible responses to this point. It might be argued that this is not a problem as such with the use of market mechanisms to resolve environmental problems, but rather with the prior distribution of assets. Moreover, there are some theoretical ways of modifying willingness-to pay-measures to respond to these distributional consequences, for example by giving differential weight to the preferences of the poorer. However, given existing patterns of inequality, the use of markets and standard unmodified willingness-to pay-measures will result in the less well-off being more adversely affected by policies than the better off. A further set of distributional problems arises from the fact that some parties affected by environmental decision making—future generations and non-human animals— cannot express a willingness to pay. Their interests can be included only to the degree that those who do express a willingness to pay are concerned for them. Again, it might be argued that this is a problem that is general to any form of representation of future generations and non-human beings in current decision making. All forms of representation will be indirect. However, for reasons I shall discuss, there are grounds for thinking that there are features of deliberative institutions, as against market institutions, which entail that the interests of future generations will be better represented in the former than the latter.

A second problem with the attempt to extend willingness-to pay-measures to capture environmental values is that there are social relations and ethical commitments associated with environmental goods that are constituted by a refusal to put a price on them. Social rela- tionships of kinship and friendship, for example, are constituted by a refusal to treat them as commodities that can be bought or sold. Given the nature of love and friendship, one cannot buy either. Similarly ethical value-commitments are also characterized by a refusal to trade. To accept a price in cases like this would be an act of betrayal, and to offer a price would be an act of bribery (Raz, 1986: 345ff; O'Neill, 1993: 118–122). Environmental goods associated with particular places can be expressive of social relations between generations. Care about non- human nature is often not merely instrumental but involves ethical commitments, for exam- ple to the well-being of non-human beings. Given those features of environmental values, it is rational to respond to requests to price the goods by a protest bid that refuses to engage in the act of monetary evaluation.

A third set of objections focuses on the kinds of preferences that are captured by willingness-to-pay measures. The measures capture the private preferences of individuals as consumers rather than their public preferences as a citizen. Sagoff in particular suggests that the conflation of consumer preferences with citizen judgments involves a category mistake (Sagoff 2008). Public judgments about the good of a community are treated as if they were private preferences about personal welfare measured through willingness to pay. As a private consumer I might get great personal benefits from the road that cuts through a rare wetland habitat in virtue of the time it saves me to get to my favorite rock climb. However, as a citizen I may judge that it should not be built. The values that represent what I believe to be good or right for the community should not be conflated with the preferences I have about my consumption opportunities. Central to the distinction being drawn is the claim that citizen judgments answer to reasoned argument in a way that private preferences need not. As such they require deliberative rather than market-mimicking procedures for the resolution of dif- ferences. Whether or not Sagoff's strict separation of citizen judgments and consumer pref- erences can be sustained, the argument does point to two important distinguishing features of market as against deliberative institutional settings (O'Neill, 2007). The first is that market exchanges and expressions of willingness to pay are reason blind. Monetary valuations at best reflect the strength and weakness of the *intensity* with which a person has a preference for some marginal change in a bundle of goods. They do not reflect the strength and weakness of the *reasons* for the preference for the goods in question. Judgments are treated as expressions of taste to be priced and weighed one with the other. They do not have to undergo the test of being able to survive public deliberation. Consequently, markets and market mimicking processes offer conflict resolution and policy formation without rational assessment and debate. Judgments about environmental goods should be expressed and resolved in the forum and not the market. Second, the publicness condition on deliberation, that reasons must be able to survive being made public, ensures that the interests of non-humans and future generations are likely to be better represented than in market or market-mimicking contexts. Forcing participants to offer reasons that can withstand public justification requires participants to appeal to general rather particular private interests. Hence, reasons for action that appeal to wider constituencies of interest—including those of future generations and non-humans—will better survive in public deliberation than in private, market-based methods for expressing preferences (Goodin 1996: 846–847; Jacobs 1997).

3 Using Market Instruments—Effectiveness, Solidarity, and Injustice

The use of market mechanisms to realize environmental ends need not, as such, entail that all values can be caught by a monetary metric. Environmental ends might be defined through scientific and deliberative institutions, without the attempt to extend monetary metrics to capture preferences for environmental goods. However, markets might still be defended as the most efficient and effective means to realize those ends. Cap-and-trade schemes to control pollution and carbon emissions are often defended in this manner. The cap on total emissions is to be set according to best-science and political deliberation. Market trading of emissions rights within the cap ensures that reductions in emissions are made efficiently and effectively. Emissions markets are more efficient than regulation, since they ensure that reductions are made where they are least costly; they are more effective than other possible solutions such as carbon taxes in that a total level of emissions is set in advance (Caney, 2010; Caney and Hepburn, 2011).

3.1 Emissions Markets

Much of the debate on the actual use of markets to achieve environmental ends has focused on their effectiveness. Emissions-trading schemes in practice have proven to be ineffective in slowing the growth of emissions in greenhouse gases. Features of existing schemes such as the practice of grandfathering, allocating the greatest number of permits to emit to those with the largest prior emissions, and the low level of the initial cap are recognized even by proponents of emissions trading to have affected the efficacy of actual existing schemes.

Existing forms of trading can also produce perverse policy incentives. Consider for example markets in carbon offsets, which allow companies that emit to compensate for their emissions by financing projects in areas such as forestation, forest protection, or the replacement of polluting factories in developing countries that are claimed reduce emissions to below levels that would have occurred had the project not been financed. The result can mean that polluting and logging activities become an asset to be maintained for future trade in markets despite existing public-good pressures to eliminate them (Lohmann, 2006). More generally, the fact that the offsetting regimes rely upon counterfactual claims about what would have been emitted without the trade means emissions savings are difficult to verify, thus rendering them open to abuse. In response, proponents of carbon trading tend to argue that these are flaws in market design. Ideal or close to ideal emissions markets, possibly without the addition of offsetting regimes, still remain the most effective and efficient means of achieving reductions (Caney and Hepburn, 2011). The shift of the debate to ideal carbon markets does raise issues about the relationship between such idealizations and actual world markets (Aldred, 2012; Spash, 2010). Moreover, questions of effectiveness can be raised even with respect to ideally designed markets. A particularly important argument is that by encouraging emissions reductions where they are cheapest, emissions trading will not break the current technological lock-in of carbon-dependent sources of energy.

In addition to these arguments about the effectiveness and efficiency of markets in achieving environmental goals, there are also a number of arguments questioning their ethical defensibility (Caney and Hepburn, 2011; Goodin, 1994; Sandel, 2005). One that has been central to both academic and popular objections to emissions trading is that there is a *prima facie* case against controlling wrongful acts by granting parties tradable rights to perform those acts. Neither individuals nor firms should be permitted to buy rights to perform wrongful acts (Goodin, 1994). For example, even if giving gangs tradable rights to extort under some capped total were an efficient way to limit extortion, it would not be an ethically defensible policy. These objections do rely upon a premise that at least some carbon emissions are morally wrongful. Any version of the moral wrongfulness objection must concede that not all emissions are morally culpable. For example, subsistence emissions cannot be avoided and hence cannot be understood as morally culpable. The defender of trading might suggest that it will be difficult to find any particular act of emission that is wrongful, even those that are luxury emissions, since no individual act will be normally in itself harmful. It is the total aggregate level of carbon emission that is harmful, not any particular act. Since the purpose of carbon trading is to bring that aggregate level below that which would cause serious harms, it cannot be ethically objectionable. One response to this argument is that the wrongness involved in luxury emissions should be understood as a form of injustice. It is unjust that the wealthy be able to buy or benefit from rights to emit in a commons at levels that would cause serious harms if all were permitted to act similarly (Goodin, 1994: 585).

Similar concerns underlie arguments that appeal to considerations of solidarity. Internationally it might be argued that emission trading allows wealthy nations to buy their way out of contributing to the solution of common problem for which historically they bear greatest responsibility (Sandel, 2005: 95–96). Domestically, the argument might run that emission trading permits the wealthy to continue a life style without contributing to the solution of the problems to which they contribute. It is inconsistent with equality of standing that the rich be exempted from a common effort to cut emissions. If each person is to play his or her part, the rich may not buy their way out of common duties. Social solidarity requires that citizens' emission rights in greenhouse gases should be rationed, as in wartime, and firms regulated directly. One response to the argument here might be to deny the assumption that equality of standing requires that each person directly does his or her part (Caney, 2010: 207ff.) The argument raises large issues about what individuals and societies owe each other when faced with a common problem. However, it has particular significance where the wealthy contribute most to that problem and are least vulnerable to its consequences. In such circumstances, demands of justice and solidarity become particularly evident.

3.2 Biodiversity Markets

The use of cap-and-trade markets as an efficient means to realize independently defined environmental ends is not confined to emissions trading. Their use has been proposed in markets employing biodiversity offsets. Landowners who create, restore, or enhance some site of biodiversity are assigned credits, which can be sold to developers to offset losses to biodiversity caused by a development. The result of the market transactions is an efficient allocation of resources for development while ensuring that there is no net loss of biodiversity.

The extension of cap-and-trade markets to biodiversity raises particular problems over and above those associated with emissions trading. In particular it makes contentious assumptions about the value of biodiversity. It assumes that sites of biodiversity are to be valued in terms of the "ecosystem services" they provide. The creation of biodiversity at one site can offset losses in another if they provide the same services, be this in terms of life support, resource provision, waste assimilation, or cultural amenities. A feature of this understanding of biodiversity is that what is valued is not the specific object or site, but rather the services they provide: "Material objects are merely the vehicles which carry some of these services, and they are exchanged because of consumer preferences for the services associated with their use or because they can help to add value in the manufacturing process" (Ayres and Kneese, 1969: 284).

Understanding the value of biodiversity in terms of service provision assumes a particular understanding of the nature of that value. A useful way of understanding the assumptions being made is in terms of the distinction between *de re* and *de dicto* valuation. Hare illustrates the distinction through joke about Zsa Zsa Gabor, who is said to have found a way of doing good, through keeping her husband young and healthy almost forever; she gets a new one every five years (Hare, 2007: 514). The joke plays upon an ambiguity about what it is for Zsa Zsa Gabor to value the health and youth of her husband. We assume a *de re* understanding—that there is a particular person, her husband, and that she values his health and youth. The joke turns on the fact that she in fact merely values the health and youth of her husband *de dicto*, that is, whoever fits the description of being her husband is young and healthy. If a site of biodiversity is valued merely as "a vehicle" to provide services then it is valued *de dicto*. Hence, one site of biodiversity, like a husband of Zsa Zsa Gabor, can be replaced by another if it provides the same services. A *de dicto* understanding of the value placed of many ordinary fungible commodities is reasonable: I don't value any particular apple (except on special occasions, say as a present from my daughter) but just that there is an apple with particular gustatory properties. Similarly I don't disvalue any particular molecule of CO_2 that contributes to climate change. Other objects demand a *de re* valuation— for example, persons. There are good grounds for placing at least some sites of biodiversity within the class of objects for which a *de re* valuation is appropriate. They are valued as places or biological systems that are valued as particulars that embody specific histories. To the extent that this is the case, then there are good reasons for holding that, whatever the defensibility of cap-and-trade markets to control pollution and carbon emissions, they are not appropriate in the sphere of biodiversity protection. Different sites are not substitutable with each other in the way required for this policy (O'Neill, 2014).

4 MARKETS, KNOWLEDGE, AND CLIMATE CHANGE

A distinct set of arguments for a market-based response to environmental problems is to be found within the Austrian tradition of economics. Sagoff's criticisms of the attempt to extend monetary prices to include unpriced environmental goods have been combined with an endorsement of a Hayekian epistemic defense of markets and criticisms of state planning. Hayek's arguments depend upon a distinction between two kinds of knowledge: (1) scientific knowledge held by experts, which consists of propositional statements of general rules, and (2) the specific knowledge held by particular individuals, which is local to a time and place and is often practical knowledge that cannot be stated in propositional form. Central planning is claimed to be based on a form of scientism that identifies knowledge with scientific knowledge and fails to recognize the local and practical knowledge dispersed across different agents in society. Much dispersed knowledge cannot be articulated in the form of general propositional statements that could be passed on to a centralized planning agency. In contrast, through the price system, the market communicates that information that allows different individuals to coordinate their particular plans and actions. On this view, Sagoff argues, the neoclassical project of placing shadow prices on environmental goods to measure welfare gains and losses associated with different projects is founded upon a mistake. Actual prices are not measures of welfare, but coordinating devices (Sagoff, 2008: 80–81). The attempt by the state to mimic markets through shadow-pricing and cost-benefit analysis is founded upon an error. Public deliberation should aim not at expert measurements of welfare, but rather the articulation of the public values that shape general laws. The solution to environmental problems lies in the definition of property rights over relevant environmental and non-environmental goods within a framework of general rules of law that will allow the market itself to coordinate the actions and plans of different individuals. A market free of the distortions of public subsidies will deliver technological solutions to resource limits and provide the best arrangement for the protection of environmental goods.

This Austrian argument for market environmentalism is distinct from the more prominent neoclassical approach that dominates most public policy. However, it faces a number of difficulties (Gamble, 2006; O'Neill, 2012). There is an internal difficulty to the Hayekian argument that is of particular significance. Hayek's argument is founded on a criticism of scientism, not of science. He recognizes that science is an important form of knowledge that matters to policymaking, particularly in the environmental sphere (Hayek, 1960: 371). The role of expert knowledge associated with climate change offers a more recent example. The observation sets up a potential conflict between the use of scientific and local knowledge, and the problem of how to call upon both. Hayek's solution is to suggest that the generic knowledge of science be dispersed among relevant actors so as to allow them to use their local knowledge (Hayek, 1960: 371). However, the dispersal of generic knowledge has the same difficulties Hayek raised against the centralization of special knowledge. If, as Hayek claims, the knowledge of scientists itself has a tacit dimension that cannot be completely articulated in propositional form, then there is more reason to assume that it can be dispersed downward to all relevant actors than specific knowledge can be centralized upward to planners. The problem of bringing different kinds of knowledge to bear on decisions is ubiquitous. While the epistemic problems Hayek raises are important, his market solution is open to the same epistemic limits he raises against centralized planning.

5 Market Economies and the Environmental Limits to Growth

A central area of dispute between market-endorsing and market-skeptical positions has been over the relationship between markets, economic growth, and environmental limits. It is possible to distinguish a number of different positions. One, found among technological optimists in the market-endorsing position, is that markets will deliver economic growth, and economic growth itself is a condition of environmental sustainability. By driving technological changes that ensure declining energy and resource intensity in the production of goods and bringing material wealth, which fosters "post-materialist" values which endorse environmental protection, market driven economic growth is best able to deliver long-term sustainable outcomes. Among skeptics of the assumption that continuing economic growth is consistent with respect for environmental limits, one can distinguish between those who claim that there is no conflict in principle between a market economy and a steady state economy and those who are more skeptical of the possibility of a market economy delivering such an outcome. Both argue that continuous economic growth is neither possible nor desirable. In a globally just world it is not possible. There are limits in the waste assimilation capacities of the atmosphere, in particular with respect to greenhouse gases; in energy production; and in the use of critical resources, including water and top soils, which are such that the levels of consumption that exist now in "advanced economies" could not be generalized globally. Nor are there reasons to believe that technological innovation can overcome all such limits. In particular, falling relative energy and resource intensity is and has been consistent with increasing absolute total energy and resource use in an unregulated market economy. Part of the reason for this concerns rebound effects, discussion of which can be traced back to Jevons' paradox (Jevons, 1866; Jackson, 2009). In a market economy, falling relative resource and energy intensity *ceteris paribus* leads to a relative cheapening of the goods, which will either increase or displace demand and hence potentially negate the claimed resource and energy savings.

At the same time neither is continuous growth desirable. There are, as Hirsch notes, social as well as environmental limits to growth. Insofar as the goods that people pursue are positional goods—goods such as status goods whose worth to a consumer is dependent on the consumption of the same goods by others—then in a market economy each individual's consumption of that good will not issue in the promised improvement in well-being, since collective consumption of that good will mean that no one will be better off (Hirsch, 1977: 26).

The classical view shared by both hedonic and objective state accounts of well being that there are limits to the goods required for a good life, has been the subject of renewed empirical defense (Easterlin, 1974; Steinberger and Roberts, 2010). These arguments against growth are not arguments against technological or cultural innovation but against the possibility or desirability of an economy requiring increasing consumption of material and energy.

Critics of growth agree on the existence of social and environmental limits on continuing increasing consumption. Where disagreement lies is in what the drivers of growth are. Those who defend the compatibility of a capitalist market economy and the respect for environmental limits often take the source of the problem to be one of the cultural values embodied in consumerism, which involve a mistake about the sources of human well-being. Correspondingly, a change in values will render a market economy consistent with the recognition of limits. While the truth of this claim is an empirical matter, arguments for this position are sometimes guilty of what might be called the ethicist's fallacy—the confusion of appraisal and explanation: that a state of affairs is appraised as deficient according to some set of values does not entail that the way to rectify that deficiency is a shift in values. Those more skeptical of the possibility of a capitalist market economy delivering sustainability argue that there are systemic features of a market economy that drive growth. The Aristotelian claim that the pursuit of wealth without limits is characteristic of the commercial world (Aristotle, 1948: book 1, ch.8) is one that is developed in the work of Marx in his account of the absence of limits in the processes of capital accumulation (Marx, 1970: ch.4) and in Polanyi in his account of the ways in which the market economy is disembedded from social and moral constraints (Polanyi, 1957: 53–55). The truth of these different perspectives is in the end a matter of empirical investigation. They will properly remain at the center of the continuing debates in political economy and political ecology about the economic preconditions of an environmentally sustainable economy.

REFERENCES

Aldred, J. (2012). "The Ethics of Emissions Trading." *New Political Economy* 17 (3): 339–360.

Anderson, E. (1993). *Value in Ethics and Economics.* Cambridge MA: Harvard University Press.

Aristotle (1948) *Politics*, E. Barker trans. Oxford: Clarendon Press.

Arrow, K. (1984). "Limited Knowledge and Economic Analysis." In *The Economics of Information.* Cambridge MA: Harvard University Press.

Ayres, R. U., and Kneese, A. V. (1969). "Production, Consumption, and Externalities." *The American Economic Review* 59: 282–297.

Caney, S. (2010). "Markets, Morality and Climate Change: What, If Anything, Is Wrong with Emissions Trading?" *New Political Economy* 15: 197–224.

Caney, S. and Hepburn, C. (2011). "Carbon Trading: Unethical, Unjust and Ineffective?" *Philosophy and the Environment Royal Institute of Philosophy,* Supplementary Volume 69.

Easterlin, Richard. (1974). "Does Economic Growth Improve the Human Lot? Some Empirical Evidence." In *Nations and Households in Economic Growth: Essays in Honor of Moses Abramovitz*, edited by P. A. David and M. W. Reder. New York: Academic Press.

Gamble, A. (2006). "Hayek on Knowledge, Economics and Society." In *The Cambridge Companion to Hayek*, edited by E. Feser, 111–131. Cambridge, England: Cambridge University Press.

Goodin, R. (1994). "Selling Environmental Indulgences." *Kyklos* 47(4): 573–596.

Goodin, R. (1996). "Enfranchising the Earth, and Its Alternatives." *Political Studies* 44: 835–849.

Hare, C. (2007). "Voices from Another World: Must We Respect the Interests of People Who Do Not, and Will Never, Exist?" *Ethics* 117: 498–523.

Hayek, F. A. (1960). *The Constitution of Liberty.* London: Routledge and Kegan Paul.

Hirsch, F. (1977). *Social Limits to Growth.* London: Routledge and Kegan Paul.

Jackson, T. (2009). *Prosperity without Growth.* London: Earthscan.

Jacobs M. (1997). "Environmental Valuations, Deliberative Democracy and Public Decision-Making Institutions." In *Valuing Nature?* edited by J. Foster. London: Routledge.

Jevons, W. (1866). *The Coal Question,* 2nd ed. London: Macmillan and Co.

Kapp, K. (1974). *Environmental Policies and Development Planning in Contemporary China and Other Essays.* Paris: Mouton.

Lohmann, L. (2006). "Carbon Trading." *Development Dialogue* 48 http://www.thecorner-house.org.uk/sites/thecornerhouse.org.uk/files/carbonDDlow.pdf.

Polanyi, K. (1957). *The Great Transformation.* Boston: Beacon Press.

Marx, K. (1970). *Capital I.* London: Lawrence and Wishart.

Martinez-Alier, J. Munda, G., and O'Neill, J. (1998). "Weak Comparability of Values as a Foundation for Ecological Economics." *Ecological Economics* 26: 277–286.

Neurath, O. (1920). "Ein System der Sozialisierung." *Archiv für Sozialwissenschaft und Sozialpolitik* 48: 44–73. Translated by R. S. Cohen and Th. Uebel as "A System of Socialisation." In *Economic Writings. Selections 1904–1945,* edited by Th. Uebel R. S. Cohen, 345–370. Dordrecht: Kluwer, 2004.

O'Neill, J. (1993). *Ecology, Policy and Politics: Human Well-Being and the Natural World.* London: Routledge.

O'Neill, J. (2004). "Ecological Economics and the Politics of Knowledge: the Debate between Hayek and Neurath." *Cambridge Journal of Economics* 28: 431–447.

O'Neill, J. (2007). *Markets, Deliberation and Environment.* London: Routledge.

O'Neill, J. (2012). "Austrian Economics and the Limits of Markets." *Cambridge Journal of Economics* 36: 1073–1090.

O'Neill, J. (2014). "Sustainability." In *Handbook of Global Ethics,* edited by D. Moellendorf and H. Widdows. Durham: Acumen Press.

Raz, J. (1986). *The Morality of Freedom.* Oxford: Clarendon.

Sandel, M. (2005). "Should We Buy the Right to Pollute?" In *Public Philosophy: Essays on Morality in Politics.* Cambridge, MA: Harvard University Press.

Sandel, M. (2013). *What Money Can't Buy: The Moral Limits of Markets.* London: Penguin.

Sagoff, M. (2008). *The Economy of the Earth,* 2nd ed. Cambridge, England: Cambridge University Press.

Satz, D. (2010). *Why Some Things Should Not Be for Sale.* Oxford: Oxford University Press.

Spash, C. (2010). "The Brave New World of Carbon Trading." *New Political Economy* 15(2): 169–195.

Steinberger, J. and Roberts, J. (2010). "From Constraint to Sufficiency: The Decoupling of Energy and Carbon from Human Needs, 1975–2005." *Ecological Economics* 70: 425–433.

Walzer, M. (1983). *Spheres of Justice.* Oxford: Blackwell.

CHAPTER 5

....

LAW, GOVERNANCE, AND THE ECOLOGICAL ETHOS

....

DANIEL BUTT

1 INTRODUCTION

....

THE last 50 or so years have witnessed rapid developments in the ability and the willingness of the state to regulate the environmental impact of those who operate within its boundaries, with some clear successes, as well as notable failures. Environmental law is, of course, not a new phenomenon, and the period of time since the Industrial Revolution, in particular, has witnessed various attempts by political communities to control the harmful side-effects of human activity, such as attempts to improve air quality in Britain by measures such as the 1848 Public Health Act on industrial emissions, and the more wide-ranging 1956 Clean Air Act that followed London's Great Smog of 1952 (Ashby and Anderson, 1981). It is common-place, however, to look to the late 1960s, and developments such as the passage of the US National Environmental Policy Act in 1969, which placed a responsibility on federal agencies to prepare environmental impact statements before undertaking actions with significant environmental effects, and the 1970 creation of the US Environmental Protection Agency, for the beginnings of modern day environmental law. Many see the subsequent creation of state-controlled regulatory regimes as a significant progressive accomplishment. Sheila Jasanoff claims that the codification of environmental law "can justly be seen as an achievement of humankind's enhanced capacity to reflect upon its place in nature", writing that, "With this body of legislation, the governments of virtually all the nations of the earth announced their intention to safeguard the environment through systematic regulatory action, and to subordinate the desires and appetites of their citizens to the needs of other species and biological systems on the planet" (Jasanoff 2001: 331). Of course, as scientific understanding has advanced, so has our appreciation of the way in which environmental impacts do not respect state boundaries, and the same period has also seen the development of an extensive and complicated body of international law through a raft of treaties and agreements between states, and as a result of the actions of a complex web of international institutions, including the United Nations and its various agencies and programs. This, again, is often viewed positively. Birnie, Boyle, and Redgwell note that the law that has emerged from this process, while not without weaknesses, is "neither primitive nor unsystematic" (2009: 1) and has provided a "framework for cooperation between developed and developing states, for measures aimed at equitable and sustainable use of natural resources, for the resolution of international environmental disputes, for the promotion of greater transparency and public participation in national decision making, and for the adoption and harmonization of a great deal of national environmental law" (2009: 2).

The development of environmental law, then, has not come about without effort or cost, and one can point to any number of examples where it has had a clear impact in relation to air and water pollution, the protection of wildlife and ecologically significant areas, the depletion of resources, and the regulation of genetically modified organisms, as well as many other policy areas. Consideration of environmental concerns has become institutionalized in many policymaking contexts, and requirements have been placed on a wide range of public and private bodies in terms of environmental reporting and audit (Weale et al., 2002: 1). However, it is equally clear that we live in a world where, these legal developments notwithstanding, grave environmental problems persist. Perhaps most significantly, the nascent environmental law regime has proved largely inadequate as a way of responding to the existential threat posed by human-induced climate change. So there is at least a perspective whereby instead of seeing environmental law as a still-developing force for good, which has made significant progress in relation to the prevention of harm and the inequitable distribution of environmental "bads," it can alternatively be viewed as having failed its most important test and as being fundamentally unfit for the purpose of furthering the cause of environmental justice: in the words of Mary Christina Wood, "modern environmental law has proved a colossal failure" (2009: 43). The point of this chapter is not to insist that the world's failure to react appropriately to climate change is the "fault" of environmental law; as Birnie et al. argue in an international context, "to say that economic or political models have as much or more to contribute than international law is merely to observe that protecting the environment is not exclusively a problem for lawyers" (2009: 1). Instead, this chapter argues that environmental law and governance face particular challenges that do not apply to other forms of legislation and regulation. This means that the relationship between environmental legislation and environmental justice is complicated, and importantly different from the case of, for example, the relation between distributive justice and state regulation of the ownership of property, or between corrective justice and the system of criminal law. The particular character of environmental justice and the failings of contemporary domestic and international environmental law regimes in relation, in particular, to anthropogenic climate change both require and legitimate different forms of action on the part of law-making institutions. Environmental justice is unlikely to be adequately realized through either command-and-control or market-based legal mechanisms, but instead, it is argued, requires a model of environmental governance more broad than law where citizens share in a widespread "ecological ethos," whereby they are willing to forego from acting on the basis of apparent short-term self-interest when such actions cause or risk environmental damage, either in isolation or when considered together with the actions of others.

2 ENVIRONMENTAL LAW AND THE STATE

For the purposes of this chapter, I will define a context as being environmentally just when (a) there is an appropriate degree of protection for the environment, and (b) where environmental burdens and benefits are distributed fairly, both within and across state boundaries and within and between different generational cohorts. Such a definition does not simply require that the costs of environmental bads be allocated in a just manner (Caney, 2005), it also requires that the production of environmental bads is itself limited to those which are deemed acceptable by one's background account of sustainable development (Hopwood, Mellor, and O'Brien 2005; see also Bryan Norton's contribution to this volume). To what extent can and should the state employ the law to pursue the end of environmental justice? Insofar as environmental law involves using the coercive power of the state to affect individual and group behavior, it is, of course, controversial from an ethical point of view. Political theorists have long debated the rights and wrongs of intervention by the state in the life of its citizens. Disagreement as to both the justification and the legitimacy of state action leads to a range of models of the scope and character of the good polity (Simmons, 1999). Thus, while some see the state as a moral agent which is justified in acting to promote ethical ends in a wide range of circumstances, others argue for a limited conception of legitimate government and maintain that the state exceeds its bounds when it steps beyond the minimal functions of a night watchman (see Goodin, 1989; Nozick, 1974, respectively). Consequently, different models of the state license different forms and degrees of state regulation.

In his book *Regulation: Legal Form and Economic Theory*, Anthony Ogus argues that there is a tension in all industrialized societies between two forms of economic organization. The first is the market system, under which individuals are largely left free to pursue their own goals, subject only to basic constraints. The legal system, he writes, "underpins these arrangements but predominantly through instruments of private law; regulation . . . has no significant role" (2004: 1) The relevant distinction between private law and regulation here is that the former is concerned with relations between particular private parties, whereas the latter additionally involves the state. The law in a market system has a "primarily facilitative function": it provides a legal framework that agents can use to manage their interactions with one another, though they have the option of agreeing to interact in different ways outside of this state-provided structure (2004: 2). The state has a role in upholding individual rights through systems of constitutional and criminal law, but social utility is seen as being furthered by voluntary contractual agreements between different parties. One obvious problem with such an approach, however, concerns externalities: the effects of such agreements on individuals or groups who are not parties to the contract. Effects on the environment are among the most important such externalities, and they are hard to address within private law. Although there are a range of possible mechanisms which can be employed, by means of contract law, property rights, and tort law, for example, these are of debatable efficacy and come with significant transaction costs (2004: 24, 204). Nonetheless, some environmental legislation has operated squarely within this paradigm as some institutions have sought to develop market-based mechanisms for protecting the environment. The development of emission quotas, for example, whereby the state sets a cap on the permissible emission of a pollutant, issues permits enabling firms to emit certain amounts of the pollutant up to this limit, and then allows a market in such permits falls within this category. (See Chichilnisky, Heal, and Starrett, 2013 on the economics; Singer, 2010; Caney, 2010 on the ethics of emission quotas; Stavins 2000 on market-based environmental policies more generally.)

By contrast, in a more collectivist system, the state plays a different, more active role: intervening to correct market deficiencies to promote the common good. This opens the door to a more extensive model of "command and control" regulation, whereby the state uses coercive force to set up penalties, backed up by civil or criminal law, which are triggered if individuals are caught breaking the rules or acting in ways that cause particular kinds of harm. This has been the dominant form of environmental legislation and has been widely employed even by states that have generally shied away from collectivist intervention and instead adopted a laissez-faire approach to the workings of markets. Hutter, for example, notes that command-and-control regulation has generally expanded even in political contexts where other aspects of state activity have been cut back and deregulated, not least on account of pressure from the environmental movement (Hutter 1999: 5). Although the command-and-control model of environmental regulation has undoubtedly had many real successes, particularly in relation to the "first wave" of environmental legislation of the 1970s and 1980s (Vandenbergh, 2001: 193), it is clear that models of environmental governance that focus solely or primarily on the coercive force of state regulation face serious limitations. Early environmental legislation sought to prevent certain forms of environmental harm, particularly in relation to pollution. In a world where the main effects of pollution were thought to be local in character and where the primacy of state sovereignty was less contested, it is not hard to see how one might be optimistic as to the potential for using the power of the state to minimize or eliminate threats to the environment. Things today are not so simple.

Contemporary states are limited in the extent to which they are able to use regulation in order to pursue the ends of environmental justice even in domestic contexts. Increased understanding of the nature of anthropogenic effects on the environment means that it is now clear that environmental justice cannot be achieved simply by preventing or reducing particularly egregious instances of pollution: instead, much more extensive change is necessary. The idea of sustainable development plays a key role in much contemporary environmental thinking. This means that choices that agents make in their daily activity are significant for the pursuit of environmental justice: on some accounts, at least, certain kinds of environmental bads can only be avoided if large numbers of individuals, groups, and companies make far-reaching changes to their ways of life. The state can legislate to encourage such choices, using its powers of taxation to incentivize and disincentivize particular choices, by increasing taxes on gasoline or creating tax breaks for corporations that use sustainable energy, for example, and penalizing those who either cause or risk certain types of harm, but its powers effectively to police behavior are limited by both the possibility and desirability of microscopic state-led scrutiny of how individuals live their lives. In many contexts, both small and large scale, there are myriad ways in which agents can flout their environmental obligations in a fashion that makes it very unlikely that anyone will ever know what they have done and be able to call them into account. Some have even disputed whether it is harmful, and so wrong, for an individual to act in an environmentally unfriendly way in many aspects of her day-to-day life, given the near certainty that her own individual contribution to, for example, anthropogenic climate change is likely to be either minute or nonexistent (Sinnott-Armstrong, 2005).

The international context complicates things further, since the powers of international legal institutions are more limited than those that states wield over their own subjects. The weakness of international legal mechanisms has been vividly illustrated by the world's collective failure properly to address climate change, as evidenced for example by the lack of effective mechanisms to ensure compliance with the 2002 Kyoto Treaty. The current state of international law, resting primarily on a patchwork of multilateral treaty agreements, means that states can flout their self-imposed obligations with relative ease, incurring penalties that consist of more demanding future targets, which will be open for negotiation at the end of the current commitment period (Gardiner, 2010: 20). It would be wrong to suggest that there is no compliance with international law or that there is nothing to be done to encourage states to comply with their self-made obligations, but it is safe to say, at least, that comparative study reveals uneven and patchy compliance in a range of different cases (Weiss and Jacobson, 2000).

It should also be noted that environmental law tends to be strongly anthropocentric in character: it is generally phrased in terms of and justified by explicit reference to human interests, with other interests and values typically seen through the prism of their instrumental utility to humans (Emmenegger and Tschentscher, 1994). Though some have put forward arguments for the extension of legal rights to natural objects, we are far from a situation where there is widespread acceptance of the justifiability or plausibility of non-human legal rights-bearers (Stone, 1974; Grear, 2012). As Birnie et al. note in an international context: "Nature, ecosystems, natural resources, wildlife, and so on, are . . . of concern to international lawmakers primarily for their value to humanity" (2009: 7). This need not, they note, be understood in narrow economic terms, since reference can also be made to aesthetic, amenity, and cultural value, but the dominant perspective is nonetheless one that reflects the 1992 Rio Declaration's statement that "Human beings are at the centre of concerns for sustainable development," particularly insofar as international environmental claims are expressed in terms of the language of human rights (UNCED, 1992).

Existing legal provision is also seriously limited in relation to intergenerational justice. Ideas of duties to future generations do admittedly find legal expression, and it is not unusual to see constitutional documents, statutes, and international agreements that make explicit reference to duties to posterity. The first Principle of the 1972 Stockholm Declaration states that man "bears a solemn responsibility to protect and improve the environment for present and future generations" (UNCHE, 1972) and, as Philippe Sands notes, recent international treaties have sought to preserve particular natural resources and other environmental assets for the benefit of future generations with reference to, inter alia, wild flora and fauna, the marine environment, essential renewable natural resources, water resources, and biological diversity (Sands, 2009: 85). It is one thing for there to be theoretical legal protection for the interests of future peoples, however, but quite another for these interests properly to be respected, despite the promise of recent work on the incorporation of the public trust doctrine, which stresses the common ownership of many natural resources, into environmental law (Wood, 2009a, 2009b). There are certainly moves in some judicial contexts to use the law to uphold the rights of future generations, as famously happened, for example, in the 1993 Supreme Court of the Philippines ruling in *Oposa v. Factorian*, which sought to cancel timber license agreements in order to preserve the country's virgin rainforest for future generations, explicitly accepting the legitimacy of actions being filed on behalf of people who do not yet exist. However, as the travails of different administrations in relation to climate change have revealed, successful interventions of this kind are relatively rare. The well-known limits of judicial policymaking mean that courts are unlikely to be able to have far-reaching effects in such cases without the active support of other political institutions (Butt, 2006). Weston and Bach note that "Clear-cutting of tropical forests continued unabated in the Philippines after *Oposa* despite the clear enunciation of intergenerational principles on paper," before concluding that although courts can play a role in the promulgation and clarification of legal principles in relation to future generations, "of the legal tools available to those seeking intergenerational justice in climate change, litigation is a very resource-intensive strategy generally of limited impact" (2009: 36). Perhaps the most important point to be made here concerns the difficulties that political actors face in seeking to further long-term goals, and, in particular, in safeguarding the interests of future persons in a way that requires sacrifices from those living in the present, particularly in contexts of risk and uncertainty. This is evidently a general problem faced when contemporary polities try to plan for their long-term future, such as determining future pension provision. All political institutions in democracies must work within the confines of public opinion, and there is good evidence to say that this is as true for supposed independent institutions such as judiciaries as for elected representatives. If mechanisms such as the constitutional protection of the interests of future persons are to be successful, they must operate within a political context where publics are sympathetic and willing to make sacrifices for the sake of those who come after them. The question that now needs to be addressed is what the state can and should do to develop and further such an attitude among its citizenry.

3 ENVIRONMENTAL GOVERNANCE AND THE ECOLOGICAL ETHOS

Although command-and-control and market based approaches to environmental protection may seem very different, they have something in common. Both models are compatible with a general outlook that places the primary responsibility for caring for the environment with the state. Both assume that firms and individuals will act in a self-interested fashion within the terms of the law in question. The aim of the law in each case, therefore, is to organize incentives and disincentives in such a fashion so that environmentally good outcomes will result from self-interested actors seeking to further their own good but playing by the rules. Of course, it will be an important question in each case whether the rules are, in fact, being followed, or whether agents are managing to get away with furthering their own good by acting in an illegal fashion. The model, however, is nonetheless one where environmental protection is thought to come about by using the power of the state to align self-interest with environmental good. Whether environmental law works by disincentivizing actions that cause environmental bads or by incentivizing actions with positive effects, and whether one assumes the existence of a global economic system dominated by growth capitalism or advocates some kind of state-led redistribution or restructuring, the picture is one whereby desired outcomes can come about as a result of the self-interested actions of agents who seek to maximize their own advantage within the law.

Is this kind of state-centered approach sufficient to bring about environmental justice? It is instructive here to look at relevantly similar debates as to the relation between state regulation and the pursuit of justice in the more deeply theorized field of distributive justice. Consider, for example, the highly influential work of John Rawls on the topic. Rawls famously developed an account of distributive justice that afforded individuals the same set of basic liberties, respected a far-reaching principle of equality of opportunity, and only permitted distributive inequalities between individuals when such inequalities were necessary to improve the position of the worst-off members of society—the "difference principle"

(Rawls, 1999). But Rawls's principles of justice only applied to what he called the "basic structure" of society: those social and political institutions which assign basic rights and duties and significantly affect individuals' lives by regulating the division of advantages that arise from social cooperation over time (Rawls, 2001: 10). Individuals have duties to obey the law and to uphold just institutions, but so long as they keep to the terms of the law, they are free to pursue their own self-interest. This feature of Rawls's theory is often misunderstood as representing a claim that individuals are inherently self-interested. This is quite wrong: the point, rather, is that there is a functional division of labor within Rawls's theory (Freeman, 2007: 100–1). The state takes care of justice: individuals can get on with living their own lives safe in the knowledge that their justice-based obligations are being fulfilled by the state. Suppose, then, that we envisage a society characterized by full compliance with Rawls's principles of justice, where the law regulated society in such a way that inequalities were only permitted when they maximized the position of the least advantaged. Would such a society be perfectly just? This is contested. G. A. Cohen draws upon the feminist claim that "the personal is political" to maintain that principles of distributive justice apply not only to the basic structure itself, but also to the choices that people make within the legally coercive rules and institutions of the basic structure (Cohen, 2000: 122). The idea here is that a society that demonstrated what Cohen terms an "egalitarian ethos," defined as a "structure of response lodged in the motivations that inform everyday life" (Cohen, 2000: 128), whereby individuals did not need the incentives provided by the difference principle in order to act in a way that improved the position of the least advantaged, would be more just than a society where inequalities had to be introduced in order to achieve the same goal. Thus, "an ethos which informs choice within just rules is necessary in a society committed to the difference principle" (Cohen, 2000: 132). Cohen's point here is not the anarchist one that we should do without the state: his egalitarian ethos functions within a context that features a substantial degree of state action to set up and regulate the basic structure of society. So the idea is not that we do not need just laws in order to achieve a just society, but that—in Rawls's model, at least—just laws are not sufficient.

This idea of a motivating ethos has obvious application in relation to environmental protection in the contemporary world. It now seems clear that state-led enforcement mechanisms will be insufficient to stave off grave environmental harms in the near and medium future. If the environment is to be protected to at least a minimally decent level, then agents must do more than seek to pursue their self-interest within a context of rules and regulations that constrain or incentivize their behavior toward environmental goods. Instead, the pursuit of environmental justice requires that an *ecological ethos* is widely shared, both domestically and internationally. Such an ecological ethos requires that groups and individuals are motivated in their day-to-day lives to act with non-self-interested concern for the environment, and so generally refrain from acting on the basis of apparent short-term self-interest when such actions either cause or risk damage to the environment, either in isolation or when considered together with the actions of others. The precise content of the ecological ethos will differ depending on the detail of one's favored model of environmental justice and sustainable development, incorporating a particular attitude to risk and the precautionary principle. It may be specifically anthropocentric in its scope, or it may stipulate a wider concern for the natural world above and beyond the interests of human beings. The key point for current purposes is that the ecological ethos goes beyond positive law: it requires that individuals act with an appropriate degree of respect and care for the environment in cases where the law is silent, and in cases where they could break the law without risk of detection. The claim here need not be that such an ethos is a necessary aspect of any environmentally just society: perhaps in different contexts, state-led enforcement mechanisms could be sufficient to ensure environmental justice. Alternatively, in other situations such enforcement may be unnecessary for the pursuit of environmental justice: the ecological ethos could motivate people to do all that was necessary without the need for any coercion at all. The scale of climate change, however, makes both positions untenable in the here and now. Precisely how the laws of the state and the ethos interact and reflect one another will be a contingent question for particular societies, but both are needed in today's world if environmental justice is to be realized.

Acknowledging the importance of such an ecological ethos helps clarify the role of the state in relation to environmental policy. The state is not able directly to legislate its way to environmental justice: it is dependent on the non-coerced cooperation of a wide range of non-state actors, ranging from individuals to non-governmental organizations, from corporations to social protest movements. The role of such actors is stressed in accounts of environmental governance: an approach which, as James Evans writes, "provides a third way between the two poles of market and state, incorporating both into a broader process of steering in order to achieve common goals" (Evans, 2009: 4; see also Jasanoff and Martello, 2004: 3) Environmental governance emphasizes both the delegation of aspects of governing to non-state actors and efforts to increase popular participation in governmental processes. This involves the state fulfilling a different role than in command-and-control contexts, whereby it does not direct but rather facilitates decision making by others. The involvement of non-state actors is not automatically good news for the environment, of course: as in the case of command-and-control regulation, governance processes can be captured by private interests and face serious challenges in their attempts to develop progressive environmental policy. Thus, for example, writers disagree as to how public participation best feeds into environmental governance. Pieter Galsbergen differentiates between "participatory" and "rejectionist" approaches, which differ as to whether the approaches view the state in broadly positive or negative terms. The participatory approach emphasizes the legitimizing effects of popular participation and draws on accounts of deliberative democracy to suggest that the practical effects of sharing in democratic governance will have beneficial effects on participants by educating them in the details of environmental policy, for example, and encouraging them to think in terms of public rather than individual good. The rejectionist approach instead sees existing state structures as having been largely captured by private interests that oppose ecological change, and it views participation "as an opportunity to correct the bias of the state and its agencies" (Glasbergen, 1998: 8). Environmental governance is not an ecological panacea, but its focus on multi-level decision-making and subsidiarity does potentially allow for interesting institutional innovations, such as the introduction of ombudsmen to look after the interests of parties who lack meaningful representation within the present day, such as future generations, as has recently happened in Hungary (Jávor, 2006).

There is scope, then, for a governance approach that looks more broadly at the making of environmental policy, and stresses the desirability of participation by a wide range of non-state actors and by the public as a whole, to rectify at least some of the limitations of state-led environmental law, while encouraging popular participation in a way that can encourage the development of an ecological ethos among the citizenry. A focus on the ecological ethos also permits a particular, interventionist role for the state in the promotion of environmental education in schooling and in public health campaigns. For some, this will obviously set alarm bells ringing, both as a result of the deeply contentious character of much contemporary debate over the environment, particularly in relation to climate change, and as a consequence of widely shared beliefs that it is inappropriate for the state to use its privileged position to promote particular doctrinaire accounts of the good. Such concerns have force, of course, but it should be noted that state interventions in relation to environmental education are already commonplace in many countries. If we conceive of the furthering of the ecological ethos as a necessary component of the pursuit of justice, it is more straightforward that the state has an obligation to seek to encourage a respect for the environment in its citizens, in the same way that it is entitled to promote respect for the rule of law and the prevention of harm to others; or to promote the civic virtue of its citizens and thus encourage democratic participation; or to go beyond the promulgation of anti-discriminatory law and actively encourage respect for cultural, racial, and sexual diversity. Given the scale of the threat posed by human-induced climate change, it is not tenable for modern day states to adopt an air of neutrality in relation to the desirability of the inculcation of an environmentally-friendly disposition within its citizenry. Duties to future generations, to some of the world's poorest people, to fellow citizens, to humanity broadly perceived, and, arguably, to the natural world as a whole require law and policymaking bodies of all sorts to do all they can to encourage the pursuit of environmental justice.

REFERENCES

Ashby, E., and Anderson, M. (1981). *The Politics of Clean Air*. Oxford: Clarendon.

Birnie, P., Boyle, A., and Redgwell, C. (2009). *International Law and the Environment*. Oxford: Oxford University Press.

Butt, D. (2006). *Democracy, the Courts and the Making of Public Policy*. Oxford: Foundation for Law, Justice and Society.

Caney, S. (2005). "Cosmopolitan Justice, Responsibility and Global Climate Change." *Leiden Journal of International Law* 18: 747–775.

Caney, S. (2010). "Markets, Morality and Climate Change: What, If Anything, Is Wrong with Emissions Trading?" *New Political Economy* 15: 197–224.

Chichilnisky, G., Heal, G., and Starrett, D. (2013). "Equity and Efficiency in Environmental Markets: Global Trade in Carbon Dioxide Emissions." In *Environmental Markets: Equity and Efficiency*, edited by G. Chichilnisky and G. Heal, 48–67. New York: Columbia University Press.

Cohen, G. A. (2000). *If You're an Egalitarian, How Come You're So Rich?* Cambridge, MA.: Harvard University Press.

Emmenegger, S., and Tschentscher, A. (1994). "Taking Nature's Rights Seriously: The Long Way to Biocentrism in Environmental Law." *Georgetown International Environmental Law Review* 6: 546–592.

Evans, J. (2009). *Environmental Governance*. London: Routledge.

Freeman, S. (2007). *Rawls*. Hoboken: Taylor & Francis.

Gardiner, S. M. (2010). "Ethics and Global Climate Change." In *Climate Ethics: Essential Readings*, edited by S. Gardiner, S. Caney, D. Jamieson, and H. Shue, 3–35. Oxford: Oxford University Press.

Glasbergen, P. (1998). "The Question of Environmental Governance." In *Co-operative Environmental Governance: Public-Private Agreements as a Policy Strategy*, edited by P. Galsbergen, 1–20. Dordecht: Kluwer.

Goodin, R. (1989). "The State as a Moral Agent." In *The Good Polity: Normative Analysis of the State*, edited by A. Hamlin and P. Pettitt, 123–139. Oxford: Blackwell.

Grear, A. (2012). *Should Trees Have Standing? 40 Years On*. Cheltenham: Edward Elgar.

Hopwood, B., Mellor, M., and O'Brien, G. (2005). "Sustainable Development: Mapping Different Approaches." *Sustainable Development* 12: 38–52.

Hutter, B. M. (1999). "Socio-Legal Perspectives on Environmental Law: An Overview." In *A Reader in Environmental Law*, edited by B. M. Hutter, 3–47. Oxford: Oxford University Press.

Jasanoff, S. (2001). "Law." In *A Companion to Environmental Philosophy*, edited by S. Dale Jamieson, 331–346. Oxford: Blackwell.

Jasanoff and M. L. Martello (2004). *Earthly Politics: Local and Global in Environmental Governance*. Cambridge, MA: MIT Press.

Jávor, B. (2006). "Institutional Protection of Succeeding Generations: Ombudsman for Future Generations in Hungary." In *Handbook of Intergenerational Justice*, edited by J. C. Tremmel, 282–298. Cheltenham: Edward Elgar.

Nozick, R. (1974). *Anarchy, State, and Utopia*. Oxford: Basil Blackwell.

Ogus, A. (2004). *Regulation: Legal Form and Economic Theory*. Oxford: Hart Publishing.

Rawls, J. (1999). *A Theory of Justice* (revised ed.). Oxford: Oxford University Press.

Rawls, J. (2001). *Justice as Fairness: A Restatement*. Cambridge, MA: Harvard University Press.

Sands, P. (2009). "Protecting Future Generations: Precedents and Practicalities." In *Future Generations and International Law*, edited by E. Agius and S. Busuttil, 83–92. London: Earthscan.

Simmons, A. J. (1999). "Justification and Legitimacy." *Ethics* 109: 739–771.

Singer, P. (2010). "One Atmosphere." In *Climate Ethics: Essential Readings*, edited by S. Gardiner, S. Caney, D. Jamieson, and H. Shue, 181–199. Oxford: Oxford University Press.

Sinnott-Armstrong, W. (2005). "It's Not *My* Fault: Global Warming and Individual Moral Obligations." *Perspectives on Climate Change: Science, Economics, Politics, Ethics* 5: 293–315.

Stavins, R. N. (2000). "Market Based Environmental Policies." In *Public Policies for Environmental Protection*, edited by P. R. Portney and R. N. Stavins, 31–76. Washington DC: Resources for the Future.

Stone, C. D. (1974). *Should Trees Have Standing? Towards Legal Rights for Natural Objects*. Los Altos, CA: William Kaufman.

United Nations Conference on Environment and Development. (1992). *The Rio Declaration on Environment and Development*. Available online at http://www.unesco.org/education/nfsu-nesco/pdf/RIO_E.PDF [accessed 22 January 2014].

United Nations Conference on the Human Environment. (1972). *The Stockholm Declaration of the United Nations Conference on the Human Environment*. Available online at http://www.un-documents.net/unchedec.htm [accessed 22 January 2014].

Vandenbergh, M. P. (2001). "The Social Meaning of Environmental Command and Control." *Virginia Environmental Law Journal* 20: 191–219.

Weale, A., Pridham, G., Cini, M., Konstadakopulos, D., Porter, M., and Flynn, B. (2002). *Environmental Governance in Europe: An Ever Closer Ecological Union?* Oxford: Oxford University Press.

Weiss, E. B., and Jacobson, H. K. (2000). *Engaging Countries: Strengthening Compliance with International Environmental Accords*. Cambridge, MA: MIT Press.

Weston, B. H., and Bach, T. (2009). "Recalibrating the Law of Humans with the Laws of Nature: Climate Change, Human Rights, and Intergenerational Justice." *Vermont Law School Legal Studies Research Paper Series* No. 10-06.

Wood, M. C. (2009a). "Advancing the Sovereign Trust of Government to Safeguard the Environment for Present and Future Generations (Part I): Ecological Realism and the Need for a Paradigm Shift." *Environmental Law* 39: 43–89.

Wood, M. C. (2009b). "Advancing the Sovereign Trust of Government to Safeguard the Environment for Present and Future Generations (Part II): Instilling a Fiduciary Obligation in Governance." *Environmental Law* 39: 91–139.

CHAPTER 6

··

THE ANTHROPOCENE!
Beyond the Natural?

··

HOLMES ROLSTON, III

1 THE ANTHROPOCENE? GEOLOGY, ANTHROPOLOGY, POLICY

··

By recent accounts, we are entering a new geological epoch: the Anthropocene (Crutzen, 2006a; Zalasiewicz et al., 2010). Taken figuratively as a metaphor for environmental policy, entering the Anthropocene is replacing the focus on sustainability that has characterized the last two decades. The term "Anthropocene" was first used by ecologist Eugene F. Stoermer, though geologists have regularly spoken of "The Age of Man," sometimes of the "Anthropo*gene*" (Allaby, 2005: 25) or the "Homogenocene" (Curnutt, 2000). Concern that we are crossing a hinge point in history has pushed it into center focus. Recall how Galileo's new astronomy triggered dramatic changes in our worldview.

What is the empirical evidence? Anthropocene enthusiasts say: Just look, anywhere, everywhere. But geologists need stratigraphic evidence. Human-dominated ecosystems cover more of Earth's land surface than do wild ecosystems (McCloskey and Spalding, 1989; Foley et al., 2005). Human agriculture, construction, and mining move more earth than do natural rock uplift and erosion. Humans are now the most important geomorphic agent on the planet (Wilkinson and McElroy 2007).

Shifting from geology to policy, there is a move from *is* to *ought*, from *facts* to *values*. We probe here the normative assumptions underlying shades of meaning in this ambiguous term. "Embrace the Anthropocene!"? "We are entering the Anthropocene inevitably!" Possibly, economists, politicians, bioscientists, environmentalists, and philosophers are using the idea to frame their axiological assumptions and are hiding, or are blind to, their framing. Possibly, we are facing a new environmental ethics, with choices about accepting or rejecting it. We can confront the Anthropocene in different moods.

1. *Anthropocene, Alas! Toxic Anthropocene.* One claim is that we are entering the Anthropocene willy-nilly, rushing into degrading environments, and should lament it. The Millennium Ecosystem Assessment concluded that over the past fifty years,

60% of all ecosystem services have declined as a direct result of the growth of agriculture, forestry, fisheries, industries, and urban areas (Millennium Ecosystem Assessment, 2005). By this account, matters will inevitably get worse, a global tragedy of the commons. A more descriptive name would be Anthropo-blitz. If one must use geological metaphors, the "seismic epicenter" of the planetary earthquake is this newly imperial man.

2. *Anthropocene. Limit and Adapt.* Another perspective is that, indeed, we inevitably are entering the Anthropocene; so we should get going and make the best of a bad situation. Humans have discovered ways of doing agriculture from the tropics to boreal landscapes, across a wider spectrum of climates than anything we are likely to experience due to global warming. We will have to adapt to shifting climates. But we also can and should push back and limit how far and with what zeal we enter the Anthropocene. We ought to shrink the human footprint; or putting another spin on the metaphor, conserve more places where humans leave nothing except their footprints. We might, for instance, pack the agriculture more productively into limited areas and preserve and rewild other areas. Even on agriculturally developed lands we can keep the wildlife in the nooks and crannies of the fence rows and woodlots.

Entering the Anthropocene is heading over a slippery slope, but we do not have to fall all the way down. Maybe we can flourish on terraced slopes. At least we can act to take the edge off of an uncertain future with unanticipated nonlinear shifts and catastrophic outcomes. Yes, humans are "the dominant animal," now in "a totally unprecedented position . . . overshooting the capacity of its planetary home." "We have utterly changed our world; now we'll have to see if we can change our ways . . . creating a sustainable future for ourselves and the rest of the living world" (Ehrlich and Ehrlich, 2008: 362, 368). Aldo Leopold was already thinking this way: "Every head of wild life still alive in this country is already artificialized. . . . The hope for the future lies not in curtailing the influence of human occupancy—it is already too late for that—but in creating a better understanding of that influence and a new ethic for its governance" (Leopold, [1933] 1948: 21).

The focus should not be resignation to catastrophe. No, write philosophers Allen Thompson and Jeremy Bendik-Keymer; rather, we should think about "how we might *flourish* in a new global climate." Discover a new kind of "excellence (*eudaimonia*)." *Mitigation* has not worked and will not work. Focus on *adaptation*, not as "reducing vulnerability" and "mere coping strategies," but to create a "*humanist view of adaptation.*" "Begin adjusting ourselves to live life well through the emerging Anthropocene Epoch." They insist that "it is also crucial that we think of human excellence *ecologically.*" But their mood is that we should adapt and embrace the Anthropocene (Thompson and Bendik-Keymer, 2012: 1–15, emphasis in original). Thompson has "radical hope" that humans, urged to find a significantly "diminished place for valuing naturalness," can produce a new kind of "environmental goodness . . . distinct from nature's autonomy" (Thompson, 2010: 43, 56).

3. *Anthropocene. Hurrah!* The way forward is to embrace an ever-increasing human domination of the landscape, a perpetual enlargement of the bounds of the human empire. Humans are in the driver's seat. The Anthropocene is "humanity's defining moment" (Seielstad, American Geosciences Institute, 2012). We are "the God species" (Lynas, 2011). *The Economist* has a cover story: "Welcome to the Anthropocene." "The challenge

of the Anthropocene is to use human ingenuity to set things up so that the planet can accomplish its 21st century task" (*Economist*, 2011: 11). Erle Ellis, celebrating what he calls the "Planet of No Return: Human Resilience on an Artificial Earth," concludes: "Most of all, we must not see the Anthropocene as a crisis, but as the beginning of a new geological epoch ripe with human-directed opportunity" (Ellis, 2011). He joins colleagues in the *New York Times*: "The new name is well deserved . . . The Anthropocene does not represent the failure of environmentalism. It is the stage on which a new, more positive and forward-looking environmentalism can be built" (Marris, Kareiva, Mascaro, and Ellis, 2011).

The argument to follow focuses on the enthusiasts, concerned that, however well intended, Anthropocene: Hurrah! has the potential to accelerate the tragic outcome of Anthropocene, Alas. That could (alas, again) prevent the possible successes of Anthropocene: Limit and Adapt. Enthusiasm for the Anthropocene bodes impending tragedy for humans and the community of life on Earth.

2 Biosphere and Technosphere

Until now, the technosphere was contained within the biosphere. Moving into the Anthropocene, the biosphere will be contained within the technosphere, the "Anthroposphere" (Baccini and Brunner, 2012). "Nature no longer runs the Earth. We do" (Lynas, 2011: 8). "The biosphere itself, at levels from the genetic to the landscape, is increasingly a human product (Allenby, 2000: 11). "The deliberate management of the environment on a global scale would, at least in part, force us to view the biosphere as an artifact" (Keith, 2000a: 277; 2000b). We live in "anthropogenic biomes" (Ellis and Ramankutty, 2008). What we must push for, according to the Royal Society of London, the world's oldest scientific society, is "sustainable intensification" of reaping the benefits of exploiting the Earth (Royal Society, 2009).

The Ecological Society of America has a different focus: "Achieving a sustainable biosphere is the single most important task facing humankind today" (Risser, Lubchenco, and Levin, 1991). A Royal Swedish Academy of Sciences research team agrees; emphasizing "reconnecting to the biosphere" (Folke et al., 2011). Such reconnecting will produce benefits for humans no doubt, but inseparably from an ongoing biosphere.

Rather than think of a biosphere/technosphere flip-flop, one can think of degrees of naturalness. The 100% natural system no longer exists anywhere on Earth, since there is DDT in penguins in Antarctica. Yet there are still areas where the human influence is minimal and the prevailing processes are spontaneous, wild nature. On Earth, the settled continents (excluding Europe) are between one-third and one-fourth wilderness (McCloskey and Spalding, 1989). Inside the dominant technosphere, we can have large natural reserves or smaller ones pocketed within islands, vignettes, colonies of wildland nature.

Even on long-settled landscapes there can be significant naturalness remaining. In Great Britain and Europe, there are native woodlands, ancient forests treasured by the owners over centuries, often with quite old trees. Think of a large country estate. There are secondary woodlands with trees fifty to a hundred years old, wetlands, moors, hedgerows, and mountains, such as the Alps or the Scottish Cairngorms (Adams, 2003). Naturalness is a continuous variable, ranging from completely natural (100% natural) to completely artificial (0% natural). One study uses an eight-point scale (Peterken, 1996). Another uses twelve landscape zones, placed on axes ranging from human "controlled" to autonomously "self-willed" and "pristine" to "novel" (Aplet, 1999). There are multiple dimensions of naturalness (Siipi, 2008). So one can claim that there are, on differing places on the landscape, various degrees of human alteration, with options about how much further into the Anthropocene we want to go.

In another survey, researchers find Earth's terrestrial surface altered as follows: (1) little disturbed by humans, 51.9%, (2) partially disturbed, 24.2%, (3) human dominated, 23.9%. Factoring out the ice, rock, and barren land, the percentages become (1) little disturbed, 27.0%, (2) partially disturbed 36.7%, (3) human dominated 36.3%. Most habitable terrestrial nature is dominated or partially disturbed by people (73.0%). Still, nature that is little or only partially disturbed remains 63.7% of the habitable Earth (Hannah et al., 1994).

Estimating degrees of transition, consider the following criteria: What is the historical genesis of processes now operating? Were they introduced by humans, or do they continue from the evolutionary and ecological past? What is the species present constitution or form compared with its prehuman makeup? How much cultural energy is required for the upkeep of the modified system? The more management requires large amounts of labor, petroleum, electricity, fertilizer, and pesticides, the further we are from a system that has ecological integrity or ongoing stability. Without humans, would the system re-organize itself, if not to the pre-human integrity then at least to a flourishing system? Planetary climate management, however, would overarch all these degrees of naturalness.

3 Planetary Managers, Geoengineers?

We manage landscapes in differing degrees in different places. Few will dispute that. But the novel claims, entering the Anthropocene, are that we must think more globally, managing the planet as a whole, not just parcels of it. "What we call 'saving the Earth' will, in practice, require creating and re-creating it again and again for as long as humans inhabit it" (Shellenberger and Nordhaus, 2011: 61). Enter the designer World.

1. *Planetary Management.* "Whether we accept it or not, human beings now shoulder the responsibility of planetary management" (Thompson, 2009: 97). "Once the planet was larger than us, but it no longer is" (Thompson, 2009: 97). Richard Alley provides us with *Earth: The Operator's Manual* (Alley, 2011). "Human beings are now responsible for some of the basic conditions supporting all life on earth" (Thompson, 2009: 79). We need to start thinking how "to adaptively manage the basic ecological conditions of the global biosphere" (Thompson and Bendik-Keymer, 2012: 15). More carefully put, humans are indeed now responsible for degrading some basic life support systems, three of nine according to one study. We have dangerously degraded Earth's climate, biodiversity and nitrogen cycles (Rockström, 2009). The Millennium Ecosystem Assessment examined

twenty-four ecosystem services and found that fifteen are being degraded or used unsustainably (Millennium Ecosystem Assessment, 2005).

Humans had nothing to do with the creative genesis of any of these basic conditions. Managing the planet, humans are not likely to reconstruct global rainfall patterns, or photosynthesis, or tropic pyramids, or genetic coding and speciation, or heterotroph-autotroph relations, or bird migrations, or what earthworms do in soils and insects do pollinating, or any other of the basic systems that nature provides. Perhaps, taking responsibility, we can limit or repair some damages we have introduced (global warming, ocean currents, toxics, extinctions), but that we might engineer these foundational grounding systems for the better is overblown fantasy.

More modestly, the managers may prefer to speak of planetary stewardship (Sanderson et al., 2002; Folke et al., 2011; Steffen et al., 2011). Even better would be humans as trustees of Earth. Stewards are still "users," trustees are more inclusive "caretakers" of values. Such management seeks to keep in place or to restore basic natural systems, not to rebuild them. We are quite sure that a Holocene environment accommodates humans.

Those who celebrate moving into the Anthropocene point out that although humans probably will not reconstruct these big-scale global systems, humans are bringing about novel ecosystems composed of new combinations of species under new abiotic conditions. Old styles of management, which focused on restoring ecosysems to a prior condition, are no longer sufficient or even possible. We need to experiment with novel outcomes or trajectories, rather than simply taking preventative or therapeutic measures (Seastedt, Hobbs, and Suding et al., 2008). We are not going back to once-upon-a-time nature, but beyond nature. Environmental policy and ethics is mostly about intelligently domesticating landscapes (Fox, 2006). More than 80% of all people live in densely populated rural, village, and urban landscapes (Ellis and Ramankutty, 2008). Natural systems are inextricably entwined with cultural systems, which introduces new levels of complexity (Liu et al., 2007). Plan for a socially reconstructed, anthropogenic nature.

At this point, Anthropocene limit-and-adapt proponents may caution: Slow down, fit in with natural systems, which we may adapt but also to which we adapt ourselves. Conservationists have always said that we need "working landscapes." They have never opposed "multiple use," though such use has been ecosystem oriented, multiple valued, more inclined to fit in with ongoing natural processes than to rebuild them. Thomas Princen advises: *Treading Softly: Paths to Ecological Order* (2010). Build an economy grounded in the way natural systems work.

Embrace limits, learn self-restraint, and seek to live well within natural processes—which is not exactly celebrating the Anthropocene. Humans manage natural environments across a spectrum of options. Leave enough nature remaining to produce biotic integrity and health on the landscapes we inhabit. Favor ecosystem management that "goes with the flow," rather than hands-on, high-tech management of environments that have to be constantly doctored and engineered. We have inherited a pro-life planet and ought to preserve it, even if we are only concerned about our own flourishing.

2. *Planetary Engineering.* Perhaps we will have to push further. Geoengineering is "the intentional large-scale manipulation of the environment" (Keith, 2000a: 245). In this mood, the Anthropocene enthusiasts are gung-ho for change. The editors of a *Scientific*

American special issue, *Managing Planet Earth*, ask "What kind of planet do we want? What kind of planet can we get?" (Clark 1989). Find ways to redistribute rainfall, stop hurricanes and tsunamis, prevent earthquakes, redirect ocean currents, fertilize marine fisheries, manage sea-levels, alter landscapes for better food production, and generally make nature more user-friendly. Edward Yoxen urges: "The living world can now be viewed as a vast organic Lego kit inviting combination, hybridisation, and continual rebuilding. Life is manipulability. . . . Thus our image of nature is coming more and more to emphasise human intervention through a process of design" (Yoxen, 1983: 15).

Typically, geoengineering is contemplated as warranted only in the face of radical emergency—"a last resort" (Victor et al., 2009). Proponents may argue that they only wish to geoengineer until humans can curb emissions, then the geoengineering will cease. Once geoengineering is in place, however, we might be even less likely to reform and quite likely to find ourselves unwilling, or unable, to return to any past conditions. Are we to suppose that the geoengineers will then take the matter into their own hands? Various nations already allow for "emergency powers," in times of national distress, such as wars. Ought the engineers, if they find themselves confronting planetary survival, to act re-building the planet without the consensus, or even consulting most of its inhabitants, on grounds that they (think they) know what is best? They might do something similar if there were a huge meteor about to crash into the Earth or if some pandemic disease were impending.

Meanwhile, none of this sounds like humans rationally planning for an Anthropocene age. It sounds more like panic on a planet that the engineers are realizing that they have messed up in ways almost beyond their control. Humans are smarter than ever, so smart that we are faced with overshoot (Dilworth, 2010). Our power to make changes exceeds our power to predict the results, exceeds our power to control even those adverse results we may foresee. Yes, true—comes the reply—but that is all the more reason to get still smarter. Fix the problem by deliberate geoengineering.

The geoengineers will find that their engineering is not just a technical problem; they have to consider the social contexts in which they launch their gigantic projects, the welfare and risks of those they seek to save, the (in)justice of geoengineering that spreads benefits and costs inequitably, the governance of geoengineering (Parson and Keith, 2013). Engineers are no better equipped to deal with transdisciplinary systems problems than were the politicians. Or with the ethical problems. They may find a majority of Earth's residents wondering: Is our only relationship to nature one of engineering it for the better? Now Thompson and Bendik-Keymer back off, more inclined to work with, rather than revise, the basic processes in ecosystems. "Far from the current rush toward geo-engineering, this kind of response would exhibit the virtue of humility" (Thompson and Bendik-Keymer, 2012: 15).

Better to think: *Harmony;* not *Control!* On larger global scales, it is better to build our cultures aligned with the way the world is already built than to rebuild this promising planet by ourselves and for ourselves. "Hands" (the root of "manage," again) are also for holding in loving care. What kind of planet ought we humans wish to have? One we resourcefully manage for our own benefit? Or one we hold in loving care? An engineered planet is a Trojan horse. Bring it in and there will be unanticipated surprises coming out of it. This is Promethean imperial anthropocentrism.

4 ANTHROPIC CLIMATE

The one human activity that might justify geoengineering is global warming. Nobody wanted it; it is an undesired side effect. Upsetting the climate upsets everything—air, water, soils, forests, fauna and flora, ocean currents, shorelines, agriculture, property values, international relations, because it is a systemic upset to the received elemental conditions on Earth. A United Nations report, *The Global Climate 2001–2010, A Decade of Extremes*, documents that the first decade of the twenty-first century was the warmest for both hemispheres and for both land and ocean temperatures since measurements began in 1850. The world experienced "unprecedented high-impact climate extremes," and more national temperature records were broken in that decade than in any other (WMO, 2013). There were fourteen environmental disasters causing greater than $1 billion of damage in the United States in 2011 alone, more than during the entire decade of the 1980s [http://www.noaa.gov/extreme2011/]. A frequent fear is that we may trigger a runaway greenhouse effect, where negative feedback processes, which tend to keep equilibrium in atmospheric and oceanic circulations, are replaced by positive feedbacks—non-linear or cascading shifts—spinning Earth into a disequilibrium over which humans are powerless.

Paul Crutzen, a climate scientist who has dramatized the term "Anthropocene," argues that geoengineering "should be explored," given the dismal prospects of any other solution (Crutzen 2006b,: 212). "The time has come to take it seriously. Geoengineering could provide a useful defense for the planet—an emergency shield that could be deployed if surprisingly nasty climatic shifts put vital ecosystems and billions of people at risk" (Victor et al., 2009: 66; Launder and Thompson, 2010). We are hedging disaster, buying insurance. There are several possibilities: Launch reflective particles into the upper atmosphere, or aerosols, or a cloud of thin refracting disks, or reflective balloons, thereby cooling the Earth, as volcanic eruptions have done in the past. Or fertilize the ocean so as to increase plankton, which absorb more carbon. Or spray fine ocean water mist into the clouds to make them brighter, reflecting more sunlight.

Others are not so sure whether geoengineering is appropriate or safe or moral. "Some scientists are seriously considering putting Earth on life support as a last resort. But is this cure worse than the disease?" (Robock, 2008: 14). "Such schemes are fraught with uncertainties and potential negative effects" (Blackstock and Long, 2010). There may be disastrous side-effects, such as changed rainfall patterns and increased droughts and floods, irreversible tipping points we do not foresee. We do not yet model global warming well, much less what these "fixes" would do on top of that. Cloud cover would change, especially cirrus clouds. The sky would be less blue. Injected aerosols would destroy ozone and increase damaging ultraviolet. The oceans would continue to become more acidic. Who controls the thermostat, especially if there are uneven benefits and harms? Engineers? Governments? Developed or developing nations? Ethicists (Bunzl 2008)?

The biggest worry is that geoengineering does not address the deeper causes of the problem. Indeed, having such a promised cure will make us more likely to procrastinate and less likely seriously to address the problem where it arises: in our relentless consumption of fossil fuels pursuing endless growth. Calling geoengineering a last resort might mask our inability to bring ourselves under self-control, making matters worse.

5 ANTHROPOCENE ETHICS/RESPECT FOR NATURE

Entering the Anthropocene forces reconsidering our ethical obligations both to the human and the non-human communities of life. Thompson encourages our taking "responsibility for the end of nature" (Thompson, 2009: 79) and, joining Bendik-Keymer, urges facing what is "fundamentally an ethical challenge of adjusting our conception of humanity, that is, of *understanding human flourishing in new ways,*" a new kind of "humanist excellence" (Thomson and Bendik-Keymer, 2012: 8–10). There is a pivotal trade-off in such a challenge: Ought we to promote such novel humanist excellence—even if this (responsibly) leaves "diminished place for valuing naturalness as autonomy from human interference" (Thompson, 2010: 43)? Will such displacement really further human excellence?

A first claim is that such power is to be welcomed ethically. For all of human history, we have been pushing back limits. Especially in the West, we have lived with a deep-seated belief that life will get better, that one should hope for abundance and work toward obtaining it. Economists call such behavior "rational." Ethicists can agree: We ought to maximize human satisfactions, the abundant life, with more and more of the goods and services that people want. We have a right to self-development, to self-realization. Such growth, always desirable, is now increasingly possible.

Here Anthropocene enthusiasts take the moral high ground. Classical conservation has been "socially unjust" (Kareiva and Marvier, 2012: 965). "Protecting nature that is dynamic and resilient, that is in our midst rather than far away, and that sustains human communities—these are the ways forward now. Otherwise, conservation will fail, clinging to its old myths." "Instead of pursuing the protection of biodiversity for biodiversity's sake, a new conservation should seek to enhance those natural systems that benefit the widest number of people, especially the poor" (Kareiva, Lalasz, and Marvier, 2011: 36–37).

The dream of living in harmony with nature is bygone. There is a more promising ambition: audacious humans manage their brave new world. Nature has been operating on the planet for five billion years. Human culture has been operating alongside and dependent on nature for something in the range of 40,000 to 100,000 years. Now the Anthropocene architects wish to displace globally systemic nature and radically shape the future as no generation before has had either the capacity or aspiration to do. And this will be a blessing in a more humane, equitable world.

Critics worry that, though the intentions sound high, they have an immoral trailer. "Forward for me and my kind!" "Save nature for people, not from people." That could be as much the problem as the answer. The subtext seems to be the "old myths" that wild life or ecosystems or biodiversity or evolutionary creative genesis have goods of their own, intrinsic value worth protecting. Essentially this puts *Homo sapiens* as the first, if not the only, location of moral relevance. Justice is just-us. This is the Anthropocene, and too bad for the non *anthropic.* Anthropocene proponents are concerned to get people fed, even if doing so drives tigers and butterflies into extinction.

Kareiva and Marvier urge us to shift "from a focus almost exclusively on biodiversity" to more attention to "human well-being. . . . Conservation is fundamentally an expression of human values. . . . Today we need a more integrative approach in which the centrality of humans is recognized." "We do not wish to undermine the ethical motivations for conservation action. We argue that nature also merits conservation for very practical and more self-centered reasons concerning what nature and healthy ecosystems provide to humanity" (Kareiva and Marvier, 2012: 963–965). Despite the caveat, ethical concern for nonhumans is soon undermined. We may be told that once-abundant species can vanish with no ill effects on humans—the bison, the chestnut, the passenger pigeon, the dodo, the tigers and butterflies.

Rebuilding the planet with humans at the center, or even protecting ecosystem services, no longer sounds like the high moral ground. This still puts the whole planet in the service of only one species—an unnatural condition. If our concern is for the poor in this new humanist excellence, then emphasize environmental justice, more equitable distribution of wealth between rich and poor on developed lands, rather than diminishing wild nature to benefit the poor. Solve the problem in the right place.

Anthropocene enthusiasts may further claim that there is no more "primal" or "pristine" nature; indeed, there has been none for the millennia humans have been agents on the planet (Karieva and Marvier 2012: 965). So we can't save what isn't there. Actually, environmentalists more often speak of "wild" nature, or nature "untrammeled" by humans, "spontaneous" nature, of values "intrinsic" to nature "in itself" or "on its own." But, comes the reply, such wild nature is a myth: "We create parks that are no less human constructions than Disneyland" (Kareiva, Lalasz, and Marvier, 2011: 31). Wilderness advocates may wonder if anyone who makes such a claim has ever done a backcountry trek in Yellowstone or the Bob Marshall Wilderness.

"The concept of Nature, as opposed to the physical and chemical workings of natural systems, has always been a human construction, shaped and designed for human ends" (Kareiva, Lalasz, and Marvier, 2011: 31). Ecologists reply that such "workings," biological as well as physico-chemical, just are "nature," the natural history of life, which they also respect. They often do know foundational processes that were ongoing in evolutionary ecosystems before humans appeared and are still ongoing. Environmentalists are not doing museum work; they study and conserve ongoing basic natural processes—trophic pyramids, energy flow, ecosystemic resilience, stability, diversity, succession and upsets, r and k selected species, capstone species, and so on. They do because they find capabilities, integrity, and a goodness that they respect in these wild communities of life.

The Anthropocene proponents may at this point reply that they do indeed wish to save tokens of such wild life in these "natural" parks that they "construct." These refugia will be useful in various ways: reservoirs of natural resources, museums of the past, parks for recreation, for environmental education, perhaps pockets of baseline processes as a reference for planetary engineering. They may even add that in these pocketed reserves they protect wild life for its intrinsic value. They meanwhile overlook the detrimental genetic effects of small, isolated populations, stressed by global warming, which cannot shift range to any suitable habitat outside their refuges. Proponents may say they will fix this with assisted colonization. They may say they are allowing biospheric nature to continue below by fixing the stratospheric sky above. There would be an unnatural umbrella layer spread over so as to protect the natural landscape layer, something like the natural ozone layer already does.

Certainly, humans are the dominant species and will become more so. Certainly, we have moral responsibilities for each other. And we ought, as well, to respect the larger communities of life on Earth. We ought to reside, flourishing on our landscapes, with domains that are urban, rural, and wild. Three-dimensional persons need experiences in all three.

But the more we become dominantly Anthropocene, the more we shrink to become one-dimensional. We hope for healthy people on a healthy planet. Alas, as likely a future as any on our present trajectory is a warmer, less biodiverse planet—weedier, more degraded, less sustainable, with a widening gap between rich and poor, with lives that are more artifacted, more artificial. We cannot be human without culture; that is our distinctive genius. Yet equally we do not want a denatured life on a denatured planet.

6 ONCE AND FUTURE NATURE

Let us not be arrogant about this Anthropocene Epoch. Nature has not ended and never will. Humans stave off natural forces, but the natural forces can and will return. In that sense, nature is forever lingering around. Given a chance, which will come sooner or later, natural forces will flush out human effects. Even if the historic wildness does not return, nature having been by humans irreversibly knocked into some alternative condition, wildness will return to take what course it may. This ought not to serve as an excuse to continue our dominance; rather it should sober us into finding a more lasting fitness for humans on Earth.

If one is thinking of a geological epoch, one needs to think big. The Holocene covers 12,000 years; there is no prospect of our contemporary, escalating Anthropocene forcing of the planet lasting twelve millennia. If we humans were to vanish from the planet (a definite possibility in view of pandemic diseases, nuclear proliferation, or environmental collapse), future visitors from space 100,000 years hence would find traces of our activity in the fossil record, particularly in massive anthropogenic extinctions at that layer, like we now find traces of some ancient meteor impact that killed the dinosaurs. But in the deposited layers above, these extra-terrestrial geologists-anthropologists, would find only the natural and have no need for the term "Anthropogenic Epoch." Is there prospect of smart humans forever reinventing the Earth again and again in search of a new humanistic excellence? Rather, given such arrogance, bacteria have a more certain future on Earth than do we.

The Anthropocene! Beyond the Natural?? A better hope is for a *tapestry* of cultural and natural values, not a *trajectory* even further into the Anthropocene. Keep nature in symbiosis with humans. Keep the urban, rural, and wild. Our future ought to be the Semi-Anthropocene, kept basically natural—with the natural basics—and entered carefully, full of cares for both humans and nature on this wonderland planet!

REFERENCES

Adams, W. M. (2003). *Future Nature: A Vision for Conservation,* revised ed. London: Earthscan Publications Limited.
Allaby, M. (2005). *A Dictionary of Ecology,* 3rd ed. Oxford: Oxford University Press.
Allenby, B. (2000). "Earth Systems and Engineering and Management." *IEEE Technology and Society Magazine* 19(4): 10–24.
Alley, R. B. (2011). *Earth: The Operator's Manual.* New York: W. W. Norton.
Aplet, G. H. (1999). "On the Nature of Wildness: Exploring What Wilderness Really Protects." *University of Denver Law Review* 76: 347–367.

Baccini, P., and Brunner, P. H. (2012). *Metabolism of the Anthroposphere: Analysis, Evaluation, Design,* 2nd ed. Cambridge, MA: The MIT Press.

Blackstock, J. J., and Long, J. C. S. (2010). "The Politics of Geoengineering." *Science* 327(29 January): 527.

Bunzl, M. (2008). "An Ethical Assessment of Geoengineering." *Bulletin of the Atomic Scientists* 64(2): 18.

Clark, W. C. (1989). "Managing Planet Earth." *Scientific American* 261(no. 3, September): 46–54.

Crutzen, P. J. (2006a). "The 'Anthropocene.'" In *Earth System Science in the Anthropocene,* edited by E. Ehlers and T. Kraft, 13–18. Berlin: Springer.

Crutzen, P. J. (2006b). "Albedo Enhancement by Stratospheric Sulfur Injections: A Contribution to Resolve a Policy Dilemma?" *Climatic Change* 77: 211–219.

Curnutt, J. L. (2000). "A Guide to the Homogenocene." *Ecology* 81: 1756–1757.

Dilworth, C. (2010). *Too Smart for Our Own Good: The Ecological Predicament of Humankind.* Cambridge: Cambridge University Press.

Economist, The. (2011). "Welcome to the Anthropocene." 399(8735).

Ehrlich, P. R., and Ehrlich, A. H. (2008). *The Dominant Animal: Human Evolution and the Environment.* Washington, DC: Island Press.

Ellis, E. (2011). "The Planet of No Return." *Breakthrough Journal,* 2(Fall). http://breakthrough-journal.org/content/authors/erle-ellis/the-planet-of-no-return.shtml

Ellis, E., and Ramankutty, N. (2008). "Putting People in the Map: Anthropogenic Biomes of the World." *Frontiers in Ecology and the Environment* 6(8): 439–447.

Foley, J. A., DeFries, R., and Asner, G. P., et al. (2005). "Global Consequences of Land Use." *Science* 309(22 July): 570–574.

Folke, C., Jansson, Å., and Rockström, J., et al. (2011). "Reconnecting to the Biosphere." *Ambio* 40: 719–738.

Fox, W. (2006). *A Theory of General Ethics: Human Relationships, Nature, and the Built Environment.* Cambridge, MA: The MIT Press.

Hannah, L., Lohse, D., Hutchinson, C., Carr, J. L., and Lankerani, A. (1994). "A Preliminary Inventory of Human Disturbance of World Ecosystems." *Ambio* 23: 246–50.

Kareiva, Peter, and Marvier, Michelle (2012). "What Is Conservation Science?" *BioScience* 62: 962–969.

Kareiva, P., Lalasz, R., and Marvier, M. (2011). "Conservation in the Anthropocene: Beyond Solitude and Fragility." *Breakthrough Journal,* No. 2(Fall): 29–37.

Keith, D. W. (2000a). "Geoengineering the Climate: History and Prospect." *Annual Review of Energy and the Environment,* 25: 245–284.

Keith, D. W. (2000b). "The Earth Is Not Yet an Artifact." *IEEE Technology and Society Magazine,* 19(4): 25–28.

Launder, B., and Thompson, J. (2010). *Geoengineering Climate Change: Environmental Necessity or Pandora's Box?* Cambridge: Cambridge University Press.

Leopold, A. [1933], (1948). *Game Management.* New York: Charles Scribner's Sons.

Liu, J., Dietz, T., and Carpenter, S. R. et al. (2007). "Complexity of Human and Natural Systems." *Science* 317: 1513–1516.

Lynas, M. (2011). *The God Species: Saving the Planet in the Age of Humans.* Washington, DC: National Geographic.

Marris, E., Kareiva, P., Mascaro, J., and Ellis, E. C. (2011). "Hope in the Age of Man." *New York Times,* December 8, p. A-39.

McCloskey, J. M., and Spalding, H. (1989). "A Reconnaissance Level Inventory of the Amount of Wilderness Remaining in the World." *Ambio* 18: 221–227.

Millennium Ecosystem Assessment (2005). *Ecosystems and Human Well-Being: General Synthesis*. Washington, DC: Island Press.

Parson, E. A., and Keith, David W. (2013). "End the Deadlock on Governance of Geoengineering Research." *Science* 339: 1278–1279.

Peterken, G. F. (1996). *Natural Woodland: Ecology and Conservation in Northern Temperate Regions*. Cambridge: Cambridge University Press.

Princen, T. (2010). *Treading Softly: Paths to Ecological Order*. Cambridge, MA: The MIT Press.

Risser, Paul G., Lubchenco, J., and Levin, Samuel A. (1991). "Biological Research Priorities: A Sustainable Biosphere." *BioScience* 47: 625–627.

Robock, A. (2008). "20 Reasons Why Geoengineering May Be a Bad Idea." *Bulletin of the Atomic Scientists* 64(no. 2, May/June): 14–18, 59.

Rockström, J. (2009). "A Safe Operating Space for Humanity." *Nature*, 461(24 September): 472–475.

Royal Society (2009). *Reaping the Benefits: Science and the Sustainable Intensification of Global Agriculture*. London: Royal Society.

Sanderson, E. W., Jaiteh, M., and Levy, M. A., et al. (2002). "The Human Footprint and the Last of the Wild." *BioScience* 52: 891–904.

Shellenberger, M., and Nordhaus, T. (2011). "Evolve: A Case for Modernization as the Road to Salvation." *Orion* 30(no. 1, September/October): 60–65.

Seastedt, T. R., Hobbs, R. J., and Suding, K. N. (2008). "Management of Novel Ecosystems: Are Novel Approaches Required?" *Frontiers in Ecology and the Environment* 6: 547–553.

Seielstad, G. A. (2012). *Dawn of the Anthropocene: Humanity's Defining Moment*. Alexandria, VA: American Geosciences Institute. (A digital book)

Siipi, H. (2008). "Dimensions of Naturalness." *Ethics and the Environment* 13: 71–103.

Steffen, W., Persson, Å., and Deutsch, L. et al. (2011). "The Anthropocene: From Global Change to Planetary Stewardship." *Ambio* 40: 739–761.

Thompson, A. (2009). "Responsibility for the End of Nature, or: How I Learned to Stop Worrying & Love Global Warming." *Ethics & the Environment*, 14(1): 79–99.

Thompson, A. (2010). "Radical Hope for Living Well in a Warmer World." *Journal of Agricultural and Environmental Ethics* 23: 43–59.

Thompson, A. and Bendik-Keymer, J., eds. (2012). *Ethical Adaptation to Climate Change: Human Virtues of the Future*. Cambridge, MA: The MIT Press.

Victor, D. G., Morgan, M. G., Apt, J., Steinburner, J., and Ricke, K. (2009). "The Geoengineering Option. A Last Resort against Global Warming?" *Foreign Affairs* 88(no. 2, March/April): 64–76.

Wilkinson, B. H., and McElroy, B. J. (2007). "The Impact of Humans on Continental Erosion and Sedimentation." *Geological Society of America Bulletin* 119: 140–156.

World Meteorological Organization (WMO) (2013). *The Global Climate 2001-2010: A Decade of Climate Extremes*. Online at: http://library.wmo.int/pmb_ged/wmo_1103_en.pdf

Yoxen, E. (1983). *The Gene Business: Who Should Control Biotechnology?* New York: Harper and Row.

Zalasiewicz, J., Williams, M., Steffen, W., and Crutzen, P. (2010). "The New World of the Anthropocene." *Environmental Science and Technology* 44: 2228–2231.

PART II

SUBJECTS OF VALUE
*What Ought to Count Morally
and How*

CHAPTER 7

···

ANTHROPOCENTRISM
Humanity as Peril and Promise

···

ALLEN THOMPSON

1 THE IDEOLOGICAL DIAGNOSIS

I<small>F</small> one had to summarize the history of environmental ethics in a single question, a good candidate would be: Is anthropocentrism the ideological source of our environmental problems?[1] A primary concern with human relationships, including the moral status of other human beings, has been so central to ethical theory in the Western philosophical tradition for so long that no term existed for this defining orientation until Lynn White, Jr.'s influential 1967 paper, "The Historical Roots of Our Ecological Crises" (Norton, 2013). A historian concerned with the impacts Western civilization was having on other species and ecological systems, White characterized Christianity as "the most anthropocentric religion the world has seen" (White, 1967).

Literally meaning *human-centered*, the critical force of this diagnosis springs from an analogy with the objectionable self-centeredness of egoism. The egoist is self-absorbed in a way that exhibits an important moral failing: failure to attend as she ought to the moral significance of others. Likewise, on the most widely held interpretation of White's seminal work, Christian theology delivers an objectionable value framework in which only human beings are ultimately morally significant.

Thus, anthropocentrism is commonly understood as a theory of value which maintains that only human beings or their experiential states have intrinsic moral value. Consequently, everything in the extra-human world—for example, non-human animals and other living organisms, species of living organisms, or complex ecological systems—bear only instrumental value for the promotion of human welfare, however the latter is understood.[2] So we have environmental crises because we treat everything in the non-human world as having no moral significance of its own. We treat nature as something to which we owe no direct moral duties.

This diagnosis appears vividly in Routley's *Last Man* thought experiment (Routley, 1973). In effect, Routley asked us to imagine that some catastrophe has left one last human alive who desires to push a button in his or her dying moments that would destroy most of the rest of life on Earth. Would there be anything morally wrong with pushing the button? If anthropocentrism is true, it seems difficult to explain how there could be anything morally wrong with such an act, since no humans or human interests would be harmed. But there is a widespread and strong moral intuition that the Last Man would act wrongly, in which case it seems that anthropocentrism must be false. Intrinsic value in the non-human world, the thinking goes, would provide the best explanation as to why the action of Last Man would be morally odious.

It would be difficult to oversell the formative influence of this diagnostic perspective. Most early work in the field operated under the presumption that an adequate environmental ethic must locate or ascribe intrinsic value to at least some part of the non-human world of nature.[3] Rejecting anthropocentrism, however, has not been universally embraced. The issue has been polemic and the battles fierce, because it has appeared to many that so much is at stake. In this chapter, I explore in more detail the concept of anthropocentrism, review the history of its central role in the field, canvas some of the controversy it has raised, and close by making some remarks about how anthropocentrism might continue to have a vital role in environmental ethics.

2 WHAT DOES IT MEAN TO BE "HUMAN-CENTERED"?

If rejecting anthropocentrism unifies much of environmental ethics, indeed amounting to what some have called a dogma (Varner, 1998: 142), it makes sense to carefully consider what it could mean to be human-centered. There are at least three forms of anthropocentrism discussed in the literature. I will refer to these as *ontological, ethical,* and *conceptual anthropocentrism.*

First, anthropocentrism is a metaphysical thesis if it articulates a view about the ultimate nature of reality that prioritizes the existence of human beings. Appearing under different guises, as a metaphysical view about the nature of being, *ontological anthropocentrism* locates humans at the center of creation, as the end or reason for which everything else in the material world exists. It is the view that human beings have an explanatory priority; it is by some appeal to human existence that all the rest of nature is to receive its proper explanation. Support for such a view has classical underpinnings in the ancient idea of the Great Chain of Being, an ordering of entities according to their degree of perfection, descending from God to angels to humans and downward to non-human animals, insects, and plants. This idea was adopted by monotheistic religions. Judaic, Christian, and Islamic traditions offer a creation story in which humans are made in the very image of God, thus sharing in his divine transcendence of nature, together with a dualistic conception of our human constitution, an immaterial soul that is essential and superior to the material body.

Such an ontological anthropocentrism is frequently offered in support of a normative corollary, *ethical anthropocentrism,* according to which human beings are morally superior to everything else in the natural order. Those lower on the Great Chain of Being are thus "naturally" morally subordinated to the more perfect ones. In the Judeo-Christian bible, God confers to Adam and Eve, and subsequently to all human beings, dominion over all things, a position reflecting value supremacy—a superior moral worth (Genesis 1:26; Psalm 8:5–8).

In Augustine's view material reality exists merely as a setting for the soul's perfection; nature exists only for the purpose of human spiritual perfection. In sum, ethical anthropocentrism is the view that human beings possess a special and unique moral importance.

Often a distinction is drawn between strong and weak versions of ethical anthropocentrism, but use of these terms varies across the literature. As I use the terms, *strong anthropocentrism* distinguishes the view that human beings alone possess intrinsic moral worth, whereas *weak anthropocentrism* recognizes that some nonhumans have at least some inherent moral worth but never as much as a human being. In either case, the moral worth of human beings always takes precedence over, or "trumps," any other values.[4]

Indeed, White's historical analysis presents Christian ontological anthropocentrism as underwriting a strong ethical anthropocentrism. But ontological anthropocentrism does not entail ethical anthropocentrism nor visa versa (Hayward, 1997: 51). So the development of scientific worldviews—including modern cosmology, astronomy, and evolutionary biology, which have significantly diminished the prospects of ontological anthropocentrism— does not necessarily count against ethical anthropocentrism. Critics will need independent arguments because ethical anthropocentrism has a long history of philosophical defense without direct appeal to metaphysics. To many it has seemed that human beings possess special properties—for example, consciousness, complex rationality, propositional language, intentionality, or moral agency—which have been offered in defense of human moral exceptionalism.

Finally, *conceptual anthropocentrism* is the idea that human beings can only comprehend the world from a characteristically human perspective—from within a human conceptual framework. This reflects a more modest self-conception that comes with rejecting ontological anthropocentrism; human beings are, like other real and particular living things, simply a product of the material universe and in this way not particularly special.[5] Our human conceptual and motivational capacities are particular, species-specific, and necessarily limited.

Foundations for conceptual anthropocentrism reach back to the Protagorean thesis that "man is the measure of all things," asserting the insight that no "measure" can be taken of anything by a human that is not at the same time intelligible to the human mind. A modern version can be found in Kant's account of the categories of understanding, according to which the limits of human knowledge are set by cooperation between sensibility and the structure of the mind in the process of forming judgments. According to Kant's Copernican hypothesis, what appears to be a property of an object, for example causation or location in time and space, is actually a condition of the subject of perception, or "experience is relative to the standpoint and capacities of the observer" (Williams, 2014).

For environmental ethics, the most significant form of conceptual anthropocentrism is not theoretical but practical: limits imposed by the structure of human normative and axiological capacities. However we appreciate value or whatever we value, our valuing must always done from a human perspective. "All human values are human values," Minteer explains, "including the intrinsic value that ethical nonanthropocentrists ascribe to nature" (Minteer, 2009). The bearing this has for environmental ethics is fundamental and inescapable but often overlooked. Answers to our normative or evaluative questions about the environment must be based in human values, writes Bernard Williams, "in the sense of values that human beings can make part of their lives and understand themselves as pursuing and respecting" (Williams, 1995: 234).

3 Developing Alternatives to Ethical Anthropocentrism

Environmental ethicists focused on rejecting and then proposing alternatives to ethical anthropocentrism.[6] Distinct versions of ethical non-anthropocentrism are commonly divided into sentiocentrism, biocentrism, and ecocentrism.

Sentiocentrists views are based on an extension of modern theories of human ethics, utilitarian or deontological theories, to include non-human animals (see Gruen, this volume). As Bentham had foreseen, if pleasure per se is intrinsically good and pain is intrinsically bad, then consistency demands we count pleasures and pains wherever they happen to occur, including in the experience of non-human animals (Bentham, 1823). Singer updated this approach with a principle requiring that the similar interests of any being must be given equal weight in moral deliberations about what one ought to do. On Singer's view, the capacity to experience pain is a necessary and sufficient condition to have at least one morally relevant interest, the interest in avoiding pain (Singer, 1975). Since many non-human animals can experience pain, the pain of these animals must be given an equal moral weight. Thus we have a form of ethical non-anthropocentrism that locates intrinsic moral value in the experiences of non-human animals and requires that they be given direct moral consideration.

A deontological approach has also been adapted to include some sentient, non-human animals. The most well known version is Regan's, ascribing moral rights to what he calls experiencing "subjects-of-a-life" (Regan, 1983). Whereas Kant's view restricts moral significance to beings capable of a rational autonomy (i.e., freedom to act on principle, even contrary to one's desires), Regan extends such status to any and all conscious beings who "have beliefs and desires; perception, memory, and a sense of the future, including their own future" (Regan, 1983, 243). Subjects-of-a-life have lives that matter at least to themselves and thus "have a distinctive kind of value—inherent value—and are not to be viewed or treated as mere receptacles" of valuable experiences. Subjects-of-a-life have a claim against all others, a moral right, not to be used merely as a means to promote the good of others (Regan, 1983: 243). Since, Regan believes, most mammals over one year old count as subjects-of-a-life, his view presents another form of ethical non-anthropocentrism.

Some have thought, however, that exclusive concern with conscious experience or subjectivity exhibits a bias in favor of what is important from the human perspective, and that the interests of sentient beings or a conscious awareness of one's own welfare may not exhaust the field of morally relevant interests. Thus, biocenteric views maintain there is a sensible way to talk about the welfare of living things, that is, how they may be benefited or harmed, that does not require a living organism to be consciously aware of its interests in order for these interests to be morally relevant. Biocentrism finds moral value in all living things, with a provenance widely attributed to Schweitzer's fundamental ethical principle of Reverence for Life, where "good consists in maintaining, assisting and enhancing life, and to destroy, to harm or to hinder life is evil" (Schweitzer, 1923/1946).[7]

Contemporary versions, such as Taylor's, focus on individual living organisms, each of which is conceived to be a "teleological center-of-a-life" that is "pursuing its own good in its own way, according to its species specific nature" (Taylor, 1986: 45). Questions of how or how much simply *being alive* operates as an intrinsic moral value, providing a relative moral significance, has given rise to distinct forms of biocentrism (e.g., egalitarian and pluralistic versions; see Palmer, this volume), but since the set of individual living organisms includes much more than human beings, biocentrism is another form of ethical nonanthropocentrism.

A biological species is not itself an individual living organism but, rather, a collection of genetically related individuals. Yet some theorists have defended the view that species per se have morally relevant interests, in the sense that different phenomena can either promote or hinder the well-being of the species as a whole, over and above the well-being of its constituent, individual members. Moral concern with a collection of living things, such as a species, marks important distinction in environmental ethics between individualistic and holistic views.[8] Holistic views attribute intrinsic value to collectives. A view that attributes intrinsic value to a species, rather than or in addition to the individual members of the species, would be a holistic form of biocentrism.

This brings us to the holistic view of ecocentrism, the view that a collection of living and non-living things, which can be identified by compositional and functional characterizations and exhibit resilience as such, constitutes an ecosystem, and ecosystems are the loci of intrinsic value and hence moral significance (see Callicott, this volume). Leopold's Land Ethic is often heralded as an early and still influential form of ecocentrism, exemplified in his principle that "a thing is right when it tends to preserve the integrity, stability, and beauty of the biotic community. It is wrong when it tends otherwise" (Leopold, 1949).[9]

Two versions of ecocentrism have long occupied center stage. Callicott develops and defends the communitarian aspects of Leopold's Land Ethic, according to which valuing ecosystems intrinsically represents a sensible, even Darwinian, expansion of the moral community (Callicott, 1979). Based in Humean moral philosophy, in Callicott's view values are essentially only projections of human sentiments. But because we do not have to value only human beings non-instrumentally, intrinsic value does not have to be *anthropocentric*. Nonetheless, all attributions of intrinsic value are *anthropogenic*: originating in and dependent upon human acts of evaluation (Callicott, 1989).

By contrast, Rolston's view exemplifies perhaps the pinnacle of an ethical nonanthropocentrism, an objectivist environmental holism according to which ecosystems possess a systemic value that is both fundamental and prior to the intrinsic value of living things, including human beings (Rolston, 1975 1994). Systemic value is associated with the productive capacities of nature, conditions of interaction and interdependence that make possible the evolution and ongoing existence of species and individual living entities that both have and pursue a good of their own. The value of systems capable of producing life and the intrinsic value possessed by living things is thought by Rolston to exist independently of either human evaluative or perceptive acts. Value is discovered in, not conferred upon, nature and thus this is a theory of value that is objective and nonanthropogenic.

4 RECOIL INTO VARIOUS FORMS OF ANTHROPOCENTRISM

What kind of progress has been made through these efforts to supersede ethical anthropocentrism? First, while proponents of nonanthropocentrism are unified in rejecting ethical anthropocentrism, there has been no convergence on a single alternative. We learn that anthropocentrism is not alone in facing significant philosophical problems; proponents of sentiocentrism raise objections to biocentrism, just as biocentrists object to sentiocentrism, on one hand, and ecocentrism, on the other, and so on. But in committing to the idea that at least individual non-human organisms possess a morally relevant good of their own, and perhaps further even species and ecosystems, in the estimation of many the field was making progress. Yet from other perspectives the field was not meeting with sufficient success. The widely shared commitment to nonanthropocentrism, it has seemed to some, involves both practical and theoretic problems.

Questioning the utility of attributing a single, non-instrumental value to nature, Norton outlined a form of broad ethical anthropocentrism. According to this view, nature is instrumentally valuable not only as a material resource for satisfying the typically consumptive, "felt" human preferences but also for the transformative power experiences with nature can have on a person's worldview and her resultant "considered" preferences (Norton, 1984). Norton's strategy involves the "convergence hypothesis" that "individuals who rely on a sufficiently broad and temporally extended range of human values . . . and nonanthropocentrists who embrace a consistent notion of the intrinsic value of nature will tend to endorse similar policies in particular situations" (Minteer and Manning, 2000: 47). Norton, along with Weston and Light, have been key figures of environmental pragmatism, a movement critical of intrinsic value attributions to nature and focused on advancing constructive discourse about protective environmental policy (Weston, 1985; Light and Katz, 1996).

Another advocate of enlightened anthropocentrism, Hargrove argued that anthropocentrism does not imply nature is only valuable instrumentally (Hargrove, 1992). He advanced four theses, a close examination of which is worthwhile: (1) the most plausible subjectivist version of so-called "nonanthropocentric" intrinsic value theory, that of Callicott, is better understood as a "weak" anthropocentric intrinsic value theory; (2) a stronger, objective nonanthropocentric theory of intrinsic value, exemplified by Rolston, actually "requires and is supplemented by" a weak anthropocentric intrinsic value theory; (3) Hargrove's own weak anthropocentric intrinsic value theory is superior to Norton's broadly anthropocentric, pragmatic instrumentalism; and (4) most "nonanthropocentric" value theories are in various ways really anthropocentric (Hargrove, 1992).

To understand these claims it is crucial to see that Hargrove uses "anthropocentrism" to mean a form of *conceptual* anthropocentrism—value judgments with behavioral significance, including ethical significance, are necessarily made from the human perspective. But he is not committed to a strong *ethical* anthropocentrism, on which only human beings bear intrinsic value. With this use, he identifies four distinct types of value. "Nonanthropocentric instrumental value" refers to value relations of use that obtain between living organisms and that can be recognized as objective fact. For example, catching prey is valuable to the predator. "Anthropocentric instrumental value," then, picks out instrumental value relations that depend on subjective acts of human evaluation. For example, that any particular shells or metal trinkets can operate as currency rests on conventional practices of human evaluative judgment.

Completing the matrix, "nonanthropocentric intrinsic value" picks out the kind of non-instrumental value posited most clearly in biocentric individualism—individual living organisms pursue the good of their own self-realization, a good that does not depend upon any evaluative judgments made by human beings. Finally, "anthropocentric intrinsic value" refers to the non-use value assignments that human beings are capable of making, but a value that essentially depends upon acts of human evaluation, which are necessarily made from a human perspective. For example, we are able to value the lives of our children, or the ongoing existence of some giant Sequoia, for their own sake.

Now, let's unpack Hargrove's four theses. First, because Callicott's ecocentrism maintains that all attributions of intrinsic value to the biotic community are necessarily anthropo*genic*, we see that (a) for Callicott, all intrinsic values depend on human valuing and thus his view is a form of *conceptual* anthropocentrism according to which human beings can value ecosystems noninstrumentally (what Hargrove calls a "weak" anthropocentrism).[10] Second, Rolston's ecocentrism posits that intrinsic value in nature exists independently of human judgments, a value that does not *arise* from human evaluative judgment but is *discovered* by it. Hargrove's position is that in order to have ethically normative implications, (b) even a strong nonanthropocentric intrinsic value theory "requires and is complimented by" a weak anthropocentrism, that is, requires people to judge that they ought to care and do something in regard to objective intrinsic value in nature.[11] This is a fundamental issue. A requirement to justify the move from "good" to "ought" has been pointed out by others. For example, John O'Neill claimed that while there is no gap between facts and values, in that some natural facts just are value facts, there genuinely is a gap between values and norms, between the existence of objective or nonanthropogenic intrinsic value in nature and what we ought to do about it (O'Neill, 1992; see also Nolt, 2006).

Hargrove develops an anthropocentric theory based in socially grounded, aesthetic judgments about nature and argues that (c) such a weak anthropocentric view, which allows for people to value nature noninstrumentally, "is superior" to Norton's view, which relies on a contingent, transformational power of experiences with nature but denies it any intrinsic value. Now, it's a question of empirical fact as to whether Hargrove's weak anthropocentric intrinsic value theory is able to advance environmental policy better than the broad anthropocentrism outlined by Norton. But even if it does, this should not bother Norton significantly, since his convergence hypothesis implies that both an enlightened ethical anthropocentrism and a consistent intrinsic value theory will have the same policy implications. In any case, Norton is agnostic regarding a "true" theory of value in nature; his ultimate concern lies with the development of a pragmatically "adequate" environmental ethic (Norton, 1984).

Finally, through the next section, I will I consider Hargrove's final claim that (d) most "nonanthropocentric" theories are, in various ways, really are anthropocentric.

5 REASSESSING ALTERNATIVES TO ETHICAL ANTHROPOCENTRISM

The significant array of alternatives to anthropocentrism gives credence to the idea that there is something problematic about strong ethical anthropocentrism. Valuing only humans does seem arbitrary and unjustifiable, but such defects can be better understood in terms other than rejection of anthropocentrism (Hayward, 1997). For example, a failure to acknowledge the moral significance of nonhumans may simply be discrimination on the basis of species membership, when species membership is not the morally relevant criterion. Analogous to sexism and racism, arbitrary discrimination on the basis of species membership is not difficult to recognize as morally unjustified.[12] A bias in favor of the human species may *motivate* instances of problematic discrimination, but it's the moral wrongness of speciesism that actually *explains* why particular behaviors are morally objectionable.

What is more difficult, however, is making an unbiased determination of what properties actually are morally relevant and thus deserving of moral consideration and respect. Usual candidates include complex rationality, propositional language, or moral agency, but a bias in favor of humans, the disposition of "human chauvinism," may corrupt our "attempts to specify relevant difference[s between organisms] in ways that invariably favor humans" (Hayward, 1997: 53). At issue here is not making an appeal to some morally arbitrary property such as species membership, but rather precisely the question of what are the "criteria in terms of which discrimination might be claimed to be arbitrary or otherwise" (Hayward, 1997: 54; see also Routley, 1973).

Let's review the concepts central to various forms of ethical nonanthropocentrism outlined earlier. Human beings have significant interests in their own conscious experience of pleasure and pain, and thus give moral consideration to the pain and pleasure of others, others who also value pleasure and the avoidance of pain. Furthermore, we are subjects-of-a-life whose own well-being, beyond the content of our experiences, matters to us. Because we believe that we deserve moral consideration and respect because our lives matter to us, consistency demands that we respect any other subjects-of-a-life. Thus it seems reasonable to extend these concerns to many sentient non-human animals.

Biocentrists, however, point out that it is not the case that the individual welfare of each and every living organism involves consciousness or subjective experience. These conditions are valuable to humans because they are significant to our welfare or deemed by us as worthy of respect, and we fairly presume that they are also significant to other sentient beings. But sentience doesn't matter to the welfare of an individual tree, for example, or to the species of *Canis lupus*. Is it human chauvinism that identifies conscious and subjective experience as morally relevant, rather than a more brute biological welfare? Does it represent an unjustified bias that could be overcome by the development of a more sympathetic moral disposition, or does concern with consciousness and subjectivity reveal something more persistent about the conceptual structure of the human moral perspective? If the former, then we may be able overcome this bias through improvement of our moral character. If the later, then even the views of the animal welfare advocates, such as Singer, may involve an ineliminable form of conceptual anthropocentrism, which is "marked by the impossibility of giving meaningful moral consideration to cases which bear no similarity to any aspect of human cases" (Hayward, 1997: 56).

We may begin to suspect that a form of conceptual human-centeredness could be involved in each successive effort to reject anthropocentrism. In each case there is a struggle to maintain concepts that we can recognize as relevant to how we understand value, ethical reasoning, and moral consideration. For example, while biocentric *individualism* rejects consciousness and subjective experience, it retains core notions of interests, health, welfare, and the persistence of somatic identity. Alternatively, biocentric *holists*, who attribute intrinsic moral value to species per se, leave behind the preservation of somatic identity, recognizing that the health or welfare of the species does not track the well-being or survival of any specific individual organism.

A *species* may be identified in terms of genotypic representation and population biology but an ecosystem cannot. The very ontology of an ecosystem may be in doubt; perhaps it rests only on human practices and convention, existing only in the sense that the constellation *Ursa major* exists. If an ecosystem is identified in terms of functional relations, composition, and structure, involving both biotic and abiotic properties, in the conceptual language of a scientific biology, it would seem impossible to separate what an ecosystem actually is from what our human interests are. How can we talk about the health and integrity of an ecosystem *for it's own sake* if we cannot identify one independently of contingent human practices, concepts, and interests? Furthermore, why should we think that welfare, health, and integrity per se are pertinent to ecosystems *for their own sake*, beyond the fact that we—sentient individual organisms—value welfare, health, and integrity?

More generally, how could we keep our ethical bearings at all without some of our very basic concepts of morality, such as the ongoing identity of a moral patient, as an object deserving respect or loci of concern for its welfare? The point is that we probably cannot, because such features may be part of foundational human moral constructs without which we simply couldn't engage in morality, as we understand it, at all.

> If the ultimate point of an ethic is to yield a determinate guide to human action, then, the human reference is ineliminable even when extending moral concern to nonhumans. . . . As long as the valuer is a human, the very selection of criteria of value will be limited by this fact. It is this fact which precludes the possibility of a *radically* nonanthropocentric value scheme. . . .
>
> Any attempt to construct a radically nonanthropocentric value scheme is liable not only to be arbitrary—because founded on no certain knowledge—but also to be more insidiously anthropocentric in projecting certain values, which as a matter of fact are selected by a human, onto nonhuman beings without certain warrant for doing so. This, of course, is the error of anthropomorphism, and will inevitably, I believe, be committed in any attempt to expunge anthropocentrism altogether. (Hayward, 1997: 56)

Returning to Hargrove's final claim, that *most* nonanthropocentric views really are anthropocentric, we may now consider it too weak. If a view is to be relevant for guiding human behavior, as an ethical view must, then *any* nonanthropocentric view, even the most radically so, cannot escape remaining conceptually anthropocentric.

6 CONCLUSION: A PROGNOSIS FOR THE ANTHROPOCENE

The diagnostic work accomplished though various attempts to reject ethical anthropocentrism has been valuable, but the moral problems thus uncovered turn out to be more precisely expressed in other terms, including an arbitrary favoritism for one's own species (speciesism) and an objectionable disposition to identify only those properties characteristic of one's own species as worthy of moral respect and consideration (human chauvinism). In this light, key problems will revolve around distinguishing the corrigible disposition of human chauvinism from an incorrigible reliance on features of our human moral perspective. If this is right, then work exploring questions about conceptual anthropocentrism would remain vital and important to the field.

There appear to be at least two distinct dimensions of conceptual anthropocentrism. One highlights subjective or communal acts of evaluative judgment, in which objects are identified and assigned value. For example, Callicott maintains that individual persons can judge ecosystems—or anything else, for that matter—as intrinsically valuable, whereas Hargrove ties the valuing of nature intrinsically to developed cultural perspectives, on analogy with aesthetic judgments. Focusing on the subject, not the object of evaluative judgments, we ask, "How do good people value non-human nature?" or "What features of human morality affect what we ought to value and how we ought to exhibit our appreciation of value?"

A second dimension pertains to questions about the very conceptual tools or architecture with which we conduct moral inquiry. Surely Williams is right with the metaethical point that questions about the environment must invoke values that humans can "understand themselves as pursuing and respecting," but what sort of consequences could this insight have? Will it limit what or how we value parts of the non-human world? It seems it must. How flexible can our human moral perspective be regarding the non-human world without breaching into an objectionable anthropomorphism? How should we understand ourselves as good in relation to the non-human world? What is more fitting, our concepts of value, duty, or virtue?

These two dimensions together illustrate how a focus on human beings as moral agents remains a promising avenue for environmental ethics (see also Hale, this volume). As I argue elsewhere, perhaps it is time to reframe ethical questions about the environment, deemphasizing conceptions of value in nature and focusing instead on the specification and development of excellence in human moral character, that is, on specifically human environmental virtues (Thompson, 2008, 2010, see also Sandler, this volume). For one, framing environmental ethics primarily in terms of obligations regarding the intrinsic value of non-human nature offers nothing to combat some of the dualistic conceptions of Modernism (e.g., human/nature, spirit/matter, morally considerable/morally irrelevant) seen by many as a driver of contemporary environmental problems (Norton and Thompson, 2014). The alternative approach of a naturalistic environmental virtue ethics enables us to conceive of human moral goodness as one instance of the wide variety of natural goodness (Thompson, 2009). Acting well could be specified in naturalistic terms concerning our specifically human form of life, not dependent on values conceived to be external of ourselves, belonging to non-human nature (Thompson, 2012). Such an approach, I believe, holds more promise for overcoming problematic dichotomies than standard fare, occasionally dogmatic rejections of anthropocentrism and subsequent attributions of intrinsic value or rights to parts of non-human nature.

Not all advocates of ethical nonanthropocentrism are dogmatic, of course. Attfield (2011) carefully examines and critically replies to various attempts at reviving anthropocentrism, including Norton's convergence hypothesis, a perspectival/conceptual anthropocentrism, and O'Neill's Aristotelian approach, discussed earlier. Attfield worries that a focus on human values will "unintentionally narrow the range of human sympathies" (Attfield, 2011: 29). Likewise, McShane worries that any form of anthropocentrism "undermines some of the common attitudes—love, respect, awe—that people think it appropriate to take toward the natural world" (McShane, 2007: 169).

Rolston is famously critical of environmental virtue ethics as overly anthropocentric, as it gives normative priority to the concept of human flourishing (Rolston, 2005). But the virtuous human being is not disposed to be overly self-concerned, nor selfish. So, Rolston, along with Attfield and McShane, seem to confuse the orientation of a theory's construction (e.g., focus on the human virtues) with the subjective perspective of the virtuous person. O'Neill illustrates this with the virtue of friendship, a human virtue that disposes one to be concerned with the well-being of others for their own sake. Justice, of course, is another important other-regarding virtue. The environmentally virtuous person, likewise, need not maintain the outlook of ethical anthropocentrism. Instead she would possess, among other virtues, a disposition toward environmental or ecological justice, which may well be accompanied by feelings of love, awe, and respect. In a virtue-theoretic approach, however, this moral judgment must be based on human-centered criteria, whether on human conceptions of responding well to "intrinsic value" in nature or simply living well as human being.

If indeed we are moving into the Anthropocene, the age of human domination (see Rolston, this volume), then perhaps environmental ethics ought to focus closely on human beings, on the species-specific environmental character traits, the environmental virtues and vices, of this particular moral animal. The well-being of all life on Earth may hang in the balance.

NOTES

1. Thanks to Ken Shockley and Stephen Gardiner for helpful comments on the text.
2. Treating intrinsic and instrumental value as an exhaustive dichotomy has since been challenged by those attracted to pluralistic conceptions of value in nature (Wenz, 1993; Stone, 1988; Callicott, 1990; Light, 1996).
3. One notable exception is *Man's Responsibility for Nature* (Passmore, 1974). Hargrove presents a slightly alternative history, according to which the first efforts were to attribute *rights* to nature. Failing that, retreat was made to attributing intrinsic value to nature, with the strongest advocates, such as Holmes Rolston, aspiring to give an objective or mind-independent account of nature's intrinsic value (Hargrove, 1992).
4. Brennan and Lo define the terms as I do here (Brennan and Lo, 2010: 11). As Norton (1984) uses the term, however, "weak" anthropocentrism denies intrinsic value to the nonhuman world, which counts as a strong anthropocentrism as I use the terms. Hargrove (1992) uses "weak" anthropocentrism differently, only to mean that the value in nonhuman nature need not be only instrumental, yet Hargrove's use does not necessarily reserve a trumping role for human intrinsic value.
5. Or as Leopold put it, *Homo sapiens* are just a "plain member and citizen" of the biotic community.
6. If strong ethical anthropocentrism is the view that *only* human beings bear an intrinsic moral value or are morally considerable, then ethical nonanthropocentrism implies that some part or parts of the nonhuman world are intrinsically valuable. If weak ethical anthropocentrism is the view that the intrinsic moral worth of human beings *always overrides* the moral significance of nonhumans, then ethical nonanthropocentrism implies that the moral value of human beings does not always trump all other values.
7. The quote is available online at http://en.wikipedia.org/wiki/Reverence_for_Life accessed January 12, 2015.

8. Bryan Norton, famous for his "weak" or broad anthropocentrism, argues persuasively that nonindividualism is what makes environmental ethics distinctive, not the rejection of anthropocentrism (Norton, 1984).

9. The Land Ethic "simply enlarges the boundaries of the [moral] community to include soils, waters, plants, and animals, or collectively: the land . . . [A] land ethics changes the role of *Homo sapiens* from conqueror of the land-community to plain member and citizen of it. It implies respect for his fellow-members, and also respect for the community as such." (Leopold, 1949).

10. Thus, Hargrove and Norton agree in finding Callicott committed to the idea that all values are the product of human valuing. Consequently, along with Hargrove, Norton believes that Callicott's position is not genuinely a form of nonanthropocentrism. Norton writes, "it can be difficult to see how such a position, asserted to be nonanthropocentric, can maintain any sense of human-independent value because nonhuman value can only exist as a result of human affect" (Norton 2013).

11. Hargrove draws the distinction in terms as defined by Taylor: "inherent worth" picks out the objective value something has in virtue of having a good of its own, while "intrinsically valued" is associated with a thing's being valued noninstrumentally by a evaluating subject (Hargrove, 1992).

12. Some have argued for the moral relevance of species membership, for example Williams (2008) and Diamond (1991). Compelling criticisms of such approaches can be found in McMahan (2005).

REFERENCES

Attfield, R. (2011). "Beyond Anthropocentrism." In *Philosophy and the Environment*. Royal Institute of Philosophy Supplement: 69, edited by A. O'Hear, 29–46. Cambridge: Cambridge University Press.

Bentham, J. (1823). *Introduction to the Principles of Morals and Legislation*, 2nd ed., chapter 17, footnote. <http://www.econlib.org/library/Bentham/bnthPML18.html> accessed March 9, 2015.

Brennan, A., and Lo, Y. S. (2010). *Understanding Environmental Philosophy*. Durham: Acumen Publishing Ltd.

Callicott, J. B. (1979). "Elements of an Environmental Ethic: Moral Considerability and the Biotic Community." *Environmental Ethics* 1 (1): 71–81.

Callicott, J. B. (1989). *In Defense of the Land Ethic*. Albany: SUNY Press.

Callicott, J. B. (1990). "The Case Against Moral Pluralism" *Environmental Ethics* 12 (2): 99–124.

Diamond, C. (1991). "The Importance of Being Human." In *Human Beings*, edited by D. Cockburn, 35–62. Cambridge: Cambridge University Press.

Hayward, T. (1997). "Anthropocentrism: A Misunderstood Problem." *Environmental Values* 6: 49–63.

Hargrove, G. (1992). "Weak Anthropocentric Intrinsic Value Theory." *The Monist* 75: 183–207.

Leopold, A. (1949). *A Sand County Almanac and Sketches Here and There*. New York: Oxford University Press.

Light, A. (1996). "Callicott and Naes on Pluralism." *Inquiry* 39: 273–294.

Light, A., and Katz, E. eds. (1996). *Environmental Pragmatism*. London: Routledge.

McMahan, J. (2005). "Our Fellow Creatures." *Journal of Ethics* 9 (3–4): 353–380.

McShane, K. (2007). "Anthropocentrism vs. Nonanthropocentrism: Why Should We Care?" *Environmental Values* 16: 169–185.

Minteer, B. (2009). "Anthropocentrism." In *Encyclopedia of Environmental Ethics and Philosophy*, edited by J. B. Callicott and R. Frodeman, 58–62. Farmington Hills: MI: Cengage Learning.

Minteer, B., and Manning, R. (2000). "Convergence in Environmental Values: An Empirical and Conceptual Defense." *Ethics, Place, and Environment* 3 (1): 47–60.

Nolt, J. (2006). "The Move from Good to Ought in Environmental Ethics." *Environmental Ethics* 28 (4): 355–374.

Norton, B. (2013). "Anthropocentrism." In *International Encyclopedia of Ethics*, edited by H. LaFollette. New York: Wiley-Blackwell.

Norton, B. (1984). "Weak Anthropocentrism and Environmental Ethics." *Environmental Ethics* 6: 131–148.

Norton, B., and Thompson, A. (2014). "Ethics and Sustainable Development: The Virtues of an Adaptive Approach to Environmental Choice." In *Handbook of Sustainable Development*, edited by G. Atkinson, S. Dietz, and E. Neumayer, and Agarwala, 105–124. Northhampton, MA: Edward Elgar.

O'Neill, J. (1992). "The Varieties of Intrinsic Value." *The Monist* 75: 191–137.

Passmore, J. (1974). *Man's Responsibility for Nature*. London: Duckworth & Co. Ltd.

Regan, T. (1983). *The Case for Animal Rights*. The University of California Press.

Rolston, H. III (1975). "Is There an Ecological Ethic?" *Ethics* 85: 93–109.

Rolston, H. III (1994). *Conserving Natural Value*. New York: Columbia University Press.

Rolston, H. III (2005). "Environmental Virtue Ethics: Half the Truth but Dangerous as a Whole." In *Environmental Virtue Ethics,* edited by Sandler and Cafaro. Lanham: Rowman and Littlefield.

Routley, R. (1973). "Is There a Need for a New, an Environmental, Ethic?" *Philosophy and Science: Morality and Culture: Technology and Man, Proceedings of the XVth World Congress of Philosophy,* Sept. 17–22. Varna, Bulgaria: Sofia [Sophia-Press].

Schweitzer, A. (1923/1946). *Civilization and Ethics*, translated by Charles Campion. Ann Arbor: The University of Michigan Press.

Singer, P. (1975). *Animal Liberation*. New York: New York Review/Random House.

Taylor, P. (1986). *Respect for Nature: A Theory of Environmental Ethics*. Princeton, NJ. Princeton University Press.

Stone, C. D. (1988). "Moral Pluralism and the Course of Environmental Ethics." *Environmental Ethics* 10 (2): 139–154.

Thompson, A. (2008). "Natural Goodness and Abandoning the Economy of Value." *Ethics, Place & Environment* 11 (2): 216–224.

Thompson, A. (2009). "Responsibility for the End of Nature, or: How I Learned to Stop Worrying & Love Global Warming." *Ethics & the Environment* 14 (1): 79–99.

Thompson, A. (2010). "Radical Hope for Living Well in a Warmer World." *Journal of Agricultural & Environmental Ethics* 23 (1): 43–59.

Thompson, A. (2012). "The Virtue of Responsibility for the Global Climate." In *Ethical Adaptation to Climate Change: Human Virtues of the Future*, edited by A. Thompson and J. Bendik-Keymer, 203–222. Cambridge, MA: MIT Press.

Varner, G. (1998). *In Nature's Interest*. Oxford: Oxford University Press.

Wenz, P., S. (1993). "Minimal, Moderate, and Extreme Moral Pluralism." *Environmental Ethics* 15 (1): 61–74.

Weston, A. (1985). "Beyond Intrinsic Value: Pragmatism in Environmental Ethics." *Environmental Ethics* 7 (4): 321–339.

Williams, G. (2014). "Kant's Account of Reason." The Stanford Encyclopedia of Philosophy (Spring 2014 Edition), edited by E. N. Zalta. <http://plato.stanford.edu/archives/spr2014/entries/kant-reason/>. (accessed Dec. 7, 2014).

Williams, B. (1995). "Must a Concern for the Environment Be Centered on Human Beings?" In *Making Sense of Humanity and Other Philosophical Papers,* 233–240. Cambridge: Cambridge University Press.

Williams, B. (2008). "The Human Prejudice?" In *Philosophy as a Humanistic Discipline,* edited by A. W. Moore, 135–154. Princeton, NJ: Princeton University Press.

White, L. Jr. (1967). "The Historical Roots of Our Ecological Crisis." *Science* 155 (3767): 1203–1207.

CHAPTER 8

....

CONSCIOUS ANIMALS AND THE VALUE OF EXPERIENCE

....

LORI GRUEN

THE field of environment ethics has contributed greatly to value theory in that it urges us to reconsider what is morally considerable and why. Once we move beyond the view that humans are the only valuable entities on the planet, we must then ask who or what else matters from a moral point of view, and that question allows us to reconsider the content, sources, and implications of different ways of valuing. A growing number of theorists have argued that what is valuable is positive experience, and thus all conscious animals, human and nonhuman, matter. Once that is acknowledged, our responsibility for preventing or contributing to positive experience then becomes a serious topic for reflection. Here I will discuss variations on the view that can broadly be called "experientialism."[1] Experientialism suggests that all beings who have conscious experiences deserve our moral attention. Conscious beings experience positive or negative impacts on their interests—they can be benefitted and harmed by having their interests promoted or set back. What interests matter and why they matter is a subject of disagreement that has affected what we judge to be permissible or impermissible treatment of other animals.

1 HAVING INTERESTS

....

Plants, trees, and other parts of nature are often said to be "benefitted" or "harmed" depending on what happens to them. Clear cutting a forest is sometimes described as harmful to the forest, and making sure that a plant has plenty of water and sunlight is thought to benefit the plant. Because plants, trees, and other parts of nature are thought to be the sorts of things that can be benefitted or harmed, some theorists have argued that all living things should be considered from an ethical point of view, not just animals [See chapter 10]. I suggest that it is more sensible to think of non-conscious living beings as having interests that can be promoted or set back, rather than thinking of them as benefitted or harmed, and reserve the concepts of harm and benefit for beings with subjective, conscious experiences.

We can distinguish two senses of interest. When we say that A has an interest in X we could mean that A is interested in X—that is, A likes X or is aiming at X. A has a subjective attitude toward X. I may be interested in starting a sanctuary for parrots who live very long lives and have nowhere to go, given how hard they are to keep as pets. I would have to carefully consider where to locate the sanctuary, making sure to find an appropriate climate for them. I might conduct research on ways to rehabilitate birds who have been kept in squalid conditions in the exotic pet trade industry. I'd need to consult with people with experience caring for parrots. This sense of interest requires my conscious attention that allows me to direct my actions in particular ways.

Another sense of the phrase "A has an interest in X" is that X is conducive to A's good. My canine companion has arthritis, a condition that is helped by taking glucosamine. But she is definitely not interested in the medication, as I have to go through an elaborate ritual to trick her into taking it. The glucosamine is in Maggie's interest, but Maggie is not interested in the glucosamine.

So X could be in A's interests, but A may not be at all interested in X. In addition, a being could be interested in something, but that may not be in his interests, as when a dog is interested in eating garbage or when I think I want to eat a whole cake. The two senses of interest are distinct. Plants and trees may have interests in the second sense, that is, they are the sorts of things that, if certain actions are taken, their existence is threatened or furthered. When a tree is chopped down, or plants are deprived of water and light, their interests are set back, but they will never be interested in these set-backs. They are not conscious of the ways in which their interests are affected, they are thus not benefitted or harmed. Animals, on the other hand, are conscious beings that can have both sorts of interest. Things can be against their interests, and they can intentionally direct their actions to seek the promotion of some of their interests. Unlike plants, both human and non-human animals can express their interests as wants or desires that can be interpreted through their actions. Of course, the content of interests differ, and many theorists have argued that what makes animals distinctly morally considerable is our interests in not experiencing pain and suffering.

2 UNNECESSARY SUFFERING

Usually, an interest in avoiding pain generates ethical concern. Experiencing physical or psychological pain is, other things being equal, something that most humans seek to avoid, and causing an individual to suffer pain unnecessarily is generally considered morally impermissible. Humans tend to strenuously object to pain, and some are so averse to experiencing pain that they have developed tendencies to rely, often heavily, on pain-relievers. But humans are not alone in their capacity for experiencing pain; in response to this recognition a powerful argument has been made to view the badness of pain consistently across all beings that can suffer, both human and nonhuman. As Peter Singer has pointed out, "If a being suffers, there can be no moral justification for disregarding that suffering, or for refusing to count it equally with the like suffering of any other being. But the converse is also true. If a being is not capable of suffering, or of enjoyment, there is nothing to take into account" (Singer 1990: 179).

How can we know what sorts of beings feel pain? If an animal has a certain physiology and a recognizable behavioral repertoire that is indicative of an awareness of pain, then we can feel confident in thinking that animal is the sort of being that feels pain. Having a central nervous system and other physiological mechanisms that register and respond to pain, such as nociceptors and opioid receptors, and crying out or struggling when subjected to noxious stimuli or seeking to avoid such stimuli, provide reasons to believe the being in question is capable of feeling pain (Allen, 2004; Jones, 2013; Varner, 1998). Of course the same painful event can produce very different responses in different animals—this may be due in part to different physiological features or it may be due to different evolutionary demands or perhaps different prior experiences. These differences combined with questions about just how the human brain processes stimuli to produce pain-responsive behaviors keep open the epistemological questions about who feels pain.

Nonetheless, there is good evidence for thinking that mammals, birds, fish, reptiles, and cephalopods, such as octopus, feel pain. Gary Varner reviewed evidence available over twenty years ago for six pain-related conditions and devised a chart laying out which animals had each condition; all the animals on Varner's chart had endogenous opioids present, including earth worms and insects, although they lacked the other conditions (Varner, 1998). Though there is good evidence to date, discussions about "where to draw the line" between beings that feel pain and those that don't will undoubtedly continue (Braithwaite, 2010).[2]

While debates about line drawing are ongoing, there should be no debate about the suffering that billions of animals currently endure in agricultural production. An estimated 10 billion animals suffer and ultimately are slaughtered to produce animal products in the United States annually; estimates put the annual number of animals suffering in intensive agriculture globally at three to five times that number.[3] Most of these animals are confined indoors for their entire lives in areas that prevent them from moving around. They are denied species-typical social interactions, including raising young, who are instead removed at birth. And they are subjected to a variety of painful procedures: tails and ears are cut off and males are castrated without anesthesia; animals are branded with hot irons; birds have their beaks cut off with hot knives; male chicks are ground up alive in the egg industry; and cows are forcibly impregnated regularly to produce milk, and they suffer from untreated infections. Slaughter often doesn't bring immediate relief from suffering, as animals are hung upside down on a conveyer belt and only occasionally are their throats slit cleanly enough that their death is instantaneous, leaving many to linger in pain, bleeding until they ultimately lose consciousness.

Given the huge numbers of sentient creatures that are suffering so intensely to provide cheap meals for humans, combined with the suffering caused by the dire environmental and climate consequences of intensive agriculture, questions about where to draw the line can often seem beside the point. Of course, at the margins of consciousness, questions about who can feel pain and suffer can be raised. But there is as little doubt that mammals and birds experience pain and suffering as there is doubt that it is unnecessary for those with affordable alternatives to cause such suffering.

3 THE PROBLEM OF PREDATION

A great number of animals have interests in avoiding suffering, and it is relatively easy for those of us who have access to plant-based foods to satisfy our interest in avoiding hunger (as well as enjoying the pleasures of eating) by foregoing the consumption of other animals.

But this isn't so for all animals who have an interest in sustenance, such as predators. Given that being ripped apart and eaten while still alive causes suffering, there is an obvious conflict between the interests of predators and the interests of prey animals. And this conflict raises difficult questions for those who recognize that suffering should be prevented and are in a position to do something about it. Is there an obligation to prevent predation? The fact of predation is thought to be a problem for any position that holds that suffering is what matters from an ethical point of view (Everett, 2001; Gruen, 2011, ch. 6; Hadley, 2006; Horta, 2013; McMahan, 2014). It is important to remember that both predator and prey have an interest in avoiding suffering—the animal who is prey has interests in not suffering by being eaten and the predator has an interest in not suffering hunger. One of the potentially troubling implications of recognizing an interest in not suffering as a condition that generates ethical obligations arises in the context of some animals violating those interests in other animals.

It might be suggested that predation is "necessary" suffering and should be considered beyond ethical demands, so we are under no obligation to do anything. But consider a scenario in which a child is being chased down by a hungry lion. If the lion catches the child then the child will be torn to bits and probably partially eaten alive. In this case it seems more difficult to simply dismiss the child's suffering as a part of the natural cycle of life and death, however tragic it may be. If it is possible to intervene to save the child, it seems uncontroversial that one should do so, even if the predation is "necessary" from the point of view of the lion. Now let's imagine the same scenario, only this time the lion is chasing a gazelle. In both cases, there is an experiencing being whose life will end in a horribly painful death. To say that one is obligated to prevent the suffering of the child and not obligated to prevent the death of the gazelle, because the child is a child and the gazelle is not, would be to invoke an unjustifiable species prejudice. Suffering, insofar as it matters, matters regardless of the kind of body it happens to be inflicted upon. Consistency demands viewing both cases as "natural" tragedies or recognizing an obligation to intervene in both.

But intervention raises a range of problems. Perhaps in order to minimize the pain the prey animals experience (whether they are children or gazelle) and to also minimize the interest frustration of predators, we could intervene by providing predators with sustenance that does not result from suffering (Stanescu, 2009; McMahan, 2008).[4] However, even if this were a possible, affordable option, interfering is risky as we humans have a tendency to create more problems than we intend to solve when we intervene in the workings of the natural world. Following Sue Donaldson and Will Kymlicka, it may be that not all "suffering in nature really should be placed in the category of 'preventable.'"(2013, 159).

Some instances of suffering, though tragic, may not be the only feature of these conflict situations to which we should direct our moral attention. When focused on all and only suffering, we tend to distort not only the lives of "wild" animals but also our own place in nature. Wild animals live their own lives in their own species-specific ways; they are sovereign beings. (Donaldson and Kymlicka, 2011). Intervention in their autonomous ways of life, even if it would prevent suffering, is paternalistic and in most cases constitutes an unjustifiable infringement on their freedom. To think of humans in a position to prevent wild suffering also may be seen as a hubristic elevation of our own powers and a misrecognition of our own place in nature. Environmental philosopher Val Plumwood, after being attacked by a hungry crocodile, recounted the humbling and cautionary lessons she learned from being prey: "the need to acknowledge our own animality and ecological vulnerability . . . lessons largely lost to the technological culture that now dominates the earth. In my work as a philosopher, I see more and more reason to stress our failure to perceive this vulnerability, to realize how misguided we are to view ourselves as masters of a tamed and malleable nature" (2000: 145–146).

4 BEYOND SUFFERING

Conscious beings have more than just interests in not suffering. Living harmoniously within the constraints of the natural world and living a good life in which one flourishes are also interests that many conscious beings share. The lives of all animals, humans and nonhumans alike, can go better or worse for them from their own points of view, even if they are free of pain and suffering, and sometimes despite suffering. But there are different ways to specify what counts as a good life and what beyond the absence of pain and suffering is necessary to achieve well-being.

Some argue that an individual has a high level of well-being if she has attained valuable things that can be represented on what has been called an "objective list" (Parfit, 1984; Crisp, 2013).[5] On objective list accounts, an individual needn't necessarily be consciously or subjectively experiencing some thing as good or valuable in order for well-being to be promoted. Having health and bodily integrity; having meaningful social relations with others with whom one can freely choose to associate; living in a healthy environment; being free to laugh, play, relax—these are the sorts of interests that when satisfied are conducive to a high level of well-being, whether or not they are actually desired. Martha Nussbaum has generated evolving lists of conditions that are required for living a dignified life for both humans and nonhumans, with significant continuity between them. The capabilities that are thought to contribute to non-human animal flourishing, according to Nussbaum, include life; bodily health; bodily integrity; freedom to engage the senses, imagination, and thought; emotional expression; practical reason, affiliation with others of their kind and other species; play; and control over one's environment (2007: 492–400).

It would be hard to argue that being healthy and having genuine friendships, meaningful work, and the like are not the sorts of things that are valuable and conducive to well-being. Although these things are generally conducive to our well-being, it is possible that the individual who has them doesn't consider herself to be at a high level of well-being, maybe because she feels sad most of the time, despite having opportunities to live without pain, to express herself, to interact with others, and so forth. Her well-being is based on her achieving a pleasurable subjective consciousness, not on whether goods or opportunities on an objective list are available to her. Objective list well-being is akin to satisfying interests of the second sort described earlier. While having certain goods and opportunities may be conducive to achieving well-being, they are neither necessary or sufficient.

While it is quite plausible to hold that well-being must be experienced, subjective theories of well-being are nonetheless open to problems. For example, a person may be deceived into believing that her well-being is achieved; she may think she is satisfied even though the basis for her subjective mental state doesn't actually obtain. Let's suppose Ann's sense of well-being is reasonably tied to feeling appreciated by her family and respected in her community. Now let's further suppose that Ann is actually being used by her family for their own ends, they don't really love and respect her, they have tricked her into thinking that the menial labors they have her doing are worthy and convinced Ann that she is cherished. But to the community it looks as if Ann is servile, lacking in any self-respect, and people sadly smile or wave as they walk past her, gestures she perceives as respectful rather than pitiful. In this case, Ann may feel like her well-being is being promoted but believing that she has achieved what she had hoped for is an illusion. She is operating under a sense of false consciousness, and while she does have positive experiences and is not obviously suffering, she is nonetheless subordinate, her interests are not actually being satisfied, and thus her well-being is not promoted, despite her feeling like it is.

Another problem, particularly in the context of other animals, is that it is hard to determine whether another has well-being because we can't really know what is going on in another's consciousness. But as was the case with pain, there are ways to determine whether an individual has well-being that combine both the experienced, conscious component and the objective conditions that factor into determinations of well-being. These conditions are important in cases of non-linguistic beings in which those seeking to determine whether they have well-being have to engage in a sort of behavior reading. What might these objective conditions be beyond avoiding pain and suffering?

Surely providing the basics for functioning are minimal conditions; these would include nutrition and hydration, health, bodily integrity, shelter, a non-toxic environment, freedom of movement, social stimulation (for social beings), and freedom of expression in its various forms. How these conditions are satisfied will vary depending on the type of animal being considered. Chimpanzees, for example, require complex social and physical environments consisting of individuals of various ages and different social and environmental problems to solve. More solitary species require solitude or at least space to be away from others. Elephants require great distances to roam. Rodents thrive when they can burrow into small spaces. An individual who is denied the opportunity to behave in these species-typical ways will generally not have well-being, although there may be exceptions. This is glaringly true for humans forced to exist in solitary confinement; even when they are fed, can walk around their cells, and are permitted to scream or sing or talk to themselves, their well-being is purposefully diminished. If, against the odds, they are able to find some contentment or satisfaction in their thoughts, they nonetheless lack well-being.

Being able to engage in certain sorts of activities, even if those activities may cause one pain or suffering, may also be important. Conscious, experiencing animals, have a phenomenology, something that it is like to be them. Even when they don't explicitly appreciate their freedoms, being able to experience their lives as their own and to do what they do, free of suffering, is also part of what matters from an ethical point of view.

5 WHAT IT IS LIKE TO BE SOMEONE

Being free to express one's self without negative repercussions and living without threat of domination through arbitrary interference, however benevolent the intentions, are also the sorts of things that contribute to well-being. Conscious beings make choices about what matters to them, and our recognizing and respecting those choices reflects on the value of our own freedoms. Allowing beings to choose what they want and not interfering as they pursue that choice is good for us and for all conscious beings. As John Stuart Mill noted, most of the time individuals are in the best position to know what will satisfy their own interests, and allowing individuals the freedom to pursue their ways of life will lead to enhanced overall well-being. Having that freedom may also be valuable in itself, even when free actions lead to frustration or suffering.

Humans and other animals make choices about what to do, when to do it, and who to do it with. Many animals make plans, as can be observed when they construct and save tools for future use or when they cache food to collect at a later time, for example. Social animals often engage in manipulation or deception to try to get what they want and to prevent others from getting it. Not all animals in a social group do exactly the same things, eat exactly the same things, or spend time with the same individuals. Chimpanzees groom each other; grooming involves one chimpanzee using his or her hands to look through another chimpanzee's coat, picking out nits and inspecting for injuries, but mostly the behavior seems to provide enjoyment for the one being groomed and the one grooming. This is a species-typical behavior. Who gets groomed, when and under what conditions and who does the grooming, is something that chimpanzees choose. Some species-typical behaviors involve lengthy migrations, but who leads the migration, when the migration begins, and exactly where the group is heading will vary. Some species-typical behaviors involve remaining with one's natal group for life and some involve leaving as soon as one is able, but the exact time one leaves, where he or she goes, and with whom, are individual choices influenced by experience and the community. Not all cats enjoy the company of others and not all dogs greet visitors in the same way; some will run and hide others will be more forward. Social animals, whether wild or domestic, respond to different animals in their communities in a variety of ways, depending on social rank, personalities, and past behavior. While there is clearly something that it is like to be a bat, a rat, a chimp, and an elephant, there is something particular that it is like to be Tailer the rat or Sheba the chimpanzee.

Of course understanding what it is like to be someone else, to understand their umwelt,[6] is quite challenging. Since humans generally share physical experiences and are familiar with a variety of similar environments it is possible to come to understand the perspectives and experiences of another. Even if some humans have very different embodied experiences and/ or live in a very unfamiliar environment, we have language that can go a long way to filling in the epistemic gaps. But, as Thomas Nagel suggests, I can't really know what it is like to be another kind of animal, like a bat; I can only imagine what it would be like for me to have bat wings, to fly around navigating by echolocation, and to sleep hanging upside down. We are, after all, limited by the resources of our human minds (Nagel, 1974). Imagining what it is like to be a particular bat or rat or chimpanzee may be beyond human imagination. The subjective experiences of non-human others seem particularly inaccessible.

Christine Korsgaard has suggested a way we can avoid the dangers of trying to imagine what it is like to be another animal by recognizing that our judgments and perceptions can be limited by misapplying human standards:

> When we try to think about what it is like to be another animal, we bring our human standards with us, and then the other animals seem to us like lesser beings. A human being who lives a life governed only by desires and instincts, not by values, would certainly be a lesser being. But that doesn't mean that the other animals are lesser beings. They are simply beings of a different kind. . . . What is important about the other animals is what we have in common: that they, like us, are the kinds of beings to whom things *can* be important. Like us, they pursue the things that are important *to* them as if they were important *absolutely*, important in deadly earnest— for, like us, what else can they do? When we do this, we claim our own standing as ends in

ourselves. But our only reason for doing that is that it is essential to the kinds of beings we are, beings who take their own concerns to be important. The claim of the other animals to the standing of ends in themselves has [the] same ultimate foundation as our own—the essentially self-affirming nature of life itself. (Korsgaard 2013)

If we carefully observe other animals and learn about their specific ways of life we can come to see that they adapt to changing circumstances, make choices and resist changes if that is what they decide, and improve their environments, often through collective action. They learn from conspecifics and modify what they learn to suit themselves and their needs. They pursue activities they find rewarding, activities that matter to them. They autonomously express their way of being, as conscious expressions of their ways of life. We may not ever have access to what it *feels* like to be them, but we are able to respect that there is something it is like to be them and pursuits that matter to them.

6 RESPECTING OTHER ANIMALS

Respecting other animals as beings with their own lives to lead in their own ways opens the possibility that there is more that is valuable than satisfying their interest in avoiding pain. Other animals have an interest in being who they are and doing what they do, and insofar as we value the capacity to be oneself and work to protect it for other humans, we should extend that respect to all animals.

Currently, the reach of human activity has expanded across the entire globe, and humans are entangled with each other and other animals in complex ways. The nature and depth of these relationships vary, but most humans view other animals as objects, tools, commodities, or obstacles. Those of us who are able to reflect on the impact of our actions, however, have an opportunity to rethink the standard view of other animals and work to make our relationships better, or at least not make them worse. When we participate in activities and institutions that directly harm others by creating negative experiences, deprive them of their well-being, or deny them opportunities to be who they are and pursue what they care about, we owe them at least our attention and probably some remedy. Since there is something that it is like to be another conscious being, we can try to empathize with these others and determine how best to improve our relationships to promote well-being.

Even though it is challenging to understand what it is like to be another, and even though we are limited by our inevitable anthropocentric perspectives, being in respectful ethical relation involves, in part, attempting to understand and respond to another's needs, interests, desires, vulnerabilities, hopes, perspectives, and so on not by positing, from one's own point of view, what they might or should be. I have argued elsewhere that through "entangled empathy" when we direct our moral attention to specific others in their particular circumstance, we can patiently come to understand them better and respectfully respond to them. Entangled empathy is a process that involves both affect and cognition. Individuals who are empathizing with others respond to the other's condition and reflectively imagine themselves in the distinct position of the other while staying attentive to both similarities and differences between themselves and their situation and that of the fellow creature with whom they are empathizing. This alternation between the first and third person points-of-view helps minimize misperceptions and overly anthropocentric judgments (Gruen, 2015, Gruen, 2013; Gruen, 2012; Gruen, 2009).

Entangled empathy involves paying critical attention to the broader conditions that may negatively affect the experiences and flourishing of those with whom one is empathizing, and this requires those of us empathizing to attend to things we might not have otherwise. It therefore also enhances our own conscious experiences and helps us to become more sensitive perceivers. When adopting a respectful perspective on the conscious experiences of other animals, the claims they make on us come into sharper focus.

Honing our skill at empathizing with different others is desperately needed as we humans, often mindlessly, destroy the planet and all of its inhabitants.

NOTES

1. Experientialism is a term that encompasses a variety of utilitarian views, including hedonistic utilitarianism, preference utilitarianism, and two-level views; it also includes views that ground "rights" in sentience or being "the subject of a life" or personhood. Peter Singer's approach (1990) can be called "experientialist," as can Tom Regan's (1983). Experientialism is sometimes referred to as "sentientism" (see Gary Varner, 2003).
2. The ongoing debate about fish and whether they feel pain (apparently they do) and whether they are conscious of the pain (apparently they are) is illustrative of how the debate has evolved. See Braithwaite (2010).
3. Food and Agriculture Organization of the United Nations.
4. There are some who believe that animals raised humanely and then painlessly killed do not suffer, but this view has come under increased scrutiny. See for example, Stanescu (2009). The production of meat that does not entail suffering is not yet an actuality; in vitro meat (meat grown in laboratories) could be a very expensive option. McMahan (2008) has us consider eating animal bodies that have been genetically modified to cause the animal to die early natural deaths.
5. For clear descriptions of theories about "what makes a life go best" see Parfit (1984, appendix I). See also Crisp (2013).
6. Jakob von Uexküll, an early ethologist, was interested in the perceptual or phenomenal worlds that organisms experienced and in which they acted. He described the unique "bubbles" in which very different types of beings experience their worlds as their umwelt. "A Stroll Through the Worlds of Animals and Men: A Picture Book of Invisible Worlds," in *Instinctive Behavior: The Development of a Modern Concept*, ed. and trans. Claire H. Schiller (New York: International Universities Press, Inc., 1957), 5–80.

REFERENCES

Allen, C. (2004). "Animal Pain." *Nous* 38: 617–643.

Braithwaite, V. (2010). *Do Fish Feel Pain?* New York: Oxford University Press.

Crisp, R. (2013). "Well-Being." In *Stanford Encyclopedia of Philosophy*, edited by E. N. Zalta. <http://plato.stanford.edu/archives/sum2015/entries/well-being/>

Donaldson, S., and Kymlicka, W. (2011). *Zoopolis: A Political Theory of Animal Rights*. New York: Oxford University Press.

Donaldson, S., and Kymlicka, W. (2013). "A Defense of Animal Citizens and Sovereigns." *Law, Ethics and Philosophy* 1: 143–160.

Everett, J. (2001). "Environmental Ethics, Animal Welfarism, and the Problem of Predation: A Bambi Lover's Respect for Nature." *Ethics and the Environment* 6: 42–67.

Gruen, L. (2009). "Attending to Nature." *Ethics and the Environment* 14: 23–38.

Gruen, L. (2011). *Ethics and Animals: An Introduction.* Cambridge: Cambridge University Press.

Gruen, L. (2012). "Navigating Difference (Again): Animal Ethics and Entangled Empathy." In *Strangers to Nature: Animal Lives and Human Ethics*, edited by G. Zucker, 213–233. Lanham, MD: Lexington Books.

Gruen, L. (2013). "Entangled Empathy: An Alternative Approach to Animal Ethics." In *The Politics of Species: Reshaping Our Relationships with Other Animals*, edited by R. Corbey and A. Lanjouw, 223–231. Cambridge: Cambridge University Press.

Gruen, L. (2015). *Entangled Empathy: An Alternative Ethic for Our Relationships with Animals.* New York: Lantern Books.

Hadley, J. (2006). "The Duty to Aid Nonhuman Animals in Dire Need." *Journal of Applied Philosophy* 23: 445–451.

Horta, O. (2013). "Zoopolis, Intervention, and the State of Nature." *Law, Ethics and Philosophy* 1: 113–126.

Jones, R. C. (2013). "Science, Sentience, and Animal Welfare." *Biology and Philosophy* 28: 1–30.

Korsgaard, C. (2013). "Getting Animals in View." *The Point* 6. http://www.thepointmag.com/2012/metaphysics/getting-animals-view

McMahan, J. (2008). "Eating Animals the Nice Way." *Daedalus* 66–76.

McMahan, J. (2014). "The Moral Problem of Predation." In *Philosophy Comes to Dinner*, edited by A. Chignell, T. Cuneo, and M. Halteman. London: Routledge.

Mill, J. S. (1978). *On Liberty*, 8th ed. Indianapolis, IN: Hackett Publishing.

Nagel, T. (1974). "What Is It Like to Be a Bat?" *The Philosophical Review* 83: 435–450.

Nussbaum, M. (2007). *Frontiers of Justice: Disability, Nationality, Species. Membership.* Cambridge, MA: Harvard University Press.

Parfit, D. (1984). *Reasons and Persons.* Gloucestershire, England: Clarendon Press.

Plumwood, V. (2000). "Being Prey." Reprinted in *The Ultimate Journey: Inspiring Stories of Living and Dying*, edited by J. O'Reilly, S. O'Reilly, and R. Sterling, 128–146. Palo Alto, CA: Travelers' Tales, Inc.

Regan, T. (1983). *The Case for Animal Rights*, Oakland: University of California Press.

Singer, P. (1990). *Animal Liberation*, 2nd Edition, New York: New York Review.

Stanescu, V. (2009). " 'Green' Eggs and Ham? The Myth of Sustainable Meat and the Danger of the Local." *Journal of Critical Animal Studies* 7: 18–55.

Varner, G. (1998). *In Nature's Interests? Interests, Animal Rights, and Environmental Ethics.* New York: Oxford University Press.

Varner, G. (2003). "Sentientism." In *A Companion to Environmental Philosophy*, edited by D. Jamieson. Oxford: Blackwell: 192–203.

CHAPTER 9

....

LIVING INDIVIDUALS
Biocentrism in Environmental Ethics

....

CLARE PALMER

ETHICAL positions on which all living individuals are valuable and worthy of respect or moral concern are normally called *biocentric*. Ethical biocentrism forms an important family of approaches to Western environmental ethics. An early kind of biocentrism, based on the idea of "reverence for life," was proposed by Albert Schweitzer in *Philosophy of Civilization* (1923). More recently, a number of competing biocentric approaches have been systematically developed. While unified by accepting the value of living individuals, these approaches differ over what characterizes a living individual; why those characteristics might be morally relevant; whether some living individuals are more valuable than others; whether the value of life is just one among a broader, plural set of values or is the only such value; and in which ethical theory the value of life should be located. In this chapter, I briefly outline key elements of these debates, then consider how biocentric ethics might respond to emerging global environmental problems, in particular to anthropogenic climate change, about which little has so far been written from a biocentric perspective (though see Attfield, 2009, 2011).

1 THE VALUE OF LIVING INDIVIDUALS

Biocentric ethics focuses on the value, or moral considerability, of individual living things. However, although most people can easily pick out examples of living things—an oak tree, a toad, a salmon—defining what *makes* something a "living thing" is more difficult. While there's no dispute about whether some things are alive, borderline cases raise problematic definitional questions. For instance, could some kinds of complex machines, insect colonies, viruses, or bodily organs (such as livers) fall into the category of "living things"? For reasons of space, I won't attempt to adjudicate this question here (but see Goodpaster, 1978; Varner, 1990; Agar, 1995; Sterba, 1998).

Despite this uncertainty about defining "living things," one widely accepted idea is that living things are distinctively goal- or end-directed, and this goal is their own good, rather than the good of another. Paul Taylor, perhaps the best known biocentric ethicist, maintains in *Respect for Nature* (1986: 45): "Each living thing . . . [is] an entity pursuing its own good in its own way, according to its species specific nature." That living individuals are distinguished by being goal-directed toward their own good has been a central idea in biocentric ethics. If one accepts this, it makes sense to say that living things are *benefited* by processes or actions that promote their good, and *harmed* by processes or practices that set back their good, where "benefit" and "harm" just mean that living things can be made better or worse off. So, an oak tree can be benefited by adequate rainfall and harmed by being struck by lightning.

Merely accepting the view that living individuals can be better or worse off, however, does not get us to biocentric ethics, which requires the further commitment that the good of living individuals *matters* ethically, not just that living things actually have a good. There's no contradiction, for instance, in accepting that plants can be harmed or benefited while denying that harming or benefiting them matters ethically. Just because a living individual has a good does not necessarily mean that we should protect or promote that good. O'Neill (1993: 23) argues: "That Y is a good of X does not entail that Y should be realised unless we have a prior reason for believing that X is the sort of thing whose good ought to be promoted."

Many ethicists argue that organisms lacking in subjective experiences—such as plants and insects—are not of direct moral concern even though they can be benefited or harmed. Since *they* can't care about anything, then (in this view) we have no reason to care about them. As Singer (1989: 154) puts it: "If a being is not capable of suffering, or of experiencing enjoyment or happiness, there is nothing to be taken into account."

Biocentrists, however, reject the view that only experienced goods matter; *life* is what is of primary significance. Goodpaster (1978: 316) for instance, argues that "sentience is an adaptive characteristic of living organisms that provides them with a better capacity to anticipate, and so avoid, threats to life. This at least suggests, though of course it does not prove, that the capacities to suffer and to enjoy are ancillary to something more important . . ." The idea that *being alive* is either a necessary or sufficient condition to matter ethically is widely held, both within and outside environmental ethics. However, this biocentric ethic generates worries, even among those who are sympathetic to it. Is it overdemanding in practice? Does it require us never to kill any living individuals? If so, how could we live? Biocentrists have several ways of responding to these concerns.

2 Biocentric Egalitarianism and Inegalitarianism

Suppose we accept that being alive is either necessary or sufficient for moral considerability. This tells us nothing about *comparative* value. Here, it is helpful to distinguish between "moral considerability"—whether something is of direct moral relevance at all—and "moral significance," which Goodpaster (1978: 311) describes as "comparative judgments of moral weight." That all living beings count for *something* does not necessarily mean that all living things are equally morally *significant*. There may be other properties that "provide bases for different kinds or degrees of moral standing" (Schmidtz, 1998: 59).

Some biocentric ethicists—most prominently, Paul Taylor (1983, 1986) and James P. Sterba (1998)—maintain that, in principle, all living things are equally morally significant, a view called *biocentric egalitarianism*. (Egalitarianism can be interpreted in different ways; see

Attfield, 2005.) Other biocentric views, in contrast, are *inegalitarian;* the possession or expression of certain capacities, such as sentience or rationality, increases individuals' moral significance (see Lombardi, 1983; Varner, 1998; Attfield, 2003a; and Schmidtz, 2011). Attfield (2003a), for instance, argues that expressions of more complex or psychologically sophisticated capacities have higher moral significance than expressions of less complex capacities. In focusing on living individuals, these inegalitarian views remain biocentric, but they endorse a kind of value pluralism in which capacities other than just being alive are morally significant.

Biocentric egalitarianism raises strong practical concerns, if understood to imply that killing or harming other organisms is always wrong. But its advocates deny this implication. Many biocentric egalitarians develop a distinction between "basic," "non-basic," and sometimes "luxury" needs. Humans are normally permitted to defend themselves against aggressors and to harm and kill others where required for their *basic* needs, but not for their *non-basic* and certainly not *luxury* needs. Of course, what "non-basic needs" means is highly contested. But the fundamental claim is that when we recognize organisms' interests as having different degrees of importance and urgency, this helps us to make decisions about actions, policies, or practices that impact on other living things. And as Schmidtz (2011) and others point out, killing to ensure one's own survival does not imply that you regard the one you kill as inferior.

Some biocentric egalitarians also argue that while different organisms are equally alive, and so have equal moral significance, additional morally relevant considerations may also apply. So biocentric egalitarianism seems to imply that there is no reason to choose to eat plants over animals. However, even leaving aside complications (such as the relative size and nutritional value of plants versus animals, and the number of plant lives needed to sustain an animal reared for food), some biocentric egalitarians argue that animal suffering *is* a relevant additional consideration. Taylor (1986: 295) maintains that "when there is a choice between killing plants or killing sentient animals, it will be less wrong to kill plants if animals are made to suffer when they are taken for food." So if two lives are equally at stake, but killing one will involve suffering, this is a reason for choosing to kill the other (though this also suggests that if killing is painless, there's nothing to choose between killing plants and animals).

However, these interpretations and modifications of biocentric egalitarianism do not satisfy its many critics, who argue that some lives really are more morally significant than others—for instance, that the complex psychological states experienced by humans and other mammals are of higher moral significance than just being alive. Schmidtz (2011: 129), while sympathetic to the idea that being alive counts for *something,* maintains that biocentric egalitarianism—contrary to Taylor's view—actually reflects a *failure* of respect for nature. It does not recognize the morally significant differences between members of different species—such as carrots and cows, mice and chimpanzees. Most recent biocentric accounts have been *inegalitarian,* maintaining that the possession of capacities such as sentience or having "ground projects", that is, a nexus of meaningful desires that make life worth living, (Varner, 1998) makes some organisms more morally significant than others.

3 LIFE AND OTHER VALUES

Biocentric *in*egalitarianism endorses a kind of value pluralism. Being alive brings moral considerability, but other capacities, such as being sentient, add to moral significance. This kind of value pluralism is, strictly speaking, still biocentric as I am using the term, because the values at stake are all carried or manifested by individual living things. However, biocentrists also adopt other kinds of value pluralism. Taylor, for instance, focuses his account on *wild* living things, not living things "in bioculture." Organisms in bioculture are not worth less; after all, they too are alive: "The living organisms being used in any society's bioculture are organisms that have a good of their own. They can be benefited or harmed. In this matter they are exactly like wild animals and plants in natural ecosystems" (Taylor, 1986: 55). Yet some of the duties he claims we have to wild organisms—such as noninterference—can't apply to biocultural organisms, since many require our support to survive. So perhaps Taylor means "wildness" to be an *additional* value that we should protect wherever it is found. However, wildness is not an organismic capacity (unlike, for instance, sentience), and he doesn't understand it as intensifying moral significance. The idea instead seems to be that we have different duties toward wild and biocultural organisms.

Another kind of value pluralism takes "being alive" as a *sufficient* condition for having value, but not a *necessary* one. On this view, ecological communities, or species, as well as individuals, are independently morally considerable in their own right. This is usually because they are thought to be "individual-like" in as much as they have a good of their own. A number of environmental ethicists have defended this broader position, including Johnson (1991), Sterba (2001), and possibly even Taylor, although in his published work Taylor (1986: 69) maintains that the good of an ecosystem just means "the median distribution point of the good of its individual members." (Evans [2005: 123] draws on unpublished correspondence with Taylor that seems to support this more holistic view.)

The view that ecological communities and/or species are goal directed toward their own good, and therefore morally considerable in their own right, raises a number of difficulties too substantial to unpack here (but see Cahen, 1988; Sandler, 2007: 76–80). For the purposes of this chapter, I'll maintain that accepting the moral considerability of species or ecosystems as well as living individuals *departs* from strict biocentrism; such views have biocentric elements but are not themselves biocentric.

4 Biocentrism and Ethical Theory

To be action-guiding, biocentric values must be located within an ethical theory. Three ethical theories are particularly relevant here: virtue biocentrism, consequentialist biocentrism, and deontological biocentrism (though each is really a family of related positions).

4.1 Virtue Biocentrism

No thoroughgoing biocentric virtue ethic has yet been developed, although both biocentric accounts in which virtues have a place and virtue ethics that contain biocentric values have been proposed. While not primarily a virtue theorist, Taylor (1986) has been most influential here; he takes the importance of virtues to be in enabling people to comply with rules. Taylor identifies general virtues of moral strength (such as perseverance) and moral concern (benevolence, compassion, care and sympathy) alongside specific biocentric virtues of considerateness, regard, impartiality, trustworthiness, fairness, and equality.

More recently, Kawall (2003) and Sandler (2007) have proposed accounts of virtue ethics in which having reverence or respect for life is understood as a virtue, and grounds other, more specific, virtues concerning living individuals. Both are, however, pluralists, maintaining that reverence or respect for life should be seen as one virtue among others; Sandler (2007: 73) also argues that respect for individual living things needs to "be informed by our form of life." So our "care towards other living organisms" cannot extend to "bacteria and viruses" because we "literally cannot live" if we take this view; and we may appropriate living things for our own use without disrespect, though this doesn't mean it's acceptable to have a "consumptive disposition." Sandler identifies a range of virtues relevant to respect for nature: care, compassion, restitutive justice, nonmaleficence, and ecological sensitivity.

In contrast with virtue ethics, much more systematic accounts of broadly consequentialist and broadly deontological forms of biocentric ethics have been developed, most prominently by Robin Attfield and Paul Taylor, respectively.

4.2 Consequentialist Biocentrism

Consequentialists generally value *states of affairs* rather than *things in themselves*. Robin Attfield argues that the *flourishing* of living individuals is what matters ethically (while recognizing that "flourishing" has different components, and that different beings flourish in different ways). Attfield's form of biocentrism is also, in certain ways, inegalitarian: although all living beings can flourish, not all flourishing is of equal value; there "is much more of value in the flourishing of a sentient creature as such than in the flourishing of an individual tree as such" (Attfield 1994: 139). He also accepts a distinction between basic, non-basic, and trivial needs. "Impacts on basic needs outweigh lesser impacts, and . . . impacts on creatures with complex and sophisticated capacities such as autonomy and self-consciousness (in cases where these capacities are themselves at stake) outweigh impacts on creatures lacking them" (Attfield, 2003a: 52). So while the basic needs of beings with complex and sophisticated capacities take priority over the basic needs of beings that lack these capacities, this doesn't mean that the trivial needs of more sophisticated beings should trump the basic needs of less sophisticated beings.

Attfield's consequentialism is also *totalizing, maximizing,* and *indirect*. He argues that the total sum of organismic flourishing should be maximized over time (Attfield, 1991). Rather than focusing directly on particular acts, he maintains that we should normally aim to bring about best consequences indirectly by following optimal policies and practices: "there are practices that general recognition of which makes for, or would make for, a much better world than would be possible either in their absence or through alternative practices" (Attfield, 1987: 107).

Clearly this is only one possible form of biocentric consequentialism; consequentialist biocentrism could be egalitarian, direct, or satisficing, for instance. There are still many unoccupied or undeveloped possible positions here. However, Attfield's position provides a useful starting point for thinking about biocentric consequentialism and climate change.

4.3 Deontological Biocentrism

Deontological biocentrism focuses on human duties toward, or the rights of, living things. In environmental ethics, this approach emerged within the Deep Ecology movement, most famously in Arne Naess's claim that "the equal right to live and blossom [for all living things] is an intuitively clear and obvious value axiom" (Naess, 1973: 96). Taylor (1986) developed deontological biocentrism in a more systematic way, focusing on four rules that those who adopt the "attitude of respect for nature" should accept: nonmaleficence, noninterference, fidelity, and restitution. These rules, Taylor argues, should govern human interactions with wild organisms, requiring us not intentionally to harm or interfere with them; not to develop their trust in us deceptively; and where harm has been inevitable, to make appropriate restitution. Of course, in practice, following these rules is complex. Taylor suggests ways of applying them and principles for prioritization in cases of conflict. He distinguishes between actions "intrinsically incompatible with the attitude of respect for nature" and actions that, while not incompatible with this attitude, nonetheless have impacts on wild living organisms (such as building art museums on wild land). In a concession that leads many critics to claim inconsistency, Taylor accepts that there may be times when we harm or interfere with wild organisms in order to promote serious human interests—though we should always attempt to minimize wrongs and carry out restitution.

Attfield's and Taylor's forms of biocentric ethics, then, are very different. Attfield's consequentialist biocentrism focuses on maximizing total organismic flourishing; the more psychologically sophisticated, the better. Taylor's deontological biocentrism, in contrast, emphasizes rules not to harm or interfere with equally valuable wild living organisms. But both approaches—and those that concern biocentric virtues—claim to have a connection to practice and to how we should behave so as to protect, promote, and prioritize living organisms or their states. Given this, we should expect biocentric approaches to ethics to have action-guiding responses to current global environmental problems, including anthropogenic climate change. As noted earlier, though, little such work yet exists. In the rest of this chapter, I will take some first steps in thinking through possible biocentric responses to climate change, focusing on consequentialist and deontological approaches. These responses may also be relevant to other aspects of anthropogenic global environmental change, but I will not discuss these broader issues here.

5 ANTHROPOGENIC CLIMATE CHANGE AND BIOCENTRIC ETHICS

5.1 Biocentric Perspectives on Climate Change

Biocentrism provides a very particular lens through which to look at the world: one that focuses on each living thing as a morally relevant individual. Suppose we look through this individual-focused lens into a future world—a world, let's first imagine, *uninfluenced* by anthropogenic climate change. This future world would be packed with trillions of living things, though if we look far enough into the future, barely any of them would be the same living individuals that currently exist. Suppose we now look through this individual-focused lens at a future world *with* climate change. This world is still filled with trillions of living things, distinct from those currently alive. But many, or most, of the individuals in this future world *with* climate change are different individuals from those that would have existed in the alternative future world *without* climate change. Where the same species exists in both future worlds, particular genetic individuals almost certainly differ (as a changing climate, for instance, affects which individuals mate and produce offspring). And in the climate-changed world, there are likely to be fewer—or perhaps no—individuals of some species. But individuals of *other* species are predicted to be more numerous, flourishing, and found in new locations; evidence of this process already exists (e.g., Walther et al., 2002). Some places in the climate-changed world may have fewer individuals of *any* species than would otherwise exist; other places, which would be sparsely populated in a climate like today's, may be saturated with living things. Some living individuals will be struggling to survive against heat, drought, flooding, or thaws; others will flourish in the warm, the dry, or the ice-free environment.

Climate change, then, pushes the world along a particular, human-influenced trajectory. On many ethical views, this human influence matters. Nolt (2011), for instance, argues that anthropogenic climate change meets four key conditions of moral responsibility: we can cause or prevent it; we can recognize it as morally significant; we can anticipate it with some reliability; and we can act in different ways with respect to it. From this perspective, a human-influenced, climate-changed world of living things is morally charged, in a way that a "wild" future world would not have been; and for biocentric ethicists, this means that climate impacts on living things will therefore matter morally. Exactly what these impacts will be is empirically uncertain, but they may include changing the *number* of individuals, the existence of *different* individuals, harm or death to some individuals, and the bringing into being or benefiting of other individuals. Different biocentric views will evaluate these changes differently. I'll briefly outline two possible, contrasting responses here: a consequentialist biocentric view, like Attfield's; and a deontological biocentric view, like Taylor's.

5.2 Consequentialist Biocentrism and Climate Change

The major ethical concern here for consequentialist biocentrists is that climate change will create a worse future world, in terms of the flourishing of living things, than would otherwise have existed.

This worry might focus on *numbers*: if a climate-changed world over time contained fewer living individuals than a world without climate change, this world would, for most biocentric consequentialists, be worse (leaving aside the quality and psychological sophistication of the lives concerned). But this outcome does not seem particularly likely—even if we restrict "over time" to a timespan meaningful to people; Nolt (2011) suggests a couple of million years. While climate change will reduce or eliminate some species populations, "an increase in weedy and opportunistic species is … expected" (Williams et al., 2008) Some ecosystems (for instance, marine ecosystems affected by ocean acidification) may contain fewer organisms over time. But others will likely contain more—studies suggest, for example, that warming soils in subarctic areas have increased density of bacteria, fungi, and nematodes (Ruess et al., 1999). While the species mix will change, there's no compelling reason yet, at least, to be seriously concerned about reducing total future numbers of organisms.

A second concern might be about *complexity*. Climate change will cause different individuals to live, and one possible outcome would be that fewer complex organisms would live. This would not be a particular concern for *egalitarian* consequentialist biocentrists, since on an egalitarian view, if there were roughly equal numbers of roughly equally flourishing organisms, the differing complexity of their capacities would not matter. But it would matter to *inegalitarian* consequentialists if fewer psychologically complex individuals existed. And climate change might have this effect. There's some current evidence of a decline in populations of large apex consumers (Estes et al., 2011) though it is unclear whether this is attributable to climate change. Plausibly, there may be fewer individuals of some psychologically sophisticated species, such as mountain gorillas, partly on account of climate change. However, in other cases, diminishing complex species populations will be superseded by populations of equally complex individuals of other species—for instance, while the Arctic fox population declines, the red fox population expands. Substitutions between different species of equal complexity don't seem to be of direct ethical concern to consequentialist biocentrism, which is, in this sense, "species-blind." But even if a climate-changed world did have fewer psychologically sophisticated organisms, humans could breed some (including domesticates). After all, it is not required that consequentialist biocentrists regard the flourishing of an organism as less valuable because humans bred it.

Some biocentrists may resist this suggestion by defending *additional* values—such as wildness—not tied to life or individual capacities; or by arguing that even if the lost organisms' *own* flourishing could be substituted for by domesticates, the lost organisms' ecosystemic role is so critical that *other* wild organisms in the ecosystem will flourish less well (see Carter, 2001, Attfield, 2003b). Some evidence for the latter argument exists; for instance, Estes et al. (2011) maintain that where large apex consumers decline, there is "trophic downgrading" in ecosystems. But while from other ethical perspectives trophic downgrading is problematic, it isn't obviously so for biocentric ethicists; it does not necessarily imply *fewer* organisms flourishing, but rather different *types* of flourishing organisms (grasses instead of trees, for instance).

Biocentric consequentialists may also worry that climate change will reduce the flourishing of individual organisms; biocentrists, primarily inegalitarian biocentrists, might additionally worry about increased animal suffering (as would other kinds of consequentialists for whom animal suffering matters). It's very difficult to predict how, over time, climate change will affect flourishing and suffering. Humans are physiologically rather similar; so we can judge whether particular climatic conditions will cause human suffering and whether such suffering can be averted or alleviated. But biocentrists are concerned with millions of species, with different climate sensitivities and different adaptive capacities. Climate change will certainly cause some suffering and some loss of individual flourishing in the short term. But over time, species composition will change; successful species are likely to be those that are highly adaptive. As adaptive species increase, climate-originating suffering and lack of flourishing should decrease; it may be that that climate change, over time, does not cause a significant uptick in total wild suffering or lack of flourishing.

So: from the perspective of many forms of biocentric consequentialism, climate change is fairly unproblematic: numbers of living things are unlikely to decline; members of struggling species will be replaced by members of more adaptive species, and humans can breed complex animals. However, some forms of biocentric consequentialism may come to different conclusions. An inegalitarian consequentialism in which human beings are highly significant—for instance Varner's (1998) account—would be likely to find climate change more troubling. Humans are relatively physiologically similar, won't be replaced by "better adapted" people, and are relatively long lived; in addition their freedom to migrate is politically restricted; some of their adaptive measures (such as air conditioning) contribute to the problem; and they are dependent on a small variety of crops. The effects on humans may be more problematic in terms of total suffering, or loss of flourishing, than the effects on nonhumans over time; while this may seem a strange view for biocentrism to adopt, it's conceivable that this could be the strongest biocentric consequentialist objection to anthropogenic climate change.

5.3 Deontological Biocentrism and Climate Change

The primary ethical concern for deontological forms of biocentrism is harm to, and killing of, individual living things. Will climate change have this effect? In the short term, the answer is "yes." Take an animal example: polar bears. Recent evidence suggests that in parts of the Arctic, where sea ice is declining, adult polar bears weigh less than a decade ago and survival is more difficult (Derocher et al., 2004) The climate is changing around the bears; without climate change, these bears' lives would have gone better. It's plausible, then, to say that polar bears have been harmed by climate change and (given human moral responsibility) that they have therefore been wronged. For biocentrists, of course, the scope of potential morally relevant harms is much wider than sentient animals; any organism that lives long enough for climate to change around it could be harmed by the change. It's currently difficult to identify many cases like this, not least because it's difficult to pick out how far climate change is a causal factor in climate-related harms to living individuals. Nonetheless, according to a deontological view, where such wrongs can be identified, they matter; and (unlike a consequentialist view) they can't be compensated for by greater benefits to other organisms. In Taylor's view, we would need to consider what would count as appropriate restitution.

However, while climate will continue to change around organisms, as already noted, it will also change which organisms actually come into existence. This may mean that as species of more adaptive organisms expand, and less adaptive species contract, there will be fewer harms and deaths from climate change. In addition, over time, climate change will become a necessary condition of existence for an increasing number of organisms. Yet these same organisms might also subsequently be killed by some manifestation of climate change. This raises the question of whether an organism can be made worse-off in a morally relevant way by a process that's necessary for its very existence. Suppose a conifer species moves its range north as temperatures warm, but then particular individual conifers—which would not have existed had this northward expansion not occurred—are killed by a climate change–influenced drought. It might be argued that these particular conifers have not, after all, been harmed—in the sense of "made worse off"—by climate change. If the climate had not changed, those particular conifers would not be better off—they would not have existed at all. This is a case of Parfit's (1984) "non-identity problem." If the non-identity problem is taken seriously here, as time goes by, the harms of climate change appear to diminish, since climate change would become a necessary condition of existence for more and more living individuals. Yet this conclusion seems counterintuitive. Many ways of dealing with the non-identity problem have been proposed, some of which reinterpret how harm is understood; unfortunately there isn't space to discuss them here (but see Harman, 2009; Hartzell-Nichols, 2012). A deontological biocentric ethic, however (like non-biocentric deontological ethical perspectives) will need at least to consider the non-identity problem when developing a thorough-going response to climate change.

6 In Conclusion

Biocentric ethicists have moved beyond many people's intuitive sense that "life matters" to construct complex, diverse ethical systems that focus on the value of living individuals. These ethical systems must develop still further to respond coherently to growing human environmental impacts. Here I've focused on climate change (although what I've said may also apply more broadly to other human environmental impacts); but important questions are also raised for biocentrists by other anthropogenic changes, and practices such as synthetic biology.

As this brief consideration of biocentric ethics and climate change suggests, some biocentrists may find responding to these issues challenging. Biocentric ethics can't, for instance, directly register homogenization of environments or biodiversity loss as ethical problems; however, the values that biocentric ethics can directly register—fewer living organisms, lower levels of individual flourishing, or less overall psychological complexity—may not be especially threatened by climate change or global ecological change more broadly. Of course, biocentric ethicists may just accept that human global environmental impacts are not as straightforwardly morally significant as might have been expected; or biocentric views that add additional values—such as wildness or diversity—could be more systematically developed (the debate between Attfield [2003b, 2005] and Carter [2001, 2005] gives a sense of these possibilities). Biocentrism is, and will remain, a central theoretical position in environmental ethics—but it is likely to change and develop significantly in the next several decades.

References

Agar, N. (1995). "Valuing Species and Valuing Individuals." *Environmental Ethics* 17(4): 397–415.

Attfield, R. (1987). *A Theory of Value and Obligation.* Beckenham: Croom Helm.

Attfield, R. (1991). *The Ethics of Environmental Concern* (2nd ed.). Athens: University of Georgia Press.

Attfield, R. (1994). "Reasoning about the Environment." In *Environmental Philosophy: Principles and Prospects,* edited by R. Attfield, 135–149. Aldershot: Avebury.

Attfield, R. (2003a). *Environmental Ethics: An Overview for the Twenty-First Century.* Cambridge: Polity Press.

Attfield, R. (2003b). "Biocentric Consequentialism, Pluralism, and 'The Minimax Implication': A Reply to Alan Carter." *Utilitas* 15(1): 76.

Attfield, R. (2005). "Biocentric Consequentialism and Value-Pluralism: A Response to Alan Carter." *Utilitas* 17(1): 85–92.

Attfield, R. (2009). "Ecological Issues of Justice." *Journal of Global Ethics* 5(2): 147–154.

Attfield, R. (2011). "Climate Change, Environmental Ethics and Biocentrism." In *Climate Change and Environmental Ethics*, edited by Ved Nandra, 31–42. New Brunswick: Transaction Publishers.

Cahen, H. (1988). "Against the Moral Considerability of Ecosystems." *Environmental Ethics* 10(3): 195–216.

Carter, Alan (2001). "Review of Robin Attfield's Ethics of the Global Environment." *Mind* 110(437): 149–152.

Carter, Alan (2005). "Inegalitarian Biocentric Consequentialism, the Minimax Implication and Multidimensional Value Theory: A Brief Proposal for a New Direction in Environmental Ethics." *Utilitas* 17(1): 62–84.

Derocher A., Lunn, N., and Stirling, I. (2004). "Polar Bears in a Warming Climate." *Integrative and Comparative Biology* 44(2): 163–176.

Estes, J. A., Terborgh, J., Brashares, J. S., Power, M. E., Berger, J., Bond, W. J., . . . Wardle, D. A. (2011). "Trophic Downgrading of Planet Earth." *Science* 333(6040): 301–306.

Evans, C. (2005). *With Respect for Nature: Living as Part of the Natural World.* New York: SUNY Press.

Goodpaster, K. (1978). "On Being Morally Considerable." *Journal of Philosophy* 75(6): 308–325.

Harman, E. (2009). "Harming as Causing Harm." In *Harming Future Persons: Ethics, Genetics and the Nonidentity Problem*, edited by M. A. Roberts and D. T. Wasserman, 137–154. New York: Springer.

Hartzell-Nichols, L. (2012). "How Is Climate Change Harmful?" *Ethics and the Environment* 17(2): 97–112.

Johnson, L. (1991). *A Morally Deep World.* Cambridge: Cambridge University Press.

Lombardi, L. G. (1983). "Inherent Worth, Respect, and Rights." *Environmental Ethics* 5: 257–270.

Kawall, J. (2003). "Reverence for Life as a Viable Environmental Virtue." *Environmental Ethics* 25(4): 339–358.

Naess, A. (1973). "The Shallow and the Deep Long-Range Ecology Movement." *Inquiry* 16(1): 95–100.

Nolt, J. (2011). "Nonanthropocentric Climate Ethics." WIRES *Climate Change* 2: 701–711.

O'Neill, John (1993). *Ecology, Policy and Politics: Human Well-being and the Natural World.* London: Routledge.

Parfit, D. (1984). *Reasons and Persons.* Oxford: Oxford University Press.

Ruess, L., Michelsen, A., Schmidt, I. K., and Jonasson S. (1999). "Simulated Climate Change Affecting Microorganisms, Nematode Density and Biodiversity in Subarctic Soils." *Plant and Soil* 212: 63–73.

Sandler, R. (2007). *Character and Environment: A Virtue-Oriented Approach to Environmental Ethics.* New York: Columbia University Press.

Schweitzer, A. (1987/1923). *The Philosophy of Civilization.* New York: Prometheus Books.

Schmidtz, D. (1998). "Are All Species Equal?" *Journal of Applied Philosophy* 15: 57–67.

Schmidtz, D. (2011). "Respect for Everything." *Ethics, Policy and Environment* 14(2): 127–138.

Singer, P. (1989). "All Animals Are Equal." In *Animal Rights and Human Obligations*, edited by T. Regan and P. Singer, 148–162. New Jersey: Prentice Hall.

Sterba, J. P. (1998). "A Biocentrist Strikes Back." *Environmental Ethics* 20: 361–376.

Sterba, J. P. (2001). *Three Challenges to Ethics: Environmentalism, Feminism and Multiculturalism.* Oxford: Oxford University Press.

Taylor, P. (1983). "In Defense of Biocentrism." *Environmental Ethics* 5(3): 237–243.

Taylor, P. (1986). *Respect for Nature.* Princeton: Princeton University Press.

Walther, G., Post, E., Convey, P., Menzel, A., Parmesan, C., Beebee, T. J. C., . . . Bairlein, F. (2002). "Ecological Responses to Recent Climate Change." *Nature* 416: 389–395.

Williams, S. E., Shoo, L. P., Isaac, J. L., Hoffmann, A. A., Langham, G. (2008). "Towards an Integrated Framework for Assessing the Vulnerability of Species to Climate Change." *PLoS Biology* 6(12): e325.

Varner, G. (1990). "Biological Functions and Biological Interests." *Southern Journal of Philosophy* 28(2): 251–270.

Varner, G. (1998). *In Nature's Interests? Interests, Animal Rights and Environmental Ethics.* Oxford: Oxford University Press.

CHAPTER 10

HOW ECOLOGICAL COLLECTIVES ARE MORALLY CONSIDERABLE

J. BAIRD CALLICOTT

IN the context of environmental ethics, "ecological collectives" may be understood to refer to transorganismic levels of biological organization: populations within species; species within biotic communities; biotic communities and associated ecosystems within landscapes; landscapes within biomes; biomes within the biosphere. These ecological collectives are among the principal objects of ethical concern among many environmentalists and environmental professionals, such as conservation biologists and ecological restorationists (Groom et al., 2006). When we hear slogans such as (a) Save the Florida Panther!, (b) Save the Marbled Murrelet!, (c) Save the Kanza Prairie!, (d) Save the Big Thicket!, (e) Save the Rainforest! we hear morally charged pleas on behalf of (a) a regional population of cougars, (b) an endangered seabird species, (c) a biotic community and its associated ecosystem, (d) a landscape (as ecologists define it, a regional mosaic of biotic communities and associated ecosystems), and (e) a biome (or major type of vegetation found around the world). As ethical concern about global climate change grows more urgent, when not specifically a concern for humans that are adversely affected by it, ethical concern about climate change is directed to the biosphere. We now realize that so-called "individual organisms" (including human organisms) are also ecological collectives, composed not only of billions of such organisms' own cells, but also of billions of microbes representing hundreds of species (Gilbert et al., 2012). Thus eventually all ethics will perforce follow the model of the ethics of ecological collectives expounded here.

1 ETHICAL THEORY

One major task of moral philosophy is to "justify" commonly felt moral concerns—sometimes called "moral intuitions." Moral philosophers do so by means of ethical theory. Among other things, an ethical theory identifies the proper objects of ethical concern— called "moral ontology" from the Greek *ontos* ("being")—and provides reasons why those entities and not others should be the beneficiaries of ethics. In the history of Western moral philosophy, going back more than 2,500 years, most ethical theory was devoted to justifying the moral intuition that individual human beings and not other kinds of beings are the rightful beneficiaries of ethics. In a word, Western moral philosophy has been predominately anthropocentric (human-centered). A task for many environmental ethicists has been to construct a non-anthropocentric moral ontology—and thus to justify recently emerging moral intuitions about other-than-human beings and the more-than-human natural world.

New theoretical developments in a science, such as astronomy or physics, build upon and are continuous with the theories that precede them, even though some theoretical developments in a science are so different from past theory that they are characterized as revolutionary (Kuhn, 1962). Similarly, new developments in moral philosophy build upon and are continuous with the ethical theories that precede them, even though some theoretical developments in moral philosophy are so different from past theory that they, too, may be characterized as revolutionary. A non-anthropocentric moral ontology constitutes such a revolutionary development in ethics. Some non-anthropocentric moral ontologies, however, diverge more radically than others from the anthropocentric ontologies that precede them. A similar circumstance exists in the case of revolutionary theories in science. For example, even though he made the Earth a planet orbiting the sun—rather than the other way around, as astronomers (with a few rare exceptions) had assumed up until the sixteenth century—Nicolas Copernicus conservatively believed that the orbits of the planets (including that of the Earth) were circular not elliptical, as later realized by Johannes Kepler (Kuhn, 1957). Kepler's was thus a more radical departure from past astronomical theory.

Just as astronomers had long assumed that the celestial bodies move in circles, ethicists had long assumed that moral ontology should be conceived in essence-and-accident terms. How can we moral philosophers justify the moral intuition that human beings are the sole proper beneficiaries of ethics? The classical way is to posit an essential characteristic unique to humans that renders humans the rightful—and exclusive—beneficiaries of ethics. Aristotle claimed that rationality was that essential characteristic. All other characteristics— color, ethnicity, gender, race, religion—are "accidents" (that is, nonessential characteristics) "*qua*" ethics (that is, so far as ethics is concerned). One had to be a natural-born, adult, male person to be a citizen of Athens, but one need only be a rational animal (which is how Aristotle defined what a human being is) to be a beneficiary of ethics—to be a "moral patient" in the jargon of contemporary moral philosophy. Just as Copernicus conservatively stuck with using circles to plot the orbits of the planets in his revolutionary non-geocentric astronomy, so some environmental philosophers conservatively stick with an essence-accident approach to moral ontology in theorizing their revolutionary non-anthropocentric ethics.

2 CONSERVATIVE NON-ANTHROPOCENTRIC MORAL ONTOLOGY

In the essence-accident anthropocentric ethic of Immanuel Kant, the class of moral agents (those capable of acting ethically) and the class of moral patients is coextensive, specified by rationality. Tom Regan (1979) pulled the linchpin holding the circle of moral patients onto the axis of rationality with what he called (somewhat insensitively) the "Argument from Marginal Cases." If rationality is not to be something purely metaphysical, believed by an act of faith to exist in all and only human beings, but something actual and empirically ascertainable, we should be able to determine its presence or absence by specifying markers of rationality and observing whether or not a being exhibits them. Some human beings—the so-called "marginal cases"—do not exhibit those markers: human infants are prerational; human adults who are severely disabled mentally are nonrational; and older humans suffering from advanced dementia are postrational. If rationality is the essential property of a moral patient, then the human marginal cases do not qualify and therefore may be treated in the same way as other beings who do not qualify as beneficiaries of ethics are treated: used as subjects of painful and often fatal medical experiments; hunted for sport; or sent to abattoirs and slaughtered for pet food. The prospect of treating orphaned human infants, the severely disabled mentally, and senior citizens suffering from advanced dementia in such ways is thoroughly abhorrent.

To avoid this repugnant conclusion, moral philosophers have three choices: (1) admit that the rationality criterion was just a ruse and that anthropocentrism is an arbitrary, unjustified restriction on the class of moral patients; (2) make of rationality a mysterious metaphysical property that cannot be empirically ascertained; or (3) abandon the rationality criterion and select and justify some other essential characteristic that qualifies a being for ethical concern, that renders a being "morally considerable." The first alternative is unphilosophical, because it provides no justification at all for anthropocentric ethics. The second alternative is dangerous, because it opens up a Pandora's box of other non-empirical properties that would narrow the class of moral patients by excluding some humans—such as the so-called "Curse of Cain," once used by racists to exclude people of color from the class of moral patients (Schwartz, 1997). There remains only the third option, and so the Argument from Marginal Cases set revolutionary moral philosophers off on a quest for a new moral essence that would admit the marginal cases into the class of moral patients. The stronger motive for such a quest, however, was the increasingly common moral intuition that using animals as involuntary subjects in medical experiments, as "game" for human hunters, and slaughtering them for food is also abhorrent. The proposed new moral essences would indeed admit the human marginal cases into the class of moral patients, but would also admit some non-human beings into it as well.

Just as Aristarchus in the third century BCE provided Copernicus with a precedent for a non-geocentric astronomy, in the eighteenth century CE Jeremy Bentham, founder of utilitarianism, provided a precedent for a non-anthropocentric ethic. While the classical utilitarians were anthropocentrists for all practical purposes, Bentham realized that in defining, as he did, good and evil in terms of pleasure and pain, respectively, utilitarianism was nonanthropocentric in theory if not in practice. Non-human animals experience pleasure and pain and thus should be regarded as legitimate beneficiaries of ethics. Accordingly, the first proposed new moral essence, "sentience" (the capacity for experiencing pleasure and pain), was not really new (Singer, 1975). Just as "animal liberation" is built on classical utilitarianism, Regan built "animal rights" on modified Kantian deontology—from the Greek *deon*, meaning (duty). He argued that being a self-conscious "subject of a life," which can go better or worse from the subject's own point of view, should be the essence of a moral patient. Being the subject of a life is a more restrictive moral essence than sentience, which would open the class of moral patients at least to all vertebrates, but would almost certainly exclude plants and microbes. Almost simultaneously, philosophers motivated by more expansive moral intuitions proposed still more inclusive moral essences: being alive (Goodpaster, 1978); being conative (Feinberg, 1974); and being a "teleological-center-of-life" (Taylor, 1981). The latter two are different ways of naming the same thing—the property of striving toward a goal (a *telos* in Greek). All three of these proposed morally essential capacities admit more or less the same beings into the class of moral patients—all organisms from microbes to plants to animals.

I will skip over the ingenious justifications that various revolutionary moral philosophers have offered, each in defense of a preferred moral essence, because doing so would exceed the scope of this chapter. I should note, however, that all the accidental (non-essential) characteristics of thus selected members of the class of moral patients are no less morally irrelevant than such characteristics as gender, race, ethnicity, sexual orientation, religious affiliation are in the essence-accident form of anthropocentric ethics. Thus all who exhibit the essential characteristic are entitled to *equal* moral consideration—whether they are human subjects of a life or simian subjects of a life; human sentient beings or reptilian sentient beings; human living beings/conative beings/teleological centers of life or insect living beings/conative beings/teleological centers of life. This is called the "principle of equality" or "principle of impartiality" (Singer, 1972).

In revolutionary non-anthropocentric ethics, while the class of moral patients becomes more inclusive, the class of moral agents must remain limited to rational beings, because we cannot expect the human marginal cases and non-human animals—let alone insects, microbes, and plants—to be morally considerate, nor can we hold them responsible for those of their actions that adversely affect moral patients (including human moral patients). Thus the principle of equality or impartiality has also been denominated a "rational principle" (Rachels, 1990). For unequally to consider morally beings that equally qualify for moral consideration is inconsistent; and consistency, the law of noncontradiction, is the most basic law of logic, the most basic rule of rational thought and action.

3 ECOLOGICAL COLLECTIVES REQUIRE A MORE RADICAL NON-ANTHROPOCENTRIC ETHICAL THEORY

This predominant essence-accident form of ethical theory cannot, however, be made to include ecological collectives, although Lawrence E. Johnson (1991) tried to do just that. He argued that species can be understood—as some philosophers of biology (Ghiselin, 1974; Hull, 1976) suggest—to be spatially and temporally protracted individual living things and that ecosystems, as Odum (1969) claimed, exhibit developmental strategies (with which human moral agents can interfere or which we can frustrate). Ecosystems, Johnson argued, were, in effect, conative (goal-seeking) entities. Johnson's species-as-legitimate-moral-patients argument, however, is based on a notion of species that is so eccentric as to have no more than a handful of adherents; and the idea that ecosystems are teleological entities has been abandoned in ecology (Pickett and Ostfeld, 1995).

Ethical concern for endangered species populations, such as the Yellowstone cutthroat trout; whole endangered species, such as the horned toad; biotic communities and their associated ecosystems, such as tamarack-sphagnum bogs; landscapes, such as oak savannahs; and

biomes, such as cloud forests, greatly exceeds the ethical concern that many environmentalists and environmental professionals feel for individual living/conative/teleological centers of
life, such as a mesquite tree or a fire ant—if for such beings they feel any ethical concern at all.
For many environmentalists and environmental professionals ethical concern for ecological
collectives also exceeds their ethical concern for individual sentient beings, such as a garter
snake, or even individual subjects of a life, such as an opossum. To justify such moral intuitions, a more radical revolution in moral philosophy is required. It cannot be done within the
constraints of the prevailing essence-accident form of ethical theory.

Fortunately, there is one ethical theory, which also hails from the philosophically fertile
eighteenth century, that does not incorporate an essence-accident moral ontology. It was
most fully and effectively articulated by David Hume. A moral agent is not compelled by
reason to accord equal consideration to equally qualifying moral patients by virtue of their
exhibiting some essential capacity or characteristic, but is motivated to act ethically by a certain special set of feelings or emotions called the "moral sentiments." Qua ethics, human
emotions may be divided into two classes—self-oriented feelings and other-oriented feelings. The latter are the moral sentiments and they are common to the human species—in two
senses: (1) all psychologically normal humans experience them; and (2), in contrast to the
self-oriented feelings, other-oriented feelings are shared.

Among the moral sentiments are sympathy, charity, and benevolence. But also among
them are feelings—such as loyalty and patriotism—that are oriented not to human persons
but to human institutions, such as religions and countries. Passions for collectives, such as
a sports team, can rise to a fever pitch. A team's complement of athletes is ephemeral; and a
gifted athlete, when traded to a rival team, goes from an object of adoration to one of scorn—
indicating that the sentiment of loyalty is directed to the collective, not distributively to its
individual athletes. Many of my fellow American patriots love their country but loathe those
of its citizens who differ racially, religiously, or politically from them.

Because the moral sentiments are the same in all psychologically normal humans, disagreements about moral particulars turn not on differing emotional constitutions, but
entirely on the subordinate, yet crucially important role that reason plays in moral deliberation, choice, action, and judgment. Therefore, if convincing reasons are offered for making
ecological collectives the objects of the moral sentiments traditionally oriented to various
human collectives—as patriotism is oriented to nations—then ecological collectives will fall
within the purview of non-anthropocentric environmental ethics.

4 THE BIOLOGICAL ACCOUNT OF THE ORIGINS AND CULTURAL EVOLUTION OF ETHICS

The theory of moral sentiments enjoyed little currency in twentieth-century moral *philosophy*. It was and still remains the theory of choice in the *biological* account of ethics initiated
by Charles Darwin in the *Descent of Man* and dialectically elaborated in the twentieth and
twenty-first centuries.

The existence of ethics among humans presented Darwin's creationist opponents with
a phenomenon that would appear to be recalcitrant to an explanation by descent with

modification and natural selection. How could actions benefitting others and costly to the actor be anything but maladaptive for individuals competing with others in the struggle for existence? It would seem that natural selection would favor selfish behavior indifferent to the welfare of others and reward those individuals who were the most devious, treacherous, brutal, and violent with survival and reproductive success. Any tendency to share resources with others or to put oneself in harm's way to defend others from attack would surely be nipped in the bud. Therefore, the only plausible explanation for the fact that humans are moral beings is that human ethics is the hallmark of Providence in the soul of man.

Darwin solved this problem simply and elegantly. For many animals and especially for *Homo sapiens*, the struggle for existence can only be successfully prosecuted collectively. Prolonged human infancy and childhood require equally prolonged parental care and nurturing, motivated and sustained by what Darwin (1874: 101) calls "the parental and filial affections." As to descent *with modification*, these affections might well chance to extend to other relatives—grandparents to grandchildren and vice versa, aunts and uncles to nieces and nephews and vice versa—in which case, an extended family or clan might form. And as to natural *selection*, in competition with nuclear family groups, extended-family bands would have the advantage—and so these more widely cast familial affections would spread throughout the species. Without moral restraint, the unity and solidarity of these ür-societies would be shattered and their erstwhile members scattered and forced to pursue life's struggle as solitaries—thus doomed to die prematurely without surviving offspring. As Darwin (1874: 120) colorfully put the point: "No tribe could hold together if murder, robbery, treachery, etc., were common; consequently such crimes within the limits of the same tribe 'are branded with everlasting infamy'. . . ."

Immediately, Darwin (1874: 120) adds, "but excite no such sentiment beyond these limits." The raison d'etre of ethics being to hold the group together, the limits of the community and the limits of ethics are coextensive. The competitive advantage of group size, degree of organization, and in-group discipline led to a merger of small clans into tribes, tribes into nationalities, and nationalities into nation states. And with the emergence of each new social collective, the scope and complexity of ethics expanded and evolved: "As man advances in civilization and small tribes are united into larger communities, the simplest reason would tell each individual that he ought to extend his social instincts and sympathies to all the members of the same nation, though personally unknown to him" (Darwin 1874: 126). That brought the state of ethical development up to Darwin's own time, when nation states were beginning to emerge from the union of fractious principalities in Europe. Presciently, Darwin (1874: 126–127) looks forward to our time when the global village is emerging: "This point being once reached, there is only an artificial barrier to prevent his sympathies extending to the men of all nations and races."

5 THE LAND ETHIC: AN EVOLUTIONARY-ECOLOGICAL THEORY OF ENVIRONMENTAL ETHICS

In "The Land Ethic," Aldo Leopold clearly alludes to Darwin's account of the origin and cultural evolution of ethics. Leopold (1949: 202) begins by noting that ethics have progressed over the 3,000 years of recorded Western civilization going back to "the wars in Troy." He characterizes "[t]his extension of ethics ... as a process of ecological *evolution* ... which has its origin in the tendency for interdependent groups to *evolve* modes of cooperation" (Leopold, 1949: 202, emphasis added). Leopold then (1949: 203–204) succinctly summarizes Darwin's account of the origin and evolution of ethics: "All ethics so far evolved rest upon a single premise: that the individual is a member of a community of interdependent parts. His instincts prompt him to compete for his place in that community, but his ethics prompt him also to co-operate (perhaps in order that there may be a place to compete for)."

Leopold (1949: 204) next notes that ecology "simply enlarges the boundaries of the community to include soils, waters, plants, and animals, or collectively: the land." This newly discovered community membership calls for "a land ethic [which] changes the role of *Homo sapiens* from conqueror of the land-community to plain member and citizen of it. It implies respect for his fellow-members, and also respect for the community as such" (Leopold 1949: 204). The land ethic is able ethically to enfranchise ecological collectives, such as biotic communities, because the moral sentiments may target social wholes (collectives) as well as fellow-members thereof, not being constrained by an essence-accident moral ontology. As to other ecological collectives, Leopold (1949: 210–211) attributes a "biotic right" to "continuance" for non-human species. When he characterizes "land" as "a fountain of energy flowing through a circuit of soils, plants, and animals" he is characterizing it as an ecosystem (Leopold, 1949: 216). So Leopold explicitly includes biotic communities, their species populations, and their associated ecosystems—three of the most commonly identified ecological collectives—within the purview of ethics.

6 THE SPECTER OF "ENVIRONMENTAL FASCISM" EXORCISED

"A thing is right," Leopold (1949, 224–225) concludes, "when it tends to preserve the integrity, stability, and beauty of the biotic community. It is wrong when it tends otherwise." Fellow members of the biotic community, initially mentioned as meriting respect, are not mentioned in this summary moral maxim of the land ethic. That would seem to license conservation biologists and ecological restorationists, guided by the land ethic, to control irruptive or invasive species that compromise the integrity, stability, and beauty of biotic communities by killing their specimens—respectfully of course. The very reason for the emergence of environmental ethics is that *Homo sapiens* is an irruptive and invasive species, compromising the integrity, stability, and beauty of biotic communities all over the world. But *Homo sapiens* is no less a plain member and citizen of the biotic community than *Rattus norvegicus* or *Odocoileus virginianus*. If the land ethic licenses environmentalists to kill invasive Norwegian (brown) rats and forest-destroying white-tailed deer, then it should also license them to kill environmentally destructive humans down to a population size that is compatible with preserving the integrity, stability, and beauty of representative biotic communities. That too is an abhorrent conclusion. For this reason, Regan (1982) accused the Leopold land ethic of "environmental fascism"—of making the good of the biotic community trump that of its individual members, including its human members.

Whether the charge of environmental fascism sticks to the land ethic or not turns on the logical interpretation of "when" in Leopold's summary moral maxim. It could be interpreted *either* as "if" *or* as "if-and-only-if." Does "when" denote merely a sufficient condition or *also* a necessary condition? If the latter, the Leopold land ethic is indeed guilty of environmental fascism and should be shunned as entailing abhorrent consequences; if the former, the land ethic is exonerated, because things other than preserving the integrity, stability, and beauty of the biotic community could also be right. That Leopold (1949, p. 205) meant by "when" just "if" (a sufficient condition) not "if-and-only-if" (also a necessary condition) is indicated by his characterization of the land ethic as an "accretion"— which means an added layer, as when each year a tree adds on a new ring. The land ethic adds a new layer of ethics over all our other ethics generated by our multiple community memberships—our familial duties, our professional ethics, our civic responsibilities, our humanitarian moral obligations. Identifying and justifying the principles guiding choice among these many community-generated ethics when their indications conflict is a complicated problem, the solution to which exceeds the scope of this chapter. Suffice it to say that the Leopold land ethic does not trump the very basic and well-established humanitarian ethical obligation not to commit mass-murder in order to preserve the integrity, stability, and beauty of biotic communities.

7 THE BIOLOGICAL ACCOUNT OF THE ORIGIN AND EVOLUTION OF ETHICS AFTER THE MODERN SYNTHESIS

Darwin's account of the origin and evolution of ethics satisfied Leopold and other biologists interested in the matter during the first half of the twentieth century. But during the 1930s and 1940s, Julian Huxley (1942) and others effected the Modern Synthesis of Mendelian genetics and Darwinian descent with modification and natural selection. Evolutionary theory became all about genes competing for representation in future generations; and Richard Dawkins' (1976) characterization of genes as "selfish" became evolutionary orthodoxy. Darwin had explicitly appealed to "group selection" in developing his natural history of ethics, but after the Modern Synthesis, group selection became anathema (Williams, 1966). Thus, the evolutionary account of the origins and evolution of ethics had to be recast in terms of the selfish gene. The question that Darwin confronted had to be asked anew: How could ethics possibly exist?—when selfish genes rule.

To simplify matters, a surrogate for ethics was posited—altruism, defined as self-sacrifice. The hypotheses offered to explain the existence of altruistic behavior throughout the animal kingdom were "kin selection" and "reciprocal altruism" (Hamilton, 1964; Trivers, 1971). Animals might be disposed to sacrifice themselves for others if those others shared a significant fraction of the altruists' selfish genes—half in the case of siblings; a fourth in that of cousins; and so on. And animals might be heritably inclined to benefit others if they could expect a return of benefits equal in value from similarly inclined others in the future. The kin-selection hypothesis seemed to be confirmed by the haplodiploidal social insects, the most altruistic animals on Earth, the females of which share three-fourths of their genes; and the reciprocal altruism hypothesis seemed to be confirmed by prisoner-dilemma game theory (Wilson, 1975).

Kin selection and reciprocal altruism, however, eventually proved to be inadequate to account for the evolution of anything like cooperative human societies and the ethics that make them possible, and so group selection returned to favor under the more general rubric of "multi-level selection" (Wilson and Wilson, 2007; Novak et al., 2010). According to Samuel Bowles and Herbert Gintis (2011: 198–199), kin-selection and reciprocal altruism are "peculiarly ill-suited to explain the distinctive aspects of human cooperation," but which can be explained only by appeal to "gene-culture coevolutionary and multi-level selection processes." Gene-culture coevolution is the idea that just as the capacity for enculturation is a heritable human trait, culture is among the environmental conditions exerting selective pressure on the human genome (Henrich and McElreath, 2007).

The evolutionary foundations of the Leopold land ethic, specifically tailored to fit ecological collectives, are thus entirely vindicated by recent developments in the biological tradition of ethical theory traceable to Charles Darwin and through Darwin to David Hume. While its evolutionary foundations have been vindicated, the ecological foundations of the Leopold land ethic are challenged by the paradigm shift from the "balance-of-nature" to the "flux-of-nature" in ecology (Pickett and Ostfeld, 1995).

8 THE VIABILITY OF THE ESSENCE-ACCIDENT ETHICAL THEORY IN TWENTY-FIRST-CENTURY MORAL PHILOSOPHY

Consider the state of play for the twentieth-century's dominant essence-accident form of ethical theory in the twenty-first-century global village. Rational moral agents are bound to give equal consideration to each and every *moral patient* whom their actions might affect, irrespective of the accidents of spatial and temporal distance and, according to many, irrespective of the accident of species (Singer, 1972; Singer, 1975). One is contemplating buying a cell phone? Can one universalize the maxim of one's action? Whose interests might one's action affect? We moral agents now live in a world in which one's every action—what clothes one wears, what food one eats, what mode of transportation one uses—affects hundreds, sometimes thousands, sometimes millions, sometimes even billions of extant and future moral patients (Asma, 2013). The prevailing essence-accident form of ethics is simply impracticable; to even try to guide one's actions by it would drive a conscientious moral agent crazy (Asma, 2013). For less conscientious moral agents, absent any other way to think about ethics, it leads to "moral corruption" (Gardiner, 2011).

Moreover, the requirement in the essence-accident form of twentieth-century moral philosophy that the essential characteristic of a moral agent is rationality and that moral actions are motivated by impartial reason, not the moral sentiments, is theoretically untenable because it does not hold up to the scrutiny of the twenty-first-century scientific analysis of ethics. In a synoptic paper published in *Science*, Jonathan Haidt (2007: 998) validates the sentiment-based theory of ethics going back to Hume: "Evolutionary approaches to morality generally suggest affective primacy. Most propose that the building blocks of human morality are emotional (e.g., sympathy in response to suffering, anger at nonreciprocators, affection for kin and allies)."

8.1 Toward a New Moral Ontology

How might we better conceive of ourselves as moral beings? I suggest we think of ourselves as nodes in skeins of social and environmental relationships. Along with one's biological endowments, they constitute the very fabric of one's being. In imagination, peal back these relationships one by one and at the end of that process there is nothing of oneself remaining. These relationships are also the very fabric of ethics. They generate a suite of nuanced moral duties and obligations—not a one-size-fits-all "principle of impartiality, universality, equality, or whatever" (Singer, 1972: 232). The duties and obligations one has to family and family members differ from those one has to neighbors and neighborhood, which differ from those one has to one's country and its fellow citizens, which differ, in turn, from those one has to the global village and its fellow denizens.

One is also a plain member and citizen of a biotic community, the duties and obligations to which were set out by Aldo Leopold in "The Land Ethic" and have been further expounded by environmental philosophers since the 1970s. As well, one is a member of mixed human-animal communities, which memberships also generate a suite of nuanced duties and obligations (Midgley, 1984). Pets are ersatz family members and are owed food, shelter, medical care, and affection. But unlike actual family members one may euthanize them when they grow old and infirm. Other animals are our associates in sport, work, and war—polo ponies, draft horses, cutting horses, work elephants, seeing-eye dogs, bomb-sniffing dogs. The revulsion that many beefeaters experience at the thought of eating horsemeat is precisely because the kind of mixed community humans have traditionally shared with horses is different from that we have shared with cattle. And although we slaughter and consume cattle and other animals for food, our communal relationships with such animals are fraught with duties and obligations that industrialized agriculture has egregiously abrogated.

With the advent of global climate change, we should become cognizant of how exquisitely we *Homo sapiens* are adapted to the climates of the Quaternary and how dependent the emergence of agriculture and human civilization has been on the climate of the Holocene. There are many moral reasons why we should do everything in our power to mitigate global climate change, but as Derek Parfit (1984) has demonstrated, giving equal consideration to the interests of *presently indeterminate* future moral patients is not among them. Unstinted, global climate change probably will suddenly bring about a new geological era with a climate like that on Earth thirty-five million years ago (Kiel, 2011). That would almost surely precipitate the collapse of global civilization. As the current custodians of global civilization, we have a fiduciary responsibility to it. Should it collapse, the human population would be decimated, its surviving members dispersed into mutually hostile bands led by warlords.

I fervently hope that my son and grandson enjoy the same Holocene climate that I have enjoyed during my lifetime. I can and will bequeath an inheritance to them and to them alone. But I cannot bequeath to them and them alone the climate to which our species is adapted and with it a viable human civilization. That we can only do collectively. So not only should we think of ecological collectives as beneficiaries of ethics—to reconceptualize ourselves as moral beings in relational, communal, and collective terms is a matter of the greatest urgency for twenty-first century moral philosophy (Callicott, 2013).

REFERENCES

Asma, S. T. (2013). *Against Fairness*. Chicago: University of Chicago Press.

Bowles, S., and Gintis, H. (2011). *A Cooperative Species: Human Reciprocity and Its Evolution*. Princeton, NJ: Princeton University Press.

Callicott, J. B. (2013). *Thinking Like a Planet: The Land Ethic and the Earth Ethic*. New York: Oxford University Press.

Darwin, C. (1874). *The Descent of Man and Selection in Relation to Sex*, 2nd ed. New York: Crowell.

Dawkins, R. (1976). *The Selfish Gene*. New York: Oxford University Press.

Feinberg, J. (1974). "The Rights of Animals and Unborn Generations." In *Philosophy and Environmental Crisis*, edited by W. Blackstone, 43–68. Athens: University of Georgia Press.

Gardiner, S. M. (2011). *A Prefect Moral Storm: The Ethical Tragedy of Climate Change*. New York: Oxford University Press.

Ghiselin, M. T. (1974). "A Radical Solution to the Species Problem." *Systematic Zoology* 23: 536–544.

Gilbert, S. F., Sapp, J., and Tauber, A. I. (2012). A sybiotic view of life: We have never been individuals. *Quarterly Review of Biology* 87: 325–341.

Goodpaster, K. (1978). "On Being Morally Considerable." *Journal of Philosophy* 75: 308–325.

Groom, M. J., Meffe, G. K., Carroll, C. R., and contributors (2006). *Principles of Conservation Biology*, 3rd ed. Sunderland, MA: Sinauer Associates.

Haidt, J. (2007). "The New Synthesis in Moral Psychology." *Science* 316: 998–1002.

Hamilton, W. D. (1964). "The Genetical Evolution of Social Behavior." *Journal of Theoretical Biology* 7: 1–16.

Henrich, J., and McElreath, R. (2007). "Dual Inheritance Theory: The Evolution of Human Cultural Capacities and Cultural Evolution." In *Oxford Handbook of Evolutionary Psychology*, edited by R. Dunbar and L. Barrett, 555–570. New York: Oxford University Press.

Hull, D. L. (1976). "Are Species Really Individuals." *Systematic Zoology* 25: 174–191.

Huxley, J. (1942). *Evolution: The Modern Synthesis*. London: Allen and Unwin.

Johnson, L. E. (1991). *A Morally Deep World: An Essay on Moral Significance and Environmental Ethics*. New York: Cambridge University Press.

Kiel, J. (2011). "Lessons from Earth's Past." *Science* 331: 158–159.

Kuhn, T. (1957). *The Copernican Revolution: Planetary Astronomy in the Development of Western Thought*. Cambridge, MA: Harvard University Press.

Kuhn, Thomas (1962). *The Structure of Scientific Revolutions*. Chicago: University of Chicago Press.

Leopold, A. (1949). *A Sand County Almanac and Sketches Here and There*. New York: Oxford University Press.

Midgley, M. (1984). *Animals and Why They Matter*. Athens: University of Georgia Press.

Novak, M. A., Tarnita, C. E., and Wilson, E. O. (2010). "The Evolution of Eusociality." *Nature* 466: 1057–1062.

Odum, E. P. (1969). "The Strategy of Ecosystem Development." *Science* 164: 262–270.

Parfit, Derek (1984). *Reasons and Persons*. New York: Oxford University Press.

Pickett, S. T. A., and Ostfeld, R. S. (1995). "The Shifting Paradigm in Ecology." In *A New Century for Natural Resources Management*, edited by R. L. Knight and S. F. Bates, 261–278. Washington, DC: Island Press.

Rachels, J. (1990). *Created From Animals: The Moral Implications of Darwinism*. New York: Oxford University Press.

Regan, T. (1979). "An Examination and Defense of One Argument Concerning Animal Rights." *Inquiry* 22: 189–219.

Regan, T. (1982). *The Case for Animal Rights*. Berkeley: University of California Press.

Singer, P. (1972). "Famine, Affluence, Morality." *Philosophy and Public Affairs* 1: 229–243.

Singer, P. (1975). *Animal Liberation: A New Ethics for Our Treatment of Animals*. New York: Avon.

Schwartz, R. M. (1997). The Curse of Cain: The Violent Legacy of Monotheism. Chicago: University of Chicago Press.

Taylor, P. W. (1981). "The Ethics of Respect for Nature." *Environmental Ethics* 3: 197–218.

Trivers, R. L. (1971). "The Evolution of Reciprocal Altruism." *Quarterly Review of Biology* 46: 35–57.

Williams, G. C. (1966). *Adaptation and Natural Selection: A Critique of Some Current Evolutionary Thinking*. Princeton N. J.: Princeton University Press.

Wilson, E. O. (1975). *Sociobiology: The New Synthesis*. Cabridge, Mass.: The Belknap Press of Harvard University.

Wilson, D. S. and E. O. Wilson (2007). Rethinking the theoretical foundation of sociobiology. *Quarterly Review of Biology* 82: 327–348.

CHAPTER 11

....

VALUING WILD NATURE

....

PHILIP CAFARO

PRESERVING wild nature has been an important goal of the conservation and environmental movements throughout their existence. This is illustrated by the creation of national parks and wildlife preserves in many parts of the world, by efforts to protect endangered species and even in modest attempts to keep a little wild nature on managed landscapes, such as butterfly gardens in city parks. The reasons given for preserving wild species and wild places sometimes focus on the benefits to human beings and sometimes on the intrinsic value of wild things themselves. In either case, more or less emphasis may be given to wildness per se as a direct value-conferring property. Instrumental and intrinsic value arguments are typically found together in the speeches and writings of conservationists. While philosophical analysis may separate them, both rhetorical effectiveness and the logic of ethical justification tend to bring them back together.

Though nature lovers have won many battles, overall we are losing the war to preserve wild nature. The twentieth century saw by far the greatest conversion of wild lands to developed lands of any time in history: a function of humanity quadrupling its population and expanding the global economy twenty-five-fold (Reid et al., 2005). This great taming was attended by the extinction of many thousands of species of wild animals and plants, a reduction in numbers and range for most remaining species, and the extension of human impacts across every square meter of the Earth's surface. While much wildness remains, humanity continues to degrade and displace wild nature and the prognosis is for its continued degradation and displacement. Little wild nature will remain a century or two from now unless humanity consciously and forcefully commits to limiting our domination of the biosphere.

For those who place a high value on wild nature, creating societies that preserve wildness on the landscape remains a key ineliminable component of a proper environmentalism. Environmentalists of a more anthropocentric bent may see preserving wild nature as at best a distraction from more pressing issues, such as reining in pollution threatening human health. Clarifying the value of wildness thus is a key task facing environmental ethics. Because human demographic and economic growth necessarily displaces wild nature, whether we value the wild will help determine whether environmentalists continue to accept conventional measures of social progress focused on growth, or replace such goals with others that are less harmful to other forms of life. Whether we value wildness per se also has important implications for a whole range of particular environmental policy decisions from forest management to geoengineering to population policies.

1 WILDNESS DEFINED

The *Oxford English Dictionary* defines the adjective "wild," in part, thus:

1. Of an animal: Living in a state of nature; not tame, not domesticated . . .
2. Of a plant (or flower): Growing in a state of nature; not cultivated . . .
4. a. Of a place or region: Uncultivated or uninhabited; hence, waste, desert, desolate . . .

Antonyms such as "tamed," "domesticated," "cultivated," "inhabited," or "developed" refer to various ways in which nature can be dominated or displaced by people: the independent activities of organisms are replaced by the goals of their human masters (horses pull plows); the spontaneous productions of a piece of land are replaced by landscapes that people find more useful (fens are drained and grow corn). At its core, "wildness" means biological nature's freedom from domination by human beings. Men and women can be free; birds and beasts, swamps and forests, can be wild.

Like human freedom, biological nature's wildness is relative rather than absolute. Sometimes it makes sense to sharply distinguish the wild from the tame. Dogs and chickens are domestic animals, we say, while wolves and golden eagles are wild, thus marking what we take to be a fundamental difference between these animals. Wolves and eagles are best understood in terms of their evolutionary histories and ecological relationships, stories in which humans play little to no role, while dogs and chickens have largely evolved through interactions and manipulations by people.

At other times it makes more sense to speak of wildness as a matter of degree. For example, there may be numerous stages on the way from a natural forest to a tree plantation, or from a wild and free flowing river to one that is heavily managed or impacted by humans. We can jump many stages at a time—tropical primary forest is cut down and planted to sugar cane or oil palm trees—or the pendulum can swing slightly in one direction, as human impacts or control increase or decrease. Here understanding and explaining the details of what one sees on the landscape is likely to be furthered by a view of wildness as graded and multivalent and by sensitivity to both human and non-human influences on the land.

Critics sometimes claim that wildness and the related concepts of nature and the natural are incoherent or systematically misleading (Nelson and Callicott, 2008), and it is certainly true that the words "wild," "nature," and "natural" have multiple, complex objective meanings and subjective overtones that can lead to obscurities in their use. John Stuart Mill noted long ago two principal meanings for the word "nature": (1) that which is distinct from the supernatural, the physical world as a whole; and (2) that which "takes place without the agency, or without the voluntary and intentional agency, of man" (Mill, 1874). To this day critics of wilderness preservation efforts sometimes object that human actions are "just as natural" as beavers building dams, so that there is no point in designating wilderness areas. But this seems willful obscurantism: a deliberate confusion of Mill's senses 1 and 2. In fact, the multiple meanings of "wild" and related terms can help people express their insights into nature. When Henry Thoreau (1906) writes in his journal for February 16, 1859 that "what we call wildness is a civilization other than our own" he is making the case that wild lands in the sense of lands "uncultivated or uninhabited" by people are *not* wild in several further senses: not "waste" places because other species make use of them and in fact need them for their survival (a moral point); not "lawless" or "disorderly" since they have their own ecological regularities, which we can study and understand (a scientific point). The wildness of our words, their protean and open-ended nature, helps generate their power and usefulness (Wittgenstein, 1973).

In an influential discussion John O'Neill, Alan Holland, and Andrew Light (2008, chapter 8) review some subtleties around the use of the term "natural," plausibly claiming that its descriptive use sometimes obscures more than it reveals about the genesis or character of specific places. Because they are particularly interested in mixed landscapes whose features owe a lot to both human and non-human causes, O'Neill et al. see a simplistic wild/humanized dichotomy as misleading. Doubting whether more rigorous or nuanced use of such concepts might help us understand the past or plan for the future in such areas, O'Neill et al. question whether "there is a significant distinction to be drawn between what humans do intentionally and everything else that happens." "To picture nature as the world from which intentional human acts have been abstracted may seem unreal," they write, "given that intentional human agents are as much products of nature [in Mill's sense 1] as are sunflowers and seahorses" (2008: 130–131).

But sunflowers and seahorses are not poised to extinguish a significant portion of the world's species in the next hundred years. Human beings are. Even were this not the case, the evolution of complex consciousness and intentionality arguably rank among the half dozen major achievements of life's three and a half to four billion year career on Earth. The widespread substitution of conscious human goals for nature's unconscious teleologies, along with the immense power, influence, and moral responsibility that flow from this substitution, mark important and essential changes in the world. Like the rise of multi-cellular organisms, the rise of complex consciousness does indeed mark a "significant distinction" in evolutionary history. Like the asteroid that probably caused Earth's last mass extinction, we deserve "significant distinction" for our role in altering life's trajectory. Whatever the metaphysical status of complex consciousness and intentionality, their ontological and ethical importance cannot be denied.

In the end it is only a concept's proven usefulness that can justify our continuing to use it. Wildness remains a useful concept ethically. It helps people create laws and institutions that let them treat the natural world with respect and restraint, such as national parks and "wild and scenic river" designations (Wuerthner et al., 2015). The concept also remains scientifically useful, helping paleontologists and ecologists consider the relative importance of anthropogenic forces in determining the phenomena they study. To note three relevant examples, there exist robust ongoing debates about the roles native peoples have played in determining the species composition of lands in the Brazilian Amazon, influencing fire regimes in different ecosystems in North America, and causing species extinctions in Australia. These debates could hardly take place without distinguishing between natural and human influences. And when we consider the broad sweep of world environmental history over the past hundred thousand years, *the* story that confronts us is the rise of humanity, and in the past few hundred years our rise to dominance over the rest of life. One can no more ignore or downplay this story line than one could accurately tell Life's story during the Mesozoic Era without mentioning the dinosaurs (or describe that era's end without the asteroid).

When we move from describing the past to prescribing actions for the future, however, "to picture nature as the world from which intentional human acts have been abstracted may seem unreal" for reasons that are less conceptual than empirical. For some critics argue that wildness is a quality that, perhaps sadly, has vanished from the landscape and for that reason has little applicability to today's environmental choices (Kareiva and Marvier, 2012). Whatever the past merits of preserving wild lands or keeping a "hands off" policy regarding other species, these positions no longer make sense. No area is really wild, so we cannot preserve areas *as* wild. Furthermore, keeping (formerly?) wild plants and animals on the landscape now often involves active management to preserve the conditions that allow them to continue to thrive. The Anthropocene Epoch is here, these critics say. Get used to it.

Any defender of wild nature must grant that there is some truth in these criticisms, since they are grounded in the very trends that we decry. I believe the proper response to them must begin by acknowledging that in some places and for some kinds of decisions the critics are correct. If a wetland providing important habitat for migrating waterfowl depends on water piped in from a reservoir, nature lovers probably should not try to make the area more natural by removing the pipe and drying out the wetlands. If native prairie plants on publicly owned lands depend on grazing and native grazers have been removed, we may sometimes support managed cattle grazing as an ecological substitute. Wild values often conflict with one another and with other important values in the crowded, damaged world humanity has created. Upholding them often involves compromise and accepting partial success.

However in many areas and for many decisions it still makes sense to try to keep nature as wild as possible, by avoiding increased human influence or actively working to decrease human impacts or control. Arguably the US National Park Service should stop culling elk in Rocky Mountain National Park and instead reintroduce wolves, thus recreating more natural conditions in a park whose stated management goals prioritize the preservation of natural processes and ecosystems. Arguably we should allow most wild fires to burn in remote areas of the US Rocky Mountains, not just because excessive control efforts are expensive and often futile, but also because fire is a natural process that belongs in these wild ecosystems and because it rejuvenates ecological conditions that benefit many native species. Whether such a laissez-faire approach to fire in the Rockies will remain the right choice one hundred years from now under a human-altered climate is a further question.

This example suggests that it also makes sense to talk about preventing *the world as a whole* from becoming more dominated by humans (Wuerthner et al., 2014). Climate change indicates an ever more pervasive human impact on the Earth, but this should not lead to complacency regarding our intrusiveness. Rather than take climate change or other massive ecological harms as justification for discarding the preservation of wild nature as an important conservation goal, we may take them as evidence that people are too intrusive now and that we should strive to reduce our impacts. It is not just that serious harms are likely to befall both people and other species due to climate change (although that appears to be true). It is that it is greedy, creepy, sloppy, and wrong for humanity to degrade the biosphere in this way. It would be even more presumptuous to compound the wrong by trying to take conscious control of Earth's atmosphere and climate. Instead we should work on controlling ourselves.

What we are asking of people when we set aside wilderness areas, limit pollution, request that folks not feed the bears, or in other ways seek to protect wild nature is that they act with respect toward these radically other beings and places, appreciate them for what they are, and let them be. There is no jettisoning the concept of the wild or the effort to preserve some nature relatively free from human interference without accepting the human conquest of the biosphere (Cafaro, 2013). And we should not accept that conquest because it is selfish and unjust: the hogging of the world's resources by one species at the expense of all the others. Better to step back from the moral abysses of mass extinction or the attempt to geoengineer Earth, show some humility and set limits to human domination. For skeptical readers who still wonder *why* it would be better to allow the world to remain partly wild, I specify an answer in what follows: first in terms of the instrumental and intrinsic values of wild nature, then in terms of the narratives that conscientious human beings would want to tell about their own lives and about humanity's career on Earth in the coming centuries.

2   INSTRUMENTAL VALUE

Looking again at the *Oxford English Dictionary*, I'm struck by the many negative connotations the word "wild" may carry, such as rude, licentious, demented, or out of control when applied to a person and wasted, unimproved, dangerous, or worthless when applied to a piece of land. Yet people in fact find wild nature instrumentally valuable in many ways (Rolston, 1989, chapters five and seven). Consider the benefits that nearby residents might enjoy from a publicly owned second- or third-growth forest on the outskirts of a suburban town in the eastern United States: "wildish" if not fully wild, about two hundred acres in extent with clearings, ponds, marshes, and a few abandoned farm buildings. To visitors it may be

- A place of beauty when the spring warblers migrate through, the fall leaves change color, or during a thousand other ordinary or extraordinary occurrences throughout the year
- A place of recreation through which they walk, jog, bicycle, cross-country ski, fish, bird-watch, or aimlessly wander
- A place of learning for elementary school children catching crawdads or college students seining pond water for a microbiology class
- A place of refuge from crowds, asphalt, noise, or other tiresome aspects of more developed landscapes
- A place to watch wildlife of all kinds, including species that may be rare or non-existent elsewhere
- A place to think about local history among the ruined buildings and stone walls piled up centuries earlier by hardworking farmers
- A place for quiet reflection in which to meditate or commune with God or the local spirits

Finding instrumental value in wild landscapes in these ways need not involve denying the instrumental value of more developed landscapes. Walkers routinely find beauty in wild forests *and* well-designed gardens; students observe natural processes in the wild *and* test hypotheses back in the lab. However, some people may obtain some instrumental benefits more easily in wilder landscapes. Even if most folks are happy to commune with God inside a church, others head to the desert for spiritual reflection. Certain experiences and certain kinds of values may be better preserved in general on wild landscapes. Many field biologists and ecologists prefer studying relatively unmodified ecosystems that better model the natural ecological interactions and evolutionary processes they seek to understand. We can experience the "otherness" of animals while playing with our cats and dogs but glimpse a more radical otherness in our fleeting sightings of wild animals. Too, there is often a greater amount or diversity of some valued quality when both wild and tame landscapes are preserved. We might live in the most beautiful town in the world yet still think that having a wild forest nearby adds important opportunities for appreciating beauty. We might still want that forest there, rather than another beautiful town.

The wild often has an important contrast value for people (Kahn and Hasbach, 2013). If you had to choose between having access to a garden and a wild forest, you might choose the garden as a more reliable source of food; in a more developed state of affairs with a grocery store down the street, you might choose the garden because you really enjoy gardening. Still, if we can have access to both, the forest provides experiences and values that enrich our existence. Aldo Leopold (1949) writes that wilderness as the cradle of human cultures "gives definition and meaning to the human enterprise," seeing in this an important cultural value best experienced directly. Holmes Rolston (1989) discovers a "dramatic contact with ultimacies" in wild lands and, like many naturalists, finds that encounters with wild creatures "stretch us out of ourselves." There is no way to put a dollar value on such experiences, but we sense that our lives would be impoverished without them. As societies become more technologically sophisticated, as crowds grow and natural landscapes shrink, these wild contrast values seem bound to increase in importance.

Instrumental values can motivate significant efforts to preserve wild nature. When fishermen oppose stocking rivers with dull, easy-to-catch exotic fish or birdwatchers purchase habitat for an endangered species that they someday hope to see, the native fish and birds are protected even if this protection comes through a selfish interest in preserving certain kinds of human experiences. Note though that many of our instrumental uses of nature point beyond themselves to an intrinsic value in wild things. It would be odd to go out to appreciate a forest's beauty and not find any value in it beyond its ability to show us beauty; odd to value ornithology as a noble pursuit if the stories that it taught about the lives and evolutionary histories of birds were themselves meaningless. Most people believe that at least some nonhuman beings or wild places have an intrinsic value beyond their instrumental usefulness to people.

3 INTRINSIC VALUE

Some of the most important arguments for the intrinsic value of wild nature have been explored in earlier chapters of this handbook. Important qualities that philosophers have appealed to in order to justify the intrinsic value of nonhuman organisms, species, or ecosystems include selfhood, sentience, conation, possession of a telos, order, complexity, creativity, diversity, uniqueness, and an ancient evolutionary genealogy. Wildness—the quality of being relatively free from human influence—can be an important value-adding quality in its own right, but it often figures in arguments for nature's intrinsic value in conjunction with some of these other qualities. Even when there is no explicit appeal to the value of wildness, it often seems to play a role in ascriptions of intrinsic value or moral considerability to wild nature.

Bernard Williams, for example, in answering the question "Must a concern for the environment be centered on human beings?" argues that in addition to straightforward worries about the fair allocation of resources among people, environmentalism is rightly based on appreciation and respect for "raw nature" itself (1995: 237). Whether manifesting as gratitude for nature's beauty or fear of its danger or indifference, these feelings point to "a value which we have good reason, in terms of our sense of what is worthwhile in human life, to preserve, and follow, to the extent that we can" (1995: 239). But it is precisely nature's otherness that grounds these feelings: the fact that it lies "outside the domestication of our relations with one another" (1995: 237). "Nature is independent of us, something not made, and not adequately controlled" (1995: 239). In this account nature's wildness is inseparable from the role Williams believes it may play in helping give definition and significance to people's lives.

Robert Elliot defends an intrinsic value in nature more directly. Arguments for nature's intrinsic value have appealed variously to "its beauty, diversity, richness, integrity, interconnectedness, variety, complexity, harmony, grandeur, intricacy and autonomy," he writes. "Doubtless these properties do provide bases for natural values. There is, however, another property which warrants most attention, because it seems, to me at least, the key to the explanation of nature's intrinsic value. It is the property of being naturally evolved or the property of naturalness" (Elliot, 1997: 59). Many of the properties Elliott mentions may be understood as aesthetic properties, and for him, "nature's aesthetic value is a basis for nature's intrinsic value because the aesthetic value in question arises independently of intentional design" (1997: 61). High aesthetic quality + wildness = intrinsic moral value. "The fact that nature's organizational complexity arises in the absence of intention and design itself contributes crucially to nature's aesthetic value. Moreover, this fact transforms the aesthetic value in question into the kind of aesthetic value that gives rise to moral value" (1997: 61). Just as we would not necessarily ascribe human rights to even the most lifelike cyborg but would certainly grant them to its builder, in Elliott's view a wild forest or desert has an intrinsic value that we are bound to respect, while a tree plantation or monocultural farm field does not.

Holmes Rolston affirms an objective intrinsic value for natural biological organisms. "Something more than [external] causes . . . is operating within every organism," he writes. Genetic information "gives the organism a *telos*, [an] end, a kind of (nonfelt) purpose" as "the genius of life is coded in genetic sets" (Roston, 1988: 98). Organisms literally affirm their own intrinsic value by seeking to instantiate a certain way of being in the world. But for Rolston the fact that organisms pursue ends *of their own* is crucial to affirming their intrinsic value. It is the *telos* plus the "own-ness" that justifies the affirmation. Like Elliott, he makes a sharp distinction between organisms and artifacts. "The values that attach to machines are . . . entirely instrumental," Rolston writes, "derivative from the persons who have created these instruments. But the values that attach to organisms result from their nonderivative, genuine autonomy as spontaneous natural systems" (1988: 105). *Teloi* + wildness = intrinsic value.

Similarly Rolston (1988) finds intrinsic value in natural communities and wild ecosystems, basing this variously on their diversity, complexity, species richness, ecological integrity, or unique histories (chapter five). But it is the fact that these qualities have been generated or maintained by the places themselves rather than imposed on them by humans that lends them their full intrinsic value. This value is diminished or lost when people manage them for their own purposes. Once again wildness is an essential component of intrinsic value. "The sequoia and bison, the mountain community or the geyser basin [are] excellent achievements in spontaneous nature" (Rolston, 1989: 136).

The fact that people value diverse qualities in wild nature combined with the fact that wildness is threatened in a variety of ways complicates our management choices. For example, we may value both the species richness and the wild, unmanaged integrity of a national park that has gradually become encroached on by human settlements. Now we may have to decide whether to periodically supplement some wildlife populations in order to keep them from going locally extinct, or leave the park alone and allow it to lose some species richness. Similarly, we may have to choose whether to put out grain and periodically flood farm fields in a heavily managed agricultural landscape to help migrating waterfowl. Doing so would arguably keep more wildness on the local landscape and help preserve a globe-spanning natural phenomenon.

In such situations lovers of the wild can make a strong case for active management. This is a function of the kind of world humanity has created: one where wild nature is diminished in many ways and threatened at every turn. It would be perverse to take the existence of such hard choices as good evidence for tossing out wildness as a value-adding category altogether. This situation should instead encourage us to create a world where such choices are forced upon us less often (Hettinger and Throop, 1999).

For example: by preserving sufficiently large core wilderness areas and undeveloped migration corridors between them, we can facilitate the natural dispersal and intermixing of populations rather than having to artificially move species in perpetuity in order to keep them from going extinct. Such large-scale habitat preservation may not be possible in many places, but where it is still possible we should pursue it. It could become possible in more places if we slowly and humanely ratcheted back human numbers with their attendant economic demands (Foreman, 2011). Similarly, people might take serious steps to reduce our carbon emissions and limit global warming. That would allow us to avoid many intrusive (and likely ineffective) efforts to preserve species threatened by climate change, such as transferring them to new locations or temporarily preserving them in zoos or botanical gardens.

By better managing ourselves, we can leave more wild nature unmanaged or lightly managed. In contrast, dismissing the possibility or value of wild nature removes a powerful incentive to humility and interspecies justice (Staples and Cafaro, 2012). It paves the way for humanity to pave over the Earth.

4 Letting Nature's Stories Continue

John O'Neill, Alan Holland, and Andrew Light have developed an argument for the importance of narrative in environmental ethics with significant implications for how we value the wild. O'Neill et al. distinguish two ways people value the world around us: "end-state or outcome-based" approaches in which we value things "simply in virtue of their displaying some cluster of properties"; and "historical or process-based" approaches in which we value things "not merely as a cluster of properties but as particular individuals individuated by a temporal history and spatial location" (2008: 144–145). O'Neill et al. claim that many of the values people find in nature are of the latter kind. "History matters . . . in our evaluations of environments," they believe, while various management choices "receive their justification through some sense of what is the appropriate continuation of the story of a place" (2008: 145–146).

I agree that historical narratives must play a role in our environmental ethics if we hope to do justice to the full range of values at stake in environmental decisions. Yet O'Neill et al. focus narrowly on the various meanings people project onto the landscape, forgetting that other species also have histories that matter. For example, they criticize descriptions of Yellowstone National Park as a wilderness because this allegedly overlooks the contributions Native Americans played in creating the landscape, ignoring the fact that legal wilderness designation best secures the continued existence and free ecological interactions of thousands of species for whom the park has been home for millennia. O'Neill et al. set up a false dichotomy by saying they favor "the historical perspective rather than an approach that advocates a return to nature" (2008: 160), overlooking the fact that history includes *natural* history. Their anthropocentric approach has room to appreciate the ecological role the Miwok Indians played by setting fires in the Yosemite Valley two hundred years ago, but not the ecological roles of Giant Sequoia trees, which evolved in the late Miocene Era six to ten million years ago and which have been helping set fires in the Yosemite region ten thousand times longer than people.

Environmental ethicists need to apply the narrative insight more broadly. We do need to respect the heritage and meanings people find "on the ground" in helping decide how the stories of different places should continue. But we can also appreciate the stories that other species have written onto the land (Monbiot, 2014). Those stories are good stories, often manifesting great beauty, complexity, and persistence. They deserve to continue, and at least in some places to continue free from human interference.

Natural species have intrinsic value in part because they are the products of unique journeys through deep evolutionary time. By nearly extinguishing the whooping crane North Americans have come perilously close to ending a journey that has lasted tens of millions of years. The details of the whoopers' physiology, life-ways, migrations, and ecological interconnections are interesting in themselves and mark these birds as well worth preserving. But the full meaning of what may be lost (or saved) only becomes clear when we remember that whooping cranes are unique in the stream of time. Nothing exactly like them will ever come again, and the same may be said for all the wild kinds that human beings threaten to extinguish.

Once again the narrative insight must be broadened: this time to encompass humanity's own role in the story of life on Earth. In *Homo sapiens* nature knows its own stories, perhaps for the first time. But rather than calling these stories "good," appreciating them and ensuring that they continue, we are on track to end many of them in the sixth mass extinction since complex life began some 650 million years ago. Paleontologists tell us that after past mass extinctions it has taken five million to twenty million years to recapture previous levels of diversity. So if we continue on our current path we will not see this lost biodiversity replaced in our lifetimes and quite likely *no* human beings will ever see it replaced. It is even possible that Earth's biodiversity might never fully recover if people sufficiently damage the resources necessary for life's regeneration. If this comes to pass our story will be one in which humanity defines itself either as a cancer on the biosphere, blindly growing in a way that destroys its host (Hern, 1999), or as a genocidal horde, extinguishing other species simply in order to create more room for itself (Gottlieb, 2009).

Thankfully there is a better way. With discipline and restraint we can allow nature's stories to continue, free from human domination in many places and graced by human understanding, appreciation, and gratitude. As Holmes Rolston notes: "Humans want a storied residence in nature where the passage of time integrates past, present, and future in a meaningful career. This does not make nature a mere instrument in a human story, any more than it makes the fellow persons in our drama merely tools. Rather, we have reached the richest possible concept of life in community, one in which all the actors contribute to storied residence" (1988: 351).

What does this mean in practice? At a minimum it means people should allow every natural species to continue to flourish in its native habitat, even if in reduced numbers, and allow some places to remain as wild as possible. To achieve these goals environmentalists need to redouble our traditional efforts to create new national parks, wildlife preserves, and wilderness areas (Noss, 2011), while working more broadly to replace our current cultures of extinction with societies that can live harmoniously with other species. That in turn means not just accepting but embracing limits to growth (Cafaro and Crist, 2012): both limits to human numbers and limits to human economic expansion. Nothing less will preserve wild nature in the long term, and in the long term that will be best for us, too. For as Henry Thoreau reminded his readers 160 years ago: "Our village life would stagnate if it were not for the unexplored forests and meadows which surround it. We need the tonic of wildness . . . We can never have enough of Nature" (1971: 317–318).

References

Cafaro, P. (2013). "Expanding Parks and Reducing Human Numbers: A Superior Alternative to Embracing the Anthropocene Era." *The George Wright Forum* (30): 261–266.

Cafaro, P. and Crist, E. (eds.) (2012). *Life on the Brink: Environmentalists Confront Overpopulation*. Athens, GA: University of Georgia Press.

Elliott, R. (1997). *Faking Nature: The Ethics of Environmental Restoration*. London: Routledge Press.

Foreman, D. (2011). *Man Swarm and the Killing of Wildlife*. Durango, CO: Raven's Eye Press.

Gottlieb, R. (2009). "Ecocide." In *Encyclopedia of Sustainability*, vol. 1, edited by W. Jenkins. Leiden: Brill Publishers.

Hern, W. (1999). "How Many Times Has the Human Population Doubled? Comparisons with Cancer." *Population and Environment* 21: 59–80.

Hettinger, N. and Throop, W. (1999). "Refocusing Ecocentrism: De-emphasizing Stability and Defending Wildness." *Environmental Ethics* 21: 3–21.

Kahn, P., and Hasbach, P. (eds.) (2013). *The Rediscovery of the Wild*. Cambridge: MIT Press.

Kareiva, P., and Marvier, M. (2012). "What Is Conservation Science?" *BioScience* 62: 962–969.

Leopold, A. (1949). *A Sand County Almanac and Sketches Here and There*. Oxford: Oxford University Press.

Mill, J. S, (1874). "Nature." In *Three Essays on Religion*. London: Longmans.

Monbiot, G. (2014). *Feral: Rewilding the Land, the Sea, and Human Life*. Chicago: University of Chicago Press.

Nelson, M., and Callicott, J. B. (eds.) (2008). *The Wilderness Debate Rages On: Continuing the Great New Wilderness Debate*. Athens, GA: University of Georgia Press.

Noss, R. (2011). "Bolder Thinking for Conservation." *Conservation Biology* 26: 1–4.

O'Neill, J., Holland, A., and Light, A. (2008). *Environmental Values*. London: Routledge Press.

Reid, W. et al. (2005). *The Millennium Ecosystem Assessment: Ecosystems and Human Well-being: Synthesis*. Washington, DC: Island Press.

Rolston, H. III (1988). *Environmental Ethics: Duties to and Values in the Natural World*. Philadelphia: Temple University Press.

Rolston, H. III (1989). *Philosophy Gone Wild: Environmental Ethics*. Buffalo: Prometheus Press.

Staples, W. III and Cafaro, P. (2012). "For a Species Right to Exist." In *Life on the Brink: Environmentalists Confront Overpopulation*, edited by P. Cafaro and E. Crist, 283–300. Athens, GA: University of Georgia Press.

Thoreau, H. (1906/1962). *The Journal of Henry D. Thoreau*: Vols. 1–14. edited by B. Torrey and F. Allen. Reprint. New York: Dover.

Thoreau, H. (1971). *Walden*. Princeton: Princeton University Press.

Williams, B. (1995). *Making Sense of History and Other Philosophical Papers: 1982–1993*. Cambridge: Cambridge University Press.

Wittgenstein, L. (1973). *Philosophical Investigations*. 3rd ed. Translated by G. E. M. Anscombe. London: Pearson.

Wuerthner, G., Crist, E., and Butler, T. (eds.) (2014). *Keeping the Wild: Against the Domestication of Earth*. Washington, DC: Island Press.

Wuerthner, G., Crist, E., and Butler, T. (eds.) (2015). *Protecting the Wild: Parks and Wilderness, The Foundations for Conservation*. Washington, DC: Island Press.

PART III

NATURE OF VALUE

*The Meaning of Value and
Normative Claims*

CHAPTER 12

TRUTH AND GOODNESS
Metaethics in Environmental Ethics

KATIE McSHANE

IN environmental ethics, philosophers have raised questions not only about what parts or aspects of the world are good and about how we ought to respond to that goodness but also about what the nature of goodness itself consists in.[1] To ask this last question is to enter the realm of metaethics. Metaethics aims to provide an analysis of our moral practices—to explain not only what we are doing when we are making or expressing moral judgments but also which features of the world, if any, might vindicate these judgments.

In some ways it is surprising that environmental ethicists have paid so much attention to metaethical issues. The most common view among philosophers recently has been that metaethics and normative ethics are distinct domains of inquiry, that is, that the truth of claims in one domain need have—and ideally should have—no implications for the truth of claims in the other domain.[2] If this is correct, then one might think that the energies of environmental ethicists would be better spent on matters with a clearer connection to substantive ethical norms (Light, 2002).

The aim of this chapter is to consider the environmental ethics literature on metaethics with an eye to determining what legitimate interest people concerned about practical environmental problems might have in metaethical issues. In section 1, I briefly describe the major positions in metaethics. In section 2, I consider the main claims that environmentalists have looked to metaethics to vindicate, or at least allow, and describe the metaethical positions that they have thought most likely to accomplish this goal. In section 3, I consider more generally the issue of the normative neutrality of metaethics and assess what remaining reasons environmental ethics might have for continuing to ask metaethical questions. Ultimately, I argue that while environmental ethicists' concerns about metaethical theories are more legitimate than critics have allowed, contemporary metaethical views have considerable resources for addressing these concerns from a number of different theoretical perspectives.

1 Metaethics

Broadly speaking, metaethics has traditionally focused on two questions:

1. What are we doing or trying to do when we make value judgments?
2. Does the world have the features it would need to have to vindicate the practices described by the answer to (1)?

Answering (1) has involved inquiry into our moral practices and the semantics of our moral discourse; answering (2) has involved inquiry into metaphysics and the sciences. These two questions have frequently been approached in conjunction with one another.

Here is one way of classifying the answers that metaethicists have offered to these questions.[3] Some theorists claim that our value judgments express cognitive states, typically beliefs. This view is called "cognitivism." Others claim that our value judgments express noncognitive states, though there is disagreement about which noncognitive states these are. This view is called "noncognitivism." Within noncognitivism, some claim that our value judgments express emotions (emotivism), others that they express prescriptions (prescriptivism), yet others that they express our acceptance of social norms (norm-expressivism) (Ayer, 1936; Stevenson, 1937; Blackburn, 1984, 1993; Hare, 1981; Gibbard, 1990). Within cognitivism, there are disagreements about whether the moral facts that purport to be the objects of moral beliefs really exist. Some claim that they do not—that even though our value judgments express beliefs about the way the world is, the world is in fact not that way. Error theory and moral fictionalism are both views of this kind (Mackie, 1977; Joyce, 2001). Other theorists claim that the moral facts that purport to be the object of our moral beliefs do—or at least can—exist. Of course, this claim opens up the question of what these facts are like. Here there are two questions we might ask. One is whether these facts are natural facts (traditionally understood as facts that can be known through the methods of the natural sciences).[4] Nonnaturalists and supernaturalists claim that moral facts are not, and are not reducible to, natural facts (Moore, 1993; Adams, 1999). Naturalists claim that moral facts are, or are reducible to, natural facts. Within naturalism, there are different views about what these natural facts are facts about. Conventionalists claim that they are facts about our social conventions (Dworkin, 1978, 1986). Constructivists claim that they are facts about our rational agreements with one another (Rawls, 1971; Korsgaard, 2008). Response-dependence theorists claim that they are facts about our subjective responses to valued objects (Smith, Lewis, and Johnston, 1989; McDowell, 1998a). Other naturalists believe that moral facts are facts about some other natural fact in the world: contribution to well-being, promotion of evolutionary fitness, and so forth (Railton, 1986; Foot 2001; Richards, 1986). Some naturalists even believe that moral facts are basic, that they aren't about anything else outside of themselves (Boyd, 1988; Sturgeon, 1985; Brink, 1989). The second question is whether moral facts are mind-dependent or mind-independent, that is, whether their truth value is at least partly determined by our opinions about their truth value.[5] The view that moral facts are mind-independent is sometimes referred to as "objectivism"; the view that moral facts are mind-dependent is sometimes referred to as "subjectivism."[6]

There is one older distinction within metaethics that sometimes still drives the classification of views. This distinction takes as its starting point the question of whether or not moral claims can be mind-independently true. The view that they can be mind-independently true has been called "realism"; the view that they cannot be so has been called "antirealism" or "irrealism" (Wright, 1988; Dreier, 2004).[7] On this distinction, antirealism/irrealism includes all of noncognitivism, error theory, moral fictionalism, and all subjectivist versions of cognitivism: conventionalism, constructivism, response-dependence theories, and the like. Realism includes everything else. The introduction of minimalist theories of truth, according to which a discourse is truth-apt if it presents assertions as true (i.e., as corresponding to the facts), if the assertions have truth-functional negations, and if their truth is independent of their justification, has made trouble for the project of distinguishing realism from antirealism/irrealism (Wright, 1992: 34). If one assumes a minimalist theory of truth, at least some versions of noncognitivism seem to satisfy the conditions for realism (Wright, 1988). This has led many metaethicists to consider realism versus antirealism/irrealism a less helpful way of classifying views than was once thought (Drier, 2004).[8]

While this description provides a rudimentary classification, it is worth noting that within contemporary metaethics, one also finds hybrid views, more fine-grained versions of the distinctions mentioned here, further subcategories, and cross-cutting classifications. Furthermore, the field has grown to consider a much broader range of issues than just the explanation of the nature of moral claims. These include questions of moral motivation, moral psychology, the nature and function of practical reason, the generality of truths in the moral domain, and moral epistemology. Some prominent views within metaethics (internalism and externalism, rationalism and sentimentalism, particularism and generalism, intuitionism, projectivism) are positions that theorists have taken about these other matters and so are not included in this classification.

For our purposes, however, the positions just described are the most important ones, as these are the issues with which environmental ethics has been most deeply engaged. Let us turn, then, to consider the range of views that environmental ethicists have argued for, as well as the motivations for them.

2 METAETHICS IN ENVIRONMENTAL ETHICS

Environmental ethicists have looked to metaethics as part of their project of formulating a philosophical approach capable of articulating the causes of and solutions to environmental problems. In general they have looked to metaethics to vindicate, or at least allow, three claims: (1) that human beings are not the source of all goodness in the world—that at least some parts or aspects of nonhuman nature are good independently of their value to us; (2) that human beings and human morality must be understood as continuous with rather than independent from the natural world; (3) that humans' moral beliefs can be foolish, ignorant, selfish, solipsistic, short-sighted, and otherwise stupid, not just individually but collectively as well—that is, that we can (and sometimes do) get morality quite wrong.

Let us first consider the claim that human beings are not the source of all value. Some environmental ethicists have interpreted this claim purely normatively as the view that humans (and/or human interests, human ends, and human experiences) aren't the only things that have value in their own right, that at least some nonhuman parts of the world have intrinsic value. Understood normatively, as a claim about how we ought to value the natural world, this claim is compatible with almost every metaethical position I have described. A subjectivist will say that by making this claim, we are expressing beliefs about certain mind-dependent facts about nature; a nonnaturalist will say that we are claiming that nature has the nonnatural property of goodness; an emotivist will say that we are expressing an intrinsically valuing attitude toward nature, and so on. Indeed, many environmental ethicists accept the compatibility of strong intrinsic value claims about nonhuman nature with these metaethical positions and on that basis have accepted subjectivist metaethical frameworks, for example, as fully compatible with normative claims about the intrinsic value of the natural world (Elliot, 1997; Callicott, 1999[9]; Jamieson, 2002; O'Neill, 1992).

Other environmental ethicists, however, have interpreted intrinsic value claims as at least partly metaphysical. Holmes Rolston, III, for example, claims that on a subjectivist account of intrinsic value, "Despite the language that humans are the *source* of value which [subjectivists] *locate* in the natural object, no value is really located there at all" (1988: 115). On Rolston's view, if the facts that vindicate our claims about an object's intrinsic value are really just facts about a perceiving subject's mental states, then the value isn't properly intrinsic to the valued object. The value isn't "in" the object at all; it is in the perceiver or perhaps in the relation between the perceiver and the object. This kind of claim only makes sense if we think that claims about intrinsic value are (or imply) claims about the metaphysics of value (O'Neill, 1992; McShane, 2007a; and Jamieson, 2008).[10] Nonetheless, some environmental ethicists have taken the view that in order for us to regard some entities in the nonhuman natural world as having intrinsic value (i.e., value independently of their relationship with us, the valuing subjects), we must be objectivists about value (i.e., we must think of value as a mind-independent property that really exists in the natural world and to which we really have a duty to be responsive). Thus we shouldn't be subjectivists of any kind—or error theorists, fictionalists, or noncognitivists.

Whether this is a position that makes any sense will take some sorting out. In one respect, it looks to be a simple mistake. Metaethics is in the business of explaining what we're doing when we're making claims such as, "Trees are intrinsically valuable." It is not in the business of assessing the content of these claims. Metaethics doesn't tell us which things are right or good; rather, it tells us what we would be saying in claiming that they are so. In this respect, any metaethical view ought to be compatible with any claim about the value of the nonhuman natural world, even intrinsic value claims. It won't evaluate these claims, of course, but that's not its job. Its job is just to explain what we mean in asserting them and what vindicating them would require (O'Neill, 2001; Jamieson, 2002).[11]

On the other hand, certain metaethical theories clearly can imply the truth or falsity of certain intrinsic value claims. A simple reductive naturalism that identifies intrinsic value with pleasure will have to deem the claim "Trees are intrinsically valuable" false, since according to this view nothing but pleasure can be intrinsically valuable. Such a view could still claim that trees tend to produce something of intrinsic value in us, and perhaps even that they do so in virtue of their own properties rather than in virtue of their relations to us, but it must technically deny the claim that trees can possess intrinsic value. Certain simple naturalistic reductions, then, might rule out particular normative views. Whether they do so in a way that seems like a "mere technicality" or whether we ought to be worried about the normative claims that would be thereby undermined depends on how metaphysically robust we think our normative claims should be. By the same mechanism, certain naturalistic reductions might guarantee the truth of our normative claims. If we identify intrinsic value with "being an organism," then we guarantee that trees will turn out to be intrinsically valuable (Rolston, 1988; McShane, 2007b). It is worth pointing out, however, that simple naturalistic reductions have very few proponents in contemporary metaethics.

The preceding analysis assumes that what intrinsic value theorists want out of a metaethical theory is for their intrinsic value claims to turn out to be true. What we have seen is that most versions of cognitivism allow for them to be true—though (a) different versions of cognitivism will interpret these claims somewhat differently, and (b) simple reductive naturalisms could have difficulty with more metaphysically robust interpretations of intrinsic value claims. On any standard version of noncognitivism, these intrinsic value claims can be at least as true as any other moral claim. (More precisely, they will be as eligible for whatever the analogue of truth is on the particular version of noncognitivism at issue—e.g., second-order endorsement, the rationality of intrinsically valuing attitudes, etc.) Because of these facts—that is, because most metaethical theories don't entail that claims about the intrinsic value of nature are false, or in any case, more false than any other value claim—some environmental ethicists have rejected the view that metaethics has any significant relationship to the normative claims that are, or at least should be, the central focus of environmental ethics (Jamieson, 2002; O'Neill, 2001).

However, one might be able to tell a more sympathetic story about why an environmental ethicist concerned to make intrinsic value claims would have preferences regarding metaethical theories. Consider a view common in environmental circles: that environmental destruction has been a result of human arrogance. The idea is that we can see this arrogance expressed in many domains, in many mutually reinforcing narratives about the world: that we are at the "top of the food chain"; that we are a unique and awesome achievement of evolution; that we alone create art, civilization, morality, and science; that we alone possess reason, and perhaps souls; that our science and technology have freed us from our biological and ecological limits; that the rest of the world is a resource for us. Many environmentalists want to challenge this arrogance by telling a different kind of story—one that views people as only a small part of what matters in the universe. This might include making claims about history (how old and large the universe is compared to human beings, how recently humans have arrived on the evolutionary scene), biology (how impressive the traits of other species are), religion (how our religious duties include care and respect for the natural world), and so on. The aim is to tell stories that decenter humanity, that don't portray human beings as the entirety or pinnacle of everything worth caring about. In the realm of morality, this might involve challenging the assumption that people are the center of the moral universe, that all of morality is ultimately about us and our interests, that all goodness in the universe must somehow have a connection to our species.

There are three points worth noting here. One is that this would explain why environmental ethicists might have worries about the human-centeredness of our metaethical theories that aren't just worries about the normative implications of metaethical views. Environmental ethicists might be concerned about the human-centeredness of metaethics in its own right, in much the same way that they are concerned about human-centered historical or scientific stories. Of course, a metaethicist might object that the fact that a story is human-centered doesn't necessarily make the story an incorrect one. (It might, for example, be a better narrative for political purposes to say that the world is made of pudding; it doesn't follow from this that we should abandon quantum mechanics in favor of pudding mechanics.) If we have a clearly true view, the metaethicist might argue, the fact that it tells an undesirable kind of story shouldn't deter us from accepting it. Likewise, if we have a clearly false view, the fact that it tells a desirable kind of story shouldn't deter us from rejecting it.

And yet our choice among theories in contemporary metaethics isn't between clearly true theories and clearly false theories. What we have instead are a range of plausible theories, each of which does a better job of explaining some phenomena and a worse job of explaining other phenomena. All of them are trying to explain our practices in the moral domain in a way that is coherent with our explanations of other aspects of the world, and there is disagreement among theorists about which kinds of coherence it is most important for a theory to establish. Some naturalists think we must make metaethical theories consistent with the belief that the only facts in the world are natural facts, some noncognitivists think it more important to explain how normative claims get their motivational grip on us; some cognitivists think we most need to explain moral disagreement or the logical functionality of moral language. Environmental intrinsic-value theorists are insisting on coherence with a different set of background beliefs: that the best explanation of the most important features of the world cannot be parochially focused on human beings. Of course, it might turn out that coherence with this kind of belief does not constitute an acceptable standard by which to assess our metaethical theories. But an argument for that claim would need to be given.[12]

The second point worth noting is that there might be relationships other than logical implicature between our metaethical positions and our normative positions that an environmental ethicist would be right to care about. Claims in one domain can make claims in other domains more probable; they can have stronger coherence relations than others; they can make claims in other domains less surprising. The aforementioned intrinsic value theorists aren't just concerned about whether the truth of a value proposition is logically possible; they care about how plausible it will look within the overall story about humans and their place in the world. In this regard, a theory that makes our subjective attitudes the truthmakers for all claims about goodness might make claims about the value of a natural world that we largely don't know about or care about seem less plausible, even if it is still logically possible for those claims to be true.

The third point is that even in cases where there aren't any probabilistic or coherence relationships between two domains when background beliefs are taken into account, claims in one domain still might have powerful framing effects on the way that we view claims in another domain. Social theorists have long noticed how assumptions about the way political or economic institutions must be organized affect the explanations that people find plausible in biology and ecology: nonhierarchical explanations seem less plausible to people accustomed to living in hierarchical social institutions; individualist explanations seem more plausible to those who understand other matters individualistically.[13] Likewise, one might think, a story about what goodness consists in that makes our attitudes toward things central might make us more inclined to see human satisfaction as the only good and less inclined to think that the natural world can have goodness in it outside of the ways that it serves our interests.

The second claim that environmental ethicists have looked to metaethics to vindicate is the claim that human beings and human morality must be understood as continuous with rather than independent from the natural world. This claim is important to some environmental ethicists because they view our belief in human exceptionalism (the view that humans are qualitatively different from and superior to the rest of nature) as part of the explanation of how we could have allowed ourselves to treat nonhuman nature so badly. Thus a metaethical position that rejects this hubris can be seen as an important corrective to human self-congratulation. To accept human beings and human morality as part of the natural world suggests that we're not as special as we might like to think. This thought has motivated some environmental ethicists to prefer naturalism to nonnaturalism and supernaturalism. If moral facts either are or are reducible to natural facts, then we can see human moral systems as just another mode of social organization that social animals have developed.[14]

And yet far from recommending any particular metaethical perspective, this concern seems to be only a mark against nonnaturalism and supernaturalism. Rejecting nonnaturalism and supernaturalism does seem to rule out at least one reason for thinking that humans are exceptional: that our moral agency connects us to a special realm of facts that differs in kind from those accessible to nonhumans, who (some claim) aren't moral agents. But metaethical naturalism is not the only alternative to nonnaturalism or supernaturalism. Error theory/fictionalism and all of noncognitivism are also fully compatible with viewing human behavior as just another kind of animal behavior.

The third claim, that humans can get morality quite wrong, has seemed an important fact about morality to those who think that on matters of our relationship to the nonhuman natural environment, we humans have in fact gotten morality quite wrong. Thus many environmental ethicists have wanted a theory that preserves the possibility of widespread—even universal—mistakenness. This has moved some theorists away from mind-dependent views of moral facts (response-dependence, conventionalism, subjectivism, etc.), since they feel the need to articulate a notion of moral truth in which what is true is independent of, and often opposed to, people's opinions. This concern has also moved some theorists away from noncognitivism and toward cognitivism, since cognitivist views have a more straightforward explanation of what it is for a moral claim to be mistaken (Attfield, 1995).

And yet, almost every metathical position these days tries to account for the way in which we talk as if people can be mistaken in their moral claims. Proponents of mind-dependent views of moral facts try to account for the fact that our disagreements about moral claims seem to presuppose that their truth is independent of our belief in them. Proponents of noncognitivism try to account for the fact that we seem to talk as if our moral claims are claims that can be true or false in the first place. These are old problems in metaethics, and every contemporary theory has something to say about them. This is not to say that all of the solutions are equally good, of course.[15] But it is important to notice the many different ways that metaethical theories have of capturing environmental ethicists' intuitions about the way that goodness exists in the world.

3 THE NORMATIVE NEUTRALITY OF METAETHICS?

What place should normative concerns have in evaluating metaethics, then? After all, metaethics needn't be thought of as a domain of inquiry separate from normative ethics. In fact, for much of the history of philosophy it wasn't. While one finds metaethical questions under discussion in Western philosophy at least as far back as Plato's *Euthyphro*, one doesn't see metaethics emerge as a field of inquiry distinct from normative ethics until the twentieth century. G. E. Moore distinguished the central questions of each in *Principia Ethica* and made the distinction central to his work (Moore, 1993). Ethical theorists who followed Moore accepted this distinction, and by midcentury it was largely taken for granted within Anglo-American analytic philosophy that metaethics is normatively neutral; its claims are logically distinct from any substantive normative position. Furthermore, the general view seemed to be that this was a good thing, as it made metaethics a proper subject for philosophy. The view, to quote L. W. Sumner, was "that the proper office of the ethical philosopher is metaethics, normative concerns being better left to such as journalists, politicians, and preachers" (1967: 95). Of course, this was in an era where appeals to ordinary language and conceptual analysis were the main focus of philosophy. That has since changed. Views about the independence of metaethics from normative ethics, for the most part, have not. So what should we think about this matter today?

One way in which metaethics might be thought normatively nonneutral is in defining the realm of "the moral," which it seeks to explain. Any metaethical theory will have to say something about what domain it is trying to explain—what the boundaries of that domain are and what distinguishes it from other domains. So, for example, one might define moral claims as claims about harm and benefit, or beliefs about moral wrongness as beliefs about the circumstances in which guilt and shame are warranted (Railton, 1986; Gibbard, 1990). How one carries out this circumscription clearly has an impact on which claims and practices can be considered part of the domain of ethics, which in turn can affect our thinking about which behaviors are subject to ethical scrutiny. For example, if one thinks that the domain of the moral includes only those actions that produce harm or benefit, then the destruction of things that have no well-being (and thus cannot be harmed or benefitted) will not in itself be a moral matter at all. On this view, an environmental ethicist who wanted to argue that species, ecosystems, or rock formations ought to be given direct moral consideration would have to show that such things have a well-being. More broadly, whether we think of environmental preservation as an ethical matter or (merely) as an aesthetic matter will turn on how we distinguish between the moral and aesthetic domains.

Another way that metaethics might be thought normatively nonneutral is if, contrary to what was claimed previously, metaethical theories themselves always imply the truth or falsity of certain normative claims. If all metaethical positions did come with substantive normative commitments of this kind, then one might think that environmental ethicists would be justified in choosing metaethical theories in part on the basis of whether the theories imply the superiority of environmentalist normative claims to anti-environmentalist normative claims. In fact, efforts have been made over the last century to show that all metaethical views do have normative implications. These arguments tend to proceed by showing that a particular seemingly neutral metaethical position has some normative implication or other. Defenders of the normative neutrality of metaethics typically respond to these criticisms by proposing a different metaethical position that does not have normative implications—thus showing that metaethical views can avoid normative implications, even if not all of them do (Dworkin, 1996; Dreier, 2002; Olafson, 1956; Taylor, 1958; Sumner, 1967). My own view is that the latter group has won the day. While some metaethical positions might have hidden normative implications, it is not a necessary truth that they must.

If some metaethical positions can avoid normative implications, then we face the question of whether we should prefer those that do to those that guarantee the truth of our normative positions. That is to say, is there any reason for preferring a more normatively neutral metaethics to a more normatively committed metaethics? The early twentieth century view that ethical theorizing is only a properly philosophical endeavor once it insulates itself from the dirty business of taking a stand on ethical matters is clearly silly. There are many different ways to do philosophy, from the detached to the evangelical, and while we might find the approach that is not our own irritating, there is no reason not to call it philosophy. But there are other reasons for wanting a metaethical story about what value is that is as inclusive as possible. A truism in contemporary metaethics is that it is the mark of a good metaethical view that it doesn't rule out substantive normative positions by fiat. That is to say, its story about what value is should not, as far as possible, prejudge the question of which things are valuable. This, one might think, is a good thing. If we're going to have a theory about what value is, let it be one that can allow as many substantive value claims as possible to be articulated, and then let conflicts among them be adjudicated on substantive grounds. Surely it is the way things are in the world, not the way we've chosen to define "value," that ought to determine which evaluations we deem acceptable. More neutral (or at least more ecumenical) metaethical views will not settle normative matters for us simply through their definition of "value." Indeed, we should not want matters settled that way, even if we can sometimes find ways to make it work in favor of our own normative positions. Instead of rigging the definitions in our favor, environmental ethicists should be talking about what the world is like, why it is so good, and why we ought to be working hard to nurture and respect that goodness. While neutrality obviously isn't the only consideration that should guide theory choice within metaethics, there is some reason to prefer metaethical views that don't guarantee the truth of one's own normative commitments to those that do.

In practical ethics, then, we shouldn't make the mistake of thinking that our metaethics can do the work of substantive normative arguments (nor, in fact, that our substantive normative arguments can do the work of political negotiating and democratic deliberating). But this is not to say that environmental ethicists should have no interest in metaethics. Metaethics is an important part of our story about the place of human beings and human practices in the larger world, and environmental ethicists are right to be concerned about how that story goes. Contemporary metaethics has many thoughtful, sophisticated ways for that story to go, and environmental ethics would benefit from a more fruitful engagement with contemporary metaethics on these issues.

Notes

1. Among the moral claims that metaethics analyzes, environmental ethicists have been particularly interested in claims about goodness, i.e., value. For this reason, I will focus on claims about goodness here, though readers should note that the same claims are made about other moral concepts, such as rightness.
2. For early articulations of this view, see Ayer (1936) and Stevenson (1937). For a more recent discussion, see Dreier (2002), and in environmental ethics, O'Neill (2001) and Jamieson (2002).
3. For less compressed overviews of metaethics, see Miller (2013), Darwall, Gibbard and Railton (1997), and Part I of Copp (2006).
4. The concern to explain morality in a way that is consistent with a broadly naturalistic worldview has been a driving force in metaethics for a long time now and has inspired

debates about what should be counted as a "natural fact" (McDowell, 1998b) and what kind of consistency with a broadly naturalistic worldview is required of metaethics (Railton, 1989, 1993).

5. While these two questions are logically independent of one another (at least in principle, both mind-dependent and mind-independent facts could be either natural or not), mind-dependent moral facts are typically taken to be natural facts, while mind-independent facts can be natural or nonnatural.

6. The terms "subjectivism" and "objectivism" have acquired a wide range of uses within philosophy, and for this reason (a) one often finds these terms used to designate views other than those described here; and (b) one sometimes finds claims about the mind-dependence or mind-independence of value designated with other terminology.

7. Technically, antirealists claim that moral claims cannot be true because there are no facts in the world that would make them true. Error theory and fictionalism would be views of this kind. Irrealists claim that they cannot be true because nonfactualism about moral discourse is correct: moral claims are not claims about facts, and so cannot be true or false. Noncognitivism would be a theory of this kind. Antirealism and irrealism are often lumped together and both referred to as "antirealism." For a discussion of the distinction, see Wright (1988) and Dreier (2004).

8. It is worth noting that other developments in metaethics have put pressure on the distinction between cognitivism and noncognitivism as well, leading some theorists to wonder how much difference is left between the two. See Dreier (2004).

9. Callicott is a Humean about value, and Hume's metaethic is notoriously difficult to categorize using contemporary category schemes. I classify it here as subjectivist, since it rejects the mind-independence of value, but Callicott himself seems to reject the subject/object distinction. It might also be a kind of noncognitivism, though neither Callicott nor Hume takes an explicit stand on the question of which mental states our value claims express.

10. Of course, what metaphysical position is implied by intrinsic value claims is difficult to sort out. Presumably the claim cannot be that value is an intrinsic property, for then value couldn't be a normative property. The position could be that value supervenes only on an object's intrinsic properties. For different ways of understanding what is meant by intrinsic value claims, see O'Neill (1992), McShane (2007a), and Jamieson (2008).

11. See O'Neill (2001) and Jamieson (2002) for arguments along these lines.

12. There are, however, discussions of a similar question in the philosophy of science: whether coherence with value judgments is a legitimate reason for accepting/rejecting a scientific theory. See, e.g., Lacey (1999).

13. See, for example, Keller (1983, 1985) and Nisbett (2003).

14. See, for example, Callicott (1989).

15. See Attfield (1995) for arguments to this effect.

References

Adams, R. M. (1999). *Finite and Infinite Goods: A Framework for Ethics*. Oxford: Oxford University Press.

Attfield, R. (1995). *Value, Obligation, and Meta-Ethics*. Amsterdam: Rodopi.

Ayer, A. J. (1936). *Language, Truth and Logic*. London: Victor Gallancz.

Blackburn, S. (1984). *Spreading the Word*. Oxford: Oxford University Press.

Blackburn, S. (1993). *Essays in Quasi-Realism*. Oxford: Oxford University Press.

Boyd, R. (1988). "How to Be a Moral Realist." In *Essays on Moral Realism*, edited by G. Sayre-McCord, 181–228. Ithaca, NY: Cornell University Press.

Brink, D. (1989). *Moral Realism and the Foundations of Ethics*. Cambridge: Cambridge University Press.

Callicott, J. B. (1989). "The Conceptual Foundations of the Land Ethic." In *In Defense of the Land Ethic*, 75–99. Albany: State University of New York Press.

Callicott, J. B. (1999). "Intrinsic Value in Nature: A Metaethical Analysis." In *Beyond the Land Ethic: More Essays in Environmental Philosophy*, 239–261. Albany: SUNY Press.

Copp, D., ed. (2006). *The Oxford Handbook of Ethical Theory*. Oxford: Oxford University Press.

Darwall, S., Gibbard, A., and Railton, P. (1997). "Toward Fin de Siècle Ethics: Some Trends." In *Moral Discourse and Practice*, edited by S. Darwall, A. Gibbard, and P. Railton, 115–189. Oxford: Oxford University Press.

Dreier, J. (2002). "Meta-Ethics and Normative Commitment." *Philosophical Issues* 12: 241–263.

Dreier, J. (2004). "Meta-Ethics and the Problem of Creeping Minimalism." *Philosophical Perspectives* 18: 23–44.

Dworkin, R. (1996). "Objectivity and Truth: You'd Better Believe It." *Philosophy and Public Affairs* 25(2): 87–139.

Dworkin, R. (1986). *Law's Empire*. Cambridge, MA: Belknap Press.

Dworkin, R. (1978). *Taking Rights Seriously*. Cambridge, MA: Harvard University Press.

Elliot, R. (1997). *Faking Nature: The Ethics of Environmental Restoration*. London: Routledge.

Foot, P. (2001). *Natural Goodness*. Oxford: Oxford University Press.

Gibbard, A. (1990). *Wise Choices, Apt Feelings: A Theory of Normative Judgment*. Cambridge, MA: Harvard University Press.

Hare, R. M. (1981). *Moral Thinking*. Oxford: Oxford University Press.

Jamieson, D. (2008). *Ethics and the Environment: An Introduction*. Cambridge: Cambridge University Press.

Jamieson, D. (2002). "Values in Nature." In *Morality's Progress*, 225–243. Oxford: Oxford University Press.

Joyce, R. (2001). *The Myth of Morality*. London: Cambridge University Press.

Keller, E. F. (1983). *A Feeling for the Organism*. New York: W.H. Freeman & Co.

Keller, E. F. (1985). *Reflections on Gender and Science*. New Haven: Yale University Press.

Korsgaard, C. M. (2008). "Realism and Constructivism in 20th Century Moral Philosophy." In *The Constitution of Agency: Essays on Practical Reason and Moral Psychology*, 302–326. Oxford: Oxford University Press.

Lacey, H. (1999). *Is Science Value Free? Values and Scientific Understanding*. London: Routledge.

Light, A. (2002). "Contemporary Environmental Ethics: From Metaethics to Public Philosophy." *Metaphilosophy* 33(4): 426–449.

Mackie, J. L. (1977). *Ethics: Inventing Right and Wrong*. London: Penguin Books.

McDowell, J. (1998a). "Values and Secondary Qualities." In *Mind, Value and Reality*, 131–150. Cambridge, MA: Harvard University Press.

McDowell, J. (1998b). "Two Sorts of Naturalism." In *Mind, Value and Reality*, 167–197. Cambridge, MA: Harvard University Press.

McShane, K. (2007a). "Why Environmental Ethics Shouldn't Give Up on Intrinsic Value." *Environmental Ethics* 29(1): 43–61.

McShane, K. (2007b). "Rolston's Theory of Value." In *Nature, Value, Duty: Life on Earth with Holmes Rolston, III*, edited by C. J. Preston and W. Ouderkirk, 1–15. Dordrecht: Springer.

Miller, A. (2013). *An Introduction to Contemporary Metaethics*, 2nd ed. Cambridge: Polity Press.

Moore, G. E. (1993). *Principia Ethica*, 2nd rev. ed., edited by T. Baldwin. Cambridge: Cambridge University Press.

Nisbett, R. E. (2003). *The Geography of Thought: How Asians and Westerners Think Differently . . . and Why*. New York: Free Press.

Olafson, F. A. (1956). "Meta-Ethics and the Moral Life." *The Philosophical Review* 65(2): 159–178.

O'Neill, J. (1992). "The Varieties of Intrinsic Value." *The Monist* 75: 119–137.

O'Neill, J. (2001). "Meta-Ethics." In *A Companion to Environmental Philosophy*, ed. Dale Jamieson, 163–176. Oxford: Blackwell Publishers.

Railton, P. (1986). "Moral Realism." *Philosophical Review* 95: 163–207.

Railton, P. (1989). "Naturalism and Prescriptivity." *Social Philosophy and Policy* 7: 151–174.

Railton, P. (1993). "Reply to David Wiggins." In *Reality, Representation, and Projection*, edited by J. Haldane and C. Wright, 315–328. Oxford: Oxford University Press.

Rawls, J. (1971). *A Theory of Justice*. Cambridge, Massachusetts: Harvard University Press.

Richards, R. J. (1986). "A Defense of Evolutionary Ethics." *Biology and Philosophy* 1: 265–293.

Rolston, H., III (1988). *Environmental Ethics*. Philadelphia: Temple University Press.

Smith, M., Lewis, D., and Johnston, M. (1989). "Dispositional Theories of Value." *Proceedings of the Aristotelian Society*, Supp. 63: 89–174.

Stevenson, C. L. (1937). "The Emotive Meaning of Ethical Terms." *Mind* n.s. 46(181): 14–31.

Sturgeon, N. (1985). "Moral Explanations." In *Morality, Reason, and Truth*, edited by D. Copp and D. Zimmerman, 49–78. Totowa, NJ: Rowman and Allanheld.

Sumner, L. W. (1967). "Normative Ethics and Metaethics." *Ethics* 77(2): 95–106.

Taylor, P. W. (1958). "The Normative Function of Metaethics." *The Philosophical Review* 67(1): 16–32.

Wright, C. (1992). *Truth and Objectivity*. Cambridge, MA: Harvard University Press.

Wright, C. (1988). "Realism, Antirealism, Irrealism, Quasi-Realism." In *Midwest Studies in Philosophy XII: Realism and Antirealism*, edited by P. A. French, Theodore E. Uehling, Jr., and Howard K. Wettstein, 25–49. Minneapolis: University of Minnesota Press.

CHAPTER 13

PRACTICAL REASONS AND ENVIRONMENTAL COMMITMENT

ALAN HOLLAND

THIS discussion of practical reasons has two main aims. The first is to distil the findings of some recent work on the topic and to draw attention to some important distinctions, especially the distinction between reasons that are *internal* and reasons that are *external* (Williams, 1981). The second is to use those findings in order to ascertain what kinds of reasons might be the most effective in promoting an "environmentalist" stance—the stance of one who, as Aldo Leopold succinctly puts it, "cannot live without wild things" (1949: vii).

1 THE NATURE OF REASONS

1.1 Some Distinctions

Practical reasons have a twofold function. Being *practical* rather than theoretical, they are reasons for doing something (or nothing), rather than reasons for thinking that something is the case. Being *reasons* for doing something, the other function of practical reasons is to make sense of what we do, both to ourselves and to others. Making sense of what we do is often understood in terms of placing and relating what we do within some wider context. But the relationship here is reciprocal. Insofar as it is the function of reasons to make sense of what we do, having reasons for what we do in turn contributes meaning to our lives.

There are reasons why we do something, there are reasons to do something, and there are reasons for doing something. How do these differ, and how are they related? As a first approximation we can say that "reasons for" are reasons that we actually have and would consciously avow—"operative reasons," as Scanlon (1998: 19) calls them. To say that they are reasons that we actually have is to say, among other things, that they form part of the explanation for our action. "Reasons why," on the other hand, while they also form part of the explanation for our action, are not necessarily reasons that we would avow, or are even aware of. They would figure in a biography, but not necessarily in an autobiography. "Reasons to" do something are different again. They do not necessarily form part of the explanation for our action, nor are they necessarily reasons that we actually have or would consciously avow. For example we might be said to have a reason to do something but fail to act for that reason due to ignorance, which means, in turn, that it will not figure as part of the explanation for our action. And this is true whether or not we perform the act that we have reason to perform. "Reasons for" both explain and justify our actions. "Reasons to" in fact do neither but are capable of doing both. "Reasons why" explain but do not justify.

1.2 Reasons and Desires

Two versions of what it is to have a reason for action go, very roughly, as follows:

(i) An agent has a reason for doing X if *he or she has reason to believe* that X-ing is a step toward or is partly constitutive of something worthwhile: this is an "internalist" reading.

(ii) An agent has a reason for doing X if *there is reason to believe* that X-ing is a step toward or is partly constitutive of something worthwhile: this is an "externalist" reading.

We shall return shortly to the distinction between the internalist and externalist readings, and to the claim, implied by the inclusion of the notion of what is worthwhile, that the ascription of reasons has a normative dimension. Already we see that reasons for action are by no means always instrumental to the achieving of some desired or desirable end, but might, for example, be experimental, creative, or expressive (cf. Holland, 2002: 28–31). And note also that whether the end is described as desired or desirable, we face a dilemma. If it is desired, then it may in addition be highly undesirable—which makes it at least a moot point whether we have reason to pursue it. If it is desirable, this is to say that there is reason to desire it, so that to include the notion of what is desirable in an account of what it is to have a reason for action is to generate a regress.

It was claimed earlier that reasons "make sense of" what we do. If this is true, and in light of the considerations just mentioned, it seems clear that bare wants or desires, which are sometimes assumed to be paradigmatic (or at least default) reasons for doing something, are not reasons at all (Raz, 1997: 113–115).[1] In the first place, to say that we are doing "what we want" does not "make sense of" what we do at all, but merely signals the fact that we are acting voluntarily rather than performing some involuntary movement. In the second place, there is no reason whatever for supposing that doing what we want achieves anything that can be described as worthwhile, or that it can supply the slightest justification for doing something.

As distinct from bare wants or desires, considered or informed desires—more usually called "preferences"—present a different case. But if considered or informed preferences provide reasons for doing something, it is not because they are preferences, but because they are considered or informed. As Joseph Raz persuasively argues (1997: 115), desires function as reasons only if there are reasons for the desires. More generally, it would seem that only of a being who is already conceived of as a voluntary agent, and who is therefore capable of action (rather than mere movement), could it be said that he or she acts for a reason (cf. Scanlon, 1998: 20–22). The task of reasons is thus to explain or justify why this action rather than that action was performed; it is not to explain or to justify, de novo, why any action at all was performed.

1.3 Internalism and Externalism

But how does what there is reason to do become a reason that we have, an operative reason, something that we have a reason for doing? In an article that has become a classic in the field, Bernard Williams provides the following answer: an agent has a reason for performing action A only if she could reach the conclusion that she should A by a "sound deliberative route" from her "subjective motivational set," which he refers to simply as "S," where S is understood to contain "dispositions of evaluation, patterns of emotional reaction, personal loyalties ... projects ... [and] ... commitments" (1981: 105).[2] He proceeds to defend this "internalist" view of reasons for action against an "externalist" view that denies the necessity for such a condition: the externalist claims that an agent can be said to have reason for performing action A even though no such deliberative route is available.

Nevertheless, as noted, for example, by both Richard Norman (2001: 17) and John Brunero (2007: 23), Williams allows considerable latitude in how we are to interpret the notions of "subjective motivational set" and "sound deliberative route." And this fact makes it a little difficult to determine where exactly the line between the internalist and externalist positions is to be drawn.[3] The problem is this: there just is no telling whether the agent could in principle, and by some conceivable deliberative route, come to believe the purportedly external reason or not. Absent belief in some strong form of determinism, this has to be a totally indeterminate matter. Suppose, for example, that an agent indulges in counterfactual deliberations as even a necessary and salutary part of her strategy in coming to a decision about what to do. Suppose, specifically, that it is part of her current motivational set to be disposed to ask herself: "What if one or more of my current motivational set were different—how would things look then?" In that event it seems possible that any purportedly external reason could turn out to be an internal reason after all. It is not obvious, at any rate, that she could not in this way reach a conclusion somewhat at odds with the one to which the balance of her current motivation set would seem to point. Nor does the indulgence in counterfactual deliberation have to be self-initiated. It might be suggested by a friend or adviser.

Williams defends the internalist position by arguing that if R is someone's reason for acting then R must figure in an explanation of that action, and that "no external reason statement could *by itself* offer an explanation of anyone's action" (1981: 106). What also needs to be true (at least) is that the agent believes R to be a reason for the action in question. But even for an agent to believe R to be a reason for the action in question, it is Williams's contention that an appropriate "actual or potential motivational repertoire" needs to be in place (1981: 107–108).

However, we cannot at this point brush off a concern that motivates many externalists and is articulated most clearly by John McDowell (1995). To express the concern bluntly, if melodramatically: we cannot countenance a theory of practical reason that has as a possible consequence that a torturer or serial killer has a perfectly good reason for what they do. For if the torturer counts among her subjective motivational set a determination to seek out that activity that best fits her particular set of skills, or if the serial killer counts the killing of anyone who should annoy him as among the most basic of his projects or commitments, then each can no doubt find a "sound deliberative route" to her or his chosen careers. Nor does it seem adequate to respond by saying that it is their morality rather than their rationality that is at fault. For it is the fact that they might claim to have a perfectly good *reason* for what they do that cannot be allowed to stand. But neither is it an adequate response to say that they are irrational, for it may be that their reasoning, as such, cannot be faulted. However, what can, perhaps, be said, is that the torturer or serial killer is exhibiting a condition that is "pathological." In itself, this is hardly an explanatory term. But it is, perhaps, symptomatic: symptomatic of the fact that those who exhibit such proclivities are considered to be answerable in some way to what we might call "the court of human sentiment."

Thus, what seems rather to be true is that ascriptions of reasons contain an external "justificatory" element: to claim that an agent has a perfectly good reason for what she does implies among other things not simply (and perhaps not at all) that she believes she is justified in what she does, but that she *really is* justified. And different accounts are, of course, available, as to what makes actions unjustified. Perhaps the action itself is judged to be morally wrong, whether for utilitarian reasons or on Kantian grounds. Perhaps it is judged to exhibit one or more of the serious vices. Or perhaps it is held, simply, to display characteristics that lie far outside the acceptable range of human responses. If any of these criticisms stand, the claim that an agent has a perfectly good reason for what she does is open to challenge. But at the same time, and even if one or more of these criticisms should stand, they do not automatically defeat the claim that an agent acts for good reason. This depends on the situation.

And here we glimpse another factor that bears on the question of whether an agent has a good reason for her action: the concrete situation in which she finds herself.[4] Our motivational repertoire, including our beliefs about what we do and do not have reason to do is, in part, a function of our external circumstances. So if, for example, an agent must steal in order to survive, she may be said to have good reason for her action. But however strongly motivated she may be, it is not this that makes her reason a good one. Whether it is or not will still depend on an external critical judgment to the effect that her situation makes the action defensible.[5] The example brings out two important, if surprising, corollaries. The first is that if it remains wrong to steal even in these circumstances, then we do not always have good reason to act morally; or, at any rate, that any reason to act morally can be outweighed by nonmoral considerations such as need, pure and simple. The second is that the external critical viewpoint can override what agents themselves believe they have reason to do.[6]

To summarize: for people to be said to have good reason for what they do, in a sense that also explains what they do, all of the features upon which internalists insist have to be in place—in particular, the appropriate motivational repertoire and the sound deliberative route. This is not sufficient, however, for the persons to be said to have good reason for what they do. For this to be the case, the action also has to withstand external critical scrutiny. Thus both internalists and externalists draw attention to features that are necessary for it to be said that agents have a perfectly good reason for what they do. But neither account is by itself sufficient.

2 HOW TO MAKE THE ENVIRONMENT MATTER

2.1 Leopold and the Land Ethic

At the very beginning of the foreword to *A Sand County Almanac*, Aldo Leopold writes: "There are some who can live without wild things, and some who cannot. These essays are the delights and dilemmas of one who cannot" (1949: vii). This comes as close as one could wish to being a definition of "an environmentalist": one who cannot live without wild things. And the essays that follow contain an uncanny anticipation of what our discussion so far has identified as some of the key elements that have to be in place if one is to give people reasons to share that point of view.

First, there is Leopold's emphasis on terms such as "community" and "health"—terms that are guaranteed to tap into most people's "actual or potential motivational repertoire," and from which they might be expected to derive an appropriate environmentalist agenda. The main competitor against which Leopold runs his notions of community and health is that of human (economic) interests. And this too, just like the notions of community and health, might be expected to tap into people's actual (rather than merely potential) motivational repertoire, and thus provide people with considerable incentive for action. Indeed, current thinking in environmental policy circles—exemplified most obviously in the emphasis on "ecosystem services"—seems to be of the persuasion that action derived from the motivation to preserve ecosystem services is the closest we are likely to get to something approaching the environmentalist agenda. Leopold, however, finds economically motivated actions inimical to the ecological community and to ecological health; and environmental philosophers tend to side with Leopold. As Eric Katz puts it: "an environmental ethic cannot be based on human interests because of the contingent relationship between human interests and the welfare of the natural environment" (1985: 242–243 n. 3).

A second, and even more interesting way in which Leopold anticipates our foregoing analysis is the "invitation" that he issues in the matter of how we should regard "the land" (soils, waters, plants, and animals): "We abuse land because we regard it as a commodity belonging to us. When we see land as a community to which we belong, we may begin to use it with love and respect" (1949: viii). This should be read not as an argument for the proposition that land is a community, but as an invitation for us to shift our motivational repertoire—to "see" land as a community. Leopold is thus adopting precisely the strategy that we attributed to our agent who asked herself: "How would I act if one or more parts of my current motivational set were different?" He is asking us to consider what it would be like to conceive of land differently. And indeed, the bulk of the essays that follow are devoted to showing what it would be like, in Leopold's view, to conceive of land as a community. We would, for example, be concerned for the "health" of land, as we are for that of a community, and might indeed see it in somewhat similar terms as "the capacity for self-renewal." We would be distressed when land became "sick"—when its formerly characteristic denizens dwindle to vanishing point, as we are when communities "die"—when village shops, schools, and even local places of worship are closed down. Above all, our criterion of right action would be focused, in all likelihood, around the beauty, integrity and stability of such a community. But although Leopold succeeds admirably in showing us *what it would be like* to share his point of view, it is not obvious that he has succeeded in giving us *reasons for* sharing his point of view.

2.2 The Appeal to Intrinsic Value

Since Leopold wrote, discussion of the reasons that might be offered in support of the environmentalists' stance has tended to revolve around the ascription of intrinsic value to nature. Protecting the natural world is worthwhile because we are protecting something that has intrinsic value. However, Jonathan Dancy has already sounded a warning note about the ability of the appeal to value to constitute a determinate reason for action: "Though value-facts are about practical relevance," he observes, "they do not themselves specify the actions concerned . . . .[t]hat something is good . . . is not an explicit answer to any question what to do or what not to do" (2006: 137). And if the appeal to value is based on the finding that both individuals and collective entities can be said to have "constitutive goods," that is, goods that are constitutive of their flourishing, then the situation is even worse. For not only do such appeals provide no determinate reason for action—they provide no reason for action at all. No doubt such constitutive goods are ubiquitous in nature, and no doubt they are as objectively real as anything is, but, as John O'Neill remarks: "That Y is a good of X does not entail that Y should be realised." He goes on to observe: "This gap clearly raises problems for environmental ethics" (1992: 132).

Taken in another sense, the "non-instrumental" sense (O'Neill, 1992: 119), the ascription of intrinsic value to nature can be read as an endorsement of Leopold's view that land is not, or should not be treated as, a commodity. But in the first place, it is difficult to imagine how one might set about showing that land *is not* a commodity. And if the claim is that land *should not* be treated as a commodity, we still lack a reason for not treating it so.

At this point, we might fall back on an extensionalist appeal to the intrinsic value that we (have reason to) attach to individual humans, and therefore, by extension, have reason to attach, albeit perhaps in decreasing measure, to all living beings.

But if the ascription of intrinsic value to humans is supposed to have Kantian authority, this strategy does not look promising. It is true that in Kant's view, humans have a special status. By virtue of their rational natures, they are said to be "ends-in-themselves" and therefore to have "intrinsic worth" or "dignity." But to claim on this basis that human beings have a "value" that is intrinsic is to imply that they have something (intrinsically) that is *of the same kind as* other things have instrumentally, which is not obviously consistent with Kant's view of their special status. Furthermore, we cannot overlook the fact that, for Kant, humans have "value" or worth solely because of their capacity to enact the moral law. Failing the discovery of this capacity elsewhere in the biosphere, therefore, the attempt to extend this concept is an attempt to deploy what is essentially a Kantian notion shorn of its Kantian roots and therefore shorn of its Kantian justification.

Holists will have their own objections to the proposal that the basis for environmental commitment is to be found in the intrinsic value of individual living things. From their perspective, it is neither necessary nor sufficient to generate the reasons that we seek. Not necessary because the environmentalist agenda cannot possibly hope to make provision for every single individual living thing. Not sufficient because collective entities—species, ecosystems, habitats and the like—have claims that cannot be disaggregated into the claims of their constitutive individual members.

But aside from the objections that holists might bring to the proposal, there is also a metaphysical objection: it assumes a one-size-fits-all understanding of the concept of "individual" that is untenable. First, there is a distinction between "individuals" that exhibit a degree of integrity and coherence, and mere "particulars," such as a piece of wood, which do not. Second, among individual organisms, there is a distinction between those that are divisible, such as delphiniums and snowdrop bulbs, and those that are not: it makes no sense, for example, to speak of half a squirrel, or three-quarters of a badger. Third, there is the problem of how to account for the micro-organisms that hang out, for example, around the roots of trees and in the guts of mammals. Are they individuals in their own right or are they simply parts of the larger organisms to whose existence they are vital? These metaphysical issues bring normative problems in their wake: Which bits of the world exactly count as individuals, for example, and therefore as "morally considerable"? Are some (kinds of) individuals more deserving of consideration than others?

2.3 Some Desiderata

If the appeal to intrinsic value is found wanting, where then are we to find the reasons for environmental commitment, and what conditions would they have to satisfy? They would not have to be reasons that are external in the sense that they would be reasons for absolutely anyone, no matter what their motivational repertoire. But they would have to be reasons that are robust enough to withstand external critical scrutiny. They would also have to be reasons for anyone judged to lie "within the court of human sentiment," and they would have to remain reasons despite the presence of irrationality, folly, intransigence, dogmatism, and insensitivity—any of which might affect any of us at any time and prevent our "seeing matters aright." In short they would be reasons for anyone judged to be displaying "practical wisdom."[7] Some have sought to find such reasons in the domain of the various relationships that bind us to the natural world.

2.4 The Appeal to Relationships

Among considerations that are inherently "relational," reasons based on an appeal to self-interest, human interests, or human sentiment will often satisfy all of these necessary requirements and will sometimes afford good (enough) reasons for taking environmental action. But it is unlikely that any of them will prove sufficiently robust or will coincide with sufficient reliability with the environmentalist agenda to form the basis of what we are looking for. Others turn to virtue ethics in the belief that if we inculcate in ourselves and others dispositions to love, care for, respect, wonder at, and be humble before the natural world, we shall find reason enough to act appropriately toward it. The approach holds some promise though it is as yet in the early stages of development. Suffice it here to identify one or two of the challenges that it faces. One is how far the attitudes to which appeal is usually made are even appropriate attitudes to hold with respect to the natural world; and conversely, how far the natural world displays features toward which it is appropriate to hold these attitudes. One thinks in particular of "love," "care," and similar attitudes. The phrase "friends of the Earth" is of course a familiar one. But if Aristotle is right, one cannot literally be a "friend" of the Earth, any more than one can be friends with a bottle of wine (1925: 194 [1155b27]). And it is surely a moot point, for example, how much of the natural world is lovable—as distinct from ugly, bleak, or downright hateful, as many artists ranging from Virgil ("lacrimae rerum"—the tears of things) to the English composer Benjamin Britten ("the cruel beauty of nature") have thought. Further, "care" is a term usually reserved for those who are perceived as in need of care, as vulnerable in some way, and hence it might not be universally appropriate. This leads directly to a second challenge arising from doubts about how widely applicable these attitudes are—how much of the natural world can plausibly be perceived as lovable or needy, for example—which is whether they could come anywhere near supporting the environmentalist agenda as a whole. A third challenge echoes the difficulty that Dancy raises regarding the appeal to value, which is to specify what actions exactly flow from the exhortation that we should love, care for, respect, wonder at, and be humble before the natural world.

A rather different approach is recommended by John O'Neill, who suggests that we might look to the requirements for human flourishing to find the reasons that we seek. The suggestion is that "For a large number of, although not all, individual living things and biological collectives, we should recognise and promote their flourishing as an end in itself" because "such care for the natural world is constitutive of a flourishing human life" (1992: 133). The appeal to human flourishing will tap into most people's motivational repertoire and will readily be recognized as a worthwhile objective, while several "deliberative routes" might be devised to take us from that set of motivations toward actions and policies that are expressive of environmental commitment. But this approach, too, is open to challenge. One has to ask how the promotion of flourishing can constitute a clear objective in an arena where "flourishing" is quite clearly a "competitive" good. In cases where A and B belong to the same species, for example, or cases where A is predator and B is prey, one often cannot promote the flourishing of A without at the same time demoting the flourishing of B. An associated difficulty arising from the fact that flourishing is a competitive good is that we can never be sure whether and how far the flourishing of non-humans might be inimical to, rather than constitutive of, the flourishing of humans. The so-called "pest" species come to mind—rats, mosquitoes, and the like. Perhaps we see here the basis of O'Neill's parenthesis "although not all." But in that case, it is less clear that we have found a basis for the environmentalist agenda, which would tend to frown on the proposal that we "play favorites" with species. A final difficulty arises from the fact that flourishing is so rare a condition of creatures in the wild, most of whom meet their end long before they reach maturity. Because of this, if human flourishing were to depend for its sustenance on the flourishing of natural beings and collections of natural beings, as is held to be the case on this approach, there would be a risk of its becoming seriously malnourished.

There are, however, other ways of developing the appeal to relationships. Recall again, and finally, our earlier claim that a primary role of reasons is to make sense of our actions. If this is true, then the very fact that we attach such significance to the giving of reasons for our actions—indeed the fact that, for some, the capacity to act for reasons is the very mark of what makes us human[8]—is testament, in turn, to the importance that we attach to having meaning in our lives, to engaging in and being witness to meaningful relationships. Elizabeth Anderson, for one, suggests that people are apt to set more store by meaningful relationships than welfare or flourishing. "People want their welfare to be achieved in the context of meaningful relationships with others," she writes (1993: 75); and again "People care about living meaningful lives, even at the cost of their welfare" (1993: 76). The suggestion is, then, that we have reason to embrace the deepest form of environmental commitment insofar as we seek to live meaningful lives, since some of the richest and most meaningful engagements are to be found both within and in our relationships with the natural world.

As before, the appeal to meaningful relationships is likely to tap into most people's motivational repertoire, and it will readily be recognized as a worthwhile objective; but in this case, it is less clear perhaps what "deliberative routes" might be devised to take us from that set of motivations toward actions and policies that are expressive of environmental commitment.

We conclude, therefore, with some suggestions about how the quest to sustain meaningful relations might be expected to yield environmental dividends:

1. The natural world provides both the context and framework of our lives: it is indeed the precondition of our being able to enjoy any meaningful relationships at all.
2. The natural world supplies the beat and rhythm of our lives through the succession of the seasons and the exchange of night and day.
3. It is through the responses of living organisms to this beat and rhythm that the inorganic natural world has this effect.[9]
4. It is the natural world rather than "man" (as Protagoras thought) that is the measure of all things—that affords the backdrop against which we can gauge the meaningfulness of our lives.
5. It is through the history of the biosphere—its temporal narrative—that we understand and can make sense of how we have come to be where we are (cf. Holland, 2011).
6. The natural world is where we dwell, which is therefore the ultimate source of our attachments to place and of our sense of belonging.
7. The meaningful engagements that are afforded by our interactions with the natural world and with the indefinite number and variety of its life forms are central to our lives.
8. More soberly, we must note that the natural world is not only a source of joy, but also of sadness, suffering, and cruelty; not only a source of beauty, but also of ugliness and bleakness; not only a source of variety, but also of monotony.

Hence, and finally, the real and underlying point of appealing to meaning as the robust and reliable source of environmental commitment is this: that, unlike many of the approaches previously canvassed, it is capable of withstanding some of the bleakest visions of the natural world to which, from time to time, mankind is capable of giving expression. If our commitment is to the natural world as such, then we cannot pick and choose. Leopold did not refer to his essays as the delights and dilemmas of one who cannot live without *some* wild things.

NOTES

1. For more detailed argument, see Raz (1997: 113–115).
2. S is perhaps better articulated by Peter Railton as an "agent's actual or potential motivational repertoire," because this does not suggest, nor is it Williams's intention that it should, something given or determinate (Williams, 1981, cf. 1995: 35; Railton, 2006: 270).
3. John McDowell's "Might There Be External Reasons?" (1995) is the starting point for the following reflections.
4. Recent empirical work to which Sendhil Mullainathan and Eldar Shafir draw attention, for example (*Scarcity*, 2013), demonstrates the extent to which scarcity (in a variety of dimensions—time, money, friends, and so forth) enters our mindset and compromises our ability to make good decisions.
5. If she is a deeply moral person she may indeed herself believe that she has no good reason for her action. She simply acts in desperation. Nevertheless, the external judgment still stands.

6. But note that in doing so it is not at odds with Williams's internalism requirement; indeed, one might argue that it rather presupposes it. For it is based on the assumption that the need to survive is indeed part of the agent's motivational set, notwithstanding its coexistence with strong moral scruples (cf. Williams's remarks about needs, 1981: 105–106).

7. The issue of scale is important here. I am not personally inclined to dispute Erasmus's charmingly argued case for the importance—indeed the value—of "practical folly" in human affairs, at least at the individual level (2004). But folly does become dangerous if practiced on a planetary scale, for example in the burning of fossil fuels, "as if there were no tomorrow," which indeed there might not be, if we persist.

8. On one interpretation of Aristotle's characterization of humans as "rational animals."

9. Understandably perhaps, it is to nature writers rather than philosophers that we must look for articulation of these meanings—thus: "Trees that you have known all your life become, to those who love them, invested with the same individuality as the household gods . . . You have wintered and summered them, known them through long years in frost and snow, in sun, wind and rain. You know which branch comes earliest into leaf in spring . . . and which tree, intolerant of cold, first casts its flaming raiment down . . . Each tree has its great moment in the year" (Haggard, 1985: 140).

REFERENCES

Anderson, E. (1993). *Value in Ethics and Economics*. Cambridge, MA: Harvard University Press.

Aristotle (1925). *Nicomachean Ethics*, translated by W. D. Ross. London: Oxford University Press.

Brunero, J. (2007). "McDowell on External Reasons." *European Journal of Philosophy* 16: 22–42.

Dancy, J. (2006). "Nonnaturalism." In *The Oxford Handbook of Ethical Theory*, edited by D. Copp, 122–145. Oxford: Oxford University Press.

Erasmus (2004). *Praise of Folly*, translated by B. Radice. Harmondsworth: Penguin Books.

Haggard, L. R. (1985). *A Country Scrapbook*. Gloucester: Alan Sutton Publishing.

Holland, A. (2002). "Are Choices Trade-Offs?" In *Ethics, Economics and Environmental Policy*, edited by D. Bromley and J. Paavola, 17–34. Oxford: Blackwell.

Holland, A. (2011). "Why It Is Important to Take Account of History." *Ethics, Policy and Environment* 14: 1–16.

Katz, E. (1985). "Ecosystem, Organism and the Substitution Problem." *Environmental Ethics* 7: 241–254.

Leopold, A. (1949). *A Sand County Almanac*. New York: Oxford University Press.

McDowell, J. (1995). "Might There Be External Reasons?" In *World, Mind and Ethics*, edited by J. E. J. Altham and R. Harrison, 68–85. Cambridge: Cambridge University Press.

Mullainathan, S., and Shafir, E. (2013). *Scarcity: Why Having Too Little Means So Much*. London: Penguin Books.

Norman, R. (2001). "Practical Reasons and the Redundancy of Motives." *Ethical Theory and Moral Practice* 4: 3–22.

O'Neill, J. (1992). "The Varieties of Intrinsic Value." *The Monist* 75: 119–137.

Railton, P. (2006). "Humean Theory of Practical Rationality." In *The Oxford Handbook of Ethical Theory*, edited by D. Copp, 265–281. Oxford: Oxford University Press.

Raz, J. (1997). "Incommensurability and Agency." In *Incommensurability, Incomparability and Practical Reason*, edited by R. Chang, 110–128. Cambridge, MA: Harvard University Press.

Scanlon, T. M (1998). *What We Owe to Each Other*. Cambridge, MA: Harvard University Press.

Williams, B. (1995). "Internal Reasons and the Obscurity of Blame." In *Making Sense of Humanity*, 35–45. Cambridge: Cambridge University Press.

Williams, B. (1981). "Internal and External Reasons." In *Moral Luck*, 101–113. Cambridge: Cambridge University Press.

CHAPTER 14

···

ENVIRONMENTAL
HERMENEUTICS AND
THE MEANING OF NATURE

···

MARTIN DRENTHEN

ENVIRONMENTAL hermeneutics is a relatively recent stance within environmental philosophy and environmental ethics. The starting point of an environmental hermeneutics is the idea that the world that humans inhabit is always already interpreted and infused with meanings. Human understandings of and encounters with environments are informed and molded by preexisting narratives—individual and collective, factual and fictional accounts of (encounters with) environments and of memories thereof. Hermeneutics starts from the assumption that people make sense of their lives by placing themselves in a larger normative context of texts and other meaningful things. An *environmental* hermeneutics will focus on the fact that environments matter to people too, because environments embody just such contexts.

Environmental hermeneutics is built on the insights and theories from hermeneutics in general. Hermeneutics began as a legal and theological methodology governing the application of law, and the interpretation of Scripture, and developed into a general theory of human understanding through the work of Friedrich Schleiermacher and Wilhelm Dilthey. Martin Heidegger developed hermeneutics into a fundamental philosophical perspective, which was worked out by Hans-Georg Gadamer, Paul Ricoeur, and others. Philosophical hermeneutics is the philosophical theory that claims that the quest for understanding is a fundamental characteristic of human existence. Hermeneutics is often focused on the understanding and interpretation of written texts, but its scope is more general and includes all those elements in the world that somehow convey meaning and yet require interpretation: literary texts but also works of art, human actions, and possibly even environments and landscapes. *Philosophical hermeneutics* is usually distinguished from hermeneutics as referring to different qualitative methods in social environmental sciences. In contrast, philosophical hermeneutics is not so much a method, but rather a fundamental perspective on human existence and human understanding (Gadamer, 1989).[1] As such, it is generally considered one of the important strains of twentieth-century continental philosophy.

Environmental hermeneutics examines the role of interpretation in human relations with environments but often combines this fundamental philosophical perspective with more empirical approaches. As such, it is part of the broader field of environmental humanities, examining concrete cases of human–environmental relationships, making explicit the role that different interpretations of environment play in these relations, and showing how conflicting interpretations of environment are intertwined with different notions of personal and social identity.

This chapter presents and discusses some key thoughts and ideas from philosophical hermeneutics and reflects on how these might bear on environmental philosophy. Special attention is paid to some central concepts in the works of Gadamer and Ricoeur, two key thinkers for the development of philosophical hermeneutics. It is important to note, however, that this chapter merely presents elements of their work that might be relevant to contemporary environmental hermeneutics.

1 Philosophical Hermeneutics as a Fundamental Perspective on Human Understanding

Philosophical hermeneutics starts with the idea that humans are essentially interpretative beings. Humans seek to understand meaning through interpretation, and this is not some accidental feature, but rather it is distinctive of humans. The world we inhabit is a reflection of this interpretative character: we live in a world that is always already interpreted. The phrase "always already" refers to the notion that we are immersed in a lifeworld and a language that predates us; the meanings that our life is intertwined with have an origin that lies before us and cannot be fully appropriated by us.

1.1 Effective History and Historically Affected Consciousness

Historically, one early strand of hermeneutics, emerging from Friedrich Schleiermacher's and Wilhelm Dilthey's work, advocates that understanding the meaning of a text amounts to knowing the intention of the author. This so-called "romantic hermeneutic" view on meaning and interpretation has been famously criticized by Gadamer. According to Gadamer, texts can mean both less *and* more than was intended by the author—less because the author may have all sorts of idiosyncratic associations with his texts, more because texts typically afford more than one reading. Moreover, to "understand what a person says is . . . to come to an understanding about the subject matter, not to get inside another person and relive his experiences" (Gadamer, 1989: 385).

In contrast, Gadamer insists that all understanding is historically situated and thus historically shaped. Our understanding is always inescapably embedded in particular historical circumstances in a way that cannot be made fully transparent to ourselves. "In fact history does not belong to us; we belong to it. . . . *That is why the prejudices of the individual, far more than his judgments, constitute the historical reality of his being*" (Gadamer, 1989: 278).

Rather than trying to liberate our understanding from preconceptions, hermeneutics stresses that preconceptions should be considered almost like transcendental conditions of understanding. It is our very belonging to a specific historical tradition that enables us to discern meanings in the first place. We are a part of the tradition in virtue of which certain things can present themselves to us as being significant and meaningful. We are always already situated in the "hermeneutic circle," in which the meanings we seek to understand are always already speaking to us. It makes no sense to ask what the "true" or objective meaning of a particular experience would be besides the cultural interpretation because this question itself would be nonsensical: we always already live in an interpreted world.

From within our place in an ongoing history, certain "texts" present themselves to us as somehow important and meaningful, yet, what this meaning is exactly is not yet clear to us. Whenever we try to understand the meaning of a transmitted text through interpretation, the historical *horizons of meaning* and our contemporary understanding enter a dialogue in which we seek to understand the text but also gain new perspectives on ourselves. Gadamer calls this mutual transformation between text and interpreter that takes place within such a continuous dialogue, a "fusion of horizons" (Gadamer, 1989, 305).[2] Understanding is less like grasping the content than like engaging in a dialogue—the "dialogue that we are," says Gadamer. Understanding is aimed at an expanding horizon of meaning. Through interpretation we come to understand the meaning of what at first appears alien and participate in the production of a richer, more encompassing context of meaning—and by doing so we gain a better and more profound understanding not only of the "text" but also of ourselves. Each understanding ultimately always includes self-understanding, indeed self-encounter.

Understanding does not just repeat historically transmitted meanings but implies entering into a dialogue with them. According to Gadamer, the basic rule for hermeneutics is to "reconstruct the question to which the transmitted text is the answer" (Gadamer, 1989, 367). The world somehow presents itself to us as being significant and meaningful; what exactly it does mean is still in need of articulation, and each particular interpretation of the meaning will inevitably be parochial, that is, shaped and determined by the particular historic situation in which we find ourselves. Whenever we understand and interpret a text, history is effectively working through us; this is known as "effective history" (*Wirkungsgeschichte*). But our understanding of the meaning of the world will inevitably always also be "closed." Hermeneutics reflects on this always particular understanding of meaning and self, shaping our understanding, not only by allowing it to understand more but also by making it more aware of its finitude, of the particularity of every understanding. The awareness of the fact that one belongs to a interpretation history that one cannot fully appropriate leads to what Gadamer calls "historically effected consciousness" (*wirkungsgeschichtliches Bewusstsein*), the realization of the historically contingent and finite nature of one's own understanding, which urges for an openness toward other interpretations. "The soul of hermeneutics," Gadamer famously said, "consists in the possibility that the *other could be right*."

1.2 The Dialectic of Distantiation and Appropriation and Narrative Identity

The fact that our understanding is always dependent on and shaped by the contingent historical and cultural context surrounding us does not mean we are imprisoned in that context. We may find that we have gotten stuck with stories and interpretations about our world that have been told before, petrified interpretations or fixed narratives that do not always properly articulate the actual meaning that these places have for us now. In these cases, we will not always be able to adequately articulate what that new meaning actually is. Gadamer points out that temporal distance can sometimes help to solve the critical question of hermeneutics: confronting our own understanding with others—from other times and other cultures as transmitted through literature, art, monuments—can make us more aware of the contingent character of the historical particularity of our preconceptions, help us reflect on the strengths and weaknesses of our own interpretation, and trigger a willingness to revise our interpretations if they prove to be untenable or too restrictive.

Paul Ricoeur (in close dialogue with Gadamer) has developed this critical hermeneutics, based on a close analysis of the relation between readers and texts. He points out that the issue of interpretation comes into play as soon as a text "emancipates from its author"— when spoken language is transformed into a *text* ("any discourse fixed by writing"; Ricoeur, 1981: 146) that assumes a life of its own. Whereas a speaker can accompany his signs and explain himself, the author is absent from the text. Without an external authoritative source to turn to, a reader can only revert to reading the text to discover its meaning. Ricoeur argues that this model of understanding texts provides a model for all those instances in which we interpret things that present themselves as significant but are not self-explanatory and therefore require interpretation (Ricoeur, 1991: 140–163, Van Tongeren, 1994).

Ricoeur points out that interpretation of texts requires active participation of the reader. Unlike living speech, with which a speaker can point to the things in the "real" world that both speaker and interlocutor are part of, a text does not so much point to or represent the world, but rather *presents a world*. To grasp this imaginary world, the reader therefore has to play an active interpretative role, using the context of his own life to fill the gaps in the text's references. Understanding not only requires an openness to the world as presented by the text, but also a willingness to place oneself—for the time being—in that world. Understanding a text means to be involved, to be present in the act of reading, to actively participate in the world of the text, use the context of one's own life to bring to life the world that is being brought forward by the text, and bring to bear the meanings of words and concepts that play a role in one's own life (*appropriation*). This does not mean that we should project our own beliefs and prejudices onto the text but rather that we "let the work and its world enlarge the horizon of the understanding which I have of myself"(Ricoeur, 1981: 178). Good reading requires appropriation, but also requires an openness to the strangeness of a text (*distantiation*) on the part of the reader and a willingness to abstract from the context of one's particular life. Hermeneutic interpretation is ultimately aimed at understanding texts that "speak of possible worlds and of possible ways of orienting oneself in these worlds" (Ricoeur, 1981: 177).

Ricoeur argues that, in order to prevent such hermeneutic interpretation from being an all-too-easy appropriation of the text, a mere projection of our prejudices, a *critical* hermeneutic interpretation should do justice to the text by first taking seriously the text as a network of signification that is closed in on itself (Ricoeur, 1981: 145–154).[3]

According to Ricoeur, the world of the text provides the reader with the means of constructing a notion of a sustained self, a *narrative identity*. Our culture provides us with a body of narratives—our holy texts, our dearest works of literature and art, and so on—that give us words and storylines with which we can tell ourselves who we are and what our life is about. As narrative beings, we know ourselves *through* the stories that are being told (*emplotment*).

If the reader answers to the invitation of the text, then the refiguration of the world by the text can bring about an active reorganization of the reader's being-in-the-world. By reading and interpreting texts, and imagining oneself in the meaningful worlds that are being opened by these texts, one gets to know "oneself as another" (Ricoeur, 1992). One's narrative identity is thus shaped by the opening horizon of new worlds that are being disclosed by texts and other meaningful things.

2 Hermeneutics and Environmental Philosophy

As a general theory of human understanding, philosophical hermeneuticists can be applied to specific issues concerning our interpretation of and relation to environments. *Environmental hermeneutics* starts out from the assumption that the world we live in always already has significance because it is always already infused with meanings. It therefore explores what it means to interpret environments, how environments can become meaningful to us, and how certain interpretations of the environment support certain understandings of oneself. Moreover, environmental hermeneutics also stresses that in order to grasp the full meaning of a particular place, one has to get involved in a process of interpretation. For that reason, many works in environmental hermeneutics tend to combine fundamental philosophical reflection with concrete case studies. Specifically, hermeneutics calls for a critical reflection on more current forms of environmental ethics. A typical hermeneutical environmental *ethics* will not start with a reflection on or identification of abstract values that people should adhere to. Rather, it will reflect on actual existing relationships with and experiences of an environment, examine the narratives in which the different interpretations are expressed, and seek to understand what they disclose about self-understandings and environmental identity. For example, it will show how "the lumber company's view of woodland as 'lumber' and 'resource' might be bound up with a frontier narrative of conquering an unruly wilderness and using it for the benefit of human 'progress,'" or how "the perspective on woodland as leisure or recreation (e.g., as a site for one's summer cottage) can take place within a narrative of original innocence (original unity with nature), fall (artificiality of modern technological society), and periodic release from big city life (weekends at the cottage)" (Van Buren, 1995: 260).

2.1 Hermeneutics and Anthropocentrism

Hermeneutics maintains that meaning only exists within the context of human understanding. Thus, even the use of the phrase the "meaning of nature" may be misleading, for it suggests that meanings can exist independently of understanding. Meaning is not an object or a feature of the objective world that understanding sets out to grasp. Moral experiences of nature and moral meanings of nature come into play as soon as *we* start articulating our relationship with the world. In this process, we transform the neutrality of space into a meaningful *place*, that is, through interpretation we make mere *Umwelt* (environment) into a *Welt* (world); that is, into a meaningful and inhabitable world that we can live in, to paraphrase Ricoeur (Ricoeur, 1991: 149). Yet from a hermeneutical perspective, the meanings we encounter in the world are not a secondary addition to an otherwise objective reality, but rather *form the very fabric* of the kind of world that matters to us.[4]

Environmental hermeneutics sees humans as essentially meaning-seeking beings. Its prime object is human understanding; it focuses on the meaning nature has *for us*. This might suggest that hermeneutics is human-centered and can therefore never provide a model for an adequate environmental ethic. However, if we take anthropocentrism to be the view that believes that the value of the natural world is determined at will by humans, then surely an environmental hermeneutic will *not* be anthropocentric. Hermeneutics believes that moral meaning exist within human understanding, but the process of interpretation is not a process of *constructing* but rather of responding to an experience of meaning.

Meanings have to be articulated in response to experiences of the world in which the world presents itself as somehow meaningful, although usually at first it is not clear what particular meaning is trying to present itself. Meaningful (moral) experiences do have to be actively appropriated and interpreted as part of a complex, integral web of references. But the world we live in is an always already interpreted world; it presents itself as other and confronts us with issues that we have to acknowledge in our interpretations of the world. Understanding the meaning of an environment is a never ending process—not just because we constantly discover new means of extracting information from a text (in this case, a particular place), but also, and more importantly, because the meaning of environments is always transcendent and only shows itself in an ongoing conversation about who "we" are and what the world is to "us." We do not always already fully know *what* places have to say to us, but we feel their appeal to us. These places present themselves as significant and beckon to be understood and interpreted—"what is it about this place?" The world outside exists, and throws its questions at us, it has a meaning that beckons to be understood but never fully can be understood (Drenthen, 1999).

2.2 Hermeneutics and Place

Moreover, environmental hermeneutics is critical of philosophical attempts to ground a sense of ethical value in nature that exists "objectively," independent of moral understanding. From a hermeneutical perspective, the very idea that meaning can exist outside the realm of human understanding and interpretation is by itself incomprehensible. What is at stake in issues of meaning is ultimately tied to understanding and is thus a historical *human* perspective (Ricoeur, 1991: 149).[5] This hermeneutical perspective also has consequences for environmental ethics. According to one representative view, human beings are not born ethical, but "gradually become informed about moral expectations that implicitly instruct us through culture, our institutions, our historical tradition, and the geographical places within which we are situated. In that sense, ethical discernment is less a matter of intellectual construction than it is one of attunement to a particular way of being-in-place" (Stefanovic, 2000: 128).

From a hermeneutical perspective, environmental ethics must therefore focus on the moral meanings and ethical commitments that people have to concrete environments. For this reason, many environmental hermeneuticists focus in the meaning and the development of an *ethics of place* (e.g., Casey, 1993; Smith, 2001; Trigg, 2012).[6]

Such a view on environmental ethics differs greatly from other forms of environmental ethics that tend to seek ethical guidelines for dealing with the environment in abstract notions such as "intrinsic value of nature" or "ecocentric egalitarianism," concepts meant to help people leave behind anthropocentrism, "speciesist rationality," and "human chauvinism." From a hermeneutical perspective, such an approach to the human perspective is deeply mistaken, because it presupposes a displaced, disembodied, and ahistorical view of our being-in-the-world that will eventually transform people into the very abstract beings that such a theoretical perspective presupposes. This focus on particular places is one of the reasons that environmental hermeneutics has been open to the empirical approaches of social environmental sciences from the early start of the field. As a qualitative method in social science, hermeneutics has played a role in social geography, architecture, archaeology, and environmental history, mostly as a method for social scientists to articulate people's different environmental understandings in concrete places. Especially in the perspectives of philosophy of architecture and philosophy of geography, one finds strong connections with philosophical reflections from phenomenology and hermeneutics.

As early as 1989 an edited volume appeared that, although mostly phenomenological in focus, also featured a few environmental hermeneutic contributions on dwelling, place, and environment (Seamon and Mugerauer, 1989). In 1995, Robert Mugerauer published a pioneering book that aimed to systematically introduce scholars from environmental studies, architecture, cultural geography, and others fields to the perspective of phenomenology and hermeneutics (Mugerauer, 1995). This book examined concrete case studies that showed how perceptions of landscapes and places evolved from earlier religious, secular, and scientific thought. Only in recent years can one find more explicit attempts to elaborate *philosophical* hermeneutics into an alternative approach to environmental philosophy and ethics to the point that one can speak of a newly emerging field (Clingerman et al., 2013).

2.3 Environmental Hermeneutics Compared to Other Approaches

Philosophical hermeneutics is built on the assumption that people make sense of their lives by placing themselves in a larger narrative contexts; *environmental* hermeneutics focuses on the fact that environments matter to people too, because environments embody just such contexts (O'Neill, Holland, and Light, 2008: 163).[7] In recent years, many environmental philosophers have argued for approaches more sensitive to issues of meaning, narrative, and history. O'Neill, Holland, and Light have criticized the dominant "itemizing approach" to environmental values (O'Neill, Holland, and Light, 2008: 167) in favor of a more historical account that does "more justice to the kinds of concern that appeals to biodiversity and sustainability are attempting to capture" (2008: 168). Similarly, King has argued for a "contextualist" view on the moral status of nature because "both the intelligibility and persuasiveness of ecocentric concepts and arguments presuppose that proponents of these ideas can connect with the narratives and metaphors guiding the expectations and interpretations of their audiences" (King, 1999: 23). Against this backdrop, the recent emergence of environmental hermeneutics can be seen as part of a broader movement in environmental philosophy.

In order to focus somewhat more on the specific nature of the hermeneutical perspective, it can be useful to compare it to similar approaches in environmental philosophy.

Hermeneutics shares a common interest with social constructivist environmental philosophers in studying conflicting interpretations of environment. A typical constructivist will claim that nature itself does not exist but is merely a social construction, a mere "projection" onto intrinsically meaningless and valueless objects (Evernden, 1992; Vogel, 1996, Rolston, 1997; Keulartz, 1998; and Peterson, 1999) and will tend to argue that conflicts between interpretations should be primarily analyzed from a political angle. In contrast, an environmental hermeneuticist will instead argue that while it is certainly true that meanings cannot exist unless there are agents (humans) in the world, there is no reason to think that meanings exist only in our minds. As Ricoeur holds, hermeneutics is a way of learning how to deal with such conflicts of interpretation (Ricoeur, 1974). Confronted with conflicts of interpretation, hermeneutics does not just take note of the different interpretations in a debate but also attempts to stage a conversation between these interpretations, a dialogue in which both parties open themselves to coming to an agreement about the matter itself (*die Sache*; Gadamer 1989) in order to find appropriate interpretations that do justice to the "text."

A hermeneutic approach to environmental conflicts of interpretation will attempt to reconstruct and articulate the ethical experiences that underlie the different interpretations of environments by following the basic hermeneutic rule that one should "reconstruct the question to which the transmitted text is the answer" (Gadamer, 1989: 367). It will then examine how the acknowledgment of the interpretative nature of our understanding of the environment and the re-articulation of normative motives in terms of hermeneutics can help further the ethical debate. It is in this vein that John van Buren has argued for a "critical environmental hermeneutics" (Van Buren, 1995). He argues that hermeneutics, on one hand, should help understand and make explicit the deeper epistemological, moral, and political ideas at stake in actual conflicts of interpretation regarding the environment, but, on the other hand and more importantly, it also has a critical role to play in environmental ethics by providing criteria with which one can determine the adequacy of particular environmental interpretations.[8]

A critical hermeneutic analysis of an environmental conflict might reveal that the actual moral conflict is not where most conflicting parties think. For example, many conflicts concerning restoration that appear to be about empirical issues actually involve "meaning of particular places and how we, both as humans in general and inhabitants of a local area, need to relate to nature and to very specific places" (Deliège and Drenthen, 2014: 109).

A critical environmental hermeneutics will not only articulate and make explicit those interpretations and meanings that are already at work in our everyday practices, bring them to light, and make them explicit but also confront existing meanings and interpretations with other, less obvious ones. Doing so will increase our sensitivity for the many different meanings that can be at stake in our dealings with a particular place, although it will also make the questions of ethics even more complex than they already are.

Another close relative within environmental philosophy is so-called environmental phenomenology (e.g., Brown and Toadvine, 2003; Foltz and Frodeman, 2004; James, 2009). Hermeneutics and phenomenology share a common interest in "rescuing the phenomena." Both aim to increase openness to experiences and other perspectives and to provide a space to articulate the kinds of meaning at play. Yet there are also some important differences. Whereas certain environmental phenomenologists will stress the virtue of clearing away one's presuppositions, hermeneuticists will emphasize the importance of having presuppositions and stress that each understanding of the world will inevitably be "closed" in a specific historic shape. From a hermeneutical perspective, our understandings of the meaning of nature will always be provisional contributions to an ongoing conversation, attempts to articulate a meaning that presents itself to us.

Seen from this perspective, an environmental hermeneutic will be critical toward the suggestion by some phenomenologists that one could have an undisturbed, unmediated understanding of the environment. Abram, for instance, grants that "there can be no complete abolishment of mediation, no pure and unadulterated access to the real" but suggests that "there's a wildness that still reigns underneath all these mediations—that our animal senses, coevolved with the animate landscape, are still tuned to the many-voiced earth" (Abram, 2010: 264). From a hermeneutical perspective, however, all meanings of nature only exist within the realm of cultural interpretations, within a historical tradition of interpretations, a dialogue between texts and readers that all revolve around the question of meaning (Drenthen, 2009).

2.4 Recent Contributions to Environmental Hermeneutics

Several ideas from the philosophical hermeneutics of Gadamer and Ricoeur have provided fresh new starting points for thinking about a wide range of issues in environmental philosophy and ethics. Environmental hermeneuticists have shown that humans understand themselves not just through texts and narratives but also through the meaningful places in which they find themselves. For that reason environmental hermeneuticists have suggested to complement Ricoeur's notion of *emplotment* with a notion of *emplacement* (Clingerman, 2004). Ricoeur's approach to narrative identity is proposed to be useful for understanding what can be called "environmental identity," that is, the way environments provide us with a context with which to understand ourselves (Utsler, 2009). Environmental hermeneutics is used as a critical theory to think through and open up dominant environmental narratives, for instance the dominant technocratic approach to landscape management or the all-too-naive romanticism of certain urban wilderness narratives.

The idea that landscapes can be considered as multilayered texts that afford different readings and therefore support different environmental identities and complex ethical relations to environments and places can provide a framework for thinking through the ethical dimension of conflicts of land management. Conflicts about rewilding in cultural landscapes, for instance, often involve a clash of ethical positions that read the landscape differently. Those who oppose rewilding out of a concern for cultural heritage landscapes and the identities that are based on those landscapes typically refer to relatively recent legible features of a landscape. In contrast, many of those who believe that we have an obligation to "rewild" our landscapes seek to restore a much older historic continuity, referring to a much deeper legible layer in the landscape palimpsest. Both readings articulate different moral meanings that complement each other (Drenthen, 2009; Drenthen, 2011).

Hermeneutics has also been shown to provide a fresh perspective on issues in environmental virtue ethics and narrativity (Treanor, 2008, Treanor, 2014), to be helpful in thinking through issues of environmental justice (Utsler, 2009), and to contribute to thinking about urban environmentalism and the ethics of care for monuments and heritage landscapes (e.g., Trigg, 2012).

Environmental hermeneutics can play both constructive and critical roles in environmental philosophy and ethics. It can be constructive in the sense that it can help moral understanding by finding new articulations and interpretations that more adequately give voice to the moral experiences that underlie any of our relations with the natural world and by reflecting on cultural sources and confronting dominant interpretations with alternative ones. It can be critical in the sense that a hermeneutical reflection on the nature of our understanding of nature will not only show us alternative modes of understanding but will also make us more aware of the contingent character of our particular understanding of nature. By confronting contemporary understandings with others that have been handed over to us through history—in the form of texts, narratives, works of art but also actions, events, and even landscapes—hermeneutics confronts contemporary understanding with other possibilities and thereby helps us deepen our understanding while making us more aware of the provisional character of each attempt to pinpoint the meaning of things. In other words, the hermeneutic approach invites us to open a dialogue, and in turn to a broadening of perspectives and a fusion of horizons in our understanding.

An environmental hermeneutics will start with the recognition that the interpretations of the places in which we live in turn provide an ongoing and ever-changing narrative context from which we can understand ourselves. By explicating the interpretational base of our being-in-the-world and articulating those preexisting meanings and interpretations that already play a role in how we act and think, hermeneutics will force us to have a second look at the meanings we often take for granted. A hermeneutical environmental ethics will articulate and make explicit those interpretations and meanings that are already at work in our everyday environmental practices and will confront existing meanings and interpretations with other, less obvious interpretations. Doing so will increase our sensitivity to the many different meanings that can be at stake in dealing with the environments we inhabit, although it will also make the questions of ethics even more complex than they already are.

NOTES

1. In *Truth and Method*, Gadamer explicitly argues that "truth" and "method" are at odds with one another.
2. The fusion of horizons does refer not so much to the way that two interpreters find a common understanding, but rather that in the fact that through the activity of interpreting meaning we gradually get introduced to the broader horizon of meanings that already preexist in the history of interpretations in which we find ourselves (Gadamer, 1989: 305).
3. This is the reason Ricoeur stresses the importance of a structural analysis of language. Cf. "What Is a Text?" Ricoeur (1981: 145–154).
4. This is even true for scientific interpretations: the world of science is the world as it is (made) intelligible to us through the scientific perspective.
5. Of course, this notion of human is not a biological but a philosophical one. Meaning is tied to the perspective of historical beings that are "suspended in language," beings that are capable of understanding. Note that there is a relevant difference between human understanding of meanings, and the kind of understanding that humans share with other animals. Animals understand the world as a correlate of their sensory apparatus; they understand functional relationships between their own sensory existence and their surroundings. Conversely, their communication forms consist of exchanging signs that

represent aspects of their relationship to their environment. Human understanding of meaning, in contrast, transcends this mere "instrumental" relationship. Human interpretations do not *represent*, but rather *present* a world; and thus they transform mere environment ('Umwelt') into a world "that one could inhabit" (Ricoeur 1991: 149).

6. It should be noted that the failure to find a meaningful relation to the places is an important topic for environmental hermeneutics. The "uncanny" (e.g. Trigg. 2012) refers to the finitude of human ability to make sense of places, but the notion of wilderness has been interpreted as a critical border concept (e.g., Drenthen, 2005).

7. "We make sense of our lives by placing them in a larger narrative context, of what happens before us and what comes after. [. . .] Particular places matter to both individuals and communities in virtue of embodying their history and cultural identities. Similar points apply to the specifically natural world" (O'Neill, Holland, and Light, 2008: 163).

8. Van Buren distinguishes four criteria for adequacy of environmental interpretations: (1) biophysical, (2) historical, (3) technical, and (4) communicative ethical-political.

References

Abram, D. (2010). *Becoming Animal: An Earthly Cosmology*. New York: Vintage.

Brown, C., and Toadvine, T., eds. (2003). *Eco-phenomenology. Back to the Earth Itself.* New York: SUNY Press.

Casey, E. (1993). *Getting Back into Place. Toward a Renewed Understanding of the Place- World.* Bloomington and Indianapolis: Indiana University Press.

Clingerman, F. (2004). "Beyond the Flowers and the Stones: 'Emplacement' and the Modeling of Nature." *Philosophy in the Contemporary World* 11(2): 17–24.

Clingerman, F. Drenthen, M., Treanor, B., and Utsler, D., eds. (2013). *Interpreting Nature. The Emerging Field of Environmental Hermeneutics.* New York: Fordham University Press.

Deliège, G., and Drenthen, M. (2014). "Nature Restoration: Avoiding Technological Fixes, Dealing with Moral Conflicts." *Ethical Perspectives* 21(1): 101–132.

Drenthen, M. (1999). "The Paradox of Environmental Ethics. Nietzsche's View of Nature and the Wild." *Environmental Ethics* 21(2): 163–175.

Drenthen, M. (2005). "Wildness as Critical Border Concept; Nietzsche and the Debate on Wilderness Restoration." *Environmental Values* 14(3): 317–337.

Drenthen, M. (2009). "Ecological Restoration and Place Attachment: Emplacing Non-Places?" *Environmental Values* 18: 285–312.

Drenthen, M. (2011). "Reading Ourselves Through the Land. Landscape Hermeneutics and Ethics of Place." In *Placing nature on the borders of religion, philosophy, and ethics*, edited by F. Clingerman and M. Dixon, 123–138. Farnham: Ashgate Publishing Ltd.

Evernden, N. (1992). *The Social Creation of Nature*. Baltimore and London: Johns Hopkins University Press.

Foltz, B., and Frodeman, R., eds. (2004). *Rethinking Nature. Essays in Environmental Philosophy.* Bloomingon and Indiana: Indiana University Press.

Gadamer. H.-G. (1989). *Truth and Method,*. 2nd rev. ed. Translation revised by Joel Weinsheimer and Donald G. Marshall. London: Continuum.

James, S. (2009). *The Presence of Nature. A Study in Phenomenology and Environmental Philosophy.* London: Palgrave.

Keulartz, J. (1998). *Struggle for Nature. A Critique of Radical Ecology.* New York: Routledge.

King, Roger J. H (1999). "Narrative, Imagination, and the Search for Intelligibility." *Ethics and the Environment* 4(1): 23–38.

Mugerauer, R. (1995). *Interpreting Environments: Tradition, Deconstruction, Hermeneutics.* Austin: University of Texas Press.

O'Neill, J., Holland, A., and Light, A. (2008). *Environmental Values.* New York: Routledge.

Peterson, A. (1999). "Environmental ethics and the social construction of nature." *Environmental Ethics* 21(4): 339–357.

Ricoeur, P. (1974). *The Conflict of Interpretations. Essays in Hermeneutics.* Evanston, IL: Northwestern University Press.

Ricoeur, P. (1981). *Hermeneutics and the Human Sciences. Essays on Language, Action and Interpretation,* translated by J. B. Thompson. Cambridge: Cambridge University Press.

Ricoeur, P. (1991). *From Text to Action. Essays in Hermeneutics II,* translated by K. Blamey and J. B. Thompson. Evanston: Northwestern University Press.

Ricoeur, P. (1992). *Oneself as Another.* Translated by Kathleen Blamey. Chicago: Chicago University Press.

Rolston, H. (1997). "Nature for Real: Is Nature a Social Construct?" In *The Philosophy of the Environment,* edited by T. Chappell, 38–64. Edinburgh: Edinburgh University Press.

Seamon, D., and Mugerauer, R., eds. (1989). *Dwelling, Place and Environment: Towards a Phenomenology of Person and World.* New York: Columbia University Press.

Smith, M. (2001). *An Ethics of Place:. Radical Ecology, Postmodernity and Social Theory.* New York: SUNY Press.

Stefanovic, I. (2000). *Safeguarding Our Common Future: Rethinking Sustainable Development.* New York: SUNY Press.

Treanor, B. (2008). "Phronesis without a Phronimos: Narrative Environmental Virtue Ethics." *Environmental Ethics* 30(4): 361–379.

Treanor, B. (2014). *Emplotting Virtue. A Narrative Approach to Envirnomental Virtue Ethics.* New York: State University of New York Press.

Trigg, D. (2012). *The Memory of Place: A Phenomenology of the Uncanny.* Athens: Ohio University Press, 2012.

Utsler, D. (2009). "Paul Ricoeur's Hermeneutics as a Model for Environmental Philosophy." *Philosophy Today* 53(2): 173–178.

Van Buren, J. (1995). "Critical Environmental Hermeneutics." *Environmental Ethics* 17: 259–275. (Reprinted 2013 in *Interpreting Nature. The Emerging Field of Environmental Hermeneutics,* edited by F. Clingerman, M. Drenthen, B. Treanor, and D. Utsler. New York: Fordham University Press.)

Van Tongeren, Paul. (1994). "The Relation Between Narrativity and Hermeneutics to an Adequate Practical Ethic." *Ethical Perspectives* 1(1): 59.

Vogel, S. (1996). *Against Nature: The Concept of Nature in Critical Theory.* New York: SUNY Press.

....

CHAPTER 15

PHENOMENOLOGY AND ENVIRONMENTAL ETHICS

....

TED TOADVINE

PHENOMENOLOGY as a philosophical tradition originated with the work of Edmund Husserl and was subsequently advanced by numerous thinkers, most notably Max Scheler, Martin Heidegger, Jean-Paul Sartre, Maurice Merleau-Ponty, Emmanuel Levinas, and Jacques Derrida. Many of phenomenology's perennial concerns have a bearing on environmental ethics, including value theory, subjectivity, embodiment, nature, animality, and technology, and since the 1980s environmental themes have been an explicit focus of phenomenological research.

Phenomenology's diversity makes it difficult to generalize about its doctrines, but it does have a narrative consistency and family resemblance of philosophical commitments and argumentative styles. These include its pursuit of philosophy as a practice that radically sets aside the assumptions of the historical tradition, common sense, and scientific explanation in order to describe in an unprejudiced fashion what is experienced, the "phenomena." This commitment is evident among "ecophenomenologists," who are generally skeptical of epistemological and metaphysical naturalism and the privileging of value theory as theoretical points of departure for environmental ethics. Instead, ecophenomenology emphasizes inquiry into the basic epistemological and ontological assumptions that frame the contemporary relationship with nature as a starting point for reevaluating ethical and political alternatives. Ecophenomenology's critique of resourcist, technological, economic, and managerial approaches to environmental problems as manifestations of a modernist instrumental rationality has often aligned it more with the "radical ecology" movements than with mainstream environmental ethics.

The formative figures of phenomenology were not environmentalists in the contemporary sense, yet their concepts and approaches have proven fruitful for current environmental discussions. Gaston Bachelard, Simone de Beauvoir, Gabriel Marcel, Jan Patočka, and Scheler offer important insights, but the most significant influences have been those of Husserl, Heidegger, and Merleau-Ponty. Husserl's contributions include his conception of intentionality, his rejection of naturalistic explanations of consciousness and values, and his account of the historical development of modern scientific rationality from the pre-theoretical life-world (Melle, 1997; Brown, 2003; Kohák, 2003). Ecophenomenologists have drawn from Heidegger's account of being-in-the-world, his diagnosis of modern technology as a mode of revealing that determines beings as "standing reserve," the retrieval of the Greek sense of *phusis* and descriptions of the "withdrawal" of earth, the critique of ethics as an extension of the metaphysical tradition, and his proposal of poetic dwelling as a more primordially ethical manner of inhabiting the earth (Zimmerman, 1983; Foltz, 1995; McWhorter & Stenstad, 2009). Merleau-Ponty's early ontology of Gestalts, studies of perception and embodiment, and ontology of flesh have shaped the development of the field (Abram, 1996; Cataldi & Hamrick, 2007; Toadvine, 2009). Ecophenomenological studies have also drawn on Levinas's ethics of alterity and description of the elemental (Llewelyn, 1991; Diehm, 2003; Sallis, 2004; Edelglass et al., 2012) and, more recently, on Derrida's attention to animality as a central philosophical theme (Lawlor, 2007; Krell, 2013).

The pervasive influence of phenomenology across the humanities and social sciences has given it a broadly interdisciplinary influence on environmental thought. Key figures such as Heidegger, Merleau-Ponty, and Derrida have shaped the development of theory in anthropology, architecture, art, cultural geography, history, literary theory, and science studies, in turn framing the approach taken to environmental issues within these disciplines. For example, one of phenomenology's most significant contributions to the broader horizon of environment thinking is the concept of "place," introduced within cultural geography in the 1970s through the inspiration of Bachelard and Heidegger, and subsequently guiding research in aesthetics, architecture, green design, and urban planning (Relph, 1976; Norberg-Schulz, 1980; Casey, 1993). The fruitfulness of phenomenology for describing and conceptualizing the lived experience of place as an integral component of human identity has led to its refinement as a qualitative empirical research method within environmental design fields (Seamon, 2000). Similarly, phenomenological concepts and approaches have guided research in biosemiotics, critical animal studies, ecocriticism, environmental history, political ecology, and other interdisciplinary fields concerned directly or indirectly with environmental ethics.

Phenomenology's distinctive contributions to environmental ethics are its focus on the epistemic and ontological revindication of experience, its critique of metaphysical and modernist assumptions, and its aim to articulate a post-metaphysical conception of the self-world relation and an alternative ethos appropriate to our experience of nature. Rather than surveying the diversity of approaches that emerge from phenomenology, I offer here a narrative overview of the philosophical foundations underpinning the ecophenomenological approach, concluding with four key concepts that offer compelling opportunities for emerging philosophical inquiry: the lifeworld, earth, chiasm, and dwelling.

1 THE REVINDICATION OF EXPERIENCE

Phenomenology may be defined preliminarily as a descriptive and interpretive study of the essential structures of experience, including both what is experienced and how it is experienced. The study of experience may be undertaken with more or less radical epistemic and ontological assumptions. Psychology studies experience within the framing assumptions of what phenomenologists call the "natural attitude"—the usual, commonsense view of the world and the self as given facts. Phenomenological psychology and the contemporary efforts within cognitive science to "naturalize" phenomenology maintain the framework of the natural attitude and consequently understand phenomenology as an introspective description of first-person experiences, which can then be contrasted with the objective state of affairs.

Transcendental phenomenology's approach to experience is distinctive because it involves suspending or "bracketing" the natural attitude in order to describe experience in an unprejudiced and radically empiricist fashion. Rather than explaining experience in terms of putative facts, "pure" phenomenology investigates experience as the field for all possible evidence, including that of logic, common sense, and empirical science. How "experience" is best understood has undergone considerable elaboration in the development of the tradition. Following Kant, Husserl identifies believing, valuing, and willing as the three main categories of intentional relations with the world, which he understands as acts of consciousness. Merleau-Ponty emphasizes a pre-reflective corporeal level of intentional relatedness that is foundational for but not explicable in terms of conscious acts, effectively broadening the category of experience. Furthermore, Heidegger describes *Dasein* in terms of being-in-the-world, our concernful engagement with the totality of involvements that constitute our horizon of intelligibility. The structure of the world consequently reflects our individual and shared interests and possibilities, as well as the recognition that we are corporeally implicated within it. Experience in this inclusive sense becomes the starting point for description of what exists and how it may be encountered.

In taking experience as its point of departure, phenomenology has traditionally distinguished itself from metaphysical naturalism, understood as the theoretical view that what exists is limited to physical reality governed by natural laws. For Husserl, our everyday natural attitude has a naive bias toward naturalism, but the explicit theoretical formulation of naturalism as the presumptive ontology of the natural sciences and the dominant worldview of modernity distorts this pre-theoretical understanding. Naturalism is self-refuting, according to Husserl, insofar as it relies on the perspective of consciousness, ideas, and norms even as it collapses these into mere physical occurrences. Later phenomenologists such as Heidegger and Merleau-Ponty, although they distance themselves from Husserl's privileging of consciousness with its subjectivist and idealistic implications, endorse the critique of naturalism as misconstruing experience's originary relation with the world. Phenomenology's critique of naturalism complicates its relationship with environmentalism, which has typically embraced a natural scientific worldview, for instance by taking scientific ecology as its literal or metaphorical model of knowledge (Evernden, 1993; Foltz & Frodeman, 2004). Some ecophenomenologists argue for a rapprochement between phenomenology and naturalism that would integrate causal and intentional accounts of experience without reducing the latter to the former (Wood, 2003), while others emphasize that, since the methodologically appropriate naturalism of the sciences does not entail metaphysical naturalism, ecophenomenology is consistent with while remaining distinct from naturalistic research and explanation (Konopka, 2008).

Phenomenology's critical distance from metaphysical naturalism sets it apart from mainstream approaches in environmental ethics but arguably provides it with resources for a richer account of the lived experience of nature than is possible within a naturalistic framework. For example, Simon James contends that phenomenology is better equipped to account for nature's independent reality than is environmental realism (James, 2009). Furthermore, to the extent that the experience of nature is taken as ontologically prior to its scientific description (in the sense that the landscape is ontologically prior to its map, in

Merleau-Ponty's analogy), then it is legitimate to recognize expressive, aesthetic, and normative aspects of the extrahuman world that a naturalistic metaphysics would rule out. If western scientific accounts of nature are understood to provide one valid and useful abstraction for understanding the natural world, rather than its definitive and exclusive explanation, room is made for place-based and traditional ecological knowledge as legitimately organizing experience according to different epistemic frameworks. Finally, phenomenology can also broaden the field of experience beyond the human, first by treating experience as a "transhuman" event that emerges at the intersection of the experiencer and the world, and second by endorsing the prospects for a description of the world as encountered from the various perspectives of nonhuman life (James, 2009).

2 THE CRITIQUE OF METAPHYSICAL AND MODERNIST ASSUMPTIONS

Phenomenology's critical contribution to environmental ethics includes its rejection of metaphysical and modernist assumptions that constrain our understanding of the human-nature relation and are culpable for its contemporary crisis, such as the fact-value split, mind-body dualism, human exceptionalism, the privileging of instrumental rationality, and the reduction of nature and human beings to the ontological status of "resources." These critiques develop insights drawn from the tradition's major figures in ways that converge with and provide theoretical elucidation for concerns raised by environmental thinkers of other stripes. Of particular importance for this critical project are Husserl's analysis of the cultural crisis in the foundation of the sciences, Heidegger's critique of metaphysics and its culmination in modern technology, and Merleau-Ponty's recovery of a corporeal level of meaning-making distinct from reflective consciousness.

In late writings such as *The Crisis of European Sciences*, Husserl identifies naturalism and reductive scientism as symptomatic of European modernity's misguided deformation of the rational legacy that had guided its cultural development since ancient Greece. For Husserl, naturalistic objectivism obscures the foundation for universal rationality, thereby devaluing the scientific perspective as an historical achievement and undermining the foundations of modern culture, with the rise of National Socialism as the most obvious of its disastrous social implications (Husserl, 1970). Although Husserl was primarily concerned with the cultural implications of this crisis, his account is a point of departure for reinterpreting the relationship between nature as the object of our culturally informed experience—with all of its evaluative, aesthetic, and practical qualities—and nature as scientifically described, which excludes these qualities.

According to Husserl, the mathematization of nature and technicization of science since Galileo have had three significant implications: first, the mathematized, ideal account of nature is taken to be nature "as it really is"; second, our own direct experiences of the world are downgraded to the status of "subjective-relative" appearances, ultimately to be displaced by objective, causal explanations; and, third, the objectivity of the sciences is understood as a decisive break with prescientific attitudes and beliefs. Husserl argues that each of these assumptions is overturned by the recognition of science's ongoing practical and theoretical dependence on the "lifeworld," the pregiven and pretheoretical horizon of all possible human experience. Rational norms and scientific objectivity must be understood as grounded on and emergent from the lifeworld. Objective science is therefore subsumed within the broader project of a phenomenological science of the lifeworld that would describe its universal and culturally specific structures, its pretheoretical methods of truth-testing and induction, and the steps by which objectivity develops as a continuation and refinement of these pretheoretical methods. To environmental phenomenologists, Husserl's account suggests that the nature with which we are ultimately concerned is not the ideal, mathematized reconstruction of nature arrived at through scientific techniques but rather nature as directly experienced, within which the distinctions between fact and value and between mind and body are not yet reified. A phenomenological account of nature-as-experienced may therefore help to avoid the dichotomies that many environmentalists have held responsible for our failure to recognize the value of nature on its own terms (Evernden, 1993; Brown, 2003; Marietta, 2003).

Following Husserl, Heidegger identifies the contemporary crisis of our technological age as the culmination of the history of metaphysics. Since the ancient Greeks, metaphysical thinking has construed being as such on the model of beings, with the consequence that, throughout the progression of epochs that define the "history of being," being itself is understood as constant presence: as idea, *substantia*, objectivity, absolute spirit, or will to power. The modern scientific conception of nature as an object that stands over against the Cartesian *ego cogito* is a moment in this history of being as presence and continues to underlie the contemporary privileging of scientific "objectivity." The culmination of this history is modern technology, not as a particular configuration of techniques and equipment, but rather as a mode of metaphysical disclosure, determining the being of what is and the manner by which beings can be encountered. In our technological era, beings are characteristically determined as "standing reserve" or "stock" constantly on call as a resource for use and manipulation. In this respect, modern technology contrasts sharply with the *technē* of the ancient Greek craftsman, which involved a kind of *poēisis* or "bringing forth" that retained much in common with the self-emergence of *phusis*.

Modern technology's challenging or provocation of nature is paradigmatically illustrated by the forced extraction of atomic energy from matter. Through this provocation, the being of nature is determined essentially as raw material fully available for domination and control. Heidegger's (1993) own famous examples distinguish the traditional agricultural techniques of the peasant farmer from those of the mechanized food industry and contrast an old wooden bridge over the Rhine with a hydroelectric power plant, the latter transforming the river into a constantly available resource for power and the tourism industry. Since these examples lend themselves to environmental interpretation, Heidegger's critiques of scientific objectivity and modern technology have been appropriated by philosophers who are critical of the framing of current environmental problems in largely scientific, resourcist, and technocratic terms. Heidegger's suspicion concerning the privileging of presence in the metaphysical tradition extends also to the concept of "values," which bears an essential reference to the modernist subject, leading contemporary ecophenomenologists to critique traditional ethical approaches to nature's "value" (Foltz, 1995; Thompson, 2004). Any genuine alternative must begin with a post-metaphysical philosophy of nature and the human-nature relation rather than with ethical analyses of nature's value (Stone, 2005).

3 KEY CONCEPTS OF ECOPHENOMENOLOGY

3.1 The Lifeworld

Among phenomenology's contributions to the study of nature and environment, several key concepts stand out for their foundational influence and promise for future research. One of the best-known and most widely appropriated of these is the lifeworld, which can be provisionally understood as the practical, pre-theoretical, and directly perceived world of everyday experience. This is the world as we encounter it in the "natural attitude," in which we take as given the objects and events of our daily lives, including other persons and living beings, cultural objects, and the natural world. The realities of this everyday world include, for instance, the roundness and sweet taste of an orange, the gloominess of an overcast sky, the beauty of an impressionist painting, or the impatient expression of a coworker. What exists within our lifeworld is a function of habitual methods of testing and verification that are appropriate to our practical aims and guided by the norms of an intersubjective community. Consequently, the lifeworld develops historically through a community's traditions as these are passed along in language, cultural training, and habitual practices. Since a lifeworld is relative to a particular historically and geographically situated intersubjective community, there is not one lifeworld but many. Furthermore, everyday reality is essentially morphological—inexact, vague, and approximative—rather than ideal and mathematizable in the manner of the exact sciences (e.g., the roundness of the orange is not that of a geometrical circle).

This preliminary characterization of the lifeworld seems to oppose it to reality as described by the exact sciences. Yet these sciences are also practical accomplishments that develop historically within the lifeworld, and their theoretical results may be absorbed into our habitual assumptions and daily practices, often making their theoretical status less obvious: we casually refer to water as H_2O and believe the earth to be round. The lifeworld is also essentially shaped by technology and transformed through its innovations (Ihde, 1990). Consequently, the lifeworld is not a static, pre-scientific, or pre-technological perspective, and its revindication does not imply any primitivism or nostalgia for pre-scientific ways of life. The lifeworld is instead the constant and indispensable background taken for granted by all theory and practice. Scientific knowledge, however abstract and exact, continually relies on the subjective-relative evidence of this everyday world of experience for its ultimate meaning and justification.

Thus far, the lifeworld has been considered ontologically, that is, as the everyday world encountered in the natural attitude. The lifeworld can also be considered transcendentally—not as something experienceable or given as a totality but rather as the pre-given conditions for any experience of the world and things within it. Since, as living beings, we are also included within the world, the lifeworld in this sense makes possible our own appearing, as well as that of objects we encounter. From a transcendental perspective, the lifeworld is both the ultimate horizon and the absolute ground of all meaning. As world-horizon, the lifeworld is the open-ended nexus of referential implications that is constitutive of the emergence of meaning. As earth-ground, the lifeworld is the pre-given and unique support or base from which physical and living bodies in space-time are generated. Viewed transcendentally as horizon and ground, the lifeworld reveals our constitutive horizons of meaning as simultaneously historical and geographical (Steinbock, 1995).

The concept of the lifeworld has a number of implications for environmental ethics and philosophy. First, it entails that nature is broader than what can be scientifically described, including aesthetic, ethical, and ontological elements that are directly apprehended in our experience (without implying that these are ahistorical, require no interpretation, or are beyond critique). Consequently, an adequate understanding of the human-nature relationship and our obligations toward nature cannot be based solely on a naturalistic worldview. Furthermore, since nature as experienced is intersubjectively constituted, there is necessarily a cultural, traditional, and historical framing for the natural world and its practical and ethical value. Since the exact sciences rely on the lifeworld as their evidential and contextual background, they inescapably take a certain cultural and historical framing for granted. Furthermore, the concept of the lifeworld allows for legitimate ways of knowing that are distinct from those of the exact sciences and that vary historically and culturally, which may include forms of traditional ecological knowledge.

3.2 Earth and the Elements

The rediscovery of the lifeworld shows that nature is essentially historical; the scientific understanding of nature as objectivity is not exhaustive but only one manner in which nature may be encountered. This opens paths for alternative and arguably more originary descriptions of nature and its role in the manifestation of the experienced world. Heidegger calls attention to an earlier and more primary sense of nature, termed *phusis* by the ancient Greeks, that is characterized by self-unfolding emergence, as in the sprouting of a plant. Correlative with the self-emergence of *phusis* is its withdrawal or self-concealment, which is not merely a hiddenness but also a source of sheltering and reserve: in order to emerge and extend itself into the openness of the air, the plant must be rooted in the dense opacity of the soil. "Earth" is Heidegger's term for this sheltering and self-concealing aspect of *phusis*, manifest not only in the literal soil, but also in the canvas and pigments of a painting, the sound of a spoken word, or the flesh of the human body. Earth here expresses the phenomenological experience of materiality as what grounds, supports, and shelters the emergence of meaning while simultaneously receding from its own disclosure. This description of earth captures the dynamic interplay between the opening of a world of referential meanings and the grounding of this world in an obdurate thingliness. The scientific understanding of matter as objectivity and the technological reduction of earth to raw materials both violate earth's withdrawal by forcing it into simple presence. One goal of a phenomenologically inspired environmental ethics would therefore be to respect the earth's self-concealing aspect. As Bruce Foltz writes, "it is this insight into the preconditions of the earth's *primary* carrying capacity of which a new understanding of nature is most in need" (1995, 15).

Bringing Heidegger's account of earth together with Levinas's (1969) description of the elements, John Sallis (2000, 2004) suggests that a return to the sensible elements offers an encounter with nature's resistance and vulnerability that avoids the difficulties of materialism. Rather than treating the elements as materials from which nature is composed, he proposes that we attend to the manifestive role of "elementals"—for example, wind, sea, earth, sky—insofar as they bound and articulate the horizon within which all things show themselves. Elementals sensibly shape our experience without themselves being experienced as things; unlike things, they are only encountered from a single edge that opens onto an encompassing expanse. Yet every experience occurs within a context framed by elementals: at a determinate location on the earth, at a time of day marked by the sun's passage through the sky, within the mood shaped by a particular season and climate, and so on. The manifestive character of elementals may, on Sallis's view, provide the basis for a renewed encounter with nature and a responsiveness to its alterity.

Phenomenological descriptions of earth and the elements contribute to the growing interest in "new materialist" approaches to the ontology of nature by articulating sensible nature's resistance to and withdrawal from conceptualization alongside its manifestive role for experience. They also develop further the implications of the fact that the natural world is always encountered from a position within it, so that it precedes and conditions our capacity to conceptualize it. Furthermore, investigations of earth and the elements reveal that our relationship with nature is essentially temporal. We noted above the historical character of the lifeworld, which mediates the meaning of nature for an intersubjective community. The investigation of earth and the elements further reveals prehistorical, material conditions for the emergence of a lifeworld. Experience and reflection are inescapably conditioned by a deep history—the immemorial past of evolutionary, geological, and cosmic time—that represents their indebtedness to the radical exteriority of sensible nature (Toadvine, 2014).

3.3 Chiasm

Phenomenology's perennial concern with overcoming the dualistic heritage of Western thought has held broad appeal for environmental thinkers, many of whom trace our alienation from nature to the conceptual severance of mind from body, value from fact, and experience from the world. Husserl's concept of intentionality, Heidegger's being-in-the-world, and Merleau-Ponty's account of the lived body suggest fruitful alternatives to such dualism. Chiasm, developed most fully in Merleau-Ponty's later work, is a promising figure for rethinking the relationship of traditional binaries such as mind and body, intelligible and sensible, human and animal, experience and nature. The term *chiasm* is a shortened form of two distinct words, one physiological (*chiasma*) and one rhetorical (*chiasmus*). A *chiasma* is a point where anatomical structures cross, especially the intertwining of the optic nerves where they meet the brain, while a *chiasmus* is a figure of speech formed by an inverted parallelism—"Beauty is truth, truth beauty" (Keats). Merleau-Ponty's chiasm combines these two senses to describe an ontological structure of reciprocal mediation, linking the reversal and circularity of the chiasmus ("there is a body of the mind and a mind of the body and a chiasmus between them," [1968, 259]) with the unity-in-difference of the chiasma ("like the chiasma of the eyes, this one is also what makes us belong to the same world" [1968, 215]; see Toadvine, 2011). The figure of chiasm thus exemplifies a general structure of mediation, operative across various relationships and levels of complexity, that avoids simple opposition as well as synthesis.

A paradigmatic example of chiasmic structure, for Merleau-Ponty, is the sensible-sentient doubling or reflexivity of the body. Husserl had already noted that, when touching an object with my hand, I can apprehend either the sensed qualities of the object (warm, firm) or the sensations that it gives rise to within my hand (warming, pressing). When I touch one hand with another, the sensations in each hand can be experienced in this double way; for the touching hand, the touched hand is never merely an object, since it also senses itself as touched. According to Husserl, this doubling of touch when the body touches itself is the condition for experiencing a body as one's own. Merleau-Ponty extends Husserl's account by identifying this self-sensing of the body as paradigmatic of three key features of chiasmic structures: First, the hand's ability to touch requires that it have a place among those things that are touchable. More generally, in order to be sentient, the body must be sensible, demonstrating an ontological continuity or kinship between sentience and sensibility. Second, the relationship between the touching hands is reversible: when one hand is the agent of touch, the other slips into the role of object touched, but with a change of attention the roles can reverse. A parallel reversibility between activity and passivity is experienced to varying degrees between the sensing body and sensed things, especially other living bodies: they touch me as I touch them. Lastly, the touching-touched relation necessarily involves an incompleteness or divergence. The touching hand never manages to touch the touching that was happening, only a moment before, in the touched hand. Consequently, the touch can never quite touch itself *as touching* but only *as touched*, which is why our two hands remain distinct even as they are joined within one sensing body. A comparable divergence characterizes all chiasmic relationships, so that they attain a unity only across non-synthesizable differences.

For Merleau-Ponty, the body, here taken as an "exemplar sensible," reveals the chiasmic structure that characterizes every being (1968, 137). We experience these chiasmic mediations corporeally in our sensible exchanges with the perceived world. Such exchanges happen through an "encroachment" that blurs the boundaries between what is joined, such that we can no longer say precisely where activity becomes passivity, where the touch becomes touched, where the self ends and other living beings or the world begins. The reversibility and encroachment of chiasmic structures informs Merleau-Ponty's ontology of "flesh," that is, of a continuity or kinship that links diverse regions of beings, not on the basis of identity, but rather as immanent divergence or nondifference. Merleau-Ponty finds in this ontology a new departure for describing the relationship between the body and the world, self and other, facts and ideas, sensibility and language, humanity and animality.

The figure of chiasm and ontology of flesh have inspired environmental philosophers on several fronts. First, by taking sensibility and embodiment as ontologically exemplary and thereby decentering the traditional emphasis on rationality, consciousness, and subjectivity, this ontology makes room for affective, habitual, and visceral dimensions of bodily relationships, inorganic as well as organic, and broadens the scope of ethics to include such relationships. Furthermore, by understanding the world as composed of relations of becoming and exchange rather than as external interactions between discrete substances or identities, this perspective reinterprets traditional dualisms as chiasmic mediations rather than binary oppositions. Such mediations are reversible and lateral rather than linear and vertical, so that instead of reproducing traditional teleologies and value hierarchies, they facilitate anarchic, creative, and hybrid becomings. Lastly, these becomings are immanent to the world, without reference to any transcendence that would escape the embodied and sensible flesh of things. Values, ideas, language, and consciousness are therefore modulations or differentiations of the world's flesh rather than dimensions that transcend it. Consequently, this ontology breaks with the traditional privileging of spirit over matter, mind over body, human over animal, or culture over nature.

3.4 Poetic Dwelling

Dwelling is one of the most important concepts in Heidegger's later writings, where it names the essence of human being: "To be a human being means to be on the earth as a mortal. It means to dwell" (1993, 349). In explaining this notion of dwelling, Heidegger reverses the everyday understanding that dwelling follows from building, that is, from cultivating the soil and erecting buildings. Our cultivation and construction are instead derivative from and dependent on our dwelling. To dwell as human beings on the earth is "to cherish and protect, to preserve and care for" what exists in its essential unfolding (1993, 349). More precisely, dwelling is the preservation and safeguarding of "earth and sky, divinities and mortals" (1993, 351). According to Heidegger, to think either of these four—for example, human beings as mortals, as beings that can die—is already to think its relation to the other three, since the four belong together in a primal unity that he terms the "fourfold." To dwell is to look after and care for the fourfold in its essence, so that our safeguarding is also fourfold: saving the earth, receiving the sky, awaiting the divinities, and initiating ourselves into our own mortality. Dwelling occurs concretely in the manner that we engage with things, by letting them be in their essence. By "thing," in contrast with the scientific "object," Heidegger here means a gathering of the fourfold, as he illustrates with such examples as a footbridge and an earthen jug. We preserve and protect the gathering of the fourfold in things when our building, in the everyday sense of cultivating the soil and constructing buildings and artifacts, is carried out in the service of dwelling. Furthermore, this everyday sense of building is derivative from the more fundamental manner of building, essential to dwelling, which is poetic creation. To create poetically is to take the measure of the span between earth and sky that is the dimension of our dwelling. That such poetic dwelling is, for Heidegger, the essence of human being does not imply that we necessarily dwell poetically today; "presumably we dwell altogether unpoetically" (1993, 227). Yet it is only by renewing the search for the essence of dwelling and heeding the poetic that we can hope for a turning point in our contemporary way of life.

By stepping back from the presuppositions of the metaphysical tradition, the notion of poetic dwelling suggests the possibility of an environmental *ethos* outside the ontological framework of modern technology and the concomitant subjectivizing of "values." In other words, it proposes a post-metaphysical understanding of the human-nature relation that provides for a responsiveness to nature in its genuine being. On this view, it is through the poetic that the being of nature is most genuinely disclosed, while its authentic conservation rests on the "saving of the earth" that takes precedence in dwelling. As Bruce Foltz, the most eloquent advocate for this view, writes, "The genuine scope of the ethical is not limited to the human or even to the sentient; it extends to the whole of entities. It concerns the bearing through which we comport ourselves toward entities, how we hold ourselves in relation to the being of entities, and how we in turn are ourselves held by our being. It concerns whether we dwell poetically on the earth" (Foltz 1995, 169).

Phenomenology opens a space for experience-based investigation of the environment, which has made it an attractive and fruitful perspective for scholars across the humanities, social sciences, and design fields. By critically assessing the epistemological and ontological assumptions that inform the historical and contemporary relationship with nature, including those of metaphysical naturalism and instrumental rationality, ecophenomenology seeks to reawaken our attention to the world as we directly experience it, with all of the philosophical consequences that such a revindication of experience would entail. The concepts of the lifeworld, the earth and elements, chiasmic flesh, and poetic dwelling illustrate directions opened by a phenomenological approach to environmental ethics, although these are far from exhaustive. By reframing our understanding of what the environment is and how we know it, phenomenology guides us toward a richer sense of the natural world and the response it invites from us.

REFERENCES

Abram, D. (1996). *The Spell of the Sensuous*. Vintage: New York.

Brown, C. (2003). "The Real and the Good: Phenomenology and the Possibility of an Axiological Rationality." In *Eco-Phenomenology: Back to the Earth Itself*, edited by C. Brown and T. Toadvine, 3–18. Albany: State University of New York Press.

Casey, E. S. (1993). *Getting Back Into Place: Toward a Renewed Understanding of the Place-World*. Bloomington: Indiana University Press.

Cataldi, S., and Hamrick, W. eds. (2007). *Merleau-Ponty and Environmental Philosophy: Dwelling on the Landscapes of Thought*. Albany: State University of New York Press.

Diehm, C. (2003). "Natural Disasters." In *Eco-Phenomenology: Back to the Earth Itself*, edited by C. Brown and T. Toadvine, 171–185. Albany: State University of New York Press.

Edelglass, W. Hatley, J., and Diehm, C. (2012). *Facing Nature: Levinas and Environmental Thought*. Pittsburgh, PA: Duquesne University Press.

Evernden, N. (1993). *The Natural Alien: Humankind and Environment*, 2nd ed. Toronto: University of Toronto Press.

Foltz, B. (1995). *Inhabiting the Earth: Heidegger, Environmental Ethics, and the Metaphysics of Nature*. Atlantic Highlands, NJ: Humanities Press.

Foltz, B., and Frodeman, R. (2004). *Rethinking Nature: Essays in Environmental Philosophy*. Bloomington: Indiana University Press.

Heidegger, M. (1993). *Basic Writings*, edited by D. F. Krell. San Francisco: HarperCollins.

Husserl, E. (1970). *The Crisis of European Sciences and Transcendental Phenomenology*, translated by David Carr. Evanston, IL: Northwestern University Press.

Ihde, D. (1990). *Technology and the Lifeworld: From Garden to Earth*. Bloomington: Indiana University Press.

James, S. (2009). *The Presence of Nature: A Study in Phenomenology and Environmental Philosophy*. New York: Palgrave Macmillan.

Kohák, E. (2003). "An Understanding Heart: Reason, Value, and Transcendental Phenomenology." In *Eco-Phenomenology: Back to the Earth Itself*, edited by C. Brown and T. Toadvine, 19–35. Albany: State University of New York Press.

Konopka, A. (2008). "A Renewal of Husserl's Critique of Naturalism: Towards the *Via Media* of Ecological Phenomenology." *Environmental Philosophy* 5(1): 37–59.

Krell, D. F. (2013). *Derrida and Our Animal Others: Derrida's Final Seminar, the Beast and the Sovereign*. Bloomington: Indiana University Press.

Lawlor, L. (2007). *This Is Not Sufficient: An Essay on Animality and Human Nature in Derrida*. New York: Columbia University Press.

Levinas, Emmanuel (1969). *Totality and Infinity*. Translated by Alphonso Lingis. Pittsburgh, PA: Duquesne University Press.

Llewelyn, J. (1991). *The Middle Voice of Ecological Conscience: A Chiasmic Reading of Responsibility in the Neighbourhood of Levinas, Heidegger and Others*. New York: St. Martin's Press.

Marietta, D. Jr. (2003). "Back to Earth with Reflection and Ecology." In *Eco-Phenomenology: Back to the Earth Itself*, edited by C. Brown and T. Toadvine, 121–135. Albany: State University of New York Press.

McWhorter, L., and Stenstad, G. eds. (2009). *Heidegger and the Earth: Essays in Environmental Philosophy*, 2nd ed. Toronto: University of Toronto Press.

Melle, U. (1997). "Ecology." In *Encyclopedia of Phenomenology*, edited by L. Embree et al., 148–152. Dordrecht: Kluwer Academic Publishers.

Merleau-Ponty, M. (1968). *The Visible and the Invisible*. Translated by Alphonso Lingis. Evanston, IL: Northwestern University Press.

Norberg-Schulz, C. (1980). *Genius Loci: Towards a Phenomenology of Architecture*. New York: Rizzoli.

Relph, E. (1976). *Place and Placelessness*. London: Pion.

Sallis, J. (2000). *Force of Imagination: The Sense of the Elemental*. Bloomington: Indiana University Press.

Sallis, J. (2004). "The Elemental Earth." In *Rethinking Nature: Essays in Environmental Philosophy*, edited by B. Foltz and R. Frodeman, 135–146. Bloomington: Indiana University Press.

Seamon, D. (2000). "A Way of Seeing People and Place: Phenomenology in Environment-Behavior Research." In *Theoretical Perspectives in Environment-Behavior Research*, edited by S. Wapner, J. Demick, T. Yamamoto, and H. Minami, 157–178. New York: Plenum.

Steinbock, A. (1995). *Home and Beyond: Generative Phenomenology After Husserl*. Evanston, IL: Northwestern University Press.

Stone, A. (2005). "Nature, Environmental Ethics, and Continental Philosophy." *Environmental Values* 14(3): 285–294.

Thompson, I. (2004). "Ontology and Ethics at the Intersection of Phenomenology and Environmental Philosophy." *Inquiry* 47: 380–412.

Toadvine, T. (2009). *Merleau-Ponty's Philosophy of Nature*. Evanston, IL: Northwestern University Press.

Toadvine, T. (2011). "The Chiasm." In *Routledge Companion to Phenomenology*, edited by S. Luft and S. Overgaard, 336–347. London: Routledge.

Toadvine, T. (2014). "The Elemental Past." *Research in Phenomenology* 44: 262–279.

Wood, D. (2003). "What Is Eco-Phenomenology?" In *Eco-Phenomenology: Back to the Earth Itself*, edited by C. Brown and T. Toadvine, 211–233. Albany: State University of New York Press.

Zimmerman, M. (1983). "Toward a Heideggerean *Ethos* for Radical Environmentalism." *Environmental Ethics* 5(3): 99–131.

CHAPTER 16

....

AESTHETIC VALUE, NATURE, AND ENVIRONMENT

....

EMILY BRADY

1 WHAT IS IT TO VALUE NATURE AESTHETICALLY?

IMAGINE wandering through a forest of giant sequoia trees. At close range, the red-brown color, thick texture of the bark, and enormous girth of the trunk will be striking to both sight and touch. High above one's head, the green, lacey shapes of the branches can be seen as they stretch out in curved forms from the towering, tapering trunk. An evergreen scent will be noticed as a light breeze passes through. Beetles can be seen scuttling around the trunk and a chipmunk darts around the back of the trunk. Repeated "peek, peek," calls from an American Robin punctuate the relatively tranquil feel of the place. Our attention may be intentionally directed, as one feels the texture of the tree's trunk, but it may also be more sharply drawn out by aspects of the environment that strike us more spontaneously; for example, the chipmunk darting into view or the arrival of a cool breeze.

Here we find an experience that can be aptly described as aesthetic. From sight to smell, many of the senses are involved. Aesthetic experience is not merely sensory, however, it is also perceptual and can thicken with a range of components or layers. Thoughts, imaginings, knowledge, and emotion may all become integrated into the experience. For example, a frequent visitor to the area may have a sense of the place and the ways a variety of aesthetic qualities or properties may be present there across different points in time. They might use this as a reference point, reflecting on some new quality that appears with a new season. An ecologist may use their considerable knowledge of *sequoiadendron giganteum* to discover features of this tree's ecosystem and the aesthetic qualities that emerge from that (e.g., teeming invertebrates). Yet another person—someone new to the place—may be so overwhelmed by the sheer size of the tree that their attention is not focused on perceptual qualities carefully discerned, but just immensity and height: a tree with a scale not yet seen before and one that evokes feelings of sublimity, perhaps of wonder too.

My aim in describing these aesthetic experiences is to try to capture how we might understand aesthetic engagement and how that grounds our aesthetic judgments and valuing of environments. The perceptual (or more layered) experience of the sequoia forest may be said to ground an overall aesthetic judgment, for example, that the tree, or perhaps the forest as a whole, is sublime. There may also be more particular aesthetic judgments arising from different episodes of the experience: the robin's song is bright or the forms and lie of the sequoia's branches are majestic. In these cases value is placed on various perceptual qualities of the tree or forest. The sharp, punctuating call of the robin has a pleasant tone, or the overwhelming scale of the trees makes one feel insignificant and small, leading to feelings of admiration for something much greater than ourselves.

Philosophers working in aesthetics of nature or environmental aesthetics (the latter covering broader subject matter) generally agree on what makes an experience distinctively aesthetic in terms of an emphasis on perceptual qualities, rather than other concerns such as knowledge, practical concerns, or economic value. It is also widely agreed that environmental aesthetics is largely concerned with the *environmental* character of natural objects as opposed to the object-centered approach typical of art, where the aesthetic object is conceived as relatively static and bounded, such as a painting or sculpture. In the sequoia forest, we have complex ecosystems involving various forms of interactions, as well as growth, decay, the effects of weather, the seasons, and so on. The more dynamic character of environments will have an effect on the range of aesthetic qualities we find and how these qualities change over time in light of various factors.

Environmental aesthetics provides an important alternative to the scenic approach, which has been subject to a couple of major criticisms. First, the scenic approach reduces aesthetic appreciation of nature to scenes, prioritizing visual qualities, and thereby treating nature more like a flat, two-dimensional painting. It is often argued that this approach is rooted in the Picturesque movement of the eighteenth and nineteenth centuries, where landscapes were judged as aesthetically pleasing according to standards of human design, e.g., landscape paintings or gardens designed to capture pictorial qualities. Although visual qualities constitute an important part of aesthetic appreciation of nature for many people, environmental aestheticians are generally wary of the scenery model (Carlson, 2000: 34; cf. Crawford, 2004). In response, they argue that a range of senses are drawn upon within a more situated, three-dimensional, environed perspective, as illustrated by the different senses drawn upon in the sequoia forest example.

Second, they claim that in reducing environments to scenes, they become viewed as relatively unchanging and static, failing to capture the dynamic and spontaneous processes that constitute nonhuman nature, such as trees moving in the wind, a flowing river, or a bumblebee moving from one flower to the next.

2 CONTEMPORARY DEBATES

Apart from these areas of general agreement, philosophical debates about aesthetically valuing nature splinter depending upon just what layers of the experience play a role and serve as grounds for our aesthetic judgments. In environmental aesthetics, theories tend to be framed at least in terms of which grounds are consistent with notions of aesthetic experience more generally, but also just what ought to ground our aesthetic judgments of nature if such judgments are to be appropriate to their objects.[1] As such, two key questions drive the debate: (1) How do aesthetic experience and judgments of nature (including modified or influenced nature) differ from artistic experience and judgments? (2) What are the grounds of appropriate aesthetic judgments of nature?

Two sets of positions have emerged in response to these questions, "scientific cognitivism" and "noncognitivism."[2] Scientific cognitivism holds that if appreciation is to reach beyond a superficial aesthetic response and issue in judgments appropriate to their objects, it must be informed by scientific knowledge. The most well-established position, Carlson's (2000) "natural environmental model," rests on an argument by analogy. In art appreciation, art history and criticism provide the foundation of informed judgments. For natural aesthetics, instead, the most legitimate and "objective" source will be the natural sciences, such as geology and biology. It is claimed that such knowledge will ensure aesthetic judgments that accord with their objects, enabling a grasp of relevant aesthetic qualities. If I were to appreciate a whale without correct knowledge, as a "fish" rather than a "mammal," for example, I might see it as a clumsy fish instead of recognizing its majesty as it moves apparently effortlessly through the ocean (Carlson, 2000, 2008).

Although noncognitivists agree that non-trivial aesthetic appreciation is essential in order to avoid judgments that might distort nature, they argue that scientific cognitivism misses some fundamental ways we experience natural and semi-natural environments. Arnold Berleant (1992) makes a strong case for a participatory, multisensory, and immersive engagement in environments, attempting to move beyond the subject-object dichotomy and "disinterestedness" often associated with artistic appreciation and historical conceptions of the aesthetic response. Through "aesthetics of engagement," we find a new starting point for aesthetics, where our aesthetic judgments are not determined by fairly passive responses to artworks or individual objects but rather by forms of situated engagement. Other non-cognitive theories can be categorized through the different ways in which they bring out some layer or component of appreciation. The "arousal model," an emotion-based account, argues that scientific cognitivism fails to capture the legitimate, non-sentimentalizing ways that emotional responses shape aesthetic appreciation (Carroll, 1993). An important component of Immanuel Kant's aesthetic theory, imagination, has been brought to the fore by some views in order to emphasize how exploratory, projective, and ampliative imaginings can enrich and deepen appreciation without at the same time distorting or humanizing nature (Hepburn, 1996; Brady, 2003).

It is important to note that both sides of the debate aim for an understanding of appreciation based on the aesthetic qualities nature actually possesses. Yuriko Saito (1998) has provided the most influential formulation of this aim, where valuing nature on its own terms will begin and end in the observable features of some natural object (Saito, 1998; Parsons, 2008). When various narratives such as folk knowledge or science figure in appreciation, she argues that we must always be guided by the object's sensuous qualities, rather than distracted away from aesthetic concerns about the object: "the molecular structure of a rock or the medicinal value of a spring seems too removed from our immediate perceptual arena to be realizable on the sensuous surface" (Saito, 1998: 144).

3 PLURALISM AND AESTHETIC VALUING OF NATURE

Notwithstanding some points of agreement, a tension arises between approaches that stress the role of knowledge and those that stress alternative components as important, such as imagination or emotion. In my view, one very good reason to side with noncognitivism is the pluralistic character of its various approaches. Before explaining why pluralism is more desirable, let me first say something about why noncognitivists might be pluralists.

In their attempt to integrate a range of both cognitive and non-cognitive layers of aesthetic responses, several non-cognitive positions move toward pluralism. Hepburn's (1984, 1996) interest in multisensory responses and participatory, reflexive engagement suggest a range of appropriate ways to approach nature, from imaginings and feelings to various kinds of narratives (from science to literature). Although special emphasis is put on the role of perception and imagination, following Kant's aesthetic theory, Brady's "integrated aesthetic" aims to be inclusive regarding potential layers of aesthetic experience, with the senses, attention to perceptual qualities, imagination, emotion, and, to some extent, knowledge playing some role, depending on the particular aesthetic situation (2003). "Syncretism" attempts to bridge the cognitivism/noncognitivism debate by weaving together various layers of appreciation, such as imagination and scientific knowledge, and making natural beauty central to the good life (Moore, 2008). The pluralistic outlook is nicely illustrated through Heyd's (2001) discussion of the "many stories" of nature and the way they can bring out various aesthetic qualities and perhaps engage us more deeply than scientific facts. Finally, some views, such as Carroll's, represent at least a weak form of pluralism insofar as it recognizes the range of responses, where scientific knowledge will sometimes be relevant and at other times our emotional responses will have more traction.

It would be incorrect to characterize cognitivism as interested only in knowledge as the foundation of aesthetic experience. Certainly, cognitivist positions try to capture some of the more traditional components of aesthetic experience, like emphasis on multisensory experience. However, they raise the concern that emotional or imaginative responses are unreliable or potentially distorting grounds for aesthetic judgment (Eaton, 1998; Brady, 2003).[3] This is at least because cognitivism, generally, strives for *correctness* rather than merely appropriateness where aesthetic judgments are concerned. For the cognitivist, we must get things right. The noncognitivist is more generous, recognizing that there may be a variety of ways we can appreciate the same thing—and in ways that still appreciate the thing as it is.

Many of the advantages of pluralism relate to how it opens up a variety of avenues for appreciation. Through this, a pluralistic stance potentially supports rich forms of aesthetic engagement with, for example, natural beauty, sublimity, the interesting as well as the ugly. First, it fits with an *environmental* approach that recognizes the myriad possibilities for appreciation beyond the arts. The implications of the dynamic and changing character of environmental, natural appreciation are significant for opening up modes of aesthetic attention that are less constrained by artistic appreciative conventions and situations. It is possible to take up a variety of appreciative positions on the ground, as it were, attending to a single aesthetic object, a combination or the whole situation. We can draw upon various senses, depending on the aesthetic qualities present, which in themselves may be determined by a set of factors, for example, time of day (morning, evening) and light, weather, movement in animals, plants, and so on. We can return to the same place and appreciate its evolving aesthetic qualities across the seasons. In response to sensory engagement, some combination of components—background knowledge, thoughts, imaginings, and emotional responses—come together in appreciation and underpin the aesthetic judgments we make.

Second, the indeterminacy of environmental appreciation signals a greater degree of *freedom* in aesthetic appreciation in contrast to the more conventional settings of many forms of artistic appreciation. Historically, such freedom has been a hallmark of the aesthetic point of view, where the senses, perception, and imagination are developed through responses that draw out more creative, poetic, and metaphorical interactions with the world, in contrast to the more knowledge-directed engagement of science and other intellectual endeavors. Such perspectives have been seen as valuable within both art and non-art aesthetics for the ways they increase and enrich the scope of our engagement with the world and enable us to practice and develop our perceptual, emotional, and imaginative capacities.

Third, the openness of pluralism also provides a way to avoid the potentially reductive lens of science while also recognizing its significance alongside other components. While scientific knowledge may enrich appreciation by providing information that enables the discovery of new aesthetic qualities, designating it as the sole reference point for correctness presents a set of problems. For example, scientific theories themselves are often in dispute, so we will need to be wary of just what claims are being made and how up to date the facts we have to hand are. Also, there is potential for aesthetic valuing that is more egalitarian in spirit if there is no requirement of such knowledge for grounding aesthetic judgments. The implication of this will be a range of aesthetic judgments deemed reasonable and relevant rather than being dismissed as uninformed. This is no small matter given the role of aesthetic value in various disputes in environmental planning and policy (the location of wind turbines presents a recent challenge).

The biggest stumbling block for pluralism is that not every story will, in fact, be appropriate, and some stories will potentially distort the aesthetic object. Parsons' (2008) interesting discussion of pluralism argues that mythological stories of the night sky, for example, can be problematic by taking us away from truthful appreciation of stars and constellations. Scientifically informed appreciation will, instead, support appreciation of nature on its own terms, appreciation that is more truthful to its objects. However, it is not clear that science does, in fact, present the best story, given my previous remarks about its narrow compass, variability, and so on. We may also find that other kinds of stories engage us more concretely and directly and provide avenues to more accessible aesthetic valuing, without distorting nature. Avoiding distortion and developing a "critical pluralism" will involve close perception and careful attention to the actual qualities of the natural object, process, and so forth, so that this will always form the center of our attention or the main ground of our valuing. Embracing diverse stories and drawing on many of our capacities is achievable within the parameters of appreciation of nature on its own terms. We can learn from eighteenth-century aesthetic theory—and the pervasive influence of Kant's philosophy on both aesthetics and environmental aesthetics—that such valuing ought to be conceived of as non-instrumental, separating the aesthetic stance from more instrumental forms of valuing, for example, practical or hedonistic concerns.

The critical pluralism I have been outlining here makes certain demands on us. It requires us to assess the extent to which our more imaginative or emotional engagements with natural objects constitute reasonable responses and just how these forms of engagement will fit with the object itself. We need not jettison more "subjective" forms of engagement, if they can be allied with the object's actual perceptual qualities and a commonsense understanding of what it is. That is, science need not provide the exclusive story of what we experience, but it can provide one story in the mix. This kind of approach will ground aesthetic judgments for which we can provide justification, that is, aesthetic judgments for which we can give some reasonable explanation. I have in mind here a form of aesthetic justification based in the discrimination of aesthetic qualities (as based in non-aesthetic qualities) and the ways in which the activity of appreciation can be communicated to others and shared among valuers (Sibley, 2001; Brady, 2003). Sorting reasonable from less reasonable responses and judgments, according to the aesthetic situation at hand, makes demands that we might usefully capture through recent discussions about virtues in aesthetics (Kieran, 2010). Appreciative virtue can be understood as working toward aesthetic appreciation that is open and informed by our different capacities, yet that also balances openness with attention to the aesthetic object for its own sake.

Adopting critical pluralism may enable the richest form of aesthetic engagement with the natural environment and lead to closer and more constructive nature-human relations. Within environmental ethics, Ron Sandler classifies aesthetic sensibility as a type of "environmental virtue" belonging to "virtues of communion with nature" (2007, 82). Through our aesthetic sensibilities we can establish meaningful relationships with the environment, which potentially underpin forms of cherishing and caring.

In light of this connection between aesthetic valuing of nature and a kind of communion or meaningful relationship, one might ask if all aesthetic experiences of nature are positive. What about forms of aesthetic disvaluing? Can they also lead to meaningful relationships? Scientific cognitivists such as Carlson have used their approach to underpin "positive aesthetics," the view that all of nature is beautiful or aesthetically good (Rolston, 1998; Carlson, 2000). Where less attractive parts of nature are concerned, the claim is that an ecological understanding of the thing in question, for example, a decomposing carcass, can be transformed or ultimately valued as something beautiful once we have a full understanding of the ecological narrative at play. That is, we can find beauty there if we understand the ecological processes of life and death at work. This approach seems to exclude aesthetic disvalue of nature and only allow disvalue where nature modified by humans is concerned. Elsewhere, I have argued that although this approach is appealing for its ecological awareness, it fails to recognize the range of aesthetic values/disvalues we do, in fact, find in nature. As I see it, ugliness is not something that can be explained away through an ecological story, rather, we ought to embrace the significance that more negative forms of aesthetic experience have for our human-environment relations (Brady, 2012). Indeed, the natural world can be beautiful, but also sublime, ugly, and so on.

My ideas here are partly inspired by moves in environmental ethics away from an exclusive focus on intrinsic value and toward discussions about how our relationships to environments shape our moral attitudes to them. This shift in emphasis, as illustrated, for example, in environmental pragmatism and work by John O'Neill, Alan Holland and Andrew Light (2007), is signaled by the recognition that many of our interactions with nature exist not only in the context of distant wild places but also within more cultural contexts, for example, rural and urban environments. In these kinds of places we may have more regular interactions with nature in ways that enable us to form meaningful relations.

Meaningful relationships also take place through more challenging or difficult aesthetic situations. Consider gentle valleys, pastoral farmlands, a calm lake, or a pretty goldfinch, compared to the more challenging features of vast mudflats, clear-cut forests, and toads. More difficult aesthetic experiences often involve a more diverse range of feelings and emotions, from anxiety and awe to fascination and aversion, as we are drawn out of more comfortable forms of appreciation. The challenges presented by aesthetic features of ugliness, terrible beauty, and to some extent, the sublime, contrast with experiences demanding less effort and those distinguished by their pleasure or delight. These categories of aesthetic value draw out more complex kinds of relationships with nature, but they can be meaningful and educative through that very complexity. For example, a great storm experienced from a position of shelter will evoke the complex mix of pleasure and anxiety characteristic of paradigm cases of the natural sublime. We may feel insignificant and puny, but at the same time, appreciate the greatness of natural forces and our capacity to (sometimes) cope with them (Brady, 2013; Shapsay, 2013). With ugliness, a form of aesthetic disvalue, we may struggle to appreciate, with pleasure, any features of some object, yet there may be educational benefits that arise from the experience. Perhaps we engage with something previously avoided due to feeling repelled (a tick), and we come to take some new interest in it, even if it remains ugly to us.

In recognizing the range of environmental values (particularly disvalue) and to build an account that extends beyond intrinsic value, Holland argues for the importance of meaningful relations as a "unifying concept that characterizes evolutionary and ecological relations as well as cultural ones" (Holland 2012: 3). Bringing the concept of meaningful relations into our aesthetic and ethical reflections can enable us to recognize the significance of a range of our interactions with environments, how they can be enriching and educative, and how they might feed into moral motivations. These ideas can also give us a more complete and generous grasp of our meaningful engagement with environments in aesthetic terms, including both positive and negative relations, as well as those which mix the two.

4 Aesthetic Value and Environmental Ethics

Some connections between aesthetics and ethics have been drawn out thus far through appreciative virtue and the notion of meaningful relationships. These ideas helpfully link ideas from aesthetics with trends in environmental ethics; however, the kinds of worries noted by cognitivists against non-cognitivists raise the general concern that aesthetic valuing lies on the more humanizing, even anthropocentric, end of the perspectives and attitudes we take to the natural world. Some philosophers have tried to address this concern more directly through (1) "aesthetic preservationism," or the idea that aesthetic valuing of nature can feed into ethical attitudes toward natural environments (Fisher 2003); and (2) condoning theories of environmental aesthetics that meet the requirements of environmentalism.

Aesthetic preservationism holds that through the sensitive perception characteristic of aesthetic attention and the discovery of beauty, majesty, and so on, we may develop care and respect for nature. In this way, a kind of aesthetic awareness potentially feeds into ethical attitudes and forms of environmental action (Hargrove, 1989; Lintott, 2006). For example, "aesthetic protectionism" argues that natural beauty can serve as an important motivation for protecting the environment, as long as we can provide sufficient justification—some kind of objectivity—for our aesthetic judgments of nature (Hettinger, 2007). To take an example with which many people will be familiar, the destruction of some natural area in order to build a parking lot, shopping center, or other development will mean the loss of plant life and habitat for insects, birds, and other animals and with that a whole set of aesthetic qualities—a place—enjoyed by people. In anticipation of the possibility of losing that place, many people will come to know it more intimately and seek to protect it for ecological, aesthetic, and other reasons. Here, the valuing of aesthetic qualities in that place may be cited as a motivating factor in any moral actions.

The second view provides the most direct defense of aesthetics in light of concerns from an environmentalist perspective. Carlson (2008: 297) puts forward five desiderata for any theory of environmental aesthetics in this regard. It must be acentric rather than simply anthropocentric; environment-focused rather than scenery-obsessed; serious rather than superficial and trivial; objective rather than subjective; and morally engaged rather than morally vacuous. Although he argues that only scientific cognitivism meets these requirements, it is certainly possible to find sufficient evidence for an environmentalist perspective from within critical pluralism, if we are satisfied with an account of aesthetic judgments as reasonable rather than "correct" or "objective." Critical pluralism meets the other requirements, embracing an environmental rather than scenic perspective that also avoids anthropocentrism and triviality. In addition to these points, it is important to emphasize, again, that in the subfield of philosophical aesthetics, aesthetic value is commonly conceptualized as noninstrumental. Although this form of value is most of often associated with delight, liking, or pleasure in beauty, it is always in response to particular qualities in natural objects, processes, and so on, which are valued for their own sake and—on the best accounts—on their own terms (cf. Lee, 1995).[4]

5 MOVING FORWARD WITH AESTHETIC VALUE AND NATURE

Environmental aesthetics has increasingly been concerned with exploring how humans engage aesthetically with forms of modified or influenced nature. Several philosophers have asked whether or not artistic engagement with environments (environmental, land, and ecological art) creates positive human-environment relationships or, rather, manipulates nature for the sake of human, artistic ends (Carlson, 2000; Parsons, 2008; Simus, 2008). Gardens and other cultural landscapes have also been highlighted as significant places where creative interactions and relationships of co-dependence between humans and nature may develop (Cooper, 2006; Arntzen and Brady, 2008). An area of managed (to less managed) environments that deserves attention from environmental aestheticians is ecological restoration, novel ecosystems, and new calls for rewilding, as these issues have so far been treated mainly from ethical perspectives (Prior and Brady, forthcoming). It would also be interesting to see environmental aesthetics engaging more with nature in urban settings, perhaps building on Diane Michelfelder's (2003) work, which looks at how aesthetic experience of non-human animals in urban places relates to issues in environmental ethics. Given that the environment includes a range of natural items, it is surprising that natural aesthetics has given little attention to non-domesticated animals and how forms of distorted aesthetic appreciation, such as anthropomorphism, might be avoided (but see Rolston, 1987; Parsons, 2007).

There are other interesting and promising areas for aesthetic reflections on nature and environment. Environmental aesthetics tends to draw largely on North American and Anglo-Saxon understandings of environment. Taking a cue from Saito (2010), there are opportunities to develop our knowledge of other global traditions. While Saito herself has discussed some interesting links between Japanese aesthetics, environmental aesthetics, and the neighboring subfield of everyday aesthetics, little has been written from the perspective of philosophical environmental aesthetics about non-western traditions. An interesting way into these studies might be to focus on the environments themselves, and from there incorporate more globally diverse perspectives, thereby complementing comparative aesthetics, a less philosophically driven, empirical area (Feagin, 2007).[5] For example, a more philosophical or phenomenological approach could be taken by starting with the aesthetic character of the frozen environments inhabited by the Inuit or the deserts of nomadic communities (Yi-Fu Tuan, 1993).[6]

Finally, there is also scope for reflecting on extreme environments and other relatively neglected places, for example, marine environments, the deep sea, the sky above, and the atmosphere. Brady (2014) has discussed issues at the intersection of environmental aesthetics, ethics, and climate change, asking whether landscapes of the future affected by anthropogenic climate change may be considered beautiful or not. What might be said about the aesthetic, let alone ethical implications, of new calls for geoengineering the planet? The "Anthropocene," the proposed geological epoch defined by humanity's pervasive effects on the earth, will introduce yet more challenges for environmental aesthetics, underlining the need to consider aesthetic issues as they arise at the nexus of nature-human interactions.

NOTES

1. My use of "objects" is intended to be broad, covering single objects which become the focus of one's attention, or a set of objects, or a place, or environment more generally, as well as natural phenomena or processes (e.g., flowing water, weather, erosion).
2. These terms are specific to the debate within environmental aesthetics and do not reflect discussions of noncognitivism in metaethics.
3. This criticism may seem outdated given recent work in philosophy that recognizes emotions as legitimate sources of knowledge. However, for discussions of aesthetic value within environmental policy debates it remains timely. In these debates, many practitioners assume that aesthetic experience is deeply subjective, and thus difficult to measure or pin down (Brady, 2003). This assumption is often based on the belief that aesthetic experience is always an emotional experience, varying from one individual to the next.
4. See Lee (1995) for a conflation of aesthetic value and hedonistic value.
5. For some theoretical, global perspectives, though more centered on the arts, see Feagin (2007).
6. See earlier work by the cultural geographer Yi-Fu Tuan (1993).

REFERENCES

Arntzen, S., and Brady, E., eds. (2008). *Humans in the Land: The Aesthetics and Ethics of the Cultural Landscape*. Oslo: Oslo Academic Press/Unipub.

Berleant, A. (1992). *The Aesthetics of Environment*. Philadelphia: Temple University Press.

Brady, E. (2003). *Aesthetics of the Natural Environment*. Edinburgh: Edinburgh University Press.

Brady, E. (2012). "The Ugly Truth: Negative Aesthetics and Environment." In *Philosophy and Environment. Royal Institute of Philosophy Supplements*, edited by A. O'Hear, 69: 83–99. Cambridge: Cambridge University Press.

Brady, E. (2013). *The Sublime in Modern Philosophy: Aesthetics, Ethics, and Nature*. Cambridge: Cambridge University Press.

Brady, E. (2014). "Aesthetic Value, Ethics, and Climate Change." *Environmental Values* 23: 551–570.

Carlson, A. (2000). *Aesthetics and the Environment: The Appreciation of Nature, Art and Architecture*. New York: Routledge.

Carlson, A. (2008). *Nature and Landscape: An Introduction to Environmental Aesthetics*. New York: Columbia University Press.

Carlson, A. and Lintott, S., eds. (2007). *Nature, Aesthetics, and Environmentalism: From Beauty to Duty*. New York: Columbia University Press.

Carroll, N. (1993). "Being Moved By Nature: Between Religion and Natural History." In *Landscape, Natural Beauty and the Arts*, edited by S. Kemal and I. Gaskell, 244–266. Cambridge: Cambridge University Press.

Cooper, D. (2006). *A Philosophy of Gardens*. Oxford: Oxford University Press.

Crawford, D. (2004). "Scenery and the Aesthetics of Nature." In *The Aesthetics of Natural Environments*, edited by A. Carlson and A. Berleant, 253–268. Peterborough: Broadview Press.

Eaton, M. (1998). "Fact and Fiction in the Aesthetic Appreciation of Nature." *Journal of Aesthetics and Art Criticism* 56: 149–156.

Feagin, S. L., ed. (2007). *Journal of Aesthetics and Art Criticism Special Issue: Global Theories of the Arts and Aesthetics* 65: 1–146.

Fisher, J. (2003). "Environmental Aesthetics." In *Companion to Environmental Philosophy*, edited by D. Jamieson, 264–276. Malden, MA: Blackwell.

Hargrove, E. (1989). *Foundations of Environmental Ethics*. Englewood Cliffs: Prentice Hall.

Hepburn, R. (1984). "Contemporary Aesthetics and the Neglect of Natural Beauty." In *British Analytical Philosophy*, edited by B. Williams and A. Montefiore, 285–310. London: Routledge and Kegan Paul, 1966. Reprinted in Ronald Hepburn. *Wonder and Other Essays*. Edinburgh: Edinburgh University Press.

Hepburn, R. (1996). "Landscape and the Metaphysical Imagination." *Environmental Values* 5: 191–204.

Hettinger, N. (2007). "Objectivity in Environmental Aesthetics and Protection of the Environment." In *Nature, Aesthetics, and Environmentalism: From Beauty to Duty*, edited by A. Carlson and S. Lintott, 413–437. New York: Columbia University Press.

Heyd, T. (2001). "Aesthetic Appreciation and the Many Stories About Nature." *British Journal of Aesthetics* 41(2): 125–137.

Holland, A. (2012). "The Value Space of Meaningful Relations." In *Human-Environment Relations: Transformative Values in Theory and Practice*, edited by E. Brady and P. Phemister, 3–15. Dordrecht: Springer.

Kieran, M. (2010). "The Vice of Snobbery: Aesthetic Knowledge, Justification and Virtue in Art Appreciation." *Philosophical Quarterly* 60(239): 243–263.

Lee, K. (1995). "Beauty For Ever?" *Environmental Values* 4(3): 213–225.

Lintott, S. (2006). "Toward Eco-Friendly Aesthetics." *Environmental Ethics* 28: 57–76.

Michelfelder, D. (2003). "Valuing Wildlife Populations in Urban Environments." *Journal of Social Philosophy* 34(1): 79–90.

Moore, R. (2008). *Natural Beauty: A Theory of Aesthetics Beyond the Arts.* Peterborough: Broadview Press.

O'Neill, J., Holland, A., and Light, A. (2007). *Environmental Values.* London: Routledge.

Parsons, G. (2007). "The Aesthetic Value of Animals." *Environmental Ethics* 29: 151–169.

Parsons, G. (2008). *Aesthetics and Nature.* London: Continuum.

Prior, J. and Brady, E. (forthcoming). "Environmental Aesthetics and Rewilding." *Environmental Values.*

Rolston, H., III (1987). "Beauty and the Beast: Aesthetic Experience of Wildlife." In *Valuing Wildlife: Economic and Social Perspectives*, edited by D. Decker and G. Goff, 187–196. Boulder: Westview Press.

Rolston, H., III (1998). "Aesthetic Experience in Forests." *Journal of Aesthetics and Art Criticism* 56(2): 157–166.

Saito, Y. (1998). "Appreciating Nature on Its Own Terms." *Environmental Ethics* 20: 135–149.

Saito, Y. (2010). "Future Directions for Environmental Aesthetics." *Environmental Values* 19 (3): 373–391.

Sandler, R. (2007). *Character and Environment.* New York: Columbia University Press.

Shapsay, S. (2013). "Contemporary Environmental Aesthetics and the Neglect of the Sublime." *British Journal of Aesthetics* 53: 181–198.

Sibley, F. (2001). "Aesthetic Concepts." In *Approach to Aesthetics: Collected Papers on Philosophical Aesthetics*, edited by J. Benson, B. Redfern and J. Roxbee Cox, 1–23. Oxford: Oxford University Press.

Simus, J. B. (2008). "Ecological Art and Environmental Citizenship." *Environmental Ethics* 30: 21–36.

Tuan, Y. F. (1993). "Desert and Ice: Ambivalent Aesthetics." In *Landscape, Natural Beauty and the Arts*, edited by S. Kemal and I. Gaskell. Cambridge: Cambridge University Press, 139–157.

PART IV

HOW THINGS MATTER

*Theoretical Perspectives on
the Way We Ought to Act*

CHAPTER 17

CONSEQUENTIALISM IN ENVIRONMENTAL ETHICS

AVRAM HILLER

WHAT is valuable?[1] How should one act? There are numerous forms of consequentialism; what they have in common is that they answer the second question by appealing to an answer to the first. Consequentialists typically claim that an act is right when it produces the best state of affairs (relative to other acts the agent could have performed; Hooker, 2008), and then they offer a theory of what makes for the best state of affairs. For instance, classical act-utilitarianism, the most traditional form of consequentialism, holds that an act is right insofar as it maximizes overall utility, where utility is understood as the optimal balance of the most pleasure and least pain. Most consequentialists nowadays believe that the utilitarian focus on pleasure and pain is too simplistic, and thus provide alternative views of what makes for better or worse states of affairs.

A full explanation and defense of consequentialism in all its forms is well beyond the scope of this chapter (though see Sinnott-Armstrong, 2011; Driver, 2012), although along the way I shall say some things both in clarification of and in defense of consequentialism in general. My main focus will be on versions of consequentialism that pertain directly to environmental ethics. Although consequentialism has had a grand history as one of the principal types of ethical theory over the last 200 years or so, relatively few environmental ethicists have been consequentialists (Elliot, 2001: 181). Why this is the case is something I will not address here (but see Hiller and Kahn, 2014); instead, my goals are to discuss the contours of possible consequentialist environmental ethical views, compare environmental consequentialism with some competing environmental ethical views, and note challenges that a fleshed-out form of environmental consequentialism must meet. I will put special emphasis on examining a *holistic* environmental consequentialism, a view that has been, in my judgment, under-developed.

Two types of consequentialist accounts of our responsibilities with regard to the non-human world should be distinguished at the outset. First, a consequentialist may hold to a traditional anthropocentric view of value (see Thompson, chapter 7 of this volume) and argue that one must promote long-term human good, but to do so one must be concerned with how our actions affect the environment. Second, a consequentialist may adopt a theory of value according to which at least some non-human entities have intrinsic value. Although most forms of consequentialism explicated by philosophers who work primarily in environmental ethics are of this second kind, it will be instructive to begin by discussing a view of the first type, especially given its historical significance.

The end of the nineteenth century and the beginning of the 20th marked a turning point in United States environmental history in that the frontier, exploited over the first part of the country's history, was no longer seen as limitless. Gifford Pinchot, the first Head of the US Forest Service (beginning with the formation of the Forest Service under the Presidential administration of Theodore Roosevelt in 1905), was an avowed utilitarian (Pinchot, 1947; Nash, 1982; Katz, 1997), and Pinchot recognized that the greatest long-term benefit for people required conservation of natural resources. Pinchot thus helped fashion regulations that restricted exploitation of the natural environment. However, Pinchot was not and still is not universally hailed by environmentalists. Notoriously, Pinchot was instrumental in the decision to dam the Hetch Hetchy Valley in Yosemite National Park to provide drinking water for San Francisco. Pinchot testified before Congress in 1913:

> I think that the men who assert that it is better to leave a piece of natural scenery in its natural condition have rather the better of the argument, and I believe that if we had nothing else to consider than the delight of the few men and women who would yearly go to Hetch Hetchy Valley, then it should be left in its natural condition. But the considerations on the other side of the question, to my mind, are simply overwhelming (Walsh et al., 2007).

Pinchot's reasons are entirely consequentialist and anthropocentric. On the other side of the debate, John Muir and the Sierra Club, which Muir founded, were adamantly opposed to the dam. [2] The official position of the Sierra Club was given in a principle: "That our National Parks shall be held forever inviolate" (Colby, 1909). Muir wrote:

> These temple destroyers, devotees of ravaging commercialism, seem to have a perfect contempt for Nature, and, instead of lifting their eyes to the God of the mountains, lift them to the Almighty Dollar. Dam Hetch Hetchy! As well dam for water-tanks the people's cathedrals and churches, for no holier temple has ever been consecrated by the heart of man (Walsh, et al. 2007).[3]

It is critical to recognize that there are two aspects of this critique of Pinchot's utilitarianism. The first is that what is held by Muir and the Sierra Club to be of value is more than just human good—Hetch Hetchy Valley itself has value. Second, certain acts of despoiling National Parks are always impermissible, regardless of the consequences of the acts. Importantly, it is possible to accept the first criticism of an anthropocentric utilitarianism without also accepting the second. Consequentialists may develop a theory of value according to which there are non-human goods, and claim that damming Hetch Hetchy is wrong because doing so does not maximize overall value. However, consequentialists will still bite the bullet in claiming that *nothing* should be held inviolate. For one can imagine circumstances in which a regulatory agency is faced with a choice of destroying one part of a National Park in order to save numerous parts from being destroyed in a like manner. Would it not be better, from the perspective of one who values nature, to commit the violation so as to maintain as much of the park as possible?[4]

This type of issue looms large in consequentialist theory. When G. E. M. Anscombe (1958) introduced the term "consequentialism," she intended it as a derogatory term. First, Anscombe argues that consequentialist views are wrong in that they to fail to distinguish between foreseeable consequences of an action from intended consequences. For Anscombe, it is appropriate to perform an act when the intended consequences are good even if the overall foreseeable consequences are not. In addition, Anscombe decries any view according to which certain acts that cause harm to innocent persons are morally right. Arguably, Anscombe is wrong on both counts (see Bennett, 1966 for an early response to Anscombe). If one intends to make a friend happy by buying him a statue made of ivory, it seems like a morally wrong act if one foresees that the purchase will lead to endangered elephants being killed. And one can imagine highly unfortunate scenarios in which harming an innocent person will end up saving numerous innocent persons from being harmed. Why do we intuitively hold that harming an innocent person is wrong? The reason, it seems, is that the outcome of doing so is that an innocent person will be harmed. But if one is so concerned about preventing innocent persons from being harmed, then it is seemingly irrational to approve of activities that lead to more such harm when one could act to minimize it. In short, *whatever* one takes to be of value—human life, human integrity, animal well-being, wilderness areas—it would be wrong to act in such a way that, *ceteris paribus*, more of what is of value is destroyed.

As I have noted, most consequentialist environmental ethicists accept that there are nonhuman goods, and in what follows I shall focus on the varieties of such non-anthropocentric views. A good place to begin is to note that Jeremy Bentham, founder of utilitarianism, argues that the welfare of nonhuman animals may be considered in moral calculus (Bentham [1789] 1996). This utilitarian view is elaborated upon in great detail by Peter Singer in his book *Animal Liberation* (1975) and elsewhere. Singer's view is *sentientism*—all and only sentient beings' experiences have value (see Gruen, Chapter 8 of this volume). Singer does argue that we should preserve natural areas and non-sentient things, but only on instrumental grounds; ecological habitats, and the non-sentient organisms in them, are necessary to support sentient animals in leading satisfying lives but are not valuable in themselves.

Arguably, Singer's sentientist consequentialist position in favor of animal welfare is more plausible than the main alternative—the rights-based approach of Tom Regan (1983). In Regan's view, animals with certain psychological attributes have rights, and this entails, for instance, that one should never conduct medical testing on animals even if it promotes the greater good. However, it seems reasonable, in some cases at least, that if the benefit of conducting testing on animals will be significant relative to the harm caused to a few animals, then it is permissible. A sentientist consequentialist approach, which tallies the good against the bad, will have this result.

One may object to sentientist consequentialism on the ground that it fails to properly respect the intrinsic values of non-sentient living things (see Palmer, Chapter 9 of this volume). Robin Attfield, in a series of works (Attfield, 1983, 1999, 2003, 2014), defends *biocentric individualism*, the idea that all and only living things have value. Although others such as Albert Schweitzer ([1923] 2008) and Paul Taylor (1986) defend the value of all living things, Attfield is unique in doing so from a consequentialist perspective. Like Schweitzer and Taylor, Attfield appeals to the fact that living things have interests and capacities in pursuing their own good, and this qualifies them as having value (Attfield, 1999: 39). However, unlike Schweitzer and Taylor, Attfield is an *inegalitarian*—he believes that although all and only living things are valuable, not all living things are *equal* in value. Some organisms have higher capacities, such as for autonomous action, and such creatures have greater value than organisms with more limited capacities. This helps biocentric individualism avoid the implausible consequence that a blade of grass is equally morally considerable to a chimpanzee or human.

Still, some philosophers, and certainly many environmentalists who are not professional philosophers, find even biocentrism to be too limited. Sentientist and biocentric consequentialism are in principle consistent with massive alteration of native ecosystems and even the extinction of many species for the purpose of maximizing positive sentient experience or maximizing the good of living things, respectively. (Some utilitarians, such as Brian Tomasik, 2014, embrace this ramification.) Instead, what matters, according to many, is the flourishing of ecosystems (see Callicott, Chapter 10 of this volume). However, unlike sentientist consequentialism, with its lengthy defense by Singer, and unlike biocentric consequentialism, with its well-developed account given by Attfield, there has not been an extensive and detailed explication or sustained defense of a fully consequentialist position that accepts ecosystemic values. I shall thus dedicate much of the remainder of this chapter to this kind of consequentialism, although the remarks I make will of necessity be a mere sketch of a position.

Famously, Aldo Leopold's "Land Ethic" is ecocentric, and it is phrased in what appears to be consequentialist terms ([1949] 1980, 262): "A thing is right when it tends to preserve the integrity, stability, and beauty of the biotic community. It is wrong when it tends otherwise." However, James Fieser argues (1992)—successfully in my opinion—that Leopold did not intend the land ethic as a primary moral principle, let alone an act-consequentialist one. As Fieser claims, Leopold either was ignorant of utilitarianism or chose not to deeply engage with it (also see Moline, 1986). Of course, Leopold's views have been adopted by philosophers who are indeed well aware of normative theory. J. Baird Callicott, for instance, accepts Leopold's Land Ethic and in his early work seems to accept some of its consequentialist implications (Callicott, 1989).

However, the charge of so-called "environmental fascism," as levied by Tom Regan (1983: 361), led Callicott to abandon consequentialism (Callicott, 1999: 172–173). Regan argues that accepting Leopold's Land Ethic as the single moral principle would absurdly entail that it is more morally appropriate to kill a human being rather than an endangered wildflower. Similar to what we saw in the case of the Sierra Club's criticism of Pinchot, the environmental fascism objection raises two distinct issues. As Clare Palmer notes (1998: 136), there is, first, the standard objection to consequentialism that it does not protect inviolable individual human rights, and second, there is an objection against the view that a wildflower, in its ecosystem, may contribute more to overall value than a human. I shall say more about environmental fascism below; for now I simply note that Callicott responds by disavowing his earlier acceptance of the Land Ethic as the single principle for right action.[5]

However, it is not hard to imagine an act-consequentialist view that upholds the spirit of Leopold's view and that can withstand the objection from environmental fascism. Elsewhere, I argue in favor of what I call *system consequentialism* (Hiller, 2014). Like other forms of maximizing act-consequentialism, it is the view that one should act so as to produce the best state of affairs. But it adds an important proviso: To determine what is the best state of affairs, one should not simply aggregate the goods that are possessed by individuals. Instead, the best state of affairs is the one that has the most systemic good. In what follows, I shall briefly explain the notion of systemic good and how it may fit within a consequentialist ethic, and I argue that a refined version of it does not succumb to the problem of environmental fascism.

A *system* may be defined as a whole with interdependent parts (Leopold, [1949] 1980: 262; Callicott, 1999: 130–131). There are many details that must be given in a full metaphysical account of interdependence, and I shall not attempt to give such an account here (though see Hiller, 2013). Still, ecosystems can be considered to be paradigm cases of systems. Organisms within an ecosystem have evolved with other organisms in the ecosystem, and thus members of the various species form an interdependent web. What makes an ecosystem valuable? Leopold's original characterization of ecosystemic goodness invokes a notion of stability, but most ecologically minded philosophers nowadays reject stability as an ecosystemic value. Because of this, it is difficult to arrive at an uncontroversial notion of ecosystemic value. Still, by defining ecosystemic health in a dynamic way, a number of philosophers still do attribute value to ecosystems (see especially McShane, 2004; also see Callicott, 1999 and Chapter 10 of this volume; Rolston, 1988, and 1991; Jamieson, 2002).

One feature of system consequentialism is that it may help explain, in consequentialist terms, what is (prima facie) wrong about cases where humans disrupt ecosystems. On a common view, disrupting an ecosystem is, in itself, a bad thing. For instance, Robert Elliot (1997) holds that when humans interfere in a natural system, the resultant area will have less value than an otherwise identical ecosystem that has not been disrupted by human action. But this type of anti-interference judgment seems at odds with consequentialism: typical consequentialists hold that what matters in the evaluation of an action is only the outcome of the action, and if two actions lead to states of affairs that are otherwise identical, then the actions should be judged equally. But if an impacted ecosystem is not as valuable as an otherwise identical one that humans have chosen not to disturb, it is hard to see how a consequentialist can account for the difference. Elliot, who himself otherwise is a supporter of a consequentialist environmental ethic, abandons consequentialism at this crucial juncture (Elliot, 1997: 113–114).

Despite initial appearances, this is not an intractable problem for the ecologically minded consequentialist. When a human acts, the act may be more or less in accord with systemic, ecological good, for some human actions are contrary to natural systems and others are not. On the assumption that we are able to make prior value judgments about the good of systems, in cases where a human action disrupts a natural system we can say that there is something about the very action itself that makes the state of affairs less valuable. This view also allows that human actions can contribute positively to overall value if they are done in accord with natural systems, in the same way that the action of *any* organism is good when it is done in accord with its natural ecosystem. But to be clear, this is merely to say that some human acts can be assessed as contributing to systemic good or bad, which is not the same as saying that such acts are, on their own, *right* or *wrong*.[6] Thus an impacted ecosystem has less value than an otherwise identical, undisturbed one simply because systemic good is greater when a system that has historically not been inhabited by humans remains free from human interference.

However, there remains the problem of environmental fascism. If we value ecosystems, and if preserving a single endangered wildflower maintains ecosystemic good more than saving a human, then it seems that we should value the flower more than the human. Yet ecosystems do not seem to be harmed when humans steal or commit murder (Fieser, 1992), but surely we should have an ethic that prohibits such actions in at least most situations.

As I just noted, there are two aspects to the charge of environmental fascism. I shall set aside further discussion of the issue of whether it is *ever* right to cause harm to one individual for the sake of the greater good, since that is a more general concern for consequentialists. Instead, I shall focus on the charge that system consequentialism may absurdly place more value on flowers than on humans (or other sentient organisms). The system consequentialist may first note that indeed a long-term reduction of the human population may be best, but this in itself would not justify murder, since there are much better ways of lowering population (such as providing increased education for women). Second, one may accept *multidimensional* consequentialism, a view developed by Alan Carter (2005).[7] In Carter's view, there is a plurality of values—anthropocentric, zoocentric, biocentric, and ecocentric. According to Carter, there is no inconsistency in claiming that ecosystems are valuable but humans are as well, and human good can in some cases outweigh ecosystemic good. Carter specifically uses this to respond to the problem of environmental fascism (Carter, 2011). For Carter, there is a plurality of goods that must be weighed against each other in determining right action.

However, there is a potential problem with Carter's view. According to Carter, the different kinds of value are independent of each other. But this seems mistaken, for arguably, ecocentric values are not independent of biocentric, zoocentric, or even anthropocentric values, given that ecosystems simply are composed of non-sentient living things, sentient animals, and in some cases humans (in addition to non-living things; see Attfield, 2014 for a similar concern). But this consideration allows for another form of response to the problem of environmental fascism. Although for the system consequentialist, the ultimate value is the value of systems, the value of a system may be taken to depend, in part, on what individuals are in the system. Ecosystems with more complex and sentient animals may be taken to be more valuable systems than functionally similar ones that have only non-sentient individuals. Thus if one were to choose to save a wildflower over a human or other sentient animal, the total value of the ecosystem would decrease even if its ecosystemic health increases. How far this modification of eco-consequentialism moves away from an original Leopoldian ecocentric vision and toward a more anthropocentric or sentientist one is a matter for investigation beyond the scope of this chapter.[8]

Having discussed various forms of environmental consequentialism, it may be instructive to compare environmental consequentialism with alternative forms of environmental ethical theory—deontology (see Hale, Chapter 18 of this volume), virtue theory (see Sandler, Chapter 19 of this volume), and pragmatism (see Minteer, Chapter 44 of this volume). Although there are stark differences between the views, there is also, perhaps surprisingly, quite a bit of common ground. I have already argued briefly that there are reasons to believe that there should be no inviolable deontological restrictions, and that what motivates deontological restrictions ought to be framed in consequentialist terms. However, maintaining that certain actions have negative axiological valence when they disturb ecosystems is a step toward deontology, and as I argue elsewhere, the system consequentialist can accept a wide range of intuitive judgments that typically are upheld by deontological views (see Hiller, 2014). Still, even though it holds that some acts have axiological valence, system consequentialism remains a consequentialist view in that it holds that whether an act is *right* can be determined only be appealing to the full range of states of affairs that ensue if one performs the act.

Both environmental virtue ethicists (see e.g., Hill Jr., 1983) and environmental pragmatists (see e.g., Norton, 2005) criticize the core notion for any consequentialist theory, the notion of intrinsic value. I will address the issue of intrinsic value momentarily, but I will briefly note at the outset that numerous defenses of claims of intrinsic value, which can be employed by consequentialists, have been made by philosophers writing on environmental ethics on both meta-ethically objectivist (Rolston, 1988) and subjectivist (Callicott, 1999; Jamieson, 2008; McShane, 2007; McShane, 2011) grounds.

There is perhaps more in common between consequentialism and both environmental virtue ethics and environmental pragmatism than one might initially think. Although Robert Elliot argues on consequentialist grounds that a version of environmental virtue ethics problematically requires some prior notion of what is good in nature (Elliot, 1997: 55–58), there are other forms of environmental virtue ethics that are not susceptible to Elliot's argument. For instance, Ronald Sandler's *Character and Environment* (Sandler, 2007)—perhaps the most complete work dedicated to explicating and defending environmental virtue ethics—is in fact quite similar to a consequentialist view, for according to Sandler's view, what makes a character trait a virtue is that it is conducive to goodness (Sandler, 2007). As Sandler himself notes (Sandler, 2007: 32), his environmental virtue ethic is quite similar to rule-consequentialism. (However, see Thompson, 2008 for a criticism of Sandler from within environmental virtue ethics.) Furthermore, all consequentialists would encourage the development of virtuous character traits in promoting overall value.

The commonality between environmental pragmatism and environmental consequentialism may be first seen by noting how both views are outcome-oriented; consequentialist views simply formalize talk of good outcomes in a way that is grounded in axiological principles. In fact, some arguments used by environmental pragmatists straightforwardly support environmental consequentialism. For instance, consider Ben Minteer's analysis of Holmes Rolston's view regarding Nepalese tigers. Minteer writes:

> Because I subscribe to a contextual and experimental approach toward intrinsic value, I cannot follow Rolston and simply decide to 'put the tigers first' in Nepal. . . [For Rolston,] our obligations become immediately obvious—we must protect the park's biological integrity at any cost, including, perhaps, the lives of the distressed citizens at its borders. (Minteer, 2012: 70)

Minteer rejects this "at any cost" ethic. Setting aside whether this is the proper interpretation of Rolston's view, there is much here with which the environmental consequentialist will be sympathetic. Consequentialists will welcome the idea that judgments about how to act must be based upon the specific decision-making context and on empirical information about long-term consequences. And of course Minteer's rejection of the idea that one must save an animal species regardless of the consequences of doing so is the same kind of argument that consequentialists have long been leveling against deontologists, which I discussed previously.

In the end, environmental consequentialists and environmental pragmatists will part company about the nature of intrinsic value. Minteer's notion of the contextual nature of judgments of value is not the same as the consequentialist's. Minteer writes: "[N]oninstrumental claims [of value] are not epistemically or metaphysically foundational. They are *contextual* and are justified in terms of their ability to contribute to the resolution of specific environmental problems" (Minteer, 2012: 67). However, a consequentialist defender of intrinsic value would claim that by placing judgments of intrinsic value secondary to a logically prior notion of the "resolution" of environmental problems, environmental pragmatists put the cart before the horse. For what counts as a *successful* resolution? Certainly many environmental problems have been "resolved" by humans simply choosing to destroy the part of nature in question. But it seems that many such ways in which people have resolved problems are *bad* resolutions due to their negative impact on the natural world. But the pragmatist, who places judgments of intrinsic goodness and badness posterior to judgments about resolutions of problems, is in no position to make such a judgment. This issue is of course complex and deserves more attention than can be given here.

There is also a more general worry about intrinsic value that environmental pragmatists have expressed. They claim that a focus on the intrinsic value of the non-human world may be ineffective or even counterproductive in promoting environmental policy (see e.g., Light, 2005). However, a consequentialist environmental ethic is immune to this concern. First, consequentialists also want their theoretical views to be put into practice to have the best overall effects; but this may simply lead one to the view that what consequentialists say in academic texts should differ from what they say publicly when making policy arguments (see de Lazari-Radek and Singer, 2010). Second, the evidence is in fact quite strong that appeals to intrinsic value have had positive influence on people. For instance, Kempton et al. (1996) show that most people, even mill workers who lost their jobs due to use restrictions from the effort to preserve habitat for the spotted owl in the US Northwest, value the non-human world intrinsically.[9]

I have attempted to show that a form of consequentialism that accepts ecosystemic value but gives more value to humans and complex sentient animals is a promising view. Still, there are challenges that a fully fledged consequentialist environmental ethic faces. As I noted earlier, the system consequentialist needs to provide a theory of what a system is, what exactly makes systems good, and to what degree different systems are good. In fact, there has never been a consensus among consequentialists about the relative weights of *any* sets of values; ever since John Stuart Mill's criticism of simplistic hedonic utilitarianism (Mill, [1863] 1998) it has been a matter of controversy exactly how to measure good states of affairs. System consequentialism, which counts the complexity and sentience of the individual beings in an ecosystem as a source of increased value for the system, exponentially increases this difficulty. There is thus reason to believe that system consequentialists will never be able to provide a theory of the good that can help with real-world decision making.

I shall note two points in response to this worry. First, this is not on its own a fatal objection against system consequentialism or consequentialism more broadly. For a consequentialist may claim that it only demonstrates that in many cases, it is extremely difficult to determine what the right action or policy is. Uncertainty about what exactly is of value is not a sufficient reason to hold that we should abandon the project of giving a theory of what is valuable, for that would simply take us even farther away from knowing which actions are right. Second, some consequentialists have attempted to show that there are still rational ways to act even when there is uncertainty about the relative values between different kinds of goods—namely, by attributing weights to different views of value in a consequentialist calculus (Bykvist, 2014). If this view succeeds, uncertainty about levels of value should not lead us to reject consequentialism.

There are also concerns that due to the long-term and multidimensional nature of environmental problems, consequentialism will never be able to provide a decision procedure for actions or policies.[10] However, a response similar to the previous one may be given. First, such a view simply shows that decisions regarding the environment are extremely difficult ones, and not that consequentialism is wrong. Second, we should still do our best to maximize expected utility, even if there is a great deal of uncertainty; to do anything else would be to act in a worse way.

Although there are still significant challenges for the development of consequentialist environmental ethics, it is in many respects a new field of inquiry, and there is hope that with further development it can be fleshed out more completely. My own view is that the fact that these outstanding questions exist should lead philosophers to work to resolve them on behalf of maximizing act-consequentialism rather than abandon it for its alternatives. For by abandoning maximizing consequentialism one will, by definition, fail to always endorse doing what has the most long-term good, whatever one takes to be good—be it human experiences, experiences of all sentient beings, ecosystems, or something else. Why should one ever prefer doing something other than what will lead to what is best?

NOTES

1. "Value," as used in this entry, denotes (except where noted) what is typically called "intrinsic value" rather than instrumental value. That is, value is what is good in itself as opposed to good for what a thing is used for.
2. See Katz (1997, ch. 16) and Nash (1982, chs. 8, 10) for helpful discussion of the dispute between Muir and Pinchot.
3. Muir, http://www.sierraclub.org/john_muir_exhibit/writings/the_yosemite/chapter_16.aspx, quoted in Walsh et al. (2007).
4. In defense of consequentialism, Robert Elliot (1997: 52) gives an example of setting fire to a certain natural area in order to create a firebreak to prevent a forest fire from spreading. Setting aside the issue of the naturalness of forest fires (many forest fires are indeed natural), in many situations it seems fully appropriate to create the firebreak even though doing so involves harming part of nature.
5. Callicott ultimately describes his own view as a *communitarian* view and claims that there is a hierarchy of duties (seemingly echoing W. D. Ross) at different levels of community, and such duties preclude harming fellow humans (1989: 172–173). However, Callicott's communitarianism leaves him open to the objection (such as in Domsky, 2006) that his view entails the implausible claim that we owe no moral consideration to sentient beings who are not members of our community. Also see Carter (2005, appendix), for another critique of Callicott.
6. As Crisp (2006: 41, fn. 7) notes, it is now common for consequentialists to claim that acts themselves have axiological valence. See also Hiller (2014).
7. It should be noted that Carter (2005: 81), in the end, is not fully consequentialist.
8. The view in this paragraph is perhaps an extension of G. E. Moore's principle of organic unities. On the one hand, Moore does not believe that the value of a unity is equal to the sum of the components. However, this still leaves open the possibility that the value of the whole is at least correlated with the values of the individuals in the whole. See Moore (1959/1903, ch. 1).
9. Kempton et al. (1996, ch. 5). Although Light (2005: 345) cites Kempton et al. to support his claim that human attitudes toward nature are anthropocentric, the overall message from Kempton et al. is that in fact humans do value nature intrinsically.
10. See Lenman (2000) for an elaboration of this issue. See Holland (2014) for an application of the problem to consequentialist environmental views. Also see Gardiner (2011, §7.5) for

a critique of utilitarian approaches that also applies to other forms of consequentialism, and ch. 8 for a critique of cost-benefit analysis.

References

Anscombe, G. E. M. (1958). "Modern Moral Philosophy." *Philosophy* 33(124): 1–19.

Attfield, R. (1991 [1983]). *The Ethics of Environmental Concern*, 2nd ed. Athens: University of Georgia Press.

Attfield, R. (1999). *The Ethics of the Global Environment*. Edinburgh: Edinburgh University Press.

Attfield, R. (2003) *Environmental Ethics: An Overview for the 21st Century*. Malden, MA: Blackwell.

Attfield, R. (2014). "Can Biocentric Consequentialism Meet Pluralist Challenges?" In *Consequentialism and Environmental Ethics*, edited by A. Hiller, R. Ilea, and L. Kahn. New York: Routledge.

Bennett, J. (1966). "Whatever the Consequences." *Analysis* 26(2): 83–102.

Bentham, J. (1996 [1789]). *An Introduction to the Principles of Morals and Legislation*, edited by J. Burns and H. L. A. Hart. Oxford: Clarendon Press.

Bykvist, K. (2014). "Evaluative Uncertainty, Environmental Ethics, and Consequentialism." In *Consequentialism and Environmental Ethics*, edited by A. Hiller, R. Ilea, and L. Kahn. New York: Routledge.

Callicott, J. B. (1989). *In Defense of the Land Ethic: Essays in Environmental Philosophy*. Albany, SUNY Press.

Callicott, J. B. (1999). *Beyond the Land Ethic: More Essays in Environmental Philosophy*. Albany: SUNY Press.

Carter, A. (2005). "Inegalitarian Biocentric Consequentialism, the Minimax Implication and Multidimensional Value Theory: A Brief Proposal for a New Direction in Environmental Ethics." *Utilitas* 17(1): 62–84.

Carter, A. (2011). "Towards a Multidimensional, Environmentalist Ethic." *Environmental Values* 20(3): 347–374.

Crisp, R. (2006). *Reasons and the Good*. New York: Oxford University Press.

De Lazari-Radek, K., and Singer, P. (2010). "Secrecy in Consequentalism: A Defence of Esoteric Morality." *Ratio* 23: 34–58.

Domsky, D. (2006). "The Inadequacy of Callicott's Ecological Communitarianism." *Environmental Ethics* 28: 395–412.

Driver, J. (2012). *Consequentialism*. London: Routledge.

Elliot, R. (1997). *Faking Nature: The Ethics of Environmental Restoration*. London: Routledge.

Elliot, R. (2001). "Normative Ethics." *A Companion to Environmental Philosophy*, edited by D. Jamieson, 177–191. Oxford: Blackwell.

Fieser, J. (1992). "Leopold and The Compatibility of Eco-Centric Morality." *International Journal of Applied Philosophy* 7: 37–41.

Gardiner, S. (2011). *A Perfect Moral Storm: The Ethical Tragedy of Climate Change*. New York: Oxford University Press.

Hill, Thomas E. Jr. (1983). "Ideals of Human Excellence and Preserving Natural Environments." *Environmental Ethics* 5(3): 211–224.

Hiller, A. (2013). "Object-Dependence." *Essays in Philosophy* 14(1): 33–55.

Hiller, A. (2014). "System Consequentialism." In *Consequentialism and Environmental Ethics*, edited by A. Hiller, R. Ilea, and L. Kahn. New York: Routledge.

Hiller, A. and Kahn, L. (2014). "Consequentialism and Environmental Ethics." In *Consequentialism and Environmental Ethics*, edited by A. Hiller, R. Ilea, and L. Kahn. New York: Routledge.

Holland, A. (2014). "On Some Limitations of Consequentialism in the Sphere of Environmental Ethics." In *Consequentialism and Environmental Ethics*, edited by A. Hiller, R. Ilea, and L. Kahn. New York: Routledge.

Hooker, B. (2008). "Rule Consequentialism." *Stanford Encyclopedia of Philosophy*. http://plato.stanford.edu/entries/consequentialism-rule/, accessed June 10, 2013.

Jamieson, D. (2002). *Morality's Progress: Essays on Humans, Other Animals, and the Rest of Nature*. New York: Oxford University Press.

Jamieson, D. (2008) *Ethics and the Environment: An Introduction*. Cambridge, England: Cambridge University Press.

Katz, E. (1997). *Nature as Subject: Human Obligation and Natural Community*. New York: Rowman and Littlefield.

Kempton, W., Boster, J., and Hartley, J. (1996). *Environmental Values in American Culture*. Cambridge, MA: MIT Press.

Lenman, J. (2000). "Consequentialism and Cluelessness." *Philosophy and Public Affairs* 29(4): 342–370.

Leopold, A. (1980 [1949]). *A Sand County Almanac*, New York: Ballantine Books.

Light, A. (2005). "What Is a Pragmatic Philosophy?" *Journal of Philosophical Research* 30(Special Supplement): 341–356.

McShane, K. (2004). "Ecosystem Health." *Environmental Ethics* 26: 227–245.

McShane, K. (2007). "Why Environmental Ethics Shouldn't Give Up on Intrinsic Value." *Environmental Ethics* 29(1): 43–61.

McShane, K. (2011). "Neosentimentalism and Environmental Ethics." *Environmental Ethics* 33(1): 5–23.

Mill, J. S. (1998 [1863]). *Utilitarianism*, edited by R. Crisp. Oxford: Oxford University Press.

Minteer, B. (2012). *Refounding Environmental Ethics: Pragmatism, Principle, and Practice*. Philadelphia: Temple University Press.

Moline, J. (1986). "Aldo Leopold and the Moral Community." *Environmental Ethics* 8(2): 99–120.

Moore, G. E. (1959 [1903]). *Principia Ethica*. Cambridge, UK: Cambridge University Press.

Nash, R. (1982 [1967]). *Wilderness and the American Mind*. 3rd ed. New Haven: Yale University Press.

Norton, B. G. (2005). *Sustainability: A Philosophy of Adaptive Ecosystem Management*. Chicago: University of Chicago Press.

Palmer, C. (1998). *Environmental Ethics and Process Thinking*. Oxford: Clarendon Press.

Pinchot, G. (1998 [1947]). *Breaking New Ground*. Washington, DC: Island Press.

Regan, T. (1983). *The Case for Animal Rights*. Berkeley: University of California Press.

Rolston, H. (1988). *Environmental Ethics*. Philadelphia: Temple University Press.

Rolston, H. (1991). "Environmental Ethics: Values in and Duties to the Natural World." In *The Broken Circle: Ecology, Economics, Ethics*, edited by F. Herbert Bormann and S. R. Kellert, 65–84. New Haven, CT: Yale University Press.

Sandler, R. (2007). *Character and Environment: A Virtue-Oriented Approach to Environmental Ethics*. New York: Columbia University Press.

Schweitzer, A. (2008 [1923]). "Reverence for Life." In *Environmental Ethics*, 5th ed., edited by L. Pojman and P. Pojman, 131–138. Belmont: Cengage.

Sierra Club (1909). "1909 Letter to Gifford Pinchot." http://www.sierraclub.org/ca/hetch-hetchy/, accessed June 10, 2013.

Singer, P. (1975). *Animal Liberation*. New York: Random House.

Sinnott-Armstrong, W. (2011). "Consequentialism." *Stanford Encyclopedia of Philosophy*. http://plato.stanford.edu/entries/consequentialism/, accessed June 10, 2013.

Taylor, P. (1986). *Respect for Nature*, Princeton: Princeton University Press.

Thompson, A. (2008). "Natural Goodness and Abandoning the Economy of Value." *Ethics, Place & Environment* 11(2): 216–224.

Tomasik, B. (2014). "The Importance of Wild Animal Suffering." http://www.utilitarian-essays.com/suffering-nature.html, accessed April 4, 2014.

Walsh, B., Barnard, E., and Nesbitt, J. (2007). "The Pinchot-Muir Split Revisited." http://www.safnet.org/fp/documents/pinchot_muri_split_07.pdf, accessed June 10, 2013.

CHAPTER 18

....

RIGHTS, RULES, AND RESPECT FOR NATURE

....

BENJAMIN HALE

THOUGH estimates vary, experts believe that nearly 80,000 acres of rainforest are destroyed daily,[1] a further 150 to 200 species of plants, insects, birds and/or mammals go extinct every day,[2] and approximately 85% of global fish stocks have already been destroyed or depleted.[3] It is tempting to assess these findings and suppose that the salient ethical problem is that nature has been degraded or devalued, that the ensuing state of affairs is less valuable or desirable than it otherwise might have been. According to this way of thinking, what makes an action right is whether it promotes or produces the good. In this respect, a preponderance of views about environmental wrongdoing are expressly consequentialist.

Such views are quite reasonable. When talking about the environment, are we not first and foremost concerned with states of affairs? Certainly one cannot believe that mountains have rights, or that one has duties to streams. But consequentialist approaches to environmental wrongdoing are subject to many of the classical concerns that have otherwise plagued non-environmental consequentialism. That is, they are subject to at least five concerns: about welfarism, aggregationism, responsibility, demandingness, and applicability.

In this chapter I would like to defend a variant view of environmental deontology that strikes me as at least less problematic than other environmental positions. I shall approach the topic first by assessing the most prevalent environmental standpoint: consequentialism. My strategy here will be primarily negative, in that I will offer five complications for environmental consequentialism, suggesting that a nonconsequentialist account may be better equipped to address environmental concerns. I will then touch on three complications for nonconsequentialist accounts with the objective of zeroing in on a plausible deontological view. At the end, I offer a few reasons as to why the account that I favor—roughly a deontological account—may be better suited to deal with environmental issues than a consequentialist account. I have little space in an essay of this length to cover the full breadth of objections to the consequentialist account, but it is important to note that consequentialist arguments of various stripes have been offered across an enormous range of environmental subfields and that very often the chink in the armor for the environmental position rests with one, if not several, of the weaknesses I will adumbrate.

1 The Consequences of Environmental Consequentialism

Criticisms of consequentialist ethical theory are legion, but in the environmental realm, these familiar problems become all the more pronounced. Consider just the five objections I mention above. First, consequentialists face the problem of welfarism: that is, How to establish the environmental good? Typically, environmental welfare positions invoke either a subjective theory or an objective theory of welfare. Subjective theories characteristically locate welfare in the subjective states of affected parties, whereas objective theories identify features of the world that are essential for welfare (Heathwood, 2014). There is huge variation within and across these two categories, so criticisms can get a little clumsy, but the basic idea is that value is either associated with some state of the mind or with some state of the world.

In the realm of environmental ethics, subjective theories tend to manifest in the guise of private or exchange valuation, which often then translate into claims about ecosystem services or the merits of cost benefit analysis. In essence, the idea is that whatever value nature may have, this value is perhaps best isolated by determining net increases in welfare for human users of the environment. These welfare improvements can be assessed through empirical means, whether experimental, hypothetical, or derivative. Take forestry as an example. Techniques like hedonic pricing and contingent valuation studies aim to demonstrate the value of nature by illustrating how consumers and users of the environment already value it. As many others have pointed out, such attempts at valuation quickly get mired in objections about comparability and commensurability (J. O'Neill, 1993), as well as objections that the very idea of "preferences," which is fundamental to many subjective theories, underdetermine the full extent of the ethical problem (Hausman and McPherson, 2009; Kawall, 1999; Sagoff, 2004). Without question, subjective theories have generated and continue to generate enormous controversy in the environmental community.

Others have therefore sought to argue the second horn of the welfare dilemma: for objective values. These objective theories of welfare present still different complications. That is, environmental positions that prioritize natural goods over other human concerns come off as, at best, unappealingly elitist and, at worst, crass and inhumane. An objective theory that places great value on recreation or aesthetics might be viewed as elitist, whereas one that places value on predation and trophic cascades might be viewed as inhumane. Moreover, it is nearly impossible to process the variety of value in nature given the multiple levels at which an objective approach might be targeted. Some things that may be very good for members of one species can be quite bad for the ecosystem as a whole, and translated across these various groups is no simple endeavor. What is good for a lobster may well not be good for a coral reef, which in turn may not be good for a crop of potatoes. So the problem of welfarism is particularly pronounced in the environmental arena, where establishing what is good is complicated by the diversity of nature. Put simply, the right set of objective values remains elusive.

Second, consider the problem of aggregationism, which also characterizes consequentialism. This is the idea that we can compare and aggregate values across value-holders. In economics, aggregating values works nicely to tabulate total benefits, as when one calculates the value of three bushels of apples and eight wheels of cheese. It works impressively well in market contexts, when a narrowly circumscribed community of actors and a fair system for comparing like-goods determines, as if by magic, the exchange price for those goods. In the environmental arena, however, these distributional questions take on a slightly different contour. As goods begin to spill out of the commodity bin and into different categories of moral value—that is, when goods cease to be mere "goods"—aggregating values becomes a much stickier proposition. It is true that the problem of aggregationism is not limited to the environment, but again due to nature's diversity and the common view that entities within the environment are best understood as resources, the full extent of the problems with aggregationism truly kick in.

When set in a market context, the problem of aggregation is therefore intimately tied to problem of welfarism mentioned above. That is, aggregation also presents the problem that it cannot easily be presumed that value commitments are held equally across all individuals. In the human arena, this sometimes manifests as claims about the separateness of persons, which on one hand regards the matter of how persons themselves should be valued, but on the other hand regards the matter of whether subjective utility schedules can be aggregated without regard for the subject holding those schedules. Rawls, most famously, defends the separateness of persons against utilitiarianism by invoking the Kantian idea that each person be treated as an end in himself, but many other notable theorists have made similar points (Kant, 1785; Nagel, 1970; Nozick, 1977; Rawls, 1971; Williams, 1973). Consequentialists tend to deny the separateness of persons, by contrast, and instead suggest that one can and ought to aggregate goods and bads across all persons, and that we ought to do so in a way that disregards distribution (Norcross, 2008).

This manifests as an environmental complication when classical welfare economics is extended into environmental valuation, which is a widely utilized approach for arguing on behalf of the environment (Gowdy, 2004). In such instances, the environmental concern is not so much about the mere moral inseparability of welfare and experience for persons, or even non-human persons, but rather with concerns about the general good. It is challenging to defend the view, for instance, that killing some number of animals of differing species is equivalent to killing the same number of different animals of the same species, particularly if killing those animals of the same species would result in a marked problem for the species. If some ecological management approach suggests that culling 500 elk from an ecosystem will benefit the system, but that none of the creatures in the system will be individually benefitted, one who holds such a position may well also be committed to the view that culling 500 wolves from the same ecosystem carries roughly the same moral valence. Moreover, without a fixed source of value—say, for instance, human welfare or animal welfare—it is all the more challenging to aggregate values. Where aggregationism requires that goods are transitive across entities, any ecologist must acknowledge that even the most basic predatory relationships cast doubt on whether goods can be aggregated across predator and prey. As Jeff McMahon provocatively asks, "If we could bring about the end of predation . . . ought we to do it?" (McMahan, 2010).

Third, it would appear that one great benefit of taking the consequentialist approach to environmental problems is that it avoids assessment of intentions or reasons for those actions. Indeed, this has been a core objective of consequentialism for centuries: to observe that failing to act may be just as morally problematic as acting. But so many of our environmental problems are presumably problems *precisely because* they are intentional or accidental anthropogenic actions. When an oil bed opens up on the ocean floor, this is generally not considered an environmental disaster. It's just the way that nature is. If a company blows open an oil bed on the ocean floor, on the other hand, this is an event of far more serious moral import. So too for most environmental problems. Winter comes and goes every year, killing billions of plants, starving countless animals and insects, and forcing millions of children to endure the humiliating indignity of wearing mittens. This, again, is just the way that nature is. If, on the other hand, human intervention were to cause an extremely harsh winter, perhaps by geoengineering, many would consider this to be a far more morally troubling matter. It's not that the ensuing states of affairs in nature are the best or the worst that could possibly be, but rather that they are good or bad by accident. There are limits to this point, of course. As states of affairs grow increasingly worse, we may come to evaluate them differently. But such concerns can be addressed by clearly understanding how we come to value things.

Fourth, environmental consequentialist theories suffer from strident demandingness objections. On one hand, consequentialism is said to demand too much of individual actors. In order to maximize or promote value, one may be required to give of oneself until little of value remains. Utilitarianism, for instance, may require that one give almost all of one's money to assist the poor. On the other hand, consequentialism may not demand enough. So long as the good is promoted, consequentialism may permit rights violations or other morally problematic practices—like, for instance, sacrificing some to save many.

In a narrowly defined universe of humans, the demandingness objection is enough of a problem, but in a universe in which one must grapple with the consumption of environmental resources and their eventual emission, the demandingness objection takes on renewed potency. Moral extensionism in environmental ethics complicates demandingness objections considerably. If faced with a decision about whether to apply pesticides to bodies of still water in order to prevent malaria and thus save human lives, some consequentialist positions, such as biocentric individualism, might hold that such spraying ought not to occur. The lives saved are fewer than the lives destroyed; thus environmental consequentialism may demand that humans live with more disease and misery. Conversely, if faced with a decision about whether to take a drive on a Saturday afternoon or contribute a miniscule amount of carbon to the atmosphere, thus contributing imperceptibly to climate change (cf. Sinnott-Armstrong), it may not be the case that consequentialism has the resources to require a shift in action. Much of how the demandingness objection cuts, of course, will depend on what theory of the good informs the view, as well as the scope of the theory.

This raises related problems. Since consequentialist theories almost all insist upon either promotion of the good or prevention of the bad, if we consider that every beneficial action generates a harmful outcome somewhere in the world, then we are in fact in quite a predicament. All actions must be considered strictly in terms of whether they do what consequentialism demands. But every single action both promotes the good and causes damage; or prevents damage and causes good. Principles like maximizing goods or minimizing harms can be quite limiting indeed when incorporating the full scope of environmental activities—as opposed to narrower-scope consequentialist theories that focus on the pleasure or suffering of sentient creatures.

Finally, one other point merits note. That is, one of the reasons that consequentialist approaches to environmental ethics are thought so attractive is that they make intuitive appeals to principles and values that are already prevalent in the policy process. Environmental advocates often enough suggest we cannot address environmental problems without "using the same language" as those who set our public policies. Thus, many are driven to answer such concerns out of a desire to see deeper philosophical commitments addressed in the policy discourse. One approach to salvaging environmentalism from the wreckage of consequentialism is obviously to seek sound responses to the objections raised earlier. Environmentalists have spilled a fair bit of ink to account for deficiencies in these views. A good portion of the work in environmental economics, conservation biology, restoration ecology, and other fields centers on describing better and worse states of affairs. But in my view this is unpromising. For every consequentialist argument in favor of the environment, there's an equally compelling argument in favor of sacrificing the environment. It is more promising to abandon the consequentialist approach entirely.

Fortunately, ethics offers other nonconsequentialist options, like deontology and virtue ethics. For reasons that I will briefly cover in the next section, I favor the deontological view over the virtue view, but a first critical step involves moving away from an emphasis on states of affairs. The nonconsequentialist view that I advocate—roughly, democratic justificatory liberalism—also has parallels in the policy arena. Indeed, many policies are forged not on the anvil of cost-benefit analysis, or on rational self-interest, but rather through reasoned—or, at least, ostensibly reasoned—public debate. The above complications, while perhaps not alone devastating for environmental consequentialism, do at least raise significant questions about the viability of a consequentialist view.

2 A Nonconsequentialist Turn toward Deontology

Given the concerns, there is reason to favor nonconsequentialist—and particularly deontological—views over consequentialist views. Nonconsequentialist theories offer wider latitude for determining what the good is, adjudicating between various conceptions of the good, assigning responsibility, and avoiding the dual horns of the demandingness objection. Where consequentialists may insist that morality demands that some good state of affairs be promoted, nonconsequentialists can speak much more broadly about obligations and permissions and rights. Consider, for instance, Paul Taylor's deontological approach to environmental respect. Taylor's biocentric egalitarianism establishes the attitude of respect for nature as morally prior to other considerations like the promotion of value (Taylor, 1986). Or consider Mark Sagoff's scathing deontological screeds against cost-benefit analysis and ecosystem services, in which he argues for democratically ratified moral permissions and constraints over appeals to utility (Sagoff, 2004, 2008). Alternatively, from the animal ethics literature, consider Tom Regan's view that all subjects of a life deserve rights (Regan, 1983). Two features of nonconsequentialism ought to make a more deontological approach attractive for the environmental theorist.

For one thing, deontologists are concerned first and foremost with right actions, not with producing a better state of affairs. Where the consequentialist proposes that the rightness of an action hangs on the eventuating state of affairs, deontologists must invoke other criteria entirely. So, for instance, they may suggest that one should defend an endangered species because it is the right thing to do, not necessarily because it will make the world a better place or be cost efficient. They can situate responsibilities and obligations in basic rights or humanity or in some other such principle. So the task for environmental deontology isn't necessarily to identify best state of affairs in nature, but rather to identify a sufficiently comprehensive source of normativity.

Moreover, as mentioned before, though it may seem strange to suggest that promoting better states of affairs ought not to be the guiding moral objective for environmentalists—how else to describe a tailings pond or a clear-cut forest but by appeal to states of affairs?—to emphasize right actions over states of affairs ought not to imply that states of affairs do not matter. Indeed, states of affairs are constituent components of actions—all of our actions are responses to states of affairs and/or behaviors that bring about new or different states of affairs. It's just that the deontologist looks more expansively on actions than simply the eventuating state of affairs. In other words, the deontologist argues rather that states of affairs are not all that matter in the determination of what qualifies an action as right. To put this colloquially: where consequentialist views place priority on the good over the right, deontological views place priority on the right over the good.

Taking a deontological approach isn't without its pitfalls. To be sure, there are many reasons that deontology hasn't been particularly attractive to environmental theorists. But there is wide disagreement among deontologists about the best theory, and a smart way to approach this question is to take a somewhat finer look at the variety of deontological positions on offer. Complicating matters, there clearly are good reasons to be skeptical of some deontological views.

To begin with a very blunt preliminary distinction, deontologists fall into either patient-centered or agent-centered camps. The first camp—patient-centered deontology—is perhaps most obvious for those seeking an inroad to environmental ethics. Those who are patient-centered focus on what sorts of obligations or permissions an agent has with regard to other entities or patients. These theories tend to isolate qualities or attributes of the moral patient, inasmuch as they aim to circumscribe the set of actions that are permissible with regard to the patients of moral concern. Patiency has historically been wedded intimately to rights and agency, which may be partly what trips up environmentalists. But this presumption is far too hasty. Much traction can be gained by turning the focus of environmental ethics back on the obligations of acting parties. The second camp—agent-centered theories—may in this vein suggest instead that it is the agent, not the patient, who has strong positive obligations to abide by principles or duties to respect others. So, for instance, they may say that the burden falls on the agent to discover, endorse, and abide by the principles of right and moral action; it does not fall on the patient to set itself apart as a subject of moral concern. Less abstractly: if we aim to better understand constraints on actions, we ought not to look to the attributes of animals, say, in order to determine whether we can completely exclude them from our moral deliberations. Rather, we rational humans must ask ourselves what obligations we must uphold; and it is out of this understanding about our obligations that we can determine how to relate to others. Since one of the key distinguishing features of environmental ethics is its emphasis on non-human nature, which is manifestly non-rational, and since agent-centered deontology ostensibly places a heavy burden rational agency, ethicists with an environmental leaning have tended to discount agent-centered deontology rather rapidly.

Return for a moment to patient-centered deontology and consider the how it might serve to illuminate obligations. If we identify dolphins and great apes as the cutoff class of entities deserving moral consideration, then we have a clear demarcation of permissions and constraints (provided that we can correctly identify the set of attributes that sets this class of entities apart). We are permitted to act upon entities falling outside the class of dolphins and great apes, but restricted from acting upon entities falling within this class (without further consideration or permission-seeking). In its narrowest contour, patient-centered deontology grounds down to a question about the scope of moral theory: what sorts of things deserve consideration; what sorts of things count as moral patients? This is a vexing question.

Humans are easy. Without them, ethics doesn't get off the ground. Matters grow far more complicated, however, once one tries to expand the circle of moral status. Widening the scope of moral theory to include first non-human animals, but then even non-animal organisms, communities of organisms, or even abiotic entities, such as rock formations, raises serious problems about criteria for moral considerability. Almost all criteria that have been suggested as necessary or sufficient for moral considerability—reason, agency, autonomy, interests, and so forth—leave a woeful cluster of entities out of the configuration. This is I think a devastating problem for the patient-centered deontological literature, where patiency is critical.

Naturally, many continue to pursue remedies to this problem, but the discussion remains saddled with terminological and conceptual complications. As Kenneth Goodpaster points out in his seminal article, moral considerability questions intercalate and overlap with other questions about rights, scope, and status (Goodpaster, 1978). Though some have sought to approach the problem in a finer-grained fashion (Warren, 2000), in my view such approaches will always be hamstrung by their inclusive/exclusive nature.

No doubt, these approaches are unacceptably narrow and rife with complications. Theorists have had little place to turn. It would appear that one either must accept that identifying deontological constraints involves only identifying the universe of moral patients, after which point one has no obligations or duties to entities that fall outside of this universe; or one can seek a wider, more comprehensive, more "environmental" view and abandon considerability questions to turn to some other agent-centered position—typically virtue ethics.

Indeed, this has roughly been the story of environmental ethics. To elide the question of moral considerability altogether, important early authors such as Aldo Leopold, who writes of a "biotic right" in the Land Ethic, sought instead to emphasize ecosystems and species (Callicott, 2001; Leopold, 1966); whereas other holists such as Arne Naess, widely viewed to be the father of deep ecology, sought to point out the basic interconnectedness of all individuals. This turn away from individualism and toward holism within environmental ethics, while much disputed among even the holists, nevertheless underscores the deep discomfort that environmental theorists have had with moral considerability and patient-centering. One could certainly characterize the holist's position as one of expansionism—that is, as one of expanding moral scope to include everything as a moral patient—but this doesn't resonate, at least to me, with the writings of these holist authors. On my read, the need to eschew the complications of patient-centering and instead turn to agent-centering has not yet been fully explored. I have argued elsewhere that the question of moral considerability gets tangled up in presumptions about moral status (Hale, 2011a).

3 AGENT-CENTERING IN A UNIVERSE OF NONAGENTS

This leaves theorists with the option of turning to agent-centering instead, which then raises somewhat separate complications. As I've mentioned, it is natural when taking an agent-centered approach to assume that emphasis must turn to the motivations or the character of the agent. Indeed, frustrations with deontological patient-centering and dissatisfaction with the reductivism of consequentialist accounts may help explain why so many environmental theorists turn to virtue ethics as the only remaining alternative. But for all of its promise, virtue ethics turns too sharply to agent-centering and tends to short circuit many, if not all, of the difficult ethical and policy questions that perplex environmentalists. As one very brief objection to turning to virtue: many environmental problems are the outcome of collective behaviors, not individual actions, and as such demand responses at the institutional level. Focusing on the character of all relevant actors seems woefully insufficient to account for or address wrongdoing. Without a robust theory of institutional character, virtue ethics is practically impotent to solve some of the most vexing environmental challenges. Fortunately, the deontologist has an alternative.

First things first, environmental ethics has tended to avoid deontological agent-centering fairly aggressively, in part because it appears to place a good deal of emphasis on agency. Since, environmentally speaking, most of the objects of concern aren't agents in the proper sense of the term, this would appear to be a dead-end. Certainly some brave advocates have sought to argue for the agency and autonomy of nature (Heyd, 2005; Ridder, 2007), where others have even gone so far as to suggest that nature "speaks" to man. But this path, while tested, has yielded few compelling openings. Steven Vogel has written superb and in-depth essays dismantling such positions (Vogel, 2006).

A further complication for agent-centering rests in the belief that it leaves little room to distinguish between doing the right thing and doing the right thing for the right reasons. It is important to note here that there are at least two different directions that agent-centered deontological views may take—either they may focus on the intentions and motivations of agents, or they may emphasize and defend the duties and responsibilities of the agent absent any concern about intentions. They may, for instance, place a good deal of emphasis on what reasons motivate an agent to act in a particular way, in which case an ethical evaluation will turn primarily on "motivating reasons." Or, they may instead emphasize justifications for the actions themselves, in which case intentions and motivations are far less of an issue. Instead what is at issue is whether there are any existing reasons that speak in favor of or against a given action.

The Kantian position that I favor, and one that many neo-Kantians favor, doesn't rely on having the right intentions so much as having the right reasons. Once one cleaves off reasons from intentions, having the right reasons doesn't entail being motivated (psychologically) by those reasons or having those reasons as intentions. It just means that the reasons in principle have to best explain the cause of the action. In these instances, deontologists will hope to distinguish between different act-descriptions, cutting a finer line between justificatory and motivational reasons. The latter approach is more fruitful for precisely the reason that it leaves enough space to distinguish between doing the right thing and doing the right thing for the right reasons. One can speak of the justification for an action and also ask whether it was that justification that motivated the agent.

Where consequentialism has the advantage of offering up agent-neutral conceptions of the good, locating value in a state of affairs that all agents have a reason to promote regardless of their circumstances, the agent-centered deontologist must give an account of why some actions are right only with regard to particular agents. Many of these approaches have come by way of Kantians and neo-Kantians who have sought, through varying strategies, to make space for animals. While Kant's famous Formula of Humanity—that one should always treat others as ends in themselves, and never as a means only—appears to restrict moral consideration to humans, several prominent Kantians have made inroads into the animals debate by arguing that it is not so limiting (Hayward, 1994; Korsgaard, 2004; Wood, 1998). Contrary to the orthodox interpretation of Kant, these theorists have argued that the Formula of Humanity places greater emphasis on the agent than on the patient. The same idea can be brought to bear on environmental questions more broadly, as Onora O'Neill has suggested (O. O'Neill, 1997).

One follow-on concern for deontologists is that even in the realm of more anthropocentric questions, deontologists must yield in part to conflicting permissions, obligations, and restrictions. Obligations to assist, for instance, may supersede prohibitions on lying. So, for instance, Jones may face a situation in which he is forced to lie in order to save a life; or Smith may face a situation in which she feels forced to embellish the dangers of a pollutant in order to facilitate the regulation of that pollutant. On one hand, such a conflict relates to the defeasibility of obligations—in other words, whether one is permitted to violate some restrictions in order to achieve more praiseworthy ends. On the other hand, it also relates again to the demandingness objection: that is, How much can morality demand of us? A rigid deontologist may argue that no violation of obligation or principle is permissible, where some others may argue that there are circumstances in which rules can be bent to achieve more intuitively good ends. Generally, such concerns can be addressed by softening the absolutism of more traditional Kantian deontological views and advancing Rossian or Pragmatist positions that admit of defeasible or *prima facie* rights or duties, but obviously once rights or duties become violable, the strength of the deontological position can more easily be called into doubt.

Our discussion offers a pathway into novel, potentially compelling deontological positions. For instance, many theorists around the turn of the twenty-first century sought to locate duties and responsibilities in contractualist agreements or interpersonal endorsements. Authors such as Jürgen Habermas (1991) with his discourse ethics, Tim Scanlon (1999) with his contractualist account of what we owe to each other, Christine Korsgaard (1996) with her practical identities, Stephen Darwall (2006) with his second-personal stance, and Rainer Forst (2012) with his right to justification, each in slightly different ways, all seek to locate morality in the arrangements between parties. These hybrid deontological approaches—some more contractualist, some more Aristotelian—hold promise over more classical deontological theories in that the root of normativity can be located in actual or hypothetical agreement or endorsements. Far from what one might anticipate, this view does not necessarily commit morality to elitist or problematic anthropocentrism. Indeed, variant hybrid approaches have been picked up by a number of recent environmental theorists (Cohen, 2007; Hale, 2011b, 2013a, 2013b; Hale and Grundy, 2009; Rowlands, 1997; Sagoff, 2004).

For one thing, these "justificatory" approaches can offer guidance on forward-looking questions about how to act. For instance, they may require that principles for action be *reasonable*, where this means that reasons for action must be subjected to the scrutiny of reasonable and rational affected parties. If reasons for action pass such a test, then this ostensibly authorizes the action. The permission for the action, in other words, emerges out of the justificatory process. Justification in this sense rests in the justify-*ing*, not in some feature of the patient or some status of the act.

If we wish to cut an acre of forest in order to build a school, say, a robust justificatory approach might require that we obtain permission for such an act by justifying the act to affected parties. We needn't in this instance appeal primarily to the moral status or value of the resident species in order to determine our permissions or constraints, but instead can draw from locally relevant standards and norms. Certainly, such public scrutiny is always subject to the perversions of self-interest, politics, information asymmetries, and so on, but justificatory approaches can appeal to ideals of justification and leave the conclusions of the justificatory process always open to revision. In this respect, the guidance may be both non-absolute and fallible, meaning that as we seek clarity on how to handle non-human nature, we can always be called upon to clarify our reasons for acting. So, perhaps we discover that this forest is habitat to a unique species. Upon such a discovery, we may need to reevaluate the reasonableness of building the school on that site.

Such approaches may also offer clarity on backward-looking assignments of responsibility for environmental wrongdoing. If looking back on an action it can be determined that actors acted without good reason, or without reason that would have passed the scrutiny of reasonable and rational affected parties, such actors might be accused of environmental wrongdoing. Through this mechanism, then, one can identify incidents of wrongdoing, and conceivably also perpetrators of wrongdoing, without first establishing that some critical environmental value has been lost or damaged.

Finally, such approaches can offer an explanatory backdrop against which to make sense of a suite of environmental conflicts. Where it might first seem that the primary problem with rampant logging, overfishing, and species depletion is that the environment is being degraded, if we look at a few basic criticisms of consequentialist theory we can see how quickly such a view falls to tatters. On the hybrid deontological view that I have been advocating, degradation of the environment only really matters if it can't be justified against other conflicting or competing moral norms and values. As I see it, the contemporary environmental predicament is at least as much about actions or practices that are taken for "no good reason" (that is, without justification, without having gone through the justificatory process) as it is about the degradation of nature. And, as it happens, if one takes a wide view of justification (as I and other theorists do), the degradation of nature fits neatly into the set of reasons that one might offer for advancing or avoiding some actions in the environment. When one construes value not as a so-called "fact about the world," but rather as a determination emergent out of shared normative commitments, as has been suggested by many of the aforementioned turn-of-the-century deontologists, then there is more space to adjudicate between conflicts of welfarism, aggregationism, responsibility, and demandingness. Moreover, this justificatory approach has parallels in political and policy life as well, since such theories dovetail neatly with justifications for democracy.

Notes

1. http://www.scientificamerican.com/article.cfm?id=earth-talks-daily-destruction
2. http://www.guardian.co.uk/environment/2010/aug/16/nature-economic-security
3. http://www.bbc.com/future/story/20120920-are-we-running-out-of-fish

References

Callicott, J. B. (2001). "Holistic Environmental Ethics and the Problem of Ecofascism." In *Beyond the Land Ethic: More Essays in Environmental Philosophy*, edited by J. B. Callicott. Albany, NY: State University of New York Press.

Cohen, A. I. (2007). "Contractarianism, Other-regarding Attitudes, and the Moral Standing of Nonhuman Animals." *Journal of Applied Philosophy* 24(2): 188–201.

Darwall, S. (2006). *The Second Person Standpoint: Morality, Respect, and Accountability.* Cambridge, MA: Harvard University Press.

Forst, R. (2012). *The Right to Justification: Elements of a Constructivist Theory of Justice*, translated by Jeffrey Flynn. New York: Columbia University Press.

Goodpaster, K. (1978). "On Being Morally Considerable." *Journal of Philosophy* 75: 308–325.

Gowdy, J. M. (2004). "The Revolution in Welfare Economics and Its Implications for Environmental Valuation and Policy." *Land Economics: A Quarterly Journal of Planning, Housing and Public Utilities* 80(2): 239–257.

Habermas, J. (1991). "Discourse Ethics, translated by C. Lenhardt and S. W. Nicholson. In *Moral Consciousness and Communicative Action*, edited by C. Lenhardt and S. W. Nicholson. Cambridge, MA: MIT Press.

Hale, B. (2011a). "Moral Considerability: Deontological, Not Metaphysical." *Ethics and the Environment* 16(2): 37–62.

Hale, B. (2011b). "Non-renewable Resources and the Inevitability of Outcomes." *The Monist* 94(1): 369–390.

Hale, B. (2013a). "Can We Remediate Wrongs?" In *Consequentialism and Environmental Ethics*, edited by A. Hiller, R. Ilea, and L. Kahn. New York, NY: Routledge.

Hale, B. (2013b). "Polluting and Unpolluting." In *Environmental Ethics*, 2nd ed., edited by M. Boylan. Hoboken, NY: Wiley-Blackwell.

Hale, B., & Grundy, W. (2009). "Remediation and Respect: Do Remediation Technologies Alter Our Responsibilities?" *Environmental Values* 18(4): 397–415.

Hausman, D. M., and McPherson, M. S. (2009). "Preference Satisfaction and Welfare Economics." *Economics and Philosophy* 25(01): 1–25. doi: 10.1017/S0266267108002253

Hayward, T. (1994). "Kant and the Moral Considerability of Non-rational Beings." In *Philosophy and the Natural Environment*, edited by R. Attfield and A. Belsey, 129–142. Cambridge, England: Cambridge University Press.

Heathwood, C. (2014). "Subjective Theories of Well-Being." In *The Cambridge Companion to Utilitarianism*, edited by B. Eggleston and D. Miller, 199–219. Cambridge, England: Cambridge University Press.

Heyd, T. (2005). *Recognizing the Autonomy of Nature: Theory And Practice*. New York: Columbia University Press.

Kant, I. (1785). "Grundlegung zur Metaphysik der Sitten." In *Practical Philosophy*, edited by M. J. Gregor. Cambridge, England: Cambridge University Press.

Kawall, J. (1999). "The Experience Machine and Mental State Theories of Well-being." *The Journal of Value Inquiry* 33(3): 381–387. doi: 10.1023/a:1004557501837

Korsgaard, C. (1996). *The Sources of Normativity*. Cambridge, England: Cambridge University Press.

Korsgaard, C. (2004). *Fellow Creatures: Kantian Ethics and Our Duties to Animals*, Vol. 25/26. Salt Lake City: University of Utah Press.

Leopold, A. (1966). *The Sand County Almanac*. New York: Oxford University Press.

McMahan, J. (2010). "The Meat Eaters," *The New York Times,* September 19.

Nagel, T. (1970). *The Possibility of Altruism.* Oxford, England: Clarendon Press.

Norcross, A. (2008). "Two Dogmas of Deontology: Aggregation, Rights, and the Separateness of Persons." *Social Philosophy and Policy* 26(01): 76–95.

Nozick, R. (1977). *Anarchy, State and Utopia.* New York: Basic Books.

O'Neill, J. (1993). *Ecology, Policy, and Politics.* New York: Routledge.

O'Neill, O. (1997). "Environmental Values, Anthropocentrism and Speciesism." *Environmental Values* 6: 127–142.

Rawls, J. (1971). *A Theory of Justice.* Cambridge, MA: Harvard University Press.

Regan, T. (1983). *The Case for Animal Rights.* Berkeley, CA: University of California Press.

Ridder, B. (2007). "The Naturalness versus Wildness Debate: Ambiguity, Inconsistency, and Unattainable Objectivity." *Restoration Ecology* 15(1): 8–12. doi: 10.1111/j.1526-100X. 2006.00184.x

Rowlands, M. (1997). "Contractarianism and Animal Rights." *Journal of Applied Philosophy* 14: 235–247.

Sagoff, M. (2004). *Price, Principle, and the Environment.* New York: Cambridge University Press.

Sagoff, M. (2008). "On the Economic Value of Ecosystem Services." *Environmental Values* 17(2): 239–257.

Scanlon, T. M. (1999). *What We Owe to Each Other.* Cambridge, MA: Harvard University Press.

Taylor, P. W. (1986). *Respect for Nature.* Princeton, NJ: Princeton University Press.

Vogel, S. (2006). "The Silence of Nature." *Environmental Values* 15(2): 145–171.

Warren, M. A. (2000). *Moral Status: Obligations to Persons and Other Living Things.* Oxford, England: Oxford University Press.

Williams, B. (1973). "A Critique of Utilitarianism." In *Utilitarianism For and Against,* edited by J. Smart and B. Williams. Cambridge: Cambridge University Press.

Wood, A. W. (1998). "Kant on Duties Regarding Nonrational Nature." *Proceedings of the Aristotelian Society* 72: 189–210.

CHAPTER 19

ENVIRONMENTAL VIRTUE ETHICS

Value, Normativity, and Right Action

RONALD SANDLER

THE practical goal of environmental ethics is to provide guidance on how we ought to inter-act with the natural environment (including the nonhuman individuals that populate it), as well as respond to environment issues more generally. Central to this practical goal are two theoretical questions:

1. Who or what matters—that is, which things ought we to care about?
2. How do things matter—that is, how ought we to take them into consideration?

These are questions about value and normativity and are the purview of ethical theory. Only when we know which things matter and how they matter are we able to develop well-justified practice and policy guidance. This is as true in environmental ethics as it is in interpersonal ethics. In this chapter, I discuss the virtue ethics approach to the second of these questions, how things matter. This is, I will argue, the distinctive feature of a virtue ethical approach to normative ethics, and it is a large part of what distinguishes an environmental virtue ethics approach to environmental ethics (Aristotle, 1985; Foot, 2001; Slote, 2001).[1]

Virtue ethics, construed as an alternative normative theory, needs to be distinguished from virtue theory. Virtue theory is an account of what makes a character trait a virtue or a vice. Deontological and consequentialist ethics often involve a virtue theory, even though they are not virtue ethics. For example, in a deontological view the virtues are (roughly) character traits that dispose their possessor to do their duty (or follow the moral law) (Kant, 1996). On consequentialist views, the virtues are (roughly) character traits the possession of which are conducive to realizing the appropriate consequences (Mill, 2001).

Virtue ethics also needs to be distinguished from character ethics or accounts of which traits are virtues and vices. In environmental ethics, virtue language abounds and perme-ates the tradition. Henry David Thoreau exemplified simplicity and attentiveness (Thoreau, 1951). Aldo Leopold called for respect and love for the land (Leopold, 1968). Rachel Carson emphasized the role of wonder in ecological engagement (Carson, 1956). More recently, environmental ethicists have advocated for friendship, humility, temperance, optimism, benevolence, gratitude, creativity, appreciation, tolerance, openness, respect, and many more virtues; while others have focused on environmental vices such as greed, selfishness, shortsightedness, arrogance, apathy, materialism, gluttony, and laziness (van Wensveen, 1999; Sandler, 2007; Cafaro, 2009).[2] It is largely uncontested in environmental ethics that the kind of people that we are, our character, is crucial to engaging well with the natural environment. It is relevant to fulfilling our ecological responsibilities, and it is vital to having beneficial relationships and experiences with the nonhuman natural world (Cafaro, 2001a; Sandler, 2007). Character ethics is thus widely recognized as crucial to environmental ethics.

This chapter is about environmental virtue ethics, rather than virtue theory or environmental character ethics. It is about how things matter. It is not possible to discuss virtue ethics without also discussing what makes a character trait a virtue or vice and referencing particular virtues and vices. However, the focus of the chapter is on explicating environmental virtue ethics as a normative theory and advocating for it as a viable approach to environmental ethics. In section one, I characterize what is distinctive about a virtue ethics approach to normativity in environmental ethics. In section two, I respond to a prominent criticism of virtue ethics approaches to environmental ethics—that they are problematically anthropocentric because they cannot accommodate the independent value of non-human nature. In section three, I describe how things matter in virtue ethics, with an emphasis on its pluralistic approach to moral status. In section four, I describe a virtue ethics principle of right action and approach to decision making based on its conception of moral status.

1 Characterizing Environmental Virtue Ethics

Theories in environmental ethics can be distinguished according to how they answer the two questions enumerated earlier: Who or what matters? And how do things matter? For example, according to one prominent view, hedonistic utilitarianism:

1. All and only sentient beings matter (because all and only sentient beings have the capacity to suffer or enjoy).
2. All suffering and enjoyments need to be considered in calculations of how to bring about the greatest balance of interest promotion over interest frustration (or pleasure over pain).

Another prominent view is ratiocentric deontology:

1. All and only robustly rational beings matter (because all and only robustly rational beings have the capacity for moral agency, reciprocal obligations, or collaborative deliberation).
2. All robustly rational beings must be treated as an end and never merely as a means.

Virtue ethics, as a normative theory, is distinguished by how it answers the second question. It is an alternative to utilitarian and deontological (and other) normative frameworks. Its distinctive feature is that how things matter is explicated through the virtues, rather than through the specification of duties or the trading off of interests. Moreover, because there are many different virtues, things matter in different ways. It is inherently pluralistic. Here, for example, are two virtue ethics–based answers to the question of how things matter (assuming, for the sake of illustration, the same answers as stated earlier to the question of which things matter):

1. All and only sentient beings matter (because all and only sentient beings have the capacity to suffer or enjoy).
2. All sentient beings are due compassion.

And

1. All and only robustly rational beings matter (because all and only robustly rational beings have the capacity for moral agency, reciprocal obligations, or collaborative deliberation).
2. All robustly rational beings are due respect.

The answers to the first question—which things matter (or have value)—are the same here as they were for hedonistic utilitarianism and ratiocentric deontology, respectively. The difference, again, is in the second question, in how things matter. They need to be treated compassionately and respectfully, rather than having duties regarding them fulfilled or their interests being included in a utility calculus.

Therefore, the distinctive and critical normative component to virtue ethics is substantive specifications of what the virtues are—what constitutes compassion, respect, honesty, loyalty, tolerance, humility, appreciation, and so on. For example, does a compassionate person respond to all suffering in the same way? In what ways are her relationships relevant to how she responds to the suffering of others? Are there contexts or conditions where she does not regard suffering as bad? Does she prioritize not causing suffering over alleviating suffering? Or alleviating suffering over providing benefits? It is not just that the virtues are conducive to doing the right thing or bringing about good consequences. What is appropriate responsiveness and what is right is articulated through the virtues. (I discuss virtue ethics principles of right action in section four.) Part of the specifications of the substantive content of the virtues has to do with the values to which the virtues are responsive. Because suffering is bad, a central component of compassion is going to involve alleviating suffering. However, that is not the only consideration, and the values at stake underdetermine the substantive content of the virtue.

There are analogs of this in other normative theories. A full specification of which types of entities have what sorts of interests does not settle what counts as "bringing about the greatest balance of interest satisfaction over interest frustration." Do the peripheral interests of many collectively outweigh the serious or basic interests of a few? Should everyone's interests be equally considered? Similarly, that something has final value or value as an end does not immediately imply that it can never be treated merely as a means. What if there are other valuable ends at stake? Why is it not sufficient that its value is given due consideration? What if obligations come into conflict? These are familiar issues in normative ethics, and I do not mean to address them here. The crucial point is that in virtue ethics, as in any ethical theory, including any environmental ethic, there is theoretical work that needs to be done when moving from value theory to normative theory. They are, to at least some extent, independent from each other. In the case of virtue ethics that work involves substantively specifying the dispositions constitutive of virtues and vices, including environmental virtues and vices. I return to this point in section three.

2 WHY VIRTUE ETHICS IS NOT NECESSARILY ANTHROPOCENTRIC

As I have argued, the value theory and normative framework components of a theory of environmental ethics can vary independently of each other. To see this, consider the ratiocentric deontological view described earlier. Several theories in environmental ethics retain the deontological normative framework but reject the ratiocentrism. This is the case, for example, with animal rights views (Regan, 1983) and even some biocentric views (Taylor, 1986). Similarly, one might maintain a utilitarian normative framework but adopt an anthropocentric account of value—that is, that all and only human beings have final (or noninstrumental) value (Pinchot, 1914; Baxter, 1974).

It is frequently argued that virtue ethics is unfit for environmental ethics because it is too human-centered or agent-focused (Rolston, 2005; Haught, 2010). There are two components to this concern. The first is that any adequate environmental ethic must involve valuing at lest some environmental entities (e.g., animals, ecosystems, or species) unconditionally, in the sense that they have value independent of their usefulness to people and independent of human evaluative attitudes—that is, their value is there in the world, discovered by us, rather than created by us (Rolston, 1986). (I have elsewhere referred to this type of value as objective final value [Sandler, 2012]. Others have referred to it as intrinsic value [Rolston, 1986, 2005.]). The second component of the concern is that a virtue ethics framework cannot accommodate such value: "Environmental Virtues, as achieved by humans, will initially involve concern for human quality of life. But our deeper ethical achievement needs to focus on values as intrinsic achievements in wild nature" (Rolston, 2005, p. 69).

Several environmental ethicists have challenged the claim that any adequate environmental ethics must involve valuing items in nature unconditionally. For example, some have argued that there is no objective final value (Norton, 1995). Others have argued that it is possible to construct an adequate anthropocentric environmental ethic (Light and Katz, 1996). Still others have argued that an adequate nonanthropocentrism can be generated based on human evaluative attitudes—that is, that environmental entities can be valued by us for their own sake (Callicott, 1989; Elliot, 1992). For present purposes, however, let us set aside this issue and focus on the claim that virtue ethics cannot accommodate unconditional values in nature (Hursthouse, 2007 also discusses this claim). Why would one think this?

The reason is that many prominent ancient and contemporary virtue theories—accounts of what makes a character trait a virtue—are eudaimonistic in that a character trait is a virtue to the extent that it is conducive to (or constitutive of) its possessor flourishing or living well (Aristotle, 1985; Hursthouse, 1999). On such accounts, it appears that the only thing that has final (or unconditional) value is the flourishing of the possessor or virtue itself. Everything else is valuable (or valued) only insofar as it contributes to the agent's being virtuous or flour-ishing. Species, nonhuman organisms, ecosystems, and landscapes are not moral agents; they do not have character traits. Therefore, they do not have unconditional or final value. Thus, even if virtue involves caring for natural environments, organisms, and species for their own sake, it is because such caring is conducive to agent flourishing—that is, the agent herself has a sort of basic value from which the value of other things flows. The concern concludes, then, that virtue ethics is inescapably anthropocentric (or, more precisely, moral agent-centric) in a way that renders it unsuitable for environmental ethics.

But the earlier discussion should make it clear why this critique is mistaken. If it is suc-cessful, it applies at most to only one particular virtue theory—a particular account of what makes a character trait a virtue. However, insofar as virtue ethics is a normative framework, it is consistent with a wide variety of values theories and virtue theories. That only agent flourishing ultimately matters is just one possible account of which things have final value, underlying one possible virtue theory, situated into a virtue ethics framework. Another pos-sible account is that moral agents and all other living things have final value. If this is so, the corresponding account of what makes a character trait a virtue is that it is conducive to (or constitutive of) its possessor, other people, and nonhuman flourishing. This is, in fact, a prominent view in environmental virtue ethics (Cafaro, 2001b; Sandler, 2007).

The concept of virtue is that of excellence (Aristotle, 1985). Human beings are both organ-isms and rational agents. So our excellence should be related to both flourishing and moral agency—that is, identifying and responding well to things that matter (Sandler, 2007). If this is right, and if nonhuman organisms or entities have final value, then human virtue should be informed by both what constitutes our flourishing (which includes being good rational agents) and what is conducive to their flourishing (or responds to their value). In fact, our flourishing would then arguably involve recognizing their flourishing as valuable for their own sake. This is another reason that the claim that virtue ethics cannot accommo-date unconditional final values in nature is mistaken. Not only does virtue ethics not have to be eudaimonistic; eudaimonistic virtue ethics does not necessarily preclude the type of value at issue. Thus, the virtue ethics normative framework is consistent with *any* account of the value of nonhuman nature.

3 How Things Matter

In the prior section, I argued that virtue ethics is consistent with any account of the value of nonhuman nature. What virtue ethics, understood as a normative theory, provides is an account of how things matter.

To see the distinction between *which things matter* and *how things matter*, consider the difference between deontological animal rights views and utilitarian animal welfare views. In both animal rights (Regan, 1983) and animal welfare (Singer, 1977, 1989) views, animals matter, they have final value, or are directly morally considerable. However, they mat-ter differently. On animal rights views, animals are to be treated as ends in themselves and never merely as a means to the ends of others. This implies very strong negative duties— duties against using animals for food, research, sport, and so on. On animal welfare views, the suffering of animals needs to be considered in calculations regarding whether the activities involving them are justified. For example, it is permissible to use animals for medical research, so long as the reasonably expected positive outcomes of the research sufficiently outweigh the anticipated harms to the animals. Frivolous research, research with a very low probability of success, or research for which alternatives are available would not be justified, but some use of animals in research would be. Thus, that animals are directly considerable underdetermines how they should be considered and, consequently, how we should treat them in some contexts—for example, hunting, research, and agriculture. (It should be noted that there are also very broad areas of convergence between animal welfare and animal rights views in practice, for example against concentrated animal feed operations.)

In virtue ethics, as discussed earlier, how things matter is explicated through substantive specification of the virtues. Aristotle describes character traits as states that decide with respect to feelings and actions (Aristotle, 1985). More contemporary virtue theorists would put this in terms of their being dispositions that have evaluative, affective, conative, and practical components (or, more generally, cognitive and psychological components). Two people have divergent character traits when they are consistently disposed to respond to the same sorts of considerations differently. For example, a person who tends to be unmoved by the suffering of others, even when he is in a position to help, is callous; whereas a person who consistently finds the suffering of others to be important (evaluative), feels for the person suffering (affective), desires to help them (conative), and takes effective steps to do so (practical) is compassionate. The two agents are disposed regarding the same thing—the condition of other people—but they are differently disposed.

Suppose someone were to ask, "Why should we be disposed to act to reduce the suffering of others?" Part of the answer to this question has to do with the value of people—that is, that all people matter, have final value, or are directly considerable—as well as the badness of suffering. However, as touched upon earlier, there has to be more to it than this, since that people matter and suffering is bad does not tell us how we ought to respond to people's suffering. Should we consider all suffering equally? Should we prioritize not causing suffering over alleviating suffering? Does the suffering of all people deserve equal responsiveness, regardless of their relationship to us? These are questions that can only be answered through detailed, substantive specifications of what compassion is and what it involves. This is not the place for such a specification (see, e.g., Blum, 1980; Sandler, 2007). What is crucial for present purposes is that a thing's having value underdetermines how it matters, and that how things matter depends upon more than the type of value that they have (e.g., instrumental or final). It also depends upon our form of life, our psychological capacities, the things of which we are (and are not) capable, our ecological/technological situatedness, and the significance of particularity and relationships in our lives. For example, it is implausible that compassion should call for equal consideration and similar responsiveness to the suffering of all people—for example, the suffering of one's own child and that of a stranger. The reason for this does not have to do with any difference between their value as individuals or in the badness of their suffering, with respect to these they are arguably the same; but rather with the role that the parent-child relationship has in the human form of life. Similarly, part of the explanation for why wastefulness of ecologically derived resources is a vice (profligacy) is that we are ecological-dependent and that ecological resources are finite and increasingly scarce. Again, the values involved underdetermine how things matter (their moral status) and are sensitive also to our form of life and our social, ecological, and technological condition.

The discussion in the previous paragraph focused on determining how things matter within the domain of a particular virtue (e.g., compassion). However, not all things with value (or that matter) fall within the domain or field of responsiveness of the same virtues. For example, let us assume that people have final (non-instrumental) value and that great works of art also have final (non-instrumental) value. Even assuming this, the way in which we ought to respond to their value is quite different. People, as rational agents capable of choosing their own ends, are due a kind of respect—respect for their capacity as autonomous choosers. Respectfulness is therefore a virtue (the details of which must of course be specified), such that it is *prima facie* disrespectful to restrict people's autonomy, enslave them, or prohibit their living according to their conceptions of the good. That people are due this sort of respect is grounded in the capacities that they have. However, great works of art lack these capacities. It would make no sense to say that we need to afford sculptures appropriate autonomy. Instead, appropriate responsiveness to them involves appreciation. Thus, it is possible for two things to matter, to both have final value, but matter in very different ways. Part of this concerns differences in types of value, but it is also related to the fact that things with value properly fall within the domain of different virtues.

There is a very wide array of environmental entities—for example, species, animals, landscapes, ecosystems, and microorganisms. One of the primary aims of environmental ethics is to articulate how these things matter, whether and how we should care about them and consider them in deliberations about which actions to perform, practices to encourage, and policies to adopt. But even if they all matter, and even if they do so noninstrumentally, it is implausible that they could all matter in the same way. Part of this has to do with the facts about the entities. For example, individual organisms have a good of their own or interests. They can be benefitted or harmed. So it is possible to care about their welfare and be disposed against unnecessary harm to them. We can be benevolent (or, less strongly, nonmalevolent) toward them. However, landscapes and ecosystems do not have a good of their own, interests, or a welfare. They are simply not the sorts of things toward which moral agents could be nonmalevolent. Similarly, compassion can only be appropriate to some nonhuman organisms, those with psychological interests or the capacity to suffer. However, these differences in capacities and value are, again, only part of the story regarding the bases for different responsiveness. Relational properties also matter. For example, some landscapes are due consideration because of their cultural, religious, or symbolic value. Similarly, we ought to respond differently to the welfare of companion animals—ones in with which we have a history and emotional connections—than to the welfare of their wild counterparts, even when they have similar psychological capacities. It may be that nonmalevolence is due to wild animals (that is, we should not cause them to suffer and should afford them space to pursue their good), but that positive beneficence is due to companion animals (that is, we have a responsibility to actively promote their good). Again, the reason is not that they have different capacities or different value, but that we ought to respond to their value differently, due to their relational properties (Sandler, 2007; Palmer, 2010).

Thus, on a virtue ethics approach to environmental ethics, the question of how things matter is pluralistic. It is articulated through substantive specifications of the domain and dispositions constitutive of a wide variety of virtues—compassion, tolerance, generosity, nonmalevolence, and so on. And those specifications are not settled by the value that things have or the capacities they have, but also include a variety of relational considerations. The process of specification might therefore be counted as one of wide reflective equilibrium, since it involves not only theoretical, logical, and value considerations, but also empirical considerations and critical evaluation of beliefs.

Pluralism in how environmental entities matter, in how they need to be considered and responded to, is crucial to environmental ethics given the tremendous diversity of environmental entities, the sorts of values that they possess, and our relationships and interactions with them. Virtue ethics is not the only view on which pluralism in moral status or moral considerability can be generated. For example, rule consequentialism can be pluralistic as well, with the different rules articulating different forms of responsiveness to different types of entities (Sandler, 2007). However, any approach to environmental ethics that is not pluralistic in this way would lack the resources to capture the richness of the natural world and the complexity of our relationship with it, and for this reason it would be inadequate.

4   ENVIRONMENTAL VIRTUE ETHICS AND RIGHT ACTION

Earlier I argued that what is distinctive of environmental virtue ethics as a normative theory is that how things matter, and by implication what responses are good or right, is explicated through the virtues. This is true for emotions, desires, and actions.

The most influential and well-know virtue ethics principle of right action is that formulated by Rosalind Hursthouse: "An action is right iff it is what a virtuous agent would characteristically (i.e., acting in character) do in the circumstances" (1999: 28). Hursthouse emphasizes that this virtue ethics principle has the same structure as familiar deontological and utilitarian principles—"An action is right iff it conforms to the moral law" and "An action is right iff it promotes the best (or good enough) consequences." In both of these cases, the principle itself is far from sufficient for determining what one ought to do in a particular situation. One also needs a substantive account of the moral law or a substantive account of what constitutes the best (or good enough) consequences. These are what provide the normative content. Similarly, with the virtue ethics principle of right action one needs an account of what the virtuous agent would characteristically do, and this is provided through substantive specifications of the virtues, since a virtuous person is distinguished by her possession of the virtues. That is to say, the normative content of a virtue ethics principle or right action is provided by substantive specifications of the virtues. This, again, is why those specifications are indispensible to virtue ethics.

Hursthouse's virtue ethics principle of right action is a qualified agent principle. It holds that an action is right if and only if it is what an appropriate qualified (i.e., virtuous) person would do in the situation. Several difficulties have been raised for such principles. For instance, the right thing for a person to do often depends upon her individual characteristics. For example, a virtuous agent who is a good swimmer might jump in the water to save a distressed child, but a nonvirtuous (or virtuous) agent who cannot swim should not do so. Thus, what is right for a person to do often is contingent on her skills, knowledge, and abilities. It is also sometimes right for people to do things that a virtuous person would not do, precisely because they lack virtue. For example, they should engage in activities to help to improve their character (Johnson, 2003). Similarly, there can be things that are right for a virtuous agent to do, which would be wrong from those who lack virtue. For example, a person who lacks the cooperativeness, commitment, and reliability to effectively lead a community environmental effort ought not do so, particularly if there is a candidate with both the requisite skills and strength of character.

These difficulties arise for Hursthouse's principle because what it is right for a person to do often depends upon their particularity—their knowledge, resources, abilities, and character. So proper responsiveness for an actual person in an actual situation is not fully determined by what a (or some) virtuous person would do. For reasons given previously, it is not even always right for a person to do what a virtuous version of herself would do.

It is possible to avoid these difficulties by moving from a qualified-agent principle of right action to a target-oriented principle, according to which an action is right if it hits the target of the operative virtues in a situation as well or better than other actions available to the agent (Swanton, 2003; Sandler, 2007). Hitting the target of a virtue involves "success in the moral acknowledgment of or responsiveness to items in its field or fields, appropriate to the aim of the virtue in a given context" (Swanton, 2003: 233). Target-oriented principles define right action directly in terms of appropriate responsiveness as determined through the virtues. They make explicit that in virtue ethics the link between how things matter and right action is the virtues.

For environmental ethics, this means that guidance on how we ought to interact with the natural environment and evaluation of what practices and policies we ought to adopt with regards to it are generated by identifying, in concrete situations, which virtues are operative and what actions of those available to the agent best hit the targets of those virtues. Thus, on a virtue ethics approach to environmental ethics the normative force of action-guiding prescriptions is drawn from the substance of the virtues. If a person ought not clear a stand of trees in her backyard in order to improve the view from her window, the reason is not that doing so would not produce the best consequences or that it violates the moral law. The reason is that doing so misses the targets of care, compassion, ecological sensitivity, or other operative virtues. (For other, more extensive examples see Sandler, 2007 and Hursthouse, 2007.)

Of course, there will be difficult cases, where it is not obvious what the operative virtues call for or there are virtues that appear to favor different courses of action. This is particularly so, given the pluralism of how things matter, argued for earlier. Some ethicists have objected to virtue ethics, including environmental virtue ethics, on the grounds that it lacks the resources to resolve these hard cases and so cannot provide adequate action and policy guidance. Defending virtue ethical decision making against this charge is beyond the scope of this chapter, and it has been done at length elsewhere (Hursthouse, 1999; Swanton, 2003; Sandler, 2007). For now, suffice it to say that no ethical theory can make difficult cases simple, unless it does so by excluding relevant considerations. Hard cases, in environmental ethics as elsewhere, arise when there are competing goods, tragic choices, and/or high levels of uncertainty. The point of an environmental ethic is not to make hard environmental decisions or evaluations easy and obvious, but to provide a framework, concepts, and resources to help to identify what is at stake (what matters) and to reason through how we ought to respond to them (how they matter). Environmental virtue ethics does this. If it turns out that there is not always a single best course of action or policy, then this reflects the complexity and indeterminacy of the case, rather than the paucity of normative and decision-making resources at the disposal of environmental virtue ethics.

5 CONCLUSION

I began this chapter by distinguishing virtue ethics from virtue theory and character ethics. As mentioned then, it is uncontroversial that virtue theory and character ethics are crucial to environmental ethics. What is contested is whether virtue ethics, understood as a distinctive type of normative theory, could provide a viable environmental ethic. In response to this concern, I have tried to (1) explicate what is distinctive about a virtue ethics approach to normativity within environmental ethics—that is, that how things matter (moral status) is explicated through the virtues; (2) demonstrate that a virtue ethics normative framework can accommodate whatever is the correct account of the value of nonhuman nature; (3) argue that a pluralistic approach to moral status, such as virtue ethics, is indispensible to environmental ethics; (4) articulate a plausible virtue ethics principle of right action and decision making. If I have been successful, then virtue ethics should be regarded as a viable approach to environmental ethics, and it should be considered alongside other, more familiar, approaches such as deontology and consequentialism.

NOTES

1. Virtue ethics is also often thought to provide a distinctive theory of value, on which value is explicated or revealed through the evaluations or responsiveness of virtuous agents, or else virtue (or virtuous activity) is intrinsically valuable and the condition or source from which other values flow. Aristotle (1985) is sometimes interpreted as advocating this sort of view, and contemporary proponents of versions of it include Michael Slote (2001) and Phillippa Foot (2001). My focus here on virtue ethics as a distinctive normative theory is not meant to preclude the possibility that virtue ethics also provides a distinctive account of the source and nature of value.
2. For a cataloging of environmental virtues and vices, see van Wensveen (1999); for a systematic categorization of environmental virtues, see Sandler (2007); and for an extended discussion of some cardinal environmental vices, see Cafaro (2009).

REFERENCES

Aristotle (1985). *Nicomachean Ethics*, translated by T. Irwin. Indianapolis, IN: Hackett.
Baxter, W. (1974). *People or Penguins: The Case for Optimal Pollution.* New York: Columbia University Press.
Blum, L. (1980). "Compassion." In *Explaining Emotions*, edited by A. O. Rorty, 507–517. Berkeley, CA: University of California Press.
Cafaro, P. (2001a). "The Naturalist's Virtues." *Philosophy in the Contemporary World* 8 (2): 85–99.
Cafaro, P. (2001b). "Thoreau, Leopold, and Carson: Toward an Environmental Virtue Ethics." *Environmental Ethics* 23: 1–17.
Cafaro, P. (2009). "Gluttony, Arrogance, Greed, and Apathy: An Exploration of Environmental Vice." In *Environmental Virtue Ethics*, edited by R. Sandler and P. Cafaro, 135–158. Lanham, MD: Rowman and Littlefield.

Callicott, B. (1989). *In Defense of the Land Ethic: Essays in Environmental Philosophy*. Albany, NY: State University of New York Press.

Carson, R. (1956). *The Sense of Wonder*. New York: Harper and Row.

Elliot, R. (1992). "Intrinsic Value, Environmental Obligation, and Naturalness." *The Monist* 75: 138–160.

Foot, P. (2001). *Natural Goodness*. Oxford, England: Oxford University Press.

Haught, P. (2010). "Hume's Knave and Nonanthropocentric Virtues." *Journal of Agricultural and Environmental Ethics* 23: 129–143.

Hursthouse, R. (1999). *On Virtue Ethics*. Oxford, England: Oxford University Press.

Hursthouse, R. (2007). "Environmental Virtue Ethics." In *Working Virtue*, edited by R. Walker and P. Ivanhoe, 166–182. Oxford, England: Oxford University Press.

Johnson, R. (2003). "Virtue and Right." *Ethics* 113: 810–834.

Kant, I. (1996 [1797]). *The Metaphysics of Morals*, translated by Mary Gregor. Cambridge, England: Cambridge University Press.

Leopold, A. (1968). *A Sand County Almanac*. Oxford, England: Oxford University Press.

Light, A., and Katz, E. (1996). *Environmental Pragmatism*. New York, NY: Routledge.

Mill, J. S. (2001). *Utilitarianism*. Indianapolis, IN: Hackett.

Pinchot, G. (1914). *The Training of a Forester*. Philadelphia and London: J. B. Lippincott Company.

Norton, B. (1995). "Why I am Not a Nonanthropocentrist." *Environmental Ethics* 17: 341–358.

Palmer, C. (2010). *Animal Ethics in Context*. New York, NY: Columbia University Press.

Regan, T. (1983). *The Case for Animal Rights*. Berkeley, CA: University of California Press.

Rolston, H. III (1986). *Philosophy Gone Wild: Essays in Environmental Ethics*. Amherst NY: Prometheus.

Rolston, H. III (2005). "Environmental Virtue Ethics: Half the Truth but Dangerous as a Whole." In *Environmental Virtue Ethics*, edited by R. Sandler and P. Cafaro, 61–78. Lanham, MD: Rowman and Littlefield.

Sandler, R. (2007). *Character and Environment*. New York, NY: Columbia University Press.

Sandler, R. (2012). *The Ethics of Species*. Cambridge, England: Cambridge University Press.

Singer, P. (1977). *Animal Liberation*. London, England: Paladin.

Singer, P. (1989). "All Animals Are Equal." In *Animal Rights and Human Obligations*, edited by T. Regan and P. Singer, 148–162. Upper Saddle River, NJ: Prentice Hall.

Slote, M. (2001). *Morals from Motives*. Oxford, England: Oxford University Press.

Swanton, C. (2003). *Virtue Ethics: A Pluralistic View*. Oxford, UK: Oxford University Press.

Taylor, P. (1986). *Respect for Nature: A Theory of Environmental Ethics*. Princeton, NJ: Princeton University Press.

Thoreau, H. D. (1951). *Walden*. New York: Bramhall House.

Van Wensveen, L. (1999) *Dirty Virtues*. New York, NY: Humanity Books.

CHAPTER 20

....

ETHICS OF CARING IN ENVIRONMENTAL ETHICS
Indigenous and Feminist Philosophies

....

KYLE POWYS WHYTE AND CHRIS J. CUOMO

OVER 40 years ago a phenomenal grassroots environmental movement was organized in the Himalayas of Uttarakhand, India, when women and men of the Chipko Andolan movement surrounded and hugged trees to protect local forests from state-approved logging companies. The Chipko movement enacted ethics of caring for trees, forests, women, and communities as valuable interdependent beings, and it initiated a national movement that embraced and publicized the potent symbol of tree-hugging as an expression of resistance to environmental exploitation (Shiva, 1988; Gottlieb, 1996). More recently, in the spring of 2003, a group of Anishinaabe grandmothers and other community members gathered and began walking around the Great Lakes in response to pollution and water misuse. Their Mother Earth Water Walk seeks to raise consciousness of water's sacredness, our interdependence with water, and the reciprocal responsibilities that connect humans, water, and other beings. Now an annual movement throughout the North American continent, the Water Walk includes persons of different heritages and nations (McGregor, 2012). Spanning several decades and a great many miles, Chipko Andolan and the Mother Earth Water Walk are connected as environmental politics grounded in ethics of caring and responsive caretaking, mindful of human and nonhuman concerns at multiple scales and aiming to protect and to shift consciousness.

"Care ethics" refers to approaches to moral life and community that are grounded in virtues, practices, and knowledges associated with appropriate caring and caretaking of self and others. In contrast to ethical theories that assume the paradigm of moral reasoning to be an isolated agent making impersonal, abstract calculations—a dominant view in western philosophy—ethics of care highlight the affective dimensions of morality, the inevitability of dependence and interdependence, the importance of caretaking and healthy attachments in the basic fabric of human well-being, and the relational and contextual nature of any ethical question or problem (Gilligan, 1982). Ethics of care understand moral agents as deeply and inextricably embedded in networks of ethically significant connections and conceive of caring as exercising responsibilities and virtues that maintain and positively influence relationships and general flourishing within those overlapping networks. As philosopher Virginia

Held has written, a fundamental premise of care ethics is that "morality should address issues of caring and empathy and relationships between people rather than only or primarily the rational decisions of solitary moral agents" (1995: 1). Proponents of care ethics describe realms of caring such as good parenting, friendship, and community membership as relationships that foster human development, social cooperation, and the basic foundation of all morality and ethics. They therefore reject the idea that caring and caretaking are trivial or irrelevant in "public" spheres. Care ethicists highlight the extent to which certain people are commonly directed to spheres and norms of feminine caretaking and compulsory service for others, and they argue that women may therefore have significant epistemic insight concerning philosophical and practical understandings of care ethics. However, most identify caring as an orientation accessible to all and eschew the notion that caring and caretaking ought to be "women's work."

Yet, as the Chipko and Water Walk movements illustrate, care ethics can be compelling foundations for environmental ethics, and the general relevance of care ethics for environmentalism is connected to matters of gender. Ethical paradigms centered around caring are able to acknowledge the significance of caring for all kinds of others, as well as the complex value of ecological interdependencies, and the limitations of worldviews that deny reliance on nature. Perspectives informed by care ethics raise crucial questions about the specific relationships involved in any particular environmental issue and highlight opportunities for developing appropriately caring actions and policies. Care ethics question canonical conceptions of nature as passive or inert and express anticolonial ethics and epistemologies based on the wisdom of relation-centered traditions and practices.

Environmental ethics nearly always stress the need for increased and improved moral regard for nonhuman others and ecological systems, and the lack of such regard is commonly cited as a fundamental cause of environmental damage and destruction. Nonetheless, in the canon of environmental philosophy, ethical caring is rarely taken seriously as a framework for guiding decision making, although emotional caring, including care for future generations, is noted as motivating environmental action. There remains an overriding tendency for theorists and policy advocates to consider caring as a pre-cognitive rather than knowledge-producing response. Liberal philosophers focus instead on ideals such as "biotic citizen," "rights-holder," and "manager," and frame moral issues in abstract, economic, and legalistic terms (Kheel, 2008; Whyte, 2014). Ironically, environmental thinkers such as Aldo Leopold, Edward Abbey, and Arne Naess, who did call for more effective caring for nature, seem to neglect or underestimate the importance of caring for other human beings as a way of caring for nature (Plumwood, 1993; Cuomo, 1998).

Environmental ethics that incorporate paradigms of caring conceive of environmental harms and the exploitation of nonhuman animals as failures to extend caring to worthy others and see those failures in relation to similar failures to care for other people. As decision-making guides, ethics of care attend to the affiliations and relationships that frame a particular moral problem and recommend actions and policies with potential to heal or create worthy affiliations and relationships. They may also call for resisting or severing relationships that are harmful or oppressive (Friedman, 1987; Hoagland, 1988; Card, 1990). Care ethics inform a distinct set of priorities and methods for environmental decision making that give voice to a range of perspectives. Here we discuss influential indigenous and feminist discourses in which care figures centrally in environmental ethics and provides guidance for ethical decision making about action and policy.

1 Care Ethics in Indigenous Environmental Movements

Indigenous peoples are among the leading environmentalists of the twentieth and twenty-first centuries and exemplars of ethical perspectives highlighting attentive caring for the intertwined needs of human and nonhuman communities. As a collective term, "indigenous peoples" refers to communities who governed themselves before a period of invasion or colonization; today they total about 370 million persons, with a presence on every continent, and continue to exercise self-government in the context of being dominated by the colonial power of nation states such as the U.S. or New Zealand. Concepts of care are often integral aspects of the communications and practices of indigenous environmental movements, although they may not use English language terms for caring, and when they do their meaning can differ from traditions of care ethics articulated by people of other cultures and heritages. We offer the view that important philosophical and practical themes related to care ethics are influential in many indigenous environmental discourses, and these provide important paradigms for caring as part of environmental ethics. Specifically, indigenous conceptions of care (1) emphasize the importance of awareness of one's place in a web of different connections spanning many different parties, including humans, non-human beings and entities (e.g., wild rice, bodies of water), and collectives (e.g., forests, seasonal cycles); (2) understand moral connections as involving relationships of interdependence that motivate reciprocal responsibilities; (3) valorize certain skills and virtues, such as the wisdom of grandparents and elders, attentiveness to the environment, and indigenous stewardship practices; (4) seek to restore people and communities who are wounded from injustices by rebuilding relationships that can generate responsibilities pertinent to current environmental challenges such as biodiversity conservation and climate change; (5) conceive of political autonomy as involving the protection of the responsibility to serve as stewards of lands, the environmental quality of which is vital for sustenance.

Indigenous environmentalists have expressed these themes in their writings and practices in response to a number of environmental problems that occur at the intersection of industrialization and colonization. Across the globe indigenous peoples have frequently been displaced by the creation of national parks and the establishment of conservation areas. They also endure harms associated with their reproductive capabilities that are linked to living nearby polluting industries, and are among the first societies who face permanent relocation due to climate change that has been triggered by the emissions of greenhouse gases from corporate activities and high levels of consumption (Grinde and Johansen, 1995; LaDuke, 1999; Shearer, 2011; Weaver, 1996; Igoe, 2004; Hoover et al., 2012; Krakoff and Rosser, 2012; Abate and Kronk, 2013). The lands and waters that indigenous peoples depend on have been degraded by extraction industries, from mineral mines to forestry to tar sands extraction, and by chemical and manufacturing industries, such as automaking and petrochemical processing. In many communities, harms associated with global environmental issues such as climate change are often compounded by other factors. For example, interest in resource extraction and the warming circumpolar region has increased the risk to indigenous people, and especially to women, of being exploited by the harmful economies that accompany intensive extraction industries (Sweet, 2014). Examples such as these are connected to large literatures that cover multiple ways in which environmental degradation associated with colonial economies disrupt relationships that are integral to indigenous livelihoods, such as indigenous gender systems (e.g., Calhoun et al., 2007) and indigenous community planning methodologies (e.g., Walker et al., 2013).

Beyond expressing or arguing for ethical commitments by writing philosophy articles, in recent decades indigenous thinkers worldwide have composed a great many political declarations and statements summarizing the viewpoints and positions of their communities regarding various environmental matters. Indigenous peoples' environmental movements almost always express normative philosophies of how humans should relate to other humans and non-humans. For example, the Kari-Oca 2 declaration, produced by a gathering of some 500 indigenous persons at the RIO + 20 Earth Summit, states that environmental policy must respect

> the inseparable relationship between humans and the Earth, inherent to Indigenous Peoples . . . for the sake of our future generations and all of humanity. . . Our lands and territories are at the core of our existence – we are the land and the land is us; we have a distinct spiritual and material relationship with our lands and territories and they are inextricably linked to our survival and to the preservation and further development of our knowledge systems and cultures, conservation and sustainable use of biodiversity and ecosystem management . . . Caring and sharing, among other values, are crucial in bringing about a more just, equitable and sustainable world (Indigenous Peoples of Mother Earth assembled at the site of Kari-Oca, 2012).

There is much to say about Kari-Oca 2, but a key theme is the importance of an awareness of the intimacy and multidimensionality of the connections linking humans, non-human beings and entities, and collectives. In particular, the relationships involve close and interdependent ties. They have intrinsic value as sources of identity, community, and spirituality but also instrumental value as sources of sustenance and usable knowledge that furnish guidance on caring for biodiversity and ecosystems. The relationships are morally weighty because they motivate responsibilities involving reciprocity, harmony, solidarity, and collectivity. The term "caring" is used to suggest a value foundational for justice and sustainability.

As enactments of complex commitments to care, indigenous environmental movements have made great strides in protecting indigenous lifeways against the parties who are responsible for the environmental problems they face, including international bodies, nation-states, subnational governments, corporations, and nongovernmental organizations. Though the struggle to reestablish indigenous peoples' rights to steward their territories continues, the positive developments stemming from indigenous environmental movements are many, and they are powerful reminders of the possibilities of applying environmental care ethics in practical political realms. For example, various indigenous parties worked to ensure that the United Nations (UN) Declaration of the Rights of Indigenous Peoples, adopted in 2007, included articles that support the environmental protection many indigenous peoples rely on for continuing their lifeways (see Articles 20 through 32; Joffe, Hartley, and Preston, 2010). Indigenous peoples have also won numerous court victories against subnational governments and corporations, from the Saramaka decision by the Inter-American Court to the Boldt Decision in North America, gaining important legal protections and strengthening their capacities for preserving and enacting traditional but dynamic models of environmental stewardship (Otis, 2012; Brown, 1994).

Indigenous environmental movements have also enacted civil disobedience and mass mobilizations in defense of their autonomy as peoples and the links between their autonomy and their deep connections with other beings. The Idle No More movement in Canada focuses on concerns about the settler government's lack of respect for indigenous environmental values and systems of stewardship that predate colonialism, and it has expressed discontent through media activism, teach-ins, and flash mob round dances (Idle No More, 2014). Indigenous environmentalists have also shaped national policies in countries that dominate indigenous communities, such as in the United States, where indigenous communities have fought hard to use treaties and federal policies to bolster political sovereignty in ways that also serve subsistence cultures and environmental protection (Wilkinson, 2005).

2 Knowledge, Responsibility, Reciprocity, and Moral Repair

Themes of indigenous knowledge, responsibility, reciprocity, and moral repair are salient in indigenous environmental movements and political discourses. In 2012, the *First Stewards Symposium: Coastal Peoples Address Climate Change* convened indigenous peoples from North America and the Pacific and produced a resolution stating that "First Stewards" have "awareness of the interconnectedness of the clouds, forest, valleys, land, streams, fishponds, sea, lakes, canyons and other elements of the natural and spiritual world, and . . . expertise and methodologies to assure responsible stewardship of them . . ." (McCarty et al., 2012). Here stewardship does not express human exceptionalism or control over nature, as it typically does in other environmental discourses. Instead, it refers to acknowledgment of one's place in a web of interdependent relationships that create moral responsibilities, and it recognizes that there are methods and forms of expertise involved in carrying out such responsibilities. The environmental ethics suggested by the First Steward's resolution involve responsibilities that flow from close and interdependent relationships. Indigenous peoples' understanding of interdependence forms the basis for justifying and motivating ethical responsibilities in human and ecological communities.

Declarations also emphasize the importance of awareness of connections across humans, non-human beings and entities, and collectives. *The Anchorage Declaration*, written in 2009 by indigenous representatives from the Arctic, North America, Asia, the Pacific, Latin America, Africa, Caribbean, and Russia, claims to "reaffirm the unbreakable and sacred connection between land, air, water, oceans, forests, sea ice, plants, animals and our human communities as the material and spiritual basis for our existence" (The Anchorage Declaration, 2009). Many declarations do choose to invoke the term "care" for describing the moral significance of interdependence. The *Water Declaration of the Anishinaabek, Mushkegowuk, and Onkwehonwe* (peoples), convened by the Chiefs of Ontario, claims the three cultures have "their own inherent responsibilities and intimate relationships to the waters" and "have the responsibility to care for the land and the waters by our Creator." It claims that these peoples "have a direct relationship with all waters—fresh and salt that must be taken care of to ensure that the waters provide for humans on a daily basis . . . [they] have ceremonies from birth to death that relate to the care of the waters . . . and our own ways to teach our children about their relationships to waters." In fact, treaties were intended "to make certain that decision making processes related to use and care of the water . . ." (Chiefs of Ontario, 2008). Relations with a settler nation such as Canada through treaties were from an indigenous perspective intended to protect caretaking. The *Indigenous Peoples Kyoto Water Declaration*, written in 2003 by indigenous participants in the World Water Forum, states that water is "sacred and sustains all life" and that indigenous "traditional knowledge, laws and ways of life teach us to be responsible in caring for this sacred gift that connects all life" (Third World Water Forum, 2003). The Declaration identifies indigenous peoples as "caretakers of Mother Earth." The Tlatokan Atlahuak Declaration, from the Indigenous Peoples Parallel Forum of the Fourth World Water Forum in 2006, claims that "We have been placed upon this earth, each in our own traditional sacred land and territory to care for all of creation and water . . . our traditional knowledge, laws and forms of life teach us to be responsible and caring for this sacred gift that connects all life" (Third World Water Forum, 2006).

In the philosophical views expressed in these declarations, responsibilities are not conceived as only the province of human beings, and water is not considered inert. In fact, several emphasize the responsibilities of water to humans and others. Anishinaabe scholar and activist Deb McGregor, who has worked closely with Mother Earth Water Walkers of the Great Lakes basin, describes the responsibilities that are derived from such a relationship as follows:

> We must look at the life that water supports (plants/medicines, animals, people, birds, etc.) and the life that supports water (e.g., the earth, the rain, the fish). Water has a role and a responsibility to fulfill, just as people do. We do not have the right to interfere with water's duties to the rest of Creation. Indigenous knowledge tells us that water is the blood of Mother Earth and that water itself is considered a living entity with just as much right to live as we have. (2009, 37–38)

McGregor's words support an approach to ethics involving relationships with diverse beings and entities. The responsibilities that maintain and strengthen those relationships are between and among active agents, and they are reciprocal, not one-directional. Here "inextricably close" and "interdependent" relationships justify and motivate responsibilities among various entities and collectives. As responsible agents, a range of human and nonhuman entities, understood as relatives of one another, have caretaking roles within their communities and networks.

Indigenous environmental movements express their environmental ethics to help people of other heritages and nations understand how to be critical about their ethical assumptions . . . Cherokee scholar Jeff Corntassel argues that an array of civil and political rights discourses are inadequate for indigenous peoples because they ignore "the cultural responsibilities and relationships that indigenous peoples have with their families and the natural world (homelands, plant life, animal life, etc.) that are critical for their well-being and the well-being of future generations . . ." (Corntassel, 2008, 107). The Kari-Oca 2 declaration calls on "civil society" to respect indigenous "values of reciprocity, harmony with nature, solidarity, and collectivity," including "caring and sharing." The declaration also claims that the idea of saving "nature by commodifying its life giving and life sustaining capacities [is] a continuation of the colonialism that Indigenous Peoples and our Mother Earth have faced and resisted for 520 years . . ." (2012). These examples express criticisms of impersonal utilitarian and rights-based ethical orientations toward the environment. Instead, characteristics of an ethics of care such as relationships, interdependency, and responsibilities are emphasized. In this vein, McGregor describes an Aboriginal perspective on environmental justice as involving more than distributive justice and critiques of power:

> Environmental justice is most certainly about power relationships among people and between people and various institutions of colonization. . . It is about justice for all beings of Creation, not only because threats to their existence threaten ours but because from an Aboriginal perspective justice among beings of creation is life-affirming. . . An Anishinaabe understanding of environmental justice considers relationships not only among people but also among all our relations (including all living things and our ancestors). (McGregor, 2012: 27–28)

In the writings discussed here, we see "care" as referring to recognizing and learning from one's place in a web of diverse relationships and being drawn by the responsibilities that are embedded in such relationships. Indigenous movements emphasize the importance of specific relationships involving reciprocal, though not necessarily equal, responsibilities among participants who understand one another as relatives. Accepting responsibilities is constitutive of realizing healthy ecosystems that already include human communities. Indigenous environmental movements also suggest to others the importance of seeing all people as in relationships with other humans and many other respected beings and entities. Finally, repair of harms is conceived as a matter of rebuilding relationships that can generate new responsibilities in contemporary times. Indigenous environmental movements therefore represent important places for conversations about the significance of caring in environmental ethics.

The moral theories explicit in indigenous environmental movements offer more than criteria of moral rightness; they also furnish guidance for decision making on action and policy in relation to environmental issues. They contend that intimate relationships of interdependence yield complex forms of moral and scientific knowledge. In addition, a large literature shows how through intimate relationships indigenous peoples express crucial ecological knowledge that is important for informing conservation strategies and climate change adaptation. Indigenous ecological knowledges have been compared to adaptive management (Berkes, Colding, and Folke, 2000) and resilience theory (Trosper, 2002) and have been valorized in theories of common pool resource management (Cox, Arnold, and Tomas, 2010). Indigenous ecological knowledges are often seen as containing insights that differ from or complement insights stemming from environmental and climate sciences (Kimmerer, 2002; Whyte, 2013). The Mandaluyong Declaration states that indigenous "mutual labor exchange systems" and "forest management practices" are effective in part because they are guided by a spirituality that connects "humans and nature, the seen and the unseen, the past, present and future, and the living and nonliving" (Mandaluyong Declaration, 2011). One implication of this literature is that any efforts to address environmental issues must take guidance from the ecological knowledge, advice, and leadership of indigenous peoples. Numerous international and national policy documents and academic literatures attest to the importance of indigenous knowledges for ethical and policy decision making on environmental issues (Nakashima et al., 2012; Berkes, 1999; Williams and Hardison, 2013; Mauro and Hardison, 2000).

Indigenous scholar Roland Trosper discusses how important guidance on ethical behavior and policy toward the environment flow out of indigenous webs of relationships, interdependency, and responsibility. In the potlatch system of some Pacific Northwest Tribes, "high grading is not allowed, consumption has an upper bound, and there is always concern

that ecosystem health should be maintained" (Trosper, 1995). Trosper argues that principles like these allow a society to buffer, self-organize, and learn in response to environmental issues (Trosper, 2009). A study by Nick Reo and Whyte describes the case of one
Ojibwe (Anishinaabe) community in which governance of subsistence hunting practices
was structured by a web of interconnected responsibilities to deer, forests, and fellow community members (Reo and Whyte, 2012). Elsewhere Reo and Jason Karl discuss how this
responsibility- and morality-based governance structure is a viable form of regulation
according to some criteria in comparison to the governance structure for hunting endorsed
by the state of Wisconsin, which emphasizes different sources of motivation and values (Reo
and Karl, 2010).

3 Feminist Care Ethics and Environmental Ethics

In feminist philosophy the deep significance of caring and caretaking for human ethics is
also emphasized, but it is understood as fundamentally gendered in oppressive contexts
and therefore requiring critical engagement and rearticulation. Feminist care ethics include
moral orientations that (1) understand individuals, including human selves and other beings,
as essentially embedded and interdependent, rather than isolated and atomistic, even if they
also exercise some degree of autonomy; (2) take mutually beneficial caring relationships to
be foundational and paradigmatic for ethics; (3) highlight the common association of care
work with females and subjugated peoples; (4) emphasize the virtues, skills, and knowledges
required for beneficial caring relationships to flourish; (5) are attentive to the contexts of
moral questions and problems; and (6) recommend appropriate caring and caretaking as
remedies for addressing histories of harm and injustice, and as necessary counterpoints to
the overemphasis in some cultures on impersonal, abstract ethical judgments. Recent discussions of care ethics in philosophy emerged from feminist perspectives, but other systems
of morality recognize the fundamental importance of caring and caretaking and encourage
appropriate caring for human and nonhuman others as a basic good and as a form of practical wisdom. Segun Ogungbemi has identified a care ethic toward the natural environment
in African traditions, and Buddhism's foundational commitment to compassion for all sentient beings places interspecies caring at the center of morality (1997). Philosophical discussions of care ethics have highlighted critical concerns about appropriate caring, including
the limits of caring as a response to violence, historical connections between colonialism
and oppressive discourses of caring, the pitfalls of caring within unequal relationships, and
the challenges of translating caring into formal systems of decision making (Code, 1991; Bell,
1993; Tronto, 1993; Narayan, 1995; Halwani, 2003; Slote, 2007). Feminist research on care ethics articulates the significance of distinct moral perspectives associated with caring work
and female socialization, while analyzing how gendered moral paradigms create and maintain hierarchies and oppressive relations.

In academic theory, a movement to claim care ethics as a distinct ethical approach was
sparked by philosopher Sara Ruddick's articulation of "maternal thinking" as an effective
and pervasive form of moral reasoning focused on attentive caring for dependent others

and by the work of psychologist Carol Gilligan, whose research questioned the view that approaches to ethical problem solving associated with masculinity and impersonal objectivity are paradigmatic or superior (Ruddick, 1980; 1989; Gilligan, 1982). Gilligan's findings indicated that even among culturally similar (white, American, middle class) subjects, two moral "voices" or paradigms of moral reasoning are evident: one focused on impersonal justice and rule-following, the other focused on appropriate caretaking and meeting responsibilities within specific relationships. Early studies indicated that these different approaches to ethics are linked to gender roles within patriarchy, although later research questioned a strong identification of ethical perspectives with gender (Gilligan 1988).

The identification of a fully developed care perspective highlighted a foundational dimension of ethical life that has been ignored or regarded as an object of disdain by western philosophy. But the moral and material strength of practical care ethics show that forms of moral reasoning associated with female social roles are not inherently immature or irrational, but instead demonstrate significant moral wisdom. Importantly, as in anti-colonial theory, the critical lens that feminist philosophers have brought to the idea of care ethics also probes the extent to which "feminine virtues" may express a "slave morality" of false ethical norms that uphold oppressive divisions and hierarchies (Deloria 1972/2003; Card, 1990; Hoagland, 1991; Cuomo, 1992; Willett, 1995). Caring labor is often assigned to and associated with females and subjugated peoples, whose social identities may be defined by self-sacrifice and service for others and whose options may be severely limited in relation to those associations. For example, overemphasizing caring virtues and self-sacrifice in girls and discouraging them in boys propagates sexist divisions, violence against women and girls, and patriarchal oppression in private and public spheres. As philosopher Michele Moody-Adams has written, within sexist societies moral capacities identified with femininity may "best suit women for domestic pursuits," and "the vision or morality that Gilligan believes to be dominant in women's thinking is bound up with rather limiting stereotypes" (1991: 201). In addition, some paradigms of caretaking that claim to be moral are actually paternalistic, hierarchical, and belittling (Narayan, 1995).

However, although relegation and socialization into the realm of caretaking labor can be a fundamental feature of oppression, caring and nurturing cannot be dismissed as only or inevitably exploitative. Rather, they are indispensable and valuable, and the virtues of caring can be understood and revised in more egalitarian ways that value caretakers and recipients of care. Caretaking positions such as "parent," "mammy," "nurse," "guide," "tree-hugger," and the like have developed and realized specific forms of ethical wisdom, virtue, and problem-solving, sometimes in resistance to hegemonic norms about what it means to be good or to do the right thing, as when the female subjects of Gilligan's early studies shared that they would bend or disregard inadequate or unjust rules and laws to benefit an innocent loved one in need. Discussions of care ethics have been influential in caring professions such as nursing, teaching, social work, and public health. The framework of care ethics that has evolved in the literature articulates modes of ethical life founded on mutually beneficial caring relationships that do not exploit caregivers, that enable and encourage responsible and healthy caring and caregiving, that highly value the input and autonomy of the cared-for, and that are promising as correctives to moral, political, and philosophical systems that neglect the significance of context, embodied emotion, and dependence in moral life (Tronto, 1987; Kittay, 2001; Held, 2007).

Feminist care-based environmental ethics are also prominent in movements focused on the value of animal others. Animal rights activists and theorists have embraced the discourse of feminist ethics, promoting caring and empathy for all animals, and linking the mistreatment of nonhuman animals to other forms of social injustice (Adams and Donovan, 1996; Gaarder, 2011). For example, Greta Gaard and Lori Gruen provide an eco-feminist analysis of the connections among the exploitation of women of color employed as chicken factory workers, the slaughter of chickens for food, and the cultural construction of chickens as a life form subjected to gross mistreatment but deserving of far more caring and justice (Gaard and Gruen, 1993). But feminist environmental ethics of care are not limited to caring for sentient beings. Grassroots women-led movements for environmental justice clearly show how environmental protection can be enlivened by women's local knowledge about communal well-being and the intermingled interests of human and nonhuman life. Their enactment of care ethics have brought new understandings of conservation and women's unique stakes in environmental protection, especially where basic rights and needs are threatened by destructive projects that generate profits for outsiders (Bahuguna, 1984).

There has been a great deal of analysis of ethics as a combination of care and justice approaches, involving levels of concern from the personal and cultural to the institutional and legalistic. Regarding global warming, feminist discussions of the gendered dimension of climate change focus on the importance of empowering communities to care for themselves and the social and ecological communities in which their lives and interests are interwoven. As a moral and practical problem, climate change evokes a range of dilemmas involving caring and caretaking, as well as demands related to justice, fairness, inclusive methods, and empowering policies—matters of legalistic morality and institutional justice (Aguilar, 2009; Tschakert and Machado, 2012; Cuomo and Tuana, 2014). Empirically and on the ground, efforts toward moral repair regarding environmental harms benefit from the integration of care ethics into institutions and collective decision making. It is noteworthy that serious attention to these issues seems to be articulated by agencies as mainstream as the US Environmental Protection Agency, which purports to address the unjust distribution of environmental harms through "community-based programs that help build capacity to address critical issues affecting overburdened populations" (USEPA, 2011: 5). Utilizing a framework of environmental justice, this language extends ethics of care in the direction required by fairness, toward the "overburdened". But when disastrous pollution and the like are inflicted on already-targeted communities, such reparative support is clearly only the beginning of what truly respectful ethical caring demands.

4 CONCLUSION

Feminist and indigenous conceptions of care ethics offer a range of ideas and tools for environmental ethics that are helpful for unearthing deep connections and moral commitments, and for guiding environmental decision making. Beyond the examples discussed here, care often figures behind the scenes in policies and practices that aim to promote both human and environmental well-being. More work is needed, however, to draw attention to the important contributions made by ethics of caring in spheres of politics and policy. Movements such as the Mother Earth Water Walk and the Green Belt Movement are ongoing examples of the effectiveness of on-the-ground environmental care ethics (Maathai, 2011). The gendered, feminist, historical, and decolonial dimensions of care ethics and related approaches to environmental ethics provide rich ground for rethinking and reclaiming the nature and depth of diverse relationships as the very fabric of personal, social and ecological being.

References

Abate, R. S., and Kronk, E. A. (2013). *Climate Change and Indigenous Peoples: The Search for Legal Remedies*. Cheltenham, England and Northhampton, MA: Edward Elgar Publishing.

Adams, C., and Donovan, J. (1996). *Beyond Animal Rights: A Feminist Caring Ethic for the Treatment of Animals*. New York: Continuum.

Aguilar, L. (2009). "Women and climate change: Vulnerabilities and adaptive capacities." *Worldwatch Institute*: 59.

Anchorage Declaration. (2009). *Indigenous Peoples' Global Summit on Climate Change. Consensus Agreement*. Anchorage, Alaska. http://unfccc.int/resource/docs/2009/smsn/ngo/168.pdf.

Bahuguna, S. (1984). "Women's Non-Violent Power in the Chipko Movement." In *In Search of Answers: Indian Women's Voices from Manushi*, edited by M. Kishwar. London: Zed Press.

Bell, L. (1993). *Rethinking Ethics in the Midst of Violence*. Lanham, MD: Rowman and Littlefield.

Berkes, F. (1999). *Sacred Ecology: Traditional Ecological Knowledge and Resource Management*. Philadelphia: Taylor and Francis.

Berkes, F., Colding, J., and Folke, C. (2000). "Rediscovery of Traditional Ecological Knowledge as Adaptive Management." *Ecological Applications* 10(5): 1251–1262.

Brown, J. J. (1994). "Treaty Rights: Twenty Years after the Boldt Decision." *Wicazo Sa Review* 10(2): 1–16.

Card, C. (1990). "Caring and Evil." *Hypatia* 5(1): 101–108.

Calhoun, A., Goeman, M., and Tsethlikai, M. (2007). "Achieving Gender Equity for American Indians." In *Handbook for Achieving Gender Equity through Education*, edited by S. S. Klein, B. Richardson, D. A. Grayson, L. H. Fox, C. Kramarae, D. S. Pollard and C. A. Dwyer, 525–552. New York: Routledge.

Chiefs of Ontario. (2008). "*Water Declaration of the Anishinaabek, Mushkegowuk, and Onkwehonwe*." Garden River First Nation. http://www.chiefs-of-ontario.org/node/76.

Code, L. (1991). *What can she know?: feminist theory and the construction of knowledge*. Ithaca, NY: Cornell University Press.

Corntassel, J. (2008). "Toward Sustainable Self-Determination: Rethinking the Contemporary Indigenous-Rights Discourse." *Alternatives: Global, Local, Political* 33(1): 105–132.

Cox, M., Arnold, G., and Tomas, S. V. (2010). "A Review of Design Principles for Community-Based Natural Resource Management." *Ecology & Society* 15(4): 38–57.

Cuomo, C. (1992). "Unravelling the Problems in Ecofeminism." *Environmental Ethics* 14(4): 351–363.

Cuomo, C. (1998). *Feminism and Ecological Communities: An Ethic of Flourishing*. New York: Routledge.

Cuomo, C., and Tuana, N. (Eds.) (2014). "Issue on Climate Change" [Special issue]. *Hypatia: A Journal of Feminist Philosophy* 29(3).

Deloria, V. (1972/2003). *God is Red: A Native View of Religion*. Golden, CO: Fulcrum Publishing.

Friedman, M. (1987). "Beyond caring: The de-moralization of gender." *Canadian Journal of Philosophy* 17(1): 87–110.

Gaard, G., and Gruen, L. (1993). "Ecofeminism: Toward Global Justice and Planetary Health." *Society and Nature* 2: 1–35.

Gaarder, E. (2011). *Women and the Animal Rights Movement*. New Brunswick: Rutgers University Press.

Gilligan, C. (1982). *In a different voice*. Cambridge, MA: Harvard University Press.

Gilligan, C. (1988). *Mapping the moral domain: A contribution of women's thinking to psychological theory and education*. Cambridge, MA: Harvard University Press.

Gottlieb, R. S. (1996). *This Sacred Earth: Religion, Nature, Environment*. New York: Routledge.

Grinde, D. A., and Johansen, B. E. (1995). *Ecocide of Native America: Environmental Destruction of Indian Lands and Peoples*, 1st ed. Sante Fe, NM: Clear Light.

Halwani, R. (2003). "Care ethics and virtue ethics." *Hypatia* 18(3): 161–192.

Held, V. (1995). *Justice and Care: Essential Readings in Feminist Ethics*. Boulder, CO: Westview Press.

Held, V. (2007). *The Ethics of Care: Personal, Political, and Global*. New York: Oxford University Press.

Hoagland, S. (1988). *Lesbian Ethics*. Palo Alto, CA: Institute of Lesbian Studies, 1988.

Hoagland, S. (1991). "Some Thoughts about Caring." In *Feminist Ethics*, edited by C. Card, 246–263. Lawrence, KS: University of Kansas Press.

Hoover, E., Cook, K., Plain, R., Sanchez, K., Waghiyi, V., Miller, . . . Carpenter, D. (2012). "Indigenous Peoples of North America: Environmental Exposures and Reproductive Justice." *Environmental Health Perspectives* 120(2): 1645–1649.

Idle No More. (2014). Manifesto. Available from http://www.idlenomore.ca/manifesto.

Igoe, J. (2004). *Conservation and Globalization: A Study of the National Parks and Indigenous Communities from East Africa to South Dakota, Case Studies on Contemporary Social Issues*. Belmont, CA: Thomson/Wadsworth.

Walker, R., Natcher, D., and Jojola, T. (2013). *Reclaiming Indigenous Planning*. Montreal, PQ, Canada: McGill-Queen's Press.

Joffe, P., Hartley, J., and Preston, J. (2010). *Realizing the Un Declaration on the Rights of Indigenous Peoples: Triumph, Hope, and Action*. Saskatoon, Canada: Purich Publishing.

Kari-Oca 2 Declaration (2012). *Indigenous People's Rio +20 Earth Summit*. Rio de Janeiro, Brazil. http://www.ienearth.org/kari-oca-2-declaration/.

Kheel, M. (2008). *Nature Ethics: An Ecofeminist Perspective*. Lanham, MD: Rowman & Littlefield.

Kimmerer, R. (2002). "Weaving Traditional Ecological Knowledge into Biological Education: A Call to Action." *BioScience* 52(5): 432–438.

Kittay, Eva F. (2001). "When Caring is Just and Justice is Caring: Justice and Mental Retardation." *Public Culture* 13(3): 557–579.

Krakoff, S. A., and Rosser, E. (Eds.) (2012). *Tribes, Land, and the Environment*. Burlington, VT: Ashgate Publishing Company.

LaDuke, W. (1999). *All Our Relations: Native Struggles for Land and Life*. Brooklyn, NY: South End Press.

Maathai, W. (2011). http://www.ecology.com/2011/10/24/wangari-maathai-quotes/.

Mandaluyong Declaration. (2011). "Mandaluyong Declaration of the Global Conference on Indigenous Women, Climate Change and Redd Plus." In *Indigenous Women, Climate Change & Forests*, edited by Tebtebba. Baguio City, Philippines: Tebtebba Foundation.

Mauro, F., and Hardison, P. D. (2000). "Traditional Knowledge of Indigenous and Local Communities: International Debate and Policy Initiatives." *Ecological Applications* 10(5): 1263–1269.

McCarty, M., Williams, M., Simonds, K., and Mears, J. (2012). *"First Stewards Resolution."* Presented at F. S. Symposium, Washington, D.C. http://www.firststewards.org/resolutions.html.

McGregor, D. (2009). "Honouring Our Relations: An Anishnaabe Perspective on Environmental Justice." In *Speaking for Ourselves: Environmental Justice in Canada,* edited by J. Agyeman, P. Cole, and R. Haluza-Delay, pp. 27–41. Vancouver, BC, Canada: University of British Columbia Press.

McGregor, D. (2012). "Traditional Knowledge: Considerations for Protecting Water in Ontario." *The International Indigenous Policy Journal* 3(3): 11.

Nakashima, D. J., McLean, K. Galloway, Thulstrup, H. D., Castillo, A. Ramos, and Rubis, J. T. (2012). *Weathering Uncertainty: Traditional Knowledge for Climate Change Assessment and Adaptation.* Paris: UNESCO and Darwin, UNU.

Narayan, U. (1995). "Colonialism and Its Others: Considerations on Rights and Care Discourses." *Hypatia* 10(2): 133–140.

Ogungbemi, S. (1997). "An African Perspective on the Environmental Crisis." In *Environmental Ethics: Readings in Theory and Application,* edited by L. J. Pojman. Belmont, CA: Wadsworth Publishing Company.

Otis, G. (2012). "The Role of Indigenous Custom in Environmental Governance: Lessons from the Inter-American Human Rights System." In *Tribes, Land, and the Environment,* edited by S. A. Krakoff and E. Rosser. Burlington, Vermont: Ashgate Publishing Company.

Plumwood, V. (1993). *Feminism and the Mastery of Nature.* London, UK: Routledge.

Reo, N., and Karl, J. W. (2010). "Tribal and State Ecosystem Management Regimes Influence Forest Regeneration." *Forest Ecology and Management* 260(5): 734–743. doi: 10.1016/j.foreco.2010.05.030.

Reo, N., and Whyte, K. (2012). "Hunting and Morality as Elements of Traditional Ecological Knowledge." *Human Ecology* 40(1): 15–27.

Ruddick, S. (1980). "Maternal thinking." *Feminist studies* 6(2): 342–367.

Shearer, C. (2011). *Kivalina: A Climate Change Story.* Chicago, IL: Haymarket Books.

Slote, M. (2007). *The Ethics of Care and Empathy.* London: Routledge.

Sweet, V. (2014). "Rising Waters, Rising Threats: The Human Trafficking of Indigenous Women in the Circumpolar Region of the United States and Canada." *MSU Legal Studies Research Paper* (12-01).

Third World Water Forum. (2003). *Indigenous Peoples Kyoto Water Declaration.* Kyoto, Japan.

Third World Water Forum. (2006). *Tlatokan Atlahuak Declaration.* Kyoto, Japan.

Tronto, J. (1987). "Beyond Gender Difference to a Theory of Care." *Signs: Journal of Women Culture and Society* 12(4): 644–663.

Tronto, J. (1993). *Moral Boundaries: A Political Argument for an Ethic of Care.* London: Routledge.

Trosper, R. L. (1995). "Traditional American Indian Economic Policy." *American Indian Culture and Research Journal* 19(1): 65–95.

Trosper, R. L. (2002). "Northwest Coast Indigenous Institutions that Supported Resilience and Sustainability." *Ecological Economics* 41: 329–344.

Trosper, R. L. (2009). *Resilience, Reciprocity and Ecological Economics: Northwest Coast Sustainability.* New York: Routledge.

Tschakert, P., and Machado, M. (2012). "A Rights-Based Approach to Gender in Climate Change Adaptation." *Ethics and Social Welfare 6* (3): 275–289.

United States Environmental Protection Agency (USEPA). (2011). *Plan EJ 2014.* Washington, D.C.: Office of Environmental Justice, US Environmental Protection Agency. http://www.epa.gov/compliance/ej/resources/policy/plan-ej-2014/plan-ej-2011-09.pdf.

Shiva, V. (1988). *Staying Alive: Women, Ecology, and Development.* London: Zed Books.

Whyte, K. P. (2013). "On the Role of Traditional Ecological Knowledge as a Collaborative Concept: A Philosophical Study." *Ecological Processes* 2(1): 1–12.

Williams, T., and Hardison, P. (2013). "Culture, Law, Risk and Governance: Contexts of Traditional Knowledge in Climate Change Adaptation." *Climatic Change 120*(3): 531–544.

Weaver, J. (1996). *Defending Mother Earth: Native American Perspectives on Environmental Justice.* Maryknoll, NY: Orbis Books.

Whyte, K. P. (2014). "How Similar Are Indigenous North American and Leopoldian Environmental Ethics?" Available at SSRN: http://ssrn.com/abstract=2022038 or http://dx.doi.org/10.2139/ssrn.2022038 (March 14).

Wilkinson, C. F. (2005). *Blood Struggle: The Rise of Modern Indian Nations.* New York: Norton.

Willett, C. (1995). *Maternal Ethics and Other Slave Moralities.* New York, NY. Routledge.

CHAPTER 21

....

THE SACRED, REVERENCE FOR LIFE, AND ENVIRONMENTAL ETHICS IN AMERICA

....

BRON TAYLOR

1 PROLEGOMENA: RELIGION AND THE SACRED

....

PERCEPTIONS regarding religion, spirituality, and the sacred have been and will continue to be deeply entwined with environmental ethics. To analyze this history and think about the future of nature/human relationships and the corresponding role of environmental values, I provide operational definitions of these terms, which have been variously understood.

Religion is often assumed to involve beliefs and perceptions related to non-material divine beings or supernatural forces. Increasingly, however, scholars consider this to be a problematic assumption, for it leaves aside a wide variety of social phenomena that have typically been understood to be religious. Consequently, increasing numbers of scholars are assuming what they call the "family resemblances" approach to the study of religion. Those taking this approach seek to illuminate the multifarious religious dimensions of human experience, indifferent to a project of discovering a strict boundary between what counts as religion and what does not (Saler, 1993). This approach has the analytic advantage of being able to consider as similar what some distinguish as "religious" and "spiritual" social phenomena. With the family resemblance approach, the commonly-made distinction between religion and spirituality—such as the former is organized and institutional and involves supernatural beings while the latter is individualistic and concerned with the quest for meaning, personal transformation, and healing—is not heuristically valuable because both "religion" and "spirituality" share most if not all of the same sorts of characteristics.

As a "family resemblance" scholar, therefore, I focus broadly on the nature and influence of a wide array of traits and characteristics that are typically associated with religious perceptions and practices, including those having to do with:

- Sacred and profane/mundane times, spaces, objects, and organisms, as well as rituals and ethical mores governing how to orient oneself and one's community with regard to them
- Food acquisition and preparation, birth, and death
- Spiritual or physical health, healing, transformation, and redemption
- Cosmologies and cosmogonies that purport to explain the origin and unfolding of the universe and the human place and future in or beyond the biosphere

Other common elements include practices and processes that are designed to:

- Evoke and reinforce proper perception, emotions, and behavior
- Recognize or establish leaders and justify their authority and governance
- Classify organisms into hierarchies of differing spiritual and moral value
- Provide meaning and community to enhance felt well-being and help people cope with fear, suffering, and death

All of the these elements reflect and influence environmental values and practices, but in the Western world and when assessing the religion-related sources and dimensions of environmental ethics, none has been more important than perceptions that environmental systems and their constitutive elements are sacred or, conversely, profane, mundane, or desecrated.

The *sacred*, however, has been understood in two main ways. For some, an experience of transformative spiritual power or of something as holy is the essence of religion. Mircea Eliade thought, for example, that an experience of the sacred is the heart of religion and involves "an uncanny, awesome, or powerful manifestation of reality, full of ultimate significance" (Chidester and Linenthal, 1995). For Eliade and his progeny, the essence of religion was the eruption of the sacred into profane space during extraordinary experiences, usually in natural surroundings and consequently being replete with nature-related symbolism (Eliade, 1959).

A contrasting perspective on the sacred—first found in the writings of Emile Durkheim's early observations (Durkheim, 1965 [1912])—has been that "nothing is inherently sacred," therefore, the term "can be assigned to virtually anything through the human labor of consecration" (Chidester and Linenthal, 1995: 6). Put differently, some understand the experience of the sacred to tap into some extraordinary but objective reality, while others (myself included) think it is the result of cultural work involving "attention, memory, design, construction, and control of place" (Chidester and Linenthal, 1995: 6; following Smith, 1987). A bearing in mind these two understandings of sacred place—what could be called the *metaphysical* and the *constructionist* approaches, respectively—can illuminate the role of religion in the contested historical unfolding of environmental ethics in America.

2 THE SACRED IN NORTH AMERICAN ENVIRONMENTAL HISTORY AND ETHICS

There has long been a deep connection between environmental history and environmental ethics. Indeed, it is hard to imagine environmental ethics without environmental history, especially as it has contrasted the religious beliefs and practices of the Europeans with that of American Indians.

The main outline of this history can be simply summarized and draws especially on the work of the pioneering historians William Denevan (1992, 2011), Perry Miller (1956), Roderick Nash (2001 [1967]), Lynn White Jr. (1967), Donald Worster (1994 [1977]), Carolyn Merchant (1980), Stephen Fox (1981), Max Oelschlaeger (1991), and Catherine Albanese (1990). By the time significant numbers of Europeans began to arrive in North America with an intention to stay rather than just raid, the diseases that the earlier arrivals carried with them had decimated the American Indian populations that had no natural immunity to them. As a result, the land they encountered was much less populated and appeared less domesticated than would have been the case otherwise (Denevan, 2011). These European settlers were, generally speaking, deeply conditioned by Christianity as well as European histories and philosophies, which had desacralized nature and promoted instrumental attitudes toward it; moreover, they had little experience with the kind of wildness they encountered. Consequently, and again generally speaking, they had fearful, negative, and exploitive attitudes toward the peoples and environments they encountered, attitudes and subsequent behavior that led to a rapid decline of the continent's biocultural diversity.

Although there were dissidents to the hegemonic cultural mainstream who appreciated their natural surrounds, it was not until the early nineteenth century that such voices became pronounced. This was due to a complex matrix of factors, including the rise and influence of European romanticism, corresponding developments in literature and the arts in America, and the rise of Transcendentalism, combined with skepticism about the supposed march of progress and its impacts on the land and on the character of Americans. Ralph Waldo Emerson's Transcendentalism was especially influential, as was his reverence for nature. For Emerson, however, the spiritual value of nature was indirect: in a way that had affinity with Plato's doctrine of correspondence, material nature was ultimately a symbol that pointed to deeper, universal, spiritual truths (Emerson, 1836). Emerson's writings nevertheless struck an experiential cord with many of his readers and promoted reverence for and value in nature, thereby providing a cornerstone for the soon-to-follow conservation movement. Emerson's greatest influence on this movement, however, was probably his mentoring of Henry David Thoreau.

In any case, while some scholars have interpreted Thoreau differently, the weight of evidence is that toward the end of his life Thoreau had left behind Emerson's Platonic vision of nature as a sacred symbol, supplanting it with a sense of material nature as sacred in and of itself—even its aspects, such as suffering and death, that are typically considered negative. Moreover, he innovatively expressed a number of ideas that would become central to environmentalism and many subsequent constructive environmental ethics: a spirituality of belonging and connection to nature, kinship feelings with non-human organisms, and an ecocentric value system in which environmental systems and species have intrinsic value. Thoreau also contended that he had nothing to learn from Christianity but much to learn from Native Americans and some of the religious traditions that originated in Asia. Most importantly, Thoreau had become a naturalist. Indeed, he had spent so much time in close observation of natural systems that by the time he first read Charles Darwin's *On the Origin of Species* (within a month of its publication), he immediately endorsed Darwin's theory. Moreover, he had become convinced that what everyone most needed was direct, visceral and sensory contact with nature; this was his spiritual epistemology. Thoreau also advanced the possibility of scientifically-informed religious and moral evolution, which in turn would depend on people developing an intimate relationship with nature (see Taylor, 2010a: 50–58, 227–247).

Not long after Thoreau's death in 1862, John Muir completed a long and difficult journey from Wisconsin to Cedar Keys, Florida. In a scathing and sardonic essay named for the place and originally written in 1867, Muir attacked what he understood to be the Christian doctrine that the world had been made for man. Such a view, according to Muir, provided theological underpinnings for anthropocentrism and indifference, if not also hostility, to non-human beings, which he considered widespread. And while later critics would point out other themes in the Abrahamic traditions that worked against environmental concern and respect for peoples with nature-based spiritualities, Muir was the first to pointedly launch such criticism. Not much more than a century later this critique would be widely held among environmentalists.

It was not only Muir's critique of anthropocentric theism, however, that took root among environmental thinkers and activists but also his constructive religious vision. For Muir, wildlands were "holy" and "sublime" places, likened often to "cathedrals" and "temples," inhabited by animals and plants who were thought of as kin. What Muir meant by the sublime reflected what, writing in the eighteenth century, Edmund Burke considered to be the experience of the sublime and the beautiful, namely, astonishment at nature's beauties and sometimes terrifying power, which he averred, leads to "admiration, reverence and respect" (Burke 1990 [1757]: 53) for specific places and sometimes also for non-human organisms in such places (see Taylor 2010a: 45–47). Nowhere did Muir express such perceptions more clearly than in this passage reflecting upon his first encounter, in 1869, with the Sierra Nevada's Cathedral Peak:

> The Sierra Cathedral, to the south of camp [at Tuolumne Meadows], was overshadowed like Sinai. Never before noticed (*sic*) so fine a union of rock and cloud in form and color and substance, drawing earth and sky together as one; and so human is it, every feature and taint of color goes to one's heart, and we shout, exulting in wild enthusiasm as if all the divine show were our own. More and more, in a place like this, we feel ourselves part of wild Nature, kin to everything (Muir, 1997 [1911]: 296–97). . . . The Cathedral itself [is] a temple displaying Nature's best masonry and sermons in stones. . . . In our best times everything turns into religion, all the world seems a church and the mountains altars (Muir, 1997 [1911]: 301).

In combination with his critique of anthropocentrism, Muir's expressions of kinship and reverence for life clearly conveyed an ecocentric ethic long before this ethical orientation was named. In religious terminology he was both a pantheist and an animist[1]—nature and indeed the entire cosmos were sacred; receptive humans could feel and be healed by the love of "mother earth"; and humans could communicate and commune with other life forms. Sacred places and animals, however, could be desecrated—and in a way that seemed to echo Thoreau—this occurs when they lose their wildness. Although for decades Muir lived a domesticated life, he nevertheless often spoke of domesticated spaces and domesticated animals, including human beings, as defiled, and he expressed outrage at those responsible for desecrating acts. Muir compared Gifford Pinchot to Satan for promoting the construction of a dam on the Tuolumne River in Hetch Hetchy Valley in Yosemite National Park, declaring "Dam Hetch Hetchy! As well dam for water-tanks the people's cathedrals and churches, for no holier temple has ever been consecrated by the heart of man" (Cohen, 1984: 330; for the

Satan comparison, see Fox, 1981: 141). This prophetic denunciation is interesting not only for its clear statement of the valley as a sacred place but also for its recognition that the designation of sacred places is a human act rooted in affective experience. This recognition was an insight that preceded by generations constructionist scholarly understandings of religions and sacred spaces that became prevalent beginning in the late twentieth century.

Reflecting the early and longstanding influence of Alexander von Humboldt, Muir also expressed and promoted an ecological metaphysics of interdependence, which would become a central tenet within the global environmental milieu. He put it poetically in what may be his most famous aphorism: "When we try to pick out anything by itself, we find it hitched to everything else in the universe." But equally representative of Muir's thought, and much environmental spirituality to follow, was his next but less-often-quoted animistic sentence: "One fancies a heart like our own must be beating in every crystal and cell, and we feel like stopping to speak to the plants and animals as fellow mountaineers" (Muir, 1997 [1911]: 245). This was only one of many animistic phrases in Muir's writings; earlier and regularly his biocentric sentiments were expressed in phrases such as "Nature's precious plant people" (Muir, 1997 [1911]: 231). Whether Muir meant his animistic writings to be taken literally or metaphorically remains unclear but their biocentric implications are clear.

Muir thus rooted his love of nature in a sacred cosmos in which wanton killing and needless destruction were sacrilegious, and efforts to prevent these evils were a profound ethical duty. Similar sentiment would become prevalent in much subsequent environmental ethics.

Muir's contemporary, John Burroughs, for example, the earliest and most prominent proponent of America's back-to-the-land and bioregional movements, perceived the cosmos and biosphere to be sacred, even though he was not in any conventional way religious: "The forms and creeds of religion change, but the sentiment of religion—the wonder and reverence and love we feel in the presence of the inscrutable universe—persists. . . . If we do not go to church so much as did our fathers, we go to the woods much more, and are much more inclined to make a temple of them than they were" (Burroughs, 2001 [1912]: 246).

Rachel Carson also had a deep sense of the sacred in nature. In her first book, for example, she imaginatively and intimately expressed biocentric values: in an animism-resembling way that even had tinges of a kind of naturalistic pantheism, she empathetically entered the world of marine organisms and expressed kinship with them, even striving to give agency to the ocean itself by making it her central character (Carson 1941).[2] In a candid lecture to female journalists in 1954, she waxed unapologetically sentimental and expressed her love of the beauties of the earth and the need for human contact with it, adding, "I believe it is important for women to realize that the world of today threatens to destroy much of that beauty that has immense power to bring us a healing release from tension." Then, presaging later essentialist versions of ecofeminist claims, she added, "Women have a greater intuitive understanding of such things" (Carson, 1998: 161). In an equally innovative way she contended, "This affinity of the human spirit for the earth and its beauties is deeply and logically rooted" because "as human beings, we are part of the whole stream of life" (Carson, 1998: 160). In this, she anticipated the biophilia hypothesis that would be advanced by E. O. Wilson a generation later (Wilson, 1984). But nowhere did she signal her own sense of the sacred more directly than through her dedication of *Silent Spring* to Albert Schweitzer, thereby expressing her affinity with his "reverence for life" ethics. In a way that resembles many other environmentalists, Schweitzer's reverence was rooted in feelings of belonging to the earth and humility about humanity's tiny place in the universe, as well as in empathy for and solidarity with all creatures, with whom we share a will to live (Schweitzer, 1936, 1969).

Aldo Leopold (1887–1948) also expressed a deep, affective connection to and reverence for the earth. He summarized his "land ethic" with these often-quoted words: "A thing is right when it tends to preserve the integrity, stability, and beauty of the biotic community. It is wrong when it tends otherwise" (Leopold, 1966 [1949]: 261). But ultimately this ethic was, for Leopold, rooted in affective experience: "It is inconceivable to me that an ethical relation to land can exist without love, respect, and admiration for land, and a high regard for its value" (Leopold 1966 [1949]: 263; cf. Callicott, 1982, 1989). And 20 years before Lynn White Jr.'s 1967 argument that Christian anthropocentrism and the tradition's antipathy to nature religions were key drivers of environmentally destructive behaviors, Leopold had already made a similar argument while simultaneously contrasting such attitudes with organicist and pantheistic understandings of the interdependence of life (Meine, 1988: 506), combining these understandings with expressions of personal feelings of belonging to nature, and biocentric, kinship ethics:

> Conservation is getting nowhere because it is incompatible with our Abrahamic concept of land. We abuse land because we regard it as a commodity belonging to us. When we see land as a community to which we belong, we may begin to use it with love and respect (Leopold, 1966 [1949]: xvii–xix).

> It is a century now since Darwin gave us the first glimpse of the origin of species. We know now what was unknown to all the preceding caravan of generations: that men are only fellow-voyagers with other creatures in the odyssey of evolution. This new knowledge should have given us . . . a sense of kinship with fellow-creatures; a wish to live and let live; a sense of wonder over . . . the biotic enterprise (Leopold, 1966 [1949]: 16–17).

Leopold's kinship ethics was rooted in a Darwinian understanding that all life is related, intimated by Darwin himself in one of his notebooks:

> If we choose to let conjecture run wild, then animals, our fellow brethren in pain, diseases, death, suffering and famine—our slaves in the most laborious works, our companions in our amusements—they may partake [of] our origin in one common ancestor—we may be all netted together (in Worster, 1994 [1977]: 180).

Of course, there are more pathways to felt empathy toward other life forms than an evolutionary understanding of biotic kinship—many Native American traditions have expressed a similar sentiment with ethics of care for "all our relations," which should be recognized in any discussion of environmental ethics in North America (see LaDuke, 1999; Callicott, 1994). And Leopold himself was doing more than articulating a scientific narrative, he was consecrating it, making it an evocative and compelling sacred story—it was an *odyssey*, an epic, a heroic journey. Leopold's language echoed the concluding passages in *On the Origin of Species*, in which Darwin offered solace to those who would leave behind traditional religious cosmogonies, by proclaiming there is grandeur in the evolutionary story of the origin and unfolding diversity of life (Darwin, 2003 [1859/1839]: 913). Leopold also presaged E. O. Wilson's use of the phrase "Epic of Evolution," who called it "the best myth we will ever have" and used it to capture the feelings of awe, wonder, and grandeur that scientific observers of nature often feel (in Barlow, 1998: 12; cf. Wilson, 1978).

But Leopold's youngest daughter provided the most revealing window into Leopold's spirituality when, not long before Leopold's death, she asked him about his religious beliefs. "He replied that he believed there was a mystical supreme power that guided the universe but to him this power was not a personalized God. It was more akin to the laws of nature.... His religion came from nature, he said" (in Meine, 1988: 506). Leopold's son added that his father, "like many of the rest of us, was kind of pantheistic. The organization of the universe was enough to take the place of God, if you like. He certainly didn't believe in a personal God" (in Meine, 1988: 506–507).

As his offspring suggested, Leopold and his progeny, both in and beyond his own family, had a deep sense that, although mysterious, there was something precious, something sacred in the world, which is a common metaphysical ground for ecocentric and biocentric ethics.

3 "Dark Green Religion and Environmental Ethics" after Earth Day

I have focused on the most important precursors and inspirations to the emergence of the discipline of environmental ethics in North America in order to spotlight how important their perceptions of the sacred were as grounding for their environmental values. I have elsewhere labeled such nature spiritualities and ethics "dark green religion," analyzing their affective and religion-resembling dimensions and the diversity of proponents and means of expression that are used to spread such spirituality and promote environmental protection (Taylor, 2010a). In addition to its critical stance toward much Western religion and philosophy, dark green religion, as I defined its key tenets,

> is generally "deep ecological," "biocentric" or "ecocentric," considering all species to be intrinsically valuable, that is, valuable apart from their usefulness to human beings. This value system is generally (1) based on a felt kinship with the rest of life, often derived from a Darwinian understanding that all forms of life have evolved from a common ancestor and are therefore related; (2) accompanied by feelings of humility and a corresponding critique of human moral superiority, often inspired or reinforced by a science-based cosmology revealing how tiny human beings are in the universe; and (3) reinforced by metaphysics of interconnection and the idea of the interdependence (mutual influence and reciprocal dependence) found in the sciences, especially ecology and physics (Taylor, 2010a: 13).

Such dark green spirituality also often involves animistic perceptions about the possibility of relationship with non-human organisms, as well as holistic, Gaian metaphysics (Lovelock, 1979).

Dark green spirituality is expressed and promoted not only by scientists such as Lovelock or through the discipline of environmental ethics but also by environmental activists, historians, and artists, nature writers and literary critics, museum and aquarium curators, and many others. Since the first Earth Day in 1970, such spirituality has grown along with the environmental movement in America and globally. I have argued that these sorts of spiritualities and ethics are grounded directly in, or at least cohere with, the senses and reason and thus are consistent with scientific methodologies and understandings; consequently, they are likely to increase their share of adherents in the increasingly global and competitive cultural marketplace. Moreover, I contend, these trends have been salutary and historically significant, even though this is as yet little recognized.

The approaches to environmental ethics that I have spotlighted, however, have been sharply criticized. One of the most influential critics has been the historian Bill Cronon, who stressed that notions such as "wilderness" were socially constructed and argued that these constructions were misleading and have perverse consequences (cf. Evernden, 1992). According to Cronon, the long-prevalent environmental story of (desecrating) anthropogenic environmental decline from a pristine nature, combined with a corresponding priority on the conservation of wildlands, has fostered a nature-humanity dualism, ironically separating people emotionally and conceptually from the environments they typically inhabit. This has hindered action toward reforming the everyday practices that negatively impact environmental systems (Cronon, 1995a, 1995b).

A chorus of scholars from different disciplines have taken Cronon's critique even further than he did, arguing that the human impact on nature is so widespread that if nature is understood as something distinct from human beings then there is no nature in that sense, using such a view to criticize those who wish to protect wildlands as naïve and misguided if not also misanthropic (for an analysis, see Sutter, 2013, for examples, see Fletcher, 2009; Kareiva and Marvier, 2011, 2012; and for rejoinders, Callicott and Nelson, 1998; Nelson and Callicott, 2008; Soulé and Lease, 1995; Butler, 2002; Noss et al., 2012; Taylor, 2013b). Still others argued that environmental narratives and objectives mask and protect elite privileges and have been indifferent to social injustices, including when the establishment of protected areas has involved the deracination of peoples who had been inhabiting them (Guha, 1989, 1997; Peluso, 1993; Warren, 1997; Spence, 1999; Jacoby, 2001; Dowie, 2009; Fletcher, 2009; Büscher, 2013).

Much such criticism is steeped in postmodern theory and postcolonial criticism, which is hostile to anything resembling a universal narrative due to its potentially authoritarian consequences. Such theorists contend that the declensionist narratives prevalent in the environmentalist milieu, as well as narratives of environmental enlightenment, are problematic if not also pernicious. In 1994 the foundational postcolonial critic Edward Said put such views starkly, calling environmentalism "the indulgence of spoiled tree huggers who lack a proper cause" (Nixon, 2011: 332, n 69).

Postmodern and postcolonial critics have astutely observed that narratives can express, reinforce, and legitimate repressive histories and social systems, and that it is difficult to "decolonize" these belief and action systems. Yet many of the critics have simplistic understandings of nature protection movements, believing they are animated foremost by recreational or aesthetic preferences or by individualistic spiritual values, whereas in fact what has united the more radical forms of such movements are efforts to protect or restore commons regimes (Taylor, 1995). Moreover, most of the critics fail to realize that since the time of Thoreau and Darwin, the rationale for nature protection has often been based foremost on the value of biodiversity (even though the term was not coined until the 1970s), which has in turn been undergirded by understandings of biotic kinship, ecological interdependence, and mutual dependence (Taylor, 2012; Butler, 2002). This latter sort of rationale has grown in importance as more has been learned about the dependence of all organisms on flourishing and diverse environmental systems. And this rationale has also been strengthened by increasing understanding of the synergies between cultural and biological diversity and by findings from the field of environmental psychology, which demonstrate the ways in which human physical and emotional health depends on or is enhanced by contact with relatively intact biological systems.[3]

That so many fail to recognize that the health of human beings and their social systems depends on flourishing environmental systems may be due in part to the extent to which such intellectuals live urban lives. What is more difficult to grasp is why so many of those who focus on human-on-human oppression fail to notice or express concern about the domination of humankind over the rest of the living world (Taylor 2013b).[4] A part of the answer might be the deep roots of human exceptionalism in the Western world, as inherited from Abrahamic traditions with their hubristic claim that the human species alone bears the image of God and properly has dominion over it (Taylor, 2010b; Taylor, 2014). Whatever the cause of such anthropocentrism, one antidote is an evolutionary and ecological worldview that stresses biotic kinship, interdependence, and mutual dependence (Callicott, 2011; Callicott et al. 2009; Taylor, 2013a). As Leopold put it when expounding his Land Ethic, this ethic "changes the role of *Homo sapiens* from conqueror of the land-community to plain member and citizen of it" (Leopold, 1966 [1949]: 240). And such values are often embedded in perceptions and expressions to the effect that the biosphere and natural systems—indeed life itself—is sacred and worthy of reverent defense.

4 THE PERSISTENCE OF THE SACRED IN ENVIRONMENTAL ETHICS

People disagree as to whether the sacred is something divine or holy that perceptive humans recognize or is a notion that humans construct to express what they feel and care about most deeply. What is certain is that environmentally concerned people often rely on religious terminology or rhetoric of the sacred, to express their feelings of connection to nature and of kinship and responsibility toward other kinds of life. Such individuals have often also viewed the destruction of living things and living systems as desecrating acts and, as some critics have asserted, this sometimes leads to binary thinking in which some places and things, but not others, are sacred and worthy of care.

Despite the criticisms that have been made of those who perceive, express, and promote understandings of nature as sacred, the impulse to invoke the sacred when expressing deeply held feelings and urging environmental protection is not going away. Rhetoric of the sacred is like profanity—sometimes only the strongest possible language can convey one's most passionately held feelings. There is also a strategic reason that rhetoric of the sacred is often invoked—if one wins the rhetoric-framing battle in environmental disputes, then one's ethical claims are rooted powerfully on sacred ground—and sacred values trump mundane concerns every time.[5]

There may be a deeper, even a logical reason, that in environmental ethics perceptions regarding the sacred, and the strategic deployment of the sacred, have been so important and are not likely to go away. If there is no metaphysical grounding for the perception that life on earth has value—regardless of how extensive that valuation is considered to be—then one could argue that any valuing of nature expresses mere emotion, as many analytic philosophers have done when analyzing emotion-based value claims (following Ayer, 1936). One way that traditionally religious individuals can respond to such a critique is to root environmental values in sacred ground by claiming that a holy being created everything. The book of Genesis in the Hebrew Bible, for example, states that God, after his creative acts, declared that it was all good. This could lead in a straightforward way to a broad ethical principle: Whatever God creates is valuable and should not be destroyed. But why do so many who are skeptical that the universe and Earth were created by some divine agent nevertheless use religious terminology to express their awe, wonder, and love for life, or conversely, dismay and outrage at its destruction?

It may be that there is a twin root for both ethics and religion, in the affective human experience of the value of life and in a corresponding supposition that, without some kind of sacred ground for this experience, the accompanying feelings and values are at best transient and at worst delusional (Ogden, 1963, Phillips, 1966; Crossley, 1978; Taylor 1997).

But ultimately, those who love and value earthly life must choose whom and what to trust. Indeed, we all face what social constructivist theorist Peter Berger once called the "heretical imperative"—which he traced to the Latin root meaning "to choose"—to argue that we must choose whether to find meaning and value in our lives and in the worlds surrounding us (Berger, 1979). Should we embrace an absolute moral relativism or even nihilism, siding with cynics and the skeptics? Or if we have experiences through which we come to value human and other life forms, should we trust those sentiments?

For many, including those who find the mystery underlying the existence of the universe and of life impenetrable, it makes sense to confess a conviction that life on earth is sacred, even if fully understanding the origins of life and the universe itself remains beyond our ken. Many if not most of those who find meaning and virtue in a life caring for and trying to protect life will continue to find sacred ground for both a meaning-filled life and for a reverence-for-life ethics. For many, these are the roots of environmental ethics and, indeed, all ethics.

NOTES

1. Animism is the perception that nature is full of spiritual intelligences, or persons, to whom one owes respect if not also reverence, and with whom one should strive to be in proper relationship if not also communion. Pantheism is the belief that the world as a whole is God or divine.
2. For evidence of Carson's biocentrism and her animism-and-pantheism-resembling spirituality, see Carson (1998: 54–62).
3. For an extended list of references see Taylor (2013b: 142, n5).
4. There are a few scholars affiliated with postmodern and postcolonial schools who are exceptions to the general tendency, including Haraway (2008), Morton (2010), Nixon (2011), Carrigan (2011), Miller (2012), Tsing (2012), and especially Helen Tiffin (Huggan and Tiffin, 2010). Some are even articulating a kind of sacred ground to their theorizing, such as Connolly (2010) and Bennett (2010).
5. Detailing these developments are beyond the scope of the present analysis but two journals have especially focused on these trends, *Worldviews*, and the *Journal for the Study of Religion, Nature and Culture* (see www.religionandnature.com). An encyclopedia and a number of books survey such phenomena (Taylor, 2005; Tucker, 2003; Gottlieb, 2006; Sponsel, 2012).

References

Albanese, C. L. (1990). *Nature Religion in America: From the Algonkian Indians to the New Age.* Chicago: University of Chicago Press.

Ayer, A. J. (1936). *Language, Truth and Logic.* London: V. Gollancz, ltd.

Barlow, C. (1998). "Evolution and the AAAS: A Leading Scientific Organization Considers Religious Interpretations and the Cultural Importance of Modern Scientific Cosmology." *Science and Spirit* 9(1): B12–B13.

Bennett, J. (2010). *Vibrant Matter: A Political Ecology of Things.* Durham, NC: Duke University Press.

Berger, P. (1979). *The Heretical Imperative.* Garden City, NY: Anchor.

Burke, E. (1990 [1757]). *Philosophical Enquiry into the Origin of Our Ideas of the Sublime and Beautiful.* Edited by A. Phillips. Oxford: Oxford World Classics.

Burroughs, J. (2001 [1912]). *Time and Change.* Amsterdam, The Netherlands: Fredonia Books.

Büscher, B. (2013). *Transforming the Frontier: Peace Parks and the Politics of Neoliberal Conservation in Southern Africa.* Durham, NC and London: Duke University Press.

Butler, T. (2002). *Wild Earth: Wild Ideas for a World Out of Balance.* Minneapolis, MN: Milkweed.

Callicott, J. B. (1982). "Hume's Is/Ought Dichotomy." *Environmental Ethics* 4: 173 f.

Callicott, J. B. (1989). *In Defense of the Land Ethic: Essays in Environmental Philosophy.* Albany, NY: State University of New York Press.

Callicott, J. B. (1994). *Earth's Insights: A Survey of Ecological Ethics from the Mediterranean Basin to the Australian Outback.* Berkeley: University of California Press.

Callicott, J. B. (2011). "The Worldview Concept and Aldo Leopold's Project of 'World View' Remediation." *Journal for the Study of Religion, Nature and Culture* 5(4): 509–528.

Callicott, J. B. and Grove-Fanning, W., Rowland, J, Baskind, D, French R. H., Walker, K. (2009). "Was Aldo Leopold a pragmatist? Rescuing Leopold from the imagination of Bryan Norton." *Environmental Values* 18: 453–486.

Callicott, J. B., and Michael P. Nelson (1998). *The Great New Wilderness Debate.* Athens: University of Georgia Press.

Carrigan, A. (2011). *Postcolonial Tourism: Literature, Culture, and Environment.* New York: Routledge.

Carson, R. (1998). *Lost Woods: The Discovered Writings of Rachael Carson.* Edited by L. Lear. Boston: Beacon Press.

Carson, R. (1941). *Under the Sea Wind.* New York: Dutton.

Chidester, D., and Linenthal, D. (1995). "Introduction." In *American Sacred Space*, edited by D. Chidester and E. Linenthal, 1–42. Bloomington: Indiana University Press.

Cohen, M. P. (1984). *The Pathless Way: John Muir and American Wilderness.* Madison: University of Wisconsin Press.

Connolly, W. E. (2010). *Pluralism in Political Analysis.* New Brunswick, NJ: AldineTransaction.

Cronon, W. (1995a). "The Trouble with Wilderness; Or, Getting Back to the Wrong Nature." In *Uncommon Ground: Toward Reinventing Nature*, edited by W. Cronon, 69–90. New York: Norton.

Cronon, W. (1995b). *Uncommon Ground: Toward Reinventing Nature.* New York: Norton.

Crossley, J. P. (1978). "Theological Ethics and the Naturalistic Fallacy." *Journal of Religious Ethics* 6(1): 121–134.

Darwin, C. (2003 [1859/1839]). *On the Origin of Species and the Voyage of the Beagle (with an Introduction by Richard Dawkins)*. New York: Knopf (Everyman's Library). Original ed., *Voyage of the Beagle* originally published in 1839 as his *Journal and Remarks; Origin of Species* first published in 1859.

Denevan, W. M. (1992). "The Pristine Myth: The Landscape of the Americas in 1492." *Annals of the Association of American Geographers 82*(3): 369–385.

Denevan, W. M. (2011). "The 'Pristine Myth' Revisited." *The Geographical Review 101*(4): 576–591.

Dowie, M. (2009). *Conservation Refugees: The Hundred-Year Conflict Between Global Conservation and Native Peoples*. Cambridge, MA: MIT Press.

Durkheim, E. (1965 [1912]). *Elementary Forms of the Religious Life*. New York: Free Press.

Eliade, M. (1959). *The Sacred and the Profane: The Nature of Religion*. New York: Harcourt Brace & World.

Emerson, R. W. (2000 [1836]). *Nature: The Essential Writings of Ralph Waldo Emerson*. New York: The Modern Library.

Evernden, N. (1992). *The Social Creation of Nature*. Baltimore, MD: John Hopkins University Press.

Fletcher, R. (2009). "Against Wilderness." *Green Theory & Praxis: The Journal of Ecopedagogy 5*(1): 169–179.

Fox, S. (1981). *The American Conservation Movement: John Muir and His Legacy*. Madison: University of Wisconsin Press.

Gottlieb, R. S. (2006). *A Greener Faith: Religious Environmentalism and Our Planet's Future*. Oxford and New York: Oxford University Press.

Guha, R. (1989). "Radical American Environmentalism and Wilderness Preservation: A Third-World Critique." *Environmental Ethics 11*: 71–83.

Guha, R. (1997). "The Authoritarian Biologist and the Arrogance of Anti-humanism: Wildlife Conservation in the Third World." *Ecologist 27*: 14–20.

Haraway, D. J. (2008). *When Species Meet, Posthumanities 3*. Minneapolis: University of Minnesota Press.

Huggan, G., and Tiffin, H. (2010). *Postcolonial Ecocriticism: Literature, Animals, Environment*. London & New York: Routledge.

Jacoby, K. (2001). *Crimes against Nature: Squatters, Poachers, Thieves, and the Hidden History of American Conservation*. Berkeley: University of California Press.

Kareiva, P. M. and Marvier, M. (2011). *Conservation Science: Balancing the Needs of People and Nature*. Greenwood Village, Colo.: Roberts and Co.

LaDuke, W. (1999). *All Our Relations: Native Struggles for Land and Life*. Philadelphia, PA: South End Press.

Leopold, A. (1966 [1949]). *A Sand County Almanac with Essays on Conservation from Round River*. Enlarged ed. New York: Sierra Club and Ballantine Books.

Lovelock, J. (1995 [1979]). *Gaia: A New Look at Life on Earth*. Oxford, England and New York, NY: Oxford University Press.

Meine, C. (1988). *Aldo Leopold: His Life and Work*. Madison: University of Wisconsin Press.

Merchant, C. (1980). *The Death of Nature: Women, Ecology and the Scientific Revolution*. San Francisco: Harper & Row.

Miller, J. (2012). *Empire and the Animal Body: Violence, Identity and Ecology in Victorian Adventure Fiction*. London: Anthem Press.

Miller, P. (1956). *Errand into the Wilderness*. Cambridge, MA: Harvard University Press. Reprint, 1986.

Morton, T. (2010). *The Ecological Thought*. Cambridge, MA: Harvard University Press.

Muir, J. (1997 [1911]). "My First Summer in the Sierra." In *Muir: Nature Writings*, edited by W. Cronon, 147–309. New York: The Library of America.

Nash, R. F. (2001 [1967]). *Wilderness and the American Mind*. 4th ed. New Haven: Yale University Press. Original ed., Yale University Press, 1967.

Nelson, M. P. and Callicott, J. B. (2008). *The Wilderness Debate Rages On: Continuing the Great New Wilderness Debate*. Athens, GA: University of Georgia Press.

Nixon, R. (2011). *Slow Violence and the Environmentalism of the Poor*. Cambridge, MA: Harvard University Press.

Noss, R. and Nash, R., Paquet, P., and Soule, M. (2012). "Humanity's Domination of Nature is Part of the Problem: A Response to Kareiva and Marvier" *Biosience* 63(4): 241–242.

Oelschlaeger, M. (1991). *The Idea of Wilderness: From Prehistory to the Age of Ecology*. New Haven: Yale University Press.

Ogden, S. M. (1963). *The Reality of God*. San Francisco: Harper & Row.

Peluso, N. L. (1993). "Coercing Conservation: The Politics of State Resource Control." In *The State and Social Power in Global Environmental Politics*, edited by R. D. Lipschutz. and K. Conca, 46–70. New York: Columbia University Press.

Phillips, D. (1966) "God and Ought." In *Christian Ethics and Contemporary Philosophy*, edited by I. Ramsey, 133–139. London: SCM.

Schweitzer, A. (1936). "The Ethics of Reverence for Life." *Christendom* 1: 225–239. (Available at http://www1.chapman.edu/schweitzer/sch.reading4.html)

Schweitzer, A. (1969). *Reverence for Life*, 1st ed. New York: Harper & Row.

Saler, B. (1993). *Conceptualizing Religion: Immanent Anthropologists, Transcendent Natives, and Unbounded Categories*. Leiden: Brill.

Smith, J. Z. (1987). *To Take Place: Toward Theory in Ritual*. Chicago: University of Chicago Press.

Soulé, M., and Lease, G. (1995) *Reinventing Nature?: Responses to Postmodern Deconstruction*. Washington D.C.: Island Press.

Spence, M. D. (1999). *Dispossessing the Wilderness: Indian Removal and the Making of the National Parks*. New York: Oxford University Press.

Sponsel, L. E. (2012). *Spiritual Ecology: A Quiet Revolution*. Santa Barbara, CA: Praeger.

Sutter, P. S. (2013). "The World With Us: The State of American Environmental History." *Journal of American History* 100(1): 94–119.

Taylor, B. (1995). *Ecological Resistance Movements: The Global Emergence of Radical and Popular Environmentalism*. Albany, NY: State University of New York Press.

Taylor, B. (1997). "On Sacred or Secular Ground? Callicott and Environmental Ethics." *Worldviews* 1(2): 99–112.

Taylor, B. (2010a). *Dark Green Religion: Nature Spirituality and the Planetary Future*. Berkeley and Los Angeles: University of California Press.

Taylor, B. (2010b). "Earth Religion and Radical Religious Reformation." In *Moral Ground: Ethical Action for a Planet in Peril*, edited by K. D. Moore and M. P. Nelson, 379–385. San Antonio, TX: Trinity University Press.

Taylor, B. (2012). "Wilderness, Spirituality and Biodiversity in North America: Tracing an Environmental History from Occidental Roots to Earth Day." In *Wilderness in Mythology and Religion: Approaching Religious Spatialities, Cosmologies, and Ideas of Wild Nature*, edited by L. Feldt, 293–324. Berlin, Germany: De Gruyter.

Taylor, B. (2013a). "Is Green Religion an Oxymoron?: Biocultural Evolution and Earthly Spirituality." In *Ignoring Nature No More: The Case for Compassionate Conservation*, edited by M. Bekoff, 352–360. Chicago: University of Chicago Press.

Taylor, B. (2013b). "Its Not All About Us: Reflections on the State of American Environmental History." *Journal of American History 100*(1): 140–144.

Taylor, B. (2014). "Dangerous Territory: The Contested Perceptual Spaces between Imperial Conservation and Environmental Justice." *RCC (Rachel Carson Center) Perspectives 1*: 117–122.

Taylor, B. (Ed.) (2005). *The Encyclopedia of Religion and Nature*. London and New York: Continuum International.

Tsing, A. (2012). "Unruly Edges: Mushrooms as Companion Species." *Environmental Humanities 1* (November): 141–154.

Tucker, M. E. (2003). *Worldly Wonder: Religions Enter Their Ecological Phase*. LaSalle, IL: Open Court.

Warren, L. S. (1997). *The Hunter's Game: Poachers and Conservationists in Twentieth-Century America*. New Haven, CT: Yale University Press.

White, L. (1967). "The Historic Roots of Our Ecologic Crisis." *Science 155*: 1203–1207.

Wilson, E. O. (1978). *On Human Nature*. Cambridge, MA: Harvard University Press.

Wilson, E. O. (1984). *Biophilia*. Cambridge, MA: Harvard University Press.

Worster, D. (1994 [1977]). *Nature's Economy: A History of Ecological Ideas,* 2nd ed. Cambridge, MA: Cambridge University Press.

PART V

KEY CONCEPTS

*Tools for Framing
and Addressing Problems*

CHAPTER 22

....

INDIVIDUAL AND CONTRIBUTORY RESPONSIBILITY FOR ENVIRONMENTAL HARM

....

KENNETH SHOCKLEY

1 CLEANING UP OUR MESS

....

OUR responsibilities are commonplace. When we make a mess we are responsible for clean-ing it up. When we break something we are responsible for fixing it, replacing it, or providing some accommodation for the loss. Nearly as clear is the intuition that if by performing some action we can prevent some harm from happening—or even make that harm less likely—we have a responsibility to perform that action. These intuitions are focused on what we might be responsible *for*, rather than the thorny metaphysical and conceptual issues associated with what it is to *be* responsible. Yet even these intuitions are not as clear in the context of environmental ethics.

In what follows, my particular focus will be on what has become a standard set of con-cerns for normal individualistic accounts of moral responsibility, collective action problems. Along the way we will briefly consider some of the distinctive challenges that environmental contexts pose for traditional accounts of responsibility. This will bring us to one of the great environmental problems of our age, climate change. Intuitively, it might seem that we each bear some responsibility for the harms of climate change. Yet Sinnott-Armstrong (2005) has argued that there is no principle on which to base an individual *obligation* to reduce emis-sions and so, to this extent, individual agents are not morally responsible for the collective harms caused by climate change. In this short chapter I will gesture toward a response to this seemingly counterintuitive position and suggest the form responsibility should take in troubling cases of responsibility for disparate environmental harms. I will suggest that our responsibilities include not just matters of what we have done but also how we might influence the wide range of institutions and practices that can influence harm and benefit. We should expect cases of direct responsibility for harm, with a clear causal chain between one agent and another, to be less prevalent features of our moral landscape than cases where individuals play contributory roles in generating conditions that lead to harms or play parts in conventions or institutions that bring about harms. These cases constitute instances of *indirect* responsibility; our connection to harm in such cases is meditated by networks of relationships, institutions, or other intermediaries.

2 RESPONSIBILITY

As traditionally understood, moral responsibility involves not only causal responsibility but also blameworthiness. The reason for this is clear: as moral responsibility involves the attribution of praise or blame, a form of ownership of an action over which one is being praised or blamed is required. An individual is *causally* responsible insofar as they brought about a state of affairs. As one's efforts to bring about that end can be more or less satisfactory, responsibilities can be more or less fulfilled (Goodin, 1986). An individual is *morally* responsible insofar as they brought about that state of affairs with a blameworthy or praiseworthy or otherwise relevant frame of mind in doing what they did. If our actions were performed negligently, or maliciously, or callously, or in some other morally salient way, then, coupled with causal responsibility, we would often be taken to be morally responsible. In short, we are morally responsible for those states of affairs we have (causally) brought about in such a way and to such a degree that we are deserving of praise or blame.

This appeal to agency and frames of mind captures the sense that if one does something for which one is morally responsible, then it would seem one must have chosen or intended to do that for which one is morally responsible. As Jamieson claims, moral responsibility typically involves cases where "an individual acting intentionally harms another individual; both the individual and the harm are identifiable" (Jamieson, 2010: 436). It is commonly thought that for one to be morally responsible one must have intentionally performed or otherwise been in possession of a potentially culpable state of mind when performing that action.

But this is much too quick. We can be responsible for states of affairs that we did not, at least directly or clearly, choose or intend to bring about. I can be responsible for omissions, for example, or for traits of character I have developed (for good or ill). I may be responsible not only for the pollution that I generate, but also for pollution I could prevent but let occur (e.g., not only the pollution generated while driving and but also pollution generated from failing to install a more efficient furnace). As Aristotle (1984: 1113b2–1114a12) made clear, I can be responsible for failing to habituate myself properly; I can be responsible for failing to generate the right sort of habitual behaviors that would motivate me to drive less or install more efficient appliances.

Indirect responsibilities are made yet more complex in the context of environmental harms, as many of those harms only exist as a result the contribution of many individuals (Shockley, 2013).[1] As we have seen, traditional accounts of individual responsibility are fairly straightforward: an individual agent is responsible for what they have done (causally) in a certain (blameworthy or praiseworthy) frame of mind. Contributory or distributive responsibility involves cases where individuals are responsible for their contribution to a state of affairs that only occurs through the accumulated effects of the actions of others. Any responsibility incurred as a result of this contribution is typically distributed according to that contribution. Whether this sort of responsibility rises to the level of moral responsibility rests on whether we take the contribution to be blameworthy or not. The difficulties associated with settling on the level of responsibility to be attributed to contributing individuals in complex cases constitutes the central challenge for understanding and applying moral responsibility in environmental ethics.

Given the typically complex relation between individual agents and environment harms, we should expect individualistic approaches to moral responsibility, where responsibility is spelled out in terms of the harms one individual does to another, to be particularly unsatisfying. In a related context, O'Neill, Holland, and Light note,

> Responsibility is individualized not simply in the sense that it is assigned to specific agents, but also because it is assigned only for particular acts in virtue of particular individual decisions or choices. If one focuses merely on the particular decisions that lead to particular acts, the primary responsibility for action is lost sight of. From that perspective, many acts of environmental damage get assigned to the category of "accidents" for which no one is held responsible; . . . The problem here lies in taking specific acts and decisions as the primary object of appraisal. (O'Neill, Holland, and Light, 2008)

In environmental contexts those things for which we can be held responsible are markedly various, diffuse, and theoretically awkward (Jamieson, 2008). Here I set aside the complicated and conceptually challenging matter of whether the environment or specific features of the nonhuman environment might be something with intrinsic value, and that therefore can be harmed in a morally relevant way (Routley, 1973; Regan, 1983; Taylor, 1986; Rolston, 1988; Elliot, 1997).[2] Regardless of whether features of the environment have intrinsic value, we might well be responsible for the condition of those features. We might be responsible for the state of an ecosystem, responding to an environmental catastrophe, protecting a resource, saving a valley . . . the familiar list continues. Often we rely on a range of principles and heuristics to provide a set of defeasible guidelines for characterizing our responsibilities. These principles—encapsulated in ideals such as polluter pays, do no harm, protect the vulnerable, provide opportunities, promote well-being, enable opportunities—capture a diffuse set of considerations that shape both our intuitive and our more reflectively informed attributions of responsibility.

A characteristic example of environmental harm can be seen in acid rain. The production of energy, through the use of power plants fueled by sulfur-containing coal, generates enormous quantities of toxic compounds. When released into the atmosphere these compounds form sulfuric acid, better known as acid rain. From the damages to forests to fisheries to limestone cathedrals and monuments, there are adverse consequences to acid rain. Regardless of how the damage is characterized, the obvious *causal* source of the damage would seem to be the power plant itself. Of course the power plant is not responsible for harm done in any *moral* sense. An agent is required for that. The usual culprits are often taken to be the principals of the companies that run the plants, or even sometimes the companies themselves.

However, those generating the power are also responding to a demand, created not only by those who have a vested interest in the growth of these industries, but also by those who use the power they generate. It is too easy to let those of us who use the products of a polluting industry or problematic practice off the hook. I do not mean to imply that operators, owners, and managers of grossly polluting plants can adequately respond to charges of responsibility with the tired, "just responding to demand" or the banal, "just doing my job." Nor do I mean to exclude or ignore the influence of powerful political, social, and economic constituencies. There is more than enough responsibility to go around; in most cases of environmental harm, responsibility is distributed widely even when there is an obvious culpable party. The broadened notion of responsibility I am here advocating responds to just this network of individual, social, and political factors. In environmental contexts, the importance of aggregate harms and collectivization problems become much more the norm in our understanding of responsibility. Indeed, Bryan Norton (1995, 2003) has argued that all environmental problems are at their root collectivization problems, versions of the tragedy of the commons, or what I have described here as problems in attributing contributory responsibility for aggregate harms.

3   THE TRAGEDY OF COLLECTIVE ACTION PROBLEMS

Assigning contributory responsibility for collectively produced harms requires a consideration of the tragedy of the commons. The modern interpretation of the tragedy of the commons comes from Garrett Hardin's (1968) analysis of the depletion of a shared resource by the individualistically rational decisions of those who utilize that resource. As any cost (damage) to the commons is distributed across all users and any benefit from using the commons is held by the individual user alone, there is a rational incentive for individuals to exploit the resource. As all members are subject to this incentive structure, the rational consequence is the depletion of that common resource—which may be a field, a fishery, a pollution sink, or most any environmental resource (Ostrom, 1990).[3] Without constraint on individual freedom to use that common resource, environmental harm is the result. What is in our common interest is not necessarily what is in an individual's interest (Sagoff, 1988).[4]

How does this affect our moral responsibilities? Surely we have a responsibility not to contribute to these environmental harms. Yet as whatever harm or damage that might occur might still occur even if our own activity stops, it seems odd to say we have a responsibility to stop that activity. Indeed, the sense in which we "contribute" to such a harm is unclear. Without the ability to prevent that harm by refraining from directly contributing to it, in what sense could we be blameworthy for contributing to it? While our contribution is causally efficacious in some indirect and limited sense, our failing to contribute will not prevent the harm from occurring. Insofar as we can only be obligated to do what we are able to do— "ought" implies "can"—and the barrier generated by such collective action problems blocks our ability to affect the relevant harm, it would seem we have no corresponding responsibilities. Or at least so concludes the critique of individual responsibility on the basis of the tragedy of the commons.

However, as a matter of practice, we *do* resolve collective action problems (Axelrod, 1984, 1997; see also Ostrom, 1990), and we *do* recognize responsibility for contributing to those resolutions (or failing to do so). Any substantial contribution seems to make us at least in part causally responsible for the harm (we *did* something that contributed to a harm) and as we intentionally performed an action knowing that a risk of harm would result, we seem morally responsible as well. So it is a mistake to think our responsibilities are dissolved simply because we are faced with a collective action problem or because we cannot evade the complex institutional intermediaries between our actions and an indirectly and diffused set of harmful consequences (Gardiner, 2011b.).[5] If one faces a tragedy, one has a responsibility to undermine the conditions enabling that tragedy. When Leopold (Leopold, 1949/1989) famously describes farmers in Wisconsin acting in their short-term interest to the detriment of their individual and common long-term interest, a typical reaction is that the farmers have some responsibility to change the framework that encourages them to sacrifice the long-term health of their land for short-term economic gain. They should do what they can to make these changes; as Leopold (Leopold, 1949/1989: 209–210) noted, they should be motivated by an ecological conscience to do so, even if they have no financial incentive to do so. They may not be so motivated, but they should be. We are responsible for doing our best to find a solution, and to say that we have no personal responsibility because the problem is too big is ethical laziness. Such laziness constitutes a vice (Thompson, 2012). The perniciousness of that vice is particularly striking in the context of climate change.

4 RESPONSIBILITY AND CLIMATE CHANGE

Climate change is a moral issue on many dimensions. Our changing climate brings with it not only the uncertainties and risks associated with a changing environment but also predictable suffering. As sea levels rise, as extreme weather events become ever more normal, and as droughts and flooding patterns change, the lives of millions will be adversely affected (IPCC, 2012; NRC, 2012). As the state of greenhouse gases in our atmosphere is both seemingly under our control and the causal source of climate change, matters of moral responsibility seem clearly relevant. Gardiner (2011a) argues that climate change constitutes one of the gravest ethical challenges facing humanity today, in large part because of the difficulties in recognizing our responsibilities across the "moral storms" of contemporary coordination problems, intergenerational buck-passing, and our inability to make theoretical sense of a problem with the scale of global climate change. Yet the scale and complexity of climate change has led some theorists (Jamieson, 1992, 2012) to claim that we need to rethink our account of responsibility. On this view, old models of responsibility, built as they are on proximate person-to-person actions, are simply not appropriate for a time when the greatest harms are done across vast geographical, temporal, and even institutional distance.

The challenge posed by climate change as a collective action problem of such a large scale has led at least one theorist, Walter Sinnott-Armstrong (2005), to conclude that given our best current understanding of responsibility we simply cannot conclude that we each have an individual obligation to reduce our contribution to climate change. Following our earlier discussion, Sinnott-Armstrong claims that because of the scale of the problem and the role of institutional actors there is no way for our individual actions to have an effect on the overall concentration of atmospheric carbon. He concludes that because changes in our individual behaviors will not have any effect on the harms resulting from climate change, there are no grounds for an individual obligation to prohibit activities that produce "excessive" amounts of carbon.

The traditional requirement that we (causally) trace the consequences of individual actions back to responsible parties presents an even greater challenge. Greenhouse gasses produced by individuals are screened, as it were, by the institutions that both make climate policy and create the framework for responding to the harms that climate change generates. As these political institutions provide the source of any substantial change in emissions, any obligation we might have to address those harms, says, Sinnott-Armstrong, must be political. We might well have an obligation to work for political change, but we do not have an obligation to reduce our individual emissions. While I do not have sufficient space to survey the many excellent arguments put forth in response to Sinnott-Armstrong, it is worth noting that most focus on the relative unimportance of the institutional barriers for matters of morality. The usual strategy taken in response seems to be that the institutions that shape and make the policies and political responses to climate change cannot reshape the moral terrain as profoundly as Sinnott-Armstrong seems to think (see, for example, Hiller, 2011; Nolt, 2011; Hourdequin, 2010). However, his retreat to exclusively political obligations, I suggest, is motivated by an account of moral obligation that is excessively individualistic and excessively tied to direct causal connections.

Sinnott-Armstrong uses the deontic term, "obligation," to point to any individual responsibility one might have for mitigating the harms produced through gratuitous emissions of greenhouse gasses. Deontic terms, the key normative elements in judgments about what one *ought* to do, carry with them an appeal to the commanding, binding, individualistic nature of obligations. Often tied to commitments like promising, or cases of interpersonal affront, they are broadly directed *at* individuals (Shockley, 2008; Darwall, 2004), commanding us to behave in accordance with morality (however construed). And they bind us as individuals. The deontic tenor points to a close tie between what one is constrained to do (say, not harming others) and the grounds (harming others constitutes a moral wrong and therefore ought to be avoided). In cases like promise keeping and personal injury, this model is compelling. However, if we apply this model to purported individual obligations for climate change, it seems much less compelling. Once this account is relaxed, a more holistic approach to our responsibilities is possible, one that encompasses both direct individual responsibilities for harms done and our capacities to have an indirect effect on the circumstances of others. In the next section I will suggest that a better response to Sinnott-Armstrong is found by reconsidering the indirect effects we can have on our emissions by influencing institutions and other collective entities as part of a larger suite of moral responsibilities. We need not revert to the political to accommodate the importance of our capacity to influence institutions.

The traditional account of responsibility is at least partly right: we need to have *some* causal influence for responsibility to take hold. But that influence might be indirect, by means of our causal influence on institutions or on the behavior of others. We should consider the different ways we might influence, indirectly, the state of the world. Perhaps our actions do not have the direct consequence of decreasing harmful emissions. But they might lead indirectly to a world with fewer emissions through changing practices and modifying institutions. A broadened notion of responsibility, one focused less on what we have done and more on what we might do, allows individuals to be more centrally involved in changing the institutions and background conditions that make climate change so problematic. Thinking of responsibility in terms of how we can positively influence current and future conditions, rather than the past actions that have given us our responsibilities, provides a better way of understanding our individual moral responsibility for complex environmental problems like climate change.

5 INDIVIDUAL CONTRIBUTION TO COLLECTIVE HARMS

Making sense of individual obligations for harms attributable to institutions and social groups engaged in some practice is exceedingly difficult. However, I suspect much of this difficulty stems from thinking of institutions and other organizational entities as ontological intermediaries, as collectives formed to resolve collective action problems.[6] Collectives, understood this way, are thought to *block* our individual responsibilities for these large-scale environmental harms. Either they make it difficult or impossible to actualize change, or they play the role of actors who are the proper bearers of responsibility, perversely offsetting individual responsibility. I suspect the complex problem of collectives-as-intermediaries, coupled with a direct-causal-influence model of responsibility, leads to Sinnott-Armstrong's rejection of certain individual responsibilites.

However, institutions and other collective entities are not just mereological compositions of individuals. They are also instruments, means by which further ends are promoted. Thinking of them as means to our individual and collective ends should lead us to a different way of understanding the relationship between institutions and individual responsibilities. Just as we can be indirectly responsible for the actions we commit because of a weakness of character we allowed to come into being, so can we be indirectly responsible for failing to generate the sorts of institutional structures and political mechanisms that would enable us to prevent predictable harm. We may be indirectly responsible for failing to put into place the right sort of institutions. Even if the challenge of bringing these alternative institutions and policies into place is great, as the most available means of avoiding a harm we have a responsibility, an *individual* responsibility, to try.

Often the most efficient available means of bringing about the reduction or even prevention of a clear and recognizable harm is by making changes in the background political system or by influencing cultural norms. Sinnott-Armstrong claims that we may well have *this* obligation, the obligation to make changes in the political framework pursuant to making changes in global emissions. But his treatment of responsibility is incomplete, as it ignores indirect moral responsibility and the moral responsibilities we have for institutional and cultural change. As agents are capable of bringing about political change, they have a responsibility to do so rooted in their own individual moral responsibility to prevent the generation of an aggregate harm. If they fail to generate those institutions, then they have failed to do all that they might do to prevent a harm from occurring. Failing to work to make changes to the background conditions enabling harm is blameworthy in just the way that one is blameworthy for failing to improve one's character, when one is able. Harms resulting from an unimproved character, which could have been improved, are harms for which we are blameworthy.

It might be objected that I have begged the question by denying precisely the point Sinnott-Armstrong was trying to make, namely, that we do not, in fact, contribute to the harms resulting from elevated emissions. For Sinnott-Armstrong, the harms of climate change will occur even without one's action; as one's action makes no difference in the harm, one cannot be responsible for that harm. Your "contribution" is not causally efficacious in the production of that harm, your contribution cannot obviously be tied, directly, to blame without rethinking the nature of the responsibilities at play. Just such a "rethinking" is what I suggest is needed. I have not presumed that individuals are blameworthy for their individual emissions. The culpability, the blameworthiness associated with individual responsibility comes from failing to do what one can to change background and peripheral conditions such that the harm fails to materialize or is mitigated. I agree with Sinnott-Armstrong that satisfying my responsibilities to prevent the harms associated with carbon emissions cannot be fully satisfied by curbing my own emissions; the risk remains even if I have done what I can to eliminate my individual emissions (see also Broome, 2012). However, as individuals, we can and should do more to ensure that the harm is prevented or minimized. We can compel our governments to generate both policies that reduce or eliminate emissions more generally and policies that help us adapt to a changing world. Admittedly in the current political climate this is a substantial task. But the harm is equally substantial. That the task is difficult can surely not, of itself, absolve us of the task. The difficulty aggravates the harm, and so should motivate us all the more.

The core principle is simply that if one can do something to prevent a harm from occurring then one has a prima facie reason to do that thing. If one has a readily available means of reducing or minimizing a substantial harm, even if the probability of successful intervention is low, one has a responsibility to pursue it. Of course, the strength of this prima facie reason is contingent on a range of contextual matters. However, the harms associated with climate change are potentially catastrophic. The effort involved with affecting the harm is small by comparison to that harm, even if the probability of one's contribution making a substantial change is small. If there is an available means of making a change for the better, then one would be doing something wrong if one failed to pursue that means. This applies to changes we might make in the political realm as much as (and as well as) those we might in our individual lives.

6 INSTITUTIONS, SOCIAL PRACTICES, AND INDIVIDUAL RESPONSIBILITY

Jamieson suggested that the scale and scope of climate change leads to a novel problem, "the possibility that the global environment may be destroyed; yet no one will be responsible" (Jamieson, 2012). This would be a terrifying state of affairs. Fortunately, the actual state of affairs is not so terrifying. It is possible to lessen or even eliminate the most severe harms of climate change (and most other related environmental harms). But thus far we have failed to bring about the means necessary to address a severe and recognized problem. This is a moral failure, both individually and collectively. The focus should be on whether we did our part, as individuals, in affecting what changes we could to minimize or remove harm. Perhaps our part includes not just political action (Sinnott-Armstrong, 2005) or institutional reform (Gardiner, 2011a) or character development (Jamieson, 2012; Thompson, 2012), but also our individual contributory acts (Hiller, 2011). There is enough responsibility to go around, at both the collective and the individual level. That there are reasons that we have trouble instituting the right sort of collective responses because we, in aggregate, failed to institute the right sort of institutions, should not let us off the hook, as individuals, for doing our part in bringing about the institutional, political, and personal changes that could prevent or mitigate great harm. If our current transportation system compels us to drive long distances to work, we can work not only to minimize our driving under the constraints of that system but also to reform that system through social and political efforts. Insofar as that system leads to substantial harm, my suggestion is that we have a moral responsibility to take both actions.

We are living in an era in which few of our actions are not moderated by institutons. Here I argue that we have a responsibility to respond appropriately to those means likely to enable a positive response to the (recognizable) harms formed by the aggregation of our individual behaviors. We have a responsibility, an *individual moral* responsibility to do what we can to install the sort of institutions and social practices capable of engendering the conditions whereby harms are avoided. This provides for a way of keeping moral responsibility in the heads of individual agents and maintaining a distinctive and robust role for individuals in addressing their contributory responsibility for massive collective harms. We have responsibility where we have a reasonable chance of undermining the production of harms, whether direct or indirect, whether certain or not. Only by acting in accordance with this broad array of responsibilities, I claim, can we address the great collective action problems that are increasingly indicative of our age.

As with many other contemporary instances of environmental harm, the responsibilities we have for addressing climate change are complex and indirect. In such cases it is only through complex institutions that our responsibilities can be satisfied. Yet the influence of institutions and collective entities is not new. Our responsibilities to ensure these institutions do what they should do are not new either. If not for our capacity to take responsibility for the institutions that coordinate our actions and inform our practices, Jamieson (1992, 2012) may be right that we are without the theoretical apparatus necessary to understand our individual responsibilities for problems like climate change. But we do have the theoretical apparatus available to address these responsibilities and to understand what we have individual responsibility to do (Shockley, 2012). The concerns about the efficacy of individual actions with respect to climate change loomed large in Sinnott-Armstrong's work. As well they should. But approaching our moral responsibilities in terms of the possible ways we might influence the production of harms (or the provision of benefits) provides a better way of addressing the complex interwoven problems of our modern world. Retrospective accounts of responsibility-as-obligation tied to strict causal models of our direct contribution to harms fail to capture the wide range of possible contributions to harm. A more comprehensive account of responsibility is needed.

While my focus here has been for the most part on climate change, the point is broadly applicable to a wide range of cases where morally innocuous actions, when aggregated, lead to harmful consequences without a clear causal chain. In issues spanning population growth, overfishing, urban sprawl, deforestation, and the loss of species, we can see these concerns reflected throughout environmental ethics. Many of our responsibilities are complex, requiring that we both make changes in our own behavior and agitate for changes in the policies and practices that regulate that behavior. These responsibilities are not easily reduced to traditional person-to-person models. Whether or not we have an obligation to change our individual behavior and practices to reduce our emissions, we certainly have an individual moral responsibility to ensure there are policies in place to restrict our behaviors such that the harms that result from our aggregated individual activities are minimized. And this lesson extends across the purview of environmental ethics. Our responsibilities may require that we do better than Leopold's Wisconsinite farmers, who had yet to integrate their scientific understanding of the world with their moral sensibilities. Let us hope that the responsibilities we acknowledge reflect a more robust ecological conscience, a conscience appropriate for the large scale problems of the anthropocene.

NOTES

1. For the contrast between individual responsibility, contributory responsibility, and collective responsibility see Shockley (2013).
2. For accounts that hold nature to have intrinsic value see Routley (1973), Regan (1983), Taylor (1986), Rolston (1988), Elliott (1997).
3. For one now classic critique of Hardin's account of the Tragedy see Ostrom (1990).
4. Compare Mark Sagoff's *The Economy of the Earth* (Sagoff, 1988) on the contrast between our roles as citizen and consumer.
5. For a discussion of this challenge and response, see Gardiner's (2011b) response to Jamieson (1992, 2012).
6. This is one theme of Gardiner's (2011b) response to Jamieson (1992, 2010, 2012).

REFERENCES

Aristotle. (1984). *The Complete Works of Aristotle: The Revised Oxford Translation, Vol. 2*, edited by J. Barnes. Princeton, NJ: Princeton University Press.
Axelrod, R. (1984). *The Evolution of Cooperation*. New York: Basic Books.
Axelrod, R. (1997). *The Complexity of Cooperation*. Princeton, NJ: Princeton University Press.
Broome, J. (2012). *Climate Matters: Ethics in a Warming World* (Amnesty International Global Ethics Series), New York: W.W. Norton.
Darwall, S. (2004). *The Second-Person Standpoint*. Cambridge, MA: Harvard University Press.
Elliot, R. (1997). Faking Nature. London: Routledge.
Gardiner, S. M. (2011a). *A Perfect Moral Storm: The Ethical Tragedy of Climate Change*. New York: Oxford University Press.
Gardiner, S. M. (2011b). "Is No One Responsible for Global Environmental Tragedy? Climate Change as a Challenge to Our Ethical Concepts." In *The Ethics of Global Climate Change*, edited by D. G. Arnold. 38–59. Cambridge: Cambridge University Press.
Goodin, R. E. (1986). "Responsibilities." *The Philosophical Quarterly* 36(142): 50–56.
Hardin, G. (1968). "The Tragedy of the Commons." *Science* 162(3859): 1243–1248.
Hiller, A. (2011). "Climate Change and Individual Responsibility." *The Monist* 94(3): 349–368.
Hourdequin, M. (2010). "Climate, Collective Action and Individual Ethical Obligations." *Environmental Values* 19(4): 443–464.
IPCC (2012). "Summary for Policymakers." In *Managing the Risks of Extreme Events and Disasters to Advance Climate Change Adaptation*, edited by C. B. Field, V. Barros, T. F. Stocker, D. Qin, D. J. Dokken, K. L. Ebi, . . . P. M. Midgley. New York: Cambridge University Press.

Jamieson, D. (1992). "Ethics, Public Policy, and Global Warming." *Science, Technology & Human Values* 17(2): 139–153.

Jamieson, D. (2008). *Ethics and the Environment: An Introduction.* New York: Cambridge University Press.

Jamieson, D. (2010). "Climate change, responsibility, and justice." *Science and Engineering Ethics* 16(3): 431–445.

Jamieson, D. (2012). "Ethics, Public Policy, and Global Warming." In *Ethical Adaptation to Climate Change: Human Virtues of the Future,* edited by A. Thompson and J. Bendik-Keymer, 139–153. Cambridge, MA: MIT Press.

Leopold, A. (1949/1989). *Sand County Almanac: And Sketches Here and There.* New York: Oxford University Press.

National Research Council (NRC) (2012). *Alternatives for Managing the Nation's Complex Contaminated Groundwater Sites.* Washington, DC: The National Academies Press.

Nolt, J. (2011). "How Harmful Are the Average American's Greenhouse Gas Emissions?" *Ethics, Policy and Environment* 14(1): 3–10.

Norton, B. (2003). *Searching for Sustainability: Interdisciplinary Essays in the Philosophy of Conservation Biology.* New York: Cambridge University Press.

Norton, B. (1995). "Ecological Integrity and Social Values: At What Scale." *Ecosystem Health* 1(4): 228–241.

O'Neill, J., A. Holland, and A. Light (Eds.) (2008). *Environmental Values.* New York: Routledge.

Ostrom, E. (1990). *Governing the Commons: The Evolution of Institutions for Collective Action.* New York: Cambridge University Press.

Regan, T. (1983). *The Case for Animal Rights.* London: Routledge & Kegan Paul.

Rolston, H. (1988). *Environmental Ethics: Duties to and Values in the Natural World.* Philadelphia, PA: Temple University Press.

Routley, R. (1973). "Is There a Need for a New, an Environmental Ethic?" *Proceedings of the 15th World Congress of Philosophy,* 1: 205–210. Sophia, Bulgaria: Sophia Press.

Sagoff, M. (1988). *The Economy of the Earth: Philosophy, Law, and the Environment.* New York: Cambridge University Press.

Shockley, K. (2008). "On That Peculiar Practice of Promising." *Philosophical Studies* 140(3): 385–399.

Shockley, K. (2012). "Human Values and Institutional Responses to Climate Change." In *Ethical Adaptation to Climate Change: Human Virtues of the Future,* edited by A. Thompson and J. Bendik-Keymer, 281–298. Cambridge, MA: MIT Press.

Shockley, K. (2013). "Collective Responsibility." *The International Encyclopedia of Ethics,* edited by H. LaFollette. Oxford: Wiley-Blackwell.

Sinnott-Armstrong, W. (2005). "It's Not My Fault: Global Warming and Individual Moral Obligations." *Perspectives on Climate Change: Science, Economics, Politics, Ethics,* edited by W. Sinnott-Armstrong and R. Howarth, 221–253. Amsterdam: Elsevier.

Taylor, P. (1986). *Respect for Nature.* Princeton, NJ: Princeton University Press.

Thompson, A. (2012). "The Virtue of Responsibility for the Global Climate." *Ethical Adaptation to Climate Change: Human Virtues of the Future,* edited by A. Thompson and J. Bendik-Keymer, 203–222. Cambridge, MA: MIT Press.

CHAPTER 23

··

JUSTICE ON ONE PLANET

··

DEREK BELL

JUSTICE is the dominant value in contemporary liberal political theories and liberalism is the dominant ideology in the contemporary world. The concept of justice is, of course, contested with many different conceptions of justice proposed by liberal theorists (Barry, 1995; Dworkin, 2002; Nagel, 1991; Rawls, 1972). Some critics of contemporary liberalism have also proposed competing conceptions of justice while others have disputed the primacy of justice (Fraser, 1997; Sandel, 1982; Young, 1990). Notwithstanding the more radical critics, "justice" and "injustice" claims remain pervasive in contemporary moral and political discourse. Therefore, it is no surprise that some parts of the environmental movement have adopted the language of justice.

The most obvious example is the environmental justice movement, which began in the United States when community activists campaigning against local pollution established national networks (Schlosberg, 1999; Shrader-Frechette, 2002). The environmental justice movement has subsequently expanded both "horizontally" to tackle environmental injustices in other countries and "vertically" to campaign against international environmental injustices (Schlosberg, 2013; Walker, 2012). Activist academics, such as Robert Bullard, played a leading role in the early development of the idea of environmental justice and, in the last 20 years, moral and political theorists, as well as sociologists, geographers, and other social scientists have developed richer theoretical conceptions of environmental justice (Bullard, 1993; Bullard, 2000; Schlosberg, 2013). The common feature of most (but not all) of these accounts is that environmental justice is an anthropocentric ideal: it is concerned with the distribution of environmental benefits and burdens among humans and fair participation for humans in decision making about how those benefits and burdens are distributed (Schlosberg, 2013; Walker, 2012). In contrast, some theorists have proposed an ideal of "ecological justice" (Baxter, 2005; Dobson, 1998). Ecological justice is non-anthropocentric: it is concerned with the fair treatment of both human and non-human entities.

This chapter has two aims. First, I consider the contribution that the concept of justice might make to environmental ethics. I outline three important issues in environmental ethics that a theory of justice is likely to address. However, I also acknowledge two reasons that might be offered for not using the notion of justice in environmental ethics. The second aim of the chapter is to think about the general characteristics of a justice-based approach to environmental ethics. My approach is to consider how taking the environment seriously might challenge contemporary liberal theories of justice. I distinguish three sets of challenges for liberal theories. The first set of challenges raises issues that are already central to debates within mainstream liberalism. The second set of challenges raises issues that have been important in debates between liberals and their (non-environmentalist) critics. The third set of challenges concerns how liberals conceive of the environment. I argue that the liberal conception of the environment is not compatible with our best scientific understanding of the environment and does not pay sufficient attention to the many morally relevant ways that we value the environment. I suggest that a theory of *justice on one planet*—that is, an environmentally or ecologically aware theory of justice whether it is, in the conventional terminology, a theory of environmental justice or of ecological justice—will be significantly different from the theories of justice that have dominated liberal political and moral theory for the last fifty years.

1 The Contribution of Justice to Environmental Ethics

The concept of justice can help us to clarify our thinking about three of the most difficult issues in environmental ethics. First, *which entities* should we treat as subjects of justice to whom we can have duties of justice (Dobson, 1998)? Most theories in environmental ethics have an account of which entities have moral status. For example, an anthropocentric ethic gives moral status only to humans, while a biocentric ethic attributes moral status to living organisms and an ecocentric ethic may also attribute moral status to ecosystems. A justice-based approach to environmental ethics requires that we decide which entities are included within the "scope" of a theory of justice so that we have duties of justice toward them (Jones, 1999: 5; Shue, 1983: 602). Given the primacy attributed to justice in contemporary moral and political theory, we might reasonably think that the claim that we have duties of justice toward an entity is the strongest moral claim that can be made on behalf of that entity.

Second, *which interests* of subjects of justice have sufficient moral significance to justify treating them as justice-relevant interests? A justice-based approach to environmental ethics requires that we distinguish interests that are justice-relevant from interests that may be morally relevant but are not sufficiently important to generate duties of justice. Our contemporary understanding of justice implies that justice-relevant interests typically generate stringent duties, whereas other morally relevant interests may generate no more than *prima facie* duties, which can be overridden by duties of justice (Barry, 1991).

Third, *what principles* of justice should we use to adjudicate between the competing claims of subjects of justice (Dobson, 1998)? The reconciliation of competing interests has sometimes been identified as a particular problem for environmental ethics (Baxter, 2005; Bell, 2006; Dobson, 2000). For example, how should we reconcile the interests of the current generation with all future generations (Dasgupta, 2005; DeGeorge, 1981)? Or how should we reconcile the interests of a human and the smallpox virus or a lion and a lamb (Baxter, 1999; Wissenburg, 2011)? A justice-based approach to environmental ethics addresses this problem because theories of justice are fundamentally concerned with the reconciliation of the competing moral claims of subjects of justice.

An account of justice that takes these issues seriously and offers answers to our three questions will take a substantive position in environmental ethics. For short, and to avoid choosing between the terms "environmental justice" and "ecological justice," I will refer to such environmentally or ecologically aware theories of justice as theories of "justice on one planet." If we adopt a justice-based approach to environmental ethics, our main concern will be to consider the relative merits of competing theories of justice on one planet.

However, a justice-based approach might be resisted by some environmental ethicists for two reasons. First, it might be considered hubristic because it implies that moral agents are capable of some form of "planetary management" (Orr, 1992: 54). Justice is a social practice. It is an ideal that we use to regulate social relations (Anderson, 1999; Tan, 2011). Ideals of environmental or ecological justice suggest that we should also seek to regulate the environment or non-human entities that are in, or part of, the environment. Some environmentalists might reasonably worry that this is hubristic (Litfin, 1997; Purser, 1997). The extension of the idea of justice to the environment seems to invert the relationship between the social and the environmental. We see the environment as part of the social world under the management of human institutions rather than social relations and institutions as existing in and shaped by the environment. I will discuss this issue further in section 3, where I will argue that a theory of justice on one planet should adopt a more modest conception of the relationship between moral agents and the environment.

The second objection is that justice is the wrong value to regulate relations between moral agents and the environment. Justice has been described as a "remedial virtue," which regulates relations between individuals when more positive virtues or values, such as love, care, fraternity, solidarity, community or belonging, are too weak to support relationships within a community (Sandel, 1982, 31). For some environmentalists, the atomism of a justice-based approach, in which moral agents are seen as separate entities whose relationships with each other require regulation, is problematic. It is a mistake to try to identify separate entities and then regulate the relations between them because the entities are not separate but rather part of a larger whole that is constituted by their mutual relationships (Leopold, 1949). On a holistic conception of the environment and our place in it the relationships between parts are based on values such as belonging or solidarity rather than justice. This is an important objection but we should be careful to avoid conflating a holistic and a systemic conception of the environment. We can recognize the systemic character of the environment without denying that the parts have independent moral significance. I discuss the implications of the systemic character of the environment for a theory of justice on one planet in section 3.

In sum, a justice-based approach will not be acceptable to all environmental ethicists, but it has sufficient merit to justify closer examination.

2 Six Challenges for Liberal Theories of Justice

The discussion of justice in contemporary political theory is dominated by liberal theorists, who have often paid little attention to environmental issues. In this section, I identify six challenges for liberal theories of justice that follow from taking the environment seriously.

First, the most important late twentieth century liberal theories of justice paid most attention to the distribution of resources, usually understood as natural resources or income and wealth, but they paid little or no attention to the distribution of many environmental benefits and burdens (Bell, 2004; Holland, 2008). Environmental justice advocates argue that environmental burdens, such as air pollution, water pollution, and the harms associated with climate change; and environmental benefits, such as access to greenspace, should also be distributed fairly (Agyeman, 2002; Bullard, 1994; Hofrichter, 1993; Shrader-Frechette, 2002; Walker, 2012). However, this challenge to the "currency" of justice in liberal theories is not unique to environmentalists (Cohen, 1989). Indeed, it has been at the center of debates about justice for over 30 years with many leading justice theorists, such as Sen (1980), Cohen (1993), and Arneson (1989), defending alternative currencies, such as capabilities, midfare, and equality of opportunity for welfare. Environmental political theorists have made some interesting contributions to this debate. For example, several theorists have argued that the fair distribution of capabilities can incorporate environmental benefits and burdens (Holland, 2008; Page, 2007; Schlosberg, 2007) while others have defended variations on Rawls's notion of primary goods (Bell, 2004; Manning, 1981; Thero, 1995; Wenz, 1988). More recently, some theorists have proposed a new currency, ecological space (Hayward, 2007; Vanderheiden, 2009). There are many important questions about which environmental benefits and burdens are justice-relevant and how the currency of justice is best formulated to include them as well as other justice-relevant benefits and burdens. However, understood in this way, it seems *prima facie* plausible to imagine that contemporary liberal theories of justice could be modified to incorporate this additional class of benefits and burdens in the currency of justice.

Second, traditionally liberal theories have discussed domestic justice or how benefits and burdens should be distributed within a single state (Caney, 2001). However, the causes and effects of environmental problems do not map neatly onto political territories. For example, the causes of acid rain, river pollution, and nuclear radiation may be in one state and the effects in another, while both the causes and effects of climate change and ozone depletion may be diffused across many states. Therefore, environmental justice advocates argue that liberal theories of justice are wrong to limit the scope of justice (i.e., the community to whom we owe duties of justice) to a single state because our actions can cause harm beyond political borders (Shrader-Frechette, 2002; Walker, 2012). Again, this challenge to the spatial scope of justice in liberal theories is not unique to environmentalists. The debate about the spatial scope of justice has been important in liberal political theory for over 30 years (Beitz, 1979). Many environmental political theorists have endorsed standard arguments for cosmopolitanism while others have argued that the trans-boundary and global character of environmental problems provides new reasons for their preferred version of cosmopolitanism (Dobson, 2006). However, advocates of non-cosmopolitan theories have offered their own accounts of inter-state environmental justice (Miller, 2008). The increasing recognition of the importance of trans-boundary and global environmental problems reinforces the need for some account of "justice beyond borders" but it might not determine the character of that account (Caney, 2005).

Third, liberal theories of justice have been primarily focused on how benefits and burdens should be distributed among contemporaries, but actions that affect the environment can have long-term consequences for future generations (Laslett and Fishkin, 1992; Mazor, 2010). We know, for example, that one-fifth of carbon molecules stay in the atmosphere for a millennium while the half-life of Plutonium-239 is 24,100 years. Therefore, environmental issues pose a challenge to the temporal scope of liberal theories of justice. It would, of course, be wrong to claim that liberals have ignored intergenerational justice, but they have tended to treat it as an addendum to, or an extension of, a theory of justice among contemporaries (Gosseries and Meyer, 2009; Rawls, 1972, 2001; Tremmel, 2006). Environmental issues have raised the profile of intergenerational justice in contemporary political philosophy (Dobson, 1999; Eckersley, 2004; Gardiner, 2011; Hiskes, 2008; Page, 2007). However, the discussion of the temporal scope of justice—and how relations of justice between noncontemporaries should be understood—remains relatively underdeveloped in comparison with debates about the spatial scope of justice.

So far, we have seen that taking the environment seriously poses three challenges for liberal theories, which are closely related to ongoing debates within liberalism about the currency and scope of justice. However, David Schlosberg, drawing on his interpretation of ideas in the environmental justice movement, poses three more challenges for liberal theories of justice, which are more characteristic of debates between liberals and their critics.

The fourth challenge is that the environmental justice movement is concerned about more than the *distribution* of environmental benefits and burdens (Schlosberg, 1999, 2004, 2007; Walker, 2012). Environmental justice advocates are also concerned about *participation* and *recognition*. Participatory or political justice requires fair participation for all in decision-making processes that determine how environmental benefits and burdens will be distributed. Justice as recognition requires that all persons, irrespective of their ethnicity, gender, religion, or class, are recognized and treated as equals by the institutional and cultural norms and practices that shape their environments and their lives. Schlosberg argues that liberal theories of justice are inadequate because they are concerned only with distribution. This criticism of liberal theories of justice is familiar from—and Schlosberg explicitly draws on—the work of feminist political theorists and advocates of the "politics of difference," such as Young (1990), Fraser (1997), and Honneth (1996), who argue that the distributive paradigm is inadequate because it fails to take seriously the misrecognition and exclusion of women, cultural minorities, and other oppressed groups in contemporary societies. Liberal responses have varied but many liberals argue that they are concerned about—and can adequately acknowledge the importance of—participation and recognition properly understood (Jones, 2006). In contrast, critics of liberalism might see victims of environmental injustice—who are statistically likely to be members of oppressed groups, such as women, ethnic minorities, and indigenous peoples—as having a common cause with other victims of injustice in liberal democratic societies.

Fifth, Schlosberg has also argued that the environmental justice movement is not only concerned with justice to individuals but also with justice to communities, including territorial communities, communities of color, and indigenous communities (Schlosberg, 2004, 2007). This is another—but more radical—challenge to the scope of justice in liberal theories. Liberals recognize only individuals as subjects of justice (i.e., individuals are the only entities to which we can have duties of justice), but Schlosberg claims that communities are also subjects of justice. This criticism is also familiar but this time from multiculturalist criticisms of liberalism. Some liberal multiculturalists have recognized the moral importance of cultural communities—for example, as a "context of choice"—but have maintained that the fundamental unit of moral concern is the individual person (Kymlicka, 1989: 166). However, some critics have rejected moral individualism so that for them fundamental moral status should also be attributed to social or political communities (May, 1987; McDonald, 1991). Schlosberg is similarly critical of liberal individualism so that for him the victims of environmental injustice are not just individuals but communities.

Sixth, Schlosberg's final challenge to liberal theories of justice concerns their anthropocentrism. The subjects of justice in mainstream liberal theories are humans. However, Schlosberg (2007) argues that we can also owe duties of justice to nonhumans. This is a fourth—and, perhaps, even more radical—challenge to the scope of liberal theories of justice. The challenge to the anthropocentrism of liberal theories of justice is familiar from arguments about the moral status of animals as well as from various strands of environmentalism, including biocentrism and ecocentrism (Clark, 1977; Dryzek, 1995; Garner, 2005; Leopold, 1949; Taylor, 1986). It is also, as Schlosberg emphasizes, a feature of the environmental justice movement, particularly among indigenous communities, who have played a leading role in the US environmental justice movement (Schlosberg, 2007). There have been some attempts to develop recognizably liberal but non-anthropocentric theories of justice (Baxter, 2005; Hailwood, 2004). However, this seems to require a fundamental reconstruction of key contemporary liberal ideas, most notably the conception of subjects of justice as "reasonable" and "rational" (Rawls, 2001, 6–7).

In this section, I have considered six challenges to liberal theories of justice. The first three challenges point us toward ongoing debates within liberalism about the currency, spatial scope, and temporal scope of justice. However, the other three challenges point us toward debates between liberals and their critics and suggest that a theory of justice on one planet might be quite different from contemporary liberal theories of justice.

3 CHALLENGING THE LIBERAL CONCEPTION OF THE ENVIRONMENT

In this section, I consider a third set of challenges that relate to how liberal theories of justice conceive of the environment. I will argue that a theory of justice on one planet requires a radically different conception of the environment and that this requires the revision of some important liberal assumptions.

The mainstream liberal conception of the environment has five important features that are problematic for a theory of justice on one planet. First, liberals assume that the environment is part of the economy rather than the economy being embedded in the environment. This assumption is clearest in resourcist theories of justice. Consider, for example, Dworkin's classic "desert island" case, which he uses to introduce his discussion of equality of resources:

> Suppose a number of shipwreck survivors are washed up on a desert island which has abundant resources and no native population, and any likely rescue is many years away. These immigrants accept the principle that no one is antecedently entitled to any of these resources, but they shall instead be divided equally among them (Dworkin, 1981: 284).

Dworkin conceptualizes the island—and by implication its ecosystem—as "resources" to be incorporated into the economy by distributing them among the shipwreck survivors. In contrast, ecologists conceive of the economy as a "subsystem" that "lives off the containing ecosystem" (Daly, 1995, 451). The ecosystem supplies the raw materials for the economy and absorbs the waste products of the economy. The economy is part of—and dependent on—the environment rather than the environment being part of the economy. Liberal theorists assume that contemporary scientific knowledge should be taken seriously in public reasoning about justice yet the liberal conception of the environment-economy relationship is not consistent with our best understanding of the science of ecology (Rawls, 2001).

The liberal inversion of the environment-economy relationship is important for a theory of justice on one planet because of the assumptions that follow from it. So the second problem is that if we assume that the environment can be incorporated into the economy as "resources," we also assume that it is passive or, at least, can be brought under the control of economic processes and institutions. However, at its most fundamental level, the environment is a matter/energy system governed by the laws of thermodynamics (Daly, 1995). On our best scientific conception, the environment is dynamic rather than passive. It may coevolve with the economy—responding to human actions as we respond to it—but it is hubristic to assume that humans, or our economic and political institutions, can control the ecosystem (Norgaard, 1995). Instead, recognizing the dynamic complexity of the ecosystem should lead us to a more modest conception of our place in it and a more precautionary approach to using (parts of) the environment. A theory of justice on one planet should assume that the environment is dynamic and beyond our control rather than accepting the liberal assumption that it can be conceived as passive, controllable resources.

Third, we have noted that the environment is a "system," yet liberal theories of justice assume that the environment can be divided up for distribution among persons. Again, Dworkin's "desert island" case is an extreme illustration of this feature of liberal theories. On his account, "each distinct item on the island" is to be distributed "unless someone . . . [has a] desire . . . for some part of an item, including part, for example, of some piece of land" in which case the item must be sub-divided to produce two or more distinct items to be distributed (Dworkin, 1981: 286). In principle, there is no limit to the division. There is no recognition of the systemic nature of local or global ecosystems. We may be able to divide land into ever smaller lots, but that does not alter the ecological fact that any piece of land is related to other pieces of land in many complex ecological ways. Dworkin's conception of the environment as indefinitely divisible natural resources ignores the relations between those "resources" (or interconnected parts of the ecosystem). Moreover, it also ignores those wholly systemic goods that it is not possible to divide, such as clean air, a stable climate, a protective ozone layer, and ecosystem resilience. A theory of justice on one planet must take seriously the systemic character of the environment and the interconnectedness between parts of the environment. Therefore, it should not assume that justice is wholly—or even primarily—about the distribution of parts of the environment. Instead, justice on one planet might be more concerned with how one person's use of the environment affects other people and their opportunities to use the environment.

Fourth, liberals assume that the environment currently provides circumstances of moderate scarcity, in which "natural and other resources are not so abundant that schemes of cooperation become superfluous, nor are conditions so harsh that fruitful ventures must inevitably break down," and these circumstances can be maintained indefinitely in the future (Rawls, 1972: 127). This assumption reflects the liberal failure to take seriously the dependence of the economy on an "earth-ecosystem" that is "finite, non-growing [and] materially closed" (Daly, 1995: 451). As Daly suggests:

> Historically these [environmental] limits were not generally binding, because the [economic] subsystem was small relative to the total [eco]system. The world was "empty." But now it is "full" and the limits are more and more binding—not necessarily like brick walls, but more like stretched rubber bands (Daly, 1995: 452).

In the past, the global economy was small enough for it to develop, increasing both population and per capita consumption, without visible limits. Now the world is "full." The global economy is "stretching" the limits of the earth-ecosystem and it may only be a matter of time before the "rubber band" springs back on us or snaps altogether. Permanent economic growth in a finite and non-growing ecosystem is not possible unless new technologies always enable us to overcome biophysical constraints. However, we have already seen that this kind of extreme technological optimism is unjustified given the dynamic complexity of the eco-system. Therefore, a theory of justice on one planet must take very seriously the possibility of circumstances of extreme scarcity, in which it is impossible to meet even the most basic needs of everyone on the planet. If justice on one planet requires anything, it must require that we avoid circumstances of extreme scarcity. So it cannot endorse the idea of permanent economic growth nor can it even remain neutral between permanent economic growth and a stationary or steady state economy (Mill, 1848; Rawls, 2001). Instead, it must acknowledge that a steady state economy, without economic growth, will at some time become (or may already have become) a requirement of justice.

Fifth, liberal theories of justice primarily conceive of the environment as property. Liberal justice requires the fair distribution among persons of property rights to parts of the environment. This is problematic for three reasons. First, there are many reasonable conceptions of the environment and how it should be valued that are not consistent with conceiving of (some parts of) the environment as private property (Bell, 2002, 2005). Therefore, conceiving of the environment merely as property is not consistent with the liberal principle of neutrality among comprehensive moral doctrines (Bell, 2005). Second, a conception of the environment as property owned by humans—either individually or in communities—is another reflection of the hubristic assumption that humans can control the environment. Property rights over parts of the environment imply that we have the right and the ability to control those parts of the environment. However, we have seen that the systemic, complex, and dynamic character of the environment makes it implausible to assume that we can control the environment. Instead, the economic subsystem is dependent on the earth-ecosystem. So a theory of justice on one planet should start by recognizing our dependence on the environment rather than assuming that we have property rights over it (Bell, 2005). Third, we have already seen that the fact that the earth-ecosystem is finite and nongrowing implies that there must be limits on the size of the economic subsystem. Therefore, a theory of justice on one planet should assume that the use or transformation of parts of the environment always requires justification (Wissenburg, 1998). If justice requires that human needs are met, the use or transformation of parts of the environment might be justified by our physical and biological dependence on using or transforming parts of the environment. Moreover, there may be other requirements of justice that justify the use or transformation of the environment. However, it seems unlikely that a theory of justice on one planet will endorse full property rights, which allow individuals or communities to use, transform and transfer parts of the environment as and when they choose. Instead, it seems likely to endorse limited and carefully specified use rights.

In this section, I have argued that liberal theories of justice make five implausible assumptions about the environment. A theory of justice on one planet, which takes our knowledge of the environment seriously, will reject these assumptions. I have suggested that this is likely to have radical implications for how we conceptualize and formulate principles of justice and for our understanding of a just political economy.

4 CONCLUSION

In this chapter, I have suggested that the concept of justice may help us to clarify our thinking about some of the most difficult issues and choices that we face in environmental ethics. Which entities have sufficient moral status to be subjects of justice? Which of their interests are justice-relevant? Which principles should regulate their competing claims? However, I acknowledged that some theorists might be concerned that a justice-based approach to environmental ethics distorts rather than clarifies environmental ethics.

In the remainder of the chapter, I considered how a theory of justice on one planet—i.e., an environmentally or ecologically aware theory of justice—might differ from the liberal theories of justice that dominate contemporary political theory. I distinguished three sets of challenges to liberal theories. The first set of challenges emphasizes the importance of ongoing debates within liberalism about the currency, spatial scope, and temporal scope of justice. The second set of challenges relates to issues that have been at the center of debates between liberals and their critics, specifically, challenges to the distributive paradigm, individualism, and anthropocentrism. The final set of challenges is specific to a theory of justice on one planet because these challenges question the liberal conception of the environment. Liberals conceive of the environment as part of the economy, passive or controllable, infinitely divisible, always able to provide circumstances of moderate scarcity, and as property. I have argued that an ecologically informed conception of justice should conceive of the environment very differently. The economy is embedded in the environment. The environment is dynamic and often beyond our control. It is systemic and interconnected. There is a serious risk of extreme scarcity. Humans are dependent on the environment and conceive of it in many reasonable and justice-relevant ways. If we conceive of the environment in these significantly different ways, we are likely to arrive at significantly different theories of justice. Justice will not be concerned with the distribution of property rights but rather with justifying our use of (parts of) the environment in light of the competing claims of other subjects of justice now and in the future.

The concept of justice has already been employed fruitfully in environmental ethics in debates about environmental justice and (to a lesser extent) ecological justice. However, the more general project of developing a theory of justice on one planet, which is informed by our best scientific and our competing moral conceptions of the environment, remains relatively underdeveloped. We have seen some debates within liberalism (about currency and spatial scope) and some debates between liberals and their critics (about the distributive paradigm and individualism) move to the center of mainstream political theory since the 1980s. As the twenty-first century progresses and environmental problems become more pressing, we might eventually see debates between theories of justice on one planet replacing debates between theories of global justice as the central focus of mainstream political theory.

REFERENCES

Agyeman, J. (2002). "Constructing Environmental (In)Justice: Transatlantic Tales." *Environmental Politics* 11: 31–53.

Anderson, E. (1999). "What Is the Point of Equality?" *Ethics* 109: 287–337.

Arneson, R. (1989). "Equality and Equal Opportunity for Welfare." *Philosophical Studies* 56: 77–93.

Barry, B. (1991). "Humanity and Justice in Global Perspective." In *Liberty and Justice: Essays in Political Theory: Volume 2*, edited by B. Barry, 182–210. Oxford: Clarendon Press.

Barry, B. (1995). *Justice as Impartiality*. Oxford: Oxford University Press.

Baxter, B. (1999). *Ecologism: An Introduction*. Edinburgh: Edinburgh University Press.

Baxter, B. (2005). *A Theory of Ecological Justice*. London: Routledge.

Beitz, C. (1979). *Political Theory and International Relations*. Princeton, NJ: Princeton University Press.

Bell, D. (2002). "How Can Political Liberals Be Environmentalists?" *Political Studies* 50: 703–724.

Bell, D. (2004). "Environmental Justice and Rawls's Difference Principle." *Environmental Ethics* 26: 287–306.

Bell, D. (2005). "Liberal Environmental Citizenship." *Environmental Politics* 14: 179–194.

Bell, D. (2006). "Political Liberalism and Ecological Justice." *Analyse und Kritik* 28: 382–402.

Bullard, R. (ed.) (1993). *Confronting Environmental Racism: Voices from the Grassroots*. Cambridge, MA: South End Press.

Bullard, R. (ed.) (1994). *Unequal Protection: Environmental Justice and Communities of Color*. San Francisco: Sierra Club Books.

Bullard, R. (2000). *Dumping in Dixie: Race, Class and Environmental Quality*, 3rd ed. Boulder, Colorado: Westview Press.

Caney, S. (2001). "International Distributive Justice." *Political Studies* 49: 974–997.

Caney, S. (2005). *Justice Beyond Borders: A Global Political Theory*. Oxford: Oxford University Press.

Clark, S. (1977). *The Moral Status of Animals*. Oxford: Oxford University Press.

Cohen, G. (1989). "On the Currency of Egalitarian Justice." *Ethics* 99: 906–944.

Cohen, G. (1993). "Equality of What: Resources, Capabilities and Midfare." In *The Quality of Life,* edited by M. Nussbaum and A. Sen. Oxford: Clarendon Press.

Daly, H. (1995). "Consumption and Welfare: Two Views of Value Added." *Review of Social Economy* 53: 451–473.

Dasgupta, P. (2005). "Three Conceptions of Intergenerational Justice." In *Ramsey's Legacy,* edited by H. Lillehammer and D. Mellor, 149–169. Oxford: Clarendon Press.

DeGeorge, R. (1981). "The Environment, Rights, and Future Generations." In *Responsibilities to Future Generations: Environmental Ethics,* edited by E. Partridge, 157–166. New York, NY: Prometheus.

Dobson, A. (1998). *Justice and the Environment: Conceptions of Environmental Sustainability and Theories of Distributive Justice*. Oxford: Oxford University Press.

Dobson, A. (ed.) (1999). *Fairness and Futurity: Essays on Sustainability and Justice.* Oxford: Oxford University Press.

Dobson, A. (2000). *Green Political Thought.* London: Routledge.

Dobson, A. (2006). "Thick Cosmopolitanism." *Political Studies* 54: 165–184.

Dryzek, J. (1995). "Political and Ecological Communication." *Environmental Politics* 4: 13–30.

Dworkin, R. (1981). "What Is Equality? Part 2: Equality of Resources." *Philosophy and Public Affairs* 10: 283–345.

Dworkin, R. (2002). *Sovereign Virtue: The Theory and Practice of Equality.* Cambridge, MA: Harvard University Press.

Eckersley, R. (2004). *The Green State: Rethinking Democracy and Sovereignty.* Cambridge, MA: MIT Press.

Fraser, N. (1997). *Justice Interruptus: Critical Reflections on the "Postsocialist" Condition.* London: Routledge.

Gardiner, S. (2011). *A Perfect Moral Storm: The Ethical Tragedy of Climate Change.* New York: Oxford University Press.

Garner, R. (2005). *Animal Ethics.* Cambridge: Polity Press.

Gosseries, A., and Meyer, L. (eds.) (2009). *Intergenerational Justice.* Oxford: Oxford University Press.

Hailwood, S. (2004). *How to Be a Green Liberal: Nature, Value and Liberal Philosophy.* Durham: Acumen Publishing.

Hayward, T. (2007). "Human rights versus emissions rights: climate justice and the equitable distribution of ecological space." *Ethics and International Affairs* 21: 431–450.

Hiskes, R. (2008). *The Human Right to a Green Future: Environmental Rights and Intergenerational Justice.* Cambridge: Cambridge University Press.

Hofrichter, R. (ed.) (1993). *Toxic Struggles: The Theory and Practice of Environmental Justice.* Philadelphia: New Society Publishers.

Holland, B. (2008). "Justice and the Environment in Nussbaum's 'Capabilities Approach': Why Sustainable Ecological Capacity Is a Meta-Capability." *Political Research Quarterly* 61: 319–332.

Honneth, A. (1996). *The Struggle for Recognition: The Moral Grammar of Social Conflicts.* Cambridge: Polity Press.

Jones, C. (1999). *Global Justice: Defending Cosmopolitanism.* Oxford: Oxford University Press.

Jones, P. (2006). "Equality, Recognition and Difference." *Critical Review of International Social and Political Philosophy* 9: 23–46.

Kymlicka, W. (1989). *Liberalism, Community and Culture.* Oxford: Oxford University Press.

Laslett, P., and Fishkin, J. (1992). "Introduction." In *Justice Between Age Groups and Generations,* edited by P. Laslett and J. Fishkin. New Haven, CT: Yale University Press.

Leopold, A. (1949). *A Sand County Almanac.* New York: Oxford University Press.

Litfin, K. (1997). "The Gendered Eye in the Sky: A Feminist Perspective on Earth Observation Satellites." *Frontiers: A Journal of Women Studies* 18: 26–47.

Manning, R. (1981). "Environmental Ethics and John Rawls' Theory of Justice." *Environmental Ethics* 3: 155–166.

May, L. (1987). *The Morality of Groups.* Notre Dame: University of Notre Dame Press.

Mazor, J. (2010). "Liberal Justice, Future People, and Natural Resource Conservation." *Philosophy and Public Affairs* 38: 380–408.

McDonald, M. (1991). "Should Communities have Rights? Reflections on Liberal Individualism." *Canadian Journal of Law and Jurisprudence* 4: 217–237.

Mill, J. S. (1848). *Principles of Political Economy: With Some of Their Applications to Social Philosophy*. Available free at: http://www.gutenberg.org/files/30107/30107-pdf.pdf

Miller, D. (2008). "Global Justice and Climate Change: How Should Responsibilities Be Distributed?" The Tanner Lectures on Human Values delivered at Tsinghua University, Beijing, March 24–25, 2008. Available at: tannerlectures.utah.edu/lectures/documents/Miller_08.pdf

Nagel, T. (1991). *Equality and Partiality*. Oxford: Oxford University Press.

Norgaard, R. (1995). "Beyond Materialism: A Coevolutionary Reinterpretation of the Environmental Crisis." *Review of Social Economy* 53: 475–492.

Orr, D. (1992). *Ecological Literacy: Education and the Transition to a Postmodern World*. Albany, NY: State University of New York Press.

Page, E. (2007). *Climate Change, Justice and Future Generations*. Cheltenham: Edward Elgar.

Purser, R. (1997). "From Global Management to Global Appreciation: A Transformative Epistemology for Aperspectival Worlds." *Organization and Environment* 10: 361–383.

Rawls, J. (1972). *A Theory of Justice*. Oxford: Oxford University Press.

Rawls, J. (2001). *Justice as Fairness: A Restatement*. Cambridge, MA: Harvard University Press.

Sandel, M. (1982). *Liberalism and the Limits of Justice*. Cambridge: Cambridge University Press.

Schlosberg, D. (1999). *Environmental Justice and the New Pluralism: The Challenge of Difference for Environmentalism*. Oxford: Oxford University Press.

Schlosberg, D. (2004). "Reconceiving Environmental Justice: Global Movements and Political Theories." *Environmental Politics* 13: 517–540.

Schlosberg, D. (2007). *Defining Environmental Justice: Theories, Movements, and Nature*. Oxford: Oxford University Press.

Schlosberg, D. (2013). "Theorising Environmental Justice: the Expanding Sphere of a Discourse." *Environmental Politics* 22: 37–55.

Sen, A. (1980). "Equality of What?" In *Tanner Lectures on Human Values*, Vol, 1, edited by S. McMurrin. Cambridge: Cambridge University Press.

Shrader-Frechette, K. (2002). *Environmental Justice: Creating Equality, Reclaiming Democracy*. Oxford: Oxford University Press.

Shue, H. (1983). "The Burdens of Justice." *The Journal of Philosophy* 80: 600–608.

Tan, K.-C. (2011). "Luck, Institutions, and Global Distributive Justice: A Defence of Global Luck Egalitarianism." *European Journal of Political Theory* 10: 394–421.

Taylor, P. (1986). *Respect for Nature: A Theory of Environmental Ethics*. Princeton, NJ: Princeton University Press.

Thero, D. (1995). "Rawls and Environmental Ethics: A Critical Examination of the Literature." *Environmental Ethics* 17: 93–106.

Tremmel, J. (ed.) (2006). *Handbook of Intergenerational Justice*. Cheltenham: Edward Elgar.

Vanderheiden, S. (2009). "Allocating Ecological Space." *Journal of Social Philosophy* 40: 257–275.

Walker, G. (2012). *Environmental Justice: Concepts, Evidence and Politics*. London: Routledge.

Wenz, P. (1988). *Environmental Justice*. Albany, NY: SUNY Press.

Wissenburg, M. (1998). *Green Liberalism: The Free and Green Society*. London: UCL Press.

Wissenburg, M. (2011). "The Lion and the Lamb: Ecological Implications of Martha Nussbaum's Animal Ethics." *Environmental Politics*, 20: 391–409.

Young, I. M. (1990). *Justice and the Politics of Difference*. Princeton, NJ: Princeton University Press.

....

CHAPTER 24

SEXUAL POLITICS IN ENVIRONMENTAL ETHICS
Impacts, Causes, Alternatives

....

CHRIS J. CUOMO

Too often environmental ethics are described as concerning "human" relationships with nature, as if human beings comprise a great monolithic "we" that acts on nature en masse, or as if simply being human is the deciding factor determining how people use and regard land, other animals, waterways, the atmosphere, and Earth's biosphere. But ecological harms are perpetrated and eco-controversies are generated by people and groups moved by distinct interests, values, and perspectives. Often people harm other people *through* harms to nature, and disregard for human communities enables ecological devastation, such as in deforestation and mining, where local people's land and labor are often jointly abused and their interests jointly ignored by those with more economic or political power.

Suggestions that there is a species-driven or characteristically "human" cause of the devastation Earth has experienced in the last two centuries neglects gendered and cultural differences in orientations toward nature, such as the fact that if we look at humanity's great historical diversity we find that many cultures have developed gentler technologies and more respectful relationships with nature. To reduce human or modern subjectivity to a violent and violating dominating tendency, or to an essential, inevitably harmful collective force, is to misrepresent a minority as all of humanity, and to identify ideologies of domination and disregard for nature as paradigmatic and definitive of all humanity. These questions must also be raised about the geological theory of the "anthropocene," which linguistically attributes the impacts of industrial capitalism and militarism to humanity as a species, a misleading misrepresentation at best. It is not species-wide human agency, but rather a particular set of cultures and players which have encouraged and allowed for the devastating and unprecedented harms to nature that we currently face. And it is particular cultures and practices that must be resisted, overturned or developed for alternative ecological and social values to gain broader influence.

Considering environmental challenges such as the impacts of industrial agriculture, animal abuse, ubiquitous toxins and plastics in human bodies, grossly polluted waterways, and transnational monopolies controlling key resources, the significance of social, political and ideological factors is unmistakable. Intentionally and unintentionally, dominating forces take advantage of the compromised agency of impoverished and disempowered communities, getting away with extraordinary environmental harms that would be avoided, protested, or punished if privileged and respected rights-holders were to suffer them. Yet even the privileged are victimized by ecologically destructive practices and technologies.

Gender roles and identities are dominant expressions of culture, creating patterns of consumption and relationships with nature that express sexual and political economies and link sex and gender norms to specific ideas about nature and other species. Culturally specific moral paradigms provide compulsory guidelines for how to live, consume, use materials, and regard oneself and others. Pervasive representations of subordinated femininity as "close to nature" reinforce the idea that to be male is to transcend or to be inherently superior to animal, Earthly nature. Similarly, racist characterizations of nonwestern cultures and people of color as inferior because they are "close to nature" asserts a hierarchy that associates whiteness with distance from nature, thereby encouraging such distance. Ecofeminist writers have highlighted the roles that dualistic sexual and colonial politics play in fueling the ideologies and technologies that wreak havoc on the natural world, showing that the domination of nature is an issue of central concern for feminism (Griffin, 1978; Kheel, 1985; Gaard and Gruen, 1993; Seager, 1993; Plumwood, 1994; Warren, 2000; Shiva and Mies, 1993/2014). While there are gendered patterns in relationships with nature, such as masculinized hunting and feminized food preparation, sex and gender are interwoven with particulars of class, race, culture and other factors, and so they are also diverse.

Differences within categories of sex and gender are often more important than similarities. For example, abiding harms caused by specific histories of violence include their effects on comfort, desire, mobility, relationships, and therefore moral agency. In her essay "Black Women and the Wilderness" Evelyn White describes a way of relating to "nature" that is mediated by astute awareness of the threat of racist violence, an awareness that is heightened in the outdoors. There, her "sense of vulnerability and exposure" is palpable and "genetic memory of ancestors hunted down and preyed upon in rural settings" disrupts her ability to feel a sense of connection with nature (White 2002, p. 1064).

> While the river's roar gave me a certain comfort and my heart warmed when I gazed at the sun-dappled trees out of a classroom window, I didn't want to get closer. I was certain that if I ventured outside to admire a meadow or to feel the cool ripples in a stream, I'd be taunted, attacked . . . because of the color of my skin. I believe the fear I experience in the outdoors is shared by many African-American women and that it limits the way we move through the world and colors the decisions we make about our lives.

There are patterns to our Earthly inhabitations as sexed beings, but "women" are not essentially "closer to nature." Rather, sexism, colonialism, racism, and harms to nature are practically, causally and conceptually linked, and specific male-dominant cultures have been and continue to be the leading drivers of modern environmental destruction and degrading social violence.

1 FEMINIST SOLIDARITY WITH NATURE: CRITICAL THEMES

In contrast with the ecofeminist idea that norms and practices of sex and gender create conditions for solidarity with nature, historically feminist philosophers have stressed women's "rising above nature" beyond realms associated with necessity and domesticity and toward equality with privileged men. From Christina de Pizan's *The Book of the City of Ladies*, published in France in the early 1400s, to Shulamith Firestone's *Dialectic of Sex* (1970), feminist philosophers often begin with an acknowledgement and immediate rejection of pervasive cultural associations between femaleness and "nature," taking those associations to be false generalizations that can only lock females into realms of subordination. However, more nuanced investigations of the complex material, symbolic and ethical relationships between women, animals, and the land have long been prominent in feminist literatures (Gilman 1915/1998, Walker 1989, Silko 2000). And as social and environmental movements have developed in tandem, women activists focused on the sexual politics of environmental health, animal rights, and agricultural reform have recast cultural associations between 'women and nature' as opportunities for solidarity and coalition-building.

Some themes that have emerged in work emphasizing the significance of sex and gender in relation to environmental ethics are: (1) the linked harms of sexism and environmental destruction, (2) the cultural and symbolic associations between femaleness/femininity and "nature," and (3) the *transformative power* of multicultural feminist approaches to environmental ethics. Drawing attention to linked harms experienced by "nature," animals, women, and other subjugated groups, asserts the importance for environmental ethics of tracing the real risks and impacts of environmental harms on particular people, and integrating questions about social justice and equality, environmental racism, violence and economic disparities into environmental ethics. Although interwoven harms are not linked in uniform or universal ways, the connections among them are often identifiable. For example, feminist environmentalists highlight the evident, and likely links between harms such as rampant breast cancer, ubiquitous plastics in Earth's biosphere, and current global climate change, referring to gendered, sexed, raced, classed (etc.) links that are accidental and intentional, practical and conceptual, abstract and material.

The social dimensions of environmental practices are central because ecological harms are often harms to people, and those who experience the most immediate and dramatic impacts of environmental harms are often the same groups or communities who have been targeted by oppression, and put in "vulnerable" physical positions and social locations by exploitative forces. Due to the feminization of poverty in its multiple guises, the inherent vulnerabilities of those who care for young children, and the geographical marginalization of poor communities into beleaguered territories, women, people of color and the poor are more often and more intensely negatively impacted by many environmental disasters, harms and degradations (Enarson, 2000, Laditka et al., 2010). Culturally constructed images of nature are also used against females and other subordinated groups in the forms of repressive and punishing norms of sexuality, beauty, criminality, and morality, confining whatever is associated with femininity or degraded nature while granting more freedom and protection to masculinity and/or privileged men.

What matters in bringing attention to such linked harms is that real harms to bodies—biological bodies, psyches, social bodies/species, pseudo-bodies (eco-regions), and Earthly bodies (bodies of water or air)—are multiplied, exacerbated, and intensified through the collaborative synergies of multiple systems of oppression. Identifying linked harms points to the need for ethics and politics that can address those interwoven systems, and integrate considerations of social justice and environmental ethics at all levels. Regarding sex and gender, which are always interwoven with other factors, the "second class" yet simultaneously exhalted nature of feminity and what is associated with female biological reproductivity is a fundamental feature shaping ideas and relationships in sexist and nature-harming cultures, as is the identification of masculinity with domination and the absence of vulnerability.

A second clear theme in work focused on matters of sex and gender in environmental ethics is investigation of the conceptual presuppositions or frameworks that inform and enable systems of oppression. In philosophy, many have argued that environmentally destructive and dismissive value systems reflect meanings and symbolic systems built on identities and conceptions of nature and nonhuman animals that create and maintain a general logic of domination (Merchant, 1982; Warren, 1990; Allen, 1992). A guiding theory has been that nature and subordinated groups are symbolically associated on the debased side of western culture's foundational hierarchies. Rather than being essentialist in an Aristotelian sense, this view emphasizes the historical material and symbolic associations between women and nature, and tracks evident patterns in who bears the brunt of the violence.

To say that women and nature have been powerfully linked in western culture, and that those association have enabled sexist, racist, colonizing intersecting oppressions and social dominations, is not to imply that all femaleness is identified with only one cultural stereotype of what or how nature is, or that all women suffer the same or similar domination. Different women are symbolically identified with different aspects or fantasies of nature and anti-nature, and those associations have distinct repercussions in exploitative social systems, such as being revered as a natural beauty or being treated as a beast of burden. And naturalness is a pliable designation, for masculinities can be associated with certain ideas about nature and naturalness (stability, physical strength), and femininity is also often characterized as a domesticating cultural force, or an enemy of nature. What matters for politics and ethics is that nature and femininity are reductively associated with each other, and the effects of the association are mutually debilitating.

Pernicious cultural and symbolic connections between women and nature as reproductive, submissive, and decorative create and maintain divisions of labor that put women in closer proximity to the material world and symbolically associate femininity with subjectable natural-ness, which can or even ought to be molded to man's needs or whims. Projected associations between "women and nature" and the like propagate subordination and the potential for victimization, for example by compulsively relegating females to the work of caring for others. Hierarchical characterizations of male/female, nature/culture, primitive/civilized are interwoven systems of exploitation that shape and inform environmental relationships at every scale. Understanding and deconstructing sex and gender critically in relation to environmental ethics, and understanding and deconstructing the roles certain conceptions of nature play in propagating social oppression, complicates one-dimensional ideas about the nature of environmental problems, and points toward fruitful areas for ethical development and exploration.

Accordingly, a third theme emphasized in work focused on the sexual politics of environmental ethics, focuses on creating or reclaiming alternative values, priorities and practices, to replace colonizing and exploitation with empowerment, healing, justice and cooperation. Along those lines feminists and ecofeminists have highlighted alternative models of ethics, politics and science that challenge the stewardship or noble hunter models of environmentalism, and instead give life to principles of mutual care-taking, co-existence, empathy and respect (Plumwood, 1994; Kheel, 2007; Gruen, 2014; Whyte and Cuomo, this volume). Unfortunately, sexism, marginalization and media conglomerates can prevent alternative efforts and paradigms from gaining ground, silencing feminist and "other" perspectives through the domination of culture and public space, including the scapegoating of women who question the status quo. In response, critical attention to sex and gender and the historical impacts of sexism brings to light to the important, undervalued contributions of figures such as Rachel Carson, Lois Gibbs, Wangari Maathai to the development of global environmental ethics, and emphasizes women-led campaigns for pollution mitigation, food security, and climate justice, as models of ethics in action.

2 LINKED HARMS AND ASSOCIATION THROUGH PROXIMITY

Where sexual double-standards relentlessly associate women with domestic and caretaking labor, women may have decision-making power concerning water and energy use, food acquisition and preparation, and other matters with dramatic environmental implications. Close proximity to nature through gendered work and responsibilities makes women important environmental experts and actors, but also puts them on the front lines of those directly impacted by environmental stresses and harms. Gender norms and responsibilities create gendered risks and harms, as when women in their roles as care workers are more burdened by environmental change and uncertainty. When extreme hardship or disaster occurs, increases in care-related workloads and gendered "vulnerabilities" reinforce subordinating gender norms, exacerbating the deprivations of those in caretaking and subordinate social positions and marginalized communities, including the elderly and LGBT folk (Enarson, 2000; Covan and Fugate-Whitlock, 2010; Alston and Whittenbury, 2012; Mortimer-Sandilands and Erickson, 2010; Egan et al., 2011). Institutions in sexist, racist societies may be slow to notice and acknowledge particular harms to marginalized or poor communities, because political disempowerment undermines individuals' and communities' abilities to advocate for themselves and their environments (Smith, 2016).

Arguing that linked harms can become sources of solidarity and revolutionary knowledge, in her influential essay "Taking Empirical Data Seriously," philosopher Karen Warren showed that women in most societies are in key stakeholder positions in relation to the world's fundamental areas of concern for environmental policy: forestry, water policy, food politics, farming, technology, and pollution (1997). Yet their central roles and efforts do not necessarily translate into economic or decision-making power. For example, "women account for almost 80% of the agricultural sector in Africa," yet "seventy per cent of the 1.3 billion people in the developing world living below the threshold of poverty are women" (Denton, 2002, p. 10). Research and political practice focused on the nexus of gender and the environment has long emphasized the synergistic impacts of sexism, colonialism, technological modernization and ecological destruction, and the need for more power in women's own hands (Agarwal, 1994, 2000; Mies, 1998; Shiva and Mies, 2014).

The question of power is crucial. Recently the idea that oppressed people can be organized in ways that ultimately promote social progress, and that this can be accomplished by advancing the agency of poor women, has been mobilized to assert the primacy of human rights in international treaty negotiations, including the UNFCCC, and it is evident in NGO campaigns that aim to uplift communities and even entire nations through col-lective female agency or empowerment (UNFCCC, 2015; CARE International, 2014). The Preamble to the Paris Agreement on climate change acknowledges international ethical obligations regarding human rights, indigenous rights, gender equality, and the empow-erment of women, and the Agreement itself states that adaptation programs should be "gender-responsive, participatory and fully transparent," and particularly attentive to "vulnerable groups, communities and ecosystems" (UNFCCC, 2015, Article 7, Section 5). Prioritizing the needs and interests of impoverished and marginalized women is thought by many to be a pragmatic necessity for moving toward greater social equality and dra-matic reductions in violence and fundamental insecurity (Kristof and WuDunn, 2010). But are environmental "development" efforts targeting females helping women and girls to be more free, knowledgeable or "self"-actualized? Familiar rhetoric such as "If you teach one girl, you teach a whole village," may not be as supportive as it sounds, if it implies that some girls should be educated *because* they will be useful to a bunch of others. As Kantians and environmental ethicists have long emphasized, to be reduced to one's use value is to be cast out of the realm of moral concern.

Attention to the gendered aspects of global injustice is crucial for grounding moral under-standing and ethical engagement. However, deeper questions must also be asked, such as why are some women and "others" so vulnerable, and how are those vulnerabilities con-structed and maintained through interwoven systems of oppressive power? What are the gendered dimensions of the ethical perspectives of those whose lifestyles maintain the envi-ronmental misery of the world's most "vulnerable"? Reducing the gendered dimensions of ecological problems to *only* the vulnerabilities of the most severely targeted and impover-ished fails to address inequality or to hold the privileged accountable in ways that lead to rep-arations or effective structural change. Instead, looking at specific mechanisms of ecological domination, and the diverse but interrelated gendered roles and concepts that support them, illuminates the practical links between systemic environmental harms and regimes of other-ing, alienated work and meaning-making that maintain them.

3   WOMEN AND NATURE: CONCEPTUAL CONNECTIONS

Since the mid-twentieth century philosophers have described the widespread disregard and abusive use of nature as expressions of a "logic of domination" that also enables sex-ism, racism and colonization (Horkheimer and Adorno, 2007; Ruether, 1975; Plumwood, 1994; Warren, 2000). Many have argued that the rampant conscious and unconscious association of femaleness with nature is part of the philosophical foundation that has allowed for so much human domination and social and ecological devastation. Writing in 1940s, in the midst of their experiences of fascism and World War II, Jewish philosophers Theodor Adorno and Max Horkheimer introduced the idea of a logic of domination to describe what they considered a pervasive "European" mindset, built on a tendency to categorize the world dichotomously and hierarchically, which creates value systems that enforce oppression, including man over nature, men over women, civilized over primitive, white over black, technology over biology, etcetera. Regarding the intertwined meanings of gender, sex, and the nature/culture separation, they locate the roots of sexism in men's relationships with nature:

> Man the ruler denies woman the honor of individuation ... male logic sees her wholly as standing for nature, as the substrate of never-ending subsumption notionally, and of never-ending subjection in reality (1947/2002, p. 87).

Echoing and elaborating on this characterization of the categorical subordination of females, Simone deBeauvoir famously explored the implications of the woman/nature association theory—the theory that the meanings of "woman," or biological femaleness, and therefore the options and real experiences of female human beings, are informed by fundamental, limiting and distorting associations between femaleness and nature. In *The Second Sex*, Beauvoir presented an origin story of women's oppression that identifies the birth of patriarchy with the subjugation of nature, describing a singular logic and mode of interaction that relegates women and nature to the realm of the consumable, usable, and dangerous. Exploring in some detail the aesthetic and symbolic associations between women and nature cross-culturally, in realms from art and literature to love letters and fashion advertising, she concluded that the very meaning of femaleness is built upon the fact that men associate women with nature, categorically reducing femaleness to object status, and in turn justifying treating nature like man's submissive possession (1949, pp. 75, 174–175). In contrast with females' reduction to nature, men in power are seen by the dominant ideology as truly human, fully capable of and drawn toward exercise of freedom and meaningful agency in a challenging world, and destined to dominate nature.

Yet Beauvoir was also sensitive to the fact that as part of its propagation of alienation, anti-nature society's insidious rules about male conformity to masculine norms can also be painfully scarring to the supposedly or paradigmatically powerful. In order conform to the ruling model of humanity, assumed to be male, boys and men must dissociate from their dependent, finite, bodily nature, which is accomplished through subjugation of their own vulnerability and femininity, and the subjugation of others (p. 86). Ordering maleness over femaleness is therefore fueled by masculine emotional and physical self-denial, and the denial of humanity's animality.

Complicating the simple dualistic logic of Beauvoir's theory, which attends more to women's presumed similarities than their actual diversities, in her popular essay "Is Female to Male as Nature is to Culture?" anthropologist Sherry Ortner argued that females cross-culturally are not simply identified with nature in a starkly dualistic system. Instead, Ortner held that in nearly every society females are cast in various roles in which they serve as mediators between nature and male-identified culture, occupying an "ambiguous status" that can be used and reshaped according to the desires of men in power. Associations with nature depict women as "lower than man in the order of things," devalued but also "circumscribed and restricted" in domestic and caretaking roles which are "mechanisms for the conversion of nature into culture" (Ortner, 1974, p. 224). But, there is also diversity and flexibility in the roles prescribed for women, and "in specific cultural ideologies and symbolizations, woman can occasionally be aligned with culture, and in any event is often assigned polarized and contradictory meanings within a single symbolic system" (1974, p. 85).

Cultural ideas about the meanings of identities and categories are created and reinforced by institutions, laws and technologies. In her canonical study *The Death of Nature: Women, Ecology and the Scientific Revolution* historian, Carolyn Merchant showed how the development of European science in the sixteenth and seventeenth centuries was fueled by misogynist and mechanistic ideologies that disempowered women economically and justified the disenchantment of nature, through scientific paradigms and practices of mastery and plunder that replaced cultural tendencies to respect nature's inherent vitality. Identifying the major moral shift that enabled the rise of cultures of severe eco-destruction with the development of modern science, Merchant argues that as science consolidated into a powerful social force, "the image of an organic cosmos with a living female earth at its center gave way to a mechanistic world view in which nature was reconstructed as dead and passive, to be dominated and controlled by humans" (1980, p. xvi). Ideas and assumptions about "nature" gradually but decisively shifted from sphere demanding respect to category of degradation. The degradation of nature comingled with a rise in economic and cultural characterizations of women's sphere as negative and therefore needing/desiring the control of violating techno-science.

Logics, technologies and institutions of domination are targeting strategies, conscious and unconscious systems of definition and understanding that align with the exploitation of particular groups and "resources." They define the powerful and the powerless, and encourage the control of subordinate others, as well as the control, suppression or hiding of qualities and affinities associated with inferiority (such as difference, dependency, and emotion). A logic of domination comprises a way of perceiving, thinking and prioritizing that encourages the exploitative use of nature, "the feminine" and those characterized as less civilized or more animalistic and therefore deserving of brutal treatment or regard:

> Women are described in animal terms as pets, cows, sows, foxes, chicks, serpents, bitches, beavers, old bats . . . Similarly, language which feminizes nature in a (patriarchal) culture where women are viewed as subordinate and inferior reinforces and authorizes the domination of nature: "Mother Nature" is . . ., mastered, conquered, mined; her secrets are "penetrated" and her "womb" is to be put into service of the "man of science" (Warren 1997, p. 12).

Ecofeminist philosophers have posited that the definitive, starkly dichotomous "Western" categories of culture/nature, civilized/primitive and heaven/earth are fundamentally interwoven with specific cultural rules and ideals about the meanings of sex, gender and sexuality (Gaard and Gruen, 1993; Plumwood, 1994; Cuomo, 1998; Warren, 2000). Indigenous and decolonial feminists describe Western metaphysics as a monism that a dualism but a monism that holds up only one ideal form of being human as valuable, and categorically excludes racialized others and nature from the realm of basic respect (Mann, 2009; Lugones, 2010). "Nature" pays a high price for its association with racialized and feminized realms of human inferiority, for the careless and violent use of nonhuman nature and animals is bolstered by claims that other animals are inherently inferior to men, and nature is the passive, lowly substrate upon which masculine culture ought to be built. The projection of similar "inferior" characteristics onto the oppressed, who are identified with nature and each other, creates resonances and repulsions among them, linking them conceptually, practically, and ambiguously. Myths about the common features the oppressed supposedly share—being vulnerable, being visceral, having feelings—are cast as threatening or strange, allowing oppressor classes to distance themselves from the oppressed, through their own fictional self-conceptions as naturally or essentially superior.

Enabling and actualizing the linked harms waged on the oppressed are conceptual frameworks that make unjust, abusive hierarchies appear normal and inevitable. Culture's sex and gender norms are particularly effective means of control in the name of morality, and they are sturdy and coercive precisely because they are described or assumed to be natural. The "naturalizing" of gender is a process through which a society's particular views about what it means to be a sex or gender are defined as natural when they are really socially specific and engineered to benefit dominant systems of privilege and order. As Val Plumwood has written, "Separate 'natures' explain, justify, and naturalize widely different privileges and fates between women and men," and the idea of separate natures makes it easier for the privileged to ignore or refuse to identify with those marked as "other" (1994, p. 337). The naturalizing of gender also expresses and redeploys philosophical and morally loaded ideas about what nature is, and why and when "being natural" is considered important, decisive, or laudatory.

Yet dominating norms of gender can be engaged, rejected and transformed. For example, along with developing alternative moral paradigms, feminist philosophers have proposed that more thorough, accurate, and ethically effective science can result through the integration of ecological and feminist values (Hallen 1987, Grasswick, 2014). Patsy Hallen proposes that if the science of ecology aims to "make peace with nature," by enabling "collective action for the ecological reconstruction of society," it needs to take into account feminist criticism of science, culture and sexuality. But as crucial as it is that we make peace with nature, the most direct and lasting routes to doing so lie in the transformation of social and political structures and relationships.

4 MONOCULTURE, GENDERED WORK, AND "FLEXIBLE" LABOR

To illustrate the usefulness of feminist analyses of linked harms, structures of exploitation, and the conceptual norms that support them, consider the significance of monoculture, a paradigm of dominating agency over nature that is detrimental to Earthly balance and enabled by social inequality. Environmentalists point out that modern chemical factory-farm monocultures result in egregious harms through pesticides, deforestation and reduction of wilderness, and more, resulting in severe collateral impacts on ecosystemic and atmospheric balance wherever they are dominant (Shiva and Moser, 1995). And as Vandana Shiva highlights in her aptly titled *Monocultures of the Mind*, the contemporary problem of monoculture is also a result of exploitation and disparity of wealth at all scales, which is intensely gendered, and propagated by neoliberal global capitalism. Understanding the politics of sex and gender in the context of colonialism and capitalism's enforcement of global monoculture systems can be crucial for understanding how harmful monocultures are maintained, and how they might be transformed.

Sociologist Deborah Barndt presents a compelling case study of gendered monoculture in her book *Tangled Routes: Women, Work and Globalization on the Tomato Trail*, which traces the creation through commodification of the supermarket tomato. Through monocultural systems of agriculture and work that are extraordinarily demanding of women, especially poor women of color, the *tomatl*, a bright delicate fruit indigenous to southern Mexico, has been converted into a sturdy pale tasteless orb suitable to shipping far north to Canada in the middle of winter. In the tomato's journey, monocropping systems and grocery store monopolies are built on female labor and buying power. At all levels women workers are at the center of the commodification of the tomato, through the transnational systems of corporate agriculture, food distribution, purchasing and cuisine through which the monocropped fruit moves. As Brandt describes,

> Women are key protagonists for their families in their triple function: as salaried workers (with varying status and wage levels), as subsistence farmers (when they have access to the land), and as domestic laborers (with a wide range of living conditions, from the horrific albergues of Indigenous migrants to the better-equipped but transient homes of the mobile packers). Globalizing agribusinesses ... have built their workforces on these historically entrenched inequalities and differences. (Barndt, 2008, p. 245)

The propagation of monoculture occurs on the back of diverse, feminized, female laborers who are farmers, farmworkers, cashiers, fast-food consumers, and shoppers. The ethics of monocropping therefore cannot be adequately addressed without investigating how particular agricultural and commercial practices are enabled by underlying politics of gender and social power. Barndt shows throughout that "Indigenous women and children are clearly in the most precarious position of all who bring us the corporate tomato," and across class and race, female positions in relation to work, family and economy are central, though rarely imbued with decision-making power (Bardnt, 2008, p. 246). Are women therefore more exploited than nourished through complex food systems in which they work?

The harms and difficulties associated with women's different work roles are specific to class and culture, although similar gendered messages and dynamics can be used to normalize increased pressures on diverse workers and consumers. Barndt's research shows how the cross-cultural discourse constructing women workers and mothers as "flexible" workers, rather than workers with inherent and respect-worthy needs regarding wages, work hours and benefits, normalizes the untenable demands placed on female laborers in contemporary food industries, and squeezes nature more and more in the process. Worker "flexibility" is a dominating theme in a dichotomized economic system that produces complicated relationships between a formal sector that is structured and regulated, and an informal sector marked by its so-called flexibility, and regulated minimally if at all. But discourses of female and worker "flexibility" are cunning linguistic reversals which repackage peoples' desperation for wages as a desire for flexible work hours. Such discourses and structures enable more and more unpleasant and low-wage part-time jobs without childcare, health care benefits, or protection for workers' rights. With women's gendered labor across classes at the core, the people and natural resources that make up the informal economy "are the internal and external colonies of capital," where "workers in the informal sector, like housewives, have no lobby and are atomized" (Mies, 1998, pp. 17, 16).

5 TRANSFORMATIVE POWER

Gendered norms, women's labor, and female workers' over-determined needs help maintain harmful systems and structures, including massive monocultures of genetically modified livestock and crops. Understanding and redressing dynamics through which certain groups are punished or relegated to the lowliest work and lowest wages in society via their projected or real "closeness to nature" brings us face to face with an array of systematic and interlocking harms that are not merely environmental or social, but both. Ethically, the realities of linked harms raise questions about the causes and interdependencies of those harms, and the possibility that there are beliefs, conceptual assumptions, and culturally/politically manufactured symbolic systems that have created or encouraged them.

Tracing the racial histories and sexual politics influencing ethics, and reflexively engaging our gendered values and presumptions, are crucial processes for developing and realizing environmental ethics. A recent global survey reported that 55% of women in the United States but only 39% of American men see climate change as a "very serious problem," and 75% American women polled (compared to 57% of men) acknowledge that significant lifestyle changes will be required to address climate change (Pew Research Center, 2015). While such statistics seem to point to the potential power of female moral leadership, closer attention to gendered patterns and experiences brings diversity and a more complex ontology of identity to the fore. People who understand the gravity of an ethical issue cannot act on their caring without political, economic or cultural power. In these times of such serious endangerment of Earthly life, the potentially transformative politics of sex, gender, race and class may be more decisive than ever.

REFERENCES

Agarwal, B. (1994). *A Field of One's Own: Gender and Land Rights in South Asia*. Cambridge, England; New York, NY: Cambridge University Press.

Agarwal, B. (2000). "Conceptualising Environmental Collective Action: Why Gender Matters." *Cambridge Journal of Economics* 24: 283–310.

Allen, P (1992). *The Sacred Hoop: Recovering the Feminine in American Indian Traditions*. Boston: Beacon Press.

Alston, M., and Whittenbury, K. (2012). *Research, Action and Policy: Addressing the Gendered Impacts of Climate Change*. New York: Springer.

Barndt, D. (2008). *Tangled Routes: Women, Work, and Globalization on the Tomato Trail* (2nd ed.). Lanham, MD: Rowman & Littlefield Publishers.

CARE International. (2014). *Fighting Poverty by Empowering Women and Girls in the Poorest Communities Around the World, Annual Report*. Geneva: CARE International.

Covan, C., and Fugate-Whitlock, E. (2010). "Emergency Planning and Long-Term Care: Least Paid, Least Powerful, Most Responsible." *Health Care for Women International* 31(11): 1028–1043.

Cuomo, C. (1998). *Feminism and Ecological Communities: An Ethic of Flourishing*. New York: Routledge.

DeBeauvoir, S. (1949/2011). *The Second Sex*. New York: Vintage Books.

Denton, F. (2002). "Climate Change Vulnerability, Impacts, and Adaptation: Why Does Gender Matter?" *Gender and Development* 10(2): 10–20.

Egan, J. E., et al. (2011). "Migration, Neighborhoods, and Networks: Approaches to Understanding How Urban Environmental Conditions Affect Syndemic Adverse Health Outcomes Among Gay, Bisexual, and Other Men Who Have Sex with Men." *AIDS and Behavior* 15(1): S35–S50.

Enarson, E. (2000). "Gender and Natural Disasters." Working paper no.1, Infocus Programme on Crisis Response and Reconstruction. Geneva: International Labour Organisation, Recovery and Reconstruction Department.

Firestone, S. (1970). *The Dialectic of Sex: The Case for Feminist Revolution*. New York: William Morrow & Co.

Gaard, G., and Gruen, L. (1993). "Ecofeminism: Toward Global Justice and Planetary Health." *Society and Nature* 4: 1–35.

Gilman, C. P. (1915/1998). *Herland*. New York: Dover Publications.

Grasswick, H. (2014). "Climate Change Science and Responsible Trust: A Situated Approach." *Hypatia* 29: 541–557.

Griffin, S. (1978). *Woman and Nature: The Roaring Inside Her*. New York: Harper Publishing.

Gruen, L. (2014). *Entangled Empathy: An Alternative Ethic for Our Relationships with Animals*. New York: Lantern Books.

Hallen, P (1987). "Making Peace with Nature: Why Ecology Needs Feminism." *Trumpeter* 4(3): 3–13.

Horkheimer, M., and Adorno, T. (2007). *Dialectic of Enlightenment: Philosophical Fragments*. Palo Alto: Stanford University Press.

Kheel, M. (1985). "The Liberation of Nature: A Circular Affair." *Environmental Ethics*, 7 (2): 135–149.

Kheel, M. (2007). *Nature Ethics: An Ecofeminist Perspective*. Lanham, MD: Rowman and Littlefield.

Kristof, N. D., and WuDunn, S. (2010). *Half the Sky: Turning Oppression into Opportunity for Women Worldwide*. New York: Vintage Books.

Laditka, S. et al. (2010). "In the Eye of the Storm: Resilience and Vulnerability Among African American Women in the Wake of Hurricane Katrina." *Health Care for Women International* 31(11): 1013–1027.

Lugones, M. (2010). "Toward a Decolonial Feminism." *Hypatia* 25: 742–759.

Maathai, W. (2004). *Nobel Lecture*, Oslo, December 10, 2004. http://www.nobelprize.org/nobel_prizes/peace/laureates/2004/maathai-lecture-text.html

Merchant, C. (1980). *The Death of Nature: Women, Ecology, and the Scientific Revolution*. New York: Harper and Row.

Mies, M. (1998). *Patriarchy and Accumulation on a World Scale: Women in the International Division of Labour*. New York: Zed Books.

Mortimer-Sandilands, C., and Erickson, B. (Eds.) (2010). *Queer Ecologies: Sex, Nature, Politics, Desire*. Bloomington: Indiana University Press.

Ortner, S. B. (1974). "Is Female to Male as Nature is to Culture?" In *Woman, Culture and Society*, edited by M. Z. Rosaldo and L. Lamphere. Palo Alto: Stanford University Press.

Pew Research Center (2015). Global Concern About Climate Change, Broad Support for Limiting Emissions.

Pizan, C. (2000). *The Book of the City of Ladies*. New York: Penguin.

Plumwood, V. (1994). *Feminism and the Mastery of Nature.* New York: Routledge.

Ruether, R. R. (1975). *New Woman, New Earth: Sexist Ideologies and Human Liberation.* New York: Seabury Press.

Seager, J. (1993). *Earth Follies: Coming to Feminist Terms with the Global Environmental Crisis.* New York: Routledge.

Shiva, V. (1993). *Monocultures of the Mind: Perspectives on Biodiversity and Biotechnology.* London: Zed Books.

Shiva, V. and Moser, I. (1995). *Biopolitics: A Feminist and Ecological Reader on Biotechnology.* London: Zed Books.

Shiva, V., and Mies, M. (1993/2014). *Ecofeminism.* London: Zed Books.

Silko, L. (2000). *Gardens in the Dunes.* New York: Simon and Schuster.

Smith, M. (2016). "Flint Wants Safe Water, and Someone to Answer for Its Crisis." *The New York Times,* January 10: A16.

UNFCCC (2015). Paris Agreement. http://unfccc.int/resource/docs/2015/cop21/eng/l09r01. pdf

Walker, A. (1989). "Am I Blue?," In *Living by the Word: Selected Writings 1973-1987.* San Diego: Harvest Books. 3–8.

Warren, K. (1990). "The Power and Promise of Ecological Feminism." *Environmental Ethics* 12(2):125–146.

Warren, K. (1997). "Taking Empirical Data Seriously." In *Ecofeminism: Women, Culture, Nature,* edited by K. Warren, 3–20. Bloomington: Indiana University Press.

Warren, K. (2000). *Ecofeminist Philosophy: A Western Perspective on What It Is and Why It Matters.* Lanham, MD: Rowmand and Littlefield, 2000.

White, E. C. (2002). "Black Women and the Wilderness." In *Nature Writing: The Tradition in English,* edited by R. Finch and J. Elder, 1062–1067. New York: W. W. Norton & Company.

CHAPTER 25

··

HUMAN RIGHTS AND
THE ENVIRONMENT

··

STEVE VANDERHEIDEN

As persons are threatened by heightened resource scarcity or degraded environmental conditions as the result of human activities, their human rights can be violated. Conceiving of this threat in terms of human rights and invoking rights on behalf of environmental protection focuses attention upon several key human interests and their vulnerability to anthropogenic environmental change. It also promises to mobilize several key legal and political powers, thereby empowering would-be victims of environmental harm to invoke such rights on behalf of stronger environmental protection, either themselves or through their advocates. Rights-based approaches to environmental protection combine the normative force of moral rights, which justify claims to certain goods or capabilities, and the political powers associated with legal rights, which mobilize procedural or institutional mechanisms designed to protect such rights.

But human rights-based approaches are also inherently limited as sources or expressions of value in environmental ethics. Foremost among such limits, human rights appeal to human interests alone and so are inescapably anthropocentric. While perhaps able to justify protection of ecosystems when the interests that are protected by human rights are at stake, thereby promoting the interests of nonhumans indirectly, their orientation toward important human interests prevents these approaches from recognizing nonhuman value in itself. In addition, human rights are, unlike domestic legal or constitutional rights, largely aspirational (Donnelly, 2002), as they lack the political mechanisms needed to ensure that the most vulnerable are protected from threats to the interests that such rights are meant to protect. Conversely, as human rights become positive law and come to more closely resemble domestic legal rights, or specifically environmental rights begin to be recognized, their protection relies upon an individualistic model of responsibility that is challenged by the nature of many environmental threats, frustrating their ability to instantiate strong norms of environmental protection.

Nonetheless, human rights offer several potentially valuable conceptual and political tools for environmental ethics and politics by linking environmental imperatives with those of international humanitarian law and politics, mobilizing legal and political mechanisms that are associated with human rights objectives, and empowering a broader constituency on behalf environmental protection than might otherwise be available through rival normative approaches. The sections to follow examine the moral foundations for human rights, their application to contemporary environmental problems such as climate change, several challenges for human rights law and theory posed by the nature of some contemporary environmental issues, and the potential advantages of viewing such issues through the lens of human rights.

1 MORAL FOUNDATIONS OF HUMAN RIGHTS

Human rights are legally protected elements of international law, albeit of a softer form of law than most domestically recognized rights, depending for their legal foundation upon the treaties and conventions through which nation-states have endorsed them and pledged their protection. Their ethical foundation, however, rests upon the corresponding moral rights of protection against threats of harm or access to important goods, which share a similar structure with those legal rights. Human rights are held by all *qua* humans, regardless of national origin or citizenship, extending the protections that are granted through constitutional rights beyond national borders. They do so through treaties and other multilateral agreements by which states pledge their protection internally and their promotion abroad, in principle offering their protections even to persons residing within states that reject human rights conventions.

Originating in the early modern social contract tradition as natural rights, first declared as elements of positive law through the 1948 Universal Declaration of Human Rights (UDHR) and later expanded through a series of subsequent conventions, human rights prescribe norms of conduct in world politics, provide a mechanism for evaluating regimes and measuring social progress, and are sometimes asserted as conditions for post-Westphalian sovereignty (Buchanan, 1991). Since they are universal in scope, human rights are presumed to protect interests that are common to all, as well as being vulnerable to interference by others. In other words, they protect against wrongs, not merely bad outcomes for which none can be identified as responsible, and offer this protection through the combination of normative force designed to prevent such wrongs from occurring and remedial processes designed to intervene when they do occur. Human rights regimes, then, disseminate the norms that rights protect and enforce their prescriptive implications where necessary, utilizing various power resources in so doing.

In general, moral rights against anthropogenic environmental harm vest those protected by them with *prima facie* claims to injunctive relief against those responsible for degrading the environment or depleting natural resources in the manner connected to that harm, as well as to compensation for injuries that they are made to suffer. Recognizing this negative right provides a very strong, if not necessarily conclusive, reason for others to cease their involvement in harmful causal processes and to rectify any experienced harm for which they are responsible. In principle, the duties associated with this right are binding upon all, although the aggregative and indirect way in which one person's rights might be violated by the acts of others presents a problem for conventional rights theories, to be further discussed in the next section. The case for wielding human rights on behalf of environmental protection turns largely upon the value of the political power and normative force that human rights invoke, which some view as useful, given the difficulty in generating international cooperation on behalf of environmental problems such as climate change, which threatens several key interests that rights protect (Caney, 2008; Shue, 2011).

The moral rights upon which human rights against environmental harm are founded, then, are not against environmental harm itself, which can result from natural disasters or other events for which human causal agency cannot be clearly established. Rather, the rights protect against harm for which some human agent can be held responsible through their acts or omissions. The question of what counts as responsible human agency, without which rights cannot be violated, requires more discussion than is possible here. Following a standard for cases of rights against environmental harm based in *contributory fault* (Vanderheiden, 2008a), human rights remedies to environmental harm require the demonstration of liability on the part of responsible parties for any rights violation. Feinberg (1970a: 222) notes that this standard form of fault-based liability contains three main components, all of which are necessary conditions:

> First, it must be true that the responsible individual did the harmful thing in question, or at least that his action or omission made a substantial causal contribution to it. Second, the causally contributory conduct must have been in some way faulty. Finally, if the harmful conduct was truly "his fault," the requisite causal connection must have been directly between the faulty aspect of his conduct and the outcome. It is not sufficient to have caused harm and to have been at fault if the fault was irrelevant to the causing.

By this standard, environmental harm that results from excusable ignorance (Bell, 2011) may bring about morally bad outcomes but does not violate rights against harm, since agents cannot be faulted for causing outcomes that they could not have reasonably foreseen and thus avoided. Because moral rights involve claims against culpable others, they cannot be violated by purely accidental injuries, or those for which contributory fault cannot be established, since these are similar in structure to those resulting from natural causes. Wielding human rights against environmental harm is thus often complicated (Woods, 2010), for reasons to be explored next.

2 CHALLENGES FOR HUMAN RIGHTS APPROACHES

Before considering reasons on behalf of viewing environmental harm through the lens of human rights, several reasons against doing so must be noted. In contrast with distributive justice-based analyses of environmental problems, which claim equal rights to environmental goods and services or assign remedial burdens for environmental protection in accordance with egalitarian principles, rights-based approaches rest upon sufficientarian principles (Miller, 1999), which often have lower thresholds for access or protection. Whereas rights protection requires that all have access only to that minimal set of resources necessary for their rights not to be violated, justice may require equal access to such resources. As this contrast is typically cast, rights are concerned with reducing absolute but not relative deprivation, focusing only upon the worst off, whereas justice is concerned with narrowing the gap between the best and worst off. Depending upon where thresholds for rights violations are set, human rights approaches may leave in place significant injustice, provided that these do not violate the rights of the affected.

Caney (2009), for example, argues for a human rights-based approach to climate change, noting that human rights to life, health, and subsistence are all threatened by human-induced climate change. In response to this threat, and contrasting his human rights-based approach to those rooted in economic cost-benefit analysis, Caney formulates three well-established human rights in negative terms, as protecting against threats to these three vital human interests that result from the acts of others. As he notes, "human rights represent moral 'thresholds' below which people should not fall" (2009: 71), but such thresholds may be lower than what would be required of distributive justice if applied to the same problem. Rights may tolerate relatively more inequality in the resource-sharing or burden-sharing dimensions of climate change mitigation efforts, compared with what is needed to avoid these rights from being threatened, and offer no reasons for preventing bad outcomes that fall short of violating rights.

Moreover, the negative formulation of such rights, along with the juridical framework that they invoke, requires the demonstration of causal relationships that are often elusive in the context of aggregative problems like climate change, with the fragmented agency and diffuse causality that it involves (Gardiner, 2011). Since climate change is only probabilistically related to the impacts that Caney cites, as it only raises the frequency and intensity of extreme weather events like storms and floods or intensifies chronic problems like drought and heat, it would be impossible to link any particular loss of life or threat to health or subsistence to any responsible action, policy, or party, given legal standards of proof. No one's emissions on their own produce discernible impacts on global climate, let alone any harmful weather event, and so cannot be causally linked to the deprivation in question (Sinnott-Armstrong, 2005). Even very large groups of relatively profligate greenhouse polluters, such as residents of developed countries, cannot be linked to specific human rights violations in the manner required of conventional legal right protections, since the phenomenon results from what humanity has done in total and over time. Absent some rights-violating act, or series of acts by an identifiable agent that can be clearly and directly linked to the harm or threat in question, the correlative duties associated with human rights claims are difficult to show as being violated, thus challenging conventional rights analysis.

In the context of global and aggregative environmental harm like that expected to arise from climate change, one could follow Caney's strategy in pointing to scientific estimates of total human impacts of climate change, arguing that x additional deaths from more frequent and intense weather events means x additional arbitrary deprivations of life, violating the human rights of those affected. Even if we cannot distinguish the anthropogenic drivers of particular weather events from otherwise similar events that would have occurred at lower atmospheric concentrations of greenhouse gases, one might reason, we can identify links between human action and the loss of life, which after all is the object of a human right to life. Although we could not say with any certainty *whose* life was lost as the result of the polluting actions that cause climate change, we could estimate the number of rights violations that a given level of warming was likely to cause, thereby showing climate change (and, by extension, the actions and policies that cause climate change) to be responsible for those additional losses of life (Nolt, 2011).

The problem with this approach is twofold. First, apart from several collective rights like those to self-determination, territory, and culture, most human rights protect individuals against threats to important human interests. The right to life is one such individual right, and it is violated when, as Caney notes, any person is arbitrarily deprived of his or her life. It cannot protect groups against deaths beyond normal mortality rates, such as those resulting from conflict or environmental change, while retaining its structure as an individual right. Indeed, rights against harm are inherently individualistic, rejecting the exercises in aggregation described earlier, which, as Rawls (1971) notes of utilitarianism, fail to take seriously the separateness of persons. While higher group mortality also entails additional individual deaths, the human right to life cannot be said to be violated by statistical deviation from normal group mortality rates. Even if climate change could be identified as the cause of x additional deaths within a group, this would not violate any right held by the group. If no identifiable persons can be shown to have lost their lives as the result of climate change, then climate change cannot be responsible for violating any identifiable person's right to life, where such identification would be crucial for granting standing or assessing damages to suffers of climate-related harm.

Second, by engaging in this sort of aggregative analysis, the human rights approach does not appear to add clarity or scope to standard climate ethics analyses of wrongful climate-related harm. Deontological approaches resting on categorical prohibitions against causing avoidable harm to innocent victims already capture the same diagnosis and suffer from the same problems of distinguishing human-caused from naturally occurring deaths. Consequentialist approaches (Singer, 2004) can capture the wrongness of causing additional deaths but reject the inviolability of persons that is characteristic of rights theories. Distributive justice-based approaches to climate change likewise enjoy an advantage over rights theories, since they focus on allocations of resource shares or the manner in which climate change exacerbates existing inequalities, both of which are more amenable to the aggregative impact strategies noted earlier. Compared to showing that some set of like acts or policies caused some bad outcome, it is relatively easy to show that some person or group has emitted more than their just share of greenhouse gases, since this analysis need not link those excessive emissions to any particular effects. If the goal is to link offending actions or policies to the criteria that some normative theory uses to identify departures from their expressed ideal, rights-based approaches appear to be least well-suited for applications to climate change, with human rights offering little improvement upon the already murky links provided by its analysis through moral rights.

Another strategy for shoring up the causal links between the human activities that cause climate change and the interests protected by human rights involves the recognition of a kind of penumbra right, implied by human rights against harm, to a safe or adequate environment. By substantiating the role that environmental hazards can play in threatening existing human rights, such a right would formalize the need for protection against environmental threats, calling attention to the instrumental relationship that environment plays in human welfare. One influential formulation of such an environmental human right can be found in the Stockholm Declaration, from the 1972 UN Conference on the Human Environment, which declares:

> Principle 1: Man has the fundamental right to freedom, equality and adequate conditions of life, in an environment of a quality that permits a life of dignity and well-being, and he bears a solemn responsibility to protect and improve the environment for present and future generations.

Elevating the interest in a safe or adequate environment to the status of a human right would confer several benefits. As Hayward notes of constitutionally protected environmental rights, which are applicable to human rights insofar as they obtain the status of legal rights, such protection

> entrenches a recognition of the importance of environmental protection; it offers the possibil-
> ity of unifying principles for legislation and regulation; it secures these principles against the
> vicissitudes of routine politics, while at the same time enhancing possibilities of democratic
> participation in environmental decision-making processes (2005: 7).

Other human rights approaches are reductionist in valuing environmental quality only to the extent that it is instrumental to the protection of human interests or capabilities that through their status as protected are deemed to be inherently valuable (Holland, 2008), but guaranteeing a safe environment by right obviates the contingency associated with this instrumental relationship. Moreover, the text of this right as expressed here pairs the declaration of the right with a charge of responsibility for protecting it and refusing to wait for violations of the right to occur before ordering remedial action or limiting legal standing to those demonstrably harmed by particular environmental impacts, both of which bolster the right's ability to protect the interests around which it is designed.

3 DEFENDING HUMAN RIGHTS APPROACHES

Despite these philosophical difficulties, human rights approaches offer legal and political resources, including institutional means of redress when persons are wronged by having their rights violated. With robustly protected legal rights, victims of environmental harm can pursue redress through the courts, often with the assistance of counsel funded by states or NGOs, and if successful have the backing of other state actors in obtaining their ordered remedies. Human rights rely upon "soft" law when not formally incorporated by states but nonetheless, in principle, offer legal and political protections against significant threats, whether through quasi-judicial bodies like human rights commissions or through the multilateral protection of states pledged with the UDHR and reaffirmed through the Responsibility to Protect (R2P) doctrine. Although less robust than legal or constitutional rights, human rights promise stronger protections than ethical proscriptions and prescriptions, which carry no sanction and thus are unenforceable, and at least attempt to bring practical enforcement to the protection against moral wrongs, aligning political power with the ends that render it legitimate.

Human rights are also important sources of norms in international politics by affirming the interests protected by them as universally held and crucial to human welfare, heralding those rights as the basis for evaluation of regimes and international institutions, and calling attention to humanity's most urgent threats. Even if not justiciable sources of legal power, the recognition of human rights against environmental harm may confer significant discursive benefits for the development of international environmental policy by linking resource depletion and degradation with other human rights imperatives. By treating environmental protection as a human rights issue rather than an economic one, as Caney argues, the case might more effectively be made for strong mitigation efforts even if these come at high costs, as rights protection is not subject to cost-benefit analysis. Human rights impacts, rather than economic costs, might more effectively be used to measure the impacts of environmental degradation and the benefits of protection and to highlight the human impacts of problems such as climate change, rather than the temperature targets that have served as the dominant objectives in policy debates (McInerney-Lankford, Darrow, and Rajamani, 2011). Linking environmental protection with human rights could help consolidate support for such protections within the human rights community by making rights protection a core objective, thus reducing worries about competition for scarce aid and development resources being diverted to nascent global conservation efforts.

In addition, human rights-based approaches may be more empowering for those suffering from environmental harm than are those based in moral suasion, given their characterization of that harm as infringing upon entitlements that can be *claimed* rather relying upon those who are culpable also being conscientious. As Feinberg suggests, "having rights allows us to 'stand up like men,' to look others in the eye, and to feel in some fundamental sense the equal of anyone" (1970b: 252), for rights enable persons to make valid claims of entitlement when they are wronged by others, rather than limiting them to moral suasion or depending upon the sympathy or charity of others. Merely being in possession of rights, even without having to invoke them before the state (where claims may be dismissed), might therefore confer some salutary benefits upon would-be sufferers of environmental harm. This empowerment may be partly dependent upon the legal or political resources that protected rights also provide, when states recognize rights holders as having valid claims against each other as well as against the state itself, but issues also partly from the formulation of claims in terms of rights and persists even as such claims are officially denied. Being in the position to demand a remedy, as opposed to merely pointing out a morally bad outcome in which one is involved, implies an equal moral status that may embolden those accustomed to disadvantage to act on behalf of their interests rather than accepting harm visited upon them as inevitable or irresistible.

Human rights challenges under international law to the policies of carbon polluting states might also mobilize support for better domestic rights protections by faulting domestic policies for human rights violations abroad. For example, a 2005 challenge by the Inuit before the Inter-American Commission on Human Rights (IACHR) alleged that the United States was violating their human rights through its contribution to climate change, which has had some of its most palpable effects in the arctic regions of Canada, Alaska, Greenland, and Russia inhabited by Inuit people. According to the petition, climate change "caused by the acts and omissions of the United States" violated Inuit human rights "to the benefits of culture, to property, to the preservation of health, life, physical integrity, security, and a means of subsistence, and to residence, movement, and inviolability of the home" (Inuit Circumpolar Conference [ICC], 2005: 5). The petition was denied without prejudice in November 2006 but if accepted would have marked a significant victory for the Inuit as well as others vulnerable to climate-related harm. Included within the petition and within the IACHR's authority to order were demands that the United States "adopt mandatory measures to limit its emissions of greenhouse gases and cooperate in efforts of the community of nations," that it assess and consider impacts of domestic emissions on Inuit people "before approving all major government actions," and that is develop and finance an a plan for Inuit people to adapt to changing climatic conditions (ICC 2005: 7–8). Again, the petition's ultimate failure might give pause concerning the strategy, but the potential for agenda setting and mobilizing support through human rights discourse ought also to be considered.

4 CONCLUSIONS

Human rights are typically viewed as aspirations rather than connoting any positive law, and indeed they are described as such in the Universal Declaration of Human Rights, which calls upon signatory states to "strive by teaching and education to promote respect for these rights and freedoms and by progressive measures, national and international, to secure their universal and effective recognition and observance." While subsequent declarations of human rights through multilateral treaties are legally binding, in principle giving them the status of legal rights and requiring enforcement by signatory states no matter where rights violations occur, in practice they enjoy a significantly weaker status than domestic legal rights (Hiskes, 2008). Some of this relative weakness issues from institutional deficits at the global level, where the judicial equivalent to domestic constitutional rights and courts is lacking, thereby leaving the enforcement of human rights largely to the discretion of states rather than impartial legal authorities. Other sources of relative weakness are legal, as for example with the US reservation to the International Covenant on Civil and Political Rights declaring its provisions not to be self-executing, which denies petitioners access to US courts and rejects normal treaty requirements that its provisions also be made a part of domestic law.

While human rights law could potentially require state parties to human rights treaties and conventions to take on more strenuous environmental protection efforts as injunctive relief for current rights violations or in the interest of rights protection, it is only one of several sources of international law that already require large polluters like the United States to take meaningful action on international environmental problems such as climate change (Rayfuse and Scott, 2012). Although the United States avoided legally binding greenhouse emissions caps under the 1997 Kyoto Protocol by refusing to ratify the treaty, it is a signatory to the 1990 Rio Declaration, through which it committed to freezing its emissions at 1990 levels pending further policy actions, along with being party to the 1979 Geneva Convention on Long-range Transboundary Air Pollution, which offers another basis in international law for requiring greenhouse emissions controls. Linking human rights to climate change mitigation and adaptation efforts, or recognizing penumbra rights like the right to a safe or adequate environment, could build upon existing international law in further defining national obligations in and goals of international regulatory regimes. Moreover, linking rights against environmental degradation with those to development, which in some cases can be compromised by aggressive protections, can help to reconcile these competing rights (Vanderheiden, 2008b).

Although both the seriousness of climate change as a global policy concern and the urgency of action to prevent climate-related suffering suggest the connection to human rights, which are properly reserved for humanity's greatest moral and political challenges, the upside of invoking such rights on behalf of climate change mitigation might best be seen as political rather than philosophical, and of the political upshots the primary benefits may reside in the recognition and empowerment of current and potential sufferers of climate-related harm rather than the legal mobilization of recognized political authorities. To be sure, there remain downside risks of a human rights approach, including potential damage to support for other human rights imperatives from linking it to politically unpopular if urgent policy issues, and compromise to the more ambitious egalitarian justice imperatives that rights approaches can only partly fulfil. Whether or not to ground such efforts in terms of justice, ethics, or human rights must be regarded in strategic rather than analytical terms, as the values or risks of various approaches turn less upon their ability to clarify the moral stakes involved and more upon their propensity for mobilizing an effective response, but these considerations may warrant at least some further work on human rights approaches, perhaps seeking to offer them as more directly normative than either analytic or authoritative, thus connecting recognized ethical commitments with nascent efforts to build those into the way the world confronts several looming environmental threats.

References

Bell, D. (2011). "Global Climate Justice, Historic Emissions, and Excusable Ignorance." *The Monist* 94: 391–411.

Buchanan, A. (1991). *Secession: The Morality of Political Divorce from Fort Sumpter to Lithuania and Quebec.* Boulder, CO: Westview Press.

Caney, S. (2008). "Human Rights, Climate Change, and Discounting." *Environmental Politics* 17: 536–555.

Caney, S. (2009). "Climate Change, Human Rights, and Moral Thresholds." In *Human Rights and Climate Change*, edited by S. Humphreys, 69–90. New York: Cambridge University Press.

Donnelly, J. (2002). *Universal Human Rights in Theory and Practice.* Ithaca, NY: Cornell University Press.

Feinberg, J. (1970a). *Doing and Deserving.* Princeton, NJ: Princeton University Press.

Feinberg, J. (1970b). "The Nature and Value of Rights." *Journal of Value Inquiry* 4: 243–257.

Gardiner, S. M. (2011). *A Perfect Moral Storm: The Ethical Tragedy of Climate Change.* New York: Oxford University Press, 2011.

Hayward, T. (2005). *Constitutional Environmental Rights.* New York: Oxford University Press, 2005.

Hiskes, R. (2008). *The Human Right to a Green Future: Environmental Rights and Intergenerational Justice.* New York: Cambridge University Press, 2008.

Holland, B. (2008). "Justice and the Environment in Nussbaum's 'Capabilities Approach': Why Sustainable Ecological Capacity is a Meta-Capability." *Political Research Quarterly* 61: 319–332.

Inuit Circumpolar Conference (ICC). *Petition to the Inter-American Commission on Human Rights Seeking Relief from Violations Resulting from Global Warming Caused by Acts and Omissions of the United States.* Submitted by S. Watt-Cloutier with support from the ICC, 7 December 2005. Accessed May 6, 2013, http://earthjustice.org/sites/default/files/library/legal_docs/petition-to-the-inter-american-commission-on-human-rights-on-behalf-of-the-inuit-circumpolar-conference.pdf.

McInerney-Lankford, S., Darrow, M., and Rajamani, L. *Human Rights and Climate Change: A Review of the International Legal Dimensions.* Washington DC: The World Bank, 2011. Accessed May 6, 2013. http://siteresources.worldbank.org/INTLAWJUSTICE/Resources/HumanRightsAndClimateChange.pdf.

Miller, D. (1999). *Principles of Social Justice.* Cambridge, MA: Harvard University Press.

Nolt, J. (2011). "How Harmful Are the Average American's Greenhouse Gas Emissions?" *Ethics, Policy and Environment* 14: 3–10.

Rawls, J. (1971). *A Theory of Justice*. Cambridge, MA: Belknap Press.

Rayfuse, R., and Scott, S. (Eds.) (2012). *International Law in the Era of Climate Change*. Northampton, MA: Edward Elgar.

Shue, H. (2011). "Human Rights, Climate Change, and the Trillionth Ton." In *The Ethics of Global Climate Change*, edited by D. Arnold, 292–314. New York: Cambridge University Press.

Singer, P. (2004). *One World: The Ethics of Globalization*. New Haven: Yale University Press.

Sinnott-Armstrong, W. (2005). "It's Not My Fault." In *Perspectives on Climate Change: Science, Economics, Politics, Ethics*, edited by W. Sinnott-Armstrong and R. B. Howarth, 285–306. San Diego: Elsevier.

Vanderheiden, S. (2008a). *Atmospheric Justice: A Political Theory of Climate Change*. New York: Oxford University Press.

Vanderheiden, S. (2008b). "Climate Change, Environmental Rights, and Emissions Shares." In *Political Theory and Global Climate Change*, edited by S. Vanderheiden, 43–66. Cambridge, MA: The MIT Press.

Woods, K. (2010). *Human Rights and Environmental Sustainability*. Northampton, MA: Edward Elgar.

CHAPTER 26

....

ECOLOGICAL SPACE
The Concept and Its Ethical Significance

....

TIM HAYWARD

ECOLOGICAL space is relevant to ethics not in virtue of being an evaluative term or referring directly to any determinate object of evaluation.[1] It is primarily a descriptive term. What is to be shown here, though, is how what the term refers to, when spelled out and thought through, has considerable and distinctive ethical significance, particularly with regard to global justice and human rights. Use of the concept allows us to capture, particularly well, something morally important about the way humans' relations with one another are mediated through multifarious *natural* relations.[2]

Ethical implications of the concept of ecological space can be drawn out from the focus it brings to issues arising from the finitude and vulnerability of habitats. In this planet's biosphere, there has always been competition of various kinds—within, among, and between species, populations and communities of organisms—for adequate environmental resources. The complexity of life, of course, also means that many organisms are themselves environmental resources for others. These natural ecological processes are hardly appropriate, or even possible, matters for ethical regulation by humans. Ethical questions do arise, however, when consciously directed activities of human beings cause harm to the environments or resources that other human beings depend on. Ethical questions also arise when humans cause harm to the environments or resources of members of species other than *homo sapiens*, or indeed when they directly harm those members themselves[3]; but for the present exposition, I shall confine attention to questions of intra-human ethics.

1 ECOLOGICAL SPACE: ITS DESCRIPTIVE MEANING

....

The ethical significance of the concept of ecological space can perhaps best be revealed through developing an understanding of how it can support and inspire a particular *way of seeing*.[4] This may be captured by considering how some basic principles of ecology can be brought to bear on the concept of space.

The concept of space, in general and in the abstract, implies nothing that can be pictured, being the pure constitutive form of appearance of extended objects in reality as we experience it. Space, as we refer to the term in any determinate context, however, is always thought of under a particular sort of description; different kinds of space can be conceptualized according to different knowledge constitutive interests—cosmological space, geographical space, psychological space, personal space, and so on. Understanding the distinctive kinds of function of *ecological* space, in relation to human interests, is the key to understanding its ethical significance.

Ecology—the science and the reality studied by it[5]—concerns the complex interrelationships between and among organisms and their environments. These interrelationships take place in extended space, to be sure, but we can distinguish ecological space from geographical and topographical descriptions. The relevant space is defined more by function than by physical dimension or magnitude.

This point and its implications can helpfully be brought out by thinking of ecological space—the generic concept—as what is provided for particular species or populations by their ecological *niche*. The niches of a variety of species may be found in the same physical location. Each niche is a particular kind of functional space that furnishes the sum of the habitat requirements that allow members of a species to persist and produce offspring. The ecological term 'niche' conveys the idea of a "space" for organisms to live in that is defined by parameters other than of physical extension.[6] We are also familiar with the idea of a niche used figuratively in other contexts—such as niche products and finding one's niche within a broader social or organizational context. We tend to use the term for more marginal institutional habitats, but that is because it is in such circumstances that we are more *aware* of the special conditions necessary for survival of the entity or enterprise in question. There are, of course, much bigger niches whose conditions are more taken for granted.

In fact, the taken-for-granted nature of so many vital environmental conditions is a major factor in bringing us to the environmental crises we now face. Human beings have expanded their (*realized*)[7] niche—that is, the niche that they actually live in—on this planet quite considerably. We can adapt ourselves to a wide variety of habitats, because—or, more exactly, in virtue of the fact that—we can adapt the habitats themselves to our needs. We do not fundamentally alter the human organism's need for nutrition, hydration, a certain air temperature and pressure range, and so on (i.e., the conditions that ecologists refer to as our *fundamental*, as opposed to realized, niche); we use technological devices to provide what is needed when the immediate natural environment does not. In this sense, as Bill Freedman observes, "humans have utilized technological innovations to greatly expand the boundaries of their realized niche. Humans can now sustain themselves in Antarctica, on mountain tops, in the driest deserts, in phenomenal densities in cities, and even in spacecraft" (Freedman, 2016).

Our relation to the rest of nature, then, is highly mediated now that very complex technological and social constructions provide settings for individual human organisms, communities, populations and—ultimately—the whole species to live in, and in ever changing ways. Indeed, humans are the species in this biosphere that has a *history*, as distinct from simply a co-evolutionary record. The distinctive history of humans, their various communities and populations, is all about their changing modes of technological adaptation to, and of, their environments in conjunction with changing modes of social organization.[8] It is also striking how, in recent times, a phenomenal expansion of humanity's realized niche has allowed a great increase in the abundance of humans. This seems to set humans apart from other species, which, for the most part, have a realized niche that is smaller than their fundamental niche due to the conditions necessary for their flourishing providing support also to predators and competitor species. But humans are not exempt from ecological constraints. As Freedman points out, "it must be understood that the remarkable technological expansions of the realized niche of humans require large and continual subsidies of energy, food, and other resources. These are needed in order to maintain the colonization of difficult environments and to continue the control of constraining ecological influences. If access to these resources is somehow diminished, then the ability of humans to colonize and manage their environment is diminished as well, or it collapses" (Freedman, 2016).

This fact—that we always ultimately remain a part of nature and subject to its constraints—is one that is not only ignored but is sometimes even denied in the way of seeing the world that has tended to dominate our culture in recent times. Having become accustomed to an expansionary vision of the world, it seems, we have failed adequately to appreciate the ecological contingency of the fine web of interrelationships on this planet. The "way of seeing" that has dominated modern Western thought includes a basic depiction of Man (advisedly gendered) as set over against the rest of nature, in a world that has a lot of empty space to be filled by his products, these being wrought through the mastering of the natural objects and processes that He discovers and invents. Man came to feel Himself "independent" of nature in important ways. It is this attitude that is perhaps most tellingly criticized as "anthropocentrism" (see Hayward, 1997b; also 1997a), whereby attributes of power and transcendence vis-à-vis nature that were once projected onto deities came to be arrogated to human beings. Indeed, green thinkers have long referred critically here to a nexus of attitudes captured by terms like Promethean, hubristic, dualistic, technocentric—as well as anthropocentric—that all capture aspects of the idea of man using "rationality" to "dominate" a nature that is ready to submit to his superior ingenuity and industriousness.

The ecological space of the human species has in modern times undergone such changes that the very fact of our critical dependence on it has been lost to view to many of us in the industrialised world. We know, though, that peoples who live in direct contact with the land and depend directly for their lives and livelihoods on the survival and flourishing of local flora and fauna see a dense, complex, and vulnerable world immediately around them. They are of necessity acutely aware that they depend on ecological space that needs to be sustained in their geographical vicinity. In the highly industrialized and technologically developed world our relationship with the ecological space we depend on has become so complex and highly mediated that hardly any of us has very much appreciation of it at all. The "imaginary" that has informed Western thinking in recent centuries has consisted of impressions of geographical space with wide open spaces, endless frontiers, outer space, and so on, with an abundance of resources that unbridled human ingenuity will ever find innovative ways to valorize. The truth, of course, is that none of the things that are treated for practical purposes as unbounded or infinite actually is; and the scale of our alterations of ecological relations has become so great that it is revealed to be mistaken to suppose they are. In fact, we are now being forced to recognize that we inhabit a contained, dense biosphere that is being put under enormous strains. Our increasing demands on its capacities make the space increasingly crowded.

The planet's biosphere is crowded in the sense that the demands placed by the world's human population on its "ecological space" are such that some members do not have enough of it for their health and well-being. One aspect of this problem is the finitude of the earth's aggregate biophysical capacity that can support a finite amount of organisms in general and human organisms in particular. Another aspect of the problem is that some humans make vastly more use of the planet's "ecological space" than others do. The very different realities of lives lived in affluence or in poverty owe their tangibility to the differential capacities to command ecological space: the wealthy have an ecological footprint that covers so much of the globe while the poor are ecologically marginalized and deprived of access to resources on their own doorstep.[9]

In fact, the discrepancies and inequalities are even more marked than what analyses of relative resource usage reveal, for the ways in which ecological space figures in institutionalized social practices go very much beyond the direct metabolism of human individuals with their ecological surroundings. To appreciate this it is helpful to reflect a little more closely on how we do things with ecological space.

2 How to Do Things with Ecological Space

Since ethics applies to the conduct of agents, and justice to the institutional framework within which they act, the full normative significance of ecological space has to be understood in relation to the things people may or may not do (i.e., are permitted, required, or forbidden to do), according to the norms of the institutional orders they belong to. When talking about ecological space in relation to the prospective normative assessment and regulation of human activities, I recommend differentiating between using, occupying, and commanding ecological space. It is in relation to these activities that deontic categories—of prescription, proscription, and permission—can be applied.

1. *Use* is the most direct relationship a human being has with ecological space and its constituent functionings. As an organism in an immediate biophysical environment, a human being uses ecological functionings in order to maintain itself in life. This endosomatic use is the most elemental manifestation of the "human metabolism with nature." Ecological space can also be used exosomatically by a human being as an intentional agent, consciously, for productive purposes that are not for the immediate sustenance of the human body.[10] Then the interaction of body and environment is mediated in various ways, as human biophysical capacities are expanded and amplified by the use also of abiotic and non-renewable resources as well as by technological innovations. Through technologies of all kinds (from the most rudimentary tools to vastly complex configurations of infrastructure)—and in consort with others of our kind (and also the secondment of creatures of other kinds)—our bodily power can be greatly amplified so that we are enabled to do all sorts of things that otherwise would be impossible. Such interventions enable us to interact with nature at a distance and to use ecological functionings from various places in various ways. They also enable us to use non-renewable resources in new and powerful ways to further amplify and consolidate our transformative power in relation to the natural world.

But we should also note that the use of ecological space in externally productive activities can be more or less efficient, depending on the quality of technique applied. Thus, considering matters from the point of view of humans, the amount of ecological space available can effectively (i.e., functionally) be increased through the development of technique: it is not so much that anything changes in external reality—for the functionings in ecological space do not necessarily change—but what happens is that we can become increasingly nuanced in

our appreciation of the qualitative constitution of it and develop correspondingly sophisticated practical skills in using it, as, for instance, with the processes involved in learning how
to get more and more computing power from the use of smaller and smaller pieces of silicon.
So by being used in different and inventive ways, ecological space can, in that sense—that is,
from the perspective of effective human intentionality—be *expanded*.[11] Any innovation that
shows us how to access functionings in the natural world that we had not previously understood can be said to do this.

Use of ecological space is also not bound by geography. For instance, the food I eat is in
proximity to me at the moment I ingest it, but it might be grown on the other side of the
world; in general, the products we use, however physically intimate they might become, can
originate from external metabolic transactions with the natural world in far-flung places. It
is this general idea that is conveyed—at least in part—by the idea of an ecological footprint
(Wackernagel and Rees, 1996).[12] And we are familiar now with the general idea that the footprint of a given population can be portrayed as larger or smaller than that population's geo-
politically designated territory. But there is also a further distinct dimension to consider in
relation to how ecological space may be used by people in one geographic location when that
space is physically located in another geographical location. This is a distinctly social dimension that does not necessarily imply anything directly to do with use.[13]

2. *Occupation* of ecological space can occur without the actual use of any of its constituent
   functionings. This possibility, however, can only be described from a social perspective,
   not a purely ecological one. It signifies a relation between people and ecological space that
   depends on acceptance of particular social norms for its possibility. An analogy would be
   the situation in which an empty theater seat is said to be occupied: the convention of
   reserving seats gives sense to what would, under a purely physical description, be a self-
   contradictory proposition: "the empty seat is occupied." When one occupies a physical
   space in this manner, what one does is retain the option for oneself to use it while excluding others from exercising such an option, as long as they share a commitment to the
   salient normative expectations. Likewise, occupying ecological space is an idea that does
   not represent any facts about the *natural* world; it is understood as a purely social, *normative*, category; it can only apply when norms with the effect of *property* incidents are
   recognized as valid.[14] But it is highly relevant when we think about claims of property and
   right that involve access for some and exclusion for others. It is a crucial part of understanding how people can acquire and control more ecological space than they could ever
   actually make use of. When vast numbers of people are ecologically marginalized by the
   activities of a relatively small number, we can only understand how this could happen by
   examining the normative relations between the different kinds of people.[15]
3. By *command* of ecological space I understand a potentiality that presupposes the possibility of occupying it but does not necessarily entail actually occupying it. Such command
   can be manifest as a power to create or extinguish rights of exclusion. One commands
   ecological space to the extent that one has the power or capacity to make an effective decision to acquire or occupy ecological space that currently is owned or used by another. This
   would be the power or capacity, as typically represented by the holding of assets (including money, bonds, promissory notes, and so on, that physically manifest no ecological
   space at all), to take possession, through a transaction, either of goods or services that
   do embody ecological space, or of rights of occupation of ecological space. In a market

economy, where most things can be exchanged, subject to agreement on price, money wealth effectively represents *command* of ecological space. At any moment, a holder of money wealth could convert the money into holdings that embody actual ecological space. This potentiality is of considerable significance: we glimpse this when abstract and speculative transactions on global commodity markets, for instance, have very dramatic effects on lives and livelihoods of very many people in ecologically marginalized situations in the world. Financial wealth represents very real power over people's lives.

Command of ecological space thus operates through the creation and exercise of property rights. As Jeremy Waldron has put it, "property is a matter of rules about access to and control of material resources." It is not necessarily about ownership, but wealth is constituted for the most part by one's property relations: one may not own many resources, but the shares one holds, the funds one is involved in, and so on, define a person's position so far as access to and control of material resources is concerned (Waldron, 1985: 325). In similar vein, I would maintain that wealth is appropriately understood as the capacity to command resources, whatever the circuitousness of the connection between paper or digitally encoded assets and the material world they can ultimately be exchanged for.

Command of ecological space does not have to take the form of financial wealth, however; nor do property rights have to be private or individual. It is possible for property rights—and this especially applies to those incidents (and combinations thereof) that come closest to providing full *dominium* with respect to their object—to be held by a people or a sovereign, for instance. Ecological space, in fact, due to its inherent territorial extension, can be commanded within a regime of territorial rights too.[16] Here, command of it is manifest not as monetized claims but in the form of ultimate powers of control over physical access to it. Typically, this is a corollary of a state having a monopoly of legitimate force within the territory under its control. In virtue of commanding what Avery Kolers (2012a) refers to as geospace, a political authority can also control the use of the ecological space that is located within it. A rich and powerful state, then, can "import" a good deal of ecological space from other territories while remaining firmly in control of the ecological space within its territorial borders. This situation, from a certain ethical perspective, would seem to be a circumstance of compound injustice (see, e.g., Shue, 1992); it is a circumstance in which the linkage between issues of poverty and environment globally is particularly stark.

3 ECOLOGICAL SPACE AS A CONCERN OF HUMAN RIGHTS

An evident ethical concern relating to ecological space is that each person should have access to use of it that is sufficient thereby to be enabled to lead at least a minimally decent life. For I presume we would find hard to recognize as an ethical proposition the contrary suggestion that it is acceptable for some people to be denied the legitimate expectation of being allowed access to what they need to live a minimally decent life. We can thus—with relatively little argumentative apparatus—derive the normative proposition: To deprive a person of access to needed ecological space is wrong.

In light of the terms in which ethical discourses are generally conducted in our times, a reasonable interpretation of that proposition is to say that it implies a human right of access to sufficient ecological space.[17] Human rights language refers to those interests, common to all individual humans, that are deemed significant enough to warrant normative protection by collective legal, political, and even more directly coercive means.[18] The individual human interest in having access to the means to support one's biological life is clearly of such a kind.

I suggest that to refer to a fundamental right of this kind is to say something about the "morality of the depths" that Henry Shue (1980) has influentially referred to; it is a *basic* right in the sense of being a precondition of enjoying any further rights. Such a right takes moral precedence, *ceteris paribus*, over less directly important rights when its enjoyment is imperiled. The human right of access to such ecological space as is biophysically necessary relates, in the first place, to the endosomatic use of ecological functionings by our organic bodies. The opportunities to engage in that use, though, can be promoted or inhibited by things that other people do: the exosomatic use of ecological space by others can, as can its occupation by others, inhibit the enjoyment of an individual human's right to its (endosomatic) use. Therefore an individual's right to sufficient ecological space can be compromised or violated in a variety of complex and mediated ways. Now the discourse of rights presupposes that there are duties to make good the claims of right; and one general issue that needs to be acknowledged is that people may sometimes find themselves without access through no fault of anyone else's; so who has any duty in such a situation? I think an appropriate answer to this and related questions is to adopt the general framing advocated by Shue. He suggests we should recognize three general kinds of duties that answer to basic rights: duties not to deprive; duties to protect against deprivation; and duties to assist those who have suffered deprivation. Duties to protect or assist would fall on those, or a subset of those, who have the ability to protect or assist.[19] But here I would like to say a little more about the duty not to deprive.

The duty not to deprive another of access to needed ecological space applies, in principle, to everyone. In practice, however, the opportunities to deprive someone else of access to ecological space depend on coordinated activities of often very complex kinds such that one's individual role or contribution in the deprivation may not be clear. Most of the ways in which we use and benefit from ecological space are such that the connection with the ecological marginalization of others is far from easy to trace. Explanatory accounts of the global political economy that would seek to reveal the connections globally between affluent classes' advantages and deprived classes' disadvantages are liable to be contentious under present circumstances. What can less controversially be shown, however, is the structure of those patterns of advantage and disadvantage, whatever its explanation may be. For it is evidenced in the sum of documentation of the system of property rights that is maintained globally and can be tested in courts of law and other legal institutions around the world.

It is property rights that secure some in the possession, occupation, and command of more access to ecological space than can be ethically justified while others remain excluded from access even to bare sufficiency. Thus the human right of access to ecological space, even for the most basic and directly necessary forms of use, can be compromised or violated by the assertion of such property rights. The radical inequalities that afflict the world today[20] are manifest in the worst off being excluded from access to ecological space, as well as to nonrenewable resources or the exchange value yielded by them as commodities.

In view of this situation, I would therefore commend one further normative proposition: in any case where the human right of access to sufficient ecological space to maintain a decent life comes into conflict with a mere right of property, the latter should yield.[21]

Notes

1. This chapter draws on research conducted with the gratefully acknowledged support of British Academy Senior Research Fellowship (SRF/2007/32) and Leverhulme Research Fellowship (RF/8/RFG/2008/0179). For helpful comments on earlier versions, thanks go to members of the University of Edinburgh's Political Theory Research Group and to the editors of this volume.
2. For an early and interesting discussion of natural relations see Benton (1993). On the specific use of the idea of ecological space in normative argument see e.g. Hayward (2006, 2007).
3. Questions of animal ethics, ecocentrism in ethics, and so on constitute important fields of inquiry in their own right. Here my aim is simply to establish how the idea of ecological space can be used in the construction of ethical arguments; it could well be used for arguments involving concern for nonhumans.
4. I find it appropriate to adopt the expression that provides the title for Berger's (1972) book here. As will become clear, I shall be contrasting this way of seeing particularly with the worldview of liberal political economy.
5. For more on the basics of ecology, particularly as they can be used to inform social and political theory, see Hayward (1995).
6. Definitions of the ecological idea go back to the early twentieth century, but it was influentially formulated by the zoologist G. Evelyn Hutchinson (1958) when seeking to account for how there can be so many different types of organisms in any one habitat. Hutchinson conceptualized the niche in terms of a "hypervolume," a multi-dimensional "space" of resources and environmental conditions (e.g., light, nutrients, structure, etc.) that are available to (and specifically used by) the organisms that require them.
7. Ecologists distinguish between the fundamental niche of a species—the general conditions functionally required for its persistence and reproduction—and its realized niche. The latter refers to the actual, realized, circumstances that pertain for a given population (see e.g. Hutchinson, 1958; Freedman, internet resource).
8. Seen in this way, the materialist view of history as adopted by Karl Marx, for instance, is a particular version of such an account. For an appreciation of the ecological insights of Marx, and also, importantly, Engels, see e.g. John Bellamy Foster (2000).
9. In the next section I shall further explain why "command" of ecological space can go even beyond measurable ecological footprints.
10. On the exosomatic, and archetypically social, utilization of ecological space see the seminal contributions to ecological economics of J. (Hans) B. Opschoor (e.g., Opschoor, 1995).
11. This is how the expansion of humans' realized ecological niche appears from the standpoint of a social scientific, as opposed to a scientific ecological, interest. The expansion is not a biophysical one; it is a function, relative to intentionality, of the capabilities humans apply. We should not think of an independently fixed "amount" of space, as if some sort of fungible stuff, but of discovering new possibilities for achieving hitherto unattainable goals. An interesting argument with parallels to this is presented by Avery Kolers (2012b)

where he talks about the expansion of *territory*—a normative category distinct from the geographical category *land*—through a variety of interstitial uses, for instance.

12. The idea of the footprint being two-dimensional and operationalized through a specific set of indicators, themselves based on various assumptions of both factual and evaluative kinds, means it only captures an aspect of ecological space—rather like a particular photograph can only capture a particular aspect of a scene. But also like a photograph, the footprint analysis can still portray a good deal.

13. I suspect, although it is not my field, that there must be interesting research questions still to ask about how the various biophysical measures used to track movements of ecological assets of various kinds through trade and dispersed production methods are related to economic and property relations.

14. On the idea of property incidents see the seminal contribution of Honoré (1961).

15. The requisite understanding can build on suggestive traditions of conceptual analysis of normative thought from, e.g., Ockham ([1332]) to Ostrom (e.g., Schlager and Ostrom, 1992).

16. This is something that Avery Kolers (2012a) has highlighted when pointing out that a political regime governing a territory can make various kinds of exploitative "use" of its ecological resources without actually consuming them.

17. The initial simple proposition does, of course, leave open a number of consequent questions, as, for instance: What if the deprivation is, in some cases, unavoidable? What is the definition of a *decent* life? How does one determine what, exactly, and how much of it, is (minimally) needed? Would it also necessarily be wrong to fail to give a person what is needed, and if so, wrong of whom? What about space that is more than is needed? But these familiar questions can in fact be asked in relation to established human rights, too. On this general question, see Hayward (2005).

18. This is not the place to engage in theoretical debates about what human rights "are," and I have tried to offer a gloss that would be reckoned a reasonable description of language use, even by critics of interest theories of rights or sceptics about the status of universalistic claims.

19. An ability to protect or assist is a necessary condition of having a duty to do so (on the principle that *ought* implies *can*); it is a matter for further debate whether some principle of causation, for instance, of benefiting or being advantaged, is also a necessary condition. (Comparable considerations are familiar from recent debates about climate justice, for a summary of which see Hayward, 2012.)

20. For seminal discussions of the idea of radical inequality see Nagel (1977) and Pogge (2002).

21. By "mere" right of property I mean any property right for which no human rights justification can directly be adduced. I do not suggest this proposition would be uncontroversial; but I do suggest it follows if my previous argument for considering a right of access to ecological space as a basic right is accepted, and if such claims of right are understood as embodying peremptory ethical demands that can trump morally less demanding claims.

REFERENCES

Benton, T. (1993). *Natural Relations: Ecology, Animal Rights and Social Justice*. New York: Verso.
Berger, J. (1972). *Ways of Seeing*. London: Penguin.

Foster, J. B. (2000). *Marx's Ecology: Materialism and Nature*. New York: New York University Press.

Freedman, Bill (2016). "Niche—What Is the Niche of Humans?" Accessed April 30, 2013. http://science.jrank.org/pages/4664/Niche-What-niche-humans.html.

Hayward, T. (1995). *Ecological Thought: An Introduction*. Cambridge, England : Polity Press ; Cambridge, MA : Blackwell.

Hayward, T. (1997a). "Anthropocentrism: A Misunderstood Problem." *Environmental Values* 6(1): 49–63.

Hayward, T. (1997b). "Anthropocentrism." In *Encyclopedia of Applied Ethics*, edited by R. Chadwick, 173–180. San Diego, CA: Academic Press.

Hayward, T. (2005). *Constitutional Environmental Rights*. New York: Oxford University Press.

Hayward, T. (2006). "Global Justice and the Distribution of Natural Resources." *Political Studies* 54(2): 349–369.

Hayward, T. (2007). "Human Rights versus Emissions Rights: Climate Justice and the Equitable Distribution of Ecological Space." *Ethics & International Affairs* 21(4): 431–450.

Hayward, T. (2012). "Climate Change and Ethics." *Nature: Climate Change* 2: 843–848.

Honoré, A. M. (1961). "Ownership." In *Oxford Essays in Jurisprudence*, edited by A. G. Guest. Oxford: Clarendon Press: 107–147.

Hutchinson, G. E. (1958). "Concluding Remarks." *Cold Spring Harbor Symposia on Quantitative Biology* 22: 415–427.

Kolers, A. (2012a). "Justice, Territory and Natural Resources." *Political Studies* 60(2): 269–286.

Kolers, A. (2012b). "Floating Provisos and Sinking Islands." *Journal of Applied Philosophy* 29(4): 333–343.

Nagel, T. (1977). "Poverty and Food: Why Charity Is Not Enough." In *Food Policy: The Responsibility of the United States in Life and Death Choices*, edited by P. G. Brown and H. Shue, 54–62. New York: Free Press.

Ockham, William of (1956/[1332]). *Opus nonaginta dierum*. In *Guillelmi de Ockham Opera politica*, Vol. 2, edited by H. S, Offler et al., 288–368. Manchester, England: Manchester University Press.

Opschoor, J. (H.) B. (1995). "Ecospace and the Fall and Rise of Throughput Intensity." *Ecological Economics* 15(2): 137–140.

Pogge, T. (2002). *World Poverty and Human Rights*. Cambridge, England: Polity Press.

Schlager, E., and Ostrom, E. (1992). "Property-Rights Regimes and Natural Resources: A Conceptual Analysis." *Land Economics* 68(3): 249–262.

Shue, H. (1980). *Basic Rights: Subsistence, Affluence, and U.S. Foreign Policy*. Princeton, NJ: Princeton University Press.

Shue, H. (1992). "The Unavoidability of Justice." In *The International Politics of the Environment: Actors, Interests, and Institutions*, edited by A. Hurrell and B. Kingsbury. Oxford: Clarendon Press.

Wackernagel, M., and Rees, W. (1996). *Our Ecological Footprint: Reducing Human Impact on the Earth*. Gabriola Island, BC, Canada: New Society Publishers.

Waldron, J. (1985). "What Is Private Property?" *Oxford Journal of Legal Studies* 5(3): 313–349.

CHAPTER 27

RISK AND PRECAUTION IN DECISION MAKING ABOUT NATURE

JONATHAN ALDRED

THIS chapter examines the normative basis for two fundamentally different approaches to environmental decision making. We begin with the orthodox "risk assessment" approach, and go on to contrast it with approaches based on some form of precautionary principle (PP). The normative basis for risk assessment lies in decision theory, and lessons from decision theory inform the analysis of the PP too. Climate change will be the environmental policy issue discussed throughout, partly for reasons of brevity, but also because so much recent thinking about risk and precaution has been stimulated by it.

Questions about risk and precaution arise when there is uncertainty about the future. With the terminology of decision theory, we shall say that the decision maker chooses between various *alternatives*; each alternative leads to one of several possible *outcomes*. The term "risk" is confusing, because common usage involves both a noun and a verb, and confuses related concepts of likelihood and harm. In what follows, a decision is taken under *risk* when an objective probability can be attached to all possible outcomes of the decision, while a decision under *uncertainty* refers to the case in which objective probability distributions are unavailable to the decision maker (Keynes, [1921] 1973; Knight, 1921). Both risk and uncertainty refer to situations in which the set of all possible outcomes is known *ex ante*. When this latter assumption is violated (or when we are unsure whether it holds),[1] we say that *ignorance* prevails.

1 RISK AND UNCERTAINTY IN ENVIRONMENTAL DECISION MAKING

The distinction between risk and uncertainty points to a key feature of orthodox approaches to environmental decision making involving various tools of risk assessment, including cost-benefit analysis (CBA). As their names suggest, these tools presume that all possible

outcomes, and their probabilities, are known; essentially these tools are practical manifestations of expected utility theory. However, this approach appears to fall silent in situations of
uncertainty or ignorance. And there are good reasons to suppose that environmental decisions often involve uncertainty or ignorance. But before exploring these reasons, it's worth
briefly discussing the influential Bayesian response to this rejection of expected utility theory: when we lack objective probabilities, we should appeal to subjective probabilities, which
express our degrees of belief.

The Bayesian response asserts that subjective expected utility theory can provide a *prescriptive* decision theory. But there is a problem here, because a prescriptive decision theory
claims to provide an objective justification for the course of action it recommends. And an
objective justification cannot be based on a subjective probability. A decision theory based
on subjective probabilities cannot tell a decision maker whether X is the right thing to do. It
can merely show what beliefs will make the decision maker *think* that X is the right thing to
do, regardless of whether it is or not (Mellor, 2007).

For example, suppose a patient is given a placebo (an inert pill), but not told that it is
inert (Mellor, 2007: 123). Instead she is told that the pill will probably work. Suppose, therefore, that her subjective probability of obtaining some desired health outcome will rise.
Sometimes this leads to an increased objective probability of that outcome: there is a "placebo effect." But of course there may be no effect, because changes in subjective probabilities do not necessarily entail changes in objective ones. Alternatively, a patient may take a
(non-placebo) pill, believing that it will be ineffective, even though it is likely to work: the
pill raises the objective probability but not the subjective one. To distinguish between these
cases, both objective and subjective probabilities are required, and a prescriptive decision
theory would need to appeal to the former. In short, the Bayesian response fails: a prescriptive expected utility theory requires objective probabilities.

However, in environmental decision making, objective probabilities may be unavailable
because of uncertainty or ignorance. One reason is that environmental threats are often
novel in some sense, so past experience is little help and probabilities cannot be inferred
from frequency data. A novel threat today may not be repeated in the future either, so we
cannot rely on a "law of large numbers" to predict that outcomes will converge to some kind
of central forecast. A deeper difficulty is that environmental threats are often systemic, and
the systems involved are typically complex (Holling, 2001). It is difficult to attach probabilities to outcomes in complex environmental systems because of, among other things, feed-
back effects, human interactions, and extreme sensitivity to parameter values—popularly
illustrated by the "butterfly effect." Rather than tending towards equilibrium, complex
systems have limited resilience, and sufficiently large exogenous shocks or repeated, accumulating "overstress" can trigger large, nonlinear, unpredictable regime shifts. Complexity
theory, then, implies a very different picture of environmental uncertainty to that suggested
by a Newtonian world of mechanical processes operating in fixed systems.

The presence of uncertainty or ignorance appears to have an obvious implication for
environmental decision making: CBA and other tools of risk assessment are unavailable,
because they require objective probabilities. But this simple conclusion can be challenged
from both ends. On the one hand, it is easy to overstate the probability information required
to facilitate a useful quantitative risk analysis. In many contexts, precise point probabilities
are unnecessary; establishing that the probability of some outcome lies in an interval is sufficient to inform decision making. According to this view, CBA can survive in a world of

partial uncertainty, where (some) outcomes lack unique probabilities, but a range of probabilities can still be associated with them. On the other hand, the uncertainty characterizing environmental decisions may not be so extensive as to rule out the derivation of sufficient probability information. For example, despite the deep uncertainties involved in climate science, the IPCC is able to present a range of forecasts for future temperatures which arguably encompass most of that uncertainty. And such forecasts are clearly useful for policymaking.

Still, these responses do little to undermine the force of the argument against CBA in conditions of uncertainty and ignorance. First, forecasts such as those produced by the IPCC reflect an attempt to achieve consensus among a group of climate scientists with differing opinions. There is nothing intrinsically wrong with such consensus forecasts, but the kind of probability information implicit in them may be better interpreted as subjective, not the objective probability information required by decision-making tools based on prescriptive decision theory. Second, many advocates of CBA claim to do much more than merely present decision makers with a range of scenarios: they claim to identify the best alternative. In the case of CBA, this requires point probabilities to calculate expected benefits and costs in monetary terms; partial uncertainty will still be too much uncertainty. Third, even if we abandon the search for a best alternative, pockets of partial uncertainty may prevent an informative scenario or simulation analysis, because the uncertainties can compound each other, and economic uncertainties can magnify scientific ones. For example, the range of monetary estimates of damage from climate change is too wide to be informative, because the scale and distribution of damage is uncertain, and there is economic uncertainty about the monetary value of any given damage outcome, further exacerbated by disagreements over the discount rate which should be used to compare impacts occurring at different times. It is for just these reasons that many economists who are otherwise strong supporters of CBA argue that it may be fundamentally misleading in environmental policy contexts characterized by uncertainty or ignorance (Dasgupta, 2008; Pindyck, 2011; Weitzman, 2011).

In reply, an obdurate Bayesian might insist, in essence, that sufficient probability information can simply be imposed on the problem at hand. And in practice we observe the extensive informational demands of CBA and related tools, and their dominance in many policymaking institutions, combining to create an overwhelming pressure to attach probabilities to all relevant outcomes, even when there is no sound basis for doing so. But this leads to policy analyses which are systematically biased. A few examples must suffice here to illustrate different aspects of this broad claim.[2] There is robust evidence that political, sociological and psychological forces lead to the systematic underestimation of risks in CBA practice, especially concerning large projects or long time horizons (Flyvbjerg, 2009; Flyvbjerg et al., 2003). May et. al. (2008) argue that even in theory, CBA and other forms of orthodox risk analysis will systematically underestimate the likelihood of unforeseen outcomes in complex systems. Weitzman (2009) presents a highly sophisticated statistical analysis of climate forecasts, showing that they are characterized by "fat tails" (nontrivial probabilities of catastrophic warming) which are ignored by almost all CBAs, which rely on "bell curve based" statistical analysis. Quiggin argues that a more pervasive form of bias in favor of risk runs through formal decision theory: from the perspective of a more general theory or model, every formal decision theory is inherently biased in favor of alternatives that are roughly speaking "riskier" (more uncertain, less well understood, or involving an increased probability of very bad outcomes; Quiggin 2009; Aldred 2012). For example, theories recommending the maximization of expected value are biased in favor of risk from the perspective of expected utility theory, which in turn arguably exhibits the same bias, in light of the more general prospect theory.

A final problem concerns the mistaken attempt to incorporate uncertainty in general, and the PP in particular, within orthodox risk analysis. Crucially, it focuses on the *elimination* of uncertainty through scientific learning. But a key insight of complexity theory is that increased scientific knowledge may not help. For example, in discussing climate science, Roe and Baker (2007: 629) explain that "the probability of large temperature increases are relatively insensitive to decreases in uncertainties associated with the underlying climate processes." In other words, greater knowledge about "the underlying climate processes" may not feed through into more information about relevant probabilities. Suppose, however, that in some important environmental problems, uncertainty *will* be eliminated or reduced over time through scientific learning. An analysis focusing on the resolution of uncertainty, rather than its persistence, will still fail to capture the precautionary principle. It is misleading to claim that "precaution aims at managing the wait for better scientific information" (Gollier and Treich, 2003: 86).

Many environmentalists draw a strong conclusion from the above discussion: CBA and other forms of risk assessment are generally unavailable in conditions of (partial) uncertainty or ignorance, because the gap between the probabilistic informational demands of CBA and the available objective probability information is too great (Jamieson, 1992). But a weaker conclusion will suffice here, one that is hard to dispute: in some environmental policy contexts, CBA is misleading when used in isolation. It must be supplemented by other decision theories, principles or procedures. An obvious supplement is some kind of PP, to which we now turn.

2 THE PRECAUTIONARY PRINCIPLE

Consider the following important political articulations of the PP:

> Where there are threats of serious or irreversible damage, lack of full scientific certainty shall not be used as a reason for postponing cost-effective measures to prevent environmental degradation. (excerpt from Principle 15 of the UN Rio Declaration; UNCED, 1993)

> When an activity raises threats of harm to human health or the environment, precautionary measures should be taken even if some cause and effect relationships are not fully established scientifically. (Raffensberger and Tickner, 1999)

> The PP provides justification for public policy actions in situations of *scientific complexity, uncertainty and ignorance,* where there may be a need to act in order to avoid, or reduce, potentially serious or irreversible *threats* to health or the environment, using *appropriate strengths of scientific evidence,* and taking into account the likely *pros and cons* of proportionate actions and inactions. (European Environment Agency, 2013: 681, emphasis in original)

There is no space here for a comprehensive discussion of common objections to the PP. But it is worth briefly addressing one influential critique. Sunstein (2005) argues that regulations, laws, and policies introduced in the name of the PP often have a by-product: they give rise to new threats, or increase the likelihood of existing ones. For example, on precautionary grounds, new drugs are only released after time-consuming clinical trials. But the resulting delay in people benefiting from the drugs is itself a threat, in some cases leading to deaths. These byproduct threats also warrant a precautionary approach. Sunstein concludes that the PP, applied consistently, is paralyzing: "it bans the very steps that it requires" (2005: 26). This is because, "as a logical matter, societies . . . cannot be highly precautionary with respect to all risks" (2005: 34).

Sunstein is right to suggest that in practice, many regulations justified by appeal to the PP have been one-sided, blind to the threats which the regulations themselves introduce. But recent statements of the PP expressly recommend a holistic awareness of threats—such as the European Environment Agency's reference to "pros and cons." Moreover, consistent application of the PP does not imply paralyzing neutrality with respect to diverse threats. On the contrary, all three statements of the PP above give greater priority to particular threats— threats of serious or irreversible damage, or threats to health or the environment. And differential treatment of threats is also warranted if our knowledge of them differs. The "threat" posed by time-consuming drug trials, for example, is less significant if the benefits of the drug are uncertain *ex ante*: very often, trials are needed not merely to ensure the drug is safe, but to test whether it is truly beneficial. These remarks do not constitute a full response to Sunstein's worries, but they are enough to suggest that the problems with the PP lie in the conditions of its application; it cannot be rejected *a priori*.

As well as the presence of particular threats, uncertainty features prominently in the above statements of the PP. A consensus is emerging in the philosophical literature that these two conditions—"uncertainty" and "particular threats"—are especially relevant to determining the applicability of the PP (Cranor, 2001; Cranor, 2004; Manson, 2007; Randall, 2011; Soule, 2000; Steele, 2006; Sunstein, 2005). But beyond that, there is little agreement. In particular, it is far from clear whether these two conditions are jointly necessary, or jointly sufficient, or neither or both, to justify the application of the PP. The most comprehensive discussion is probably that of Gardiner (2006a).

Gardiner argues that, at least in the contexts he is concerned with, a precautionary decision can be interpreted as one which obeys the *maximin decision rule*; this tells the decision maker to choose the alternative with the best "worst-case" outcome—the alternative the worst possible outcome of which is superior to the worst outcome from all other alternatives. Hence, maximin ensures that the worst possible outcomes are avoided, and in this sense is "precautionary." In discussing the maximin aspect of the difference principle, Rawls identifies three conditions under which maximin might be a sensible approach. First, uncertainty, with Rawls's definition following the Keynesian/Knightian definition set out above. Second, some possible outcomes are unacceptable, simply intolerable. Third, the potential additional gains to be made by following a decision rule other than maximin are relatively unimportant to the decision maker. Gardiner endorses these three conditions, and adds a background restriction: "that the range of outcomes considered are in some appropriate sense "realistic," so that, for example, only credible threats are considered" (Gardiner, 2006b: 51).[3] Taken together, Gardiner proposes a Rawlsian Core Precautionary Principle (RCPP), a modified version of which may be stated as follows:

Rawlsian Core Precautionary Principle

Considering only realistic possible outcomes, *if* (i) the outcomes are uncertain, *and* (ii) some outcomes are unacceptable, *and* (iii) additional gains from nonmaximin choices have relatively little value, *then* the decision maker should follow the maximin rule.

The formulation here makes the three Rawlsian conditions jointly sufficient to invoke precaution-as-maximin, but leaves open whether they are also necessary. Gardiner's view is not entirely clear. Gardiner (2006b: 48) states: "on the way I am employing them, the Rawlsian conditions pick out sufficient conditions for precaution, not necessary conditions." However, elsewhere he envisages the three conditions operating as necessary conditions, suggesting that one of their functions is to "restrict its application" (Gardiner, 2011: 412). For example, Gardiner (2006b: 49) responds to Harsanyi's main objection to maximin by arguing that "the RCPP will not apply" in situations where the uncertainty condition is not satisfied. We return to this issue below.

Conditions (ii) and (iii) are nicely illustrated by a climate change example, which Gardiner regards as a paradigmatic case:

> Second, the "unacceptable outcomes" condition is met because it is reasonable to believe that the costs of climate change are likely to be high, and may possibly be catastrophic. Third, the "care little for gains" condition is met because the costs of stabilizing emissions, though large in an absolute sense, are said to be manageable within the global economic system, especially in relation to the potential costs of climate change (Gardiner, 2006b: 55).

The idea that the PP is concerned with "particular threats" is reflected in the RCPP: it is concerned with threats satisfying conditions (ii) and (iii). But what exactly makes some outcomes unacceptable, and relatedly, some gains relatively unimportant? A detailed analysis is beyond my scope here, but one plausible interpretation appeals to some notion of lexical priority (Aldred, 2012). Avoiding unacceptable outcomes, then, is lexically prior to the gains which might be had. For example, in the context of climate change, it might be claimed that avoiding catastrophic outcomes is lexically prior to other goals. The ethical concept underpinning such claims is incommensurability. Outcomes are *incommensurable* when they cannot be compared along some common cardinal scale of value, such as utility. This need not prevent comparability: outcomes can still be ranked as better or worse, but we cannot say "how much" better or worse.[4] Thus, we might say that catastrophic outcomes for the global climate are different-in-kind or "incommensurably" worse even than other bad outcomes which may obtain. As interpreted here, then, the RCPP applies when there are incommensurable values at stake.

Incommensurability is relevant to leading political statements of the PP too. Claims regarding the distinctiveness of threats of serious or irreversible damage, or threats to health or the environment, are implicitly appealing to incommensurability: they claim that some losses are qualitatively distinct and hence cannot be "traded off" against other losses or gains on a common cardinal scale of value. For example, without an incommensurability claim, any particular instance of irreversible damage would by definition be equivalent in value to larger, but reversible, damage of the same type. The notion of irreversibility collapses to be merely an amplifier: the significance of "irreversible damage" would be no more than just "the damage is more serious than it would be otherwise." And the phrase "serious and irreversible damage," despite its widespread adoption in many carefully considered statements of the PP, would involve needless repetition. In short, the significance of irreversibility appears to rest on an appeal to incommensurability (Aldred, 2012; Goodin, 1992; Martin, 1979; Sunstein, 2008).[5]

These remarks raise two more general issues. First, we are reminded that objections to the PP often raise parallel problems for rival approaches to decision making, such as CBA. Widespread ignorance may be a difficulty for the RCPP, but it is *more* of a difficulty for CBA.

Another instance: it is hard to explain in general terms the RCPP background condition that only "credible" or "realistic" outcomes are considered. But again, CBA faces this challenge too, because it presupposes a background set-up specifying the set of outcomes to be considered. Second, it is hard to give a plausible description of practical decision scenarios involving ignorance, without also raising the possibility of second-order uncertainty (uncertainty about whether all possible outcomes are known or not). Once the possibility of surprise is entertained, we are often forced to concede that the boundaries of these pockets of ignorance are vague. We are not certain about the extent of our ignorance. And in practice, problems of second-order uncertainty seem almost as prevalent in situations of first-order uncertainty as under ignorance. For example, even if a climate science or economic model assumes away the possibility of "downside surprises," implying downside uncertainty rather than ignorance, the modeler may well be doubtful about this assumption. Second-order uncertainty can pose major difficulties for most decision making approaches, including quantitative methods and the PP. We must leave aside any further consideration of ignorance or second-order uncertainty, simply because of the breadth and depth of the issues involved.

Summing up, the precautionary approach discussed so far holds that precaution-as-maximin is justified in decision contexts involving both uncertainty and incommensurability. We have left open whether uncertainty and incommensurability are necessary conditions too. An obvious way of addressing this question is to consider the two cases—uncertainty but no incommensurability, and incommensurability without uncertainty. But there are many other possibilities to consider too. There is a spectrum of intermediate cases, because both uncertainty and incommensurability are matters of degree.

Consider first the "extreme case" of complete uncertainty, but no incommensurability. In defending maximin, Rawls appeals to the axiomatic decision theory of Arrow and Hurwicz (1972), arguing that it provides a "formal proof" of maximin, albeit a "suggestive" one (Rawls, 1999: 248). Recent, more general, axiomatic decision theories which include both expected utility theory and Arrow-Hurwicz as special cases typically show that, under complete uncertainty, maximin is implied by the axioms. Thus, given the usual interpretation of these axioms as minimal requirements of rationality, maximin is not merely legitimate, but a requirement of rationality. Objections to maximin in this case mostly involve denial of the possibility of uncertainty.

At the other extreme, there is incommensurability but no uncertainty. That is, there is a situation of risk or certainty but a pervasive inability to value outcomes on a single cardinal scale. A defense of maximin can be constructed for this situation, given strong assumptions about incommensurable outcomes. For example, in the context of climate change policy, it is widely held that potentially catastrophic outcomes from climate change are in some sense different-in-kind worse than the economic costs of adaptation and mitigation, so that precautionary action is justified to reduce the likelihood of catastrophe, regardless of the economic costs. This argument does not rely on any appeal to uncertainty: one can imagine many of its supporters continuing to adhere to it even if we had full probabilistic information about the likelihood of catastrophe.

These two extreme cases suggest that uncertainty and incommensurability are not both necessary to justify maximin; one alone is sufficient. But the artificial nature of these extreme cases pushes us to consider the intermediate cases which may have more practical relevance: choices involving partial uncertainty and "pockets of incommensurability" (Griffin, 1977, 1986). Still, the analysis here stops short of analyzing real-world environmental problems directly. They are messy and complex; in order to probe intuitions, it is worth considering some simplified, hypothetical scenarios.

In each of the scenarios, the government is faced with an intractable environmental problem and must choose between two alternatives, both of which may lead to a bad outcome. Sometimes the government has reliable probability information, as described. Otherwise there is uncertainty.

> Choice A. *Under alternative A1, 600 people will die with probability 90%. 400 people will die with probability 10%. Under A2, either 700 or 300 will die, but probabilities are unknown.*

The maximin choice A1 may unsettle some supporters of the PP, if maximin choices are interpreted as precautionary. The cost of taking precautions to avoid the unknown chance of 700 deaths is high—a 90% probability of 600 deaths is incurred. But the RCPP need not recommend maximin here, because both conditions (ii) and (iii) appear to be violated. Condition (iii) seems to be violated because the potential gains from nonmaximin choices *are* valuable: by choosing A2, some additional deaths under A1 may be avoided. The potential gains from the nonmaximin choice A2 are *not* relatively less valuable than the gains from the maximin choice A1, because the outcomes from A2 are not qualitatively different from the A1 outcomes. For the same reason, condition (ii) may be violated too: arguably, it requires that only some (a subset) of outcomes are unacceptable, not all of them. But in choice A, all outcomes seem equally (un)acceptable, because they are not different-in-kind. In other words, there is no incommensurability in choice A. This feature, combined with limited uncertainty (all outcomes in A1 have known probabilities), suggests insufficient justification for maximin.

> Choice B. *B1: either 600 or 400 will die, but probabilities are unknown. B2: either 700 or 300 will die, but probabilities are unknown.*

In choice A, the doubts about maximin rest on probability information—the 90% chance that 600 people will die, almost as many as the 700 deaths in the worst-case scenario. In choice B these doubts disappear. In the absence of probabilities, it seems legitimate to prioritise the second problem because its worse-case is more severe. This supports the general claim that increased uncertainty will, *ceteris paribus*, increase the plausibility of maximin.

The arguments suggesting that conditions (ii) and (iii) are violated in choice A appear to apply in choice B too, so if maximin is warranted in choice B, conditions (ii) and (iii) cannot be necessary conditions. Put another way, choice B illustrates an extreme case of uncertainty but no incommensurability in which maximin seems justified.

> Choice C. *C1: 600 people will be paralyzed from the neck down with probability 90%. 400 people will be paralyzed from the neck down with probability 10%. C2: either 600 or 200 will die, but probabilities are unknown.*

Comparing choice C with choice A, both alternatives are less bad in choice C. But there is an important distinction between choices A and C. In choice C, it might be legitimate to regard the outcome involving 600 deaths as different-in-kind worse than the outcomes involving paralysis, and hence invoke the maximin rule to select C1 on the basis of this incommensurability. The difference in kind between the outcomes may license the use of the maximin rule in a way that was unavailable in choice A. In short, the introduction of incommensurability increases the plausibility of maximin, *ceteris paribus*.

Choice D. D1: 600 people will be paralyzed from the neck down with probability 90%. 400 people will be paralyzed from the neck down with probability 10%. D2: 600 people will die with probability 70%. 200 people will die with probability 30%.

In choice D, there is no longer uncertainty, so insofar as maximin can be defended here, its justification rests entirely on the incommensurability claim that outcomes involving death are different-in-kind worse, and so avoiding them must be given priority. Otherwise, there is no obvious obstacle to using some form of CBA to commensurate the badness of death against that of paralysis. The reduction in uncertainty in choice D, compared to choice C, appears to reduce the appeal of the maximin rule.

In sum, the analysis lends support to the following intuition: roughly speaking, with "more" uncertainty, "less" incommensurability is required to justify following maximin, and vice versa.[6] Although the idea that maximin can be justified by a flexible combination of uncertainty and incommensurability appears to track our intuitions, there is of course much more work to do to defend this approach to the PP. But even with these details undeveloped, it seems that maximin can be justified in some circumstances where not all three RCPP conditions hold.

3 CONCLUSION

In counterposing risk and precaution, we have imposed a narrow focus on the discussion of precaution: the PP was introduced as a decision-making procedure which supplements or even replaces risk assessment in some environmental policy contexts. Specifically, if the PP is to serve as a *replacement* for risk assessment if the latter falls silent in the presence of uncertainty or ignorance, then the PP must provide an operational decision rule rather than, say, a set of guidelines for decision making. This perspective explains the focus in this chapter on the PP as a decision rule; space constraints prevent discussion of informative broader conceptions of precaution as a set of substantive and/or procedural guidelines for decision making (European Environment Agency, 2013; Fisher et al., 2006; Hansson, 1999; O'Riordan et al., 2001; Raffensberger and Tickner, 1999; Stirling, 2009). However, the distinction between decision rule and mere guidelines should not be overstated. As Gardiner has emphasized, the PP should not be regarded as a universal, top-down, stand-alone decision rule. Peterson (2007: 306–307) rightly argues that the PP is *not* a decision rule "that tells us what to do and what not to do for each possible input of qualitative information," but he is wrong to reject the PP on that basis. In order to apply an approach like the RCPP to an environmental policy problem, supplementary context-specific value judgments of definition and interpretation are required—but that is equally true of the practice of risk assessment.

The relationship between the PP and risk assessment needs further clarification. The PP might replace risk assessment altogether in conditions of uncertainty or ignorance, but can it *co-exist* with risk assessment in other contexts? For the RCPP to give an affirmative answer, it must be possible to satisfy conditions (ii) and (iii) in contexts of choice under risk or certainty where tools such as CBA make sense. This requires a commensurabilist interpretation of conditions (ii) and (iii), because CBA rules out incommensurability (Aldred 2002). Although I adopted an *in*commensurabilist interpretation, Gardiner appears to do otherwise, remarking "it is not clear that proponents of expected utility theory should resist the Rawlsian criteria" (2006: 53). What would a commensurabilist interpretation of conditions (ii) and (iii) look like in Gardiner's paradigmatic example of climate change? Setting aside the possibility of uncertainty, we might say that conditions (ii) and (iii) are satisfied because the expected benefits of avoiding catastrophic climate change are large while the expected economic costs of mitigation are relatively low. But this commensurabilist interpretation makes support for substantial mitigation contingent on low (expected) economic costs. In sharp contrast, most advocates of the PP see it as making a much stronger claim: substantial mitigation is warranted *even if* the costs are certain to be high, as a precaution against catastrophe. Some kind of incommensurabilist interpretation of conditions (ii) and (iii) seems essential to support this claim. This paradigmatic example suggests incommensurability is doing much of the work in justifying precautionary action. It suggests the PP is parasitic upon deeper claims about environmental values, rather than marking out an independent justification for environmentalism. In an influential early discussion, O'Riordan and Jordan (1995: 200) claim that the PP is "the political basis of sustainability." The discussion here points in the opposite direction: sustainability is the basis for the PP, not the other way round.

NOTES

1. In most real-world decisions, decision makers are not absolutely certain that they know all possible outcomes in advance: there is always the possibility of surprise or "unknown unknowns." Rather than concluding that ignorance is almost universal, it may be more useful to add some threshold to the definition—such as requiring that there are reasonable grounds for suspecting that unknown unknowns exist.
2. See Randall (2011: chapter 5) for further discussion.
3. See also Cranor (2001, 2004).
4. The definition here follows Chang (1997), although other usages are common. For discussion of CBA and maximin in the presence of incommensurability see Aldred (2006) and Hansson (1997), respectively.
5. Humphrey (2001) discusses some problems with appeals to irreversibility.
6. For a more detailed defense see Aldred (2013).

REFERENCES

Aldred, J. (2002). "Cost-Benefit Analysis, Incommensurability and Rough Equality." *Environmental Values* 11: 27–47.
Aldred, J. (2006). "Incommensurability and Monetary Valuation." *Land Economics* 82: 141–161.
Aldred, J. (2013), "Justifying precautionary policies." *Ecological Economics*, 96: 132–40.
Aldred, J. (2012). "Climate Change Uncertainty, Irreversibility and the Precautionary Principle." *Cambridge Journal of Economics* 36: 1051–1072.
Arrow, K., and Hurwicz, L. (1972). "An Optimality Criterion for Decision Making under Ignorance." In *Uncertainty and Expectations in Economics: Essays in Honour of G. L. S. Shackle*, edited by C. F. Carter and J. L. Ford. Oxford, England: Blackwell.
Chang, R. (1997). "Introduction." In *Incommensurability, Incomparability, and Practical Reason*, edited by R. Chang. Cambridge, MA: Harvard University Press.

Cranor, C. (2001). "Learning from the Law to Address Uncertainty in the Precautionary Principle." *Science and Engineering Ethics* 7: 313–326.

Cranor, C. F. (2004). "Toward Understanding Aspects of the Precautionary Principle." *Journal of Medicine and Philosophy* 29: 259–279.

Dasgupta, P. (2008). "Discounting Climate Change." *Journal of Risk and Uncertainty* 37: 141–169.

European Environment Agency (2013). *Late Lessons from Early Warnings II: Science, Precaution, Innovation.* Copenhagen: European Environment Agency.

Fisher, E., Jones, J., and von Schomberg, R. (2006). *Implementing the Precautionary Principle.* Cheltenham, England: Edward Elgar.

Flyvbjerg, B. (2009). "Survival of the Unfittest." *Oxford Review of Economic Policy* 25: 344–367.

Flyvbjerg, B., Bruzelius, N., and Rothengatter, W. (2003). *Megaprojects and Risk.* Cambridge, England: Cambridge University Press.

Gardiner, S. (2006a). "Protecting Future Generations." In *Handbook of Intergenerational Justice.,* edited by J. Tremmel, 148–169. Cheltenham, England: Edward Elgar.

Gardiner, S. (2006b). "A Core Precautionary Principle." *Journal of Political Philosophy* 14: 33–60.

Gardiner, S. (2011). *A Perfect Moral Storm: the Ethical Tragedy of Climate Change.* Oxford: Oxford University Press.

Gollier, C., and Treich, N. (2003). "Decision-making under Scientific Uncertainty: The Economics of the Precautionary Principle." *Journal of Risk and Uncertainty* 27: 77–103.

Goodin, R. (1992). *Green Political Theory.* Cambridge, England: Polity Press.

Griffin, J. (1977). "Are there Incommensurable Values?" *Philosophy and Public Affairs* 7: 39–59.

Griffin, J. (1986). *Well-Being.* Oxford: Clarendon Press.

Hansson, S. (1997). "The limits of Precaution." *Foundations of Science* 2: 293–306.

Hansson, S. (1999). "Adjusting Scientific Practices to the Precautionary Principle." *Human and Ecological Risk Assessment* 5: 909–921.

Harsanyi, J. (1975). "Can the Maximin Principle Serve as a Basis for Morality?" *American Political Science Review* 69: 594–606.

Holling, C. (2001). "Understanding the Complexity of Economic, Ecological and Social Systems." *Ecosystems* 4: 390–405.

Humphrey, M. (2001). "Three Conceptions of Irreversibility and Environmental Ethics: Some Problems." *Environmental Politics* 10: 138–154.

Jamieson, D. (1992). "Ethics, Public Policy, and Global Warming." *Science, Technology, and Human Values* 17: 139–153.

Keynes, J. ([1921] 1973). *A Treatise on Probability.* London: Macmillan.

Knight, F. (1921). Risk, Uncertainty and Profit. Chicago: Chicago University Press.

Manson, N. (2007). "The Concept of Irreversibility." *Electronic Journal of Sustainable Development* 1: 3–15.

Martin, J. (1979). "The Concept of the Irreplaceable." *Environmental Ethics* 1: 3–48.

May, R., Levin, S., and Sugihara, G. (2008). "Complex Systems." *Nature* 451: 893–895.

Mellor, D. H. (2007). "Acting under Risk." In *Risk: Philosophical Perspectives,* edited by T. Lewens. London: Routledge.

O'Riordan, T., Cameron, J., and Jordan, A. (2001). *Reinterpreting the Precautionary Principle.* London: Cameron May.

O'Riordan, T., and Jordan, A. (1995). "The Precautionary Principle in Contemporary Environmental Politics." *Environmental Values* 4: 191–212.

Peterson, M. (2007). "The Precautionary Principle Should Not Be Used as a Basis for Decision-Making." *EMBO Reports* 8: 305–308.

Pindyck, R. S. (2011). "Fat Tails, Thin Tails, and Climate Change Policy." *Review of Environmental Economics and Policy* 5: 258–274.

Quiggin, J. (2009). "The Precautionary Principle and the Theory of Choice under Uncertainty." Working Paper, School of Economics, University of Queensland.

Raffensberger, C., and Tickner, J. (1999). *Protecting Public Health and the Environment: Implementing the Precautionary Principle*. Washington, D.C.: Island Press.

Randall, A. (2011). *Risk and Precaution*. Cambridge: Cambridge University Press.

Rawls, J. (1999). "Reply to Alexander and Musgrave." In *John Rawls: Collected Papers*, edited by S. Freeman. Cambridge, MA: Harvard University Press.

Roe, G., and Baker, M. (2007). "Why Is Climate Sensitivity So Unpredictable?" *Science* 318: 629–632.

Soule, E. (2000). "Assessing the Precautionary Principle." *Public Affairs Quarterly* 14: 309–328.

Steele, K. (2006). "The Precautionary Principle: A New Approach to Public Decision-Making?" *Law, Probability and Risk* 5: 19–31.

Stirling, A. (2009). "The Precautionary Principle." In *A Companion to the Philosophy of Technology*, edited by J. Olsen, S., Pedersen, and V. Hendricks. Oxford: Blackwell.

Sunstein, C. (2005). *Laws of Fear*. Cambridge: Cambridge University Press.

Sunstein, C. (2008). *Two Conceptions of Irreversible Environmental Harm*. Washington, D.C.: AEI Center for Regulatory and Market Studies.

UNCED (1993). *The Earth Summit: the United Nations Conference on Environment and Development*. London: Graham and Trotman.

Weitzman, M. L. (2009). "On Modeling and Interpreting the Economics of Catastrophic Climate Change." *Review of Economics and Statistics* 91: 1–19.

Weitzman, M. L. (2011). "Fat-Tailed Uncertainty in the Economics of Catastrophic Climate Change." *Review of Environmental Economics and Policy* 5: 275–292.

CHAPTER 28

CITIZENSHIP AND (UN) SUSTAINABILITY

A Green Republican Perspective

JOHN BARRY

"Activism is the rent I pay for living on this planet," Alice Walker

1 ACTUALLY EXISTING LIBERAL DEMOCRACY: A VIEW FROM THE FOOTHILLS OF POWER

ONE dominant theme in green and indeed other radical/progressive analyses of contemporary citizenship theory and practice is the reduction of "citizen" to "voter" and/or "taxpayer" under liberal political theory and liberal democratic political practice. This reduction is often used to explain the dominance of consumer (and producer) identities, interests, and valued practices over those of (active and participatory) forms of democratic citizenship.

I have direct political experience of the dominance of the taxpayer identity and framing of citizenship within local politics. As a local government councilor in Northern Ireland (for the Green Party), I said in one council meeting that I had noticed that all the other councilors regularly spoke of local people as "rate payers" and "tax payers" rather than referring to them as "citizens." I said that this struck me as odd, since while paying rates is part of what local citizens do, this does not exhaust their political identity. I suggested that viewing them as citizens with rights spoke to local government as an essential element of democracy, and that in my view the role of the local government cannot and should not be reduced merely to a service delivery mechanism. This, I went on, would be to reduce the essentially *political* relationship between local elected representatives and local governance institutions (in this case the local council) to a simple exchange relationship. In other words, to essentially view the relationship as an economic one between those who pay for a service (local rate payers) and the service provider (the council).

The reaction of my fellow councilors was telling. Universally I was criticized and ridiculed for daring to suggest such an idea. I was mocked for my comments, called a "radical," a "Marxist," and other names. One councilor dismissed my position on the grounds that it would be ridiculous to go around calling local people "citizen" when we meet them (though interestingly the reverse of this position was not explored by this councilor, i.e. greeting people as "rate payer"). What does this small experience tell us about the state of democracy and citizenship? And what may it tell us of the connection between citizenship and sustainability? Does a lack of engagement with and care for democracy lead to a similar lack of concern and care for the nonhuman world? And more importantly, does this then also lead to a lack of democratic, collective decision making over human-nonhuman relations? If the crisis of unsustainability is also a crisis of democratic politics (Gore, 2007), does this mean that more democracy is the solution? If passive forms of citizenship or practices of noncitizenship are somehow causally implicated in unsustainability, does that mean simply encouraging more active forms of citizenship will have the opposite effect and help move societies away from unsustainability?

This chapter will seek to explore some of the connections (causal and other) between the decline in active citizenship, the displacement of citizenship by consumer identities and interests, and the shift to a transactional mode of democratic politics and how and in what ways these are connected with the rise of unsustainability. It will also suggest possible responses, proposing an account of "green republican citizenship" as an appropriate theory and practice of establishing a link between democracy and democratization and the transition from unsustainability. The chapter begins from the (not uncontroversial) position that debt-based consumer capitalism (and especially its more recent neoliberal incarnation) is simply incompatible with a version of democratic politics and associated norms and practices of citizenship required for the transition away from unsustainable development (Barry, 2012). This chapter also outlines an explicitly "green republican" conception of citizenship as an appropriate way to integrate democratic citizenship and the creation of a more sustainable political and socio-ecological order.

2 Liberal Clientelism, Green Republicanism, and Citizenship

In terms of the "notes from the foothills of power," a key feature of a green republican conception of citizenship can be discerned in its antipathy to the "dependent clientelism" at the heart of the views of the councilors who rejected viewing local people as citizens. Clientelism here is understood as the selective distribution of public or other resources in exchange for voting or party support, and it has been long documented as a feature of most liberal representative democratic systems (Piattoni, 2001). While clientelism does encompass forms of corrupted citizen-party/politician relationships, there is a more mundane, less dramatic clientelism that is equally, if not more, corrupting of a healthy democratic politics. This is clientelism based on citizens not being informed about or feeling disempowered to navigate the political and policy process (to find benefits, question public officials or statutory agencies, make their views known, for example). And this of course places political parties or politicians in the position as "gatekeepers" in providing that information to citizens and offering a service to citizens as clients, in exchange, implicitly or explicitly, for political or electoral support. And in creating this sense of dependence, such clientelism also creates *unequal* citizens who are in some cases reduced to pre-modern status of being a contingent and insecure recipient of goods or services. An International Labor Organization report on "economic security" picks up on this issue: "It has often been said that the modern movement for human rights represents the painful evolution from clientelism to citizenship, where 'the citizen' is someone with individual and collective rights, rather than merely someone who relies on charity, welfare, or paternalistic gestures . . . Well meaning paternalism easily blurs into discretionary and arbitrary coercion" (International Labor Organization, 2004: 7).

Thus, from a democratic and republican point of view this clientelism leaves the opportunity for abuse of power, for arbitrariness to establish itself where equality and giving people what they are due should be the guiding principles. The avoidance and protection from arbitrary coercion and domination are key defining features of a green republican political vision of democratic citizenship. But why should this matter from a sustainability or green political point of view? Several reasons can be given for this, and indeed there has been much research on the topic over the last two decades (Doherty and de Geus, 1996; Barry, 1999; Smith, 2003 Dobson, 2003). For reasons of space I will outline three.

First, clientelism can undermine democratic politics by reducing the citizen to a passive consumer/client/voter/tax-payer and by creating a political culture that does not encourage or reward citizens becoming interested and involved and participants in the governance of their society. To put it provocatively (here viewing exaggeration as when the truth loses its temper), in so doing it effectively "infantilizes" citizens and creates interests and passive political identities.

Second, clientelism can become a key feature of a "captured" democratic system that is controlled by elites and special interest groups and is therefore a corruption of democracy as "rule by the people, of the people, for the people." On both conceptual and empirical grounds there is a strong correlation between sustainable policies and collective actions and more democratic, participative, and inclusive norms of democratic decision making. For example, there is some evidence of a disjuncture between elites and citizens when it comes to certain risky technological policies in relation to promoting economic growth. Results from deliberative citizens' experiments seem to indicate that the general public is more risk adverse and more inclined to support precautionary approaches to risky technological innovations than political and economic elites (Dryzek et al., 2009). As they note, "If precautionary worldviews are as pervasive in reflective publics as we suggest, then the generally Promethean positions of governing elites cannot be legitimated by deliberative means—at least when it comes to issues of technological risk" (Dryzek et al 2009: 34). This is suggestive of the view that the more open and deliberative the political process with active encouragement and involvement of citizens in decision making, the less likely we are to see policies for technologically risky economic growth policies. This suggests that alternatives to unsustainable economic growth as a permanent feature and objective of an advanced economy, such as "economic security" or notions of well-being, may enjoy more democratic support (Barry, 2012: 161)—but if, and only if, such decisions about the economy, for example, are democratized and made the subject of citizen rather than elite or expert decision making.

Third, and related to the last point of elite and expert domination, the apolitical, consumer logic of clientelism (itself simply being used here as a focal point for the undermining of active citizenship in capitalist-consumer liberal democracies) increases the prevalence of apolitical or often anti-political market-based "solutions" to the problems of unsustainability. These are usually technological in nature and while of course technological innovation is to be welcomed in the transition from unsustainability, part of the danger of such "techno-fix" solutions is in mostly focusing on the "ecological" or resource aspect of unsustainability; they tend to offer narrow apolitical, often individualistic, and resolutely non-collective analyses and responses (Maniates, 2002).

In this way, as Beck puts it, technologically orientated economic growth is presented and perceived by most citizens as "legitimate social change without democratic political legitimation" (1992: 214). This naive notion would be worrying at the best of times, but when such social change is wreaking wholesale ecological destruction on current and future generations, it is ecocidal to assume such "progress" is natural or automatic or safe being managed by elites (corporate and state). On the other hand, citizens under these circumstances are not offered the opportunity to consider that the choice to live in a less unsustainable society is, from a green republican point of view, the choice to live in a *different type of society* (Barry, 2014). Not the *same* society with low-carbon light bulbs or more recycling, i.e. an environmentally sustainable and resource efficient capitalism with unequal power relations, socioeconomic inequalities, and so forth still intact. Thus, essential features of a green republican citizenship (indeed of any "green" conception of citizenship I would suggest) are that it is politically transformative and transgressive, radical and emancipatory-critical (Scerri, 2013). In the next section I outline what, on first gloss, looks like an odd candidate or vehicle for such a transformative, emancipatory form of green republican citizenship practice, namely compulsory "civic sustainability service".

3 THE GREEN REPUBLICAN CASE FOR COMPULSORY CIVIC SUSTAINABILITY SERVICE

One of the reasons for seeking to explore the civic republican tradition relates to recent discussions about the "greening" of citizenship (Scerri, 2012; Barry, 2012; Trachtenberg, 2010; Gabrielson and Paredy, 2010; Gabrielson, 2008; Latta, 2007) and the greening of the state within green political theory (Eckersley, 2003; Barry and Eckersley, 2005). An obvious concern here is that the heavily duty-based conception of republican citizenship would be too burdensome, reducing the many other possible identities, interests, and activities individuals have to a dominant or master identity. Another is the "perfectionism" or imposition of one view of the "good life" that some suggest underpin the republican stress on active citizenship. However, while republicanism certainly emphasizes the importance of active citizens doing their duties, participating and defending the collective way of life of their free community, green republican politics does not require that there be one commonly held view of the good life (Honohan, 2002). Indeed, for republicanism, pluralism and contestation are as (if not more) important for democratic politics than consensus and agreement.

At the same time, prominent contemporary republican theorists such as Philip Pettit are clear that the republican promotion of and stress upon active political citizenship is not based on the ethical or metaphysical superiority of politics and political activism over other modes of life. Rather, citizenship is a means to securing liberty as nondomination, not necessarily an end it itself (Pettit, 1997). *Freedom as nondomination* (as opposed to the liberal conception of *freedom as noninterference*) is institutionalized independence from arbitrary power. This requires active citizenship and involvement in public life and defending and contesting the common good, a central part of which is ecological sustainability. Such activism is central and constitutive of a political order in which freedom can be created and sustained. In this way, green republicanism therefore sees no significant problem in holding a view of citizenship as both *instrumentally and intrinsically* valuable.

Civic sustainability service—forms of compulsory service (enforced by the state) for sustainable (including but not limited to strictly *ecological or environmental*) goals—is similar in form to the national service we find in many states today. This service could take the form of all citizens having to give up some proportion of their time to engage in a range of sustainability activities. These activities could include cleaning up a polluted beach or river, working in community-based recycling schemes, working in socially deprived areas, assisting campaigns to decrease social inequality and social exclusion, participating in public information initiatives about sustainability or environmental education, working on community farms or community wind-farms, becoming a development worker or human rights activist overseas, and so on. Such forms of "citizen work" could be integrated with educational or self-reflective activities to enable citizens to discuss and experience such activities as forms of social learning. Such forms of work/service could help, for example, citizenship education (of the type we have in many curricula in different countries) to become both more real and more meaningful. In this way distinctly "green" dimensions of citizenship could be cultivated. The amount of time given up to sustainability service could range from one year (posteducation) in the service of the common good to a couple of hours each week over a longer period.

One might view it in terms of Marx's notion of "socially necessary labor", that is labor which has to be done in order for society and its members to flourish. Or Michael Walzer's argument, updating Marx's point, in his *Spheres of Justice* where he argues that equal citizenship and the creation and sustaining of a healthy democratic community requires *all* citizens undertake an equal share of the grueling work that makes society function (Walzer, 1983). The distribution of work in all its forms (i.e., not just formally paid "employment" but also unwaged and informal/community or domestic work, including gendered reproductive labor or political work in being an active citizen) is of central concern for green politics (Barry, 2013). And as Crabtree and Field suggest, "A free society often makes claims on its people, from compulsory schooling to paying taxes and defending the nation in a time of peril. Civic service can be just such a legitimate demand" (Crabtree and Field, 2009).

The idea of compulsory sustainability service exhibits an obvious state-focused conception of green citizenship, perfectly in keeping with the republican tradition, which classically is very state-centric (or rather city-state centered. More importantly, any positive connotations of such compulsory citizenship practices seem to depend in part on whether the state that demands and enforces such obligatory work/time is a "green" or "greening" one (Eckersley, 2003). On the face of it, it does seem less objectionable (though of course not without other grounds for objection) if such compulsory forms of green citizenship are authorized by a green state that is working toward sustainability. As Dagger notes, "To paraphrase Edmund Burke, we should be sure that our country is deserving of service before we require or recommend that someone serve it" (Dagger, 2002: 27). For this reason, sustainability citizenship service should not be viewed simply as citizens obeying state injunctions; it also can require, as will be discussed in section 5, forms of resistance citizenship activism *against* the state (and other vested anti-sustainability interests; Barry, 2005).

Another possible objection to compulsory sustainability service is that in a grossly unequal society, the operation of such schemes would result in the unemployed, the poor, and the marginalized being the ones who do the bulk of this compulsory work. Therefore, a precondition for the justification of compulsory public service for sustainability ends requires the creation of a more equal society. That is, a precondition for such practices of "green republican" citizenship is some degree of "rough equality" that is not only in keeping with the egalitarian ethos of green republicanism but is also a constitutive aspect of democratic citizenship itself.

4 Forms of Sustainable Economic Citizenship—The Social Economy and Cooperatives

How the economy is conceptualized, managed, and institutionalized is one of the key issues, if not the key issue, for the transition away from unsustainability. The reasons for this are rather simple. The first is that the human economy represents the material metabolism between humanity and the nonhuman world (energy, resources, pollution, etc.), thus how it is viewed and the principles or objectives by which is it organized determines whether our species is sustainable or not. The second is that the manner in which the human economy is organized determines, in whole or part, how unequal (or not) the society is, the distribution of power and resources, and the dominant view of the "good life." And, pertinent to the discussion of citizenship here, the organization of the economy determines the extent to which notions and practices of solidarity, individual and collective autonomy and self-direction and determination, democratic decision making, and so forth are included or excluded within the economic-productive sphere of society.

Within that extremely broad issue of green political economy (Barry, 2012; Cato, 2012; Boyle and Simms, 2009), I wish to focus on arguments for the growth of the "social economy" and cooperative forms of economic activity as both a necessary feature of any sustainable economy and a way of achieving non-ecological (specifically citizenship) goals of green politics. One of the reasons for focusing on the social economy is that the current dominance of a free market capitalist organization of the economy and a still existing, but shrinking, state/public sector economy is both ecologically irrational (unsustainable largely because of the imperative of carbon-fueled economic growth; Barry, 2012) and socially irrational (creating greater socio-economic inequalities, eroding quality of life, and undermining active democratic citizenship; Wilkinson and Pickett, 2009).

For Smith, one of the reasons for a strong link between the social economy and sustainability is that, "The *ethos* of the social economy orientates organisations towards mutual, communal or general interests ... Ethos is complemented by a second characteristic of social economy organizations—their democratic *structure* ... the social economy offers a number of interesting institutional designs within which different forms of participation can be practised" (2005: 278–279). Thus, unlike either state-bureaucratic or private-capitalist forms of economic organization, the social economy, *ceteris paribus*, provides a better institutional "fit" for green democratic, egalitarian, solidarity, and active citizenship goals (Barry, 2012; Barry and Smith, 2005).

The social economy can act as a site enabling important citizenship skills and experiences to be developed. Indeed, an emerging aspect of green political economy scholarship is the claim that the achievement of these positive extra-economic benefits requires linking the growth of the social economy explicitly to the creation of a "post-growth" economic order that can effectively provide the space for the reduction and transformation (including democratization) of both the state and capitalist spheres of economic production, distribution, and consumption (Barry, 2012).

The social economy, by virtue of its cooperative and democratic potentials, can also contribute to cultivating and supporting more active senses of citizenship (Barry and Smith, 2005: 257–259). That is, the social economy and principles of "co-production" (Cahn, 2000; Stephens, Royle-Collins, and Boyle, 2008) can foster a sense of the individual qua economic/productive agent as an active citizen rather than passive consumer (market economy) or welfare recipient (public sector economy). As Iris Marion Young has argued, the self-organizing and self-directed character of the social economy is such that "[d]emocracy and social justice would be enhanced in most societies if civic associations provided even more goods and services" (2000: 166), a point also echoed by Smith, (2005: 276). The upshot of this is that such self-organizing activity involves learning and practicing skills of conflict resolution, awareness of and resistance to prevailing power relations, and, perhaps above all, the experience that collective action works and that economic production does not have to be always located in either the state or formal market economy.

Going further into some specific forms of social economic organization, a strong connection can be made between the ecological and non-ecological goals of sustainability and worker cooperatives (Carter, 1996) as a form of social economy organization that ought to be favored by green and sustainability advocates. As Tom Malleson has cogently put it,

> "in the 20th century the democratic movement crashed headlong into the locked factory gate. This is why *my democratic totem is that of a worker cooperative, since the expansion of democracy into workplaces, and throughout the economy more generally, represents the next major step in the expansion of human freedom.* The old fight for the franchise continues today in the form of the struggle for economic suffrage and economic citizenship." (Malleson 2013)

Two other reasons present themselves as to why worker cooperatives should be favored by those interested in the transition from unsustainability. The first is that beyond a certain level of production and per capita profit, a worker-managed firm will seek to limit its size and production capacity, as opposed to an inexorable competitive "grow or die" business strategy. As Rosen and Schweickart point out, "since worker-self-managed firms want to maximize profit per worker rather than total profits, they are inherently less expansionary than are capitalist firms ... Increasing the number of employees also dilutes the democratic influence within the firm of the existing members" (Rosen and Schweickart, 2006: 23). At the same time it is likely (and the evidence is there to demonstrate this) that worker-managed firms will achieve "work-life" balance patterns that encourage any productivity gains being translated into more free time (Schor, 2010) as opposed to more wage income and consumption. Or to put it simply, a green republican economy aims *to have more people working less, rather than fewer people working more*. This would enhance human flourishing, a vital component of which is meaningful free time for people. But it would also provide more people with the opportunity to be involved in democratic politics.

5   RESISTANCE IS FERTILE: GREEN CITIZENSHIP AND CONTESTATORY POLITICS

A final area for discussion in relation to citizenship within green/sustainability debates relates to what might be called "contestatory" collective political action. "Sustainability service" could also be interpreted as meaning that there is an obligation within "sustainability citizenship" to engage in forms of political struggle against underlying structural causes of ecological degradation, socio-economic inequality, poverty, ill-health, and other non-ecological components of unsustainability.

In other words, one can think of the "necessary work" that is a constitutive aspect of "sustainability citizenship" as including politically orientated "resistance work" and as not simply equated with "compliance" to state-backed forms of sustainability service and work (Barry, 2012, 2005). In casting sustainability citizenship service in this contestatory form, we move toward both the agonistic politics of republicanism and a more radical politics of green citizenship. Such contestatory forms of citizenship action fit within what Honohan outlines as republican notions of civic virtue—which she suggests "takes various forms, from more passive self-restraint to active public service and even to resistance. It does not mean simply more *obedience or deference to authority* than in a liberal system. It should be noted that it is an obligation between citizens rather than to any central authority" (Honohan, 2002: 166; emphasis added).

Arguing for a conception of what might be called "sustainability necessary resistance work" trades on the same argument often found in debates about injustice. Namely, in the face of prevailing injustices there is a need to recognize these injustices as injustices but also to seek to remedy through appropriate political action. That is, just as we can say that the first demand of justice is to fight against injustice (Simon, 1995), as well as comply with the demands of maintaining a system of justice, equally we can say that the first demand of sustainable development is to fight against unsustainable development, as well as comply with the demands of sustainable development.

It is rather telling that in official "citizenship studies" within mainstream education in most countries, official reviews of citizenship provision (Tonge and Mycock, 2010), political analysis of the importance of citizenship in modern democracies (Crick, 2005), including arguments for greening the citizenship curriculum (Dobson 2003), or forms of "education for sustainable development" (Hume and Barry 2014), resistance and practices of political struggle such as non-violent direct action (NVDA) as valued forms of citizenship action are conspicuous by their absence. Official citizenship education typically views NVDA as a historically interesting but "abnormal" form of citizenship, not fitting within a "normal" understanding of citizen identity. Thus, from a green republican view of citizenship, *agonistic* political action, *contesting* existing state or social norms or laws, does not become seen as a normal and healthy element of a vibrant democratic society. Yet this contestatory mode of citizenship should be valued and encouraged (as opposed to being either neglected or reluctantly tolerated and endured).

6 CONCLUSION

Citizenship is a central feature of green political and ethical theory. From the green republican perspective outlined here it is an indispensible element of the democratic promise of the transition from unsustainability. Citizenship is not simply of instrumental or strategic benefit in the sense that more active and resistance forms of citizenship action and collective agency are required for this transition. Citizenship, especially when viewed and presented in green republican terms, is also a deeply ethical status, practice, and identity. Active democratic citizenship is a precious gift, vulnerable, artificially created, socially maintained, and always contingent. It requires, like freedom itself, constant vigilance and protection from those forces (including internal, psychological ones) that would erode or leech it of its ethical (and activist) core. This ethical core of citizenship is both recognition of it as a legitimate way to structure and acknowledge our codependence on one another and acknowledgment of the status and identity of citizenship as bestowing dignity upon individuals in their expression of autonomy as free moral and politically creative and imaginative agents. This creative capacity for choice is a constituent element of citizenship—to see that the transition from unsustainability is not some automatic transmission mechanism but a creative, political-ethical choice to live in a different type of society.

As theorists as different as Hannah Arendt and Paulo Friere have noted, citizens cannot be "created" in the classroom but rather must be made and remade in actual political action. And perhaps a starting point in relation to contemporary citizenship action (and inaction) in relation to unsustainability is just that: to recognize that our current situation is marked by unsustainability and to make unsustainability rather than sustainability the focus of citizenship action. And from there to think through changes and struggles required to collectively chart a transition away from unsustainability, and in the process to accept our own responsibility and choice to maintain unsustainability or choose and struggle for sustainability. And ultimately, to accept that this form of green/sustainability citizenship action cannot be done for us, but only by us. And finally to ask ourselves the simple question: What if we are the people we've been waiting for?

REFERENCES

Barry, J. (1999). *Rethinking Green Politics: Nature, Virtue, Progress.* London: Sage.
Barry, J. (2005). "Resistance Is Fertile: From Environmental to Sustainability Citizenship." In *Environmental Citizenship: Getting from Here to There?*, edited by D. Bell and A. Dobson, 21–48. Boston: MIT Press.
Barry, J. (2012). *The Politics of Actually Existing Unsustainability: Human Flourishing in a Climate Changed, Carbon Constrained World.* Oxford: Oxford University Press.

Barry, J. (2013). "Post-growth: A Green Republican Political Economy." *OpenDemocracy*, Available at: http://www.opendemocracy.net/ourkingdom/john-barry/post-growth-green-republican-economy (accessed 3/08/13)

Barry, J. (2014). "Ecologism." In *Political Ideologies: An Introduction*, 4th ed., edited by V. Geoghegan et al. London: Routledge.

Barry, J., and Smith, G. (2005). "Green Political Economy and the Promise of the Social Economy." In *International Handbook of Environmental Politics*, edited by P. Dauvergne, 249–270. Cheltenham: Edward Elgar.

Barry, J. and Eckersley, R. (eds) (2005), *The State and the Global Ecological Crisis*. Boston: MIT Press.

Beck, U. (1992). *Risk Society*. London: Sage.

Boyle, D., and Simms, A. (2009). *The New Economics: A Bigger Picture*. (Cheltenham: Edward Elgar.

Cahn, E. (2000). *No More Throwaway People: The Co-production Imperative*. Washington, DC: Essential Books.

Carter, N. (1996). "Worker Cooperatives and Green Political Theory." In *Democracy and Green Political Thought: Sustainability, Rights and Citizenship*, edited by B. Doherty and M. de Geus, 55–77. London: Routledge.

Cato, M. S. (2012). *The Bioregional Economy: Land, Liberty and the Pursuit of Happiness*. London: Earthscan.

Crabtree, J., and Field, F. (2009). "Citizenship First: The Case for Compulsory Civic Service." *Prospect* 156, June.

Crick, B. (2005). *Essays on Citizenship*. London: Continuum.

Dagger, R. (2002). "Republican Virtue, Liberal Freedom, and the Problem of Civic Service." Paper presented at the annual meeting of the American Political Science Association, Boston, MA.

Dobson, A. (2003). *Citizenship and the Environment*. Oxford: Oxford University Press.

Doherty, B., and de Geus, M. (1996). *Democracy And Green Political Thought: Sustainability, Rights, and Citizenship*. London: Routledge.

Dryzek, J., Goodin, R., Tucker, A., and Reber, B. (2009). "Promethean Elites Encounter Precautionary Publics: The Case of GM Foods." *Science, Technology, and Human Values* 34: 263–288.

Eckersley, R. (2003). *The Green State: Rethinking Democracy and Sovereignty*. Boston: MIT Press.

Gabrielson, T. (2008). "Green Citizenship: A Review and Critique." *Citizenship Studies*, 12 (4): 429–446.

Gabrielson, T., and Paredy, K. (2010). "Corporeal Citizenship: Rethinking Green Citizenship through the Body." *Environmental Politics* 19 (3): 374–391.

Gore, A. (2007). *The Assault on Reason*. London: Penguin.

Honohan, I. (2002). *Civic Republicanism*. London: Routledge.

Hume, T., and Barry, J. (2014). "Environmental Education and Education for Sustainable Development." In *International Encyclopedia of Social and Behavioral Sciences*, 2nd ed., edited by J. Wright. Oxford: Elsevier.

International Labor Organization (2004). *Economic Security for a Better World*. Geneva: International Labor Office.

Latta, P. A. (2007). "Locating Democratic Politics in Ecological Citizenship." *Environmental Politics* 16: 377–393.

Malleson, T. (2013). "Democratic Imagination." Available at: http://www.democraticimagina-tion.com/exercising-imagination.html (accessed 30/7/13).

Maniates, M. (2002). "Individualization: Plant a Tree, Buy a Bike, Save the World?" *Global Environmental Politics* 1(3): 31–52.

Pettit, P. (1997). *Republicanism: A Theory of Freedom and Government.* Oxford: Oxford University Press.

Piattoni, S. (ed.) (2001). *Clientelism, Interests, and Democratic Representation.* Cambridge: Cambridge University Press.

Rosen, R. and Schweickart, D. (2006). *Visions of Regional Economies in a Great Transition World.* Boston, MA: The Tellus Institute.

Scerri, A. (2013). "Green Citizenship and the Political Critique of Injustice." *Citizenship Studies* 17(3–4): 293–307.

Scerri, A. 2012. *Greening Citizenship: Sustainable Development, the State and Ideology.* London: Palgrave.

Schor, J. (2010). *Plenitude: The New Economics of True Wealth.* New York: Penguin.

Simon, T. (1995). *Democracy and Injustice: Law, Politics and Philosophy.* Boston, MA: Rowman and Littlefield.

Smith, G. (2003). *Deliberative Democracy and the Environment.* London: Routledge.

Smith, G. (2005). "Green Citizenship and the Social Economy." *Environmental Politics* 14(2): 273–289.

Stephens, L., Royle-Collins, J. and Boyle, D. (2008). *Co-production: A Manifesto for Growing the Core Economy. London: new economics foundation.* [Online] Available: http://www.new-economics.org/sites/neweconomics.org/ les/Co- production_1. pdf (accessed 2/2/11).

Tonge, J., and Mycock, A. (2010). "Citizenship and Political Engagement Among Young People: The Workings and Findings of the Youth Citizenship Commission." *Parliamentary Affairs* 6 (1): 182–200.

Trachtenberg, Z. (2010). "Complex Green Citizenship and the Necessity of Judgment." *Environmental Politics* 19 (3): 339–355.

Walzer, M. (1983). *Spheres of Justice: A Defense of Pluralism and Equality.* New York: Basic Books.

Wilkinson, R., and Pickett, K. (2009). *The Spirit Level: Why More Equal Societies Almost Always Do Better.* London: Allen Lane.

Young, I. M. (2000). *Inclusion and Democracy.* Oxford: Oxford University Press.

CHAPTER 29

FUTURE GENERATIONS IN ENVIRONMENTAL ETHICS

JOHN NOLT

1 TAKING FUTURE PEOPLE SERIOUSLY

FUTURE generations are composed of future people. (There are also future generations of non-humans; we'll return to them later.) A *future person*, at a given time, is one who is not alive then but will be later. Someone who could exist but never actually will is not a future person.

Semantically, "future" is an indexical term. It characterizes, not the kind of a thing, but rather the point of view from which it is being described. In that respect it is like the term "foreign." From our perspective, here in our homeland, we are not foreigners. But from the perspectives of people of other lands we are. Similarly, from our perspective we are not future people, but from the perspectives of our predecessors we are. It follows that future people are not, as such, inherently different from us.

It might be objected that future people *are* inherently different from us, since we exist and they do not—at least not yet. But the sort of existence that this objection invokes is likewise a matter of perspective. Einstein and Minkowski showed that space and time are not absolute, independent continua as Newton thought, but rather that both are perspective-relative aspects of a single space-time. Existence in a place or at a time is thus not an inherent property of an object, but rather a matter of its spatiotemporal relations to other things. Future people do not exist *now* in the same way that inhabitants of the Andromeda galaxy (assuming that there are some) do not exist *here* (on Earth). Both sorts of nonexistence amount to the same thing: spatiotemporal separation from us. (For a fine non-technical account of the relations of objects to space-time, see Thorne, 1994, chs. 1, 2.)

Nor do future people differ from us in being an undifferentiated collective, rather than individuals, as the terms "future generations" and "posterity" may suggest. We cannot *know* future people as individuals, but that is what they are. Just so, we cannot know the Andromedans as individuals, though (again, assuming they exist) that is what they are. And just so, our predecessors could not know us as individuals, although that is what we are.

We understand future people best when we consider things not merely from our own spatiotemporal standpoint, but also, insofar as we can reasonably extrapolate, from theirs.

I call this "taking future people seriously." In doing so, it is natural to use untensed verbs, as I did when in the previous paragraph I said that future people "are" (rather than "will be") individuals.

Economic approaches to policymaking typically fail to take future people seriously. Consider, for example, the notion of acceptable risk, which is used in environmental policymaking to establish spending priorities. To calculate acceptable risk for an environmental hazard, economists determine how much money people would be willing to pay to reduce that risk by a certain amount. A risk is deemed acceptable to a group if the cost of reducing it exceeds what the group's members in aggregate are willing to pay.

Risks are valued in terms of willingness to pay because that is economically convenient, because it is assumed that willingness to pay accurately measures people's preferences, and because people's preferences are assumed to determine value. But willingness to pay is assessed only for people who are alive here and now. Risk assessment neglects the likely preferences of future people who will be affected by long-term hazards such as climate change. If it accounts for their preferences at all, it does so only indirectly, via the preferences of present people who care about them. It therefore does not take future people seriously.

It might be supposed that such indirection is the only possible way to value the welfare of future people, since we cannot know their preferences directly. But this presumes that preference satisfaction is the only possible measure of human welfare. Preference satisfaction and welfare are, however, quite distinct; we often prefer what is not good for us.

It is somewhat better to define welfare as satisfaction of *considered* preferences—those that are fully informed and rationally endorsed. This also has the advantage of revealing a fairly stable core of consensus. Nearly all thoughtful people value such conditions as health, longevity, safety, wealth adequate to needs, opportunities for learning, and freedom from oppression.

Arguably, however, such conditions are rationally preferred because they are *objectively* good for people—that is, good regardless of their preferences. If so, it would be better to define human welfare directly as the realization of such objective values, rather than indirectly via considered preferences. Yet even if the goodness of these conditions is not objective, but rather an artifact of rational consensus, it is a consensus from which future people are hardly likely to dissent. Such a conception of welfare is therefore compatible with taking future people seriously.

2 THE MORAL IRRELEVANCE OF SPATIOTEMPORAL SEPARATION

In the previous section I argued that future people are not, per se, inherently different from us. This section contends, further, that their spatiotemporal separation from us is in itself of no moral relevance.

We tend to value future people and their welfare less the further into the future they live. But their welfare is no less important from their own perspective than our welfare is from ours. Why then should we count it less? To account value for others less than value for us and our circle (e.g., family, friends, or compatriots), and to do so without justification, is mere bias. The aim of this section is to show that in the case of future people, we do so without justification.

This does not mean that our moral responsibilities to future people are the same as those to our contemporaries. But it does mean that where responsibilities to these two groups differ, mere spatiotemporal separation is not the reason for the difference.

We generally have special responsibilities to people to whom we are related by family or community ties, friendship, shared purpose, promises, and so on. Such relationships are either absent or attenuated between us and future people. Hence we have fewer such special responsibilities to them. But it is the absence or attenuation of such relationships, not the spatiotemporal separation, that makes the difference.

To see this, remove the relationships and ask whether the spatiotemporal separation makes any difference. It is just as wrong, for example, to plant a bomb that will reliably kill a perfect stranger in the far future as to plant a bomb that will equally reliably kill a perfect stranger today. And just as the spatial distance between us and the contemporary stranger is morally irrelevant, so is the temporal distance between us and the future stranger.

Of course, detonation of the bomb in the distant future may be improbable. But the detonation of today's bomb may be equally improbable. If the probability in each case is the same, the culpability is the same. Thus although probability may affect our responsibility, temporal separation does not. Probability, moreover, is not reliably correlated with temporal distance. Some event types (intense storms due to climate change, for example) become increasingly probable the further we look into the future—over the next few centuries, at least. Others become less probable. The probabilities of still others are unaffected.

Though improbability does not, in general, increase with spatiotemporal separation, ignorance does. Ignorance can, moreover, if innocent, diminish our moral responsibility. Those who burned large quantities of fossil fuels before it was known that this would exacerbate climate change were, for example, less to blame than we are today. But unwitting harm to future strangers is morally excusable only to the extent that similarly unwitting harm to contemporary strangers is. Once again, spatiotemporal separation per se is morally irrelevant.

Our tendency to discount future costs and benefits has been institutionalized by economists in the form of an annual percentage known as the social discount rate. This practice is justified in various ways, most of which—though appropriate for economic decisions that affect only contemporaries—fail to take future people seriously. Two such justifications, however, are at least consistent with taking future people seriously and hence worthy of mention here.

The first is that we may defer certain costs to the future—the costs of nuclear waste disposal or climate adaptation, for example—because future people, being richer than we are and having better technology, will be better able to bear them. These costs, in other words, matter less to them than to us. This takes future people seriously, but it gives them too much credit. Future people several decades from now *may* be richer and technologically more adept than we are. But civilizations rise and fall. How likely is it that all the generations during, say, the next millennium will be better off than we are? Yet that time span is, as we shall see, well within the scope of intergenerational ethics.

The second justification for discounting that is at least compatible with taking future people seriously is that beyond a certain date there may not be any future people. Some calamity, in other words, might extinguish the human species. In his work on the economics of climate change, Nicholas Stern (2008) adopts a "pure time" annual discount rate of 0.1%, a figure that reflects his estimate of the probability of human extinction. Suppose, for example, that in the year 2015 we estimate annual economic losses from climate change to amount to $100 trillion by 2100—if humans survive that long. (If they don't, then there will be no economic loss in 2100.) Given Stern's 0.1% rate, the probability of human survival to 2100 is 0.915. Hence from our perspective in 2015 the expected loss in 2100 is $100 trillion × 0.915 = $91.5 trillion. But, of course, if humans do survive to 2100, the actual loss to them that year will be $100 trillion. To see that is to take future people seriously. To recognize only a $91.5 trillion loss is not. Thus users of Stern's method *can* take future people seriously, but only if they do not conflate actual future losses with expected (that is, probability-discounted) losses calculated from our spatiotemporal standpoint.

Many economists use a higher pure time rate, which some justify in terms of the preferences of present people for gains sooner rather than later. That justification obviously does not take future people seriously. The difference in rates is politically important. Using Stern's lower rate, massive and immediate spending to mitigate climate change is economically justified. Using the higher rates it is not. The difference comes down, essentially, to whether we take future people seriously.

To summarize: alleged justifications for discounting the value of people or their welfare merely according to the degree of their temporal separation from us fail, either because they confuse temporal separation with improbability, ignorance, or the like, or because they do not take future people seriously. If we take future people seriously, then we will value them and their welfare no less than us and ours.

3 INTERGENERATIONAL ETHICS

What, then, are our responsibilities to future people? Strict Kantians have a ready answer: since future people are not inherently different from us, the categorical imperative commands the same respect for them as for our contemporaries. In particular, it forbids treating them merely as means—that is, as mere objects. Kantian ethics encode duty in a system of rules. The Rawlsian, and hence Kantian, intergenerational political theory developed by Steve Vanderheiden, for example, has two fundamental principles: "the moral duty to avoid causing predictable harm to others" and "a basic principle of equality that refuses to discount harm simply because it accrues in the future" (Vanderheiden, 2008: 137).

For utilitarians, the outlines of our responsibilities to future people are also clear. Since the welfare of each future person counts equally with the welfare of each of us and since our duty, according to classical utilitarianism, is to maximize overall welfare, we should, to a first approximation, aim for total welfare that is as high as can be indefinitely sustained.

But ethics of reciprocity falter in the intergenerational arena. Take, for example, the Golden Rule, which exhorts us to do unto others as we would have them do unto us. This exhortation is inapplicable to others born after we are dead, who can do nothing unto *us*—as distinguished from our reputations and continuing projects (see O'Neill, 1993). For intergenerational application, a more appropriate rule might be: do unto your successors as you would have had your predecessors do unto you. But that ideal is no longer one of reciprocity.

Conceptions of reciprocity are also fundamental to contractualist ethical theories, which regard morality as an idealized social contract to which all who respect persons can rationally assent. But, unsurprisingly, when contractualists consider intergenerational problems they tend to resort to non-contractualist solutions. John Rawls, for example, impressed by the impossibility of reciprocity among members of widely separated generations, envisions the negotiations that establish his hypothetical just society as occurring among contemporaries. But in his later work he appends the stipulation that the negotiators accept the contract only "subject to the further condition that they must want all *previous* generations to have followed it" (Rawls, 1993: 274). The result is presumably salutary; they will produce rules that could reasonably be endorsed by members of any generation. The signers of the contract are agreeing, in other words, to do unto their successors as they would have had their predecessors do unto them. But what yields this result is not reciprocal agreement among generations. It is, instead, Rawls' somewhat ad hoc stipulation that the contract signers think of themselves as future people relative to hypothetical past contract signers. This, at bottom, is a device for taking future people seriously.

Contractarians—who see ethics as a strategy of cooperation adopted by rationally self-interested and similarly powerful persons to maximize attainment of their ends—have great difficulty extending this idea intergenerationally (Gardiner, 2003, 2009). It is, in the first place, impossible to enter into a cooperative contract with people who will be born after we die. And, in the second, even if it were possible, it is difficult to find purely self-interested reasons not to betray such people, since they have no power to enforce a contract against us.

Communitarian ethics do better in this regard. They also require reciprocity—between citizen and community—but since communities typically last longer than people, such ethics are naturally intergenerational. Intergenerational communitarian ethical theory was pioneered by Avner de-Shalit (1995). Communities, according to de-Shalit, are of many kinds: professions, political parties, religions, nations, and so forth. Individuals are usually members of several. Membership in a community entails reciprocal privileges and responsibilities. In addition to tangible benefits, the privileges include enjoyment of a context of meaning that is larger and longer-lasting than individuals and that is fundamental in making each of us who we are as individuals. In return, the community requires of us contributions of time, talent, or treasure, which it uses to maintain itself and its members, not only in the present but often into the future. Our duties to communities are thus in part duties to the future, but they are enforceable by the community at present.

Still, de-Shalit's communitarianism is not wholly adequate as an intergenerational ethic. Communities, too, have life spans, and among the people we ought to take seriously are those who do not belong to our community, including those who will be born after its demise. One can avoid this objection by thinking of the "community" as encompassing everyone, past, present, and future—perhaps even all life. Norton (Sustainability as the Multigeneraltional Public Interest, this volume) moves in this direction. But such an ethic, though holistic, is communitarian only in a highly attenuated sense.

4 THE NON-IDENTITY PROBLEM

Different intergenerational choices may create different people, or even wholly distinct populations. Decisions among such choices are known as non-identity cases (Parfit, 1984, ch. 16). A simple non-identity case arises when a couple chooses between conceiving a child now and conceiving it a few years hence, for with each option (assuming that conception is by natural means) different gametes will unite, producing a different person.

Public policy decisions are often non-identity cases on a grand scale. One reason for this is that they affect employment patterns. After a policy is changed, many young adults take different jobs, meet different mates, and have different children than they would have had otherwise. Their children in turn produce different children, and these differences ramify. Thus, after many generations, the resulting population may be composed of wholly different people from the one that would have resulted had the policy not been changed.

Non-identity cases are philosophically puzzling. Consider, for example, a choice between two policies: greenhouse gas emissions as usual, on the one hand, and a steep and permanent reduction, on the other. Suppose that, regardless of which policy we choose, by 2300 none the people alive would have been born had we made the other choice. Suppose further that if we continue emissions, people in 2300 will suffer much and die early. Hence we may call them the post-apocalyptic people. And suppose, finally, that their travails will not be worse for them than if they had never been born. If we reduce emissions, however, people in 2300 (not the same people, of course) will be fine.

Now here is the puzzle: If we continue emissions, then apparently we do nothing wrong to the post-apocalyptic people, even though we cause them to suffer much and die early, for

*An action can be wrong only by making someone worse off than she would have been otherwise.

But had we not continued emissions, the post-apocalyptic people would never have been born; and, by supposition, they are not worse off than that. Therefore continuing our emissions was not wrong—at least as regards them.

More generally, such reasoning seems to show that it is not wrong to inflict suffering and early death upon innocent future people, provided that their lives are still worth living and the only alternative is for them never to be born. That conclusion would eviscerate intergenerational ethics.

The argument hinges crucially on the assumption marked *. This, and similar theses, are known as "person-affecting principles." Classical utilitarians reject person-affecting principles and so are not threatened by the non-identity problem, for they choose actions with regard only to aggregate welfare, not to how they affect individual people. But for theories that predicate the wrongness of actions on the wronging of individuals (e.g., rights theories), person-affecting principles are at least initially plausible.

Fortunately, however, * is false; for an action may be wrong simply because it injures or kills a person, even if it does not make her worse off than she otherwise would have been (Nolt, 2013). Consider the perspective of a post-apocalyptic woman living in 2300. She has a generally happy life but then suffers much and dies at age 20 from a drought brought on by our greenhouse gas emissions. Our choice to continue those emissions produced two consequences for her: her existence and her suffering and death. Many ethical theories, including most rights theories, can consistently maintain she was wronged by the latter consequence, even though the action that produced it also produced her existence and so did not make her worse off than she would have been without that action. These theories are therefore not committed to * and so, like classical utilitarianism, they can evade the non-identity problem.

5 The Repugnant Conclusion

So far classical utilitarianism seems to provide a plausible intergenerational ethic. But it is widely believed to be tainted by what Derek Parfit has dubbed the Repugnant Conclusion (1984, ch. 17). The gateway to this conclusion is the realization that there are two ways to increase welfare. If we think of welfare as happiness, the first and most usual way is to make people who are now alive happier. The second is to make more happy people. Making more happy people can increase total happiness even if the happiness of existing people *decreases*— so long as the decrease is less than the happiness of the additional people. Thus under special circumstances, classical utilitarianism counsels us to produce more and more people while already existing people become less and less happy. That is the Repugnant Conclusion.

Parfit (1984, sec. 122 ff.) felt its repugnance so strongly that he rejected classical utilitarianism and launched a quest for an alternative, "Theory X." But no widely endorsed Theory X has emerged. This has prompted some to reconsider the Repugnant Conclusion.

Each of us might prefer living in a world whose population is small and happy over living in a world of whose population is large and less happy. Michael Huemer (2008) reminds us, however, that that does not make the first world the better choice, for our preference takes account only of *our* happiness in the two worlds, ignoring the happiness of the additional people in the second world, who matter just as much as we do. Moreover, if the greatest happiness can be created only by some of us sacrificing some of our happiness to bring additional happy people into the world, it is not wholly obvious that we should not do so. Older generations have always had to sacrifice some of their happiness for younger ones.

6 The Need to Reduce Population

Even if we grant the theoretical validity of the Repugnant Conclusion, however, it does not follow that we should increase population here and now. On the contrary, we now ought to reduce population, at least so long as we continue to burn fossil fuels.

Four hundred thousand people now die annually from the effects of anthropogenic climate change, the chief cause of which is the burning of fossil fuels. That figure is expected to reach 700,000 by 2030 (DARA, 2012). Extrapolating, John Broome (2012: 33) infers, quite reasonably, that by 2100 the cumulative death toll from climate change will be in the tens of millions. Many more will suffer. The Intergovernmental Panel on Climate Change (IPCC) predicts that "climate change over the next century is *likely* to adversely affect hundreds of millions of people through increased coastal flooding, reductions in water supplies, increased malnutrition and increased health impacts" (IPCC 2007: 65). The adverse effects include homelessness, injury, illness and death.

Climate change will not, however, end in 2100. Its storms, droughts, floods, and other damaging effects will, given high emissions and the likely climate sensitivity of 3°C for doubling of CO_2, continue for tens of thousands of years (Zeebe, 2013). Ocean acidification and resultant depletion of marine life will last for thousands (IAP, 2009). Biodiversity loss, perhaps amounting to a mass extinction, can last for millions (Barnosky et al., 2011; Kirchner and Weil, 2000).

Thus a great many people are likely to suffer and die annually as a result of our fossil fuel use, for a very long time. Total casualties (including serious harms as well as deaths) may well reach into the billions (Nolt, 2011a, 2013).

More people burn more fossil fuels. Therefore, the higher the population in the coming decades, the greater the total emissions, and hence—since ultimate temperature is roughly proportional to cumulative total emissions (Stocker, 2013)—the greater the total long-term suffering and death. Pretty clearly, therefore, adding population today will not increase total happiness. Nor, if we increase the number of people now, will we be able to compensate for all the misery later by adding still more happy people then; for our actions are reducing Earth's carrying capacity. The chances of the planet's being able to support large populations later are greater if it has a smaller population now, while we are still unable to quit fossil fuels.

To summarize: the Repugnant Conclusion, whether defensible or not, is irrelevant to our present situation. We urgently need to reduce population. The reason for this is that the more people there are now the more fossil fuels we will burn; and the more fossil fuels we burn, the more harm we will do, and the less total welfare there will be, over the coming millennia. Implicit in this reasoning, of course, is the premise that we ought to take future people seriously.

7 The Need to Keep Fossil Fuels in the Ground

It might be objected that it doesn't matter how many people we have now or how fast we burn fossil fuels because we will eventually burn all the fossil fuels anyway (Hale, 2011). We might, but burning all of the remaining fossil fuels would result in an eventual global average temperature increase of as much as 16°C, rendering most of the planet uninhabitable by humans (Hansen, et al., 2013).

Thus another clear implication of taking future people seriously is that we must quickly eliminate the burning of fossil fuels. We *may* someday be able to render their emissions harmless, but it would be foolish to count on that.

The need to eliminate the burning of fossil fuels has a corollary. Fossil fuels are highly concentrated and hence extremely valuable energy sources. Once removed from the ground they will almost inevitably be burned. Hence to stop burning them, we must keep them in the ground.

The responsibility to keep fossil fuels in the ground does not relieve humanity of the previously mentioned responsibility to reduce population. History suggests that we are unlikely to do well at either. Therefore we had better try our best at both.

8 Future Generations of Nonhumans

So far, by "future generations," this essay has meant future generations of humans. But intergenerational ethics in a broader sense considers future nonhumans as well. If it considers them only insofar as they contribute to or detract from the goods of present and future humans, it is anthropocentric. If it regards them as having goods that are themselves morally significant, it is non-anthropocentric. I'll discuss only non-anthropocentric theories, since the anthropocentric ones add nothing fundamentally new.

Non-anthropocentric theories differ regarding which entities have morally considerable goods. Individualistic theories count only individual organisms, and often only some of these—sentient animals, for example. Holistic theories count aggregate entities such as species or ecosystems, and usually individuals as well. Intergenerational versions of each are distinguished by their greater temporal scope.

Non-anthropocentric theories further decrease the repugnance of the Repugnant Conclusion. The worry in the anthropocentric case is that utilitarianism might impel us toward a world bereft of nature and populated by many barely happy humans. But when we add consideration of the welfare of nonhumans, then the strategy of increasing welfare by adding new welfare-bearers would instead, given the plausible assumption that high welfare entails high diversity, yield a modest human population and a rich nonhuman one. Non-anthropocentric ethics also bolster the case for eliminating fossil fuels.

Non-anthropocentric responsibilities may be greater in temporal scope than anthropocentric responsibilities. Many scientists fear that climate change, coupled with habitat destruction, will produce Earth's sixth mass extinction. (A mass extinction is an event in which the earth loses most of its species in a geologically short interval. The fifth was the end-cretaceous event about 65 million years ago that eliminated the dinosaurs.) It takes biodiversity millions of years to recover from a mass extinction (Barnosky et al., 2011; Kirchner and Weil, 2000). This is longer than the likely duration of the human species. Continuing damage and depletion of that duration must have some moral significance. But if so, only a non-anthropocentric theory can account for it (Nolt, 2011b).

9 THE TEMPORAL SCOPE OF ETHICS

What, then, is the temporal scope of ethics? It is commonly accepted that we have no responsibility for events whose occurrence we can in no way predictably alter. But our acquisition of knowledge and power has been so rapid that we are now able to initiate a mass extinction, whose predictable ramifications last for millions of years. Beyond that distant limit, however, we have no responsibility for anything.

Moral theories differ regarding the extent of our responsibility on this side of that limit. Even the literature on intergenerational ethics seldom looks farther than a few centuries ahead. But given that a mass extinction could limit quality of life for humans as long as there are any, our anthropocentric responsibilities arguably now span the duration of the human species, however long that is. Our non-anthropocentric responsibilities may extend further.

Some regard such a conception of ethics as too demanding. Tim Mulgan argues that even far more modest anthropocentric intergenerational ethics leave "the agent too little time, resources and energy for her own projects or interests." He regards this "demandingness objection" as a conclusive reason to reject such theories (Mulgan, 2006). I hold, to the contrary, that intergenerational ethics presents us with demandingness *theorems* that accurately gauge the moral burdens of our godlike knowledge and power.

REFERENCES

Broome, J. (2012). *Climate Matters: Ethics in a Warming World*. New York: W. W. Norton.

Barnosky, A. D., et. al. (2011). "Has the Earth's Sixth Mass Extinction Already Arrived?" *Nature* 471: 51.

De-Shalit, A. (1995). *Why Posterity Matters: Environmental Policies and Future Generations*. London: Routledge.

Development Assistance Research Associates (DARA) (2012). *Climate Vulnerability Monitor*, 2nd ed., http://daraint.org/climate-vulnerability-monitor/climate-vulnerability-monitor-2012/report/.

Gardiner, S. M. (2003). "The Pure Intergenerational Problem." *Monist* 86 (3): 481–500.

Gardiner, S. M. (2009). "A Contract on Future Generations?" In *Intergenerational Justice*, edited by A. Gosseries and L. Meyer, 77–119. Oxford/New York: Oxford University Press.

Gosseries, A., M., and Lukas, H., (eds.) (2009). *Intergenerational Justice*. Oxford/New York: Oxford University Press.

Hale, B. (2011). "Nonrenewable Resources and the Inevitability of Outcomes." *The Monist*, 94 (3): 369–390.

Hansen, J., Sato, M., Russell G., and Kharecha, P. (2013). "Climate Sensitivity, Sea Level and Atmospheric Carbon Dioxide." *Philosophical Transactions of the Royal Society A* 371: 20120294, http://dx.doi.org/10.1098/rsta.2012.0294.

Huemer, M. (2008). "In Defense of Repugnance." *Mind* 117, 468: 899–933.

IAP (Interacademy Panel on International Issues) (2009). "IAP Statement on Ocean Acidification." http://www.interacademies.net/File.aspx?id=9075.

IPCC (Intergovernmental Panel on Climate Change) (2007). *Climate Change 2007: Synthesis Report*. Cambridge: Cambridge University Press.

Kirchner, J., and Weil, A. (2000). "Delayed Biological Recovery from Extinctions throughout the Fossil Record." *Nature* 404 (9): 177–180.

Mulgan, T. (2006). *Future People: A Moderate Consequentialist Account of Our Obligations to Future Generations*. Oxford: Clarendon Press.

Nolt, J. (2011a). "How Harmful Are the Average American's Greenhouse Gas Emissions?" *Ethics, Policy and Environment* 14 (1): 3–10.

Nolt, J. (2011b). "Nonanthropocentric Climate Ethics." *WIRES Climate Change* 2: 701–711.

Nolt, J. (2013). "Response to Critics of "How Harmful Are the Average American's Greenhouse Gas Emissions?"" *Ethics, Policy and Environment* 16 (1): pp. 1–9.

Norton, B. G. (2016). "Sustainability as the Multigenerational Public Interest." In this volume.

O'Neill, J. (1993). "Future Generations: Present Harms." *Philosophy* 68: 35–51.

Parfit, D. (1984). *Reasons and Persons*. Oxford: Clarendon Press.

Rawls, J. (1993). *Political Liberalism*. New York: Columbia University Press.

Stern, N. (2008). "The Economics of Climate Change." *American Economic Review* 98 (2) (2008): 1–37; reprinted in Gardiner, Stephen M., Caney, S., Jamieson, D., and Shue, H., eds. (2010). *Climate Ethics: Essential Readings*. Oxford/New York: Oxford University Press.

Stocker, T. F. (2013). "The Closing Door of Climate Targets." *Science* 339: 280–282.

Thorne, K. S. (1994). *Black Holes and Time Warps: Einstein's Outrageous Legacy.* New York: W. W. Norton.

Vanderheiden, S. (2008). *Atmospheric Justice: A Political Theory of Climate Change.* Oxford/New York: Oxford University Press.

Zeebe, Richard E. (2013). "Time-dependent Climate Sensitivity and the Legacy of Anthropogenic Greenhouse Gas Emissions." *Proceedings of the National Academy of Sciences* 110. doi:10.1073/pnas.1222843110.

CHAPTER 30

....

SUSTAINABILITY AS THE MULTIGENERATIONAL PUBLIC INTEREST

....

BRYAN G. NORTON

1 SUSTAINABILITY AS A CONTESTED CONCEPT

....

SUSTAINABILITY is perhaps the most important concept in environmental policy discussions today, despite its lack of a clear definition in academically acceptable terms. This lack has led to a turf war among several disciplines, as practitioners contest to "own" the term by virtue of defining it in terms of their own disciplinary theories and terminology. Prominent are economists, who offer definitions of sustainability based in the principles of mainstream economic growth theory, and ecologists, who attempt to understand sustainability by linking it to "resilience," emphasizing the importance of system-level concepts appropriate to conceiving sustainability as a path forward in a complex, dynamic system. Conservation biologists often connect the concept of sustainability with the goal of protecting biological diversity. Philosophers, on the whole, have been less engaged in the conversation about how to define this key term, as will be discussed in section 4.

Interestingly, there is a considerable literature by ethicists on obligations of presently living persons to future generations, but few philosophers have used these writings to elucidate the concept of sustainability in particular, despite the apparent implication that urging humans to live sustainably *is* to propose an obligation to future generations.[1] In this chapter I explore the intellectual territory in which the concept of sustainability is contested. I show that differing disciplinary attempts to define sustainability can be associated with different philosophical assumptions and definitions, and that developing a unified conception of sustainability will involve taking some strong positions on controversial philosophical positions in both ethics and in socio-political philosophy.

At the center of the contest over the term "sustainable" and its companion term, "sustainable development," is a separation between two basic strategies for understanding sustainability, often referred to as *strong* versus *weak sustainability.* In section 2, I explain how these two strategies and their disciplinary foundations differ and explore these strategies by applying them to Garrett Hardin's (1968) much-discussed parable, "the tragedy of the commons."

This exploration, applied in section 3, encourages an understanding of sustainability as requiring obligations that go beyond obligations to current persons and to protect system-level aspects of ecological systems. In section 4, I respond to the troublesome paradox of Derek Parfit, noting that it can provide an independent argument for the necessity of recognizing communal values in multigenerational communities. Finally, drawing on recent and earlier work on the notion of the "public interest," I show how the public interest, extended to apply to the interests of an ongoing, multigenerational "community," can provide a reasonable ideal for guiding a procedurally based notion of sustainability.

2 Strong and Weak Sustainability

It is common to divide sustainability definitions according to a distinction between "weak" and "strong" definitions, as compared in Figure 30.1 (after Norton, 2005). While there are many nuances and variations in definitions of sustainability, this particular divide is very important because it exhibits key differences in disciplinary models proposed, and it thus traces the line between economic and other approaches to sustainability. According to weak sustainability, a given generation has lived sustainably provided it passes on as much accumulated wealth (capital) to future generations as it inherited from its ancestors (Solow, 1993). The reasoning of weak sustainability theorists is that if future generations are as wealthy as we are they will be as able as we are to pursue their individual welfare. This reasoning requires a constant measure that can be compared across time, such as monetary valuation in present dollars; and since economists believe that resources are universally "fungible" (substitutable for each other), sustainability can be determined by comparing the total, undifferentiated wealth of successive generations of society across time. A generation will have lived sustainably if its bequest of general capital to subsequent generations is at least as great as the bequest of capital it inherited. This definition is referred to as "weak" because the demands it makes upon a given generation are apparently not onerous; working toward sustainability on the weak approach is simply to make good decisions that will contribute to economic efficiency over time.

"Strong" sustainability, on the other hand, makes stronger demands on the present by accounting for more values than economic ones. Its characterization of a sustainable path

	Weak Sustainability	Strong Sustainability
Home Discipline	Mainstream economics	Systems ecology
Paradigm	Welfare economics	Complex dynamic systems theory / adaptive management
Definition	Maintenance of undifferentiated capital	Weak sustainability + maintenance of resilience
Key Concepts	Nondeclining wealth	Maintaining resilient ecosystems
Key Advocates	R. M. Solow (1993)	Gunderson and Holling, 2001; Lee, 1993

FIGURE 30.1 Comparing Sustainability Definitions

into the future requires more specific and more demanding levels of protection for particular resources (see, for example, Walker and Salt, 2006). Strong sustainability is often advocated by ecologists, who argue that simply counting and comparing human economic welfare across generations is inadequate to track sustainability, because major natural systems and their resilience are seen as essential to the well-being of future people, no matter how wealthy they are. Strong sustainability is thus understood as placing more stringent standards on those who try to live sustainably in the present, and it proceeds to identify values that cannot be expressed in terms of fungible measures such as dollars. Strong sustainability theorists are often distinguished from weak sustainability advocates because the former identify objects of value that cannot be measured in terms of economic markers of welfare but must be described in physical terms (Norton, 2005, 2015). Advocates of strong sustainability thus distinguish "natural capital" (values that are exemplified in aspects of the physical world) from "human-built capital," and they insist that a sufficiently strong set of requirements for sustainability must go beyond simply requiring that earlier generations not impoverish their successors economically.[2]

One way to explore this conceptual conflict regarding sustainability is to apply these different approaches to the arguments surrounding what is called "the tragedy of the commons."[3] Although Hardin's actual target was overpopulation, he developed an argument that can be applied to a wide range of "environmental" problems, an argument that applies to use and destruction of any resource, as long as certain assumptions are made about the situation and the users. The key assumptions that generate tragedies are

1. Some resources are "owned" by private individuals living in a community; other resources are held in common by the community.
2. Individuals in the community always act to maximize their own, individual interests when making decisions.

These assumptions govern a "model" for resource use (where a model is understood as a set of assumptions that will generate a particular outcome as long as conditions and assumptions hold). The model is validated to the extent that the predicted outcome affecting a particular resource use is inevitable, given the assumptions in question.

Hardin applies his model metaphorically by asking his reader to imagine a pasture that is common property and members of the community who own cattle and graze them on the common pasture. Individuals, as private owners of cattle, can add animals to their herd. But since the "carrying capacity" of the pasture is finite (some number of cattle will cause degradation of the pasture and its ability to support grazing animals), the model tells us to expect the following behavioral pattern: individuals will add more and more animals to their personal herd, grazing them on the pasture until the pasture is destroyed by overgrazing. Hardin emphasizes the inevitability of the degraded outcome by noting that all owners of cattle, based on assumptions 1 and 2, will reason as follows: If I add an animal that I own to the communal pasture, whatever profits come from that animal will accrue to me. If there are costs imposed by my decision to add another animal, those costs will be distributed throughout the members of the community. Under the assumptions, it is always individually rational for a herder to add one more animal.

Reasoning such as this is relevant to understanding "sustainability." If individuals in a community of private owners will predictably act to increase their own well-being at the expense of resources commonly owned, then all unowned resources—from fresh air and clean water to pastures and amenities—will be degraded over time. The tragedy of the commons thus stands as a challenge to any approach to sustainability, and we can better understand the approach of weak sustainability by examining how economists deal with the tragedy.[4]

First, it is necessary to clarify one point that Hardin confused. His reasoning does not directly address *ownership* of the pasture—it is not who owns the pasture that is crucial; rather it is the fact that, lacking private ownership, he assumes there is no right to exclude others from use or increasing use, a fault that derives from *open access* to the resource, not from who owns it. For example, if an authoritarian government used its army to exclude all but minimal use of the pasture, degradation would not occur; the problem derives from open access, not from the mode of ownership.

Economists have generally addressed this challenge to wise use of resources by arguing that the pasture should be privatized (enclosed).[5] Since private ownership, by definition, includes the right to exclude nonowners from use of the pasture, they argue that assigning the pasture to private owners will result in protection of the pasture, an apparent contribution to sustainable use of resources. The private owners, recognizing that they will experience the costs as well as the benefits of overgrazing, will, the economist reasons, refrain from overgrazing their owned pasture. Indeed, economists generally respond to dangers to the sustainability of resources by exploiting or creating private markets in resource use. Most economists writing on the subject would assert, when faced with a possible tragedy of the commons, that privatization of the resource in question is both necessary and sufficient to protect that resource across time: individual owners, given the right of exclusion and a perceived self-interest in future income from the pasture, will not overgraze.

Before returning to a discussion of sustainability, I first question the economists' twin claims that (A) privatization is necessary to prevent tragedies of the commons, and (B) privatization is sufficient to protect common resources currently at risk. I have already noted that it is possible to distinguish a "common" resource from an "open-access" resource. Given this distinction, it is possible to reject Claim A, that privatization is necessary for protection of a commonly owned resource. There exists an alternative: individuals can join together to form institutions to regulate access and use of a common resource, and observers have reported many examples of commonly owned resources that have been responsibly managed for centuries (Ostrom, 1990). Examples include a number of local fisheries that are managed by excluding foreigners and by carefully regulating the methods or the take of local participants. Similarly, communities in the valleys of the Alps have shared—and protected through stringent rules and strict enforcement—the summer pastures of the high Alps. Since open access is the real problem leading to inevitable degradation, there is an alternative to privatization: community-based institutions that develop rules and enforce those rules effectively. Admittedly, these institutions can be difficult to establish and fragile in their continuance— especially in facing global problems with multigenerational consequences, but the large number of successful examples refute claim A as a generalization.[6]

Claim B, that privatization will be sufficient to shift the pattern of rational decisions by selfish herders so as to protect the pasture, is hardly ever questioned by mainstream economists, since they think self-interest—when directed at an owned resource—will lead herders to limit the size of their herd. Unfortunately, this generalized reasoning is faulty, as has been demonstrated by the mathematical bioeconomist, Colin Clark (1973). Clark drew a distinction between "rent" and "profit" derived from a resource. Rent is income derived from sustained use of the resource—the rent in any given year is the amount of income that can be derived from the resource without degrading it. Profit, by contrast, is the total amount of income-minus-expenses that can be accumulated in one year or in a series of years.

Now, consider a situation in which a given owner has exclusive use of a resource and also that the owner adopts a relatively short temporal frame.[7] Also, suppose that as our owner surveys the situation there are a number of alternative investment possibilities, some of which would create more income annually than the present herding operation. Under these circumstances, the self-interested owner would reason as follows: Debilitating damage from overgrazing usually occurs during droughts, and so forth, which are unusual, so it is rational for me to accept some risk, increase my herd grazing my owned pasture dramatically, generate a much greater income for a couple of years, and take those profits and invest them in another business opportunity. Since the owner has increased available capital and transferred that capital into another business, even if the pasture is degraded over several years, the owner will be able to walk away from the degraded pasture and enjoy the greater profits that were derived from a policy of "economic overexploitation." So, Claim B, that privatization is always sufficient to avoid degradation of resources, is not defensible, at least not on a theoretical/conceptual level.

It is, of course, an empirical question as to how often the conditions leading to economic overexploitation occur in reality—a question beyond the scope of this chapter—but it would seem that such conditions are common. Surely, there are many individuals who adopt a short time frame in making economic decisions, and there does not seem to be a shortage of investment opportunities that promise high returns on investment in most free-market societies. Therefore, if the assumption of economists that individuals will always act to improve their welfare, and if higher profits are what determines individual welfare, it would seem that Clark's model—and its outcome of degradation for privately owned resources—is as plausible as that of the economists. Conclusion: privatization is neither necessary nor sufficient to protect resources across time; privatization of resources provides no guarantee that resources will be sustained.

This important argument has quite general implications. Return to the metaphorical pasture and assume that since the reasoning showing the rationality of economic over-exploitation depends on nothing other than the original assumption of universal self-interestedness and a plausible distinction between rent and profit, that reasoning will guide each herder as the common pasture is transformed into owned plots. Now suppose that each of the herders (subsequent to enclosure) reasons in the way just discussed: the entire pasture will be destroyed by "rational" entrepreneurs who own a part of the resource. If each owner chooses overexploitation and is rewarded for their risk, *each of the individuals is better off (derives more profit) than they would by limiting their herd to carrying capacity.* Under conditions described by Clark, pursuing economic growth would apparently destroy key resources. Privatization cannot ensure the strong sustainability and protected resources necessary for a viable future.

3 STRONG SUSTAINABILITY

The argument of the last section apparently leads to a pessimistic conclusion: Assuming selfish and short-sighted actors with open access to a resource, the resource will be destroyed.

But privatization provides no adequate remedy. If all environmental values are thus inter-preted as fulfilling some individual preference, rational individuals will (in some situations, at least) have a reason to act unsustainably, regardless of the ownership regime.

Weak sustainability is expressed in economic terms, exploring value tied to individual preference-fulfillment. When one adds to the analysis a viewpoint from ecology that com-plex ecological systems require "overhead," some productivity must be devoted to the main-tenance of the resilience of the system itself. Space does not allow a detailed discussion of the exact nature of the characteristics of a system that would allow us to determine whether it is being used sustainably. Ecologists have insisted, however, that in order to know what to pro-tect for the future it is important to understand, identify, and measure key system-level vari-ables that correspond to important ecological processes (Walker and Salt, 2006; Gunderson and Holling, 2001). This has led ecologists to develop theory around key concepts such as *resilience* and *productivity*; conservation biologists place great emphasis on *within-habitat-diversity* and *cross-habitat diversity*. Others follow the great conservationist Aldo Leopold and emphasize his metaphors of *ecological integrity* and *ecosystem health*. Actors, motivated by self-interest and with a short time frame, will undermine system resilience by concentrat-ing only on production for individual consumption, which will lead to system degradation even if individuals are careful to maintain the productivity of their own piece of the pasture.

To apply this reasoning directly to the problem of understanding sustainability, it seems to follow that if individuals in a given generation wish to live sustainably—without degrading productive resources and the resilience of systems over time—they cannot generate, explain, or justify that wish on the economic models used to explain weak sustainability. Human welfare, understood as aggregated individual values, varies independently of resource pro-tection because resources will only be protected if the resilience of the system is protected. Concern with individual welfare does not provide protection for system-level features that emerge beyond the temporal horizon of individual actors. The negative conclusion, then, is weak sustainability interprets sustainability in terms of impacts on welfare of individuals, but the model implied by this interpretation implies that selfish herders may destroy their grazing resource by undermining the resource-producing system regardless of whether or not they engage in enclosure and privatization.

A positive conclusion can also be stated, however: in order to act rationally so as to pro-tect resources for future generations, sustainability requirements must refer to the condi-tion, present and future, *of the resource itself, especially the resilience of the resource systems involved.* Tracking and ensuring human welfare across time will not protect the resilience of the resource-producing system. A definition of sustainability capable of requiring adequate policies to protect resource systems across time must, in addition to paying attention to human welfare levels, pay attention to the health and resilience of the resources themselves. Such definitions are definitions of "strong sustainability."

In the process of developing these concepts, ecologists and conservation biologists began with attempts to define and model (conceptually and mathematically) these key concepts. The technical discussions, in the meantime, masked an equally important trend, which went largely unnoticed. As ecologists and conservation biologists discussed, quantified, and mea-sured characteristics of systems, they began almost imperceptibly to treat diversity, resilience, and health as important *values*. Reluctant to explicitly announce these value commitments, these scientists implicitly embraced the viewpoint that important social goals, including sus-tainability, can only be understood by incorporating requirements that such system-level characteristics be protected. We can refer to definitions of sustainability that include require-ments stated in terms of physically measured traits as providing definitions of "strong sustain-ability." Definitions of *sustainability* that do not refer to such system-level characteristics as important and valuable (weak sustainability definitions) are inadequate to capture the nature of the damage that led Hardin to characterize the outcome on the metaphorical pasture as a "tragedy."

4 ETHICS AND INTERGENERATIONAL OBLIGATIONS

In section 3, it was argued that, in order to reverse negative environmental trends it will be necessary to pay attention to more than human, individual welfare. Weak sustainability sets out to understand the concept in the standard terms of mainstream economics, which in turn measures values in terms of individual human preference fulfillment. Ethically, this approach to sustainability rests upon the idea that protecting and enhancing individual human well-being is the central obligation of ethical behavior. Strong sustainability, how-ever, builds on an important ethical insight: Protection of resources for the future will not be accomplished if policies are designed only to protect individual welfare for today's persons. True protection, as defined in strong sustainability, must depart from a concentration on cur-rent individual, human welfare (a position that can be called "anthropocentric presentism"), in order to criticize and avoid the tragedy of destruction entailed by business-as-usual.

Many controversies in the field of environmental ethics have generally dealt with the question: Must our ethics become nonanthropocentric? I will not engage this argument, as I have done so elsewhere (Norton, 2003; Norton, 2005; Norton, 2015). Here I note that the near-obsession with extra-human interests in environmental ethics has directed attention away from intertemporal ethics and, although there is a substantial literature in social and political philosophy on possible obligations to future generations, this literature has, for the most part, not been connected to current discussions of sustainability.[8] Regardless of one's viewpoint on obligations to other species, much can be learned by exploring obligations to future generations, a topic to which I now turn.

John Nolt (Future Generations in Environmental Ethics, this volume) does attempt to bring the philosophical literature on obligations to future generations to bear upon issues of sustainability. Nolt clearly takes concerns for the future seriously, and he struggles to inter-pret these obligations in a way that would impose significant obligations to change our cur-rent business-as-usual activities. He mentions, but dismisses, any attempt to base obligations to the future on a communitarian ethic, and then he sets out to examine whether it is pos-sible to make sense of obligations to the future in individualistic (human) terms.

Following Derek Parfit (1984), Nolt considers a paradox regarding two societies (call one "conservers" and the other "depleters").[9] Conservers, on the one hand, are careful to pro-tect resources for the future. Depleters, on the other hand, profligately waste resources and, in doing so, significantly reduce the well-being of future people—but not to the extent that those actually born wish they would not have been born. The paradox arises because, given the long time frames and the radically differing policies involved, the choices made by mem-bers of either group will change conditions under which individuals make their procreative decisions. Within a small number of generations, entirely different individuals would be born in the two scenarios. He asks whether depleters do anything wrong. Since the individuals who are born under the depleters' scenario are happy to be born rather than not, bringing about their existence is a benefit to them. But those who would have been born if the society had chosen a conserver path will then never be born—since they never exist, they cannot be harmed. No one is harmed if a generation pursues an overexploitative, depleting policy.

As Nolt and other commentators have noted, this counterintuitive result depends crucially on a key premise, which is referred to as the "person-regarding principle": No harm has occurred unless at least one human individual has been harmed. Given the situation as set up by Parfit, and applying this principle, no ethical harm has occurred because no individual who actually exists is harmed.

But there is a very simple (if somewhat radical) solution to Parfit's paradox. We say that, while no individuals have been harmed, the *community itself* has been harmed. The community that results from individuals pursuing the overexploitative policy on their pasture is worse off because, in the future, if some member of the community desires to develop a herding operation, the essential resource—healthy grass—is no longer available. An important opportunity has been destroyed by selfish pursuit of private profit. The community has been harmed by the loss of what Amartya Sen calls "opportunity freedom" (Sen, 2002; also see Norton, 1991: "Epilogue," 249–255). Opportunity freedom refers to the range of meaningful and effective possibilities available to individuals within communities. A community with restricted opportunities as a result of unsustainable practices that undermine the resilience of resource-producing systems is worse off than it would have been if prior generations had conserved.

Treating Parfit's paradox as a *reductio ad absurdum* of individualistic rights and interests as the basis for obligations to the future, and as providing a strong argument for a communitarian interpretation of intergenerational ethics, honors the intuition that depleters cause harm without facing the daunting task of figuring out how to characterize the individuals who are harmed (Norton, 1984). As for individuals who might exist, we can say that, whoever exists will exist in a community with diminished opportunities. We can further strengthen this communitarian approach by following Edmund Burke (1910), who described a society as "a partnership not only between those who are living, but between those who are living, those who are dead and those to be born."

One might raise an objection here.[10] Might Parfit's paradox reappear at the community level? Might it be argued that, over multiple generations, communities also change characteristics, and one might, in analogy with Parfit's reasoning, argue that over time differing policies at an earlier time will lead to different communities in subsequent generations? Could one argue convincingly that the communities that actually do come into being as a result of depleting behaviors will differ from the community emerging under a policy of conserving? If so, no actually existing community will be harmed as a result of earlier generations pursuing a depleting policy, analogous to Parfit's conclusion that no future individual is harmed by depletion today.

This objection can be rejected, however, because although human individuals have very strict criteria of identity—if two individuals differ in a single characteristic they cannot be the same individual—communities, especially Burkean communities, do not have such strict identity criteria over time. For example, if a given community were to suffer a famine in the future, it would still be the same community—and it would have remained the same community if the famine were avoided. There is no analogue in the case of communities to the strict identity criteria associated with the person-regarding principle that applies to human individuals as in Parfit's argument. Therefore, we can talk sensibly about harming communities in the future by depleting resources because, unlike individuals, communities maintain their identity even when circumstances change over time.

Nolt also states that communitarian approaches are inadequate because characterizing obligations to the future as community-bound obligations would only capture obligations to other members of "our" community. In continuing to emit greenhouse gases, he suggests, we are harming far more individuals than those in our "community." Here, admittedly, the concept of community is being used rather loosely and Nolt is justified in demanding more explanation. Perhaps Nolt fears the narrowness of communitarian obligations because he has a mainly *cultural* conception of a community, which is the approach of Avner de Shalit (1995), who links intertemporal communities through common culture and institutions, independent of a broader, Leopoldian community that includes "the land" or what some call a "place." The land, or a place, in the sense I'm suggesting is a manifestation of inter-twined natural and cultural forces, a mixed system of interacting humans and natural forces. But valuing and protecting a place requires awareness and caring also for the "space around the place" (Norton and Hannon, 1998). And thus, ecologically grounded cultures live within many embedded scales of space and time. If one considers the communities participating in this organic, multi-layered interaction of people and nature, Nolt's concern for narrowness seems easily answered by endorsing an expansive, system-based understanding of humanity in which all must live in the same "community" that exists on this fragile planet.

Notice how this "solution"—to attribute goods and bads to communities—can also help us respond to the earlier problem that each herder is better off for having overexploited his/her enclosed resource, but the pasture has nevertheless been ruined. Parfit's Paradox bites because our environmental *and our fairness* intuitions insist that overexploiters, whether in the commons or on private property, apparently do something harmful. The communitarian can honor this strong intuition by showing the exploitative pattern of behavior is harmful to the community in question because opportunities have been lost. The community is less diverse in resource bases; future members of the community will not have an entrepreneurial, economic opportunity that could have been available. This is the feature ecologists call "functional diversity," and it is a contributor to the resilience of complex systems, ecologically (Walker and Salt, 2006: 69). Politically and ethically, the recognition of the good of a community provides a foundation supporting opportunity freedom.[11]

5 THE PUBLIC INTEREST OF SUSTAINABLE COMMUNITIES

I am advocating a specific version of strong sustainability, one that posits values beyond economics and human individual welfare and that emphasizes community values, those durable, multigenerational values that connect a people to an ecological system and constitute the identity of the denizens of a place. These values and the activities associated with them depend upon processes and features of natural systems as the latter present opportunities to humans to enjoy a range of choices—opportunity freedom. Communities can be harmed even as individuals do well by drawing profits from either public or private overexploitation. Recognition that in addition to private goods and public goods there are communal goods buttresses the idea that there is a public interest, and that it involves more than aggregated individual interests.[12]

Space does not allow a full treatment of the idea of the public interest here, but Barry Bozeman has recently provided a re-interpretation—joining Dewey's idea of an "emergent public" as the voice that guides democracy into the future with Lippmann's definition, which says that the public interest is "what men would choose if they saw clearly, thought rationally, acted disinterestedly and benevolently" (quoted in Bozeman, 2007). Imagine a community that seeks to learn how to live sustainably, and that it does so by initiating a process that aspires to fulfilling Lippmann's conditions. If members of this community, also following Burke, see their community as multigenerational, and they accept responsibility to protect not just wealth and individual well-being but also attempt to protect the communal goods that community members now enjoy, then we can say that such a community is developing a deliberative process capable of achieving strong sustainability.

Given my approach to understanding sustainability as an intergenerational moral imperative to develop educational and deliberative processes that will protect communal goods into the foreseeable future, I think it is reasonable to suggest that the core idea of sustainability as exemplified in a multiscalar community is best captured thus: Sustainability and sustainable development refer to the search for the multigenerational public interest of a multigenerational community.

NOTES

1. Although there are notable exceptions, most environmental ethicists have not entered the specific debate about sustainability and how it should be defined. I hypothesize that most environmental ethicists do not engage the sustainability literature because they take the emphasis on economic development goals for humans among political actors and scientific advocates of sustainability as revealing a commitment to anthropocentrism. In fact, it would be possible to challenge this emphasis and to advocate a nonanthropocentric version of sustainability, which would argue for the sustenance of natural processes for the good of all living things.
2. Despite its popularity, the concept of "natural capital" has resisted clear definition, but the concept of strong sustainability can be defined independently of it, as I shall explain.
3. Although others, including Gordon (1954), had noticed the argument Hardin exploits, I discuss Hardin's version because it is so widely known and discussed.
4. As pointed out by Stephen Gardiner (2011, chapters 5, 6), all forms of the tragedy inevitably involve intertemporal relationships between present users of the pasture and implications for possible future users. Economists deal with this problem by "discounting" both costs and benefits across time, which favors present users over future users. This practice masks another huge ethical problem: moral relationships across generations.
5. See Coase (1960), in which the author analyzes economic externalities as best dealt with through negotiations among owners, which is often cited as supporting enclosure.
6. The argument, here, is only that there exist successful cooperative solutions to open access problems. How broadly these apply could be questioned. Gardiner (private correspondence) worries that this model will not apply to large-scale, global problems. Better

understanding the role and scope of cooperative institutions in solving environmental problems is surely one of the most important challenges in environmental policy today.

7. Technically, this condition is referred to by economists as "having a relatively high discount rate." The discount rate is a percentage by which a value is decreased over time in order to capture the fact that humans universally exhibit a time preference for the present (individuals systematically prefer that good experiences occur sooner, while negative experiences are delayed if possible).

8. For exceptions see Norton (2003, 2005, 2015) and Gardiner (2011).

9. It would be possible, to gain integration with Clark's argument, to refer not to "depleters" but to "overexploiters." I use the former in order to connect this problem to the philosophical literature following on Parfit's arguments.

10. As was suggested to me by Justin Biddle.

11. See Norton (2005) for an argument that "communal" goods differ from both individual and public goods and that understanding obligations to the future requires paying attention to communal goods.

12. Public goods are goods enjoyed by individuals, but produced by an agency such as government. Communal goods are goods enjoyed or harmed as communities protect or fail to protect the ecophysical and political processes that support opportunities to enjoy those values.

References

Bozeman, B. (2007). *Public Values and Public Interest: Counterbalancing Economic Individualism.* Washington, D.C.: Georgetown University Press.

Burke, E. (1910). *Reflections on the French Revolution and Other Essays.* London: JM Dent & Sons, Ltd.

Clark, C. W. (1973). "The Economics of Overexploitation." *Science* 181(4100): 630–634.

Coase, R. (1960). "The Problem of Social Costs." *Law and Economics* 3: 1–44.

de Shalit, A. (1995). *Why Posterity Matters: Environmental Policies and Future Generations.* London: Routledge.

Gardiner, S. (2011). *A Perfect Moral Storm: The Ethical Tragedy of Climate Change.* New York: Oxford University Press.

Gordon, H. S. (1954). "The Economic Theory of A Common-Property Resource: The Fishery." *Journal of Political Economy* 62: 124–142.

Gunderson, L. H., and Holling, C. S. (2001). *Panarchy: Understanding Transformation in Human and Natural Systems.* Washington, D.C: Island Press.

Hardin, G. (1968). "The Tragedy of the Commons." *Science* 162(3859): 1243–1248.

Lee, K. (1993). *Compass and Gyroscope: Integrating Science and Politics for the Environment.* Washington, D.C.: Island Press.

Nolt, J. (2016). "Future Generations." In this volume.

Norton, B. G. (1984). "Environmental Ethics and Weak Anthropocentrism." *Environmental Ethics* 6(2): 131–148.

Norton, B. G. (1991). *Toward Unity among Environmentalists.* New York: Oxford University Press.

Norton, B. G. (2003). *Searching for Sustainability: Interdisciplinary Essays in the Philosophy of Conservation Biology.* Cambridge, UK: Cambridge University Press.

Norton, B. G. (2005). *Sustainability: A Philosophy of Adaptive Ecosystem Management*. Chicago, IL: University of Chicago Press.

Norton, B. G. (2015). *Sustainable Values, Sustainable Change: A Guide to Environmental Decision Making*. Chicago, IL: University of Chicago Press.

Norton, B. G., and Hannon, B. (1998). "Democracy and Sense of Place Values in Environmental Policy." *Philosophy and Geography* 3: 119–146.

Ostrom, E. (1990). *Governing the Commons: The Evolution of Institutions for Collective Action*: Cambridge, UK: Cambridge University Press.

Parfit, D. (1984). *Reasons and Persons*. Oxford: Clarendon Press: Oxford.

Sen, A. (2002). *Rationality and Freedom*. Cambridge, MA: Belknap Press of Harvard University Press.

Solow, R. M. (1993). "Sustainability: An Economists' Perspective." In *Economics of the Environment: Selected Readings*, edited by R. Dorfman and N. Dorfman. New York: Norton.

Walker, B., and Salt, D. (2006). *Resilience Thinking: Sustaining Ecosystems and People in a Changing World*. Washington, D.C.: Island Press.

PART VI

CENTRAL ISSUES

Specific Areas of Environmental Concern

CHAPTER 31

....

THE ETHICS OF ENVIRONMENTAL POLLUTION

....

KEVIN C. ELLIOTT

1 DEFINITION AND MAJOR SOURCES

IN the simplest sense, pollution consists of energy or substances that are released into the environment and that cause harm to humans or other living organisms. Major examples include air pollution, water pollution, and soil contamination caused by the release of toxic chemicals, particulates, or radioactive substances. Less well-known examples include noise pollution (noise that is loud enough to be physically harmful or annoying), thermal pollution (changes in water temperature that affect aquatic life), genetic pollution (the introduction of genes into new biological contexts in ways that cause harm), and light pollution (light from cities that interferes with animal life or astronomical observations).

While pollution initially appears fairly easy to define, a number of difficult issues lie beneath the surface. For example, there is evidence that some normally toxic chemicals could actually have beneficial effects at low doses (Elliott, 2011). Therefore, one faces the question of whether the release of such chemicals counts as pollution when they are emitted at "safe" or even beneficial dose levels. Even if these emissions did not cause physical or biological harm, one might classify them as pollution if they caused some other form of harm (e.g., economic or aesthetic) or if the emissions expressed a lack of respect for others (Hale and Grundy, 2009). In other cases, chemicals might have harmful effects on some organisms or systems while having beneficial effects on others. For example, sulfate aerosols contribute to acid rain and human lung irritation, but they also have a "global dimming" effect that inhibits climate change; similarly, ground-level (tropospheric) ozone causes respiratory problems, but it may also have some of the same beneficial effects as stratospheric ozone in protecting organisms from ultraviolet radiation. In these sorts of cases, the decision of whether or not to classify a chemical as a pollutant appears to depend on which effects or systems one decides to focus on.

A further challenge to this definition of pollution is that it does not fully capture the cultural significance of pollution concepts in human society. Anthropologist Mary Douglas

(1966) famously argued that pollution concepts, like taboos, developed as symbolic systems for maintaining order and safeguarding social categories. As she puts it, "Dirt offends against order. Eliminating it is ... a positive effort to organise [sic] the environment" (Douglas, 1966: 2). While one might think that this symbolic aspect to pollution applies only to primitive societies, contemporary social scientists have found that people's cultural viewpoints (e.g., whether they hold a more individualist or a more communitarian worldview) have a significant impact on how they perceive environmental risks, including those associated with pollution (see, e.g., Kahan et al., 2006; Kahan, 2010). More strikingly, these cultural influences on risk perception appear to influence not only ordinary citizens but also expert scientists.

The cultural underpinnings of the pollution concept can also be observed in current debates about genetic pollution from genetically modified organisms (GMOs). As Paul Thompson (2003) points out, when gene flow occurs from a transgenic plant into its wild relatives, it is not clear whether this phenomenon should count as a form of pollution. Some figures classify this gene flow itself as a hazard, whereas others classify it only as a mechanism that could potentially contribute to harmful effects but that is not by itself a hazard. Thus, culturally influenced value judgments play an important role in deciding whether this form of gene flow should be classified as an instance of pollution.

Nevertheless, while a fully comprehensive approach might require attention to the ways in which people's perceptions of pollution are underwritten by cultural categories and assumptions, many contemporary pollution problems can be characterized in terms of fairly uncontroversial physical and biological harms. Some of the most significant sources of pollution include agriculture, transportation, electricity generation, and other industrial activities (Resnik, 2012). In the case of agriculture, fertilizer run-off contributes to algae blooms that have caused serious damage to fisheries in the Gulf of Mexico and the Chesapeake Bay. Meanwhile, agricultural pesticides pose risks to the environment, as well as to farmers and their families. They appear to be a contributing factor in declining amphibian and bee populations, as well as reproductive problems in birds, amphibians, reptiles, and fish (Resnik, 2012). In humans, pesticides have been linked to numerous types of cancer, especially among children, as well as developmental damage to the nervous and immune systems (Shrader-Frechette, 2007).

Combustion of hydrocarbons for transportation and electricity generation releases nitrogen and sulfur oxides, carbon dioxide, and particulate matter. These pollutants contribute to problems such as acid rain, climate change, and cardiovascular and respiratory damage to living organisms. Because of its potential to cause agricultural failure, biodiversity loss, water shortages, flooding, and other severe forms of social disruption, climate change is one of the most serious environmental issues of the twenty-first century. But the other effects associated with pollution should not be underestimated; scientists estimate that particulate air pollution alone contributes to more than 50,000 deaths per year in the United States (Shrader-Frechette, 2007). Other industrial processes release heavy metals such as lead, mercury, and arsenic, which can contribute to a variety of neurological and developmental problems. Emerging areas of technology such as nanotechnology and geoengineering also generate pollution risks that are receiving increasing attention (Hale and Grundy, 2009; Royal Society, 2004, 2009).

Finally, in addition to these obvious sources of pollution, people are exposed to numerous chemicals through everyday exposures to upholstery, carpet, computers, cans and plastic containers, receipts, tap water, and food. A Canadian study of people's "body burdens" of toxic substances found that "No matter where people live, how old they are or what they do for a living, they are contaminated with measurable levels of chemicals that can cause cancer and respiratory problems, disrupt hormones, and affect reproduction and neuro-logical development" (Cranor, 2011: 22). These chemicals include polychlorinated biphenyls (PCBs), polybrominated diphenyl ethers (PBDEs), phthalates, synthetic estrogens, and per-fluorinated compounds. The precise health effects of many of these chemicals continue to be debated, but this is partly because chemical manufacturers in the United States have not been required to collect toxicity data for products other than pharmaceuticals and pesticides (Cranor, 2011).

2 SIGNIFICANCE OF POLLUTION FOR ENVIRONMENTAL ETHICS

Historically, pollution played a particularly important role in the development of the envi-ronmental movement. For example, Rachel Carson's book *Silent Spring* (1962), which high-lighted the risks associated with pesticide pollution, played a central role in galvanizing citizens to address environmental problems. The famous 1969 fire caused by water pollu-tion in Ohio's Cuyahoga River was also a crucial symbol for the environmental movement. Pollution worries have continued to garner massive media attention because of incidents like the nuclear meltdowns at Chernobyl in 1986 and at Fukushima Daiichi in 2011, the deaths of several thousand people from the release of methyl isocyanate gas at a Union Carbide plant in Bhopal, India, in 1984, and the oil spills from the Exxon Valdez in 1989 and from the Deep Water Horizon rig in 2010.

Nevertheless, some environmental ethicists have argued that the focus on issues like pollution and resource depletion constitutes a relatively "shallow" form of environmental-ism that focuses on the needs and concerns of people in developed countries. For example, Arne Naess (1973) argued that a "deep" ecological mindset requires moving beyond mere pollution concerns and adopting a nonanthropocentric value system. A strong case can be made, however, that addressing pollution should still be a high priority for nonanthropo-centrists and those who advocate for disadvantaged groups. In developed countries such as the United States, studies indicate that minorities tend to be exposed to higher levels of toxic waste facilities than other groups, even when controlling for income (Steel and Whyte, 2012). And in developing countries, citizens are exposed to particularly severe pollution threats from sources such as agricultural chemicals, air pollution, mining, and electronic waste (Shrader-Frechette, 2007). Finally, the pollution that contributes to climate change raises serious problems not only for humans but for other living organisms and ecosystems across the globe.

In order to address contemporary pollution issues, however, it may be necessary to move beyond traditional paradigms. Pollution has often been conceptualized as a sort of "waste" that escapes from the private domain into the public domain. Viewed in this way, the obvi-ous response to the problem is to collect it and prevent it from causing harm to others. Unfortunately, contemporary pollution problems such as climate change raise challenges for this paradigm. The pollutants cannot be easily seen, their effects are difficult to identify precisely, and their consequences are often very distant in time and space from their origin (Gardiner, 2006; Spence et al., 2012). Therefore, it is often difficult to assign responsibility for pollution-related harms or to motivate citizens to address these problems.

While it is not entirely clear what a new paradigm for conceptualizing and addressing pollution would look like, a variety of suggestions have recently been offered. One important proposal is to adopt a "cradle-to-cradle" industrial design strategy that mimics biological metabolism (McDonough and Braungart, 2002). Rather than attempting to minimize waste or pollution, this design approach attempts to eliminate waste completely by creating cycles in which old products can either be biodegraded or can serve as feedstock for new products. Similarly, efforts at "green chemistry" attempt to identify new processes for chemical synthesis that do not generate harmful products or byproducts (Anastas and Warner, 2000). New regulatory systems that discourage the use of entire classes of worrisome chemicals (e.g., persistent chlorinated pollutants) and encourage research into alternatives could play a valuable role in promoting a more widespread shift toward green chemistry (Frickel et al., 2010). In order to generate public support for addressing the pollution problems that remain, social scientists are exploring ways to frame pollution problems in ways that make their significance more salient to people (Kahan, 2010; Maibach et al., 2010). Finally, given how difficult it can be to trace causal responsibility for the public-health effects of toxic chemicals, regulatory policies may need to be changed to force manufacturers to demonstrate the safety of their products before they market them (Cranor, 2011).

3 IDENTIFYING AND ASSESSING POLLUTION RISKS

One might be inclined to think that the major ethical issues related to pollution are isolated to the policy sphere, where decisions are made about how best to regulate pollutants. However, many of these issues find their way "upstream" into the scientific processes of identifying pollutants and assessing the risks associated with them. Environmental ethicists can play a valuable role by highlighting the presence of these often implicit ethical and political value judgments, which might otherwise go unnoticed (Brown, 2009).

Many of the ethical issues associated with identifying pollutants and assessing their toxicity arise because of pervasive scientific uncertainties. For example, when scientists perform studies on experimental animals, they typically expose them to very large doses of toxic substances so that they can more easily obtain statistically significant results. Then, they face difficult decisions about how to extrapolate from high-dose effects to low-dose effects, from animals to humans, and from humans in general to particularly sensitive humans such as children and pregnant women (Elliott, 2011). They also frequently have to evaluate conflicting data from multiple studies (which may employ a range of different methodologies) in an effort to decide where the "weight of evidence" lies (Douglas, 2012). When faced with these sorts of uncertainties, ethical considerations are relevant to deciding whether to draw scientific conclusions that err on the side of public health or on the side of industry (Cranor, 1993; Elliott, 2011).

The US National Research Council (NRC) attempted to address this intertwining of science and ethics in its seminal publication *Risk Assessment in the Federal Government* (NRC,

1983). First, it suggested that the process of risk *assessment* (which involves *scientific* questions about, say, the degree to which exposure to a toxic chemical will increase cancer incidence) should be clearly distinguished from the process of risk *management* (which involves *ethical* and *political* questions about, say, how high a level of cancer incidence is socially acceptable). Moreover, the NRC argued that any remaining ethical or political issues that cannot be entirely eliminated from risk assessment (e.g., decisions about how to extrapolate from high-dose toxic effects to low-dose effects under uncertainty) should be settled in a uniform manner by creating predetermined policies or "inference guidelines" to be followed in every case. By doing so, the NRC hoped that they could maintain risk assessment as a consistent, relatively objective process that would not be swayed by political debates in specific cases.

While this effort to keep scientific reasoning relatively distinct from ethics and politics is appealing in many ways, subsequent experiences with risk assessments have shown that they can be influenced by a wide variety of subtle, value-laden choices that cannot be isolated as standardized "inference guidelines." These include decisions about the initial framing of the risk situation, the specific questions asked, the collection and characterization of data, and the interpretation and communication of evidence. Even the language used for describing scientific phenomena can have ethically significant effects on how citizens and scientists respond to them (Elliott, 2009; Elliott, 2011; Larson, 2011). Therefore, the NRC proposed a different approach to handling the influences of ethical and political values on risk assessment in its later volume, *Understanding Risk* (1996). It suggested that risks should be assessed using an iterative process that moves back and forth between technical *analyses* (which involve straightforward procedures that can be performed by experts) and broad-based *deliberation* (which incorporates interested and affected parties in discussions about what analyses to undertake and how to interpret them). The NRC hoped that by incorporating deliberation among interested and affected parties throughout the process of risk assessment, any value-laden choices would be brought to light and addressed in a democratic fashion.

Unfortunately, most research on pollution is not performed in such a transparent and democratically responsive manner. Because it is difficult to establish compelling evidence that particular pollutants cause specific human or environmental problems, there are significant financial incentives for polluters to manipulate scientific research in ways that support their products. One particularly egregious example of this phenomenon is the effort by the fossil-fuel industry to mislead the public about the scientific evidence for human-induced climate change (Oreskes and Conway, 2010). But the strategies used for manipulating and suppressing evidence about climate change have also been employed by industry in a wide variety of other cases in an effort to lessen public concerns about pollutants such as lead, asbestos, vinyl chloride, benzene, chromium, beryllium, and dioxin (Elliott, 2016; Michaels, 2008). Another strategy for influencing research on pollution is to preferentially fund some projects rather than others. For example, agricultural research is dominated by funding for high-tech strategies that are likely to generate profits for agribusiness but that are much less likely than novel "agro-ecological" strategies to alleviate pollution risks (Elliott, 2013).

A multi-pronged approach is needed for responding to these influences on research (Elliott, 2011). An initial task for ethicists is to clarify which sorts of ethical and political influences on science are appropriate and which sorts are not (see, e.g., Steel and Whyte, 2012). Given the problems that are often associated with pollution research funded by those with financial or political interests in the outcome, it is also crucial to maintain ample independent funding for research on pollution, both to assess the toxicity of pollutants and to investigate less-polluting alternatives to current practices (Elliott, 2016; Shrader-Frechette, 2007). Nevertheless, because industry funding will undoubtedly continue to play an important role in research on pollution, it is important to find ways to make this research more reliable. One possible strategy would be to funnel industry funding through a governmental or nongovernmental body that would contract out research to universities or other research laboratories (Volz and Elliott, 2012). Another possibility would be to promote public trust and research reliability by creating research collaborations between industry and citizen groups or environmental NGOs (Elliott, 2014). A variety of legal reforms could also help to mitigate financial influences on science by making more of the data from safety studies publicly available and by enabling those who are threatened by pollution to more effectively challenge polluters in court (McGarity and Wagner, 2008: 283; Soranno et al., 2015).

4 REGULATING POLLUTION

While the impacts of ethical and political values on scientific research are often fairly subtle, their influences on decisions about how to regulate pollution are much more obvious. One approach to regulating pollution is to view it as a fundamentally economic issue. On this view, there is an optimal level of pollution that can be identified by determining when the marginal costs of eliminating more pollution become high enough to diminish overall human satisfaction (Baxter, 1974). From this perspective, pollution becomes a problem when "external" costs are not adequately priced by the market. For example, when a power plant emits carbon dioxide, the plant operators do not bear the costs that arise because of its contribution to global climate change. Therefore, the power produced by that plant will be underpriced in the market relative to its full social costs and will therefore be overproduced relative to less polluting approaches such as energy conservation and renewable energy technologies (Sagoff, 2004: 104). The typical economic solution to this problem is to find ways to measure the external costs of pollution so that they can be "internalized" through taxes or fees or other forms of regulation.

This approach raises ethical worries, however. One problem is that economic measurements of the social costs of pollution are influenced by factors that seem ethically irrelevant. This is vividly illustrated by a well-publicized incident in which an internal World Bank memo was leaked to the public ("Let Them Eat Pollution," 1992). The memo, which was signed by the bank's Chief Economist Lawrence Summers, included a controversial aside stating that developed countries ought to export more pollution to developing countries. The rationale was that the economic costs of pollution-related deaths and injuries are lower in developing countries, because wages are so much less. This reasoning might make sense from an economic perspective, but from an ethical perspective it seems to violate principles of justice and equity.

Another problem with the economic approach is that efforts to measure the social costs of pollution and to compare those costs with pollution's benefits are sensitive to numerous assumptions, such as the types of costs and benefits that are included in the analysis, the ways in which monetary values are assigned to them, and probabilistic estimates of their likelihood. Because of all this room for judgment, interest groups can manipulate cost-benefit analyses to obtain results that they desire (Sagoff, 2004; Shrader-Frechette, 1985). Nevertheless, these analyses can also be valuable as a way of making regulatory decisions more transparent and explicit (Schmidtz, 2001; Shrader-Frechette, 1985). Furthermore, policymakers can supplement these analyses with ethical principles that prevent violations of justice or equity (Schmidtz, 2001). Therefore, the merits of cost-benefit analyses arguably depend a great deal on whether they can be employed in a manner that includes adequate critical scrutiny and attention to additional ethical principles.

Other approaches to regulating pollution place less emphasis on economic analyses. For example, most ethicists would argue that pollution is not merely a source of external social costs but is in fact a violation of individual rights. These could involve rights not to be harmed or rights to give consent to any interference with one's body or property (Hale and Grundy, 2009). Unfortunately, once one views pollution as a violation of one's personal or property rights, it becomes unclear how to draw the line between acceptable and unacceptable levels of pollution. In principle, one could argue that it is never acceptable to violate other people's property rights by emitting pollution without their consent, but a policy of that sort could be unrealistic and economically disastrous. Therefore, this approach is typically weakened in some fashion. One option is to argue that risks from pollution are ethically acceptable as long as they remain below a *de minimis* threshold, where risks below that threshold are considered small enough to be ignored. Another option is to insist that pollution risks should be eliminated to the extent that is feasible using the best available technology (BAT).

A final ethical issue regarding the regulation of pollution is the question of who should bear the burden of proof for showing whether particular chemicals are harmful or not. In the United States, manufacturers have to provide evidence that pharmaceuticals and pesticides are safe before they can market them. (Of course, as illustrated by ongoing debates over the safety of pesticides such as atrazine and the neonicotinoids, it is not clear that these safety studies are always adequate.) For other chemicals, which have been regulated under the Toxic Substances Control Act (TSCA), manufacturers have not been obligated to prove the safety of their products before marketing them. Therefore, of the 50,000 chemicals proposed for manufacturing since 1979, there appears to be little or no toxicity information for about 85% of them (Cranor, 2011: 148). This policy is in contrast with the European Union's Registration, Evaluation, Authorisation, and Restriction of Chemicals (REACH) legislation, which requires manufacturers to submit information about the safety of industrial chemicals to regulatory authorities before they are marketed. Carl Cranor (2011) has argued that the US regulatory system under TSCA plausibly violated medical ethics guidelines, which require that appropriate prior research be performed before exposing people (and especially children) to potentially toxic substances. Partly in response to these failures, in 2016 the US Congress passed new legislation, the Frank R. Lautenberg Chemical Safety for the twenty-first Century Act, which gave the Environmental Protection Agency more power to determine whether chemicals were safe before allowing them to be marketed.

5 THE PRECAUTIONARY PRINCIPLE

In recent years, one of the most commonly discussed approaches for addressing the range of ethical issues associated with identifying, assessing, and regulating pollutants is to adopt the "precautionary principle" (PP). Many analysts argue that the PP consists not so much of a single principle as a family of related approaches. The Wingspread Declaration of 1998 illustrates its basic form: "When an activity raises threats of harm to human health or the environment, precautionary measures should be taken even if some cause and effect relationships are not established scientifically" (Raffensperger and Tickner, 1999). In order to implement this principle, it is necessary to specify at least three issues: (1) the precise kinds of threats that justify precautionary action; (2) the amount of knowledge needed about the threats to justify action; and (3) the sorts of precautionary measures appropriate in specific circumstances (see, e.g., Manson, 2002; Sandin, 1999). Some proponents of the PP argue that this flexibility is valuable, because different countries and cultures can decide how much precaution they want to demand (von Schomberg, 2006).

One of the strengths of the PP is that it is geared toward developing creative responses to the pervasive uncertainty surrounding the identification, assessment, and regulation of pollutants. For example, many proponents of the PP argue that, instead of encouraging endless wrangling over the precise probability that particular chemicals will cause harm at specific dose levels, the PP encourages the search for alternatives to suspect chemicals. There are also a number of ways in which scientific research might be performed differently in order to support the PP: (1) asking broad questions about potential harms from pollutants (even if the questions cannot be easily addressed using current research methodologies) and pursuing multidisciplinary strategies for addressing them; (2) studying the interactive and cumulative effects of multiple hazards in real-life contexts; (3) accepting qualitative data about pollution threats when quantitative data are difficult to collect; (4) engaging in strategic monitoring and surveillance so as to uncover potential threats as quickly as possible; and (5) lowering the standards of evidence required for identifying potential pollution hazards (see, e.g., Tickner, 2003). Many proponents of the PP also argue that it calls for depending less on expert judgment and more on democratic deliberation about how to handle pollution threats that are difficult to quantify (see, e.g., Raffensperger and Tickner, 1999).

Despite its strengths, the PP has come under fire from a number of critics. Some argue that it faces the dilemma of either being too strong (in which case it is paralyzing) or too weak (in which case it is trivial; see, e.g., Sunstein, 2005). On one hand, if one interprets it as calling for a ban on any actions or policies that could potentially cause serious harm, then it would seem to block almost all innovation. On the other hand, if one interprets it only as calling for prudent steps to be taken to avoid or minimize catastrophic scenarios, then it hardly seems to be particularly new or groundbreaking. In the background of these criticisms is the worry that society cannot afford to take aggressive actions against all potential threats without prioritizing them based on their likelihood and severity. But once one attempts to collect this sort of information, the PP seems to reduce to something akin to traditional cost-benefit analysis.

But these criticisms are too quick (Steel, 2014). One can take a variety of precautionary actions without going bankrupt or obtaining the sorts of precise quantitative information that traditional cost-benefit analyses require. One way to conceptualize the PP is in terms of "robust" policymaking. Policies are robust if they produce satisfactory results across a very broad range of potential future scenarios. Robust policies are not designed with the aim of getting the best possible results under the assumption that the future turns out to be exactly the way we expect; instead, they are designed to yield *satisfactory* results over a very wide range of possible future scenarios (Mitchell, 2010; Steel, 2014). In the case of pollution risks, for example, robust policies might include not only the precautionary approaches to scientific research discussed above but also the following strategies: (1) developing "rough and ready" toxicity tests and models that can rapidly assess the potential for substances to be toxic; (2) developing pre-market testing schemes that require manufacturers to employ these sorts of tests; (3) creating disincentives for using potentially toxic chemicals and incentives for developing safer alternatives; and (4) developing plans to minimize worker and consumer exposure to potentially worrisome chemicals.

6 ONGOING ISSUES

In the future, the most difficult ethical issues related to pollution are likely to revolve around striking an appropriate balance between promoting innovation, on one hand, while protecting human health and the environment, on the other hand. Tens of thousands of chemicals are currently in commerce, and relatively little is known about the biological effects of most of these chemicals (Cranor, 2011). Until fairly recently, scientists did not even recognize many of the potential neurological, developmental, and immunological effects associated with common pollutants. Therefore, society faces a great deal of uncertainty about pollution risks. Even when safety tests have been performed, as in the case of pharmaceuticals, pesticides, and GMOs, the adequacy of these tests is often in doubt. The introduction of new technologies such as geoengineering and nanotechnology raise even more pollution concerns.

In response to these worries, it is tempting to insist that new products should not be allowed onto the market without very stringent pre-market safety testing performed by independent regulatory bodies. But this is very difficult to accomplish politically, and the benefits of highly stringent safety tests must be weighed against the costs of slowing technological developments that could yield significant social and environmental benefits. Some of the strategies for robust policymaking discussed in the previous section of this chapter could be helpful for addressing these difficulties. These include the development of expedited testing schemes for assessing potential hazards and the creation of better safeguards for minimizing worker and consumer exposure to toxic substances.

But we also need to promote a new paradigm for industrial activity, as suggested earlier in this chapter. Rather than regarding pollution as an unavoidable cost of doing business, we need to promote the idea that waste should be eliminated in favor of a "cradle-to-cradle" model for industrial activity (McDonough and Braungart, 2002). We also need to encourage green chemistry and efforts to engineer "safety by design" into new products. Therefore, new legislation to control pollution should focus not solely on identifying hazardous substances and keeping them off the market but also on incentivizing businesses to avoid the production and release of potential pollutants from the outset. For example, the Massachusetts Toxic Use Reduction Act of 1989 required companies using suspicious chemicals to report how much of those chemicals they were using and to explore whether there were feasible alternatives. Instead of promoting endless debates about the safety of these chemicals, this legislation encouraged companies to reflect on why they were using particular substances and design processes; in many cases, it turned out that the available alternatives were both safer and less expensive (Raffensperger and Tickner, 1999). These are just small examples of the efforts that we can undertake to address pollution by encouraging a new industrial paradigm that is not only better for the environment but that actually takes the processes found in the environment as models for eliminating pollution and waste.

References

Anastas, P., and Warner, J. (2000). *Green Chemistry: Theory and Practice.* New York: Oxford University Press.

Baxter, W. (1974). *People or Penguins: The Case for Optimal Pollution.* New York: Columbia University Press.

Brown, D. (2009). "The Importance of Creating an Applied Environmental Ethics: Lessons Learned from Climate Change." In *Nature in Common?*, edited by B. Minteer. Philadelphia: Temple University Press.

Carson, R. (1962). *Silent Spring.* Boston: Houghton Mifflin Company.

Cranor, C. (1993). *Regulating Toxic Substances: A Philosophy of Science and the Law.* New York: Oxford University Press.

Cranor, C. (2011). *Legally Poisoned: How the Law Puts Us at Risk from Toxicants.* Cambridge, MA: Harvard University Press.

Douglas, H. (2012). "Weighing Complex Evidence in a Democratic Society." *Kennedy Institute of Ethics Journal* 22: 139–162.

Douglas, M. (1966). *Purity and Danger: An Analysis of the Concepts of Pollution and Taboo.* London: Routledge and Kegan Paul.

Elliott, K. (2009). "The Ethical Significance of Language in the Environmental Sciences: Case Studies from Pollution Research." *Ethics, Place, and Environment* 12: 157–173.

Elliott, K. (2011). *Is a Little Pollution Good for You? Incorporating Societal Values in Environmental Research.* New York: Oxford University Press.

Elliott, K. (2013). "Selective Ignorance and Agricultural Research." *Science, Technology, and Human Values* 38: 328–350.

Elliott, K. (2014). "Financial Conflicts of Interest and Criteria for Research Credibility." *Erkenntnis* 79: 917–937.

Elliott, K. (2016). "Environment," in A. J. Angulo (ed.), *Miseducation: A History of Ignorance Making in America and Abroad.* Baltimore: Johns Hopkins University Press.

Frickel, S., Gibbon, S., Howard, J., Kempner, J., Ottinger, G., and D. Hess (2010). "Undone Science: Charting Social Movement and Civil Society Challenges to Research Agenda Setting." *Science, Technology, and Human Values* 35: 444–473.

Gardiner, S. (2006). "A Perfect Moral Storm: Climate Change, Intergenerational Ethics, and the Problem of Moral Corruption." *Environmental Values* 15: 397–413.

Hale, B., and Grundy, W. (2009). "Remediation and Respect: Do Remediation Technologies Alter Our Responsibility?" *Environmental Values* 18: 397–415.

Kahan, D. (2010). "Fixing the Communications Failure." *Nature* 463: 296–297.

Kahan, D., Slovic, P., Braman, D., and Gastil, J. (2006). "Fear of Democracy: A Cultural Evaluation of Sunstein on Risk." *Harvard Law Review* 119: 1071–1109.

Larson, B. (2011). *Metaphors for Environmental Sustainability: Redefining Our Relationship with Nature.* New Haven: Yale University Press.

"Let Them Eat Pollution." (1992). *The Economist* 322: 66.

Maibach, E., Nisbet, M., Baldwin, P., Akerlof, K., and Diao, G. (2010). "Reframing Climate Change as a Public Health Issue: An Exploratory Study of Public Reactions." *BMC Public Health* 10: 299.

Manson, N. (2002). "Formulating the Precautionary Principle." *Environmental Ethics* 24: 263–274.

McDonough, W., and Braungart, M. (2002). *Cradle to Cradle: Remaking the Way We Make Things.* New York: North Point Press.

McGarity, T., and Wagner, W. (2008). *Bending Science: How Special Interests Corrupt Public Health Research*. Cambridge, MA: Harvard University Press.

Michaels, D. (2008). *Doubt Is Their Product: How Industry's Assault on Science Threatens Your Health*. New York: Oxford University Press.

Mitchell, S. (2010). *Unsimple Truths: Science, Complexity, and Policy*. Chicago: University of Chicago Press.

Naess, A. (1973). The Shallow and the Deep, Long-Range Ecological Movement. *Inquiry* 16: 95–100.

NRC (National Research Council) (1983). *Risk Assessment in the Federal Government: Managing the Process*. Washington, D.C.: National Academy Press.

NRC (National Research Council) (1996). *Understanding Risk: Informing Decisions in a Democratic Society*. Washington, D.C.: National Academy Press.

Oreskes, N., and Conway, E. (2010). *Merchants of Doubt: How a Handful of Scientists Obscured the Truth on Issues from Tobacco Smoke to Global Warming*. New York: Bloomsbury.

Raffensperger, C., and Ticker, J. (eds.) (1999). *Protecting Public Health and the Environment: Implementing the Precautionary Principle*. Washington, D.C.: Island Press.

Resnik, D. (2012). *Environmental Health Ethics*. Cambridge: Cambridge University Press.

Royal Society (2004). *Nanoscience and Nanotechnologies*. London: Royal Society.

Royal Society (2009). *Geoengineering the Climate: Science, Governance, and Uncertainty*. London: Royal Society.

Sagoff, M. (2004). *Price, Principle, and the Environment*. Cambridge, England: Cambridge University Press.

Sandin, P. (1999). "Dimensions of the Precautionary Principle." *Human and Ecological Risk Assessment* 5: 889–907.

Schmidtz, D. (2001). "A Place for Cost-Benefit Analysis." *Philosophical Issues* 11: 148–171.

Shrader-Frechette, K. (1985). *Risk Analysis and Scientific Method: Methodological and Ethical Problems with Evaluating Societal Hazards*. Dordrecht: Kluwer.

Shrader-Frechette, K. (2007). *Taking Action, Saving Lives: Protecting Environmental and Public Health*. New York: Oxford University Press.

Soranno, P., Cheruvelil, K., Elliott, K., and Montgomery, G. (2015). "It's Good to Share: Why Environmental Scientists' Ethics Are Out of Date," *BioScience* 65: 69–73.

Spence, A., Poortinga, W., and Pidgeon, N. (2012). "The Psychological Distance of Climate Change." *Risk Analysis* 32: 957–972.

Steel, D. (2014). *Philosophy and the Precautionary Principle: Science, Evidence, and Environmental Policy*. Cambridge: Cambridge University Press.

Steel, D. and K. P. Whyte (2012). "Environmental Justice, Values, and Scientific Expertise." *Kennedy Institute of Ethics Journal* 22: 163–182.

Sunstein, C. (2005). *Laws of Fear: Beyond the Precautionary Principle*. New York: Cambridge University Press.

Tickner, J. (ed.) (2003). *Precaution, Environmental Science, and Preventive Public Policy*. Washington, D.C.: Island Press.

Thompson, P. (2003). "Value Judgments and Risk Comparisons. The Case of Genetically Engineered Crops." *Plant Physiology* 132: 10–16.

Volz, D., and Elliott, K. (2012). "Mitigating Conflicts of Interest in Chemical Safety Testing." *Environmental Science and Technology* 46: 7937–7938.

von Schomberg, R. (2006). "The Precautionary Principle and Its Normative Challenges." In *Implementing the Precautionary Principle: Perspectives and Prospects*, edited by E. Fisher, J. Jones, and R. von Schomberg. Northampton, MA: Edward Elgar.

CHAPTER 32

POPULATION AND ENVIRONMENT

The Impossible, the Impermissible, and the Imperative

ELIZABETH CRIPPS

WHATEVER else they include, our duties of environmental ethics require us to organize ourselves to tackle global climate change, habitat and biodiversity loss, and pollution. So much, at least, I will take for granted. We also know that human population growth is a factor in all of these woes. As humans, our impact on the environment is determined by a combination of population, consumption, and technology (or the limits thereof; Ehrlich and Holdren, 1972: 20; also see Grooten et al., 2012: 41; Bernstein et al., 2007: 37).[1] Moreover, population is growing fast. Humans are expected to number 8.5 bn by 2030, 9.7 bn by 2050 and 11.2 bn by 2100, compared with 2.5 bn in 1950 and 7.3 bn in 2015 (United Nations, D.o.E.a.S.A., 2015; see also Gerland et al., 2014). In low-income countries, rapid population growth is, at least on paper, the primary driver of an increasing ecological footprint (Grooten et al., 2012: 56).

Thus, political meteorite though it may be in practice, it is barely more than common theoretical sense to suggest that policies to reverse human population growth could be key to fulfilling our environmental duties. I agree that such policies not only could but almost certainly must, as a matter of urgency. I will return to the reasons for this conviction in section 4.

However, there is a danger to be avoided in taking this line: that of defending a population policy that fits some narrow environmental ethics criteria but comes at a morally unacceptable cost to individual human beings. This danger is not that of falling into a debate on antiprocreative policies unconstrained by *any* consideration of their moral limits. This is, I hope, already widely recognized, and section 1 will outline two levels of population policy that are at least conditionally permissible. But if environmental ethics is interpreted too restrictively, there is a risk of implicitly sanctioning, or even incentivizing, the impermissible. This is a danger not only in general terms (to be filled out in section 2) but also in terms of policies to distribute the costs of fulfilling globally collective environmental duties fairly across states (section 3).

I am taking environmental ethics in this narrower sense as focusing exclusively on our impact on the natural world, the implications this has for nonhumans, and its immediate impact on ourselves (so-called environmental harms or hazards to humans). There are, of course, more or less anthropocentric versions, but I would stress that I am not taking even a narrow environmental ethics to be concerned only with nonhumans. The "narrow" implies simply this: there is no requirement that no human be avoidably deprived (by whatever cause) of the ability to secure her basic needs or fundamental human interests. In other words, although there may well be overlapping duties, the approach does not include basic human cosmopolitan justice as a general requirement.

1 Where to Begin: Population Policies and Permissibility

Let us start by building on the extensive philosophical debate on procreative rights to establish a few baselines (Callahan, 1972; Conly, 2005; Dyck, 1973; Kates, 2004; Wissenburg, 1998).

For those who choose to engage in it, parenting is so central an element of a human life that it is reasonable to consider it a fundamental human interest to have the option to reproduce. To be deprived of the chance to enjoy this unique relationship—and this stab at immortality—is, to put it in less teleological terms, an affront to human dignity. Accordingly, the onus would be on any opponent to demonstrate that the opportunity to have and rear at least one child is not a fundamental interest, or, if such a framework is preferred, that there is no human right not to be deprived of it. Moreover, any system of duties or norms requiring some people to forsake parenting altogether could reasonably be rejected as overdemanding.

However, this is insufficient to establish an all-powerful, "conversation-stopping" moral entitlement to have as many children as one might want. On the one hand, our exercise of many rights may legitimately be curtailed, beyond some basic level, if it would (individually or in combination) prevent others from exercising certain of theirs (Mill, 1859: 14; Cafaro, 2012: 50–51). This is widely conceded. On the other hand, there is no reason to believe that the valuable human experiences involved in parenting are secured only by having lots of children. As Sarah Conly puts it, women should not be valued, or value themselves, "like a Better Boy tomato plant," according to the total number of their offspring. "It is the activity of mothering, rather than an inventory count, which gives mothering meaning" (Conly, 2005: 107). Thus, while it is very plausibly a fundamental interest deprivation to be without all opportunity to reproduce, it is not necessarily such, in itself, to be without the opportunity to go on and on having more children.

This comes, however, with two significant caveats (Carter, 2004: 353–358; Gerwith, 1979: 152; Sen, 1996: 1047–58). First, not having a big family can indirectly deprive individuals of fundamental interests. Where infant mortality is high and social security nonexistent, having many children may constitute a couple or individual's only chance of security in old age. If a woman has no other career opportunities and children are her only route to any kind of social position, limiting procreative opportunities can deprive her of her only available plan of life. (I am deliberately leaving aside for this short piece the question of religious reasons for continuing to procreate. I will note only that it is not clear in general that freedom of religion should extend to freedom to perform actions that in combination are harmful to others or threaten their—equally basic—interests or rights.)

Second, while a policy to limit procreation need not itself deprive individuals of fundamental interests, any attempt to enforce such a policy through direct coercion would do so. Coercive prevention of procreation would involve mass violation of privacy (policed abstinence) or violation of women's bodily integrity (forced sterilization or abortions). As such, it is clearly beyond the pale on almost any view of what is central to human well-being or dignity. Garrett Hardin's call for "mutual coercion, mutually agreed upon" has largely been eschewed: not only by theorists who have linked environmental ethics with population, but also by the more nuanced campaign groups (Hardin, 1968; Carter, 2004; Gardiner, 2001; Sen, 1996; Population Matters, 2015).

There is also the question of the impact on the child. Nobody is responsible for her own birth. It can, I hope, be taken for granted that each individual human being, however numerous her siblings, is born with the same moral entitlements as anyone else: the same call for respect and consideration *qua* human being. If our basic rights include rights to the core elements of a decent human life, they include them for everyone (Attfield, 1998: 297). However, many incentive-changing policies could undermine the prospects of the children. Consider, for example, stringent financial penalties.

With all this in mind, I suggest that there are two tiers of at least sometimes permissible population policy. The first consists of *choice-providing policies*. They include the education of women and the reduction of gender inequality, as well as the wide provision of contraception. They include also the provision of social security and health care to give couples and individuals alternative means of providing for their old age. These policies, providing meaningful choice over procreation, are clearly permissible. They are also a key part of meeting the demands of the basic cosmopolitan justice to which I alluded earlier.

The second are *soft incentive-changing policies*. These range from public education campaigns on the link between population and environmental damage—the active cultivation of a culture of procreative restraint as part of being a responsible "green" citizen—to tax breaks or other positive financial incentives to stop at one or two children. The latter are acceptable only insofar as they can be implemented without significant interest deprivations for any of the affected children.

However, it is clear from the observations noted earlier that even soft incentive-changing policies are permissible only where choice-providing policies are already in place. Where a woman has no other educational or career options, to demand that she refrain from having a large family may be to ask her to give up the only plan of life and means to social esteem available to her. Where there is no social guarantee against destitution in old age and only a moderate chance of any given child surviving to adulthood, being asked to have only one or two children amounts to being asked to jeopardize what scant security one can acquire for oneself.

2 IMPLICATIONS: THE TRUE COST OF THE NARROW VIEW

Armed with this two-tier model of permissible population policy, we can bring out the unpalatable implications of approaching population from too narrow an environmental ethics perspective. It is all too easy for those in western states to believe that the extent of their responsibility vis-à-vis population is to stop population growth at home. (Perhaps including, as at least two environmental ethicists have advocated, by curbing immigration; Cafaro and Staples, 2009). The idea would be that is then "up to" the rest of the world to do the same.

Rhetorical support—for this and for more overtly unpalatable "lifeboat ethics" solutions—can be found in the apparently plausible notion that it is as environmentally irresponsible to have many children in a poor, overpopulated state as it is to overconsume in the developed world (Hardin, 1974; Rolston, 1996). After all, population growth is a key driver of ecological footprint in low-income countries. Moreover, the Living Planet Index (LPI), which tracks biological diversity, is in rapid decline in many such countries (Grooten et al., 2012: 56). Detached from the perspective of even basic global justice, it might be demanded that *all* states introduce at least soft incentive-changing population policies from the current status quo. (It might even—as section 3 will discuss—be considered appropriate to penalize them for failure to do so in the global assignment of the burdens of tackling environmental harms.)

Two observations point to the flaws in such reasoning. First, low-income countries may be unable to implement even choice-providing policies, such as providing social security, without assistance. However, choice-providing policies are themselves prerequisites for the morally permissible implementation of soft incentive-changing policies.

Accordingly, to consider it "up to" the developing world to set its house in order on population, without also deeming it the duty of those in richer states to enable it to do so, is to expect the poorest states to do either the impossible or the impermissible. The latter, in this case, would involve asking their own poorest citizens to sacrifice their fundamental interests. Any suggestion that it is "as irresponsible" of such citizens as it is of the empowered middle-class UK couple to have more than two children (or for the rich western couple to have regular holidays abroad) becomes the bleak stuff of *Catch-22* satire if it would be either impossible or fundamentally costly for them *not* to do so.

The second point cuts more fundamentally at the argument. By focusing on *growth* in ecological footprint, it neglects the fact that that footprint is still small in low-income countries. Total as well as per capita detrimental environmental impact is often considerably lower than for many so-called developed states (Data from Global Footprint Network, 2015; United Nations, 2015). As Stephen Gardiner puts it, "the raw numbers suggest that the climate problem would not be much affected by many more Indians, Bangladeshis, and Africans living as they currently do" (Gardiner, 2011: 454). As this reminds us—and we shouldn't need reminding, given how obviously it follows from the IPAT equation—the damage at a global level is not done by population alone (Gardiner, 2001; Hardin, 1968; at least, it is not *currently* so, a caveat to be explained in section 4). Rather, it results from human numbers in combination with consumption and the limitations of technology.

In terms of biodiversity, low-income countries do score badly. However, it would be a mistake to put too much blame on population growth. Rather, according to the Worldwide Fund for Nature (WWF), the comparatively high developed world biodiversity rates are

> likely to be due to a combination of factors, not least of which being that these nations are able to purchase and import resources from lower-income countries, thereby simultaneously

degrading the biodiversity in those countries while maintaining the remaining biodiversity and ecosystems in their own "back yard." (Grooten et al. 2012).

In other words, the greater decline in biodiversity in poor as opposed to rich countries is in part because the latter export environmental hazards to the former. (Thus, many commentators would point out, far from occupying some sustainable moral high ground, the world's rich owe an ever-increasing ecological debt (Hayward, Chapter 26 this volume).

It is worth spelling this out. We are reducing their biodiversity in order to preserve our own without giving up our own much higher standards of living. In the process, we threaten basic resources such as water. This makes it even less likely that low-income states can secure the guarantee of subsistence and the opportunities for women that are a key component of choice-providing procreative policies and a necessary condition for the permissibility of soft incentive–based policies. Thus, we both worsen their biodiversity loss and contribute to depriving them of their only permissible means of tackling its other driver: population. Under those circumstances, appealing to those same biodiversity statistics as grounds for demanding immediate, unassisted action on population would be more than a dubious bit of reasoning. It would be morally outrageous.

3 More Implications: Population-Tied Schemes

The dangers of the narrow approach to environmental ethics and population extend to certain schemes for distributing the costs of fulfilling our environmental duties across states. One possibility is that "shares" of permitted environmental impact be assigned to states on a per capita basis but tied to a fixed population level. These are often shares of carbon emissions but could potentially be formulated in terms of ecological footprint more generally (Singer, 2002: 43–49; Jamieson, 2001: 301). Taken in isolation, such a scheme could, in effect, penalize failure to introduce impermissible population policies. Moreover, I will argue, some progress is needed toward global basic justice before even a modified version can be defended.

As an aside, this is not to assume that distributive schemes must—and certainly not that they should—be formulated only in terms of states. Nor is it even to assume that the current state system is an inevitable part of our future. However, this is how the world *is* currently organized and how much of the debate has been framed, especially that on allocating the costs of tackling climate change. Accordingly, we should consider the implications of extending that debate to include population.

Far from fairly distributing the costs of fulfilling globally collective duties, population-tied policies would, without further caveats, penalize states for failing to take *all* effective action on population. Thus, they risk incentivizing the introduction of just such coercive policies as were rejected in section 1 as incompatible with universal respect for basic human rights or interests: enforced abstinence, enforced temporary or permanent sterilization, or forced abortions.

To avoid this, population-tied policies would have to be modified. At one level, a condition might be introduced ruling out such impermissible means. (Indeed, among basically just states, it might simply be *expected* that the effect would be limited to avoiding incentivizing population growth policies, and encouraging permissible policies to curtail it. That, surely, must be what the policies' cosmopolitan proponents intended.) However, I doubt that this modification goes far enough. It might render the scheme compatible with the minimal notion of basic global justice outlined in introducing this chapter, but serious unfairness would remain.

Suppose some global body has introduced a population-tied scheme. Equal per capita ecological footprints are allocated to states, tied to some fixed (historic or predicted) population levels, but with a clause forbidding impermissible population policies. Call this the Moderate Policy. Suppose further that all states have since introduced all permissible population policies: all have equal opportunities for women and a minimal welfare state, contraceptives are widely available, and public education campaigns call for couples to "Stop at Two," with some positive financial incentives.

Suppose, finally, that State A has higher than average population growth despite these policies. Maybe it includes a large (though not state-affiliated) religious group with an anti-contraception ideology. Maybe its more affluent citizens just happen to want big families, and are unmoved by soft incentive-changing measures.

Under the Moderate Policy, State A would see its permitted per capita ecological footprint fall. In other words, the policy would penalize its increase in population, even though that increase resulted entirely from the aggregated decisions of some of its members or subgroups. Because State A's only means of redressing this disparity would now be to introduce impermissible measures, the policy would be penalizing a collective for something that it not only could not permissibly control *qua* collective but was expressly banned, by that very scheme, from so controlling. In other words, all members of State A would be penalized for the unconstrainable choices of only some of them.

The objection might be denied, as Clare Heyward has argued, on the grounds that we standardly pay a price for living in a just society and it is not unfair that we should do so. Consider, for example, the increased tax burden of the welfare state: "acceptance of [these] costs," according to Heyward, is simply "part and parcel of what it means to act in accordance with the requirements of justice" (Heyward, 2012: 715).

However, there is a difference between the two following scenarios. In one, a society acts collectively with fixed resources at its disposal. It refrains from enacting a morally objectionable policy at the price of increased inroads into those resources. In the other, some larger collective (a global decision-making body or combination of states) decides collectively to institute a system that penalizes its subcollective units for failure to do something that could only be done by impermissible means. In other words, it penalizes them for retaining key elements of basic justice. In the former, Heyward is perfectly right. The state can still reasonably be expected to make that decision despite the increased cost to its citizens. In the latter, however, it is as unacceptable of the wider collective actively to incentivize acting impermissibly as it would be of the state to do so.

To avoid such unfairness, only a very limited population-tied scheme could be defended: one that tied national allowances (of carbon emissions or ecological footprint more generally) to a fixed population *only if* the state in question had failed to implement all permissible policies to prevent population growth.

Whichever of the two modifications is accepted, however, there is a second difficulty with population-tied policies. As sections 1 and 2 pointed out, poor states may be unable to implement genuine choice-providing population policies without some transfer of resources. Moreover, also following section 1, soft incentive-changing population policies are permissible only where choice-providing policies are already in place. Given this, it is worth considering what exactly a global-level distributive scheme would be doing in (effectively) penalizing the poorest states for not having implemented all permissible population policies. It would be penalizing them not only for not doing the impossible (introduce choice-providing policies) but also for not doing that (introduce soft incentive-changing policies) which, *without* having done the impossible, would be impermissible. This—to put it mildly—does not strike me as particularly fair. Thus, some progress toward global basic justice is a prerequisite of even a modified population-tied scheme for allocating the costs of fulfilling environmental duties.

4 THE OTHER SIDE: WHY WE STILL NEED TO TALK ABOUT POPULATION

So far, I have highlighted the dangers of taking too narrow a view of environmental ethics, and the demands it puts on us collectively as human beings, in responding to the population component of the IPAT equation. To attempt to address population from too narrow an environmental ethics perspective is to risk—paraphrasing Henry Shue—not so much asking the global poor to give up their blankets so we may keep our jewelry, as clinging to our diamonds while demanding that they choose between those blankets and their only source of food. And blaming them—just for good measure—for the fact that they have to do so (Shue, 1992: 397).

However, it would be equally dangerous to neglect population altogether: to set it aside as too morally intransigent or as only a secondary consideration until basic global justice has been secured. Indeed, the very demands of that basic global justice count against such a strategy, especially if it is seen as part of a broader environmental ethics. It is because it lies on this knife-edge between two equally unpalatable alternatives that population policy presents us with such a moral quandary.

Three points must be stressed. First, of course it is true that from a properly global perspective, population alone is not "the problem." This has been emphasized throughout this chapter. However, it also follows from the IPAT equation that, for a large enough population, it could be impossible to secure environmental sustainability by reducing consumption without leaving some human beings without even the most basic necessities. According to the 2010 Living Planet Report, sustainably to maintain a population of 9.2 bn on even the diet of the average Malaysian would require 1.3 planets (Pollard et al., 2010: 86). Recall that the human population is predicted to be higher than that as soon as 2050.

In other words, with enough people, the fulfillment of our collective environmental duties without undermining all possibility of global basic justice would become contingent on as-yet-hypothetical technology. This is technology not only currently unavailable but which we have no guarantee can be developed and are currently dramatically underfunding. Renewables (wind, biomass and waste-to-power, solar, marine and small hydro technologies, and geothermal) made up only 8.5% of global electricity in 2013. Although renewable investment grew in 2014 and 2015, this followed two years of decline (Frankfurt School—UNEP Centre/BNEF, 2014: 11–12; 2016: 12).

Even the 2011 World Economic and Social Survey, which calls for a radical transition to green technology, hardly makes optimistic reading. It points out that this green energy revolution must take place at unprecedented speed (40 years, compared to the 70 to 100 for previous such transitions) and against a background of decades of failure to generate any "visible shift." Moreover, technical change is, by its nature, highly uncertain, there are huge costs associated with the necessary infrastructural change, and there may be limits to how far renewable energy technologies can be "scaled up" or their use rendered energy-efficient (United Nations, D.o.E.a.S.A., 2011: x–xiv).

Nor is so-called green energy the only technological challenge. It is the current *diet* of the average Malaysian that would that require 1.3 planets, even assuming a very low carbon footprint. (For that of the average Italian, this would be nearly two planets; Pollard et al., 2010: 86.) On these figures, the maintenance of even the 2050 predicted population at fairly modest levels would be contingent also on technology to make land massively more productive.

That is not to suggest that potential technological improvement should be ignored. On the contrary, what Heyward has argued at the state level applies (in my view more obviously) globally. Alongside whatever policies are permissible on population, it is imperative to invest further in developing technology, with the aim of sustaining such population growth as could only be prevented by impermissible means (Heyward, 2012: 722–723).

However, the "T" in IPAT is not some magic button: the mere possibility of technological development is no reason to treat the population challenge with any less urgency. Just as the precautionary principle would dictate cutting carbon emissions even given reasonable disagreement on climate science, so it mandates seriously attempting to prevent such population growth as would *without* as-yet-hypothetical technology render it impossible simultaneously to achieve basic global justice and fulfill duties of environmental ethics (Aldred, Chapter 27, this volume). The higher the human population—and the more extensive our duties to nonhumans—the less likely it becomes that technology could make the impossible feasible.

Moreover, the harms to be prevented are harms to others—future generations, the global poor, other species—which result at least in part from our combined actions. This makes the moral mandate all the more forceful. As this generation's global elite, taking a "technology will save us" attitude is equivalent to my selling all the malaria drugs for a holiday to a mosquito-infested swamp, then telling my companions that this is fine because I have invested a few pounds in a company investigating potential cures.

The second reason we cannot ignore population growth is as follows. I have endeavored to show how narrow-sighted it is to equate the "irresponsibility" of those having many children in the developing world with those in the west who do so or who overconsume. On the one hand, the environmental impact of such children in combination will, on current trends, be extremely low. On the other, it is highly problematic to describe someone as "irresponsible" for doing something to which they have no basically acceptable alternative. However, it is equally problematic to assume that population growth among the global poor can be ignored precisely because its per capita ecological footprint is so low. To do so is to assume that those children, and their children, and so on ad infinitum, will continue to have minimal ecological footprints. This, in turn, means assuming either that improved living standards will be secured without increasing environmental damage or that those individuals and their descendants will continue to endure severe poverty. In other words, it means either another high-stakes gamble on technological development or accepting that even basic global justice will continue not to be done (Cafaro, 2012: 54).[2]

Third, recalling section 1, there is a particularly repellent aspect to our delaying global action on population. In so doing, we gamble on as-yet-hypothetical technology to save future generations from a decision between introducing appallingly impermissible coercive population policies and moving outside the circumstances in which it is even theoretically possible simultaneously to secure basic global justice and fulfill duties of environmental ethics (Cafaro, 2012: 51; Gardiner, 2001; Wissenburg, 1998: 97–98). Whatever else we owe to our children and grandchildren, we surely owe it to them that we take all permissible measures to avoid bequeathing such a tragic choice.

Where, then, are we left? With a path between the currently impermissible and the ultimately tragic, which may or may not prove navigable but will only become more perilous the longer it remains untaken. Our best hope lies in immediate introduction of choice-providing and soft incentive–providing policies wherever they are both possible and permissible, combined with equally urgent action toward basic global justice without (as a bare minimum) worsening environmental impact. Through reduced emissions by and transfer of resources from the global elite, we must enable the speedy implementation in the developing world of those choice-providing policies which are not only imperative in themselves but also necessary for the permissible introduction of soft incentive–providing policies. Both of these are imperative moral duties for the global elite: weakly collective duties in the sense that they are duties whose fulfillment requires us to organize ourselves for immediate, effective action.

There is also, of course a case for immediate investment in technology, but not at the expense of such policies. Given how long this has already been left, this technology might well be necessary to render global justice and almost any kind of environmental sustainability simultaneously possible. It would certainly render it considerably less painful.

Notes

1. The IPAT equation is Impact = Population × Affluence × Technology.
2. Cafaro argues that anyone committed to so-called greenhouse development rights, or even to a universal human right against poverty, "*must reject a right to unlimited procreation and support humane measures to reduce the global human population.*"

References

Attfield, R. (1998). "Saving Nature, Feeding People and Ethics." *Environmental Values*, 7: 291–304.

Bernstein, L., et al. (2007). "Climate Change 2007: Synthesis Report." (Valencia: Intergovernmental Panel on Climate Change). <http://www.ipcc.ch/pdf/assessment-report/ar4/syr/ar4_syr.pdf>.

Cafaro, P. (2012). "Climate Ethics and Population Policy." *WIREs Climate Change*, 3: 45–61.

Cafaro, P. and Staples, W. (2009). "The Environmental Argument for Reducing Immigration into the United States." *Environmental Ethics* 31: 5–30.

Callahan, D. (1972). "Ethics and Population Limitation." *Science* 175: 487–494.

Carter, A. (2004). "Saving Nature and Feeding People." *Environmental Ethics* 26(4): 339–360.

Conly, S. (2005). "The Right to Procreation: Merits and Limits." *American Philosophical Quarterly* 42(2): 105–115.

Dyck, Arthur J. (1973). "Procreative Rights and Population Policy." *The Hasting Center Studies* 1(1): 74–82.

Ehrlich, P. R., and Holdren, J. P. (1972). "A Bulletin Dialogue on 'The Closing Circle': Critique." *Bulletin of the Atomic Scientists* 28(5): 16–27.

Frankfurt School-UNEP Centre/BNEF (2014). "Global Trends in Renewable Energy Investment 2014." Frankfurt am Main: Frankfurt School of Finance and Management.

Frankfurt School-UNEP Centre/BNEF (2016). "Global Trends in Renewable Energy Investment 2016." Frankfurt am Main: Frankfurt School of Finance and Management.

Gardiner, S. M. (2001). "The Real Tragedy of the Commons." *Philosophy and Public Affairs*, 30(4): 387–416.

Gardiner, S. M. (2011). *A Perfect Moral Storm: The Ethical Tragedy of Climate Change.* Oxford & New York: Oxford University Press.

Gerland, P., et al. (2014). "World Population Stabilization Unlikely This Century." *Science* 346(6206): 234–237.

Gerwith, A. (1979). "Starvation and Human Rights." In *Ethics and Problems of the Twenty-first Century*, edited by K. E. Goodpaster and K. M. Sayre. Notre Dame, Ind.: University of Notre Dame Press.

Global Footprint Network. (2015). "Footprint for Nations." <http://www.footprintnetwork. org/en/index.php/GFN/page/footprint_for_nations/>, accessed 15 March.

Grooten, M., et al. (2012). *Living Planet Report.* Gland: World Wide Fund for Nature.

Hardin, G. (1968). "The Tragedy of the Commons." *Science,* 162(3859): 1243–1248.

Hardin, G. (1974). "Living on a Lifeboat." *Bioscience* 24(10): 561–568.

Heyward, C. (2012). "A Growing Problem: Dealing with Population Increases in Climate Justice." *Ethical Perspectives,* 19(4): 703–732.

Jamieson, D. (2001). "Climate Change and Global Environmental Justice." In *Changing the Atmosphere: Expert Knowledge and Environmental Governance*, Clark A. Miller and Paul N. Edwards, 287–307. Cambridge, Mass.: The MIT Press.

Kates, C. (2004). "Reproductive Liberty and Overpopulation." *Environmental Values,* 13: 51–79.

Mill, J, S. (1859/1991). "On Liberty." In *John Stuart Mill: On Liberty and Other Essays,* edited by J. Gray. Oxford, England: Oxford University Press.

Pollard, Duncan, et al. (2010). *Living Planet Report.* Gland: WWF International.

Population Matters (2015). "Population & Ethics." <http://www.populationmatters.org/about/ values/population-ethics>, accessed 30 March.

Rolston III, H. (1996). "Feeding People versus Saving Nature?" In *World Hunger and Morality,* edited by W. Aiken and H. LaFollette, 248–267. Englewood Cliffs, NJ: Prentice-Hall.

Sen, A. (1996). "Fertility and Coercion." *University of Chicago Law Review* 63(3): 1035–1061.

Shue, H. (1992). "The Unavoidability of Justice." In *The International Politics of the Environment,* edited by A. Hurrell and B. Kinsbury. Oxford, England: Oxford University Press.

Singer, P. (2002). *One World: The Ethics of Globalization.* New Haven and London: Yale University Press.

United Nations Department of Economic and Social Affairs (2011). "World Economic and Social Survey 2011: The Great Green Technological Transformation." New York: United Nations.

United Nations, Department of Economic and Social Affairs, Population Division (2015). "World Population Prospects: The 2015 Revision." New York: United Nations. <http://esa.un.org/unpd/wpp/index.htm>.

Wissenburg, M. (1998). "The Rapid Reproducers Paradox: Population Control and Individual Procreative Rights." *Environmental Politics* 7(2): 78–99.

CHAPTER 33

....

ETHICAL ENERGY CHOICES

....

KRISTIN SHRADER-FRECHETTE

In Spring 2013, the World Health Organization (WHO) warned that Chinese air pollution, mostly from the combustion of fossil fuels (Wong, 2013), kills 1.2 million Chinese each year and is increasing. Globally, the WHO (2011) says air pollution kills about 3.2 million people per year, deaths that otherwise could be avoided.

Generating energy has historically been one of the worst sources of planetary pollution. In the British Isles, for instance, since Roman times inhabitants have faced health hazards from burning coal. Since the early 1200s, monarchs have tried to ban it. They always failed because coal was cheap and the violators were so numerous. Not until a London coal-smoke fog killed more than 3,000 people did the British Parliament enact the Clean Air Act in 1956 (Shrader-Frechette, 2011: 34).

CHAPTER OVERVIEW

....

This chapter helps explain why energy ethics has not prevailed, despite the evidence of thousands of years of energy pollution–caused deaths. Section 1 outlines the harms created by fossil fuels and nuclear energy. Section 2 surveys environmental ethicists' responses to these harms. Because energy harms are so obvious and well established, most environmental ethicists have not spent time arguing against them. Instead, as section 3 explains, most environmental-ethics work on energy has been at the level of third-order analyses—responding to those who attempt to justify continued use of dirty energy, often by saying other power sources are unavailable or too expensive. Sections 4 through 8 provide brief, third-order ethical analyses of five major, second-order, ethical excuses for not moving to clean, renewable energy. These are, respectively, the readiness, intermittency, expense, regulation, and intention excuses. Finally, section 9 outlines how future energy-related ethics research is likely to develop. Because other chapters in this volume discuss climate change, this one does not do so.

1 HARMS OF FOSSIL FUELS AND NUCLEAR ENERGY

Apart from climate change, energy choices present serious ethical problems because of their pollution stances, their centralization, their inequitable impacts, and their military connections. For example, oil addiction is an ethical problem partly because many nations must import the oil they use, and oil drilling is a massive source of environmental injustice to indigenous peoples. Because the United States, for instance, imports more than 60% of the oil it uses, it has spent billions of dollars, many lives, and military force to try to secure its oil imports. Not counting losses of human lives, the direct costs of the Iraq War have been about $100 billion/year, equivalent to about $100 for each barrel of oil imported by the United States from the Persian Gulf region. Thus, economists say the real price of gas is about $13 per gallon, just to offset the cost of the Iraq War. In the United States, the ethical and economic disparity between real gas costs and gas-station prices is massive. It includes more than $1 trillion annually in US-taxpayer gasoline subsidies, besides health and environmental costs, for neither of which consumers pay at the pump. Economists say that in 2006, the last year for which data are available, the total unpaid costs of US gasoline, including subsidies, health effects, and so on, were up to $1.49 trillion annually (Earth Policy Institute, 2009).

Even without accidents, fossil fuels and nuclear energy cause massive increases in cancer, heart disease, and other ailments. There is no safe dose of ionizing radiation, for instance, yet every one of thousands of US nuclear installations is allowed to release ionizing radiation—one reason that children's cancer rates are higher near commercial reactors. The US government also admits that a nuclear accident could kill 150,000 people, and that the core-melt probability for all existing and planned US commercial reactors is 1 in 4 during their lifetimes. Yet to protect the nuclear industry, US citizens are prohibited by law from obtaining compensation from negligent nuclear utilities for more than 1–2% of losses from a worst-case, commercial nuclear catastrophe. In fact, in most of the world, citizens have no commercial nuclear insurance protection. It would be too expensive, and nations know accidents are likely. Unsurprisingly, a majority of people in all nations, except North Korea, reject commercial nuclear energy as unsafe. They are likely correct. US reactors have had at least 5 core melts in roughly 50 years, and global reactors have had at least 26 core melts in roughly 50 years. New York Academy of Sciences data indicate that the Chernobyl nuclear accident is causing one million premature cancers—and the Fukushima, Japan accident may be worse. Because many of these deaths are not immediate, however, polluters can misrepresent their real causes (Yablokov et al., 2009; Shrader-Frechette, 2011, ch. 4).

Fossil-fuel harms are just as serious, even without considering climate change. Even if carbon were removed from coal, it would not be clean because of its other numerous, seriously harmful pollutants. A ground-breaking 2010 report by a major physicians' association warned that coal pollutants contribute to four of the five top causes of mortality in developed nations, and most of those deaths are not merely carbon-related; a 2009 US National Academy of Sciences report placed US coal-plant health and climate costs at more than $120 billion/year, even before all costs were counted (NAS, 2009). Together, gas-powered vehicles and coal-fired plants are responsible for most of the particulates, nitrogen oxides, reactive hydrocarbons, and ozone that foul the air, and most have no safe dose (Shrader-Frechette, 2007, ch. 1; WHO, 2005).

Nuclear-weapons proliferation likewise is an energy-ethics problem because any nation with atomic energy plants faces greater risks of nuclear terrorism and proliferation. The more reactors a nation has, the more terrorist targets it has. Already the United States has uncovered terrorist hideouts containing diagrams for attacks on US reactors.

2   ENERGY ISSUES IN ENVIRONMENTAL ETHICS

Despite the many problems associated with various energy sources, little has been done about them. For instance, scientists have long known the hazards of air pollution caused by fossil fuels, yet government has mostly ignored them, partly because of special interests. More than 40 years ago, economists writing in *Science* showed that a 50% reduction in air pollution—mostly caused by fossil fuels—could cut annual US health costs by 5% and illness and death by at least $2 billion (Lave and Seskin, 1970). Yet fossil fuel–caused air pollution remains a serious problem in much of the world.

Energy-related pollution problems continue partly because burning anything in order to produce power puts risky, no-safe-dose incineration byproducts into the air, such as particulates and nitrogen oxides (Schneider and Banks, 2010). Burning biofuels releases ultra-fine particulates, even more dangerous than coal-fired particulates (Booth, 2012). While nuclear power requires no burning, its fissioning of dangerous, radioactive materials both pollutes air and water and creates hazardous wastes that will remain lethal in perpetuity.

Given the obvious problems with dirty technologies such as biomass, coal, oil, gas, and nuclear energy, most scholars doing environmental ethics have not made ethical arguments against them because their harms are obvious. Instead, ethicists have made related arguments about human responsibility to stop such harms (Pogge, 2008; see also Chapter 23, this volume), extend environment-related rights (see Chapter 29, this volume), and avoid environmental injustice (e.g., the fact that the bulk of energy-related pollutants disproportionately harm children, minorities, and poor people; see "Justice," Chapter 24, this volume; Makhijani, Smith, and Thorne, 2006; Shrader-Frechette, 2003). Still other authors have showed that green-energy choices are essential to sustainability (see Chapters 31 and 40, this volume) and to avoiding environmental risk (see Chapter 28, this volume), pollution (see Chapter 27, this volume), and climate change (see Chapters 39–42, this volume). Ethicists likewise have argued that duties of citizenship require promoting clean energy (see "Citizenship," Chapter 26, this volume; Ayres and Ayres, 2010; Shrader-Frechette, 2007).

3   THIRD-ORDER ANALYSES IN ENERGY ETHICS

Given the obvious harms created by dirty energy and the obviously inequitable ways that energy-related pollution burdens fall most heavily on children, indigenous people, people of color, and poor people (Shrader-Frechette, 2003), most arguments about energy-related environmental ethics have a specific focus. They make heavily factual, third-order responses to second-order defenses of dirty-energy technologies. A typical first-order, energy-ethics argument might be that no energy technology should impose disproportionate burdens on any person or generation. A second-order response might be that it is impossible to implement any energy technology that does not impose inequitable burdens. A third-order reply might be to distinguish different types of energy-related inequities and then argue for implementing the least-inequitable technology, all other things being equal.

Insofar as environmental-ethics questions about energy are normative and applicable to real-world decision making, they rely heavily on science, and they tend not to belabor obvious first-order arguments such as that sustainable energy is desirable. Instead, because fossil fuels and nuclear energy obviously are both more dangerous and more obviously inequitable than solar photovoltaic and wind energy, normative energy-ethics debates often focus on criticizing second-order "excuses" for not using renewable energy. Hence the main disputes in environmental ethics over energy concern whether, *ultima facie*, society has duties to use clean, renewable energy, given that "ought implies can"—and given that energy producers ought to be required to do only what they are able to do.

Following the ought-implies-can principle, dirty-energy producers typically argue against clean-energy "oughts" by providing various second-order arguments that clean energy is unable to do the job required. These arguments include claims such as the following:

- The readiness excuse: Clean energy is not ready, not developed enough to replace fossil fuels and nuclear energy.
- The intermittency excuse: Because clean energy is intermittent, it cannot supply baseload power.
- The expense excuse: Clean energy is too expensive.
- The regulations excuse: Clean-energy regulations would harm the economy and indirectly kill people.
- The intention excuse: Citizens and industry are not responsible for avoiding dirty-energy harms because they intend to do no wrong.

This chapter focuses on third-order responses to the preceding five second-order ethical excuses for not using clean, renewable energy. Consider them in order.

4 THE READINESS EXCUSE

In 2013, coal executive Robert Duncan gave an illustration of the readiness excuse. Claiming renewables are too undeveloped to meet energy needs, he said electricity "demand cannot be met without coal" <https://www.washingtonpost.com/opinions/an-america-without-coal-plants/2013/03/02/f43c7a1e-80f9-11e2-a671-0307392de8de_story.html>. In a recent Internet-roundtable exchange <http://thebulletin.org/nuclear-energy-different-other-energy-sources/low-carbon-low-cost-electricity-247> Tony Pietrangelo, vice-president of the nuclear-industry lobby group, the Nuclear Energy Institute, made similar excuses. He said that because trying to move to renewables would "risk unmet energy needs," there is no ethical imperative to do so.

An obvious ethics problem with such excuses, however, is their being made by those with conflicts of interest, those either who profit from dirty energy or who are paid by dirty energy to do special-interest science—science with predetermined conclusions that is funded to advance funders' profit interests (Shrader-Frechette, 2007). Instead, top science journals show the readiness excuse fails. The classic Princeton University article, published in *Science* and updated in 2011, says that only 6 of 9 renewable or efficiency technologies, "already deployed at an industrial scale," could easily address climate change by 2050 (Socolow, 2011; Pacala and Socolow, 2004). The pro-nuclear US Department of Energy (DOE) also rejects the readiness excuse. It says already-available renewable technologies could provide 99% of US electricity by 2020; even by 2005, the annual global growth rate of non-hydro-renewable energy was 7 times greater than nuclear (Shrader-Frechette, 2011: 81).

Indeed, both coal and nuclear energy are declining, while wind and solar-photovoltaic (PV) energy are growing explosively. By 2013, BTM Consultants (2009) say wind alone will have 340 gigawatts installed globally, with continuing massive growth. Why? The pro-nuclear and pro-coal International Energy Agency show that nuclear and coal costs have continued to escalate. Yet it says that for every doubling of installed solar-PV capacity, solar costs drop 35%, and for every doubling of installed wind capacity, wind costs drop 18%. Because of a variety of new manufacturing techniques, thin-film cells, and increased manufacturing scale, solar-PV is already $0.15/kWhr. As mentioned, DOE says solar-PV costs will drop to $0.05–0.10 by 2015 and that US solar-PV manufacturing capacity will increase 12 times in the next five years—making solar-PV competitive in all markets nationwide by 2015. Yet already solar-PV is much cheaper than nuclear (Shrader-Frechette, 2011: 59, 232).

Throughout the developed world, wind is growing faster than any other energy installations (DOE, 2010). In fact, the American Wind Energy Association (2011) says that since 2007 wind has added twice the new capacity of coal and nuclear combined. Offshore-wind-business reports say that more than half of the new global-wind installations were added outside Europe and North America (Offshorewindbiz, 2011). For years, Germany, Spain, and India *each* have annually added more wind than the *entire world* added in fission. The Danes use wind to generate 21% of electricity; by 2030, it will generate half. By 2020, the EU says renewables will generate up to 49% of total EU energy and an even higher percentage of electricity (Shrader-Frechette, 2011: 225–232).

Together, all these data show that the readiness excuse fails, and the transition to completely renewable, almost-zero-carbon energy is achievable by 2050. Details of this transition are clear (e.g., Boxwell, 2009; Shrader-Frechette, 2011, Makhijani, 2007), partly because renewables are already widespread and inexpensive. Hence the "can" of renewable energy is able support the "ought" of implementing it.

5 THE INTERMITTENCY EXCUSE

Another excuse for not implementing renewable energy is that it allegedly provides only intermittent, not baseload, electricity. Hence, the excuse-makers say society needs fission and coal. Recently formulated by MIT engineer Charles Forsberg (2011) <http://atomicinsights.com/nuclear-fission-energy-is-superior-to-other-energy-sources/> and Nuclear Energy Institute lobbyist and vice-president Tony Pietrangelo (2011), in the Internet roundtable <http://the-bulletin.org/nuclear-energy-different-other-energy-sources/low-carbon-low-cost-electricity-247> their claim is that renewables are inferior to coal and nuclear fission because they produce power intermittently, whereas coal and nuclear plants can operate around the clock.

Can coal and nuclear plants operate around the clock? No. Although coal plants are slightly better, current US and UK lifetime-average-reactor load factors (percentages of time that reactors operate) are 71%. Despite 25 years of commercial-fission experience, nuclear lobbyists admit that, by 1980, this load factor was only 56%. Reactors were "down" nearly half the time (WNA, 2012a, 2012b).

Why? Given reactors' high temperatures, radioactive bombardment, and short materials lifetimes, plants have shutdown requirements for maintenance, parts replacement, safety inspections, and refueling. The US Government Accountability Office (GAO) warns that thorough safety inspections require the reactor to be shut down. The US DOE says at least 1% of reactor components must be replaced annually, costing at least $120 million/reactor. To avoid costly shutdowns, GAO says plants defer safety inspections and maintenance, thus cause near-catastrophes, like the pineapple-sized cavity in the plant's carbon-steel reactor vessel head that caused a two-year, Davis-Besse reactor-shutdown (GAO, 2004).

The US Nuclear Regulatory Commission (NRC 2006) warned that, in the 5 years since 2001, 75% of US reactors have violated safety regulations. NRC (2011) also reported that at least 28% of US nuclear operators have covered up, not reported, defective nuclear-plant parts. Such regulatory failures illustrate why only fleet-lifetime-average—not annual—nuclear-load factors are reliable. Otherwise, violators inflate load factors by deferring maintenance and causing safety threats. At best, claims that reactors "operate around the clock" are false. At worst, they indicate regulatory misconduct and potential disaster.

However, DOE says some renewables, like offshore wind, have little "down time" and therefore no need for storage capacity—yet could economically supply four times current US electricity (Musial and Ram 2010). Hence, the "can" of renewable energy again is able to support the "ought" of implementing it.

6 THE EXPENSE EXCUSE

Coal and nuclear proponents also say renewables are too expensive. For instance, the coal industry said in 2013 that, without coal, consumers will pay more for electricity <http://www.cleancoalusa.org/research>. The nuclear industry likewise says atomic energy is the lowest-cost way to produce base-load electricity <http://www.nei.org/News-Media/Media-Room/News-Releases/Nuclear-Power-Plants-Maintain-Lowest-Production-Co>.

However, both claims are false. The coal industry claims its power is cheap because it ignores the $120 billion/year in uncompensated health harms—including fatalities—from US coal plants (NAS, 2009). Nuclear-energy proponents do something similar. They ignore most nuclear costs and most carbon releases from the nuclear-fuel cycle. Once all 14 fuel-cycle stages are considered, fission is as carbon-intensive as natural gas. Reactors themselves do not release carbon-equivalent emissions, but the nuclear-fuel cycle does. Carbon-equivalent nuclear emissions are roughly nine times greater than those from wind, and more than four times higher than those from solar-PV:

coal 60: gas 9: nuclear 9: solar 2: wind 1 (Sovacool, 2008; Shrader-Frechette, 2011.)

Regarding nuclear-energy *costs*, credit-rating firms say nuclear electricity is much more expensive than that from natural-gas or scrubbed-coal facilities—at least 15 cents/kWhr and increasing, even before counting massive subsidies that pay most nuclear costs, including construction, reactor decommissioning, permanent waste storage, full insurance, and other expenses (Moody's, 2008; Kennedy et al., 2006).

Just as nuclear-energy proponents unethically typically trim their carbon emissions, they also massively trim most fission costs. Of the 29 major international nuclear-cost assessments done since 2000, all that were done or funded by the nuclear industry (18 of them) trim cost data by making at least five counterfactual assumptions that artificially lower fission costs by 700%. Five of these counterfactual assumptions are that (1) full nuclear-liability costs are assumed to be 0 (when in reality, EU studies show they would triple nuclear costs); (2) interest charges for capital during the 12-year reactor-construction period are assumed to be 0 (not the actual 15% market rate for risky projects); (3) reactor-construction times are assumed to be 0 years (rather than at least 10 years, the historical average); (4) nuclear-load factors—or percentage of time a reactor operates—are assumed to be 90–95% (rather than the actual 71%); and (5) nuclear lifetimes are assumed to be 40–60 years (rather than the actual 22 years). Once one uses actual empirical data to correct the counterfactual "projected" values in these five assumptions, nuclear costs can be shown to be nearly $1.05 / kWhr—which is 700% higher than the $0.15 per kilowatt-hour (/kWhr) that industry typically claims. Such false claims explain why all nuclear plants run "over budget" by hundreds of percent (Shrader-Frechette, 2011: 69–109; see Makhijani, 2007: 188–190, 444; Smith, 2006: 70).

Although fission costs are increasing, the US government says current median, market-based, wind and solar-PV costs are dropping massively. US government–calculated wind costs are $0.03 /kWhr, often dropping to $0.01 /kWhr. As mentioned, in 2007 DOE—officially responsible for promoting atomic power—said full solar-PV costs would be $0.05–0.10 by 2015, largely because of improved technology. As of January 2012, solar-PV costs were $0.15, including full costs such as amortization, interest, battery, and so on, and these costs are rapidly dropping (Solarbuzz, 2012). Once one begins to include continuing taxpayer subsidies, the cost gap between fission and renewables like wind and solar-PV widens, and the real cost of nuclear power reaches at least $1.50 per kilowatt-hour (Shrader-Frechette, 2011: 69–109, 232; UCS, 2011).

Despite high nuclear prices, MRG Consultants says that over the last half-century, the US has given 33 times more subsidies ($165 billion) to commercial fission than to wind and solar combined ($5 billion)—if one counts only direct subsidies and three indirect subsidies, namely, for construction incentives, accident liability, and tax credits (Goldberg, 2000). However, if one counts all direct and indirect subsidies, the late MIT Nobel Laureate Henry Kendall (1991: 9) says US commercial-fission subsidies have been 200 times greater ($20 billion annually or $1 trillion over 50 years) than those for wind and solar combined. The Union of Concerned Scientists (2011) agrees. It says commercial-reactor subsidies, over 50 years, have been so large—in proportion to the relatively little energy they have produced—that it would have cost taxpayers less to simply buy electricity on the open market and give it away. Hence, there is no reason that the "can" of renewable energy is unable to support the "ought" of implementing it.

7 THE REGULATIONS EXCUSE

Anti-regulatory ethical and political theorists like Harvard attorney Cass Sunstein, administrator until 2012 of the US Office of Management and Budget's Office of Information and Regulatory Affairs, however, have another excuse for using dirty fuels. Sunstein, whose research has been funded by industry think tanks, like the American Enterprise Institute, says that allowing dirty energy contributes to preserving human life. He claims that because (1) monies spent on regulations (like the Clean Air Act, to cut fossil-fuel pollutants) "produce less employment and more poverty," and because (2) "wealth buys longevity," therefore health-related regulations cost money, "increase risk," and thus kill people (Sunstein, 2002).

However, Sunstein's alleged-free-market objection to fossil-fuel regulation and replacement is invalid. It commits three logical fallacies of false cause in premises (1–2). The first fallacy consists of assuming in premise (1) that regulations reduce employment. Yet health-related regulations are neither necessary nor sufficient for reduced employment. Instead, health-related regulations typically increase overall employment or shift it from one sector or industry to another, with no net job loss. For instance, workers often move from old, dirty to new, clean technologies, with no overall job loss—partly because clean technologies typically are more labor intensive per kilowatt of electricity produced. Cleaner technologies also often save lives and therefore jobs (Morgenstern et al., 2002; Dwoskin and Drajem, 2012).

A second false-cause fallacy in Sunstein's premise (1) is the assumption that industrial profits are always spent to increase employment, an assumption falsified by the last half-century of US economic history. A third false-cause fallacy occurs in premise (2), that "wealth buys longevity." On the contrary, research shows mortality is very strongly associated with societal income-inequality, not with either per-capita or median income (Kaplan et al., 1996).

These three false-cause fallacies arise partly because alleged free-market environmentalists ignore relevant facts and norms, such as that higher employment has little value for people increasingly made ill by fossil-fuel pollutants, just as higher employment does not excuse injustice to innocent children harmed by coal particulates, and just as higher employment does not excuse injustice to innocent children harmed by drugs. If it did, one could justify employing many people as "pushers" to children, and one could justify employing many people in the fossil fuel industry, despite its harms. This supposed free-market argument likewise is invalid in begging the question that cost-benefit analysis is the sole test for regulations. A simple counterexample shows it is not: law requires expensive trials and possible prosecution, incarceration, and death for accused murderers. Yet criminologists agree these requirements are rarely cost-effective because most murders are not serial offenders, and hence pose no future threat to society. Instead, society tries them because justice requires it. If so, justice trumps cost-effectiveness.

The regulations excuse also fails scientifically as well as ethically. Adam Smith and virtually all economists say economically efficient market transactions require full information and fully voluntary exchanges. Otherwise, Coase's theorem is inapplicable. (This theorem is a key basis for economic analysis of government regulation. It guarantees that, regardless of how property rights are initially apportioned, if there are no transaction costs, and if people can trade in an externality, then bargaining will lead to an economically efficient outcome.)

Yet obviously consumer-market behavior regarding fossil-fuel pollutants is neither fully informed nor fully voluntary, partly because polluters often mislead people about harm (Trasande et al., 2005; Beder, 2002; Michaels, 2008; Wagner and McGarity, 2008). If so, fossil-fuel use generates no economically efficient outcomes. Indeed, poor or poorly educated consumers often have neither equal bargaining power nor ability to correct disinformation and skewed market forces. If not, the regulatory excuse is a wolf's argument in sheep's clothing. The sheep is market reasoning; the wolf is "might makes right," defending conclusions that allow harm to poor or innocent people on false grounds that harming them increases overall wealth and employment. Besides, consistent free-market economists reject the regulation excuse and claims that regulations kill people (Hahnel and Sheeran, 2009). They realize that regulations save lives. If so, the "can" of renewable energy—its cost-effectiveness—is able to support the "ought" of implementing cheaper, safer, and cleaner energy.

8 The Intention Excuse

Still other excuses for not helping to prevent dirty energy–related harms may focus on lack of personal responsibility. Citizens may ask: "If I don't intend to cause harm by my use of nuclear energy and fossil fuels, how can I be responsible for it?" Yet as Aristotle noted, people also are responsible when their intended act, culpable ignorance, or inaction causes harm. They are responsible for what they should know and who they allow themselves to become. Just as Karl Jaspers (1961; Shrader-Frechette, 2007) and Jean-Paul Sartre (1950) asked why people failed to stop Hitler, then ascribed this failure to "metaphysical guilt," something similar applies here. Those who fail to try to help stop dirty-energy harms are likewise guilty. Jaspers and Sarter would say they are guilty for not creating themselves, through their attitudes, choices, and acts, as the sorts of people who could help protect others. Thus, to the degree that people's own inaction and insensitivity have allowed them to become passive, compassionless, or weak—to live in "bad faith"—they are culpable for inaction in the face of great harms, like energy-related deaths.

The intention excuse also fails because most citizens contribute to—and benefit from—harms caused by nuclear and fossil fuels. Thus they have duties to try to stop them and to promote renewable energy. The ethics is basic: if you broke it, you should fix it—regardless of what you intend. Moreover, democracy is not a spectator sport. All citizens are responsible for being politically active and exercising their duties of citizenship, so as to help stop public harms. Citizens also have duties to help alleviate energy-related harms, proportional to their unearned advantages from society. All other things being equal, the greater a citizen's wealth, intelligence, freedom, health, and so forth—the greater her unearned advantages—the greater her responsibility to help alleviate these harms. Obviously, however, different citizens' duties to stop energy-related harms differ, *ultima facie*, as a function of factors such as one's fractional contribution to them, knowledge, profession, time, expertise, and so on (Pogge, 2008; Shrader-Frechette, 2007).

Citizens, and especially wealthier citizens, likewise bear justice-based responsibilities to help stop energy-related harms insofar as they benefit from them. Just as people have saved money by purchasing sweatshop-produced goods, and just as wealthier people are likely to purchase more sweatshop goods and therefore have greater responsibility for the harms they cause, something similar holds for energy-related harms. At least in Europe and the United States, *fossil-fueled vehicles* cause massive health risks because they are responsible for roughly half of all ozone and particulates, neither of which has a safe dose, both of which are especially harmful to children (EEA, 2006; Wahlin and Palmgren, 2000). Although asthma is a complex disease with multi-factorial, multi-level origins, fossil-fuel-caused particulates alone cause at least $2 billion annually in environmentally attributable asthma harms to US children, apart from possible developmental decrements. Particulates are at least part of the reason that US pediatric-asthma rates have doubled in the last 10 years (Wahlin and Palmgren, 2000). Yet drivers of fossil-fueled vehicles never compensate their child victims for harms they cause.

Something similar holds regarding *fossil fuel–generated electricity*. Although coal-fired plants produce roughly 45% of US and 41% of global electricity—and are the largest US source of SO_2, mercury, air toxins, and major NOX, ozone, and particulates sources—virtually all citizens benefit unfairly from this pollution. Why? Coal-generated electricity users impose neuro-developmental risks on children from pollutants such as mercury, yet they never compensate victims—like US newborns who suffer $9 billion/year in IQ and discounted lifetime-earnings losses from coal-plant mercury pollution (Landrigan et al., 2002). Instead, fossil-fueled vehicles and electricity plants impose many of their health and economic costs—unpaid by users—on society's most vulnerable members, children.

Moreover, wealthier people may be most responsible for these uncompensated economic benefits, gained at the expense of harm to children. People in the highest-income decile appear to cause about 25 times more fossil-fuel pollutants than those in the lowest-income decile (Rabinowitz, 2012). If so, wealthier people may (unintentionally) cause disproportionate injustice from uncompensated energy harms, like asthma.

In his classic UK government report, British economist Nicholas Stern (2006) estimated that each person in the developed world causes an average of 11 tons per year of carbon-equivalent emissions—roughly $935 per year in weather-related effects that kill a total of about 150,000 people per year. Yet global fossil-fuel pollution deaths are at least 10 times greater than these 150,000 climate-related deaths (WHO, 2011). Thus, instead of perhaps causing $900 per year in climate-related harms, the average person also may cause (10 × $900) or $9,000 per year in fossil-pollution deaths. The top 10% of wage earners (2010 earnings per year of at least $82,500) thus might cause (25 × $9,000) or $225,000 per year in fossil-fuel pollution damages (Rabinowitz, 2012), mainly to children—for which they never compensate anyone. By benefitting from fossil fuels, most citizens are unintentional "free riders" who save money and health by imposing their risks on poor children. If so, the intention excuse is no reason that the "can" of renewable energy is unable to support the "ought" of implementing it.

9 ENERGY ETHICS AND THE FUTURE

Responses to the previous five excuses—for failing to stop nuclear and fossil-fuel energy harms and not promoting renewable energy—suggest that important energy-ethics arguments are not about *prima facie* principles, such as "clean energy is more ethical." Such principles are obvious. Instead, crucial arguments are about *ultima-facie*, third-order justifi-cations for specific energy choices, given second-order "excuses" for rejecting clean energy.

If so, future energy-ethics debates are likely to continue to focus on science, including tox-icology, medicine, and economics, more than ethics. One reason is that *prima facie*, energy-ethics principles are obvious. A second reason for the science emphasis is that science is trump. Regardless of what is ethically desirable regarding energy, if it is not technically and scientifically possible, there is no obligation to follow it. A third and related reason that sci-ence is likely to dominate energy-ethics in the future is that "ought implies can." Science is what circumscribes the "can."

Even social-sciences "cans" circumscribe ethical "oughts." Dirty-energy defenders, in fact, often appeal to psychology and political science to challenge whether it is humanly possi-ble to persuade people to overcome their addictions to oil, coal, and nuclear. To challenge alleged scientific findings that people cannot be mobilized to promote radical institutional restructuring, ethicists need to make ethical arguments that help people recognize their per-sonal responsibility for energy change. Just as Tom Pogge (2008) and Peter Singer (2002) have used ethics to encourage people to end poverty, we shall need to use ethics to motivate people to end dirty energy.

References

American Wind Energy Association (AWEA) (2011). *US Wind Industry Continues Growth, Despite Slow Economy and Unpredictable Policies.* New York: American Wind Energy Association.

Ayres, R. U., and Ayres, E. H. (2010). *Crossing the Energy Divide.* Upper Saddle River, NJ: Prentice-Hall.

Beder, S. (2002). *Global Spin.* Glasgow: Green Books.

Booth, M. S. (2012). *Biomass Air Pollution.* Springfield, MA: Partnership for Policy Integrity. Accessed 4-20-13 at http://www.pfpi.net/air-pollution-2.

Boxwell, M. (2009). *Solar Electricity Handbook.* Warwickshire, UK: Greenstream, 2012.

BTM Consult Aps. (2009). *International Wind Energy Development—World Market Update 2008.* Ringkøbin, Denmark: BTM, 43–61.

Dwoskin, E., and Drajem, M. (2012). "Regulations Create Jobs Too." *Bloomberg Businessweek,* February 09.

Earth Policy Institute (2009). "The Real Price of Gasoline, 2007 Update." In *Plan B 4.0: Mobilizing to Save Civilization,* edited by L. Brown. New York: W.W. Norton.

European Environment Agency (EEA) (2006). *Air Quality and Ancillary Benefits of Climate-Change Policies.* Copenhagen: EEA.

Forsberg, C. (2011). "Nuclear Fission Energy is Superior to Other Energy Sources," *Bulletin of the Atomic Scientists*; accessed 9-15-15 at http://atomicinsights.com/nuclear-fission-energy-is-superior-to-other-energy-sources.

Goldberg, M. (2000). *Federal Energy Subsidies.* New York: MRG Associates, 2000.

Hahnel, R., and Sheeran, K. A. (2009), "Misinterpreting the Coase Theorem." *Journal of Economic Issues* 43: 215–238.

Jaspers, K. (1961). *The Question of German Guilt,* translated by E. B. Ashton. New York: Capricorn Books, 36.

Kaplan, G. A., Pamuk, E. R., Lynch, J. W., Cohen, R. D., and Balfour, J. L. (1996). "Inequality and Income and Mortality in the United States." *British Medical Journal* 312: 999–1003.

Kendall, H. (1991). "Calling Nuclear Power to Account." *Calypso Log* 18: 9–10.

Kennedy, J., Zsiga, A., Conheady, I., and Lund, P. (2006). *Credit Aspects of North American and European Nuclear Power*. New York: Standard and Poor's.

Landrigan, P. J., Schechter, C. B., Lipton, J. M., Fahs, M. C., and Schwartz, J. (2002). "Environmental Pollutants and Disease in American Children." *Environmental Health Perspectives* 110: 721–728.

Lave, L., and Seskin, E. O. (1970). "Air Pollution and Human Health." Science 169 (3947): 723–733.

Makhijani, A. (2007). *Carbon Free and Nuclear Free*. Takoma Park, MD: IEER.

Makhijani, A., Smith, B., and Thorne, M. C. (2006). *Science for the Vulnerable*. Takoma Park, Maryland: Institute for Energy and Environmental Research.

Michaels, D. (2008). *Doubt Is Their Product*. New York: Oxford University Press.

Moody's Corporate Finance (2008). *New Nuclear Generating Capacity*. New York: Moody's.

Morgenstern, R. D., Pizer, W. A., and Shih, J. S. (2002). "Jobs versus the Environment." *Journal of Environmental Economics and Management* 43: 412–436.

Musial, W., and Ram, B. (2010). *Large-Scale Offshore Wind Power in the United States*. Golden, CO: National Renewable Energy Laboratory.

Offshorewind.biz. (2011). "Global Wind Capacity Increases by 22% in 2010—Asia Leads Growth." Accessed June 25, 2012 at http://www.offshorewind.biz/2011/02/02/global-wind-capacity-increases-by-22-in-2010-asia-leads-growth/.

Pacala, S., and Socolow, R. (2004). "Stabilization Wedges." *Science* 305: 968–972.

Pietrangelo, A. (2011), "Fact Check," *Bulletin of the Atomic Scientists*; accessed May 15, 2015 at http://turnbacktheclock.org/nuclear-energy-different-other-energy-sources/fact-check-nuclear-energy-has-important-role-us-energy.

Pogge, T. (2008). *World Poverty and Human Rights*. Cambridge: Polity Press.

Rabinowitz, D. (2012). "Climate Injustice: CO2 from Domestic Electricity Consumption and Private Car Use by Income Decile." *Environmental Justice* 5: 38–46.

Sartre, J.-P. (1950). *What Is Literature*, translated by Bernard Frechtman. London: Methuen, 45.

Schneider, C. S., and Banks, J. (2010). *The Toll from Coal: An Updated Assessment of Death and Disease from America's Dirtiest Energy Source*. Washington, DC: Abt Associates.

Shrader-Frechette, K. (2003). *Environmental Justice*. New York: Oxford University Press Lester Brown.

Shrader-Frechette, K. (2007). *Taking Action, Saving Lives*. New York: Oxford University Press.

Shrader-Frechette, K. (2011). *What Will Work: Fighting Climate Change with Renewable Energy, Not Nuclear Power*. New York: Oxford University Press.

Singer, P. (2002). *One World*. New Haven: Yale University Press.

Smith, B. (2006). *Insurmountable Risk*. Takoma Park, MD: IEER Press.

Socolow, R. (2011). "Wedges Reaffirmed," *Bulletin of the Atomic Scientists*; accessed April 20, 2013 at http://www.thebulletin.org/web-edition/features/wedges-reaffirmed.

Solarbuzz (2012). *Solar Market Research and Analysis, Solar Electricity Prices*. Port Washington, NY: NPD Group.

Sovacool, B. K. (2008). "Valuing the Greenhouse Gas Emissions from Nuclear Power." *Energy Policy* 36: 2940–2953.

Stern, N. (2006). *The Economics of Climate Change*. London: HM Treasury.

Sunstein, C. (2002). *Risk and Reason*. Cambridge: Cambridge University Press.

Trasande, L., Landrigan, P. J., and Schechter, C. (2005). "Public Health and Economic Consequences of Methyl Mercury Toxicity to the Developing Brain." *Environmental Health Perspectives* 113: 5990–5996.

Union of Concerned Scientists (UCS) (2011). *Nuclear Power Subsidies: The Gift that Keeps on Taking.* Washington, DC: UCS. Accessed June 1, 2012 at http://www.ucsusa.org/nuclear_power/nuclear_power_and_global_warming/nuclear-power-subsidies-report.html.

United States Department of Energy (DOE) (2010). *Electric Power Annual 2010.* Washington, DC: DOE. Accessed June 1, 2012 at www.eia.doe.gov/cneaf/electricity/epa/epa_sum.html.

United States General Accounting Office (GAO) (2004). *Nuclear Regulation: NRC Needs to More Aggressively and Comprehensively Resolve Issues Related to the Davis-Besse Nuclear Power Plant's Shutdown.* Washington, DC: GAO.

US National Research Council and National Academy of Sciences (NAS) (2009). *Hidden Costs of Energy.* Washington, DC: National Academy Press.

United States Nuclear Regulatory Commission (NRC) (2011). *Audit of NRC's Implementation of 10 CFR Part 21, Reporting of Defects and Noncompliance.* Washington, DC: Office of the Inspector General.

United States Nuclear Regulatory Commission (NRC) (2006). *Oversight of Nuclear Power Plant Safety Has Improved, but Refinements Are Needed.* Washington, DC: United States Government Accountability Office.

Wagner, W., and McGarity, T. (2008). *Bending Science.* Cambridge: Harvard University Press.

Wahlin, P., and Palmgren, F. (2000). *Source Apportionment of Particles and Particulates (PM10) Measured by DMA and TROM in a Copenhagen Street Canyon.* Roskilde, Denmark: National Environmental Research Institute.

Wong, E. (2013). "Air Pollution Linked to 1.2 Million Premature Deaths in China." *New York Times,* April 2, 2013; accessed April 20, 2013 at http://www.nytimes.com/2013/04/02/world/asia/air-pollution-linked-to-1-2-million-deaths-in-china.html?_r=2&.

World Health Organization (WHO) (2011). *Air Quality and Health.* Copenhagen: WHO.

World Health Organization (WHO) (2005). *WHO Air Quality Guidelines for Particulate Matter, Ozone, Nitrogen Dioxide and Sulfur Dioxide: Global Update 2005.* Geneva, Switzerland: WHO, 5.

World Nuclear Association (WNA) (2012a). *Essential Roles Supporting a Fast-Globalizing Nuclear Industry.* London: WNA. Accessed June 4, 2012 at www.world-nuclear.org/about.html.

World Nuclear Association (WNA) (2012b). *Nuclear Power in the World Today.* London: WNA. Accessed June 4, 2012 at http://www.world-nuclear.org/info/info1.html.

Yablokov, A. V., Nesterenko, V. B., Nesterenko, A. V., and Sherman-Nevinger, J. D. (2009) *Chernobyl.* Malden, MA: John Wiley.

CHAPTER 34

NARRATIVES OF FOOD, AGRICULTURE, AND THE ENVIRONMENT

DAVID M. KAPLAN

THE environmental ethics literature has made important contributions to food and agricultural ethics by extending the moral domain beyond humans to include animals, ecosystems, the land, and climate. The underlying conviction in environmental ethics is that the natural world has value that should be viewed apart from our narrow, human-centered concerns. This basic commitment to nature has bearing on our understanding of food production: because agriculture uses the land (and often animals), it raises ethical questions about how we should act, what deserves moral consideration, and what kind of obligations we might have to both humans and nonhumans. Although the environmental ethics literature has sometimes viewed agriculture a human affair that encroaches upon nature (Knobloch, 1996; Mason, 2005; Merchant, 1990) and been at odds with animal ethics (Callicott 1980; Callicott 1990 Regan 1983),[1] the current relationship is much more symbiotic. Environmental ethics takes food production and agriculture seriously, and agricultural ethics embraces the environment as among its central concerns. The *Journal of Agricultural and Environmental Ethics* (established in 1988) attests to the overlap and mutual concern of these two fields.

Of course, concern for agriculture and the environment is not reserved for academics. Public opinion surveys show that Americans and Europeans are well aware of the connection between the two (W. K. Kellogg, 2012; *Eurobarometer*, 2013).[2] People are generally skeptical about large-scale, industrialized food production and believe that small family farms produce safer food, more nutritious food, and are more likely to protect the environment. Both American and European consumers are overwhelmingly willing to pay more for food grown on farms that care for the land (Kellogg, 2012: 17–19).[3] The percentage of those willing to pay more in the United States has nearly doubled since 1990 (Kellogg, 2012: 30).[4] One explanation for the increased awareness and concern about food production and environment is the prevalence of food scares. Everyone surveyed in a recent Kellogg Foundation survey was familiar with one of more stories about contaminated strawberries from Mexico, e-coli in ground beef, Mad Cow disease, dolphin by-catch in tuna fishing, and other such issues (Kellogg, 2012: 49).[5] These food scares explain how agriculture and food production work—and sometimes fail. Although the effects are short-lived and we all quickly return to our routines, food scare stories teach people about food systems, regulatory oversight, health and environmental hazards, animal welfare, and other things we usually ignore (Kellogg, 2012: 49–52).[6] They provide teachable (albeit fleeting) moments.

One the reasons food scares resonate might be because they tap into familiar narratives about the consequences of overindustrialization. The public has grown accustomed to these stories; the main actors and settings are almost interchangeable plot elements. The modernization narrative is about large-scale industry that has snowballed out of control—and we are helpless to do anything about it. It is like a run-away train or Frankenstein's monster: there is no stopping it even though we know it is broken. For example, the problems of Mad Cow disease, pesticides, or antibiotic overuse are seen as yet another case of industry gone awry. Each new food scare seems oddly familiar, as if we've heard this story before. Perhaps that is why the public quickly only pays attention for so long.

According to a Kellogg Foundation study, the typical response to a food scare is resignation and helplessness. Although the modernization narrative explains the problem, it also explains away the problem. That is to say, people believe either industrialization has gone too far (e.g., farming relies too much on pesticides) or not far enough (e.g., safe pesticides have not been invented yet). Either way, the public accepts a generic story of the forces of modernization that are beyond our control as the dominant framework for understanding how food systems work (Kellogg, 2012).[7] This is unfortunate because other stories are available to help us understand how agriculture and food production work, their effects on us, and what we might do about them.

This chapter examines the role of narratives in our understanding of the relationship between food, agriculture, and the environment. Narratives are the most comprehensive way of representing things that have a historical dimension. They focus on the central actors, select the key events, and create meaningful accounts of what happened and what could happen. They are crucial for putting events into context, portraying characters, and depicting scenarios. I argue that environmental ethics needs to embrace the "narrative turn" in order to account for the diversity of ethical issues surrounding food, agriculture, and the environment, as well as to connect overarching stories about food systems to our everyday lives. I then identity several narratives commonly seen in the United States that frame the way we understand food and environmental issues. A shift from theories to narratives might lead us away from top-down, covering-law models in environmental ethics toward more practical, non-academic approaches that focus on actual problems and solutions—from theory to casuistry.

1 NARRATIVE, FOOD, AND THE ENVIRONMENT

Food and agricultural issues involve a vast range of actors, objects, animals, and environments. Each stage of food's lifecycle poses different issues, involves different agents and patients, occurs in different natural and social settings, and affords different moral choices. Each food item (and sometimes ingredient) poses different issues, involves different actors, relates to different environments, and so on. It is difficult enough to analyze and assess single food items, much less the thousands of different things we typically eat—everything from plants and animal parts to things manufactured in factories. The environments to which each food relates are often quite different. Any attempt to reckon with the all of the different ways our food and agricultural practices relate to the environment under a single theoretical framework inevitably oversimplifies. The diversity of food items is too vast (fruits and vegetables, animal products, and processed foods), the environments are too dissimilar (production, distribution, and consumption taking place in countless different settings), and the range of issues too divergent (from sustainable development and factory farming, energy usage and pollution, erosion and water usage, to public policy and ethical consumerism). There are simply too many salient empirical and normative considerations for any single ethical theory to account for, much less any theory that simplifies, the relationship between food, agriculture, and the environment as such.

This is where a narrative approach might be helpful. Narratives put things into context by organizing parts into meaningful wholes. Anything that takes place in time can be recounted in a story that connects otherwise unrelated characters, events, and things. Stories create meaningful accounts of what happened by answering basic journalistic questions—who, what, where, why, and how—and by configuring sequences into episodes. Narrative can create more nuanced and textured meanings than descriptions or explanations because they can take a longer, broader, more encompassing view. They can simply do more than any shorter unit of meaning.

There is, of course, little consensus among philosophers and literary theorists about the precise relationship between a story, narrative, and plot. On some reckonings, a narrative and story are identical (Ricoeur, 1984)[8]; on others, they are different (Genette, 1983).[9] Both stories and narratives rely on plots to configure parts into wholes. I will use *stories* to refer as any organization of a sequence of events into a coherent episode. I will use *narrative* to refer to patterns or recurring themes that organize not only characters, events, and objects but also stories. A narrative, on this reading, is like a frame or worldview. Stories transform series of decisions and actions into an account; narratives transform series of stories into an interpretive frame.

There are five key functions of non-fictional stories relevant to understanding how food, agriculture, and the environment are related:

1. Stories interpret events. Stories are told from a perspective. Any account of what happened is ultimately an interpretation, not an objective representation. This is not to say that all interpretations are equally valid or reliable but rather to note that other interpretations are always possible. Unlike simple propositions about states of affairs or logical necessity, which can be understood without stories, human affairs and historical events have an essentially narrative form. They unfold in time, occur in episodes, and are always understood in a partial, limited, and prejudiced manner. Stories create cases, depict events, and give meaning to series of actions and events. Narratives organize stories into interpretive frameworks that influence how we understand and evaluate things. Part of the task of interpretation is to analyze the narratives commonly told in order to determine their reliability. Narratives can misguide as much as they guide interpretation. But they are always operative and actively (albeit subtly) prejudicing experience.

2. Stories portray characters. A story can flesh out a character and detail both the inner life and outer manifestations of one's personality and disposition. We come to see who someone is by how he or she relates to others and responds to situations. The

answer to the question "who?" is not merely a set of identifying references but a person whose life is made up of chapters. We don't really know the identity of someone until we see how he or she initiates actions, responds to events, and relates to others. An identity unfolds over time, even a lifetime, with all of the beginnings and endings, successes and failures, digressions and subplots, and everything else that make up our stories. We understand the life of person—like any historical occurrence—in a story. A narrative builds on stories to create a broader, overarching account of who someone is. We live our lives in terms of the narratives we tell ourselves and that others tell about us. These narratives pattern our actions and responses.

3. Stories depict scenarios. Stories not only recount the past but also depict what might happen. They are not only interpretive; they are also inventive. Scenario analysis—basically predictions that try to take as many social variables into account as possible—have become a standard practice in fields that require strategic planning. Small stories and large narratives are the glue that holds together projected events and possible outcomes. Scenarios are prescriptive as well as descriptive. We tell stories about what happened in order to highlight a moral dimension—particularly choices that were made or could be made. We can also test out possible responses in a scenario by imagining how events might play out. Often moral deliberation involves telling stories in order to flesh out the ethical dimensions of real and imaginary characters and situations.

4. Stories make arguments. History, case studies, impact assessments, and other forms of nonfiction claims to be true and, often, morally right. Stories can enhance and even stand in for an argument. A narrative framework delimits a context of relevance, depicts situations, portrays characters, and imagines consequences in defense of truth claims and normative claims. In turn, arguments rely on stories (and broader narratives) for illustration. For example, Thurgood Marshall argued for *Brown v. Board of Education* by weaving together stories of the effects of segregation on the lives of African American children coupled with appeals to justice and fairness. The resulting narrative-argument was a more forceful case than if he had appealed only to life histories or to principles. President Reagan perfected the art of using the stories of "real people" in his speeches in support of his policy agendas. For example, he famously recounted the welfare queens who allegedly leached off the system. In these cases, stories and arguments worked together. It is often difficult to identify where precisely the argument lies within a story—and how precisely non-literal, creative uses of language help make arguments stronger. But the two relate to each other, as Kant might say, as concepts relate to experience: arguments without stories are empty; stories without arguments are blind.

5. Stories humanize characters and make events relatable. Perhaps the greatest virtue of stories is that they can engage us in ways that utterances and theories cannot. They bring us into their world and let us see things from the perspectives of other characters. Stories can draw us in and make us care about persons and things we otherwise might never have considered. And they can do it in ways that are related and accessible—even to those who have no specialized expertise. Martha Nussbaum is particularly eloquent on the importance of the stories to the cultivation of humanity. According to her, reading fiction helps develop a "narrative imagination," a propaedeutic for moral interaction that helps us understand the perspectives of others,

appreciate how circumstances shape actions, consider what could happen, and see oneself as another. Stories help us identify with others, comprehend other people's motives and choices, and challenge conventional wisdom and values (Nussbaum, 1998). Stories have the unique ability to connect us.

The case for the epistemic and normative function of narratives is not new. In the last 50 years, we've seen the importance of narratives for epistemology (MacIntyre, 1981; Ricoeur, 1984; Danto, 1985; Swirski, 2007), ethical theory (Blum, 1980; Nussbaum, 1992; Walker, 1998), bioethics (Frank, 1995; Nelson, 1997; Charon and Montello, 2002), personal identity (Ricoeur, 1992), and philosophy of mind (Fireman et al, 2003; Hutto, 2008). Narratives have become a part of the methodological diet of the social sciences, education, and psychotherapy. Their role is well established.

2 NARRATIVES ABOUT FOOD AND THE ENVIRONMENT

Although environmental ethics has, to some extent, recognized the importance of narratives (Cheney, 1989; King, 1999; Liszka, 2003), very little of this work has been applied to food and agriculture (Sanford, 2011; Frasier, 2001). This is unfortunate. The relationship between food, agriculture, and the environment is well suited to be framed in terms of narratives because of the countless particulars, various actors, and changing circumstances that can never be fully captured in detail by theories, descriptions, or explanations.

The goal of a narrative analysis of food and the environment is to identify the narrative (or narratives) in which events are framed and then to assess its adequacy in relation to an expectation, interest, or question; that is to say, to interpret and evaluate the narrative. We can ask whether the overarching narrative is true, if it is slanted, if it is useful, and so on. There are advantages and disadvantages to narratives because they are always partial in both senses: as incomplete and as prejudiced. Part of the challenge of reading (and writing) narratives is to be faithful to reality but also add to it—to contribute new insights into things. There is, of course, no recipe for a good story or good interpretation. There are, however, patterns: recurring narratives about food and the environment that are common in academic literature, the media, and advocacy outreach. With practice, we can become attuned to these underlying/overarching narratives and recognize how they interpret actors and events, what they reveal and what they conceal, and what they presuppose about who actors are, how the world works, and, above all, how we should act.

Here are some the most common narratives found in the United States that relate food and agriculture to the environment.

The scientific narrative. The dominant approach to questions concerning food and environment is a scientific discourse of explanations and predictions governing causal interactions of physical matter. The scientific narrative is based on the presumption that methodological precision and empirical evidence are the only ways to secure not only objectivity but also reasoned consensus about human actions on the environment. The main actors are the scientists themselves; the narrative arc begins with questions and ends with certainty; the main conflict is with either nature itself, which seemingly hides its truths, or the forces of ignorance that stand in the way of reason. The scientist and her methodological precision rescues us; hard facts redeem us. This narrative is found wherever data-driven analyses and scientific expertise are privileged, including environmental impact assessments and lifecycle analysis. The science narrative underlies the dominant utilitarianism and risk assessment discourses, both of which rely on research and experimentation to establish better or worse outcomes for humans, animals, and environments. Science alone, on this reckoning, has to power to understand the workings of nature and to solve our practical problems.

We find this story in, for example, scientific attempts to resolve the controversies surrounding genetically modified foods (Freedman 2013). What many see as a political issue of labeling, choice, and food sovereignty is translated into a technical issue of food safety and environmental risks (*Eurobarometer*, 2013). Although facts matter, the genetically modified food debates are legitimately political and, therefore, reasonably contested on the grounds of moral and political convictions as well as established facts. The scientific narrative, however, treats it as an exclusively scientific matter, where the main actors are clear-minded scientists educating a naïve public.

The techno-utopian narrative. The techno-utopia narrative underlies optimistic assessments of our technical prowess to make food production as environmentally sound as possible. The promise of technology is to make our lives better. Whatever practical or political obstacles we face, we believe that there will eventually be a device, an app, or material to save the day. We find the techno-utopian narrative in the discourses on genetically modified foods, in vitro meat, renewable energy, and some accounts of sustainable agriculture: optimistic assumptions about the ability of technologies to solve our problems and improve our lives. The techno-utopian narrative has faith in progress. Although we might not have the technical capabilities now, we will eventually engineer whatever is needed to fix (Dyson, 2000; Despommier, 2011). Private industry and pro-development interests typically invoke techno-utopianism. Monsanto's website (www.monsanto.com) is filled with optimistic assessments of what new technologies can do to feed the hungry and clean the environment. So does the Archer Daniels Midland website and "Corporate Responsibility Report" (http://www.adm.com/en-US/responsibility/2013CorporateResponsibilityReport/).[10]

The technophobic narrative. Fear of technology run amok often underlies concerns about the specter of new technologies or criticism about old ones. According to the technophobic narrative, technology is out of control; humans no longer control it, instead it controls us. Technological development is an independent force that follows its own rules and imperatives; we have no choice but to adapt to it. This narrative sometimes animates the discourses that criticize new technologies, such as genetically modified food, in vitro meat, aquaculture, and other proposed technical solutions to social and environmental problems. According to this reckoning, the problems we face are due to increasingly complex technical systems that are geared toward efficiency, higher yields, profit, and convenience. The solution is to try to live more simple, wholesome, and natural lives free from artifacts and chemicals. Food scares often follow a technophobic narrative—or what the Kellogg survey calls the modernization narrative. The alarmism that surrounds the genetically modified food debates often relies on a technophobic narrative (Jefferson, 2003).

The Center for Food Safety (www.centerforfoodsafety.org) website features several stories that have a predictably grim take on agricultural biotechnologies. For example, in their story, "Tell Pop Secret to Stop Killing our Bees!" we are told that the popcorn industry uses bee-killing chemicals in their seeds. Another story titled "Unregulated Tricks in Your Nano Treats" warns that "there's a threat to your child so small, you can't even see it coming." Even if there is truth to their warnings, the website tends to commerce in techno-dystopian fears.

The Romantic narrative. The technophobic narrative often evokes Romantic themes of man versus nature, life out of balance, and the desire to restore lost harmony with nature. According to the Romantic narrative, science and technology assume a detached, objectifying perspective that corrupts our food and pollutes the environment. The more we tamper and tinker with traditional food, the more nature, society, and the quality of food suffers. In this reckoning, connection with nature is good and alienation from it is bad. The Romantic narrative, however, is about more that just the folly of science and technology. It is a holistic worldview about the virtues of an emotional or spiritual connection with nature and each other and the vices of disconnection. We find this narrative in the local food movement and a lot of the organic food literature, as well as other calls to eschew industrial agriculture and processed food in favor of sustainable living and traditional foodways.

Michael Pollan's food writing relies on the Romantic narrative. He often makes a strong distinction between wholesome natural foods (tied to a traditional diet) and unwholesome processed foods (tied to industrial agriculture). The reason that traditional diets are healthier and better for the environment is because they treat food as more than its chemical parts. It is always a part of a diet and a lifestyle. His oft repeated mantra is to "eat food, not too much, mostly plants"—to eat the kinds of things our grandparents might have grown up eating and to avoid new developments in agriculture and food processing. Food is culture, not science (Pollan, 2009). For Pollan, a broad, holistic view of nature is good, and a narrow reductivist view is bad. It's another retelling of the Romantic narrative.

The agrarian narrative. Pollan's characterization of food and agriculture also relies on the agrarian narrative. Agrarianism stresses the role of farming and ranching in the formation of moral character and in preserving culture and traditions. By living a rural lifestyle connected to the climate and soil, we acquire a sense of identity and place that can only come about by direct contact with the land. Agrarianism was an early twentieth century response to the social and environmental costs of industrialization and urbanization, premised on the conviction that social life, food production, and the health of the land are inseparably related. That is to say, communities and the environment thrive only when farming is done properly; both suffer when farming is done poorly. The agrarian narrative celebrates the virtues of an agricultural lifestyle, such as care for the land, animals, and each other, which should be recovered to mitigate the social and economic blight, pollution, and destruction of traditions brought about by large-scale industrial agriculture.

Wendell Berry is perhaps the best-known contemporary agrarian. "Eating," he famously says, "is an agricultural act" (Berry, 1991: 145). We are all involved in agriculture because our daily food choices affect how the land is treated. People, food, and the environment are all connected in the act of eating—and when we eat the right foods in the right way, we strengthen these connections. The agrarian narrative often underlies the discourses in support of local food, farmers markets, community-supported agriculture, and sustainable agriculture. The bumper sticker that exhorts us to "know your farmer!" is agrarian sloganeering. Intimate connections are putatively superior to alienation and detachment (Freyfogle, 2001; Wirzba, 2004).

The economic narrative. The economic narrative treats food as a commodity within a global economic system. This narrative frames food and the environment in relation to notions such as profit motives, expanding markets, and business models. It highlights the winners and losers, the supply and demand, and instabilities and contradictions that characterize marketplaces. The main actors in the economic narrative include workers, investors, regulators, lobbyists, and other players in the food economy. According to this telling, when agriculture and food production are subject to market forces, the plot thins: capitalism will always seek to maximize profits in rather predictable ways. Wages will be cut, regulations disregarded, the environment polluted, food cheapened, animals suffer, costs externalized while benefits are privatized. Food scares are retellings of the familiar story of the indifference of capitalist industrial power. We find this narrative more in journalism and advocacy literature than in the philosophical literature (Hauter, 2012; Robin, 2012; Kirby, 2010).[11] For example, the heartless corporation narrative animates a lot of recent food documentaries, such as *Cowspiracy, Hungry For Change, and That Sugar Film.* These films tell stories about agribusinesses willing to cut any corner and influence any political process that stands in the way of their vampire-like thirst for profits—even if they endanger health, torture animals, or destroy the environment. It is a potent narrative.

The developing world narrative. The developing world narrative highlights the affects of the global economy, the fate of women in poor countries, and the stark contrasts to life in Western nations. It serves as a counter-weight to the typically bourgeois narratives we encounter in the United States that tend to focus on consumer choice urban anonymity. The developing world narrative focuses on the lives of the roughly 2.5 billion or 40% of the world's population who are farmers in developing countries and who produce most of the world's food, including 90% of the food produced in Africa. The life expectancy, literacy, and standard of living of these farmers are low; the technologies, access to markets, and available infrastructure is poor (Rome, 2013).[12] The environmental problems in developing countries include overuse of natural resources, inability to invest in sustainable technologies, and poor environmental protections. In addition, most of these farmers are women (FAO, 2013).[13] The developing world narrative is rarely heard in United States except for the advocacy and outreach literatures. The narrative also is underrepresented in food and agriculture documentaries, where the focus is usually on the problems of industrialized agriculture and what we in the West might do about it. However, the website of the Food and Agriculture Organization of the United Nations (www.fao.org) is replete with information from a global perspective. So is the website for the non-profit organization Heifer International (www.heifer.org).

The travelogue. The story of food begins on the farm and ends at the table. Along the way there is change, development, and transformation at every stage: planting, harvesting, rearing, slaughtering, processing, transporting, preparing, serving, spoiling, and so on. This kind of narrative follows the development of a food item in relation to the environment in order to highlight the key events or actors along the way. Often it serves a critical function by revealing what is hidden from consumers: we learn what actually happens on farms, ranches, processing plants, and other places most of us are ignorant of. The narrative works in two directions: as we witness the path that food takes from farm to table, we are invited to other worlds, where we might empathize with other humans and animals and to see for ourselves how our seemingly private acts of shopping and eating are connected to broader social and environmental issues. Pollan's *Omnivore's Dilemma* is a travelogue. He brings us to places we've never been so that we might be amazed and horrified by the origins and consequences of our food choices (Pollan, 2007).

All these narratives are by no means the only ones that shape our understanding of food, agriculture, and the environment. Others include religious narratives (for Christian narratives, see Fick, 2008; Davis, 2004; for Hindu, see Sandford, 2011; for Jewish, see Zamore, 2011)[14]; Marxists narratives (Foster, 2000; Magdoff, Foster, and Buttel, 2000); underdog justice narratives (Hesterman, 2011; Ackerman-Leist, 2013); and cautionary tales (Chiles, 2002; Tenner, 1997). These interpretive frameworks are not mutually exclusive; it is possible for events to be framed by more than one narrative at a time. Nor are narratives incompatible with traditional philosophical theories, moral judgments, or scientific explanations. At very least, narratives set the stage and determine the background context of relevance for actions and events. They complement but never replace judgments of truth or moral right. They are necessary but not sufficient in determining what things are, what took place, who was involved, and how we should act. Stories are, therefore, inseparable from establishing facts and making judgments about characters, historical events, and things that unfold over time (Kaplan, 2003; Griffin, 2013).[15]

The challenge of a narrative analysis of the relationship between food, agriculture, and the environment is to examine how they influence philosophical debates, public discourse, policymaking, consumer behavior, or any other topic about which stories might influence thought and action. A valuable research project would uncover implicit food narratives to assess their truth and moral claims, their strengths and weaknesses, their advantages and disadvantages, and their prejudices and presuppositions; that is to say, to interpret them. Such a research project will inevitably lead one outside of philosophy to other disciplines in the humanities, social and natural sciences, but so be it. The relationship between food and the environment is, after all, more than a philosophical issue.

NOTES

1. Baird Callicott called Tom Regan's view that biotic communities are best preserved when the rights of individual animals are respected "ecological illiteracy." The moral worth of an individual being should be assessed in relation to the ecosystem. Regan called Callicott's view "ecofascism" because it subordinated the rights of individuals to the whole. Callicott later attempted to reconcile individualistic animal ethics with holistic ecological ethics. See J. Baird Callicott, "Animal Liberation: A Triangular Affair," *Environmental Ethics* 2(1980): 311–388; Tom Regan, *The Case for Animal Rights* (Berkeley: University of California Press, 1983); J. Baird Callicott, *Beyond the Land Ethic: More Essays in Environmental Philosophy* (Albany: SUNY Press, 1990).
2. "Perceptions of the U.S. Food System: What and How Americans Think about Their Food." *W.K. Kellogg Foundation*, 2012; "Europeans, Agriculture, and the Common Agricultural Policy," *Eurobarometer* 80(2), 2013.
3. "Perceptions of the U.S. Food System," p. 29. "Report on the Results of the Public Consultation on the Review of the EU Policy on Organic Agriculture," *European Commission Directorate-General for Agriculture and Rural Development*, 2013, pp. 17–19.
4. "Perceptions of the U.S. Food System," 30.
5. "Perceptions of the U.S. Food System," 49.

6. "Perceptions of the U.S. Food System," 49–52.

7. "Perceptions of the U.S. Food System," 49–52.

8. For Ricoeur, narratives and stories, narrating and storytelling are more or less identical. Paul Ricoeur, *Time and Narrative,* Vol. 1, trans. Kathleen McLaughlin and David Pellauer (Chicago: University of Chicago Press, 1984).

9. For Genette, a plot organizes events into a story whose presentation takes place in a narrative, which can create various rhetorical effects. See Gerard Genette, *Narrative Discourse: An Essay in Method*, trans. Jane E. Lewin (Ithaca: Cornell University Press, 1983).

10. http://www.adm.com/en-US/responsibility/2013CorporateResponsibilityReport/

11. For example, Wenonah Hauter, *Foodopoly: The Battle over the Future of Food and Farming in America* (New York: New Press, 2012). Maria-Monique Robin, *The World According to Monsanto* (New York: New Press, 2012). David Kirby, *Animal Factory: The Looming Threat of Industrial Pig, Dairy, and Poultry Farms to Humans and the Environment* (New York: St. Martin's Press, 2010).

12. "FAO Statistical Yearbook 2013: World Food and Agriculture," The Food and Agriculture Organization of the United Nations (Rome, 2013).

13. "FAO Policy on Gender Equality: Attaining Food Security Goals in Agriculture and Rural Development," The Food and Agriculture Organization of the United Nations (Rome, 2013).

14. For Christian narratives, see Gary W. Fick, *Food, Farming, and Faith* (Albany: SUNY Press, 2008). Ellen F. Davis, *Scripture, Culture, and Agriculture: An Agrarian Reading of the Bible* (Albany: SUNY Press, 2004). For Hindu, A. Whitney Sandford, *Growing Stories from India: Religion and the Fate of Agriculture* (Lexington: University of Kentucky Press, 2011). For Jewish, Mary L. Zamore, ed. *The Sacred Table: Creating a Jewish Food Ethic* (New York: CCAR Press, 2011).

15. On how narratives relate to truth and judgment, see Ricoeur, *Time and Narrative*, vol. 1; Hilde Nelson, ed. *Stories and Their Limits.* David M. Kaplan, *Ricoeur's Critical Theory* (Albany: SUNY Press, 2003). Lisa Kern Griffin, "Narrative, Truth, and Trial." *Georgetown Law Journal* 101(281): 1–51.

References

Ackerman-Leist, P. (2013). *Rebuilding the Foodshed: How to Create Local, Sustainable and Secure Food Systems.* White River Junction, VT: Chelsea Green Publishing.

Berry, W. (1991). "The Pleasures of Eating." In *What Are People For?*, 145. New York: Counterpoint.

Blum, L. (1980). *Friendship, Altruism and Morality.* London: Routledge and Kegan Paul.

Callicott, J. B. (1980). "Animal Liberation: A Triangular Affair." *Environmental Ethics* 2: 311–388.

Callicott, J. B. (1990). *Beyond the Land Ethic: More Essays in Environmental Philosophy.* Albany: SUNY Press.

Charon, R., and Montello, M. (2002). *Stories Matter: The Role of Narratives in Medical Ethics.* New York: Routledge.

Cheney, J. (1989). "Postmodern Environmental Ethics: Ethics as Bioregional Narrative." *Environmental Ethics* 11: 117–134.

Chiles, J. R. (2002). *Inviting Disaster: Lessons from the Edge of Technology.* New York: HarperBusiness.

Danto, A. (1985). *Narration and Knowledge.* New York: Columbia University Press.

Davis, E. F. (2004). *Scripture, Culture, and Agriculture: An Agrarian Reading of the Bible.* Albany: SUNY Press.

Despommier, D. (2011). *The Vertical Farm: Feeding the World in the 21st Century.* New York: Picador.

Dyson, F. (2000). *The Sun, the Internet, and the Genome.* New York: Oxford Press.

"Europeans, Agriculture, and the Common Agricultural Policy," *Eurobarometer* 80.2, 2013.

"Report on the Results of the Public Consultation on the Review of the EU Policy on Organic Agriculture," *European Commission Directorate-General for Agriculture and Rural Development,* 2013.

"FAO Statistical Yearbook 2013: World Food and Agriculture," The Food and Agriculture Organization of the United Nations. Rome.

Fick, G. W. (2008). *Food, Farming, and Faith.* Albany: SUNY Press.

Fireman, G. D., McVay, T. E., and Flanagan, O. J. (eds.) (2003). *Narrative and Consciousness: Literature, Psychology, and the Brain.* New York: Oxford University Press.

Foster, J. B. (2000). *Marx's Ecology: Materialism and Nature.* New York: Monthly Review Press.

Frank, A. (1995). *The Wounded Storyteller: Body, Illness, and Ethics.* Chicago: The University of Chicago Press.

Frasier, V. (2001). "What's the Moral of the GM Food Story?" *Journal of Agricultural and Environmental Ethics* 14(2): 147–159.

Freedman, D. H. (2013). "The Truth about Genetically Modified Food." *Scientific American* 309(3): 80–85.

Freyfogle, E. T. (ed.) (2001). *The New Agrarianism: Land, Culture, and the Community of Life.* Washington, DC: Island Press.

Genette, G. (1983). *Narrative Discourse: An Essay in Method,* translated by J. E. Lewin. Ithaca: Cornell University Press.

Griffin, L. K. (2013). "Narrative, Truth, and Trial." *Georgetown Law Journal* 101(281): 1–51.

Hauter, W. (2012). *Foodopoly: The Battle over the Future of Food and Farming in America.* New York: New Press.

Hesterman, O. B. (2011). *Fair Food: Growing a Healthy, Sustainable Food System for All.* New York: Public Affairs.

Hutto, D. B. (2008). *Folk Psychological Narratives: The Sociocultural Basis for Understanding Reasons.* Cambridge: MIT Press.

Jefferson, V. (2003). "An Overview of the Genetically Modified Food Debate." In *Genetically Engineered Foods,* edited by N. Harris. San Diego: Greenhaven Press.

Kaplan, D. M. (2003). *Ricoeur's Critical Theory.* Albany: SUNY Press.

King, R. (1999). "Narrative, Imagination, and the Search for Intelligibility in Environmental Ethics." *Ethics and the Environment* 4(1): 23–38.

Kirby, D. (2010). *Animal Factory: The Looming Threat of Industrial Pig, Dairy, and Poultry Farms to Humans and the Environment.* New York: St. Martin's Press.

Knobloch, F. (1996). *The Culture of Wilderness.* Chapel Hill: University of North Carolina Press.

Liszka, J. (2003). "The Narrative Ethics of Leopold's Sand County Almanac." *Ethics and the Environment* 8(2): 42–70.

MacIntyre, A. (1981). *After Virtue: A Study in Moral Theory.* Notre Dame: University of Notre Dame Press.

Magdoff, F., Foster, J., and Buttel, F. H. (eds.) (2000). *Hungry for Profit: The Agribusiness Threat to Farmers, Food, and the Environment.* New York: Monthly Review Press.

Mason, J. (2005). *An Unnatural Order: Roots of our Destruction of Nature.* New York: Lantern Books.

Merchant, C. (1990). *The Death of Nature: Women, Ecology, and the Scientific Revolution.* New York: Harper Books.

Nelson, H. (ed.) (1997). *Stories and Their Limits: Narrative Approaches to Bioethics.* New York: Routledge.

Nussbaum, M. (1992). *Loves Knowledge: Essays on Philosophy and Literature.* New York: Oxford.

Nussbaum, M. (1998). *Cultivating Humanity: A Classical Defense of Reform of Liberal Education.* Cambridge: Harvard University Press.

Pollan, M. (2007). *The Omnivore's Dilemma: A Natural History in Four Meals.* New York: Penguin.

Pollan, M. (2009). *In Defense of Food: An Eater's Manifesto.* New York: Penguin.

Regan, T. (1983). *The Case for Animal Rights.* Berkeley: University of California Press.

Ricoeur, P. (1984). *Time and Narrative,* Vol. 1, translated by Kathleen McLaughlin and David Pellauer. Chicago: University of Chicago Press.

Ricoeur, P. (1992). *Oneself as Another,* translated by David Pellauer, 143. Chicago: University of Chicago Press.

Robin, M.-M. (2012). *The World According to Monsanto.* New York: New Press.

Sandford, A. W. (2011). *Growing Stories from India: Religion and the Fate of Agriculture.* Lexington: University of Kentucky Press.

Sanford, W. (2011). "Ethics, Narrative, and Agriculture: Transforming Agricultural Practice Through Ecological Imagination." *Journal of Agricultural and Environmental Ethics* 24(3): 283–303.

Swirski P. (2007). *Of Literature and Knowledge.* New York: Routledge.

Tenner, E. (1997). *Why Things Bite Back: Technology and the Revenge of Unintended Consequences.* New York: Vintage.

Walker, M. U. (1998). *Moral Understandings: A Feminist Study in Ethics.* New York: Routledge.

W. K. Kellogg Foundation (2012). "Perceptions of the U.S. Food System: What and How Americans Think about Their Food."

Wirzba, N. (ed.) (2004). *The Essential Agrarian Reader: The Future of Culture, Community, and the Land.* New York: Counterpoint.

Zamore, M. L. (ed.) (2011). *The Sacred Table: Creating a Jewish Food Ethic.* New York: CCAR Press.

··

CHAPTER 35

WATER ETHICS
Toward Ecological Cooperation

··

ANGELA KALLHOFF

WATER is the "bloodstream" of our planet (Ripl, 2003). This life-sustaining resource is endangered by processes of industrialization, population growth, and climate change. A water ethics discusses normative challenges inherent in the effects of pollution and scarcity. Yet this is only one side of the debate. Since water services are necessary for the survival of many organisms, not of humans alone, the relation between human interests and needs of non-human animals needs to be addressed, too. In particular, water is a common pool good. It is the material that constitutes groundwater and freshwater reservoirs, the seas, the lakes, and the rivers. Therefore, one of the most intriguing questions in water ethics is how two normative claims can simultaneously be met, even though they pull in two opposite directions. The first claim addresses legitimate interests of persons to utilize water as a life-sustaining resource; the second claim, instead, insists on the protection of a vulnerable good—even in the case that this does not meet human interests in utilizing water.

In this contribution, I shall respond to this situation in first discussing an approach to water ethics that focuses on its life-maintaining services to human beings. This is the discussion of water rights. Second, I shall outline an ecocentric water ethics. Cultural traditions and religious sources as well as recent approaches to ecological virtues underpin this line of thought. The first two approaches to water ethics represent what might be called extreme options: the first focusing exclusively on human interests, the second on non-instrumental values of water. The third section is dedicated to a discussion of water justice. In accordance with theories of environmental justice, a theory of water justice reaches beyond the distributive paradigm, which has dominated recent approaches to interpersonal justice. It defends a more comprehensive notion of justice, including interspecies and intergenerational fairness. This theory widens the focus of research, yet it still does not pay tribute to the tensions resulting from conflicting interests in a shared resource.

The fourth section develops an alternative perspective in water ethics by defending a common-goods approach to water. For two reasons, this is particularly convincing. First, it responds to the characteristics of water as a common good. Second, this approach does not rest on a singular normative principle, but addresses a triangle of normative claims instead, including fairness, care, and respect for water. Due to this complexity, the proceeding sections also serve as a preparation of this more comprehensive approach to water ethics.

1 A Human Right to Water

Access to clear and fresh water is a necessity for human beings. Presupposing that persons have a right to satisfy exigencies, a right to water will be included. In his defense of basic rights, Henry Shue (1996) follows this line of thought. He argues that rights are basic when "enjoyment to them is essential to the enjoyment of all other things" (Shue, 1996: 19). Basic rights comprise, inter alia, subsistence rights, whereas subsistence means unpolluted air, unpolluted water, adequate food, adequate clothing, adequate shelter, and minimal preventive public health care (Shue, 1996: 23). Following Shue, a right to unpolluted water is a basic human right. Moreover, it includes "justified demands for social guarantees against standard threats" (Shue, 1996: 34). Recently, water rights have also been reasoned as self-standing rights, belonging to a new group of environmental rights (Scanlon, Cassar, and Nemes, 2004; Gleick, 1998).

The approach to water rights combines two aspects. First, it implies that the right to water is a human right in the sense of something that each person is justified to claim for herself. A human right expresses universal, yet personal entitlements. Moreover, the right to water does not have to be glued to more fundamental rights, but instead meets the criteria of a self-standing group of rights, reasoned by means of "paramount moral importance" (Hayward, 2004: 47). Second, a right to water correlates with duties of political institutions; even though classified as a moral right, its consequences are political. This approach provides the justificatory background for soft and hard law sources, which translate a right to water into legal obligations, both on a national level and in international law—whereas customary law plays an important role (Kravchenko and Bonine, 2008: 113–146).[1]

Moreover, the content of a right to water has been spelled out in detail. Three dimensions have been highlighted: water needs to be *accessible*, that is: water resources need to be in safe reach for all, they need to be affordable to all, and they need to be accessible in law and fact; water needs to be given in *adequate quality*, it must be safe; water must be *accessible in a certain quantity*, granting sufficient and continuous measure for personal and domestic use (Scanlon, Cassar, and Nemes, 2004: 28). Even though the precise content is important for rendering a right to water precise, three arguments *against* a right to water also need to be acknowledged.

First, scholars criticize that a right to water rests on a resource-oriented approach to a natural good. While it highlights the needs of persons, it neglects two further perspectives: It remains silent on the needs of living beings that are non-human beings; and it remains silent on the necessities that result from keeping a complex natural system intact. In contrast to classical rights, environmental rights have two sides: they express justified claims of persons; simultaneously, they address environmental goods as intact resources (Shelton, 1991: 109, 117). This second aspect has been neglected. Second, the declaration of a right to water is not very helpful, unless "water" has been given further qualifications. Fresh water management is only a part of the problem of a fair water management system. Water materializes as freshwater resources, groundwater, water basins, rivers, the deep sea, and water cycles. In short: a water ethics needs to deal with different conflicts resulting from the diversity of water systems and water reservoirs. Third, the discussion of a right to water misses the point in another respect, too. Does a right to water include that each person—independently of her living place and her living conditions—has a right to clean water or merely unpolluted water? The focus on "safe water" appears to imply this: Persons have a right to "sufficiently clean" water; as long as pollution is below a level of safe water, this appears to be the case.

Even though these objections contribute to regarding a right to water in a critical light, the concept of a right to water still provides a baseline that defines a minimum moral requirement. It claims that to some degree all persons should have access to safe water as a life-sustaining resource. Yet the critical assessment also says that another perspective has not been taken seriously enough: this is the perspective which I shall address now. Water is more than a life-sustaining resource.

2 RESPECT FOR WATER

Water has been addressed in the narratives of cultures and religions (Shaw and Francis, 2008). They respond to water as a life-sustaining gift, yet in a different way than moral theory does. Some narratives contribute to regarding water as something very precious; other narratives point to the unique power of water. In many of the Western world's oldest myths such as those of ancient Mesopotamia and Greece, water is regarded as sacred. It gives birth to life. In Islam religion, water is explicitly considered to be a blessing from God. Until today, these presumptions have an influence on water law in the Arabic world (Naff and Dellapenna, 2002). Overall, water gives life and it is a blessing to humankind.

Drawing attention to water as a valuable resource has not been reserved to cultural narratives and to religions. Instead, it has also been reasoned in recent approaches to environmental ethics. Some scholars defend the view that water deserves an attitude that includes "compassionate retreat" (Brown and Schmidt, 2010), which is a reasonable attitude toward a good that has a value of its own (Armstrong, 2006). Yet presupposing something like an "intrinsic value" of water is difficult to reason. In the remainder of this section, I wish to highlight two ways of claiming respect for water that forgo a notion of "value" but might instead be a little closer to experiences with water.

Bernard Williams reminds us of a reasonable attitude to nature that responds to the fact that persons only have limited control of nature (Williams, 1995). The enormous destructive powers of water in flooding the land, in tsunamis and in extreme rainfalls, should not be forgotten here. Yet, it is not only fear, but also aesthetic appreciation that generates an attitude of respect, as for instance the beauty of waterfalls and of the seas. Captured by an experience of the sublime, the adequate response is profound respect. An attitude of respect has also been reasoned in the context of recent approaches to environmental virtues (Cafaro and Sandler, 2010; Leopold, 1949; Sandler, 2007). The virtue of humility, for instance, expresses respect for a natural good.

Theories claiming respect for water counterbalance anthropocentric theories that focus on human interests and human needs. They remind us of the powers, the beauty and the complexity of water. In particular, they provide an alternative to a resource-oriented approach, which acknowledges the value of water in terms of countable benefits. Yet one weakness of these theories is that they rely on premises that are not necessarily shared by many people. Cultures and religions, as well as ecocentric worldviews and virtue-ethics approaches, are not neutral but depend on sources that support a distinct set of values.

Recent approaches to environmental virtues contribute to transcending cultural lines and borders. Yet it is still an open question whether or not virtue theory can carry the weight of normative claims of a moral theory speaking about justice. In particular, a virtue ethics would have to define best practices in profiting from water. Possibly, a thorough discussion of how greed could be avoided and which role anti-domination might play in addressing water resources could accomplish this. At the very least, an approach to respect for water is an important reminder of aspects of nature that in industrialized societies have continuously been rendered invisible—maybe even inaccessible: the beauty of water, the specific qualities of water reservoirs, and the complexity of hydrological cycles.

3 WATER JUSTICE

So far, two general approaches to a water ethics have been discussed in terms of a right to water and in terms of respect for water. Another important aspect of water ethics is due to the fact that conflicts over water raise distinct distributive challenges. One answer to this has been the turn to theories that are more pragmatic in style and respond to situational exigencies (Kowarsch, 2011; Norton, 2005). Yet this does not render theories of justice superfluous. Instead, they can also be interpreted as supporting a modest, yet crucial role of ethics in addressing water shortages.

Unfortunately, there is no straightforward way to apply theories of justice to distributive principles for water resources. Instead, there are three major difficulties in applying approaches of justice in the context of water ethics: a misfit of the distributive paradigm, the need of local and temporal extension, and the need to rethink justice in terms of anti-dominion. I shall recall these difficulties in turn in order to explain how theories of distributive justice have been overhauled in order to address these issues; these extensions also prepare a theoretical shift in the next section, focusing on water as a common pool good. There are three major aspects in overhauling the distributive paradigm.

First, authors who discuss environmental justice challenge the distributive paradigm in that an approach to single items that can be produced and distributed does not fit the overall situation (Schlossberg, 2007: 11–44). In particular, natural resources are not products of cooperation, nor does the precondition of moderate scarcity apply (Baxter, 2005).[2] In many regions of the world, water is not scarce, but extreme scarcity and droughts, as well as extreme flooding, are frequent events; climate change is contributing to this development and to incidents of extreme weather events and water scarcity (Feldman, 2007: 1–22).

A second critique relates to the rather limited perspective of distributive justice in local and temporal terms. Some basic environmental problems are global problems. As a consequence, water justice needs to be reasoned in the context of an international and in the context of a cosmopolitan approach to ethics (Caney, 2005a; Pogge, 2001). Comparable to approaches to climate justice which defend a fair share of each person in a common resource (Caney, 2005b; Vanderheiden, 2008), a cosmopolitan approach to water justice will discuss principles of justice as related to a "global commons" (Buck, 1998). Moreover, the negative effects of mismanagement of water resource in the presence for future generations also need to be addressed. Therefore, an approach to intergenerational justice has to discuss forms of injustice that have been analyzed as "intergenerational buck-passing." This is a situation in which current generations benefit from resources, yet in benefiting they produce costs that all later groups of persons have to bear (Gardiner, 2011: 148–160). In order to avoid severe intergenerational injustice, it is obligatory to develop regimes that protect rivers, lakes, and the seas from overexploitation now.

A third critique says that distributive justice is right in addressing justice, yet the scope is ill-set. Justice in participating in natural resources needs to be addressed in terms of correcting unfair power-relations first. In particular, the claim of water justice is closely related to claims of the ending of unfair power-relations in exploiting nature (Martínez Alier, 2003). Ecofeminists connect that request with a comprehensive critique of a dualist and a dissociative worldview that results from male domination in the sciences and in politics (Plumwood, 1993). In order to prevent future water wars, feminists also recommend to account for the services of women in water supply adequately (Gaard, 2001; Shiva, 2005).[3] These claims for water justice are related to a more general theme, also traded under the name of "anti-dominion." In order to prevent status injuries (Schlossberg, 2007: 136–145), unfair power relations that favor access conditions to natural resources of select groups of persons need to be disclosed and corrected.

The outcome of the attempt to address water shortages and mismanagement of water resources in terms of distributive justice is twofold: First, the distributive paradigm is not particularly convincing in addressing conflicts over resources that cannot be resolved by distributing water resources. This critique also resonates with the discussion of water rights in section 1. Second, more attention needs to be paid to the fact that water systems and water resources are qualitatively distinct goods.

4 Ecological Cooperation

In order to come closer to the concrete challenges that a water ethics needs to address, the first step is an acknowledgment of the fact that the normative challenges cover a wide range of different scenarios. Examples comprise conflicts in freshwater supply, overexploitation of the fishing stocks in rivers and lakes, groundwater shortages caused by overexploitation by the private sector and by agriculture, transboundary water conflicts concerning lakes and rivers, the pollution of water reservoirs as in-pool pollution, and insufficient water management in areas of dense population (Kowarsch, 2011).[4] In order to measure critical limits of shortages and of degradation of water resources, a variety of indices has been developed. These indices include the "water footprint" (www.waterfootprint.org) measuring the amount of water needed for specific practices and processes of production; a "water poverty index" paying specific tribute to the close relationship between water supply and food safety (Lawrence, Meigh, and Sullivan, 2002), and the "aridity index" measuring the interdependence of climate data and water shortages (Thornthwaite, 1948; Vörösmarty et al., 2000). In addressing water as a systemic good, a key insight is the following: A water system can only be kept intact if the capacity to display ecofunctions that a water system is ready to display is not set at risk. In other words: the limits of resilience of water as a complex system need to be taken seriously (Falkenmark and Folke, 2002).

The conclusions from this description need to be drawn with caution. The shift from a general perspective to a context-sensitive perspective is not necessarily paramount to the

shift from a principled account of water ethics to a pragmatic or straightforwardly political account (Broome, 2012; Posner and Sunstein, 2008; Posner, 2004).[5] Instead, water ethics
takes into account an analysis of the drivers for the depletion of water resources on a more
general level. Threats to the resilience of water resources and water systems do not necessarily result from climate change or from overconsumption. Instead, they also result from either
mutually incompatible or straightforwardly hazardous practices in profiting from water,
including in-pool pollution. Because of indivisibility and a lack of regular entrance barriers,
water resources are particularly vulnerable to the "tragedies of the commons" (Hardin, 1968;
Jamieson, 2008: 14–15). The analysis of water in terms of a public good (Kallhoff, 2011, 2012)
is particularly helpful not only in understanding the existing shortfalls in protecting water
from environmental hazard, but also in developing a future-looking normative approach to
water ethics.

Persons and institutions that are captured in a dilemmatic structure of collective action
cannot escape the "tragedy of the commons," unless they subscribe to rules that define best
practices in addressing the good (Petrella, 2001).[6] Following proposals in social philosophy,
joint agency provides an alternative to self-interest actions of individuals and groups. In particular, collective agency differs in basic respects from the actions of individuals (Gilbert,
2006; Tuomela, 2002, 2012). A shared vision of an intended good, an *ethos*, is a central element in processes of group formation. Once persons have constituted a group, the ethos has
also reason-giving power for future action (Tuomela, 2003, 2012).[7] Members of a group are
likely to engage in activities that count as "working together"; by doing their activities, they
contribute to realizing a shared end.

This model can also be reasoned in the context of cooperation that aims at profiting intelligently from a joint resource and at paying respect to non-instrumental values of a natural
good. A precondition is that persons are aware of their dependency on water and, moreover, of their mutual dependency (Poteete and Janssen, 2010). This supports a framework
that might not contribute to an equal share but to fair practices in profiting from a shared
resource. Moreover, it contributes to rethinking practices of justified enclosure as well as
cooperative schemes for outcomes that persons can also accept for normative reasons
(Kallhoff, 2012, 2014).

A water ethics has an important role to play in explaining this model of joint agency as
well as in informing the ethos. The ethos exposes a normative vision of best current and
future practices in profiting from a shared natural good. It has three pillars. First, it declares
the integrity of a water system as a core value that deserves moral respect. "Integrity" has an
empirical side in terms of essential ecofunctions (Costanza et al., 1998). Integrity is endangered by severe incidents of stress, overexploitation, or pollution. Second, the ethos says that
caring for a shared natural resource is the right attitude of all profiteers from that resource.
Care includes a thorough and mindful appreciation of water in profiting from it. It relates to
the experiences and the knowledge of persons and groups of persons who are accustomed
to a common good (McEwan and Goodman, 2010). In particular, it addresses dependency
of a shared good and appreciation for that good in normative terms. Third, the ethos claims
fairness in profiting from water resources in two respects: as procedural fairness in decision-
making processes (Engel and Westra, 2010) and as a fair share in terms of a basic right to
water (see section 1). The ethos does not give strict principles, but instead includes basic normative yardsticks in profiting from water. It is left to team reasoning (Sugden, 2003) within
the group to develop a fine-grained approach to a specific water resource or water cycle. Yet

it says that it is necessary to recall a triangle of normative perspectives in order to succeed in ecological cooperation, namely integrity of a shared good, care for it, and fairness in profiting from it.

This approach to water ethics provides a distinct focus. It says that ecological cooperation is possible in resolving conflicts within the group of profiteers; its precondition is the willingness to comply with a shared ecological ethos.[8] It is particularly important to invite persons and parties to join the group that identifies with an ecological ethos. A necessary prerequisite is that the claims of the "ethos" are fair and not overdemanding. Moreover, the deep dependency on a critical resource needs to be rendered continuously visible.

5 CONCLUSION

In this contribution, I have discussed four alternative approaches to a water ethics. First, a theory of water rights lays emphasis on a fair share of each person in safe water supply. A critical assessment comes to the conclusion that this perspective on water as a resource is important; yet it is too limited in addressing the complexities of water supply, water hazard, and water scarcity. Second, a theory of respect for water, instead, focuses on the values of water—not as a resource, but as something that deserves appreciation, perhaps even the attitude of humility. It is one of the central questions of whether or not that approach can be translated into a virtue ethics that pays respect to cultural differences. Third, I have argued that approaches to justice are important, yet they undergo major theoretical transformation if applied to environmental goods. They need to integrate an extended temporal and local frame; they need to respond to claims of justice in terms of correcting unfair power-relations; and they need to get beyond a simplistic distributive paradigm. Fourth, I have outlined an approach to water that focuses on the characteristics of a common good.

The fourth approach teaches an important lesson about the debate on water ethics. There is no reason to think of the sketched approaches to water ethics as mutually exclusive programs. Instead, these approaches are interrelated in many different ways. In particular, an approach to water as a common good resonates with basic principles of fairness, with care as an environmental virtue, and with respect for the integrity of water as a common pool good. The major shift that a theory of collective agency provides is the following: An ecological ethos that is reasoned in the context of a water ethics provides the backdrop both for processes of group-formation and for acting together. As the examples at the end of section 4 demonstrated, this ethos is not the only driving force for collective agency. Instead, persons would be wise to work together in addressing a resource that provides important services, both in terms of life-supporting services and in terms of services for sustaining cultural and economic practices.

Two further lessons that go beyond water ethics can also be learned from these discourses. In water ethics, it is obligatory to substitute distributive justice by a more content-rich idea of justice. The latter includes concepts of the integrity of water systems and its manifold value, water as a living space and nutrient of many diverse living entities. Moreover, water ethics contributes to the insight that the overall perspective on natural goods needs to be overhauled consequently. Neither human interests nor preferences figure as exclusive backdrop for addressing best practices. Instead, scholars are asked to draw a normative map related to values and interests in nature first—a map that highlights vulnerabilities of natural resources as well as the sources of value of these goods in concrete scenarios. The corresponding ethos is not one-dimensional; instead, it includes the value of integrity as well as approaches to an attitude of care and procedural fairness.

NOTES

1. A right to water has recently been enshrined in the "General Comment No. 15 (2002): The Right to Water (arts. 11 and 12) of the International Covenant on Economic, Social and Cultural Rights" (Committee on Economic, Social and Cultural Rights, 2003). The "Human Right to Water and Sanitation" has been accepted by the United Nations General Assembly. See www.un.org/ga/search/view_doc.; access: December, 16, 2013.
2. As a response, authors have worked on a theory of ecological justice that breaks with the distributive paradigm, as for instance (Baxter, 2005).
3. Scholars who defend a feminist approach to water justice also demand the overhaul of existing law in favor of women's rights and the rights of indigenous people, i.e., in stopping privatization of water resources (Shiva, 2005).
4. For an overview over the main fields of water problems and an empirical analysis of these fields, see (Kowarsch, 2011).
5. The two most important accounts that support this step are theories focusing on cost-benefit-analysis in developing policy instruments and theories that subscribe to an over-all utilitarian framework. Theories that subscribe to one of the two strategies have been developed by Broome (2012), Posner and Sunstein (2008), and Posner (2004).
6. For an example, see rules and principles in the "Water Manifesto" (Petrella, 2001).
7. Note that the approach to group agency does not necessarily presuppose existing groups; instead, it works on a looser term of "working together." In particular, the shift from a perspective on persons to groups is not a mystical fact, but rather can be explained as a shift from I-reasoning to We-reasoning (see Tuomela, 2003; Tuomela, 2012).
8. A similar shift has already been reasoned by Elinor Ostrom; yet Ostrom lays emphasis on two different facts: she draws on the capacity of local communities to develop rules that govern a common natural good; and she draws on a situation in which the community is dependent on a resource in terms of food production and lifestock (Ostrom, 1990).

REFERENCES

Armstrong, A. C. (2006). "Ethical Issues in Water Use and Sustainability." *Area* 38(1): 9–15.

Baxter, B. (2005). *A Theory of Ecological Justice*. Routledge Research in Environmental Politics. London, New York: Routledge.

Broome, J. (2012). *Climate Matters. Ethics in a Warming World*. Amnesty International Global Ethics Series. New York, London: W. W. Norton & Company.

Brown, P. G., Schmidt, J. (2010). "An Ethic of Compassionate Retreat." In *Water Ethics: Foundational Readings for Students and Professionals*, edited by P. G. Brown, G. Peter, and J. Schmidt, 265–286. Washington, D. C., Covelo, CA, London, England: Island Press.

Buck, S. J. (1998). *The Global Commons: An Introduction*. Foreword by Elinor Ostrom. Washington, D. C., Covelo, CA: Island Press.

Cafaro, P., and Sandler, R. (eds.) (2010). "Virtue Ethics and the Environment." Repr. from *Journal of Agricultural and Environmental Ethics*, 23 (1–2), 2010. Dordrecht: Springer.

Caney, S. (2005a). *Justice beyond Borders: A Global Political Theory*. Oxford, England, New York, NY: Oxford University Press.

Caney, S. (2005b). "Cosmopolitan Justice, Responsibility, and Global Climate Change." *Leiden Journal of International Law* 18(4): 747–775.

Committee on Economic, Social, and Cultural Rights (2003). General Comment No. 15 (2002): "The Right to Water (arts. 11 and 12 of the International Covenant on Economic, Social and Cultural Rights" (www.unhchr.ch/tbs/doc.nsf/0/a5458d1d1bbd713fc1256cc40038 9e94/$FILE/G0340229.pdf; access: December 16, 2013).

Costanza, R., et al. (1998). "The Value of the World's Ecosystem Services and Natural Capital." *Ecological Economics* 25(1): 3–15.

Engel, J. R., and Westra, L. (2010). *Democracy, Ecological Integrity, and International Law*. Newcastle: Cambridge Scholars Publishing.

Falkenmark, M., and Folke, C. (2002). "The Ethics of Socio-Ecohydrological Catchment Management: Towards Hydrosolidarity." *Hydrology and Earth System Sciences* 6(1): 1–9.

Feldman, D. L. (2007). *Water Policy for Sustainable Development*. Baltimore: Johns Hopkins University Press.

Gaard, G. (2001). "Women, Water, Energy: An Ecofeminist Approach." *Organization and Environment* 14(20): 157–172.

Gardiner, S. M. (2011). *A Perfect Moral Storm. The Ethical Tragedy of Climate Change*. Oxford, New York: Oxford University Press.

Gilbert, M. P. (2006). "Rationality in Collective Action." *Philosophy of the Social Sciences* 36(1): 3–17.

Gleick, P. H. (1998). "The Human Right to Water." *Water Policy* 1: 487–503.

Hardin, G. (1968). "The Tragedy of the Commons." *Science* 162 (3859): 1243–1248.

Hayward, T. (2004). *Constitutional Environmental Rights*. Oxford/New York: Oxford University Press.

Jamieson, D. (2008). *Ethics and the Environment: An Introduction*. Cambridge: Cambridge University Press.

Kallhoff, A. (2011). *Why Democracy Needs Public Goods*. Lanham, Md: Lexington, a division of Rowman & Littlefield.

Kallhoff, A. (2012). "Addressing the Commons: Normative Approaches to Common Pool Resources." In *Climate Change and Sustainable Development: Ethical Perspectives on Land Use and Food Production*, edited by T. Potthast and S. Meisch, 63–68. Wageningen: Wageningen Press.

Kallhoff, A. (2014). "Water Justice: A Multilayer Term and Its Role in Cooperation." In *Analyse & Kritik*, 36 (2): 367–382.

Kowarsch, M., ed. (2011). Water Management Options in a Globalised World. Proceedings of an International Scientific Workshop, 20–23 June 2011, Bad Schönbrunn. Institute for Social and Developmental Studies (IGP) at the Munich School of Philosophy.

Kravchenko, S., and Bonine, J. E. (2008). *Human Rights and the Environment: Cases, Law, and Policy*. Durham, NC: Carolina Academic Press.

Lawrence, P., Meigh, J., and Sullivan, C. (2002). *The Water Poverty Index: An International Comparison*. Keele Economics Research Papers. Newcastle-under-Lyme: Keyle University.

Leopold, A. (1949). *A Sand County Almanac*. Oxford: Oxford University Press.

Martínez Alier, J. (2003). *The Environmentalism of the Poor: A Study of Ecological Conflicts and Valuation*. Cheltenham: Edward Elgar.

McEwan, C., and Goodman, M. K. (2010). "Pace Geography and the Ethics of Care: Introductory Remarks on the Geographies of Ethics, Responsibility, and Care." *Ethics, Policy & Environment* 13(2): 103–112.

Naff, T., and Dellapenna, J. (2002). "Can There Be Confluence? A Comparative Consideration of Western and Islamic Fresh Water Law." *Water Policy* 4: 465–489.

Norton, B. G. (2005). *Sustainability: A Philosophy of Adaptive Ecosystem Management*. Chicago: University of Chicago Press.

Ostrom, E. (1990). *Governing the Commons. The Evolution of Institutions for Collective Action*. Cambridge, New York: Cambridge University Press.

Petrella, R. (2001). *The Water Manifesto: Arguments for a World Water Contract*, translated by P. Camiller. New York: Palgrave.

Plumwood, V. (1993). *Feminism and the Mastery of Nature*. London, New York: Routledge.

Pogge, T. (2001). "Eradicating Systemic Poverty: Brief for a Global Resources Dividend." *Journal of Human Development* 2(1): 59–77.

Posner, R. A. (2004). *Catastrophe: Risk and Response*. Oxford: Oxford University Press.

Posner, E., and Sunstein, C. (2008). "Climate Change Justice." *Georgetown Law Journal* 96: 1565–1612.

Poteete, A. R., and Janssen, M. A. (2010). *Working Together: Collective Action, the Commons, and Multiple Methods in Practice*. Princeton: Princeton University Press.

Ripl, W. (2003). "Water: The Bloodstream of the Biosphere." *Philosophical Transactions of the Royal Society of London, Biological Sciences* 358: 1921–1934.

Sandler, R. L. (2007). *Character and Environment: A Virtue-Oriented Approach to Environmental Ethics*. New York: Columbia University Press.

Scanlon, J., Cassar, A., and Nemes, N. (2004). *Water as Human Right?* IUCN Environmental Policy and Law Paper 51. IUCN—The World Conservation Union.

Schlossberg, D. (2007). *Defining Environmental Justice. Theories, Movements, and Nature*. Oxford, New York: Oxford University Press.

Shaw, S., and Francis, A., eds. (2008). *Deep Blue: Critical Reflections on Nature, Religion, and Water*. London: Equinox.

Shelton, D. (1991). "Human Rights, Environmental Rights, and the Right to Environment." *Stanford Journal of International Law* 28(103): 103–138.

Shiva, V. (2005). *Globalization's New Wars: Seed, Water, and Life Forms*. New Delhi: Women Unlimited.

Shue, H. (1996). *Basic Rights. Subsistence, Affluence, and U. S. Foreign Policy*. Princeton: Princeton University Press.

Sugden, R. (2003). "The Logic of Team Reasoning." *Philosophical Explorations: An International Journal for the Philosophy of Mind and Action* 6: 165–181.

Thornthwaite, C. W. (1948). "An Approach Toward a Rational Classification of Climate." *Geographical Review* 38: 55–94.

Tuomela, R. (2002). *The Philosophy of Sociality: The Shared Point of View*. Cambridge: Cambridge University Press.

Tuomela, R. (2003). "The We-Mode and the I-Mode." In *Socializing Metaphysics: The Nature of Social Reality*, edited by F. Schmitt, 93–127. Lanham, Md.: Rowman & Littlefield.

Tuomela, R. (2012). "Group Reasons." *Philosophical Issues* 22(1): 402–418.

Vanderheiden, S. (2008). *Atmospheric Justice: A Political Theory of Climate Change.* Oxford: Oxford University Press.

Vörösmarty, C. J., Green, P., Salisbury, R., and Lammers, R. (2000). "Global Water Resources: Vulnerability from Climate Change and Population Growth." *Science* 289: 284–288.

Williams, B. (1995). "Must a Concern for the Environment Be Centred on Human Beings?" In *Making Sense of Humanity and Other Philosophical Papers*, 233–240. Cambridge: Cambridge University Press.

CHAPTER 36

....

ANTHROPOGENIC MASS EXTINCTION

The Science, the Ethics, and the Civics

....

JEREMY DAVID BENDIK-KEYMER
AND CHRIS HAUFE

1 Mass Extinction

....

ONE of the most striking features of the fossil record is how it registers the sudden and geographically widespread extermination of higher taxonomic groups, extinguishing effectively unrelated groups simultaneously. These are the so-called *mass extinctions*, a handful of biologically destructive events in the history of life that have been precipitated by environmental perturbations on a global scale.

The understanding of mass extinction as a distinctive phenomenon began to accumulate in the 1950s, accelerating with the 1980 discovery of a catastrophic impact event that killed the dinosaurs. We can now point to 18 mass extinction events in the fossil record (Bambach, 2006), five of which have seen the number of species on Earth reduced by 75% or more.

The last of these "Big Five" mass extinction events took place 65 million years ago (mya) at the end of the Cretaceous period. The dominant opinion is that a meteorite more than 6 miles (10km) in diameter struck the Yucatan peninsula and set off a chain reaction that would eventually drive the dinosaurs and 76% of all species then living to extinction. However, none of the other Big Five mass extinctions can be directly linked to rocks from the sky, and paleontologists generally agree that extraterrestrial causes are not necessary to produce the level of destruction witnessed at the end of the Cretaceous. Indeed, the primary cause of the end-Permian extinction (~251 mya)—which left only 4% of species alive—is currently thought to have been a series of effusive volcanic eruptions that took place in Siberia over about one million years (Erwin, 2006, chapter 2).

How do mass extinction events work, and how do they differ from "background" times in which extinction still occurs regularly but not on the scale that characterizes these events? There is no consensus for any of the Big Five as to what factors triggered the sharp acceleration in extinctions (even the Cretaceous impact hypothesis has its skeptics (e.g., Keller,

2008), but there is wide agreement that the unique form and scale of extinction seen during mass extinctions is of a special kind.

One feature of that kind is the extinction of widespread species (Raup, 1991: 182). Call this the *widespread extinction criterion*. Ecological and paleontological evidence both suggest that the extinction of a species with a large geographic range is a biologically rare event—indeed, ecologist Daniel Simberloff has called species that are widespread "effectively immortal" (Simberloff, 1994: 165). Normally, a genus composed of widespread species will long outlive one composed of a more range-restricted species. But not during mass extinctions. Having widespread species at in the end-Cretaceous did not prolong a genus's life (Jablonski, 1986).

Another feature of mass extinction is the sheer magnitude of species extinctions. Call this the *magnitude criterion*. Raup (1991) produces a "kill curve" for Phanerozoic marine life, showing how often an extinction event of a given magnitude comes around. On average, there has been an extinction event every million years in which roughly 5% of species are wiped out. In contemporary terms, that would be like 100,000 of the named, extant species going extinct in a single event. But that would be mild by comparison to even the smallest clearly identifiable of the Big Five mass extinctions, the Pliocene event. The time between truly epic mass extinctions, like the end-Cretaceous extinction, is upward of 100 million years. Something like the end-Permian extinction can be expected to happen just once every several billion years (Raup, 1991: 44). These numbers suggest that the circumstances required to produce the number of species deaths suffered during the Big Five mass extinctions are not something the Earth has an easy time generating.

The third and last feature is the peculiar form of extinction that we find only during mass extinctions, which typically see the simultaneous extinction of many ecologically dissimilar and effectively unrelated higher taxonomic groups: genera (sets of species), families (sets of genera), and orders (sets of families).[1] Call this the *dissimilar groups criterion*. In the general case, we know that the odds of chopping off an entire branch of the evolutionary tree are very low unless the species on that branch are very similar ecologically (Green et al., 2011). We also know that the odds of ecological similarity are lower if species are unrelated. Since extinguishing a higher-level taxonomic group (which would be more deeply branched according to the tree metaphor) means extinguishing every member of every species in that group, we know that the extinction of a higher-level/more deeply branching group is a very special event. Yet each of these is part of the standard mass extinction. The impact that killed over 1,000 dinosaur genera also killed 60% of calcareous sponge genera—two groups that have separated by almost a billion years of evolutionary history with nothing in common ecologically (Bambach, 2006: 140). It is important to appreciate how difficult this is to do. As Raup (1991: 183) observes, "Even extinction mechanisms that cause the collapse of a whole ecosystem rarely affect more than one basic habitat." By contrast, the sort of perturbations required to extinguish groups as phylogenetically and ecologically distinct as sponges and dinosaurs in a single event disrupt very different ecologies and very distant ecosystems.

Each one of these phenomena—extinction of geographically widespread species, extinction of very high numbers of species, and extinction of phylogenetically and ecologically distinct higher taxonomic groups—is a low-probability event. The fact that all three are routine features of mass extinction events should give the reader a sense not only of the extreme improbability of generating these types of events, but also of the breadth and magnitude of the catastrophe required to do so. This is particularly true of the Big Five. Only five times in the last 540 million years has life on Earth been so difficult that >75% of species went extinct. During the end-Permian, a Siberian region roughly the size of Mexico had to be covered in lava nearly a mile thick in some places to make the atmosphere inhospitable enough to extinguish some 95% of species (Erwin, 2006, chapter 2). In the end-Cretaceous event, a meteor the size of a city had to crash to Earth. Generally speaking, it takes something historically unprecedented or extremely violent to achieve the extinction rates that characterize these events. But in the case of the end-Permian extinction event, a million-year ooze of lava sufficed: Earth's ecology was not prepared for it.

Are we today at the outer edge of a mass extinction event caused by *homo sapiens'* population growth and industrial economy, with all the effects that these two stressors on habitat and the climate involve? One difficulty involved in answering this question concerns the historical formation of the scientific discourse around mass extinctions, which evolved alongside paleontology as one of the discourses that brought paleontology into its own as a discipline. Technically, a mass extinction—understood as a paleontological concept—depends on an evidentiary basis in the fossil record of durably skeletonized marine invertebrate genera. This means that other indicators of elevated extinction rates are normally not considered relevant to the determination of a mass extinction (cf. Barnosky et al. 2011). But the fossil record of our time is still in the process of sedimenting. We do not have it yet. Given that we cannot know the fossil record of durably skeletonized marine invertebrate genera for our present time, we seem to have no short-term, immanent method for judging whether we are entering an anthropogenic mass extinction.

1.1 Industrialism

Be that as it may, the current rates of extinction among other forms of life are alarming enough to suggest to many scientists that we are uncomfortably close to entering a new mass extinction event. Gorke (2003) lists a number of causes of anthropogenic elevated extinction, which he appears to link generally to humankind, but the main cause is habitat destruction from a variety of causes related to the deadly intersection of (a) human population growth with (b) an extractive and polluting economy. Both (a) and (b) are the result of the massive, technological potential of modern industrial economies—here, no fundamental difference between capitalism and the late, state-centric communism are noticeable (Jonas, 1984). Earlier technology (e.g., weapons for killing at a distance some 11,000 years ago or agriculture beginning at the dawn of recorded human history) contributed to elevating extinction rates on Earth. But nothing has made mass extinction more likely than the unintended effects of the industrial age, now expanded globally in the age of information through a system of extractive, polluting, corporate, capitalist production (Castells, 1996).

It is important to embed the ethical considerations we address within this social framework, a framework we call for short *industrialism*. Societies that resist or minimize (with difficulty) their relation to mass-scale, industrial extraction and pollution are not to blame for contributing to the risk of mass extinction. At the same time, any society that benefits from such an economy, growing in population exponentially for instance, is still part of the dynamic contributing to mass extinction and in that sense is still to blame. We should also realize that most nations of the globe contribute in some way to global, industrial economy.

Today, we are faced with a global economy that, by being collectively mismanaged and by misconstruing its ethical relation to life on Earth and to future human beings is prospering in the present while risking a mass extinction in the future. Gardiner (2011) calls this "front-loading." Until we manage to change the form of economy that currently manifests our industrial mismanagement—changing, too, the short time scales, lack of collective action, abstract form of value, and other related structural and conceptual problems of corporate capitalism in the context of actual Earth ecologies—we will continue headlong into a mass extinction (Bendik-Keymer, 2012). The ethical reasoning this handbook offers should be used to explain why changing our political economic form on a planetary scale is so important.

1.2 Autodestruction

When a mass extinction takes place, the ecosystems that enable the current round of life on Earth disintegrate as food chains collapse. The systems of life enabling civilization change. Houses of cards fall down. The planetary disintegration of the ecosystems enabling life as we know it undermines what we might call *the standard conditions* for human life, and the question is whether the result of this undermining also undermines a safe operating space for humankind (Rocktröm et al., 2009). Some paleontologists think that it would, while other scientists who work on the issue think (1) that we know too little of how the extinction would unravel the current age of life on Earth and (2) that human technological capacity is remarkably quick to develop. Nonetheless, the range is dire—from the mass extinction involving an extinction event for *homo sapiens* to the mass extinction involving a serious undermining of the carrying capacity of the ecosystems on which we have historically depended. All this leaves to the side, as well, the status of non-human species, which many have value on their own (Rolston III, 2012).

A number of issues arise around the threat of mass extinction that are addressed elsewhere in this handbook.

1. *The conditions of agency.* Seemingly many necessary conditions of human agency are threatened by the cascade into a mass extinction and *mutadis mutandis* by an elevated extinction event as it becomes more and more severe. We need only to consider threats to food supplies and the ecosystem services on which we depend to imagine this (cf. Holland, 2012). The process leading to a mass extinction involves the elimination of biological families and orders, some of which can be crucial to human life as we know it. The wealthy may be able to survive, but the global poor (who exist within highly developed nations as well as in underdeveloped ones) may find themselves increasingly hard pressed to find food, materials for living, and to continue many traditional ways of life. The flourishing of the global poor is likely to be challenged in many ways, and this even more given intensified competition and violence over dwindling resources. Insofar as there are ethical issues arising from a threat to health, happiness, human development, or the ability to exercise substantive freedoms, anthropogenic mass extinction and even elevated extinction events raise them (cf. Nussbaum, 2011). Accordingly, the environmental threats to human agency discussed in many other places in this handbook should be brought to bear on

any discussion of the ethics surrounding anthropogenic mass extinction, with a clear sense of the scale and irreversibility of the extinction event in mind.

2. *Cultural value.* In so far as there are ethical questions around the cultural (including aesthetic or religious) value of biological and even geological nature, anthropogenic mass extinction matters. Periods of mass extinction effectively reshape the biosphere which, being in concert with Earth's geology, affects the geosphere as well. In so far as people hold parts of either the biosphere or geosphere to be valuable for aesthetic or cultural reasons, anthropogenic mass extinctions threatens much of value. Remember how Leopold (1948) noticed that culling wolves led to the erosion of topsoil when uncontrolled elk ate away trees whose roots held the soil firm? Imagine this kind of dynamic on a massively larger scale. Accordingly, one should apply the axiological concerns addressed elsewhere in this handbook to anthropogenic mass extinction, keeping in mind as always the scale and irreversibility of mass extinction.

3. *Environmental justice.* Insofar as any of the matters of agency or of cultural value are also concerns of justice, anthropogenic mass extinction raises significant questions of justice. Problems of intergenerational justice or of global justice resulting from a global environmental problem that is itself caused by our contemporary industrial economy apply to anthropogenic mass extinction. If we industrial humans cause a mass extinction, we affect people globally and, irreversibly, into the rest of the future of humankind. This effect is categorically different in the case of mass extinction than in the case of making individual, valuable species go extinct. Mass extinction produces ecological chaos. This is an effect of a different kind than the loss of individually valuable species, although their loss can also involve issues of justice. Accordingly, the discussions relating to these issues of justice discussed elsewhere in this handbook should be consulted when considering the ethics of anthropogenic mass extinction. Mass extinction is an *amplifier* of many kinds of environmental problems and is itself a severe matter of justice: what right have we industrial beneficiaries to enjoy an Earth that can easily support us when our actions going forward risk an Earth whose ecosystems have disintegrated on a planetary scale?

4. *The moral corruption of techno-optimism.* Will technology provide us with the silver bullet to overcome a trophic level cascade into mass extinction? The promise of a technological solution that will be able to stop mass extinction raises speculative questions that are addressed under the current technological fix of climate change by geoengineering. Even more so than with geoengineering currently, reversing a trophic level collapse at a global scale is mere science fiction at present. We would be morally corrupt to expect it.

Autodestruction. The four previous issues are common in environmental ethics. But not the most extreme case that attends the threat of mass extinction: anthropogenic mass extinction risks the unintended destruction of the human species. Clearly, there are ways some form of technology could kill the human species—for example, nuclear holocaust or bioengineered pandemic. But of the major environmental issues discussed in this handbook, perhaps only mass extinction involves the plausible risk of killing our kind and this due not to a bomb or a virus but to the grinding, massive operations of a form of economy and of society—something entirely banal. What is at stake ethically in killing ourselves as a species due to a banal social form?

The first question we have to face is whether there is anything ethically specific involved in putting an end to humankind, that is, our life form, above and beyond the wrongs that may be involved in the death of each individual. We are searching for whether there is an order of wrong that shifts in scale and focus to the level of the species (cf. Sandler, 2012). Would human species autodestruction shift the kind of wrong akin to the shift when we move from, for example, interpersonal crimes to crimes against humanity? Human species autodestruction would appear to be a *wrong in its own category*. The wrong is the wrong of putting an end to humankind and all that is of value in it. This is a *cataclysmic wrong*. It is a wrong at the level of the whole, not concerning individuals. Much work could be done to conceptualize and specify the logic of this kind of wrong in the context of mass extinction studies (cf. Hatley, 2012).

2 THE BANALITY OF EVIL

Whereas moving headlong into an elevated extinction event with the prospect of increasing the magnitude, range, and taxonomic reach of the extinction we cause is most *disturbing* when one speculates as an alarmist about human species autodestruction, moving headlong into our elevated extinction event is the most *morally objectionable* when one considers what it shows about our global economy. Our current global order appears as immoral when one considers it as leading plausibly to the edge of a mass extinction. Neiman (2002) understands evil as whatever threatens the sense of human life as a whole. To be evil, a form of society—including what it permits and pursues economically—must threaten the sense of human life as a whole. Threatening anthropogenic mass extinction does this.

It destroys the conditions of sense. First, an anthropogenic mass extinction would undermine the sense we make of human life by risking human species autodestruction unintentionally. There can be no sense of human life if there is no human life.

It destroys the backgrounds, sites, and objects of sense. Second, anthropogenic mass extinction would undermine all the ongoing meaning (including the valuable meaning) associated with the species and ecologies that are extinguished or collapse during a mass extinction event. As discussed above, mass extinction events reshape the entire biological fabric of the Earth and bear on many geological processes as well. The current system of life changes. Mass extinction events result in an unfamiliar Earth. This is sense-undermining, and it would be all the more so in that we have unintentionally caused it while trying to live a life that makes sense in the world. It is important to note, too, that many—in our view legitimate—concerns about the intrinsic value of non-human nature reside here as well; for the bearers of intrinsic value extinguished in a mass extinction would take much meaning with them. We would lose so many life forms that are good in themselves. Moreover, any ongoing meaning that is associated with how we should relate to such intrinsically valuable life forms would disappear also. All we would have would be historical memory—a ghost story and its shadow. So much ritual, literature, and music and so many family albums would become dead forms, dusty memories. If it is callous, thoughtless, unkind, violent, wanton, or selfish of us to extinguish intrinsically valuable life, then anthropogenic mass extinction would also undermine the meaning of our character, showing us to be callous, thoughtless, unkind, violent, wanton, or selfish toward them and toward ourselves. Even self-hatred cannot produce such deracinating effects.

It destroys the sense of ourselves. Third, anthropogenic mass extinction would contradict any view of ourselves as relatively benign. If original sin has become a special metaphysical belief of only some religious believers, anthropogenic mass extinction raises the specter of our society being unintentionally but *characteristically destructive*. Our immoral flaw would then not reside in being human but in remaining passive to the lack of social regulation needed to produce a *postindustrial* global economy based on stable human population and renewable energy and products (the technosphere not extracting from the biosphere; Braungart and McDonough, 2002). It would reside in our failing to be active citizens who find a way to self-regulate on enough scales to keep ourselves globally within justifiable norms (cf. Scruton, 2012). The destruction most of us cause is senseless destruction in that we unintentionally do it by way of remaining docilely complicit in our existing system of production and waste and in our dominant unrestrained view of population growth, with little or no awareness, with no good justification, and with many ethical problems produced as a result, possibly including our own extinction. Such characteristic, senseless destruction undermines the sense of human life by introducing *societal level doubt* and overwhelming the capacities of individual human agents (cf. Gardiner, 2011).

The threefold evil we risk causing—of our own extinction, of destroying much of value in the bio- and geospheres, and of our society's characteristic destructiveness—is banal (Arendt, 2006). Evil is banal if and only if it arises, not from ill intentions or even obvious individual flaws but from everyday, seemingly acceptable social organization. Accordingly, banal evil is superficial, not demonic or deep. It arises from a social or institutional system, not an individual. The system of behavior that constitutes it appears familiar, acceptable, or even common sense. The things that go into making a banal evil can be trivial for an individual or even a locality. They can appear as routine duties for a functionary. On this formulation, environmental problems such as running headlong—business as usual—into a more and more widespread, massive, and taxonomically wide-reaching extinction event display the banality of evil. And we—certainly not as depersonalized as Adolf Eichmann—display how ordinary complicity in that evil can be. What the (not unreasonably) speculative risk of anthropogenic mass extinction shows us is that we have a civilizational disorder and that each of us in it who remain complicit within it suffer for want of a sound conscience (Bendik-Keymer, 2010).

3 ANTHROPONOMY

Faced with this diagnosis, one clear response is for us to learn to act collectively on a number of scales so as to be able to shape local, regional, and national government in such a way that we internalize responsibility for our unintentional consequences and deepen the sense of human life. This is a *civic* task. Anthropogenic mass extinction, like many planetary environmental problems, presents us with problems in science, in conservation, in ethics, and ultimately in politics. One of the merits of considering it is to underline the task of *anthroponomy*.

Anthroponomy is a civic task demanding the construction of institutions—market, public, and civil societal—on a number of scales that can collectively reform our global economy so that *humankind* as an aggregate collective lives up to what basic humanity demands. For starters, this would be the maintenance of a world that makes sense to us, that does not become evil. Anthroponomy is the big game in town when it comes to dealing with mass extinction, as well as with other planetary scale environmental changes such as climate change and ocean acidification. No serious environmentalist or scholar of environmentalism can neglect it. To deemphasize it is to give up on the only realistic long-term solution to contemporary environmental problems.

Our first ethical priority as people concerned with the risk of anthropogenic mass extinction must accordingly be political: to demand political, market, and civic societal institutions on a number of scales, from the local to the national, and involving international networks of governance that are collectively capable of regulating our economy eventually on a planetary scale, even if the primary site of regulation is local, regional, or national (cf. Scruton, 2012; Brenner, 2013). Given the driving cause of the risk of anthropogenic mass extinction, anthroponomy will have to be anchored in an economic form beyond the communism and corporate capitalism of the modern age, toward a postindustrial civilization (Jonas, 1984, Braungart and McDonough, 2002). This multiscaled, multisited anthroponomy rooted in a network of norm-bearing institutions will have to address many risk factors causing our current elevated extinction event: overpopulation, ecologically destabilizing pollution, human settlement sprawl and widespread habitat destruction (cf. Davis, 2007), and the big problems of climate change and ocean acidification—basically any problems straining our planetary boundaries (Rockström et al., 2009). In addition, none of these institutions will be ultimately viable until we arrive at an effective international order, the precursor to any possible global governance (not government). Accordingly, citizens concerned with anthropogenic mass extinction should focus on conservation, certainly; support scientific advances in extinction studies as well; but not let any of these overshadow the essentially political-economic task of anthroponomy. Local governance appears to be the most effective form on the planet for fostering accountability and maintaining self-governance, that is, for keeping us as a collective within norms that make sense and do not undermine sense (Scruton, 2012). A very basic challenge of anthroponomy therefore appears in how we will link the local scale to international governance, which is to this day essentially idealistic and unstable. It may be in intensified work on our nation states, and it may also be through transnational networks of governance, be they economic or appearing in the realm of affiliation-specific, transnational civil society—as in the case of Rotary Clubs, conservation societies, or activist networks against unaccountable multinational corporations.

4   LARGE-UNIT / DEEP BRANCHING CONSERVATION

If today's accelerating extinction rates were to be part of a mass extinction event, we can look forward to the same sort of fundamental reorganization of the biosphere that took place during previous mass extinctions. Mass extinctions, in Jablonski's (2001: 5397) words, "remove successful incumbents," fundamentally altering the adaptive success of existing evolutionary strategies and demolishing the evolutionary status quo. Before the K-Pg mass extinction, mammals were an unimpressive lineage composed of small things eating even smaller things (bugs, worms, baby dinosaurs; Hu et al., 2005). By the end of the recovery period (~ 5 my), they were well on their way to being the dominant form of terrestrial life. Mass extinctions reorganize the system of the biosphere, with no guarantee that currently successful taxa—like us—will be part of the new order on Earth.

If we're ultimately concerned with preserving the ecological relationships that currently characterize life on Earth, then the threat of mass extinction compels us to revise our thinking about what constitutes meaningful conservation biology. We need to consider mitigation of the elevated extinction rate event we're in with an eye to keeping it as far as we can from becoming a mass extinction. We've known for at least a generation that practical constraints (e.g., on our knowledge, on our resources) mean that we will have to prioritize when it comes to what we decide to save (cf. Sandler, 2012). But the threat of mass extinction adds a new dimension to the prioritization process. The destabilization caused by mass extinctions stems from the destruction of higher-order/deeper branching biological entities that is a unique and characteristic part of the mass extinction process. If preserving the current form of ecological stability matters to us, then that suggests a shift in the sort of biological entities that qualify as having ethical significance. On the scale of mass extinction, saving particular, individual species no longer seems as important. If the stability of the biosphere itself is in question, then the biological entities that seem to matter are the ones that can preserve that stability—for example, ecosystems, large-scale communities, geographic regions that generate much of the planet's biodiversity (so-called "biodiversity hotspots"). As to individual species, those preserving deep branching lineages would seem more important (Pinet et al., 2013). But if the biosphere's general stability depends on the stability of those large-scale biological units, and if the stability of those units is independent of their particular constituents, then our efforts should focus on those larger-scale units, since they make a difference to general stability.

Of course it's not news to most readers that preserving ecosystems and communities is important. But the independence of these entities from their current inhabitants may not be common knowledge, and it has significant ethical implications for how we ought to organize our conservation efforts. To take one example, large-scale biological communities are thought to be composed of a random draw from the regional species pool. From the perspective of the community's persistence, the collection of species that composes it at any given time is not especially significant. Individual species will come and go as time passes, but the community will remain unperturbed. If that's true, it's not clear that we have an ethical imperative to focus conservation efforts on any of the incumbent species of a given community, even if our primary concern is the preservation of the community of which they are a part. Rather, what we ought to be ensuring is that the regional species pool has sufficient reserves to reconstitute that community, along either functional or structural dimensions.

The point of this example is not to recommend a specific conservation strategy, but rather to emphasize the more important fact that mass extinctions threaten levels of the biological hierarchy that are much higher up and more deeply branching than we're accustomed to thinking about in ethical terms. We need to retrain our moral sense (and our scientific research priorities) to reflect the biological facts that are significant for the preservation of the life as we know it. Should a new mass extinction be occurring, the complex dynamics of it will very likely undermine conservation efforts aimed at particular species. But thinking toward the kind of things that happen in a mass extinction can guide us toward mitigating the elevated extinction rate event that *is* occurring so that we resist falling into a mass extinction while our efforts at anthroponomy lag behind. Perhaps an anthroponomic test for the moment is to see how well we can support regional conservation of large-scale biological units, even transnational ones.

NOTE

1. For example, dogs belong to the genus *canis*, in the family *Canidae*, which is part of the order *Carnivora*, a group that also contains walruses.

REFERENCES

Arendt, H. (2006). *Eichmann in Jerusalem. A Report on the Banality of Evil.* New York: Penguin Classics.

Bambach, R. K. (2006). "Phanerozoic Biodiversity Mass Extinctions." *Annual Review of Earth and Planetary Science* 34: 127–155.

Barnosky, A. D., Matzke, N., Tomiya, S., Wogan, G. O. U., Swartz, B., Quental, T. B., et al. (2011). Has the Earth's Sixth Mass Extinction Already Arrived? *Nature* 471(7336): 51–57. doi:10.1038/nature09678

Bendik-Keymer, J. (2010). "Species Extinction and the Vice of Thoughtlessness: The Importance of Spiritual Exercise for Learning Virtue." *Journal of Agricultural and Environmental Ethics* 23: 61–83.

Bendik-Keymer, J. (2012). "The Sixth Mass Extinction Is Caused by Us." In *Ethical Adaptation to Climate Change: Human Virtues of the Future,* edited by A. Thompson and J. Bendik-Keymer, ch. 13. Cambridge, MA: MIT Press.

Braungart, M., and McDonough, W. (2002). *Cradle to Cradle: Remaking the Way We Make Things.* San Francisco: North Point Press.

Brenner, N., ed. (2013). *Implosions/Explosions: Toward a Study of Planetary Urbanization.* Berlin: Jovis Verlag.

Castells, M. (1996). *The Rise of the Network Society (Information Age Society, vol. 1).* New York: Wiley-Blackwell.

Davis, M. (2007). *Planet of Slums.* New York: Verso.

Erwin, D. (2006). *Extinction.* Princeton, NJ: Princeton University Press.

Gardiner, S. M. (2011). *A Perfect Moral Storm: The Ethical Tragedy of Climate Change.* New York: Oxford University Press.

Gorke, M. (2003). *The Death of Our Planet's Species: A Challenge to Ecology and Ethics,* translated by Patricia Nevers. Washington, D.C.: Island Books.

Green, W., Hunt, G., Wing, S., and DiMichele, W. (2011). "Does Extinction Wield an Axe Or Pruning Shears? How Interactions Between Phylogeny and Ecology Affect Patterns of Extinction." *Paleobiology* 37(1): 72–91.

Hatley, J. (2012). "The Virtues of Temporal Discernment: Rethinking the Extent and Coherence of the Good in a Time of Mass Extinction." *Environmental Philosophy* 9(1): 1–21.

Holland, B. (2012). "Environment as Meta-capability: Why a Dignified Human Life Requires a Stable Climate System." In *Ethical Adaptation to Climate Change: Human Virtues of the Future,* edited by A. Thompson and J. Bendik-Keymer, ch. 7. Cambridge, MA: MIT Press.

Hu, Y., Meng, J., Wang, Y., and Li, C. (2005). "Large Mesozoic Mammals Fed on Young Dinosaurs." *Nature* 433 (7022): 149–152.

Jablonski, D. (1986). "Background and Mass Extinctions: The Alternation of Macroevolutionary Regimes." *Science* 231(4734): 129–133.

Jablonski, D. (2001). "Lessons from the Past: Evolutionary Impacts of Mass Extinctions." *Proceedings of the National Academy of Sciences* 98: 5393–5398.

Jonas, H. (1984). *The Imperative of Responsibility: In Search of an Ethics for a Technological Age.* Chicago: University of Chicago Press.

Leopold, A. (1948). *A Sand County Almanac and Sketches from Here and There.* Many editions available.

Keller, G. (2008). "Cretaceous Climate, Volcanism, Impacts, and Biotic Effects." *Cretaceous Research* 29 (5–6): 754–771.

Neiman, S. (2002). *Evil in Modern Thought: An Alternative History of Philosophy.* Princeton, NJ: Princeton University Press.

Nussbaum, M. (2011). *Creating Capabilities. The Human Development Approach.* Cambridge, MA: Harvard University Press.

Pinet, P., Pikitch, E., and Stager, K. (2013). "The Ongoing Extinction Event: A Deep Time, Eco-Evolutionary Perspective for Mitigation and Reconciliation Management." In *Ecosystems and Sustainable Development IX*, edited by A. Marinov and C. Brebbia. London: WIT Press.

Raup, D. M. (1991). *Extinction: Bad Genes or Bad Luck?.* New York: Norton.

Rockström, J. et al. (2009). Planetary Boundaries: Exploring the Safe Operating Space for Humanity. *Ecology and Society* 14(2): 32.

Rolston, H. III (2012). *A New Environmental Ethics: the Next Millennium for Life on Earth.* New York: Routledge.

Sandler, R. (2012). *The Ethics of Species.* New York: Cambridge University Press.

Scruton, R. (2012). *How to Think Seriously about the Planet: The Case for Environmental Conservatism.* New York: Oxford University Press.

Simberloff, D. (1994). "The Ecology of Extinction." *Acta Palaeontologica Polonica*, 38: 159–174.

Thompson, A., and Bendik-Keymer, J., eds. (2012). *Ethical Adaptation to Climate Change: Human Virtues of the Future.* Cambridge, MA: MIT Press.

CHAPTER 37

PHILOSOPHY OF TECHNOLOGY AND THE ENVIRONMENT

PAUL B. THOMPSON

THE human species' ability to inflict damage upon the habitat of other species and on planetary ecosystems is, in an obvious sense, a function of the tools and techniques that human beings deploy for all manner of diverse purposes. Singular environmental catastrophes such as the Dust Bowl, Love Canal, the depletion of the Aral Sea, the *Exxon Valdez* oil spill, and the *Deepwater Horizon* spill were all caused by mismanagement of a technical apparatus, while dispersed pollution effects from agricultural pesticides, chlorofluorocarbons, and greenhouse gases are unintended effects from the widespread use of modern technologies. Technologies with significant environmental impact range from refrigeration to the internal combustion engine. It is indeed difficult to imagine an environmental crisis on the magnitude of our present situation *without* the mechanical, power, biological, and chemical technologies that have proliferated since the industrial revolution. Although human impact on the natural environment may be caused as much or more by expansion of the global population as by technologically based pollution and resource consumption, technological advances in agriculture, medicine, and energy are themselves largely responsible for the growth in human population.

Perhaps *because* the role of technology in environmental decline is so obvious, philosophical analyses of technology's role in the environmental crisis are elusive. This chapter provides a necessarily brief and selective survey of work in the philosophy of technology that is of particular significance to environmental philosophers.

1 PHILOSOPHY OF TECHNOLOGY

The kind of technology that gave rise to the industrial revolution began to be the subject of philosophical reflection over 200 years ago. In one sense, the philosophical vision of an industrial revolution based on applied science was articulated by Francis Bacon (1561–1626), but Carl Mitcham (1994) has argued that writings by largely unknown eighteenth century figures articulated the vision in detail that science must be wedded to a set of social needs and underpinned by a clear expression of the economic possibilities and the social forces that would need to be mustered in order to realize them. Fully formed philosophical analyses of such clusters would be provided in the nineteenth century. Auguste Comte (1798–1859) argued that science and technology could indeed produce the kind of utopia envisioned by Bacon, whereas Karl Marx (1818–1883) exposed the dark side of this vision. Indeed, Marx himself argued that unchecked capitalist tendencies would lead to the overexploitation of natural resources and environmental decline (Mitcham, 1994).

In the twentieth century, Martin Heidegger attempted to describe how industrial technology had begun to distort *Dasein*—or being-in-the-world that is characteristic of human individuals. Heidegger suggested that technological rationality leads us to view everything, including our own thinking, as a resource, a theme that has now been extended directly into environmental philosophy (Zimmerman, 1983; Foltz, 1995). Theodor Adorno, Max Horkheimer, and Herbert Marcuse began to develop critiques of Western science and liberal political philosophy that drew upon Marx's analysis and wove sharply critical discussions of modern technology into their work. Adorno and Horkheimer developed a penetrating analysis of how technology of mass media permit the transformation of art and culture into instruments of capital accumulation (Adorno and Horkheimer, 1947; Adorno, 1954), while Marcuse developed the idea of "technological rationality" as a pervasive form of twentieth century consciousness (Marcuse 1941; 1964). While neither Marcuse nor Adorno had deep engagement with environmental themes, their break with liberalism signaled the onset of new work in the philosophy of technology that eventually *would* take on important environmental issues.

Like environmental philosophy itself, recent philosophy of technology has only emerged as a field of specialization during the last 50 years. The student resistance movements that gave rise to the first Earth Day in 1972 also played a key role in the development of philosophical work on technology. Most clearly, philosophers and social activists influenced by the critique of liberalism developed visions of alternative technology as a form of less impactful and more democratic means for achieving human flourishing, (Winner, 1979; Hannay and McGinn, 1980). This line of thought has matured into a *critical theory of technology* that draws heavily on Marx and the first generation critical theory of Adorno, Horkheimer, and Marcuse. A second strand in late twentieth century follows Heidegger's attempt to characterize how technology transforms human experience, and draws upon *phenomenology* as practiced by Heidegger, Edmund Husserl, and Maurice Merleau-Ponty.

A third strand in the philosophy of technology followed work by another German, Hans Jonas. At first emphasizing questions in bio-medical practice that had been generated by life extension and reproductive technologies, Jonas developed an approach that eventually gave rise to *the empirical turn*. Here, a number of contemporary scholars in the philosophy of technology concentrate on the empirical details of specific tools and techniques, sometimes conjoining their descriptive work with traditional ethical theories and sometimes drawing on American pragmatism. Finally, some philosophers have either opposed or ignored the German schools and have approached technology as applied science. This approach combines assumptions from mainstream ethics and political theory with *applied philosophy of science* to produce analyses of technology that emphasize risk analysis, on the one hand, and internalizing the social and environmental costs of technological innovation, on the other. Although these four themes intersect and fail to capture the complexity of recent work in the philosophy of technology fully, they nonetheless provide an entrée into the intersection of technology and environment.

2 CRITICAL THEORY OF TECHNOLOGY

As noted above, the protest movements of the 1960s provided an impetus to both the philosophy of technology and to environmental ethics. Works such as Rachel Carson's *Silent Spring* (1962) brought the negative environmental impact of chemical technology into public consciousness, and environmentalism joined the women's movement and civil rights as a key element of 1960s counterculture. In this sense, alternative technology is more of a social movement than a philosophical school of thought. Borrowing ideas from Jean-Jacques Rousseau, Percy Bysshe Shelly, and Henry David Thoreau that had already been reinterpreted by earlier twentieth-century figures such as Scott and Helen Nearing, Buckminster Fuller, and Ralph Borsodi, the 1960s and 1970s saw a rash of experimentation with putatively low technology alternatives, especially in food, housing, and energy. Key ideas included communal living and the development of decentralized and locally controlled technology. Advocates saw themselves equally rejecting capitalism and the environmental excesses of the industrial revolution (see Smith, 2003).

The work of first-generation critical theorists provided a platform for more rigorous philosophical articulation of the foundations for this social movement. The scholarly journal *Capitalism, Nature, Socialism* has been a continuing venue for work by a large number of social theorists, but two exemplars deserve special mention. Articulating a perspective he named "social ecology," Murray Bookchin argued that environmental problems are in fact the result of underlying social causes associated with the rise of corporations and the welfare state. The incorporation of profit-seeking enterprises creates incentives for exploitation of natural resources and undercuts institutions that would preserve the integrity of ecosystems for the purpose of community longevity and the benefit of future generations. At the same time, the rise of the welfare state has neutered the ability of democratic politics to redress these problems. Bookchin thus advocated a form of libertarian anarchism that would, he believed, restore an environmentally benign social order (Bookchin, 1995).

Andrew Feenberg is the most influential contemporary advocate of critical theories of technology. Like Bookchin and the original critical theorists, Feenberg argues that existing social relations distort incentives for development and application of modern technology. Breaking with Marcuse, who had argued that this distortion was inherent in the worldview of modern science, Feenberg argues that capitalist technologies reflect a "secondary rationalization": among the diverse potentials or availances implicit within a cluster of technical possibilities, only those that are amenable to capital accumulation tend to be selected and realized. Using the work of Barry Commoner, Feenberg argues that environmental resource depletion and disruption of vital ecosystem processes is a predictable result of secondary rationalization under the social conditions of capitalism. Feenberg also undertakes detailed discussions of how social movements organized in conjunction with information and health technologies have successfully resisted these impulses. Feenberg views the philosopher's task as one of giving voice to alternative potentials that lie dormant within technology in order to mobilize more effective social resistance (Feenberg, 2002).

A rather large literature in social theory can be aligned with the critical theory of technology, especially when it is viewed as heir and handmaiden to alternative technology social movements. Bookchin's social ecology has been succeeded by geographers and others working under the rubric of political ecology (Zimmerer and Bassett, 2003). This work tends to view the link between ecology and political institutions through a dialectical lens: ecologies shape institutions, but as stressed by Bookchin and Feenberg, institutions—including technological practices—shape the social incentives that have long been understood to have dramatic ecological effects. Other theorists working in this broad tradition continue to explore alternatives to the existing capitalist configurations of industrial technology. Recent work by Thomas Princen on limiting human wants emphasizes the notion of sufficiency (Princen, 2005). Still more have explored possibilities for altering the trajectory of science and industrial development, arguing for an *ecological modernization* thesis that stresses the way that technology and market forces are now working for environmental healing and restoration (Spaargaren and Mol, 1992 Mol, 1996.

3 Phenomenology of Technology

Stimulated by Heidegger, but eventually drawing more heavily on Husserl, Don Ihde developed a phenomenological analysis of the impact that instruments have on sensory perception, and subsequently on social ontology and epistemology. Tools and techniques have the effect of amplifying some interpretive possibilities that are latent in the perceptual field, while simultaneously reducing others. Experience based on a perceptual engagement with the world is thus mediated by whatever tools and techniques happen to be in widespread use. Ihde's work thus stands in dialog with poststructural philosophies that fixate on the seemingly infinite permutations of linguistic meaning. The experiential possibilities made available through technologically mediated engagement have a multi-stable character: although not infinitely flexible and contingent, there are nonetheless many possibilities that tend to be neglected and underdeveloped. Unreflective engagement with technology then leads to naïve investment in a much narrower set of ontic possibilities than are strictly necessary. Ihde's work (which he calls "postphenomenology") thus provides a link between Feenberg's thought of "availances" and traditional metaphysics.

Ihde's work has been brought into dialog with environmental themes by some of his students, including Evan Selinger and myself. My work has explored how agricultural and food technologies structure a form of consciousness that leads to profound disengagement with nature (Thompson, 2010), while Selinger has explored the ethical implications of "choice architecture" (Selinger and Whyte, 2011) and the phenomenon of poverty tourism (Selinger, 2009). Peter Paul Verbeek has argued that Ihde's postphenomenology can be married to recent scholarship in the social studies of science that stresses how tools and techniques function as social actors, embroiled in networks that have complex and sometimes unpredictable environmental effects (Verbeek, 2005). Verbeek is also linking this work to product design and the theme of sustainability. These moves connect postphenomenology to the ideas of ecological modernization and alternative technology (Verbeek and Slob, 2006).

Albert Borgmann is arguably the most influential adaptor of Heidegger's thought in the philosophy of technology. Borgmann frames his work as a study of the failed promise of modern technology—a failure experienced both in the fragmentation of modern life and in the environmental consequences of industrial development. Borgmann reconstructs Heidegger's analysis of technology as "the device paradigm." Modern technology seeks to displace inconvenience and waste with devices: efficient tools and techniques that require little or no skill, attentive engagement or reflection on the part of their users. However, in eliminating the annoyances of less effective methods, devices have a dual effect., In the first instance they render life devoid of meaning. It is, in fact, the distractions and detours of traditional ways of living that were the basis for deep and enduring relationships with other people and with the natural world. A world dominated by devices can be easily negotiated, but it provides no opportunity for true engagement. In addition, as reflective engagement declines, people become inured to the consequences of living in a device-filled world. The results can be seen in the decline of both community life and the natural world (Borgmann, 1987, 2010).

Borgmann's work has been extensively applied in environmental philosophy by David Strong and by Eric Higgs. Strong's book *Crazy Mountains* develops an extended application of Borgmann's device paradigm to environmental ethics. He shows how projects of technological development that destroy natural areas proceed from a mentality that fails to acknowledge the significance and meaning-giving dimensions of nature, while continuing to pursue efficiencies and uses typical of the device paradigm (Strong, 1995). Higgs has defended ecological restoration efforts as an application of focal practice, Borgmann's response to the failure of technology. A focal practice is one that eschews the device paradigm to pursue continuing engagement with things—realities that (unlike devices) are replete with meaningful possibilities. Higgs has argued that restoration efforts achieve a philosophical rationale less in terms of their ability to replace the properties of naturally existing ecosystems than in the way that they provide focal practices restoring a connection with nature and an appreciation for community life (Higgs, 1991; 2005). Borgmann's focal practice is interpreted as a way to conceptualize sustainability as a moral virtue in my book, *The Agrarian Vision* (Thompson, 2010).

4 THE EMPIRICAL TURN

The phrase "empirical turn" was used in the title of a Dutch volume examining work in the philosophy of technology by Borgmann, Feenberg, and Ihde, as well as Hubert Dreyfus, Donna Haraway, and Langdon Winner. Contributors to this collection were noting how this generation of American philosophers had turned away from a European model exemplified by Heidegger and the first-generation critical theorists, all of whom had tended to analyze technology as if it were an abstract ideal, rather than as a material assemblage of tools and techniques. In contrast, the Americans peppered their writings with discussion of specific tools and techniques and tended to approach their subject matter as one that presupposed some acquaintance with the use and application of these tools and techniques within practical contexts (Achterhuis, 1997). The empirical turn is thus a theme that cuts across others, rather than existing as a distinct methodological thrust.

As noted previously, it was actually Hans Jonas who began to both call for attention to empirical matters in the 1970s and to exemplify this call both in his work on biomedical research (Wolpe, 2003) and in his book *The Imperative of Responsibility.* The latter might be viewed as a bridge between old-style metaphysics and the empirical turn. Jonas constructed the work as a critique of both capitalism and socialism, arguing that neither political system was proving itself capable of coping with the unwanted impact of chemical and industrial technology. Instead, Jonas argued that ethics must now begin to employ technical means, by which he meant the use of applied science and technical capabilities, to anticipate and manage the unwanted consequences of modern technology. It would no longer be adequate to view ethics as a purely abstract endeavor: any effective ethics would need to be equipped with the predictive abilities of applied science and engineering. Jonas was clear that environmental impacts were at the forefront of his thinking (Jonas, 1979).

Jonas also argued that there would be circumstances in which society should forego the opportunity to take up technical means altogether because the potential consequences would be catastrophic and/or the technology simply could not be subjected to social control. He cited nuclear energy and genetic engineering as possible examples (Jonas, 1979). This theme of Jonas's work emerged some 30 years later in the form of a "precautionary approach." As articulated in the Rio Declaration giving rise to the Convention on BioDiversity, the precautionary approach enjoins states as follows:

> Where there are threats of serious or irreversible damage, lack of full scientific certainty shall not be used as a reason for postponing cost-effective measures to prevent environmental degradation.

This statement conforms closely to the formulation articulated by Jonas in the 1970s. It continues to be one of the more hotly debated philosophical principles for evaluating the environmental implications of new technology (van den Belt, 2003).

Among figures included in the Dutch volume on "the empirical turn," it is Donna Haraway who has the most immediate significance for environmental philosophy. Trained and practicing within the social studies of science, Haraway arrived on the scene as a feminist critic of methods and approaches in the biological sciences. Her work on women primatologists noted how they were more willing to undertake detailed and highly specific empirical observations than men, and how they were able to rely on emotion to develop more penetrating analyses of their subjects (Haraway, 1989). Since this pathbreaking work, Haraway has developed a philosophically rich understanding of the way that human perception and communication are deeply affected by the technical means that are deployed (Haraway, 1997) and has continued her work on animals by challenging the assumption that the human/animal dichotomy can be presumed as a metaphysically meaningful categorical disjunction (Haraway, 2008).

5 APPLIED PHILOSOPHY OF SCIENCE

Some of the philosophers of technology who are best known in environmental ethics have done work on technological risks. Like others who represent an empirical turn, they have argued for systematic attention to the impact of technologies as they are deployed on a case-by-case basis (Shrader-Frechette, 1980). Those philosophers who have approached the problems of environmental risk have treated it as a special case of rational decision making. Kristen Shrader-Frechette is the environmental philosopher whose work in this vein is best known, though important contributions have also been made by Carl Cranor and Sven Ove Hansson. Shrader-Frechette's early work on nuclear power and nuclear waste emphasized the way that risk assessment methodologies in use tended to ignore or underestimate the significance of key biological hazards, often associated with incomplete or uncertain data (1983). Her more recent work on environmental justice has emphasized the way that hazards to women, minorities, and the poor tend to be ignored or undervalued in political decision making (2002). These themes are linked by her work on political institutions that would be more democratic in the sense that they would more adequately reflect omitted and under-valued hazards (1991).

Cranor has emphasized problems created by scientific uncertainty. His work on chemical hazards has argued that the scientific treatment of Type I and Type II statistical errors creates an inappropriate burden of proof for risk assessment. In science, the epistemic rule has been to minimize the chance of accepting a causal link when none exists. Cranor argues that in toxicological risk assessment for regulatory purposes, it is more appropriate to minimize the chance of allowing a harmful substance to slip through the regulatory approval process (1993). Cranor has argued that this approach provides an epistemologically rigorous way to interpret the main ideas behind the precautionary principle (1999). Both Cranor and Hansson have argued against the view that risk assessment can be value-free, as some scientists and risk assessors have suggested. The very idea of hazard presumes some dimension of adverse outcome or value. Risk analysis is thus an inherently normative or value-laden activity (Cranor, 1990; 1997; Hansson, 1989, 2003).

All three of these philosophers have portrayed their work in terms of rational decision making regarding potentially hazardous technology. Although they have been critical of the way that regulators and the promoters of technology have approached the assessment of new technology, they have not questioned the assumption that human conduct is ethically proper and justifiable only when it aligns with norms of rationality. This stance militates against any strong identification with anti-technology activism: one must arrive at one's view on the acceptability of a given technology through careful evaluation of its benefits, risks, and the way in which it is being implemented. In this respect, philosophers who have approached technology using the concepts and methods of the philosophy of science have tended to reject or at least ignore the more radically based approaches that had their origins in the thought of Marx and Heidegger.

6 CONCLUSION: TECHNOLOGY, ENVIRONMENT, AND DEMOCRACY

The four themes or strands of thought within the philosophy of technology that are surveyed in this chapter intersect and cross with one another in numerous ways. Although they represent the main approaches developed by contemporary philosophers, they in no sense engage the full range of social theorists that have conjoined work on technology and the environment. Indeed, one might, with little exaggeration, claim that the dominant way that non-philosophers have approached the key environmental questions of our era are through social theories that formulate resource depletion, pollution, and environmental decline as technological problems. Economists, political scientists, sociologists, and geographers, as well as the policy analysts aligned with each discipline, tend to presume that social institutions such as property rights, regulation, education, and political culture establish "the rules of the game" that shape human opportunity, incentives, and behavior, but they have also come to recognize that technological innovations can transform opportunity, incentives, and thus behavior in sudden, dramatic, and often unanticipated ways. The forms of production and consumption that are viewed as the source of environmental problems from pollution to climate change reflect the dominant technical means as much as they reflect contingent policies or constants of human nature.

Thus, in addition to the philosophical themes listed already, many scholars working at the intersection of environment and technology have joined in a search for ways to improve our collective foresight with respect to technology's consequences. This can be viewed as a development of Hans Jonas's work from the 1970s, or as an implementation of Feenberg's secondary rationalization and Ihde's postphenomenology. Alternatively, it can be interpreted as liberal politics as usual, as an evolutionary development of regulatory policy implementations that have been in place for over a century. Experiments in foresight go by many names: boundary organizations (Guston, 2001), consensus conferences (Grundahl, 1995), scenario planning (Guston and Sarewitz, 2002), anticipatory governance (Barben, et al. 2008), constructive technology assessment (Rip, 1986, 2003), and democratizing technology (Sclove, 1995; Durant, 1999). Many of these analyses have roots in Langdon Winner's work from the 1980s. What they have in common is the attempt to engage a broader cross-section of affected parties in the decisions about which technologies to actually develop and how to deploy them.

Much of the impetus toward these participatory methods arose in response to environmental social movements against emerging technologies such as biotechnology, nanotechnology, synthetic biology, and, to a significant extent, nuclear power. Such social movements are among the most characteristic forms of environmental activism. Philosophers *have* been engaged in the scholarship of these emerging technologies, with me writing on biotechnology (Thompson, 2007) and Shrader-Frechette (1983) among the forefront of those who have written on nuclear power. Significant work is currently being developed on nanotechnology and synthetic biology. Philosophers who have undertaken such work have tended to view themselves as enabling and encouraging the kinds of public debate and deliberation associated with participatory methods. However, if one defines oneself as an activist through one's opposition to these emerging technologies, there may be little room to stand back and evaluate them philosophically, and there may be significant risk in participating social activities designed to generate consensus. For such a perspective, regard for the intrinsic value of nature may have more immediate utility.

In conclusion, it is not clear whether those environmental philosophers who have chosen to develop the field in terms of debates over ecocentrism and anthropocentrism, and over the contrast between instrumental and intrinsic value, will ever find much reason to engage the questions concerning technology. Philosophers of technology have pictured humanity as less than fully free with respect to the question of valuation and its underlying metaphysics. They have stressed how tools and techniques penetrate deeply into human perception and practice, informing experience and conscious processes of evaluation or choice at the level of habit and routine. This perspective might be more happily conjoined with an environmental virtue ethics (see Sandler, 2009), but it is less clear that it will be congenial to philosophies that treat value—intrinsic or instrumental—as the outcome of choice. The obvious environmental implications of technology to the contrary, philosophy of technology and environmental ethics may or may not be a match made in heaven.

REFERENCES

Achterhuis, H., Ed. (1997 [2001]). *American Philosophy of Technology: The Empirical Turn*, translated by Robert Crease. Bloomington: Indiana University Press.
Adorno, T. W. (1954). "How to Look at Television." *The Quarterly of Film Radio and Television* 8(3): 213–235.
Adorno, T. W., and Horkheimer, M. (1947 [1972]). *Dialectic of Enlightenment*, translated by John Gumming. New York: Herder and Herder.
Barben, D., Fisher, E., Selin, C. and Guston, D. (2008). "Anticipatory Governance of Nanotechnoiogy: Foresight, Engagement, and Integration." In *The Handbook of Science and Technology Studies*, 3rd Ed., Edward J. Hackett, Olga Amsterdamska, Michael Lynch and Judy Wajcman, eds. Cambridge, MA: The MIT Press, pp. 979–1000.
Bookchin, M. (1995). *The Philosophy of Social Ecology: Essays on Dialectical Naturalism*. Montreal: Black Rose Books.
Borgmann, A. (1987). *Technology and the Character of Contemporary Life: A Philosophical Inquiry*. Chicago, IL: University of Chicago Press.
Borgmann, A. (2010). *Real American Ethics: Taking Responsibility for our Country*. Chicago, IL: University of Chicago Press.
Carson. R. (1962). *Silent Spring*. Boston: Houghton-Mifflin.
Cranor, C. F. (1990). "Some Moral Issues in Risk Assessment." *Ethics* 101 (1): 123–143.
Cranor, C. F. (1993). *Regulating Toxic Substances: A Philosophy of Science and the Law.* New York: Oxford University Press.
Cranor, C. F. (1997). "The Normative Nature of Risk Assessment: Features and Possibilities." *Risk* 8: 123.
Cranor, C. F. (1999). "Asymmetric Information, the Precautionary Principle, and Burdens of Proof." In *Protecting Public Health and the Environment: Implementing the Precautionary Principle*, edited by C. Raffensparger and J. A. Tickner, 74–99 Washington, DC: Island Press.
Durant, J. (1999). "Participatory Technology Assessment and the Democratic Model of the Public Understanding of Science." *Science and Public Policy* 26(5): 313–319.
Feenberg, A. (2002). *Transforming Technology: A Critical Theory Revisited*. New York: Oxford University Press.
Foltz, B. V. (1995). *Inhabiting the Earth: Heidegger, Environmental Ethics, and the Metaphysics of Nature*. Atlantic Highlands, NJ: Humanities Press.
Guston, D. H. (2001). "Boundary Organizations in Environmental Policy and Science: An Introduction." *Science, Technology, and Human Values* 26(4): 399–408.
Guston, D. H., and Sarewitz, D. (2002). Real-Time Technology Assessment. *Technology in Society* 24(1): 93–109.
Grundahl, J. (1995). "The Danish Consensus Conference Model." In *Public Participation in Science: The Role of Consensus Conferences in Europe*, 31–40. London: Science Museum.

Hannay, N. B., and McGinn, R. E. (1980). "The Anatomy of Modern Technology: Prolegomenon to an Improved Public Policy for the Social Management of Technology." *Daedalus* 109(1): 25–53.

Hansson, S. O. (1989). "Dimensions of Risk." *Risk Analysis* 9(1): 107–112.

Hansson, S. O. (2003). "Ethical Criteria of Risk Acceptance." *Erkenntnis* 59(3): 291–309.

Haraway, D. J. (1989). *Primate Visions: Gender, Race and Nature in the World of Modern Science* New York: Routledge.

Haraway, D. J. (1997). *Modest-Witness@ Second-Millennium. Femaleman [Copyright]-Meets-Oncomouse [Trademark]: Feminism and Technoscience.* New York: Routledge.

Haraway, D. J. (2008). *When Species Meet* Minneapolis: University of Minnesota Press.

Higgs, E. S. (1991). "A Quantity of Engaging Work to be Done: Ecological Restoration and Morality in a Technological Culture." *Ecological Restoration* 9(2): 97–104.

Higgs, E. S. (2005). "The Two-Culture Problem: Ecological Restoration and the Integration of Knowledge." *Restoration Ecology* 13(1): 159–164.

Jonas, H. (1985 [1979]). *The Imperative of Responsibility: In Search of an Ethics for the Technological Age.* University of Chicago Press.

Marcuse, H. (1941). "Some Social Implications of Modern Technology." *Studies in Philosophy and Social Science* 9(3): 414–439.

Marcuse, H. (1964). *One Dimensional Man.* Boston, MA: The Beacon Press.

Mitcham, C. (1994). *Thinking Through Technology: The Path Between Engineering and Philosophy.* Chicago, IL: University of Chicago Press.

Mol, Arthur P. J. (1996). "Ecological Modernisation and Institutional Reflexivity: Environmental Reform in the Late Modern Age." *Environmental Politics* 5(2): 302–323.

Princen, T. (2005). *The Logic of Sufficiency.* Cambridge, MA: MIT Press.

Rip, A. (1986). "Controversies as Informal Technology Assessment." *Knowledge* 8(2): 341–379.

Rip, A. (2003). "Constructing Expertise: In a Third Wave of Science Studies?" *Social Studies of Science* 33(3): 419–434.

Sandler, R. L. (2009). *Character and Environment: A Virtue-Oriented Approach to Environmental Ethics.* New York: Columbia University Press.

Sclove, R. (1995). *Democracy and Technology.* New York: Guilford Press.

Selinger, E. (2009). Ethics and Poverty Tours. *Philosophy and Public Policy Quarterly* 29(1/2): 2–7.

Selinger, E. and Whyte, K. (2011). "Is There a Right Way to Nudge? The Practice and Ethics of Choice Architecture." *Sociology Compass* 5(10): 923–935.

Shrader-Frechette, K. S. (1980). "Technology Assessment as Applied Philosophy of Science." *Science, Technology, and Human Values* 5(4): 33–50.

Shrader-Frechette, K. S. (1983). *Nuclear Power and Public Policy: The Social and Ethical Problems of Fission Technology.* Dordrecht: D. Reidel Publishing Company, 1983.

Shrader-Frechette, K. S. (1991). *Risk and Rationality: Philosophical Foundations for Populist Reforms.* Berkeley: University of California Press.

Shrader-Frechette, K. S. (2002). *Environmental Justice: Creating Equality, Reclaiming Democracy.* New York: Oxford University Press.

Smith, K. (2003). *Wendell Berry and the Agrarian Tradition: A Common Grace.* Lawrence: University of Kansas Press.

Spaargaren, G., and Mol, Arthur P. J. (1992). "Sociology, Environment, and Modernity: Ecological Modernization as a Theory of Social Change." *Society and Natural Resources* 5(4): 323–344.

Thompson, P. B. (2007). *Food Biotechnology in Ethical Perspective* 2nd ed. Dordrecht, NL: Springer.

Thompson, P. B. (2010). *The Agrarian Vision: Sustainability and Environmental Ethics.* Lexington, KY: University of Kentucky Press.

Van den Belt, H. (2003). Debating the Precautionary Principle:" Guilty until Proven Innocent" or "Innocent until Proven Guilty"? *Plant Physiology* 132(3): 1122–1126.

Verbeek, P. P. (2005). *What Things Do: Philosophical Reflections on Technology, Agency, and Design.* University Park, PA: Penn State Press.

Verbeek, P. P., and Slob, A. F. Eds. (2006). *User Behavior and Technology Development: Shaping Sustainable Relations Between Consumers and Technologies.* Dordrecht, NL: Springer.

Strong, D. (1995). *Crazy Mountains: Learning from Wilderness to Weigh Technology.* Albany, NY: SUNY Press.

Winner, L. (1979). "The Political Philosophy of Alternative Technology: Historical Roots and Present Prospects." *Technology in Society* 1(1): 75–86.

Wolpe, P. R. (2003). Not Just How, but Whether: Revisiting Hans Jonas. *American Journal of Bioethics* 3: 7–8.

Zimmerer, K. S., and Bassett, T. J., Eds. (2003). *Political Ecology: An Integrative Approach to Geography and Environment-Development Studies.* New York: Guilford Press.

Zimmerman, M. E. (1983). "Toward a Heideggerean Ethos for Radical Environmentalism." *Environmental Ethics* 5(2): 99–131.

....

CHAPTER 38

THE ETHICS OF ECOSYSTEM MANAGEMENT

....

MARION HOURDEQUIN

ENVIRONMENTAL philosophy focuses centrally on human relationships to the natural world, including the ethics of managing, manipulating, and restoring nature. Yet with a few notable exceptions (e.g., Norton, 2005; cf. Rolston, 1988, ch. 5), environmental philosophers have given little sustained attention to the concept of ecosystem management. Perhaps this is because ecosystem management is a relatively new and evolving idea, or perhaps it is because many environmental philosophers find the idea of "managing" nature inherently problematic (see Rolston, 1994: pp. 223–228). Nevertheless, ecosystem management has become the dominant approach to management of protected areas and natural resources in North America and internationally. Thus, ecosystem management—as a particular management philosophy—deserves the attention of environmental philosophers. This is especially the case because ecosystem management is rapidly evolving, and certain aspects of its current trajectory warrant ethical concern. In particular, while ecosystem management has grown to encompass new aspects of ecosystem health with its increased focus on "ecosystem services," the pricing and marketing of ecological functions and services may lead to narrower and more reductive modes of valuing nature.

1 FROM RESOURCES TO ECOSYSTEMS: THE EVOLUTION OF ECOSYSTEM MANAGEMENT

....

Over the course of the twentieth century, a whole new grammar for understanding, studying, and managing ecosystems emerged. The term "ecology" entered the lexicon in the late nineteenth century, but it wasn't until the 1930s that British biologist Sir Arthur Tansley coined the term "ecosystem." During these years, the science of ecology emerged as a distinct discipline that integrated and built upon the practice of natural history, but it soon moved beyond observing and describing plants and animals. Taking physics and chemistry as exemplars, ecologists began to use experimentation and modeling, aiming to develop scientific theories that could explain and predict the interaction between organisms and their environments.

Ecology developed concepts that made it possible to consider properties and relationships at multiple levels of biological organization: from individual organisms to populations, communities, and ecosystems.

As ecological theory developed, so did its application. For example, in the 1970s and 1980s, forest management by the US Forest Service drew on models of vegetation succession that reflected a model of plant communities developed by ecologist Frederic Clements (Cook, 1996). Clements (1905) suggested that plant communities were analogous to individual organisms and that they developed in a predictable pattern over time until they reached a mature, stable, climax state. Managers employed this model of vegetative succession in "habitat typing," which used successional patterns to predict forest development at particular sites over time. This approach relied on indicator species to classify sites and predict their climax state, and it was used extensively by the US Forest Service in the development of plans for logging and forest management until the "new ecology" challenged the assumptions of consistency and predictability on which it was based.

The Clementsian model reflected a "balance of nature" view that prevailed in ecology until the 1980s, when the scientific paradigm shifted. The new ecology emphasized not balance, but disturbance, contingency, and multiple equilibria in ecological systems. This view challenged the assumptions of stability built into natural resource management. Not only did traditional habitat-typing models need to be adapted to take account of multiple potential successional trajectories; equilibrium models of plant and animal population dynamics also required adjustment. Just as foresters historically assumed predictable patterns of vegetative development, wildlife and fisheries managers under the balance paradigm assumed that many species maintain relatively stable population sizes over time, and they set harvest targets that failed to account for fluctuations and non-equilibrium population dynamics.

The evolution in ecological theory helped catalyze a shift from single-species to ecosystem-based management. Ecosystem management gained further traction as approaches focused on small areas or single species began to fail. Biologists studying grizzly bears in the Greater Yellowstone Ecosystem, for example, argued for coordination among agencies across jurisdictions, since bears (and other animals) don't respect political boundaries (Grumbine, 1994). Over time, the important role of top predators in regulating ungulate populations became increasingly clear, leading to the reintroduction of wolves to the Yellowstone ecosystem in 1995.

Critical to ecosystem management is the idea that the ongoing integrity of the system as a whole takes precedence over other goals:

> "Sustainable strategies for the provision of ecosystem goods and services cannot take as their starting points statements of need or want such as mandated timber supply, water demand, or arbitrarily set harvests of shrimp or fish. Rather, *sustainability must be the primary objective, and levels of commodity and amenity provision must be adjusted to meet that goal*."(Christensen et al., 1996: 666, emphasis added)

From this perspective, the extraction and use of natural resources must respect ecological limits, and long-term sustainability is prioritized over short-term resource use. Although ecologists developed many of the fundamental ideas that informed the ecosystem management approach, the US Forest Service played a central role in the development and implementation of ecosystem management on the ground. By the 1990s, the Forest Service was moving from an emphasis on maximizing yields of timber and other resources to a focus on the ecosystem as a whole—with watersheds, wildlife, and forests considered as integral and interacting elements of an overall system.

2 KEY IDEAS IN CONTEMPORARY ECOSYSTEM MANAGEMENT

Although ecosystem management has been defined in various ways, Gary Meffe and Ronald Carroll (1997) characterize it like this:

> "[Ecosystem management is] an approach to maintaining or restoring the composition, structure, and function of natural and modified ecosystems for the goal of long-term sustainability. It is based on a collaboratively developed vision of desired future conditions that integrates ecological, socioeconomic, and institutional perspectives, applied within a geographic framework defined primarily by natural ecological boundaries."

This definition emphasizes sustainability through time, thinking beyond political boundaries, and collaborative engagement in ecosystem planning. Other definitions of ecosystem management focus on ecological interrelationships (Grumbine, 1994), incorporation of social values (Grumbine, 1994), collaboration (Keystone National Policy Dialogue on Ecosystem Management, 1996), sustainability (USDI—BLM, 1994), and ongoing, adaptive learning (Norton, 2005).

Common to many contemporary visions of ecosystem management are three themes: integrative *ecological systems thinking, adaptive management*, and incorporation of social values through *collaborative engagement*. These elements can be understood in contrast to "command and control" approaches to natural resource management, which focus on resource extraction, assume thorough knowledge of ecosystem functioning, and favor bureaucratic or expert-driven decision making (Meffe et al., 2002). Because of their narrow focus, command and control strategies often fail to achieve their desired ends, such as sustained annual harvests of natural resources. In addition, because they make little space for collective deliberation and collaborative decisions, command and control strategies can produce polarization and gridlock, such as the conflicts of the 1990s between loggers and environmentalists over protection of the Northern Spotted Owl.

Both social and ecological developments prompted a shift away from single species or single resource management strategies and toward a more holistic approach. The critical *social* lesson was that "decide, announce, defend" approaches often frustrate the public by failing to take their perspectives fully into account (see Duane, 1997). The critical *ecological* lesson was that ecosystems are significantly more complex, dynamic, and unpredictable than we thought. Management focused on a single species or maximum yield of a particular resource thus may overlook effects on other organisms and the long-term stability and resilience of ecological systems. Ecosystem management attempts to remedy these problems by taking a more integrative, tentative, and inclusive approach.

2.1 Ecological Systems Thinking

As noted, ecological systems thinking emphasizes interconnection and dynamism in ecological systems. It considers multi-species interactions, multiple spatial and temporal scales, and system-level properties over time. Whereas single resource management focuses on maximizing production of a particular good—timber, hunting opportunities, or an annual harvest of fish—an ecosystems approach considers more holistically the ecological relationships that sustain and are sustained by particular species or ecosystem processes.

The emphasis on both spatial and temporal dynamics is key (Wallington et al., 2005). In the temporal realm, systems thinking focuses on the role of disturbance in ecosystem dynamics, the contingency of ecosystem trajectories on specific environmental conditions or chance events, and the possibility of multiple stable states for a given system. As Wallington et al. (2005) explain:

> "Rare events, management disturbances, and resource exploitation can all unpredictably shape system structure at critical times or at locations of increased vulnerability, and may even cause the system to 'flip' into a new, irreversible state."

From a spatial perspective, an ecosystem approach stresses that a system's dynamics are shaped by interactions at multiple scales, so managing a particular area or species requires understanding its broader landscape context. Animal and plant species rarely exist in fully discrete populations; instead they form metapopulations (groups of populations) whose interactions depend on the character and connectivity of the landscapes they inhabit. Thus, the viability of a songbird population in the prairies of Saskatchewan may depend not only on the quality of their North American breeding grounds but also on pesticide use and habitat fragmentation in Argentina, where they migrate when the weather turns cold in the northern plains.

2.2 Adaptive Management

Adaptive management emphasizes that our knowledge of ecological systems is partial, incomplete, and evolving, and it integrates responsiveness to new information or changing conditions. *Active* forms of adaptive management explicitly incorporate learning into the management process, treating management strategies as experiments from which we can learn (Walters and Holling, 1990). Thus effective adaptive management is a recursive process, in which strategies are tested, evaluated, and modified based on new knowledge, then tested and evaluated again.

Bryan Norton (2005: 95) suggests that adaptive management can be understood not only as an approach to the *scientific* management of natural systems but also as a template for social learning more generally:

> "[T]he same philosophy that governs the search for scientific understanding also governs the search for better management solutions and guides revisions of values and evaluations when observation and experience indicate the need for such revisions. Adaptive management is as much a search for the right thing to do as it is a search for the truth."

Norton (2005: 92) argues that adaptive management is grounded in three key ideas: experimentalism, multi-scalar analysis, and place sensitivity. The first two ideas reflect standard approaches to adaptive management, while the third explicitly incorporates the social realm, linking to issues of collaborative engagement, discussed in the next section.

As Norton understands adaptive management, it does not merely partner with collaborative engagement but also necessarily *encompasses* community participation. This enables an understanding of adaptive management in which we consider how human communities can "[develop] practices and institutions that are responsive to, and sustainable in, their local environment" (Norton, 2005: 94). On Norton's view, adaptive management is best understood as a form of human adaptation to particular places, or as he puts it, "a negotiation between the land and a human culture" (Norton 2005: 94). This approach integrates scientific understanding with community values to enable us to develop better strategies to live well in particular places; it is, therefore, "a normative science" (Norton, 2005: 95).

2.3 Collaborative Engagement

Not all conceptions of adaptive management incorporate community participation; however, collaborative decision making is a third key element of ecosystem management more generally. Twentieth-century command and control approaches to natural resource management not only focused on maximum short-term yield; they also employed expert managers to set targets and determine management priorities (see Carr, Selin, and Schuett, 1998). Because the priorities of professional land management agencies do not always match those of the public, expert-driven management can generate conflict and resistance. Challenges and appeals often land in court, further entrenching the conception of natural resource management as a zero-sum game in which one group's loss is another's gain.

In the 1990s, in response to increasing polarization and gridlock, the US Forest Service, along with other land management agencies, began to adopt collaborative processes, bringing diverse stakeholders together to deliberate about alternatives and build greater consensus around management goals. The need for community-sensitive land management and robust forms of public engagement is now broadly recognized. There remain concerns, however, that collaboration may exclude the voices of those who are not members of the collaborative group, or who participate but are marginalized or lack equal power in the deliberations. As compared to traditional public participation processes (hearings, public comment on management documents, etc.), which favor shallow and wide engagement by the public, collaboration favors deeper but narrower involvement by committed stakeholders (Hourdequin et al., 2012).

3 ETHICAL AND CONCEPTUAL ISSUES IN ECOSYSTEM MANAGEMENT

As compared to its predecessors, ecosystem management appears a promising and progressive approach to the management of forests, parks, wilderness, and other natural areas.

With increasing attention to public engagement, along with the recognition that natural and social systems are often intertwined, ecosystem management seems well prepared to extend beyond its primary testing ground on federal public lands in the United States and into new contexts and locations. Yet ecosystem management is not without its own set of ethical and other conceptual challenges.

3.1 Conceptual Challenges

Ecosystem management—like all forms of land management—depends on complex, contested, and value-laden concepts, beginning with the ecosystem concept itself. A number of authors have identified problems with the ecosystem concept (O'Neill, 2001; Sagoff, 2003; Currie, 2011). Ecosystems historically have been conceived as biotic communities along with their associated abiotic environments, and ecosystems have been treated as spatially defined entities (Currie, 2011). However, ecosystems are not closed systems. Any effort to spatially delimit ecosystems faces the "problem of partial communities" (Currie, 2011: 24), in which populations of various plants and animals extend beyond any defined ecosystem boundary. Some have suggested on these grounds that we consider ecosystems as *processes* rather than spatially defined *entities* (Currie, 2011).

Concerns about the ontological status of ecological systems are tied to conceptual and empirical challenges concerning the *properties* of ecological systems. Properties such as *stability, integrity*, and *health*—all of which play normative roles in ecosystem management—are notoriously controversial and difficult to define, and without defensible, operational definitions of these concepts, ecosystem management may founder.

Despite these difficulties, ecosystem management may help us move toward a broader environmental ethic, taking seriously Aldo Leopold's proposal that we extend our ethical framework to incorporate the land. Leopold (1949) emphasized the need to "think like a mountain," considering longer time scales and developing an integrated systems view. In "The Land Ethic," Leopold (1949) anticipated key aspects of contemporary ecosystem management philosophy, stressing the value of the biotic community and the long-term health of the land. Leopold further argued that we should seek to preserve the "integrity, beauty, and stability" of the biotic community. These ideas resonate strongly with the shift to a more holistic and integrated perspective.

Stability and integrity remain central concepts in ecosystem management today. Even as emphasis on the "balance of nature" has faded, ecologists continue to seek to understand the properties of ecological systems that produce some degree of stability over time. The central role of the diversity-stability hypothesis in ecological theory (cf. McCann, 2000) is a testament to this fact, and Robert O'Neill (2001: 3279) argues that a critical purpose of ecosystem concept itself is to advance our ability to study and understand stability as an ecosystem property. Yet O'Neill thinks that the traditional ecosystem concept, with its emphasis on clearly defined boundaries, is problematic in understanding stability. Many of the factors that determine ecosystem dynamics extend beyond any single boundary. Thus, "[a]t the minimum, the spatial context of the system and all its component populations must be included in the specifications of the ecosystem. The stability properties of an ecological system cannot be explained by a paradigm that only considers dynamics occurring within the ecosystem boundaries" (O'Neill 2011: 3277). Moreover, there is no consensual understanding of ecological stability. Grimm and Wissel (1997) identify 70 distinct stability concepts and argue that the concept is extremely vague: it can refer to "staying essentially unchanged," "returning to the reference state after disturbance," "persisting through time," or "staying unchanged despite the presence of disturbances," among other meanings.

Like stability, the concept of ecological integrity can be difficult to pin down. In general, ecological integrity emphasizes the *wholeness* of ecological systems (Westra, 2005) and resonates with the Leopoldian idea that "[t]o keep every cog and wheel is the first principle of intelligent tinkering" (Leopold, 1972). Some definitions of ecological integrity thus emphasize constancy in species composition or a full complement of native species (Noss, 1990: 242; cited in Woodley, 2010), while others add a focus on structure and function (Karr and Chu, 1999; cited in Westra, 2005), and still others stress the importance of social values in determining what counts as integrity (Regier, 1993).

The idea of integrity is closely linked to that of *ecosystem health*. Health is frequently invoked in ecosystem management through reference to healthy forests, healthy watersheds, and healthy wildlife populations, along with discussions of ecosystem health more broadly. The idea of ecosystem health seems intuitive: a polluted, lifeless stream is unhealthy, whereas a clear, cold, salmon-filled creek is healthy. From a philosophical perspective, however, ecosystem health seems to rely on an analogy between ecological systems and individual organisms, which may be problematic. Harley Cahen (1988) argues that individual organisms are integrated, teleological (goal-directed) systems, but ecosystems are not. According to Cahen's view, ecosystem features that seem to indicate goal-directedness—such as stability—are mere *byproducts* of the individual elements that comprise them. Ecosystems are not organism-like; they are amalgamations of organisms of various species, along with their abiotic environments (Cahen, 1988; De Leo and Levin, 1997). Cahen believes that this precludes the possibility of ecosystems' having interests. This view of ecosystems also challenges the notion of ecosystem health, insofar as health relies on the idea of an integrated subject. McShane (2004), however, argues that health does not require organismic integration. Instead, it requires only structure, functional parts, and the ability to be better or worse off, and these are features that ecosystems possess.

Despite debates about the meaning and significance of stability, integrity, and ecosystem health, ecologists and land managers often create operational definitions that serve in setting goals and guiding decisions. For example, various indices of biotic integrity (e.g. Karr. 2002) and ecosystem health (e.g., Costanza, 1992, 2012) have been developed. Nevertheless, fundamental normative questions remain in ecosystem management, and the challenges of dynamism and directional change in ecological systems have brought these questions to the fore. Although ecosystem management emerged in parallel with the shift to a dynamic, non-equilibrial systems perspective in ecology, ecologists, land managers, and philosophers continue to grapple with implications of that paradigm shift.

3.2 Losing Our Balance: The Challenges of Dynamism and Directional Change

Like the Leopoldian land ethic, ecosystem management invites a transition from human-centered to ecosystem-centered management, in which the good of the land itself plays a central role. Yet, as we have seen, it is not easy to define the "good of the land" or the health of an ecosystem. The "balance of nature" view implicitly assumed a built-in normativity of nature. As Jonathan Wiener (1996: 7) puts it, the dominant view of the "old ecology" was that "nature is in balance, and human action disturbs that balance." As the new ecology challenged this idea, land managers sought new normative guidance in nature through the idea of *dynamic balance*. Hence, in the 1990s, managers began to rely heavily on the "natural range of variation," or "historic range of variation," for setting goals in conservation, restoration, and land management (Keane et al., 2009). This approach retains the idea that "nature knows best" (or "ecological history knows best") but adapts it to account for the role of disturbance and patch dynamics in ecological systems over time.

However, we are now facing a second destabilizing challenge. In an era of rapid, anthropogenic global change, systems are not only changing in ways consistent with historical patterns of disturbance and recovery; they are also undergoing significant *directional* changes. Climate change, land use changes, and invasive species are all contributing to these shifts. Ecologists have begun to talk about "novel ecosystems" and "no-analog" biological communities: assemblages of species with no historical precedent (Seastedt, Hobbs, and Suding, 2008; Hobbs, Higgs, and Harris, 2009; Williams and Jackson, 2007; Hobbs, Higgs, and Hall, 2013). Since ecosystem management often relies on historical or undisturbed analogs to assess health and other ecosystem properties, new approaches may be needed to establish goals and evaluate success in the face of persistent, directional change.

Perhaps nowhere is the role and relevance of history in land management more explicitly contested than in the field of ecological restoration. Early in its development, ecological restoration focused on recreating a site's historic species composition and structure, bringing back the array of native species that occupied the site prior to human disturbance. The Society for Ecological Restoration, founded in 1988, first characterized restoration like this:

> Ecological restoration is the process of intentionally altering a site to establish a *defined, indigenous, historic ecosystem*. (Quoted in Higgs 2003: 107, emphasis added)

Philosophers raised qualms about restoration from the beginning, however. Robert Elliot (1982, 1997), for example, argues that restoration "fakes nature." Even if restoration returns the appearance and function of a natural system, the new system is a human creation: it lacks a natural genealogy and is thus of less value than the original it aims to replace (Elliot 1982, 1997). Similarly, Eric Katz (1997) argues that restoration creates artifacts, not nature, and that restoration is merely another mode of human manipulation and domination of the natural world.

Even setting aside these fundamental worries, we face challenges in defining and justifying the traditional goal of "historical fidelity" in restoration. If ecosystems are dynamic, then why should we attempt to restore a site to its condition a century ago? What makes the historic state of a system the right state to restore? In response to these questions, some have suggested that we return ecosystems not to their historic *states*, but to their historic ecological *trajectories* (Aronson and Clewell, 2013). This approach aims to incorporate dynamism and change, focusing not on what historic ecosystems looked like, but what they *would* look like today, had humans not intervened.

Others suggest that it is not historic species that should be restored, but rather ecological *processes* that existed prior to disturbance. Still others argue that in light of dynamic ecosystem processes and directional change, historical baselines may no longer be relevant, and we should embrace "futuristic restoration," which sets goals based on the needs and values of human communities today and in the future (Choi, 2004, 2007). Without natural baselines to tell us what to restore, it is up to us to decide. Consonant with this approach is the acceptance of "novel ecosystems," "designer ecosystems," and "intervention ecology" (e.g., Hobbs, Higgs, and Harris, 2009, Hobbs et al., 2011). The Society for Ecological Restoration's current definition of restoration attempts to remain agnostic on many of these issues, describing restoration as "the process of assisting the recovery of an ecosystem that has been degraded, damaged, or destroyed" (SER, 2004), without specifying in much detail what "recovery" requires.

The debate over the significance of historical baselines in restoration is far from settled. Although many continue to advocate for traditional goals of composition-centered "historical fidelity" (Egan, 2006), others suggest that being faithful to history involves considering how social and ecological histories are intertwined and seeking to preserve natural and cultural features that carry social meaning and reflect the "narrative" of a place (Holland and O'Neill, 2003; O'Neill, Holland, and Light, 2008; see also Hourdequin, 2013). Still others are happy to jettison history and embrace novel ecosystems that serve the goals and values of contemporary society. What seems clear, at this point, is that nature itself can't provide an uncontested normative standard for ecosystem management. In some cases, maintaining or restoring historic ecosystems is simply impossible due to changes in climate or in the broader landscape context. Yet even where it is possible, there is often disagreement about whether that is the right thing to do.

3.3   The Turn to Resilience and Ecosystem Services: Anthropocentrism Rising?

Two ideas—resilience and ecosystem services—seem to be filling the void left by the demise of the "balance of nature" approach and the specter of directional change. Both ideas focus primarily on ecosystem processes. *Resilience*, although subject to many of the same worries about conceptual clarity discussed earlier, measures "the capacity of a system to absorb disturbance and reorganize while undergoing change so as to retain essentially the same function, structure, identity, and feedbacks" (Folke et al., 2004: 558; Walker et al., 2004). More simply, resilience is the ability of a system to maintain or return to a particular stable, integrated, or healthy state after perturbation. Resilience is of interest from a social perspective because human communities rely on particular stable states of ecological systems to provide key goods and services.

Herein lies the link between resilience and ecosystem services. Regimes shifts in ecological systems involve changes that move the system from one state to another. Often a regime shift involves radical alterations in a system's compositional and functional characteristics. Lakes, for example, are subject to two main regimes: clear water and turbid water, which differ from one another in phosphorus cycling and phytoplankton biomass (Folke et al. 2004: 562). Similar alternate states are possible for coral reefs, savannas, wetlands, and boreal forests (Folke et al., 2004). As resilience declines, ecosystems tend to behave less predictably and reliably in the production of ecosystem services (Folke et al., 2004: 568), and regime shifts can radically change the kinds and rates of services that a particular system provides.

As human activities degrade the capacity of ecological systems to bounce back from disturbance, resilience has become an important concept. More generally, there is hope that by focusing on sustaining the ability of ecosystems to provide the services we need, we can develop new foundations for conservation and restoration. As Jackson and Hobbs (2009: 568) explain, in an era of global change, "[e]cological restoration finds new moorings in emphasizing restoration of ecosystem function, goods, and services" rather than traditional goals of historic species composition.

This approach raises important ethical and philosophical concerns, however. Ecosystem management currently risks straying from its initial promise as a broader and more holistic successor to single-resource, maximum-yield management. Efforts to quantify and maximize the provisioning of ecosystem services point to a narrower and more reductionistic view. The idea of ecosystem services, when first introduced, served to awaken us to the wonder of the natural world. Discussions of the pollination "services" of bees and other insects, for example, drew our attention to the surprising and remarkable ways in which we depend on nature. Yet dominant contemporary approaches to ecosystem services aim to tame, control, optimize, and market those services.

Kent Redford and William Adams (2009) issue a series of concerns regarding attempts to establish markets and payments for ecosystem services. They worry that a focus on economized ecosystem services will crowd out other, non-economic rationales for conservation, lead us to favor only those aspects of ecosystems that benefit humans, undermine protection of historic or native biodiversity (especially if non-native species can provide the requisite services), and reduce resilience by engineering ecosystems to provide optimal services of one or two kinds (Redford and Adams, 2009: 785–786). What's more, there are challenges in accurately pricing ecosystem services, and if ecosystem services are privatized, questions about justice and access to services may arise (Redford and Adams, 2009: Luck et al., 2012).

The core worry here is that our focus may shift from ecosystems in all their complexity and as carriers and generators of diverse forms of value (Rolston, 1988) to what various parts or configurations of ecological systems can do for us now or in the near future. This is ironic, given the supposed focus of ecosystem management on long-term sustainability. Insofar as ecosystem management seeks to carry on the Leopoldian legacy, the shift toward the provision and marketing of ecosystem services seems particularly incongruous. Leopold (1949: 210) strenuously emphasized the limitations of economically based conservation, noting that such an approach passes over many members of the biotic community that lack economic value. Rather than "invent subterfuges to give [the land and the organisms it sustains] economic importance," Leopold recommended that we reconsider why reasons for conservation must be framed in economic terms to count as legitimate (Leopold, 1949: 210). As discussions of ecosystem services and resilience evolve, there is a risk that all forms of value may be narrowed to a single currency, and this is an outcome that Leopold would advise we guard against.

4 CONCLUSION: ECOSYSTEM MANAGEMENT IN A RAPIDLY CHANGING WORLD

Ecology is a young science, and the concept of ecosystem management is even younger. Since its inception, ecosystem management has faced the challenge of finding its moorings in the world of post-equilibrium ecology. Efforts to anchor ecosystem management in stability, integrity, resilience, and ecosystem health remain active but fraught with conceptual and normative challenges. The hope that ecosystem management might be remoored in concepts of dynamic balance—historic range of variation and natural range of variation—is also under significant pressure. As ecosystems undergo directional changes, both the relevance of the past and concepts of naturalness have been called into question (Cole and Yung, 2010). From the perspective of environmental ethics, critical questions include (1) whether a philosophy of ecosystem management adequately values the natural world and all that exists within it, and (2) how practices of ecosystem management are shaping nature and our relationship with it. These questions are particularly pressing as discussion proceeds over whether we have entered a new geologic epoch, the Anthropocene. It has been suggested that the dawn of this "human age" warrants extension of our role as ecosystem managers to that of *planetary* managers (Thompson, 2012; Thompson and Jackson, 2013). Whether we can undertake such a responsibility while continuing to acknowledge the value of the natural world independent of human beings and their needs remains an open question.

References

Aronson, J., and Clewell, A. F. (2013). *Ecological Restoration: Principles, Values, and Structure of an Emerging Profession*. Washington, D.C.: Island Press.

Cahen, H. (1988). "Against the Moral Considerability of Ecosystems." *Environmental Ethics* 10: 196–216.

Carr, D. S., Selin, S. W., and Schuett, M. A. (1998). "Managing Public Forests: Understanding the Role of Collaborative Planning." *Environmental Management* 22(5): 767–776.

Choi, Y. D. (2004). "Theories for Ecological Restoration in Changing Environment: Toward 'Futuristic' Restoration." *Ecological Research* 19: 75–81.

Choi, Y. D. (2007). "Restoration Ecology to the Future: A Call for New Paradigm."*Restoration Ecology* 15: 351–353.

Christensen, N. L., Bartuska, A., Brown, J., Carpenter, S., D'Antonio, C., Francis, R., Franklin, J. F., MacMahon, J. A., Noss, R. F., Parsons, D. J., Peterson, C. H., Turner, M. G., and Woodmansee, R. G. (1996). "The Report of the Ecological Society of America Committee on the Scientific Basis for Ecosystem Management." *Ecological Applications* 6(3): 665–691.

Clements, F. E. (1905). *Research Methods in Ecology*. Lincoln, NE: University Publishing.

Cole, D. N., and Yung, L., eds. (2010). *Beyond Naturalness: Rethinking Park and Wilderness Stewardship in an Era of Rapid Change*. Washington, D.C.: Island Press.

Cook, J. E. (1996). "Implications of Modern Successional Theory for Habitat Typing: A Review." *Forest Science* 42(1): 67–75.

Costanza, R. (1992). "Toward an Operational Definition of Ecosystem Health." In *Ecosystem Health: New Goals for Environmental Management*, edited by R. Costanza, B. G. Norton, and Benjamin D. Haskell, 239–256. Washington, D.C.: Island Press.

Costanza, R. (2012). "Ecosystem Health and Ecological Engineering." *Ecological Engineering* 45: 24–29.

Currie, W. S. (2011). "Units of Nature or Processes across Scales? The Ecosystem Concept at Age 75." *New Phytologist* 190(1): 21–34.

De Leo, G. A., and Levin, S. (1997). "The Multifaceted Aspects of Ecosystem Integrity." *Conservation Ecology* 1(1): 3. Available at: http://www.consecol.org/vol1/iss1/art3/ [accessed April 1, 2014].

Duane, T. P. (1997). "Community Participation in Ecosystem Management." *Ecology Law Quarterly* 24: 771–797.

Egan, D. (2006). "Authentic Ecological Restoration." *Ecological Restoration* 24: 223–224.

Elliot, R. (1982). "Faking Nature" *Inquiry* 25: 81–93.

Elliot, R. (1997). *Faking Nature: The Ethics of Environmental Restoration*. New York: Routledge.

Folke, C., Carpenter, S., Walker, B., Scheffer, M., Elmqvist, T., Gunderson, L., and Holling, C. S. (2004). "Regime Shifts, Resilience, and Biodiversity in Ecosystem Management." *Annual Review of Ecology, Evolution, and Systematics* 35: 557–581.

Grimm, V., and Wissel, C. (1997). "Babel, or the Ecological Stability Discussions: An Inventory and Analysis of Terminology and a Guide for Avoiding Confusion." *Oecologia* 109(3): 323–334.

Grumbine, R. E. (1994). "What Is Ecosystem Management?" *Conservation Biology* 8(1): 27–38.

Higgs, E. (2003). *Nature By Design*. Cambridge, MA: MIT Press.

Hobbs, R. J., Higgs, E., and Harris, J. A. (2009). "Novel Ecosystems: Implications for Conservation and Restoration." *Trends in Ecology & Evolution* 24(11): 599–605.

Hobbs, R. J., Hallett, L. M., Ehrlich, P. R., and Mooney, H. A. (2011). "Intervention Ecology: Applying Ecological Science in the Twenty-First Century." *BioScience* 61(6): 442–450.

Hobbs, R. J., Higgs, E., and Hall, C. M., eds. (2013). *Novel Ecosystems: Intervening in the New Ecological World Order*. Hoboken, NJ: Wiley-Blackwell.

Holland, A., and O'Neill, J. (2003). "Yew Trees, Butterflies, Rotting Boots, and Washing Lines: The Importance of Narrative." In *Moral and Political Reasoning in Environmental Practice*, edited by A. Light and A. De-Shalit, 219–235. Cambridge, MA: MIT Press.

Hourdequin, M., Landres, P., Hanson, M., and Craig, D. R. (2012). "Ethical Implications of Democratic Theory for US Public Participation in Environmental Impact Assessment." *Environmental Impact Assessment Review* 35: 37–44.

Hourdequin, M. (2013). "Restoration and History in a Changing World: A Case Study in Ethics for the Anthropocene." *Ethics and the Environment* 18(2): 115–134.

Jackson, S. T., and Hobbs, R. J. (2009). "Ecological Restoration in the Light of Ecological History." *Science* 325: 567–569.

Karr, J. R., and Chu, E. W. (1999). *Restoring Life in Running Waters*. Washington, D.C.: Island Press.

Karr, J. R. (2002). "Understanding the Consequences of Human Actions: Indicators from GNP to IBI." In *Just Ecological Integrity: The Ethics of Maintaining Planetary Life*, edited by P. Miller and L. Westra, 98–110. Lanham, MD: Rowman and Littlefield.

Katz, E. (1997). "The Big Lie: Human Restoration of Nature." In *Nature as Subject: Human Obligation and Natural Community*, 93–108. Lanham, MD: Rowman & Littlefield.

Keane, R. E., Hessburg, P., Landres, P., and Swanson, F. (2009). "The Use of Historical Range and Variability (HRV) in Landscape Management." *Forest Ecology and Management* 258(7): 1025–1037.

Keystone Center (1996). *The Keystone National Policy Dialogue on Ecosystem Management*. Keystone, CO: The Keystone Center.

Leopold, A. (1949). *A Sand County Almanac and Sketches Here and There*. New York: Oxford University Press.

Leopold, A. (1972). *Round River: From the Journals of Aldo Leopold*, edited by L. Leopold. New York: Oxford University Press.

Luck, G. W., Chan, K., Eser, U., Gómez-Baggethun, E., Matzdorf, B., Norton, B. and Potschin, M. (2012). "Ethical Considerations in On-Ground Applications of the Ecosystem Services Concept." *BioScience* 62(12): 1020–1029.

McCann, K. S. (2000). "The Diversity–Stability Debate." *Nature* 405 (6783): 228–233.

McShane, K. (2004). "Ecosystem Health." *Environmental Ethics* 26(3): 227–245.

Meffe, G. K., and Carroll, C. R., and contributors. (1997). *Principles of Conservation Biology*, 2nd edition. Sunderland, MA: Sinauer Associates.

Meffe, G. K., Nielsen, L., Knight, R., and Schenborn, D. (2002). *Ecosystem Management: Adaptive, Community-based Conservation*. Washington, D.C.: Island Press.

Norton, B. G. (2005). *Sustainability: A Philosophy of Adaptive Ecosystem Management*. Chicago: University of Chicago Press.

Noss, R. F. (1990). "Can We Maintain Biological and Ecological Integrity?" *Conservation Biology*: 241–243.

O'Neill, R. V. (2001). "Is It Time to Bury the Ecosystem Concept? (With Full Military Honors, of Course!)" *Ecology* 82(12): 3275–3284.

O'Neill, J., Holland, A., and Light, A. (2008). *Environmental Values*. New York: Routledge.

Redford, K. H., and Adams, W. M. (2009). "Payment for Ecosystem Services and the Challenge of Saving Nature." *Conservation Biology* 23(4): 785–787.

Regier, H. A. (1993). "The Notion of Natural And Cultural Integrity." In *Ecological Integrity and the Management of Ecosystems*, Vol. 1, edited by S. Woodley, James Kay, and George Francis, 3–18. St. Lucie Press.

Rolston, H. III (1988). *Environmental Ethics: Duties to and Values in the Natural World*. Philadelphia, PA: Temple University Press.

Rolston, H. III (1994). *Conserving Natural Value*. New York: Columbia University Press.

Sagoff, M. (2003). "The Plaza and the Pendulum: Two Concepts of Ecological Science." *Biology and Philosophy* 18(4): 529–552.

Seastedt, T. R., Hobbs, R., and Suding, K. N. (2008). "Management of Novel Ecosystems: Are Novel Approaches Required?" *Frontiers in Ecology and the Environment* 6(10): 547–553.

Society for Ecological Restoration, Science & Policy Working Group (SER) (2004). *The SER International Primer on Ecological Restoration*. Available at: http://www.ser.org/ resources/resources-detail-view/ser-international-primer-on-ecological-restoration [accessed November 16, 2015].

Thompson, A. (2012). "The Virtue of Responsibility for the Global Climate." In *Ethical Adaptation to Climate Change: Human Virtues of the Future*, edited by Thompson and Bendik-Keymer, 203–222. Cambridge, MA: The MIT Press.

Thompson, A., and Jackson, S. T. (2013). "The Human Influence: Moral Responsibility for Novel Ecosystems." In *Designer Biology* edited by J. Basl and R. Sandler, 125–152. Lanham, MD: Lexington Books.

United States Department of the Interior, Bureau of Land Management [USDI—BLM]. (1994). *Ecosystem Management in the BLM: From Concept to Commitment*. U.S. Department of the Interior, Bureau of Land Management, Washington, D.C., USA.

Walker, B., Holling, C., Carpenter, S., and Kinzig, A. (2004). "Resilience, Adaptability and Transformability in Social-Ecological Systems." *Ecology and Society* 9, no. 2: 5. [online] URL: http://www.ecologyandsociety.org/vol9/iss2/art5

Wallington, T. J., Hobbs, R. J., and Moore, S. A. (2005). "Implications of Current Ecological Thinking for Biodiversity Conservation: A Review of the Salient Issues." *Ecology and Society* 10(1): 15, available at http://www.ecologyandsociety.org/vol10/iss1/art15/ [accessed March 30, 2014].

Walters, C. J., and Holling, C. S. (1990). "Large-Scale Management Experiments and Learning by Doing." *Ecology* 71(6): 2060–2068.

Westra, L. (2005). "Ecological Integrity." In *Encyclopedia of Science, Technology, and Ethics, Vol. 2*, edited by C. Mitcham, 574–578. Detroit: Macmillan Reference.

Wiener, J. B. (1996). "Beyond the Balance of Nature." *Duke Law and Environmental Policy Forum* 7(1): 1–24.

Williams, J. W., and Jackson, S. T. (2007). "Novel Climates, No-analog Communities, and Ecological Surprises." *Frontiers in Ecology and the Environment* 5(9): 475–482.

Woodley, S. (2010). "Ecological Integrity: A Framework for Ecosystem-Based Management." In *Beyond Naturalness: Rethinking Park and Wilderness Stewardship in an Era of Rapid Change*, edited by D. N. Cole and Laurie Yung, 106–124. Washington, D.C.: Island Press.

PART VII

....

CLIMATE CHANGE

*The Defining Environmental
Problem of Our Time*

....

CHAPTER 39

....

MITIGATION
First Imperative of Environmental Ethics

....

HENRY SHUE

BEGINNING with the upsurge in the burning of coal in the steam engines that drove the Industrial Revolution, humans have been generating greater quantities of greenhouse gases (GHGs), especially carbon dioxide, than the earth's climate system had needed to handle during the previous millennia of the human era. Unfortunately for humans and many other species of animals and plants that are adapted to the planetary surface conditions of those previous millennia, the climate system is forced by its own dynamics to deal with these additional gases through adjustments that lead to higher surface temperature, more volatile and extreme weather, sea-level rise, and the other phenomena that we call climate change, plus the acidification of the oceans from the absorption of carbon dioxide. Thus, these "radiative forcing agents," as scientists term anthropogenic emissions, make life on the surface of the planet more difficult and more dangerous for humans and many other living things that cannot change as quickly as human activities are changing the climate. Contrary to alarmist claims otherwise, it is still entirely possible to hold the warming of the average global temperature compared to the temperature level prior to the Industrial Revolution, which is the standard indicator of climate change, below 2° C (Hare, Cramer, Schaeffer, et al., 2011; Schaeffer, Hare, Rahmstorf, and Vermeer, 2012). To hold the temperature rise below 2° C, we must engage in prompt and rigorous mitigation—act now.

"Mitigation" is the name that has come to be applied to preventative actions designed to cut back on the human forcing of climate change with the ultimate goal of keeping climate change within a range to which humans can adapt. "Adaptation," by contrast, reduces human vulnerability to climate changes that occur in spite of mitigation, including changes that are already occurring and changes that are already locked in to the climate system by past emissions. The intermediate goal of mitigation is to reduce net human injection of GHGs into the atmosphere, which can be accomplished in either of two ways: reducing the sources of GHG emissions or increasing the "sinks" into which emissions can safely go. The glossary of the 2014 report by Working Group II of the Intergovernmental Panel on Climate Change (IPCC) defines mitigation of climate change as "a human intervention to reduce the sources or enhance the sinks of greenhouse gases" (Agard, Schipper, Birkmann, et al., 2014). Net additional emissions—sources minus sinks—are what count.

An unavoidable complication, unfortunately, is that all explanations of what counts as a "sink" are normatively charged because they must assume a specific answer to the question, safe for whom? Carbon dioxide, the most important GHG, is absorbed by the atmosphere, the oceans, vegetation (including trees), and the soil. Because limiting climate change depends on controlling the additional amounts of GHG emissions that reach the atmosphere, all destinations other than the atmosphere, including the oceans, are usually counted as sinks. Ocean acidification is thereby treated as a separate matter from climate change. But to consider the oceans as sinks for carbon emissions is to ignore the mounting danger posed by increasing acidification to the fish, coral, plants, and other life in the sea, which play vital roles in the overall planetary economy and specifically in the human food system (Potsdam Institute for Climate Impact Research and Climate Analytics, 2012).

If one focuses narrowly on climate change as phenomena that result from the injection of additional GHGs only into the atmosphere, then the oceans are a sink for carbon dioxide. Thus, the glossary of the same 2014 IPCC Working Group II report defines "sink" as follows: "any process, activity, or mechanism that removes a greenhouse gas, an aerosol, or a precursor of a greenhouse gas or aerosol from the atmosphere" (Agard, Schipper, Birkmann, et al., 2014). On the other hand, if one considers troubling planetary changes resulting from emissions produced by human activity more broadly, then the oceans are not a safe sink but another element of the world to which much life was previously adapted that is now being progressively and rapidly disrupted by excessive emissions. We should not, then, welcome the injection of additional levels of carbon dioxide into the oceans either. Ocean absorption of carbon may be a partial cure for one problem (atmospheric distortion), but it is the central cause of another major problem. In light of this, the main genuinely safe sinks are soils and vegetation, especially the immensely important forests, which must be protected against further deforestation and enhanced by reforestation and afforestation. Otherwise, the emphasis in mitigation ought to be on reducing emissions, especially of carbon dioxide.

Overall, mitigation is much preferable to adaptation. While mitigation is like the prevention of an affliction, adaptation is more like rehabilitation from the affliction, or in some cases, successful adjustment to it while it persists. In general, it is better to prevent a problem from occurring than to cope with it after it occurs. But the relationship between mitigation and adaptation is considerably more complicated than this suggests.

First, some adaptation is vital because some climate changes have already occurred—for instance, sea-levels have already risen—and other changes have been locked-in by past emissions—sea-levels will continue to rise, and extreme weather events will continue to increase in frequency and intensity (Blunden, Arndt, Scambos, et al., 2012). The threats to human well-being posed by some of these current and certain future changes are too severe to be safely ignored.

But if humans can successfully adapt to some types of climate change, economists will ask why we do not use one of their techniques, such as cost-benefit analysis (CBA), to distinguish between risks that it would be cheaper to prevent and those it would be cheaper to adapt to, and then prevent only the former. If sea walls can be built to protect against sea-level rises of a certain amount, and the prevention of sea-level rises of that amount would cost more than the sea walls, why don't we simply invest in the sea walls and only worry about preventing even higher sea-level rises?

But the arguments against deciding between mitigation and adaptation on economic grounds are overwhelming. Even leaving aside the fact that economic values, like efficiency, are only a small subset of human values and that techniques like CBA involve enormous amounts of arbitrary valuation, including arbitrary choices of discount rates, any such proposal would depend on a hopelessly simplistic set of assumptions about the underlying science. Most important, it rests on the false assumption that climate changes are predictably linear and unlikely to involve any sharp thresholds. Not only do we have no reason to believe that all climate change is gradual, but we have compelling evidence that abrupt changes, including abrupt reversals (from severe warming to severe cooling) have occurred a number of times in the past, for example, in the Younger Dryas (National Research Council [U.S.], 2002; Schellnhuber, Cramer, Nakicenovic, et al., 2006). If we decided to try to allow change up to, but not beyond, some point we specified, we would have no guarantee whatsoever that between here and that point there is no threshold beyond which changes would abruptly accelerate because of unexpected positive feedbacks (for example, additional carbon dioxide emissions lead to additional warming that melts permafrost and releases methane, which sharply accelerates additional warming). "As global warming approaches and exceeds 2° C, the risk of crossing thresholds of nonlinear tipping elements in the Earth system, with abrupt climate change impacts and unprecedented high-temperature climate regimes, increases" (Potsdam Institute for Climate Impact Research and Climate Analytics, 2012a). IPCC predictions, for example, have generally underestimated changes. The uncertainties about thresholds and unpredictable positive feedbacks increase sharply as one ventures farther from what humans have experienced.

Second and third—two points combined—an example like a choice of the degree of sea-level rise to which "we" would be willing to adapt assumes a simplistic managerial model of our relationship with the climate system, according to which "we" could pick and choose the effects of climate change "we" wanted to deal with. While sea level was rising to the level we chose to tolerate and adapt to, what would have happened to the South-Asian monsoon, the droughts and forest-fires in the southwestern United States, and the rains in Australia and Europe? It might be that for any given amount of climate change as measured by rise in average global temperature, say by 1.5°C over pre-Industrial Revolution temperatures, some selected threats, such as sea-level rise along the Atlantic Coast of the United States, would be such that adaptation would be the more efficient response compared to prevention, but what about all the other phenomena that would also accompany the temperature rise of 1.5° C—would they all be equally manageable for whoever had to manage them? Could the West Coast manage the forest fires as well as the East Coast could manage the Atlantic sea-level rise? How should the Indians and the Pakistanis manage either drought or flooding that resulted from concurrent disruption of the monsoon? The second point, then, is that climate change comes in large packages of disparate but interrelated phenomena: sea-level rise generally, but drought here and flooding there, unseasonal warmth here and unseasonal cold there, and disruption and volatility generally—could we all adapt to all, or even most, of the various phenomena in any one package? We cannot isolate the manageable phenomena from the others. And third, who after all is "we"? Suppose a wealthy nation like the United States could afford to build the necessary sea walls (or whatever adaptation involved)—will every other nation be able to adapt to whatever phenomena befall it at the same level of climate change? How are the costs and the benefits at that level distributed, and can those upon whom costs would fall bear them?

This question of who are the "we," or how are the goods and bads distributed, points to an argument in favor of the importance of guaranteeing the capacity for adaptation, even if one is primarily concerned about mitigation. Poorer states do not have sufficient resources to fund mitigation as well as adaptation, and the poorest lack the resources to fund even their own adaptation to climate change of any severity. It would be utterly irrational for these poorer states to divert scarce resources into bearing a share of the global cost of mitigation through their use of lower-carbon but more expensive energy than they otherwise would when, as a result, they would be left with less adequate resources for their own adaptation, in the absence of commitments by richer states to fund an adequate share of their adaptation costs (Shue, 1992/2014). But some of the poorer states, notably, India, will cause inordinate amounts of carbon emissions by burning their own abundant coal, the worst (most carbon-intensive) fossil fuel (Helm, 2012) if they do not cooperate with global plans for mitigation. One reasonable way through the dilemma between their depriving themselves of resources for adaptation by cooperating with mitigation and their not cooperating with mitigation is for richer states, which in any case bear far more responsibility for the occurrence of climate change, to contribute substantially to their costs so that they can afford both to mitigate and to adapt.

The recognition of the need for the larger of the poorer states, like India and Indonesia, to cooperate with mitigation brings us to the further complication constituted by the relation between mitigation and sustainable development. Is it incumbent upon such states to forego further development if the only development they can afford unassisted would need to rely upon the worst fossil fuels such as coal? Certainly not, for a compelling mix of empirical and moral reasons. On the one hand, mitigation is not a luxury that a state like India can choose to decline; India is one of the world's most vulnerable states to climate change (Brecht, Dasgupta, Laplante, et al., 2012; Parikh, Jindal, and Sandal, 2013). Successful mitigation is strongly in India's interest, so it is in India's interest to cooperate with multilateral agreements to mitigate if they do not demand unreasonable sacrifice. On the other hand, suspending or postponing justly distributed development that benefits India's poorest citizens would be precisely such an unreasonable sacrifice, for at least three reasons.

First, hundreds of millions of India's poorest do not enjoy their basic rights to subsistence, and they are entitled to pursue improvement in their position. Second, it would be extremely unfair to deny minimal development to the very poor when it is primarily the GHG emissions from the processes that yielded rapid economic development for the now-wealthy that have made climate change as urgent a threat to everyone as it is. Third, it would also—independently—be extremely unfair to expect the poor to sacrifice necessities when many of the richest, for example, citizens of the United States and Canada, are yet to sacrifice even luxuries in order to contribute to climate mitigation (Shue, 1993/2014).

But it would be misguided for the poorest to insist on developing by means of burning fossil fuels, which tend to be the most affordable sources of energy but are far and away the most harmful to the climate, for at least two reasons. First, it would be self-defeating. Climate change can undermine the preconditions of many elements of sustainable development, especially the weather conditions for reliable agricultural production (Porter, Xie, Challinor, et al., 2014). This is essentially another way of stating the earlier point that some of the poorer developing states are highly vulnerable to climate change and need mitigation to constrain the costs—and assure the feasibility—of adaptation, if indeed adaptation is possible, which depends on the severity of the climate change, which in turn depends on the rapidity of mitigation. Second, developing by means of the old unsustainable carbon regime that enabled the now-wealthier to develop would "lock-in" precisely the energy infrastructure that we must eliminate in order to get a grip on GHG emissions. If a state builds coal-fired electricity-generating plants because coal is its cheapest source of energy for electricity, it will have made an investment in capital stock that will pay off what it cost to build it only over decades of use. So it will have painted itself into a corner in which it must continue to burn coal long after safer energy sources are available because it would be so uneconomic—too uneconomic for a poor state—to abandon coal-fired plants early in their useful lives.

If states containing many citizens whose basic economic rights are not secure are to engage in sustainable development, and they are to avoid long-term investment in facilities dependent upon fossil fuels, which is independently required by both genuinely sustainable development and adequately robust mitigation, they obviously must have increased capacity to use non-carbon energy. Happily we encounter a fortunate conjunction here: both energetic mitigation and non-self-defeating development can be promoted by making non-carbon energy available and affordable in the poorer states—the same strategy advances both climate mitigation and enduring development and therefore ought to be the focus of international transfers (Shue, 2013/2014).

The preceding discussion of the relation between mitigation and sustainable development is a more concrete approach to the debates that in the literature have mostly been formulated as more abstract arguments about how to understand justice in mitigation: What is a fair sharing of the benefits and burdens of cooperation on mitigation (together with, I have suggested above, adaptation)? Often these arguments have been framed around the question: What is the morally best justified interpretation of Article 4 of the *Framework Convention on Climate Change*, which allocates burdens by imposing "common but differentiated responsibilities" (Rajamani, 2012)? Philosophers have tended to focus on a set of middle-level principles for the just distribution of the effort and expense of mitigation, often including an ability-to-pay principle (APP), a beneficiary-pays principle (BPP), and a contributor-pays principle (CPP; Page, 2012). The "contribution" invoked by the last is specifically contribution to the problem of climate change; it is thus a version of the general polluter-pays principle and is often operationalized as total cumulative emissions, leading to its being described as "historical responsibility." Many positions assume that the question is simply, which of the principles is the right one? and then argue for the superiority of one principle over the others. Others maintain that more than one consideration is important and argue for particular combinations of principles (Caney, 2005/2010; Kartha, Athanasiou, and Baer, 2012).

The most important point about mitigation is implicit in some earlier sections but remains to be fully explained: mitigation ought to focus in the immediate future on carbon dioxide, not the other GHGs instead, especially on preventing increased burning of coal by China, India, and other developing states that possess large domestic supplies, while they nevertheless continue to develop. It is an empirically groundless hope that reducing GHGs other than carbon dioxide instead of reducing carbon dioxide will "buy time." This point is critical, but politically contentious. For example, "methane first" is an inferior strategy to "carbon first" (Solomon, Pierrehumbert, Matthews, et al., 2013), for two important reasons, although simultaneous reductions in both without trade-offs is unobjectionable. First, as we have already noted, ocean acidification will worsen until carbon emissions are radically reduced. Acidification is caused by the absorption of carbon dioxide, and it will not stop worsening until the carbon dioxide emissions drop sharply—reductions in other GHGs have no effect on ocean acidification. The classificatory quibble about whether ocean acidification is part of climate change proper or should be considered a distinct problem has already been mentioned, but either way ocean acidification is a monumentally significant danger to life in the seas. Acidification's cause, carbon emissions, is also the primary cause of climate change in the narrower sense, which is the second reason for the overwhelming importance of carbon dioxide.

But before we look at how carbon dioxide becomes the most important factor in producing climate change, we need to see why the problems in comparing the various GHGs to each other have not already been solved by the widely accepted notion of global warming potential (GWP), which was used for comparisons in the *Kyoto Protocol*. On the one hand, the atmospheric residence time of carbon dioxide is far longer than that of any other major natural GHG; a couple of relatively minor chemicals synthesized by humans also have extremely long residence times. Less than half of the carbon dioxide emitted ever enters the atmosphere; the bulk is absorbed by soil, vegetation, and, above all, the oceans. But of the carbon dioxide that reaches the atmosphere, most stays for more than a century, much remains for more than a millennium, and some remains for tens of thousands of years (Ciais, Sabine, Bala, et al., 2014)! For as long as the carbon dioxide remains in the atmosphere it continues to contribute to increased warming on the surface, where life resides. Specifying the atmospheric residence time of carbon dioxide is made especially difficult because the fraction that remains in the atmosphere after being emitted increases with the magnitude of the total cumulative emissions (Eby, Zickfeld, Montenegro, et al., 2009). It is, of course, bad news in itself that the larger the cumulative emissions, the longer additional emissions stay and enhance warming.

On the other hand, for the relatively briefer period that methane, for example, remains active as a GHG, a unit of methane is a more powerful GHG ("radiative forcing agent") than a unit of carbon dioxide (25 times more powerful over one century). Some GHGs act longer, while others have briefer residence times but are more powerful. Policymakers have attempted to create a common metric for dealing with the different climate-forcing potencies and the different atmospheric residence times by calculating GWP, taking both potency and residence time into account. However, the weakness in any calculation of GWP results from its being relative to a specific time horizon: the shorter the horizon, the more dangerous methane looks (because it is more powerful while it acts); the longer the horizon, the more dangerous carbon dioxide looks (because it acts for much longer). GWP is therefore not neutral among different timescales, and what timescale to take seriously is a crucial normative premise of any calculation (Solomon, Pierrehumbert, Matthews, et al., 2013). Since there is no neutral way to calculate GWP, it solves fewer problems than one might have hoped (and the equivalences between GHGs built into the "single basket" of six gases in the *Kyoto Protocol* are tendentious in ignoring future centuries).

If one takes a long view and considers climate change over several centuries or a millennium, carbon dioxide is clearly the most dangerous GHG. Two factors, one relatively widely understood and one only recently documented, reveal how. First, it has the longest atmospheric residence time of any significant radiative forcing agent, as is generally known. A significant percentage of the carbon dioxide that reaches the atmosphere will contribute to increased warming for millennia, and this would be true even if, by magic, all further carbon dioxide emissions totally stopped (Ciais, Sabine, Bala, et al., 2014). One cannot overstate the importance of the fact that even when injections of carbon dioxide into the atmosphere completely cease, the carbon dioxide that reached the atmosphere earlier will continue to make warming and the other aspects of climate change worse for a mixture of additional time periods ranging from a century to thousands of millennia because it remains active in the atmosphere!

And indeed multiple studies have now confirmed that the single factor that correlates most strongly with maximum temperature rise (and other measures of the likely severity of climate change) is total *cumulative* emissions of carbon dioxide from the time when the Industrial Revolution first began to expand the atmospheric concentration until the time when the atmospheric concentration ceases to expand because net injections into it have stopped—"net" meaning beyond those absorbed elsewhere, namely by oceans, vegetation, and soil (Allen, Frame, Frieler, et al., 2009; Allen, Frame, Huntingford, et al., 2009; Bowerman, Frame, Huntingford, et al., 2011; Matthews, Solomon, and Pierrehumbert, 2012; Meinshausen, Meinshausen, Hare, et al., 2009). *Cumulative carbon* is becoming widely accepted as the best metric for likely temperature rise.

The second factor that makes carbon dioxide so dangerous, which is much more recently being grasped, is that, basically because of the inertia of the climate system, the surface temperature of the earth will not peak and begin to decline when the cumulative atmospheric concentration of carbon dioxide peaks and begins—very, very slowly—to decline. The carbon dioxide itself lasts longer (first factor) and the effects it leaves behind themselves continue longer after the carbon dioxide is gone from the atmosphere (second factor). An adequate explanation of this second factor is beyond our scope here (and beyond my capacity), but a central element is once again the oceans (Solomon, Pierrehumbert, Matthews et al., 2013). Because the atmospheric carbon dioxide will contribute to greater warming for such a long time, the amount of heat retained on earth as a result will be enormous, and much of this heat will over this long time very gradually find its way into the deep oceans (obviously adding rising temperature to greater acidification as threatening challenges for the life in the seas). The good news for those who live on the land is that the heat that is absorbed by the deep oceans will not add to the warming on the surface of the earth in the short run, but the bad news is that this fact will initially mask, by in effect temporarily hiding much of the heat, how serious the situation of the surface will eventually become.

And then as chemical processes and other factors slowly over the years and decades reduce the size of the cumulative atmospheric concentration of carbon dioxide, which would, other things equal, reduce the amount of global warming, the deep oceans will, through a process of equilibration, gradually release the heat that they have been storing to add to the heat available on the surface of the planet, effectively cancelling out for a considerable period the beneficial effect of the decline in atmospheric carbon dioxide. Life on the surface, including humans, who did not initially need to cope with the heat that entered the deep oceans on its way down, so to speak, will in the end have to cope with much of it on its way back up out of the ocean. A much less superficial explanation is in Solomon, Pierrehumbert, Matthews, et al.; Susan Solomon was Co-Chair of IPCC Working Group I for the 2007 report, and her coauthors are also outstanding scientists from three countries. They conclude: "the long-term legacy of anthropogenic greenhouse gases will be primarily determined by CO_2-induced warming."

The point, of course, is that because of both the long atmospheric residence time of carbon dioxide and the long response time of the climate system to all the heat retained on the planet during that residence time, radical reductions in carbon dioxide emissions to the very low level at which injections into the atmosphere totally cease are absolutely urgent, so that the cumulative atmospheric carbon concentration will, first, stop expanding and, then, slowly diminish. Choosing to reduce methane emissions, or emissions of any other GHG, *instead of* reducing carbon emissions does not "buy time"—it wastes time while the cumulative carbon total mushrooms for the very, very long term. The main task of mitigation, therefore, is to arrange the earliest possible exit from the now-dominant fossil-fuel regime and to make the transition to affordable non-carbon energy. Mitigation, besides prompt and rigorous, needs to be focused—focused on eliminating carbon emissions.

References

Agard, J., Schipper, L., Birkmann, J., et al. (2014). "WGII AR5 Glossary." In *Climate Change 2014: Impacts, Adaptation and Vulnerability, Contribution of Working Group II to the Fifth Assessment Report of the Intergovernmental Panel on Climate Change* edited by V. Barros and C. Field. New York: Cambridge University Press. ipcc-wg2.gov/AR5/images/uploads/WGIIAR5-Glossary_FGD.pdf.

Allen, M., Frame, D., Frieler, K., et al. (2009). "The Exit Strategy." *Nature Reports Climate Change* 3: 56–58. doi: 10.1038/climate.2009.38.

Allen, M., Frame, D., and Huntingford, C., et al. (2009). "Warming Caused by Cumulative Carbon Emissions toward the Trillionth Tonne." *Nature* 458: 1163–1166. doi: 10.1038/nature08019.

Blunden, J., Arndt, D., Scambos, T., et al. (2012). "State of the Climate in 2011." *Bulletin of the American Meteorological Society* 93: 1–264.

Bowerman, N., Frame, D., Huntingford, C., et al. (2011). "Cumulative Carbon Emissions, Emissions Floors and Short-Term Rates of Warming: Implications for Policy." *Philosophical Transactions of the Royal Society A* 369: 45–66. doi: 10.1098/rsta.2010.0288.

Brecht, H., Dasgupta, S., Laplante, B., et al. (2012). "Sea-Level Rise and Storm Surges: High Stakes for a Small Number of Developing Countries." *Journal of Environment & Development* 21: 120–138. doi:10.1177/1070496511433601.

Caney, S. (2005/2010). "Cosmopolitan Justice, Responsibility, and Global Climate Change." *Leiden Journal of International Law* 18: 747–775; reprinted in S. Gardiner, S. Caney, D. Jamieson, and H. Shue, eds. (2010). *Climate Ethics: Essential Readings*. New York: Oxford University Press, 122–145.

Ciais, P., Sabine, C., Bala, G., et al. (2014). "Carbon and Other Biogeochemical Cycles." In *Climate Change 2013: The Physical Science Basis. Contribution of Working Group I to the Fifth Assessment Report of the Intergovernmental Panel on Climate Change*, edited by T. Stocker, D. Qin, G-K. Plattner, et al., 465–570. Cambridge, Cambridge University Press. at Box 6.1 [472-3]. http://www.climatechange2013.org/images/report/WG1AR5_ALL_FINAL.pdf.

Eby, M., Zickfeld, A., Montenegro, A., et al. (2009). "Lifetime of Anthropogenic Climate Change: Millennial Time Scales of Potential CO_2 and Surface Temperature Perturbations." *Journal of Climate* 22: 2501–2511. doi:10.1175/2008JCLI2554.1.

Hare, W., Cramer, W., Schaeffer, M., et al. (2011). "Climate Hotspots: Key Vulnerable Regions, Climate Change and Limits to Warming." *Regional Environmental Change* 11 (S1), 1–13. doi:10.1007/s10113-010-0195-4.

Helm, D. (2012). *The Carbon Crunch: How We're Getting Climate Change Wrong—and How to Fix It*. New Haven: Yale University Press.

Kartha, S., Athanasiou, T., and Baer, P. (2012). "The North-South Divide, Equity and Development—The Need for Trust-Building for Emergency Mobilization." *What Next? Climate Development and* Equity, 3: 47–71. http://www.whatnext.org/Publications/Volume_3/Volume_3_articles/Volume_3_articles.html.

Matthews, D., Solomon, S., and Pierrehumbert, R. (2012). "Cumulative Carbon as a Policy Framework for Achieving Climate Stabilization." *Philosophical Transactions of the Royal Society A* 370: 4365–4379. doi: 10.1098/rsta.2012.0064.

Meinshausen, M., Meinshausen, N., Hare, W., et al. (2009). "Greenhouse-gas Emission Targets for Limiting Global Warming to 2° C." *Nature* 458: 1158–1163. doi: 10.1038/nature08017.

National Research Council (U.S.), Committee on Abrupt Climate Change (2002). *Abrupt Climate Change: Inevitable Surprises.* Washington: National Academy Press, 24–36.

Page, E. (2012). "Give It Up for Climate Change: A Defence of the Beneficiary Pays Principle." *International Theory* 4: 300–330.

Parikh, J., Jindal, P., and Sandal, G. (2013). *Climate Resilient Urban Development: Vulnerability Profiles of 20 Indian Cities.* New Delhi: IRADe.

Porter, J., Xie, L., Challinor, A., et al. (2014). "Food Security and Food Production Systems." In *Climate Change 2013: Impacts, Adaptation and Vulnerability, Contribution of Working Group II to the Fifth Assessment Report of the Intergovernmental Panel on Climate Change*, edited by V. Barros and C. Field. New York: Cambridge University Press. http://ipcc-wg2.gov/AR5/images/uploads/WGIIAR5-Chap7_FGDall.pdf.

Potsdam Institute for Climate Impact Research and Climate Analytics (2012). *Turn Down the Heat: Why a 4° C Warmer World Must Be Avoided*, A Report for the World Bank. Washington, D.C.: World Bank, *xv*, 24–26.

Potsdam Institute for Climate Impact Research and Climate Analytics (2012a). *Turn Down the Heat: Why a 4° C Warmer World Must Be Avoided*, A Report for the World Bank. Washington, D.C.: World Bank, *xvii*, 59–63.

Rajamani, L (2012). "The Changing Fortunes of Differential Treatment in the Evolution of International Environmental Law." *International Affairs* 88: 605–623.

Schaeffer, M., Hare, W., Rahmstorf, S., and Vermeer, M. (2012). "Long-term Sea-level Rise Implied by 1.5° C and 2° C Warming Levels." *Nature Climate Change* 2: 867–870. doi: 10.1038/nclimate1584.

Schellnhuber, H., Cramer, W., Nakicenovic, N., et al. (eds.) (2006). *Avoiding Dangerous Climate Change.* Cambridge: Cambridge University Press.

Shue, H. (1992/2014). "The Unavoidability of Justice." In *The International Politics of the Environment: Actors, Interests, and Institutions*, edited by A. Hurrell and B. Kingsbury, 373–397. Oxford: Oxford University Press; reprinted in *Climate Justice: Vulnerability and Protection*, edited by H. Shue, 27–46. Oxford: Oxford University Press, 2014, 27–46.

Shue, H. (1993/2014). "Subsistence Emissions and Luxury Emissions." *Law & Policy* 15: 39–59; reprinted in *Climate Justice: Vulnerability and Protection*, edited by H. Shue. Oxford: Oxford University Press, 2014, 47–67.

Shue, H. (2013/2014). "Climate Hope: Implementing the Exit Strategy." *Chicago Journal of International Law*, 13, 381–402; reprinted in *Climate Justice: Vulnerability and Protection*, edited by H. Shue. Oxford: Oxford University Press, 2014, 319–339.

Solomon, S., Pierrehumbert, R., Matthews, D., et al. (2013). "Atmospheric Composition, Irreversible Climate Change, and Mitigation Policy." In *Climate Science for Serving Society: Research, Modeling and Prediction Priorities*, edited by G. Asrar and J. Hurrell. Dordrecht: Springer Netherlands, 415–436.

CHAPTER 40

....

ETHICS AND CLIMATE ADAPTATION

....

CLARE HEYWARD

1 INTRODUCTION
....

THROUGHOUT history human beings have adapted to their environmental conditions. This chapter is about adaptation as it appears in discussions about anthropogenic climate change. Human beings have also changed the environmental conditions in which they live, sometimes intentionally, sometimes unintentionally, and sometimes in a very profound way. Anthropogenic climate change, brought about by the increasing atmospheric concentrations of greenhouse gases (GHGs)s particularly carbon dioxide, is a paradigm example. Climate change is projected to have vast environmental impacts, including temperature rises, precipitation changes, rising sea levels, and increased ocean-acidification. These projected changes have significant implications for human well-being across the world.[1] Responding to climate change is a pressing global political challenge, one that so far shows little indication of being resolved.

The idea of adaptation in discussions of climate change differs from the idea of adaptation as imported from evolutionary biology, where any change that contributes to the continued survival of the species in its ecological niche is "adaptive" and those that do not are "maladaptive." In this latter understanding, any response to climate change that avoids harm and allows survival and even flourishing of natural or human systems might be regarded as "adaptive" (Thompson, 2016).[2] In the context of climate change, adaptation does not refer to any response to climate change but to actions directed toward successfully living with the environmental changes associated with climate change, rather than those directed at preventing or limiting those changes.

Historically, adaptation was contrasted with mitigation. Mitigation refers to actions to stabilize atmospheric GHG concentrations (primarily by reducing GHG emissions), thus limiting temperature increases and other features of climate change such as precipitation changes, rising sea levels, and increased ocean-acidification (see Shue, this volume).

Achieving adequate levels of mitigation dominated discussions in the early decades of the United Nations Framework Convention on Climate Change (UNFCCC). During that time, adaptation was sidelined, even almost taboo (Pielke et al., 2007: 597–598). Lisa Schipper outlined several reasons for this (Schipper, 2006: 82–92). Those who advocated mitigation regarded talking of adaptation, variously, as (1) defeatist—an admission that mitigation would be insufficient or ineffective, (2) as indicating or creating unwillingness to partici-pate in mitigation efforts, and (3) as a distraction from mitigation. In addition, adaptation "was implicitly linked with discussion on liability and compensation, which developed countries were keen to avoid" (Schipper, 2006: 85). However, after a decade of the UNFCCC process, it became almost universally accepted that adaptation has an integral role in cli-mate policy. The need to give adaptation efforts equal priority to mitigation is now recorded in the "Cancun Agreement," the outcome of the Sixteenth Conference of the Parties to the UNFCCC (UNFCCC, 2010).

Whether to respond to climate change, how much priority to accord to mitigation and to adaptation, and who should respond have been at the heart of the climate negotiations. Most fundamentally, these are questions of values. Philosophical work on climate eth-ics and climate justice investigates questions encountered and debated in international politics but in a different context, where greater clarity, rigor, and systematicity can (it is hoped) be attained. However, as an applied discipline, discussions in climate ethics or climate justice often track developments in global politics. Perhaps for this reason, there have beeen more discussions of "justice in mitigation" than "justice in adaptation." Where the latter is debated, the questions typically concern the distribution of *responsibility*—duties to engage in adaptation efforts or to facilitate or to financially support the efforts of others. Typically, such debates are focused on the merits of three principles: "the ability to pay principle", the "contribution to problem principle" ' (both implicitly invoked in the UNFCCC's concept of "common but differentiated responsibility"), and the 'beneficiary pays principle' (Shue, 1999: 531–545).[3] Various combinations of these principles have been offered (Caney, 2010; Page, 2011; Grasso, 2010).[4] There has also been some debate about whether duties concerning adaptation should be distributed differently from duties con-cerning mitigation (Duus-Otterström and Jagers 2008: 576–591).[5] This chapter will not review the debate about the fair distribution of duties concerning adaptation. That has been done elsewhere (Hartzell-Nicholls, 2011: 287–700). Instead, it focuses on the issue of how should adaptation be understood for the purposes of a theory of climate justice. That is, (1) what is adaptation to climate change and how does it differ from other responses to climate change, (2) what should be the aim of adaptation, and from this, (3) what might adaptation measures involve? In the case of (2) and (3), the discussion of adaptation in this chapter considers the question of why should we care about climate change. That is an issue that arises prior to the questions of which parties should bear duties concerning adaptation, but it is not discussed as often. In this chapter I wish to foreground the ques-tion of why we should care about climate change. I will argue that harm to one type of important concern—an interest in cultural identity—has frequently been overlooked in the prevailing political and academic debates on climate justice.

Section 2 introduces the concept of adaptation more fully and compares it to other pos-sible responses to climate change. Section 3 considers the questions of what interests and aims adaptation measures should seek to secure. In particular, it will argue that a proper account of adaptation to climate change should take into account possible cultural loss. This has implications for what measures might count as adaptation to climate change and how adaptation is implemented.

2 ADAPTATION AND OTHER RESPONSES
TO CLIMATE CHANGE

Adaptation is used here to denote one of five analytically distinct strategies of responding to anthropogenic climate change. The others are *emissions reduction, sink enhancement, solar radiation management,* and *rectification* (Heyward, 2013: 23–27).[6] These strategies are distinguishable according to the point at which they intervene in the process between the emission of GHGs and the loss of an important element of (human) well-being. As climate change is caused by GHGs accumulating in the atmosphere, one strategy is to reduce GHG emissions. A second strategy is to protect, or increase GHG (especially carbon) sinks. Both of these address climate change by tackling atmospheric concentrations of GHGs. Until recently, these were discussed under the term *mitigation,* although in practice, greater attention was paid to the reduction of GHG emissions. Sink enhancement is, however, beginning to creep back up the policy agenda. As well as initiatives to protect forests, some scientists and businessmen are arguing that there should be more research into potential carbon dioxide removal (CDR) technologies, that is, technologies aimed at creating or increasing carbon sinks (Shepherd et al., 2009). A third possible strategy also getting increased attention is solar radiation management (SRM). SRM techniques allow increases in atmospheric GHG concentrations but aim to reduce global temperatures by increasing the amount of solar energy that is reflected back into space. Several suggestions have been made as to how it can be achieved, but no SRM (or, for that matter, CDR) technology has yet been fully developed.

Emissions reduction, sink enhancement, and SRM all aim at preventing undesirable physical changes to the global climate (Shepherd et al., 2009)[7]. However, for various reasons, ranging from lack of political will to commit to emissions reductions to increased deforestation to the fact that certain responses do not yet exist, global action on climate change has been slow in coming. The Intergovernmental Panel on Climate Change (IPCC) projects that under a "business as usual" scenario, i.e. in the absence of any specific mitigation target, average global temperatures will be 1.5 degrees centigrade higher than above preindustrial temperatures by 2035 and there is a roughly equal chance of the temperature increase exceeding 4 degrees by 2100 (IPCC 2013: 18). Only if emissions were to peak in the next decade and be rapidly reduced, is there any chance of avoiding at least a 1.5 degrees centigrade increase by 2100 (IPCC, 2013: 18). Therefore, a fourth response, adaptation, will be necessary at least to some degree to prevent serious and possibly widespread harms resulting from a warming world. Adaptation strategies do not aim at preventing build-up of atmospheric GHG concentrations (unlike emissions reduction and sink enhancement), nor preventing temperature increases (unlike SRM). Instead, actions and policies assigned the label of adaptation primarily aim at ameliorating the harmful *effects* of those temperature increases and other aspects of climate change (IPCC, 2007).[8] For example, climate change is projected to affect food and water sources, cause drought and flooding, and influence the spread of tropical diseases. Corresponding adaptive measures thus include replacing crops or developing new strains of plants, finding new food sources, adjusting water management and building practices, building flood defenses, vaccinating against diseases, and distributing mosquito nets. Migration is sometimes regarded as a form of adaptation (Webber and Barnet, 2010). The exact measures necessary will depend on the specific impacts of climate change: what environmental conditions are manifest in any given area. Adaptation is thus a (proactive or reactive) response to new or anticipated environmental conditions in a particular place. To put it very simply, adaptation seeks to ensure that any climate change manifested does not result in harm; that is, to take the "danger" out of dangerous climate change.

Should adaptation become necessary but unsuccessful for any reason, the result will be the compromising of one or more key human interests. In such circumstances, *rectification* might come into play. The aim of rectification is to make up, insofar as possible, for harms sustained. It is one of the subjects of the "loss and damage" discourse that was officially initiated in the Cancun negotiations (UNFCCC, 2010), and developed further at the nineteenth Conference of the Parties to the UNFCCC, by means of the adoption of the Warsaw International Mechanism for loss and damage (UNFCCC, 2014).[9]

In climate politics, adaptation increasingly appears among a constellation of related concepts. The first is *vulnerability*, defined by the IPCC's Working Group II as "[t]he propensity or predisposition to be adversely affected." The definition goes on to state that the idea of vulnerability itself "encompasses a variety of concepts including sensitivity or susceptibility to harm and lack of capacity to cope and adapt" (IPCC 2014a, 1775).

Both the nature and magnitude of the environmental change and prevailing social conditions contribute to the degree of vulnerability to climate change and affect whether adaptation is successful. The same physical event might be severely detrimental to some, but barely noticed by others. As Lauren Hartzell Nicholls writes, "a decrease in annual rainfall may not be a huge loss to American homeowners with municipal water supplied to their home, but the same decrease could be devastating to a subsistence farmer in Africa" (Hartzell-Nicholls, 2011: 689). The latter is said to be more vulnerable to climate change. Adaptation strategies seek to reduce vulnerability to environmental changes. Adaptation is also sometimes characterized in terms of *increasing resilience*. Broadly speaking, resilience is the ability of a system to maintain its basic functions and structures, despite any environmental changes. A resilient system (natural or social) will be able to absorb changes, in that it will operate as it did before the changes occurred. The less resilient a system is, the less it will be able to continue its normal functions. Here we might link back to vulnerability and say that such a system is more likely to be harmed. Most recently, the idea of adaptation as not only decreasing vulnerability or increasing resistance but also involving *transformation* has been adopted by the IPCC. In its latest *Assessment Report*, the IPCC defined two types of adaptation:

> **Incremental adaptation** Adaptive actions where the central aim is to maintain the essence and integrity of a system or process at a given scale. **Transformational adaptation** Adaptation that changes the fundamental attributes of a system in response to climate and its effects. (IPCC 2014a: 1758)

Incremental adaptation, the understanding of adaptation dominant in the last 25 years, is tied closely to resilience of an existing system (natural or human). Transformational adaptation, by contrast, indicates a change of system: for example, a shift from savannah to desert or, in the case of human systems, the reconstituting of a society or the "drawing up of a new social contract" (Pelling, 2010).

In the case of climate change, adaptation—however understood—is purposive; its aim is to secure a certain outcome. This is usually cashed out in terms of avoiding or ameliorating certain kinds of harms or adverse effects, but it can be conceived more broadly as aiming to secure certain outcomes or states of affairs. In either case, we need to ask what kinds of interests should be taken into account. What counts as a significant harm or adverse effect of climate change? What kinds of interests should be taken into account in vulnerability assessments, and what adaptation measures should we seek to protect or secure them? Discussions of adaptation often proceed with an implicit answer to this question, but failure to render it explicit can be behind many disagreements concerning the objectives, the relative priority, and even the very concept of adaptation in climate politics.

To illustrate, consider the most recent turn to adaptation as "transformation." The motivation for those who have proposed this understanding of adaptation, in addition to or even as a replacement for adaptation understood as "increasing resilience," is that "there is a danger that adaptation policy and practice will be reduced to seeking preservation of an economic core" (Pelling, 2010: 3). In Pelling's view, if adaptation is understood as resilience, it will simply preserve the status quo of neo-liberal capitalism (which, as well as not guaranteeing social justice, is also a key factor in creating climate change). A great opportunity for social reform will be missed. Hence we should look to adaptation as transformative.

Pelling's views are shared widely enough to be included in the latest IPCC report. However, we should be wary of jettisoning the conception of adaptation as resilience. The real complaint is not that adaptation is a conservative concept per se, but that it *could* be used to conserve the *wrong things*—that is, for Pelling, neo-liberal capitalist institutions. However, adaptation measures need not be centered on measures to protect economic growth. They can—and frequently do—include measures to protect or promote human development, not only economic development characterized in terms of GDP growth.

To illustrate this, consider the following. In 2011, the Saudi Arabian government submitted a proposal that it should be able to access monies from the $100 billion "Climate Aid" fund, established in during the COP-16 negotiations in Copenhagen to fund adaptation schemes across the developing world (Government of Saudi Arabia, 2011).[10] The Saudis argued that they were due financial assistance because they were being asked to change their economic practices in light of global climate change. If, for example, subsistence farmers were due financial assistance when switching crops or even abandoning their farming methods in order to adapt to environmental changes, then the Saudis should be due assistance when switching from an economy that is heavily dependent on fossil fuels. Both kinds of change are costly and inconvenient for those having to undergo them.

However, the Saudi submission did not achieve its objective. It might seem somewhat bizarre that a state with high record of GHG emissions that cause climate change should ask to access funds intended for the victims of climate change. In a sense, though, the submission presented the Saudis as potential victims of climate change. It can be interpreted as making two claims. The first claim is that Saudi Arabia's GDP would be diminished. Perhaps we could say that the Saudi economy is insufficiently resilient to withstand a global shift in energy provision. This first claim by itself is not enough to make the case for access to the international funds. We need a second claim: that national GDP is an interest important enough to be subject to protection or support in the form of adaptation funds provided by the international community. Adaptation funds cannot be expected to protect or support all kinds of interests that might be adversely affected by climate change. Hence, priorities must be set. Protecting Saudi Arabia's GDP was not awarded priority status.

Whether we talk about adaptation in terms of increasing resilience or as being transformative, some kinds of interests must be prioritized over others. When discussing resilience, it is necessary to consider what interests should be preserved. When discussing transformation, it is similarly necessary to consider the kinds of interests that are not yet protected or supported, but which should be the object of transformative measures.

If we understand this, then we can see that adaptation conceived as resilience is not necessarily committed to capitalism of any variety. Interests other than those best served by capitalism might be the focus of adaptation measures. Nor is transformation necessarily good. A society might not wish—or need—its social contract to be redrawn. Indeed, as I shall argue in the next section, in some cases, preservation of some things might be regarded as valuable whereas some changes to the social fabric might be considered harmful, not beneficial. Whether adaptation in the form of increasing resilience or transformative adaptation is to be preferred in any particular case depends on what interests are considered important or valuable, how well a society is supporting those important interests, and how climate change will affect its ability to do so in the future.

In the next section, I turn to the question of what might be included in this set of important interests.

3 ACKNOWLEDGING THE CULTURAL DIMENSION
TO ADAPTATION

Enabling adaptation is usually presented as a solution to climate change and the potential harms and injustices associated with it. In this section, I want to argue that in some cases, the fact that it is now necessary to make certain changes, to instigate certain adaptive measures is itself an injustice. This has consequences for the concept of adaptation.

Consider the case of Inuit groups (Macchi et al., 2008).[11] Arctic temperatures are rising twice as quickly as the global average, with the consequences that the permafrost is being lost, ice is thinning in many areas, and coastal erosion is being observed. Due to these physical changes in the environment, many traditional Inuit practices have been put at risk. For example, traditional food sources are under threat. The health and numbers of traditional Arctic game species have decreased, plus the migratory patterns of the caribou have changed and thinning ice makes it more difficult to land whales. The availability of wild berries and greens is reduced. Traditional methods of food preservation and storage are becoming less viable. Increased salinity threatens traditional sources of drinking water. Travel is also becoming more dangerous. Some Inuit members have fallen through thinning ice, and the igloo—an emergency shelter as well as one of the most important symbols of the Inuit—is harder to make as the deep and dense type of snow needed for building is less widespread. As many Inuit live in costal areas, their homes and important cultural sites are at risk from erosion and more storm surges. Such changes have been documented in a petition submitted in 2005 by the Inuit Circumpolar Conference (ICC) to the Inter-American Court of Human Rights.[12]

The ICC petition listed how the Inuit members have changed their practices according to these new environmental conditions. Overall, the practice of hunting and gathering is diminishing, and more food is purchased at shops. Travel by boat is replacing overland travel in areas where ice has thinned. Tents, rather than igloos, are used for temporary shelters. We might think that the Inuit are adapting to their new environmental conditions: their core interests in food, shelter, water are still being met. However, a core complaint of the Inuit petition is that these kinds of adaptive measures are necessary in the first place. Traditional practices are becoming unviable, and this is in itself experienced as a significant loss (Adger et al., 2009).[13] The social relations that co-constitute these practices are changing, too: for example, the role of the elders as teachers and guardians is being diminished as their traditional knowledge becomes less applicable (ICC 2005: 48). We might say that Inuit societies are undergoing a transformation, but rather than being a positive development, this is something to be regretted—a loss of a valuable way of living.

The Inuit are described in terms of "a common culture characterized by dependence on subsistence harvesting in both the terrestrial and marine environments, sharing of food, travel on snow and ice and a common base of traditional knowledge and adaptation to similar Arctic conditions" (Lynn et al., 2013).[14] The changes in the Arctic environment are making these traditional practices unviable and traditional knowledge (for example weather prediction and prediction of caribou migration) obsolete. For the Inuit, adaptation—in the form of changes in food production, travel, and so on—is not part of the solution to climate change, but part of the problem. That the Inuit are being required to initiate these kinds of adaptive measures—and will probably have to make more—is regarded as a loss of their way of life and could "seriously *threaten . . . the Inuit's continued survival as a distinct and unique society*" (ICC, 2005: 67, emphasis added).

What consequences does this have for the concept of adaptation? Adaptation has usually focused on material needs and interests, and adaptation has been regarded as making and enabling a society to make material and technological changes. The case of the Inuit suggests that this is not enough. Other kinds of interests are affected by climate change, including an interest in maintaining one's cultural identity.

If adaptation is the strategy of maintaining certain core interests in the face of environmental changes associated with global climate change, and there is a core interest in maintaining one's cultural identity, then adaptation strategies should include measures to maintain the distinctive cultural identity of vulnerable groups such as the Inuit.[15] Accepting this has implications for the limits of adaptation and thus the desired balance between mitigation, adaptation, and other responses to climate change. It also has implications regarding the kinds of measures and activities that might be might be counted as means of adaptation to climate change. In the next section I shall outline some of these.

4 RE-IMAGINING ADAPTATION

The first point to note is that including cultural identity as a core interest means that adaptation has greater limits. Rather than being limited simply by human ingenuity and the availability of substitute goods and technologies, the cultural element means that adaptation has limits that are, as Adger et al. put it, "subjectively experienced but nevertheless real" (Adger et al., 2009). Successful adaptation now requires more than ensuring that substitute material goods are available. It also requires that individuals do not become alienated from their cultural identity. This will not always be possible. Unwelcome changes from without are generally perceived as alienating. Going back to the ICC's petition, it is clear that the changes that are having to be made are regarded as loss of valued traditional ways of life and even as jeopardizing the Inuit's continued existence as a distinct society. Perhaps the greatest threat is still to be encountered: as noted earlier, sea levels are rising, which means that some coastal communities will probably have to relocate. Even if the communities are able to relocate en masse, relocation will require great upheaval and change. If the communities end up being dispersed, then their members' sense of identity must be compromised. For the Inuit, therefore, full adaptation—the maintaining of all important material interests and cultural identity—seems far from achievable, given the extent of changes already undergone in the Arctic Circle and impacts projected in the future.

As well as constituting new limits on adaptive capacity, acknowledging the importance of the interest in cultural identity also entails that the limits to adaptation are harder to ascertain, being rooted in individuals' psychology and communities' history and ethos. This understanding of adaptation might be more demanding in terms of effort and resources. In particular, adaptation should not be seen as a matter of simply providing substitute resources, but doing so in a way that is broadly continuous with the community's past. Cultural change due to climate change might be inevitable, but maintaining a sense of continuity with the past can be invaluable in ensuring that the changes are seen as a development of the community's distinctive way of life, rather than the end of it.

One striking example of the importance of even minimal continuity can be found in Jonathan Lear's book *Radical Hope* (2008). Lear describes the plight of the Crow, who, like the Inuit, were faced with the loss of their traditional practices of hunting buffalo (albeit from more directly perceived human causes). In some moving passages, Lear describes the disorientation and despair that the Crow members suffered. While the material basis of the Crow culture and most traditional conceptions of Crow life disappeared, the Crow leader, Plenty Coups, drew on his tribe's intellectual resources and values (the myth of the chickadee, a bird who learns from others and new situations) in order to maintain a sense of Crow identity and destiny throughout this profoundly distressing era. Here, the invocation of a traditional and distinctly Crow myth provided a thin thread of continuity and comfort, even as Crow members' lives changed from being part of a nomadic tribe centered on hunting and war to that of sedentary farmers.[16]

If continuity is key to maintaining cultural identity, it follows that relevant adaptation initiatives should aim at ensuring it. This will require much greater effort, both from community members who have to adapt and individuals and agencies that might be involved in facilitating it. Community members might have to reflect on their cultural beliefs and values and attempt to develop new understandings of the community and its way of life. For those who are charged with financing or delivering assistance, it is not appropriate to insist only on the most cost-effective or economically efficient changes consistent with realizing material interests of the community's members. Adaptation measures should, to the greatest degree possible, be congruent with community beliefs and values and aim at ensuring what Kyle Powys Whyte terms "tribal collective continuance" (White, 2013: 526).

Once this is recognized, we can begin to re-imagine adaptation. Some of the development literature, especially the literature concerning human development and participatory development could provide some guidance for formulating a more culturally sensitive conception of adaptation. Sabina Alkire describes a participatory development initiative in which a group of villagers in India were given funding by a non-governmental organization (NGO) to set up a business (Alkire, 2002). They chose to plant and sell roses. This scheme was successful in generating an income for the group members, although other options, such as rearing goats, would have been more economically successful. The villagers, however, were content with the financial returns and furthermore enjoyed or appreciated other, non-financial aspects of their business. For example, Alkire reports that some villagers gained some spiritual satisfaction from the scheme, knowing that the rose garlands produced would be offered in religious ceremonies (Alkire, 2002: 271–277). Therefore, although the rose-growing business was not the most economically efficient option, Alkire concludes that it was nevertheless worthy of support because of the broad array of interests that it served: material, aesthetic, and spiritual. Similarly, adaptation initiatives should not be focused exclusively on economic efficiency but at ensuring that all important interests are secured—even if this means that more resources are required from international adaptation funds than would otherwise have been the case.

Another notable feature of this example is the community involvement and participation in the initiative. The need to encourage greater participation in communities affected by climate change is increasingly acknowledged. Indigenous communities have a deep understanding of their local environment and are observing the changes firsthand. Their understanding can obviously facilitate adaptive measures. More importantly, the community is the only entity that can decide what changes are both best suited to their new environmental conditions and most congruent with their way of life, beliefs, and values.

Moreover, if group members can engage fully in responding to the climate impacts that they are experiencing, then even if changes are necessary, the changes made will be instigated by the group's members. Ensuring that group members control the processes of adaptation does not mean that there is no cultural loss—the old ways of life will remain unviable. However, even if one regrets—even resents—the loss of goods due to circumstances beyond one's control, being able to decide what course of action to take in response means that one can at least reassert one's sense of identity. *How* one responded to an adverse situation can, at a later stage, be part of the story one tells about oneself, thus helping to maintain a sense of agency and a distinct cultural identity.

There is an outward-looking element too. For others to acknowledge that it is up to the community members to decide how to engage in adaption to climate change means at least that the group's status as a distinctive entity is recognized. As Kyle Powys Whyte argues, "[c]limate change impacts should not be an excuse for weakening progress towards adequate [US] government—[tribal] government relations" (White, 2013: 526). This is not to say that ensuring community participation is a magic bullet, but simply that community participation in and control over adaptation schemes is necessary (albeit insufficient) for adaptation, in its fullest sense, to be possible.

The more interests are deemed relevant for adaptation policy and the more adaptation requires change, the harder it is to achieve. Thus it is harder to adapt fully to climate change if the interest in cultural identity is included. This has several implications. First, even greater financial and human resources might be required—which could cause revision to prevailing accounts of "climate burden sharing." Second, it might be necessary to reconsider the balance between adaptation and the other responses to climate change. The current 2 degrees centigrade threshold of "dangerous climate change" depends on generalized assumptions about adaptive capacity. If adaptation is harder to achieve, that is, adaptive capacity is lower, that could give more reason to try to prevent climate change. The Inuit might have a "right to keep cold" (Adger, 2004: 1711–1715). If that right is violated or infringed, rectification will have to play a much bigger part in the future, as failure to adapt fully means that much more is lost.

5 CONCLUSION

The aim of this chapter has been to invite reflection on what adaptation to climate change means. It has considered the relationship between adaptation and other types of response to climate change. Adaptation—along with emissions reduction, sink enhancement, solar radiation management, and rectification—is a possible response to climate change. Specifically, adaptation aims to deal with the potential or manifested effects of the physical changes associated with global climate change. It does not attempt to reduce GHG concentrations or avert temperature increases.

There are many ways in which a person or a society might be vulnerable to the effects of climate change. Therefore, it is necessary to consider what kinds of things—what interests—should adaptation seek to protect from the effects of climate change? Any account of justice in adaptation must take a position on what interests adaptation measures should protect. The increasing convention in discourses on adaptation is to assume that protection of basic individual material interests is the proper goal of adaptation, and sometimes it has been mooted that the safeguarding of economic interests can also count as adaptation. I have suggested here that an interest in a secure cultural identity is also relevant. The fact that some kinds of adaptations are already necessary can be interpreted a potential cultural injustice: causing the loss of cultural identity is an important interest. However, this injustice might be ameliorated if adaptation measures are conceived of and implemented in ways that foster collective continuance. I have suggested that this might require extra resources from the international community, but it certainly requires that those cultural groups who experience cultural loss due to climate change should have the greatest possible degree of control in deciding how to change their practices in ways that will ensure their collective continuance. Future research and adaptation policies could—and should—consider how this can be achieved.

NOTES

1. For the most up to date review of the current and projected impacts of climate, see the IPCC's *Fifth Assessment Report*, which comprises reports from the IPCC's three working groups, plus a Synthesis Report (IPCC 2013; 2014a; 2014b; 2014c).
2. Some think that contrary to its current use in the general discourse about climate change, "adaptation" should be used to refer to any (sustainable) response to climate change. For such a view see Allen Thompson (2016). Whatever the merits of that case, it would still remain the case that (as I will argue) that there are five analytically distinct ways of responding to climate change, the fourth of which is aiming to ensure that people can live decent lives despite the effects of climate change, rather than trying to prevent certain physical changes or rectify for losses. This chapter is concerned primarily with normative questions that occur when considering the response of ensuring that people can live (well) in a world where climate change has altered the physical environment and environmental systems.
3. To my knowledge, Henry Shue first identified the three principles, although he did not assign these exact labels. See Shue (1999).

4. See, for example Simon Caney (2010) and Edward Page (2011). For an account of distributing duties applied to adaptation, see Marco Grasso (2010).
5. For an explicit discussion of this, see Goran Duus-Otterström and Sverker Jagers (2008).
6. The following paragraph draws upon the typology presented in Clare Heyward (2013).
7. See John Shepherd et al., (2009). It should be noted that SRM, if workable, could only prevent temperature increases. Ocean acidification would still be a major problem. Thus it should be seen as a partial response.
8. Occassionally adapation is defined with reference to exploiting benefits of climate change. For example, in the IPCC's *Fourth Assessment Report*, Working Group 2 defined adaptation as "adjustment in natural or human systems in response to actual or expected climatic stimuli or their effects, which moderates possible harm or exploits beneficial opportunities" (IPCC 2007: 869). In practice, however, discussions of adaptation have focused on the avoidance of possible harms.
9. See the texts of the Cancun Adaptation Framework and the Warsaw International Mechanism (respectively UNFCCC 2010; 2014). Debates about loss and damage are encountering similar concerns about the admission of liability and compensation to those found in the earlier debates on adaptation.
10. See the Government of Saudi Arabia (2011).
11. I focus on the Inuit here as the most prominent example, but other indigenous groups, especially those living in delicate environments, face similar plights. For an overview, see Mirjam Macchi et al. (2008).
12. Inuit Circumpolar Conference (ICC) (2005). For academic research, see for example the various articles in a special issue of *Climatic Change* (Maldonado et al. (eds) 2013).
13. Neil Adger et al. (2009) also draw attention to this case.
14. For example, traditional foodstuffs have symbolic significance, as well as being a source of nourishment. See Kathy Lynn et al. (2013).
15. Some might dispute that a stable cultural identity is an interest worth safeguarding. I cannot debate this here, but it seems that those who dispute it do so primarily because of the potential for conservatism and oppression of individuals. See for example Susan Moller Okin's essay and responses in Okin et al. (eds.) (1999). This is a reasonable concern, but the potential for abuse need not lead us to reject outright the idea that many individuals value and/or need a stable cultural identity.
16. See Allen Thompson (2010) for an account of adapting environmental virtues by reference to the story of Plenty Coups and Jonathan Lear's conception of the virtue of "radical hope."

REFERENCES

Adger, N. (2004). "The Right to Keep Cold." *Environment and Planning A* 36(10): 1711–1715.
Adger, N. et al. (2009). "Are There Social Limits to Adaptation to Climate Change?" *Climatic Change* 93(2): 335–354.
Alkire, S. (2002). *Valuing Freedoms: Sen's Capability Approach and Poverty Reduction*. Oxford: Oxford University Press.
Caney, S. (2010). "Climate Change and the Duties of the Advantaged." *Critical Review of Social and Political Philosophy* 13(1): 203–228.
Duus-Otterström, G., and Jagers, S. (2008). "Climate Change Responsibility: On Moral Divergences between Adaptation and Mitigation" *Environmental Politics* 17(4): 576–591.

Government of Saudi Arabia (2011). "Submission by Saudi Arabia: View on Different Elements of the Cancun Agreement Decision 1/CP16." (February 21, 2011) Available at https://unfccc.int/files/adaptation/application/pdf/saudiarabia_submission.pdf.

Grasso (2010). "An Ethical Approach to Climate Adaptation Finance." *Global Environmental Change* 20(1): 74–81.

Hartzell-Nicholls, L. (2011). "Responsibility for Meeting the Costs of Adaptation." *Wiley Interdisciplinary Reviews: Climate Change* 2(5): 287–700.

Heyward, C. (2013). "Situating and Abandoning Geoengineering: A Typology of Five Responses to Climate Change." *PS: Political Science and Polices* 46(1): 23–27.

Inuit Circumpolar Conference (ICC) (2005). "*Petition to the Inter American Commission on Human Rights Seeking Relief from Violations Resulting from Global Warming Caused by Acts and Omissions of the United States.*" (7 December), available at http://www.ciel.org/Publications/ICC_Petition_7Dec05.pdf.

Intergovernmental Panel on Climate Change (IPCC) (2007). *Climate Change 2007: Impacts, Adaptation and Vulnerability. Contribution of Working Group II to the Fourth Assessment Report of the Intergovernmental Panel on Climate Change,* edited by M. L. Parry, O. F. Canziani, J. P. Palutikof, P. J. van der Linden and C. E. Hanson. P. Cambridge; England and New York, NY.

IPCC (2013). *Climate Change 2013: The Physical Science Basis. Contribution of Working Group I to the Fifth Assessment Report of the Intergovernmental Panel on Climate Change,* edited by T. F. Stocker, D. Qin, G.-K. Plattner, M. Tignor, S. K. Allen, J Boschung, A. Nauels, Y. Xia, V. Bex and P. M. Midgely. Cambridge, England and New York, NY: Cambridge University Press.

IPCC (2014a). *Climate Change 2014: Impacts, Adaptation, and Vulnerability. Part A: Global and Sectoral Aspects. Contribution of Working Group II to the Fifth Assessment Report of the Intergovernmental Panel on Climate Change,* edited by C. B. Field, V. R. Barros, D. J. Dokken, K. J. Mach, M. D. Mastrandrea, T. E. Biliar, M. Chaterjee, K. L. Elbi, Y. O. Estrada, R. C. Genvoa, B. Girma, E. S. Kiseel, A. N. Levy, S. MacCracken, P. R. Mastrandrea and L. L. White. Cambridge; England and New York, NY: Cambridge University Press.

IPCC (2014b). *Climate Change 2014: Mitigation of Climate Change. Contribution of Working Group III to the Fifth Assessment Report of the Intergovernmental Panel on Climate Change.* Edited by O. Edenhofer, R. Pichs-Madruga, Y. Sokona, E. Fhahrani, S. Kander, K. Syboth, A. Adler, I. Baum, S. Brunner, P. Eickemeier, B. Kriemann, J. Savolainen, Schlömer, C. von Stechow, T. Zwickel and J. C. Minx. Cambridge; England and New York, NY: Cambridge University Press.

IPCC (2014c). Climate Change 2014: Synthesis Report. Contribution of Working Groups I, II and III to the Fifth Assessment Report of the Intergovernmental Panel on Climate Change. Edited by the Core Writing Team, R. K. Pachauri and L. A. Meyer, Geneva, Switzerland: IPCC.

Lear, J. (2008). *Radical Hope: Ethics in the Face of Cultural Destruction.* Cambridge MA: Harvard University Press.

Lynn, K., Daigle, J., Hoffman, J., Lake, F., and Michelle, N. (2013). "The Impacts of Climate Change on Tribal Traditional Foods." *Climatic Change* 120(3): 545–556.

Macchi, M., Oviedo, G., Gotheil, S., Cross, K., Boedhihartono, A., Wolfangel, C., and Howell, M. (2008). *Indigenous and Traditional Peoples and Climate Change.* Gland, Switzerland: International Union for the Conservation of Nature.

Maldonado, J. K., Pandya, R. E., and Colombi, B. J., eds. (2013). "Climate Change and Indigenous Peoples in the United States: Impacts, Experiences and Actions." *Climatic Change* 120(3): 509–682.

Okin, S. M., Cohen, J., Howard, M., and Nussbaum, M., eds. (1999). *Is Multiculturalism Bad for Women?* Princeton, NJ: Princeton University Press.

Page, E. (2011). "Climate Justice and the Fair Distribution of Atmospheric Burdens." The Monist 94(3): 412–432.

Pielke, R. Jr., Prins, G., Rayner, S., and Sarowitz, D. (2007). "Lifting the Taboo on Adaptation." Nature 455: 597–598.

Pelling, M. (2010). *Adaptation to Climate Change: From Resilience to Transformation.* London: Routledge.

Schipper, E. L. F. (2006). "Conceptual History of Adaptation in the UNFCCC Process." *RECIEL* 15(1): 82–92.

Shue, H. (1999). "Global Environment and International Equality." *International Affairs,* 75(3): 531–545.

Shepherd, J., Caldeira, K., Cox, P., Haigh, J., Keith, D., Lauder, B., Mace, G., MacKerron, G., Pyle, J., Rayner, S., Redgwell, C., Watson, A. (2009). *Geoengineering the Climate: Science, Policy and Uncertainty.* London: The Royal Society.

Thompson, A. (2010). "Radical Hope for Living Well in a Warmer World." *Journal of Agricultural and Environmental Ethics* 23(1): 43–59.

Thompson, A. (2016). "Adaptation, Transformation, and Development." In *Ethics for the Anthropocene,* edited by K. Shockley and A. Light. Cambridge, MA: MIT Press.

United Nations Framework Convention on Climate Change (UNFCCC) (2010). "Report of the Conference of the Parties in its sixteenth session held in Cancun from 29th November to 10th December 2010." (FCCC/CP/2010/7/Add.1), § 2b.

UNFCCC (2014) 'Report of the Conference of the Parties on its nineteenth session, held in Warsaw from 11 to 23 November 2013. Part two: Action taken by the Conference of the Parties at its nineteenth session' (Geneva: UNFCCC). Available at: http://unfccc.int/resource/docs/2013/cop19/eng/10a01.pdf.

Webber, M., and Barnet, J. (2010). "Accommodating Migration to Promote Adaptation to Climate Change." Washington D.C.: World Bank, http://dx.doi.org/10.1596/1813-9450-5270.

White, K. P. (2013). "Justice Forward: Tribes, Climate Adaptation and Responsibility." *Climatic Change* 120(3): 517–530.

CHAPTER 41

....

CLIMATE DIPLOMACY

....

ANDREW LIGHT

THIS chapter reviews the relatively brief history and the ethical terrain of diplomatic efforts to form a global agreement on climate change. While in the past it has often been assumed that such efforts have yielded few results, I will make a case that climate diplomacy to date has in fact resulted in some important successes within a vexing political environment, culminating with the adoption of the Paris Agreement on climate change in 2015.

I proceed as follows. First, I offer a brief overview of the history of the primary multilateral climate negotiation body, involving nearly all UN member states, and distill from it a set of some of the core but nonetheless contentious moral elements of these negotiations. This will not be an attempt to summarize the commentary from ethicists and other observers about what the moral dimensions of an international climate agreement should be, but rather what moral elements have become embedded in the negotiations through the process of trying to create a global climate regime. Second, I take up the transformation in these negotiations since 2009, especially the move away from attempts to negotiate common mitigation targets for blocks of participating parties within a legally binding and punitive framework. A key question is whether this transformation in the preferred architecture for a global agreement is morally responsible in light of the challenges we face. Finally, I take a step back and review the current state of climate diplomacy against the backdrop of broader diplomatic priorities and argue that the elevation of climate diplomacy alongside other top-tier foreign policy issues will be critical in bringing about the kind of international cooperation needed to achieve any modicum of climate stabilization.[1]

1 MORAL DIMENSIONS OF THE UN CLIMATE NEGOTIATIONS

....

As is well known, the primary body responsible for negotiating an international treaty to limit greenhouse gas emissions is the United Nations Framework Convention on Climate Change or UNFCCC. The Convention itself was agreed upon and opened for signature at the 1992 UN Conference on Environment and Development, otherwise known as the Rio Earth Summit. By 1994 the treaty had enough signatories to enter into force. As of December 2015 it has 197 participating parties including the European Union.

The parties to the Framework Convention have met annually since 1995 in Conferences of the Parties (COPs) of the UNFCCC to try to negotiate an agreement to limit greenhouse gas emissions. In between the annual meetings, which are usually held for two weeks every year in November or December, interim negotiating sessions are held to try to advance the agenda of the previous COPs. The UNFCCC has no permanent home, so the meeting moves to a different country every year. The outcomes of each COP usually refer to the city in which they were agreed: for example, Copenhagen Accord (2009), Durban Platform (2011), Warsaw International Mechanism on Loss and Damage (2013).

Because the parties could not agree on procedural rules for these meetings, any political or legal decision must be made by consensus. This effectively means that, with very rare exceptions, all parties to the Convention have a veto on all decisions of the COP. While not originally adopted as a principled mechanism, this default consensus rule has come to represent the first important moral dimension of this forum: since climate change will impact all countries, the consensus rule effectively protects the interests of smaller and less powerful parties, who may experience both the first and the worst impacts of global warming, against the interests of larger countries that could more easily adapt to a changing climate. Although the consensus rule also allows larger parties to block the demands of the smaller parties, the necessity of consensus tends to drive the parties toward some form of compromise in order to accomplish anything. Absent this rule, smaller parties would have precious little leverage that they could exert over larger parties.

For example, beginning formally in 2009, larger and wealthier countries, like the G8 parties during their 2009 summit, began arguing that the appropriate target for some form of "climate safety" should be to hold temperature increase caused by humans to two degrees Celsius (2°C) over preindustrial levels (G8, 2009). There was, however, ample evidence in the scientific literature that even a 2°C increase in global average temperature could still cause very bad impacts both on small island states and those least developed countries with significant populated territories at or below sea level (EU Climate Change Expert Group, 2008). The consensus rule helped ensure that poor and vulnerable countries were able to push for consideration of a more stringent target at the Copenhagen COP in 2009 and get language in the ensuing Copenhagen Accord requiring an annual review of whether this target could be strengthened to holding temperature increase at 1.5°C. By the time of the Paris Agreement in 2015, all parties agreed to "pursue efforts to limit the temperature increase to 1.5°C above pre-industrial levels" (United Nations, 2015, 21, article 2.1). While it is no doubt true that some powerful countries resisted the adoption of a form of voting other than the default consensus rule to protect their own interests (which preserves their veto), the result is a process that at least aspires to be equally protective of all interests. Unfortunately however, it also simultaneously hinders collective ambition in the negotiations by sometimes driving consensus to the lowest common denominator.

Whether any particular party pushed for the default consensus rule for moral reasons, certainly the foremost explicit moral principle in the Convention is that commonly represented by the acronym CBDR for "common but differentiated responsibilities." While vauge, it is appealed to as providing some of the most explicit guidance for how burdens for mitigation should be distributed between developed and developing countries. In full, the original articulation of this principle in the Framework Convention reads:

> The Parties should protect the climate system for the benefit of present and future generations of humankind, on the basis of equity and in accordance with their common but differentiated

responsibilities and respective capabilities. Accordingly, the developed country Parties should take the lead in combating climate change and the adverse effects thereof (United Nations, 1992, 8, article 3.2).

What this passage means has been the subject of a 20-year controversy that has spread well beyond climate change to impact nearly every major UN-based international negotiation (see Leong, 2014). Within the climate framework, however, it is most often taken to mean (though nowhere has this ever been explicitly agreed to) that (1) a party's historical emissions and (2) their development needs should count in differentiating the responsibilities of developed and developing countries in response to climate change.

In very general terms, proponents of the strongest versions of CBDR argue that rich, high-emitting countries, like the United States—which was the largest carbon dioxide emitter in the world in 1992 and is still the largest historical emitter—are primarily responsible for climate change. Their emissions have been the principle drivers of accelerated anthropogenic global warming especially given the long life of CO_2. In addition, many poorer developing countries, which still have millions of people in extreme poverty, need to continue burning fossil fuels in order to reduce the harms associated with that poverty (Shue, 1993). These two ideas have been combined to argue that developed countries should make deeper cuts in their emissions first, along with absorbing the cost, for example, of transitioning to renewable energy or improving energy efficiency, followed by cuts from developing countries. This simple formulation has effectively served over the past 20 years as a very rough baseline to argue which parties should cut their emissions the most and to what level of stringency those parties making cuts should be bound.

What this effectively means in practice, however, about the differences in obligations among the parties to the Convention varies widely. In its most extreme form, this reading of CBDR has been used to argue that only developed countries should be legally required to cut their emissions. Developing countries, no matter what their emissions growth profile, should, at most, make voluntary cuts to their emissions, but only if supported in doing so by developed countries.[2] Extreme interpretations of CBDR have tended to create a deadlock in the negotiations, which, while recently showing significant signs of eroding, have historically been a critical hurdle to producing an effective global climate agreement (see Aldy and Stavins, 2008). The United States, the EU, and many other developed country parties argue that although CBDR itself must be recognized as an agreed upon starting point for assessing relative responsibility for mitigation and, with some limitations, provision of finance and technology to developing countries, a sharp bifurcation of all duties of parties to respond to climate change based on development status should not follow (see e.g. Stern, 2014).

Even with this principle of CBDR however, the original UNFCCC treaty did not bind any party to reduce emissions but only asked signatory parties to make voluntary reductions. In relatively short order for a diplomatic process, the parties created the first treaty to emerge from the Framework Convention, the Kyoto Protocol, which was finalized in 1997 and went into force in 2005. Its most controversial element, effectively expressing CBDR in a concrete form, required most developed country parties (or "Annex 1" parties as they are identified under the Convention—primarily the parties of the Organization for Economic Cooperation and Development [OECD] as of 1992) to initially achieve a 5–8% reduction in greenhouse gas emissions below 1990 levels by 2012. In this "top-down" agreement—which set a required level of legally binding emission reductions on some parties within an agreed upon compliance and enforcement regime—developing country parties (or "non-Annex 1" parties under the Convention), no matter the size or projected growth of their emissions, were not required to reduce their emissions. However, a set of project based "flexibility mechanisms"—the Clean Development Mechanism and the Joint Implementation program—were created to encourage non-Annex 1 parties to reduce their emissions by allowing Annex 1 parties to offset some of their obligations under Kyoto by paying for or co-implementing mitigation projects in developing countries (United Nations, 1998; Aldy and Stavins, 2008).

Although this outcome can be seen as a consistent application of CBDR, it unfortunately did not produce an agreement that did very much to advance meaningfully ambitious international cooperation on climate change. The United States symbolically signed the Kyoto Protocol, but the Clinton administration never submitted the treaty for ratification largely because of this application of CBDR, which severely constrained the Protocol's reach and impact. Before the treaty was even finalized in Kyoto, the United States Senate, which must ratify any foreign treaty by a two-thirds majority of the 100 members, voted 95–0 in favor of the Byrd-Hagel Resolution that stipulated that the Senate would not consider a treaty based on this kind of division of responsibilities between Annex 1 and non-Annex 1 parties embodied in the Protocol (US Senate, 1997).

Although Byrd-Hagel primarily cited economic competitiveness arguments against the United States joining Kyoto, the resolution also identified an important physical limitation of the Kyoto Protocol, that has since been embraced by virtually all Annex 1 parties, effectively introducing another moral element to the negotiations: without some reductions from the major emitters in the developing world, we cannot hope to achieve the 2°C goal. In a sense it argued that all polluters must pay something, including those whose pollution is more recently on the rise. Evidence for this claim has been mounting. The largest quantity and growth in emissions by far is now in developing countries (IPCC, 2014: 43), and those trends will no doubt continue, given global population demographics. These trends are evident not only in the case of current emissions. Shortly into the next decade, China is predicted to become the world's largest historical emitter of CO_2, and sometime in the current decade all developing countries combined, led by China, India, Brazil, Indonesia, Mexico, South Africa, and Turkey, are likely to exceed the cumulative historical emissions of developed countries (den Elzen et al., 2013).[3]

For this reason, even if developed countries achieved significant emission reductions, on the order of an 80% decrease by 2050—as they also agreed was an appropriate mitigation target at the 2009 G8 summit—and the largest emerging economies continued at current projected rates to 2050, the world would almost certainly exceed the 2°C goal (Light, 2013: 113). This does not mean that all major emitters must achieve the same reductions regardless of their development needs. It does, however, mean that all must contribute something substantial to the solution.

At the thirteenth meeting of the COP in Bali, Indonesia in 2007, the parties did manage to agree on the Bali Action Plan, which was designed as a first step past the deadlock that emerged after Kyoto with the United States refusing to join the Kyoto Protocol until countries like China agreed to emission reductions as well.[4] The Bali plan attempted to cut a tit-for-tat deal whereby developing countries would agree to nationally appropriate mitigation actions, or NAMAs, in exchange for finance and access to clean energy technology. The NAMAs would be subject some form of measurement, reporting, and verification (so-called "MRV"). Unlike the project based flexibility mechanisms under Kyoto, this is not an offset mechanism for Annex 1 parties, but assistance to help non-Annex 1 parties achieve reductions of their own.[5]

The landscape of the negotiations has significantly changed since 2009, aimed primarily at creating a new architecture for a global agreement that is more "bottom-up" than "top-down" (to be discussed in the next section). Nonetheless, these basic moral elements of the negotiations have remained in place. To summarize, they include

(1) A principle of procedural justice embedded in the consensus rule recognizing the common risk of all parties to the threat of climate change regardless of their size or political power.

(2) A basic formula for distributive justice, embodied in CBDR, usually understood to be based in an assessment of (a) each parties' current and historical emissions profile, and (b) their relative development needs.

(3) A responding call for a tempering of CBDR, through a forward looking "polluter-pays" principle, as exemplified in the US objection to Kyoto, focusing on the physical limitations of achieving long-term mitigation goals without the participation of all major emitters.[6]

(4) The basic elements of a "tit-for-tat" agreement through the institution of NAMAs for developing countries contingent on delivery of (a) technology assistance and (b) financing from developed countries, though requiring proof of these reductions through a system of MRV.

Certainly other moral elements could be teased out of the history of the negotiations as well. Foremost among these would be the explicit mention of a right to sustainable development and the articulation of a precautionary principle in the Convention; the numerous, though largely undefined, references in this process to obligations to future generations; as well as the less common but nonetheless potentially potent recent references in the agreements to protect "the integrity of Mother Earth" (for example in the 2013 "Lima Call for Climate Action"). The problem with many of these appeals to substantive moral claims, however, is that they have never found a way to be operationalized in the agreement because there is no consensus on what they mean.[7] At best, they express the views of some parties about what motivates their calls for climate action.[8]

2 MOVING BEYOND KYOTO

As already mentioned, since 2009 most of the parties to the UNFCCC have been working toward a new basic architecture for the climate negotiations, one that does not seek to create a top-down assigned schedule of mitigation commitments by parties divided according to the 1992 annexes to the Convention. In part, this was a move designed to try to pull the process out of the impasse that was created by Kyoto that did not include the emissions of the world's largest emitter (China, by design) or the world's second largest emitter (the United States, by choice). This new bottom-up architecture involves each party putting forward its own commitments for mitigation to an agreed upon year and then further agreeing to some system of MRV and voluntary compliance. In its most basic form, failure to meet one's targets does not result in any punitive consequence, such as a penalty or fine defined under the agreement. Parties are held to their targets through a form of international peer pressure, charitably referred to in international policy circles as "pledge and review," and somewhat uncharitably as "shame and blame." In truth however, both descriptions are accurate. Parties put forward pledges that are reviewed by their peers, but the consequences of putting forward a bad pledge come largely through the reputational consequences of appearing to be a bad actor, combined with whatever legal retribution other parties, or the larger community, are willing to enact in response to irresponsible action outside of the agreement. More sophisticated versions of this system, such as the 2015 Paris Agreeement, have legally binding provisions on MRV and schedules of successive pledges that significantly enhance the basic pledge and review system. I will briefly run though the history of the development of this new system before connecting it to the four moral elements of the negotiations identified at the end of the previous section.

In 2009, the parties to the UNFCCC convened to create a new climate agreement more adequate to the task of producing full participation by the largest emitters, something that was not achieved in the Kyoto Protocol. While most observers were disappointed with the result, and six small countries blocked the agreement from achieving a consensus outcome, the 2009 "Copenhagen Accord" set the template for the architecture for the new global agreement achieved at the 2015 COP in Paris.

Without getting into the very contentious dynamic of Copenhagen, the important upshot was that it succeeded in trying a new bottom-up architecture and instigated a process whereby 62 countries, responsible for approximately 75% of global emissions, officially registered what they were willing to do unilaterally to reduce their emissions by 2020, including, for the first time, the United States, China, and India. Added to this, and most important for any hope of getting significant commitments for emission reductions from non-Annex 1 parties, was a commitment by developed countries to raise $30 billion in "fast start" finance for developing countries between 2010 and 2012 for mitigation and adaptation and to mobilize $100 billion a year from both public and private sources for climate finance by 2020, primarily to flow through the creation of a new Green Climate Fund (United Nations, 2009).[9] In 2010, the Cancún COP successfully secured a consensus outcome around this new architecture (the Cancun Agreements) and added to it a fleshed out version of MRV for the 2020 mitigation commitments, though with separate and weaker provisions for developing countries (Podesta and Light, 2010).

Impressive as it is that so many countries made mitigation pledges in this period, altogether they were not sufficient to keep us on a cost-effective global emission reduction pathway that can eventually achieve the 2°C target (Light, 2013). At the Durban COP in 2011, partially in response to the ambition gap in the Copenhagen and Cancún mitigation pledges, an effective reset was called, and the parties agreed to start a new four-year process initiating the Ad-hoc Working Group on the Durban Platform for Enhanced Action to create a new comprehensive climate agreement by 2015, which would go into force by 2020. This new agreement would be designed to replace both the Kyoto Protocol and the Copenhagen Accord and Cancún agreements.[10]

After the 2011 Durban COP, a broad consensus emerged through the COPs in Doha (2012), Warsaw (2013), and Lima (2014) that the most viable path toward a new global agreement was a continuation of the Copenhagen bottom-up architecture—entailing that parties would set their own targets for the next period of post-2020 commitments—though significantly amended to make it more robust and more reliable for securing ambitious mitigation commitments adequate to meet climate stabilization goals. In the resulting Paris Agreement

(United Nations, 2015) the mitigation commitments of each party are not legally binding, while the other elements around those commitments, involving MRV, accounting rules, and the like, as well as the creation of cycles for renewing and potentially improving commitments on regular five year cycles (to be explained later in the section), are legally binding.

There are many reasons that parties have become attracted to this kind of agreement, but primarily it is practical. By the time of the Durban COP only about 15% of global emissions were covered by Kyoto. Even if the parties bound to reduce their emissions under Kyoto had zeroed their emissions, it would not have made a significant difference toward long-term global temperature trajectories. On the other hand, as was mentioned earlier, the Copenhagen pledges approximately 75% of global emissions (Light 2011), even though their ambition was not as high as would have been hoped.

In contrast, Paris achieved very high rates of participation. Before the first word was spoken at the start of the Paris COP, 188 countries representing over 95% of global emissions, had submitted their targets, or as they were termed, Intended Nationally Determined Contributions, to reduce their emissions beyond their Copenhagen pledges either to 2025 or 2030. These contributions are highly differentiated and reasonably ambitious (Taraska, 2014). For example, the European Union pledged to reduce its greenhouse gas emissions 40% below 1990 levels by 2030. The United States pledged to reduce its emissions 26–28% below 2005 levels by 2025, thus doubling its rate of decarbonization. China has announced that it will peak its CO_2 emissions in 2030, and earlier if possible, and increase the share of non-fossil fuels in its primary energy consumption to 20% by 2030. India announced a 30–35% emissions intensity target and a 40% target for installed capacity of non-fossil electricity generation by 2030.

Still, one limitation of this first round of intended contributions only going out to 2025 or 2030 is that altogether they are not yet sufficient to hit the 2°C goal. The most optimistic estimates are that the cumulative pledges could stabilize temperature increase at 2.7°C over pre-industrial levels. One of the improvements of the Paris Agreement over Copenhagen and Cancún however is to require that parties come back to the negotiating table at regular five year cycles to scrutinize their targets and compare them against a regular global stock taking exercise providing an assessments of where the world needs to be with respect to aggregate ambition. Under the Paris Agreement parties will then submit new targets for the next five years with an expectation that they not backslide but instead continually increase their ambition over time. This will make it more likely that the long-term temperature stabilization goals can be met.

One final question remains: Does this new architecture substantially change the common though contentious moral elements of the negotiations identified earlier? As for (1) procedural justice, nothing in this new approach changes the essential dynamic that every party is allowed a veto in the process. One thing that is weakened though, to which I will return, is an inherent limitation with bottom-up pledges: no party can effectively block another party's mitigation pledge as being part of the agreement.[11]

With respect to (2) the formula for distributive justice embedded in CBDR, this approach appears to allow for ultimate differentiation. Each party determines for itself what it will contribute toward global mitigation based on its own assessment of its national circumstances. But rather than being determined by one's placement in a category such as the Annexes to the UNFCCC, this is self-determined for each party. The problem is that there is no guarantee that developed country parties will "take the lead" in mitigation efforts as stipulated in article 3.2 of the Convention. While this worry was ameliorated in Paris by requirements for constant and progressive updating of pledges over time, the only recourse if a developed country party puts forward a low initial pledge, and then follows it with only incremental improvements, is to call them out for being irresponsible (i.e., "shame and blame").

The forward-looking polluter pays principle (3) is intact here by raising the expectation that all major parties will put forward some kind of contribution, although again there is no punitive consequence for failing to put forward an extremely low pledge as of yet. But the tit-for-tat structure (4) from the NAMAs is intact, and it will help to encourage more developing country parties to reduce their emissions, assuming that adequate assistance through finance and technology can be maintained.

3 Raising the Stakes on Climate Diplomacy

I will turn shortly to the complications just raised over the compatibility of the bottom-up architecture in the Paris Agreement and the moral elements of the climate negotiations. But first we should keep in mind that the UNFCCC negotiations are not the only form of climate diplomacy happening today. There is also a vast array of bilateral and plurilateral climate-related initiatives (diplomatic endeavors involving more than two but fewer than the full array of UN state parties). The latter include forums designed primarily to advance the core negotiations among a smaller group of parties—such as the Major Economies Forum and the Cartagena Dialogue—and those focused on specific sectors—such as the Clean Energy Ministerial and the Climate and Clean Air Coalition on Short-Lived Climate Pollutants. Almost all major parties have some kind of bilateral climate change track—for the United States this includes Climate Change Working Groups with China and Brazil and the Joint Working Group on Combating Climate Change with India—and there is a vast array of individual agreements that have been made between larger and smaller parties to assist them in their clean energy transitions and adaptation plans.

This is to say that the full terrain of climate diplomacy today is quite rich and varied, and we do not need to rely on the Framework Convention as the only forum for fulfilling what we may see as demands of justice with respect to the global response to climate change. Those issues that the Framework Convention has not been able to grapple with as of yet—such as ramping up cooperative programs to address greenhouse gas emissions in agriculture or creating a forum for addressing the prospect of waves of climate refugees—are already being addressed by voluntary associations of developed and developing countries.

This state of affairs should give us some solace when considering the future of the UNFCCC. Even if the negotiations, and the cycles of continual pledging established in Paris, broke down at some point in the future with a change in a major party's domestic circumstances, it would not mean that all climate diplomacy had stopped.[12] Nonetheless, even with this varied environment, compared to other critical issues of foreign policy—such as international security, trade, development assistance, or even the protection of human rights—from my perspective as a climate diplomat, climate change is only now emerging as a cross-cutting arena for international leverage, where an issue in one of these areas can be used by a party or coalition of parties to force an outcome in another. A bottom-up climate system will work best when states begin actively using non-climate carrots and sticks to achieve better climate outcomes in the same way, for example, that we have recently seen trade sanctions used to forge a deal with Iran over their nuclear weapons program.[13] There are promising signs however that all of the activity over the last four years along the road to Paris is driving us to a moment in history when we can create both an effective and stable international climate regime and raise expectations that a party's participation in advancing that regime is a key part of its profile as a good international actor.

The stability of this regime will be aided by the fact that the Paris Agreement, unlike the Kyoto Protocol, Copenhagen Accord, and Cancún Agreements, was designed to not need constant re-negotiation. If this stability persits, then parties can use the standards and timetables in the agreement to focus on continually updating their own pledges and refine opportunities for cooperative action. This will not guarantee success for achieving some level of climate stability, but it will create an environment in which that will be more likely. But a system driven by bottom-up mitigation pledges of necessity will only succeed if there are greater consequences for a party to shirking their broadly considered responsibilities than how they are received in the siloed halls of the UNFCCC negotiations. An essential element of overcoming the weaknesses I identified earlier with respect to a bottom-up architecture of self-differentiated pledges should be expanding the consequences of acting irresponsibly.

All the problems I identified with respect to the first three moral dimensions of the climate negotiations relative to a bottom-up architecture share a common element: they all involve the possibility of a party shirking some notional understanding of their proper responsibilities in the face of this global challenge, either with respect to mitigation or support for other parties. This concern begins to be mitigated by recognizing that a pledge and review system requires a system of transparency. The Paris Agreement stipulates the creation of a new common transparency and MRV system for all parties which will be built out over the next year or more. But the shame and blame part of it is not effective if the only consequence of shirking is confined to the somewhat constrained community of climate actors.[14] If, however, parties pay a broader reputational price for being bad climate actors—and it hinders their ability to seek the agreements they wish in non-climate areas—then this will put more pressure on them even if they don't pay a direct penalty under the Paris agreement. What will also help avoid the problems identified earlier with the bottom-up approach is the reverse: moving to a point where parties will actively seek international credibility and leadership for being good actors on climate change. I do not have the space to go into a full analysis of what it will mean to bring climate change into the top-tier of foreign policy to encourage this transition, but anecdotally it appears that we are getting close to this kind of world, and possibly for reasons instigated by the current negotiating process. The biggest example of this emerging trend toward parties seeking greater global credibility for action on climate change is surely the dynamic that evolved since late 2014 between the United States and China.

In the run-up to Copenhagen in 2009, these two parties were engaged in a very public and acrimonious debate over who was responsible for the lack of progress toward success in Copenhagen. Given the legacy of Byrd-Hagel, the new Obama administration did not want to appear to be soft on China. As a result, neither the United States nor China was willing to signal what reductions they would be willing to make under a new agreement until the last few weeks before the meeting started. Each was essentially waiting for the other to go first, and as a result holding back other parties from making pledges as well. This left no time to scrutinize the adequacy of either pledge, or the cumulative impacts of all of the pledges that eventually came forward, which became conclusive evidence for many that a bottom-up architecture could never generate sufficient ambition for mitigation.

Fast forward to 2014 and the world has dramatically changed. In the weeks before the Lima COP, China and the United States surprised the world by announcing in Beijing, a year before the Paris climate summit, their aforementioned top-line numbers for their post-2020 pledges (US-China Joint Announcement, 2014). The fact that these two parties made their announcement together does not prove in itself that their post-2020 mitigation pledges are morally responsible given their respective contributions to emissions. It does, however, demonstrate that both parties thought that there was something to be gained by making this announcement together, both with respect to advancing toward a new global climate agreement and for their larger geopolitical interests. While not universal, this announcement reverberated throughout the climate world, spurring other parties to put forward their own pledges well in advance of the Paris COP. This allowed for much greater scrutiny of the individual and collective adequacy of these pledges before the start of the Paris negotiations, as opposed to the secretive dynamic ahead of Copenhagen.

Potentially even more impressive in this regard was the follow-up announcement almost a year later in Washington, when President Xi and President Obama once again released a joint statement on climate change (US-China Joint Presidential Statement, 2015). Although the US side of the announcement largely reiterated pledges it had made previously, China shocked the world by announcing that it would create a national cap-and-trade program by 2017, and make available ¥20 billion (approximately $3.1 billion) from their China South-South Climate Cooperation Fund to support other developing countries, including enhancing the capacity of other developing countries to access the Green Climate Fund (paragraph 15). The dynamic here is notable. Unlike the 2014 statement, China did not clearly get anything in return for making these pledges except the international credibility of making these announcements in Washington, as opposed to at home or at the UN, in part demonstrating that they have capacity that the United States does not, especially with respect to creating a national pricing mechanism on carbon. What is emerging here is arguably a dynamic race to the top for climate leadership between the world's two superpowers. Whether generated by geo-political self-interest or a sense of global responsibility, these kinds of larger reputational benefits for ambition will have positive benefits for the climate.[15]

Given the constraints of the UNFCCC as described in this chapter, the fact that we succeeded in creating what appears to be a durable and ambitious agreement out of this process in Paris is a remarkable accomplishment of diplomacy in and of itself. But no matter one's views on the relative success of this process so far, continued work to advance on the framework achieved in Paris is essential, and should be a priority for environmental ethics, if we are to see any hope for a just outcome to the problems we now face. The unfortunate alternative is waiting for the day when a climate crisis emerges of such magnitude that we have no choice but to throw together a fragmented array of international coalitions to manage what can only be imagined as an effort at global triage. Such a day can be avoided, but only with sustained attention to this important area of climate ethics and international cooperation.

Notes

1. The following chapter is based in part on the review of the scholarly literature on climate diplomacy but also in large measure on my own experiences. I have been deeply involved in climate negotiations for the past ten years, primarily through non-governmental organizations and think tanks (where I advised a variety of government and non-government actors) and in the last three years as a senior climate change official in the U.S. Department of State. All opinions expressed herein are my own and do not represent the positions or policies of the United States government.

2. See for example the submission of the "Like-Minded Developing Countries" regarding pre-2020 ambition and mitigation commitments (United Nations, 2013), which places all responsibility for any further reduction in global emissions before 2020, above and beyond what had already been pledged in Copenhagen and Cancun by 2010, solely on developed countries.

3. It is important that these figures do not overshadow other relevant measurements such as per-capita emissions, in which the United States emits significantly more than other countries, a fact that has also been taken into account by many parties and commentators in assessing responsibilities for emission reductions.

4. Between Kyoto and Bali, there were different attempts to get the United States to reconsider its position and join Kyoto. One of the options proposed was to create a system of "graduation" for the Annexes so that, for example, China could move onto the list of Annex 1 parties and the criticisms raised about Kyoto in the US Senate could be answered. Unfortunately, however, criteria for graduation have never been agreed to, so this idea has effectively been shelved in favor of the current system of self-differentiated mitigation commitments, to be discussed further on in this chapter.

5. Disagreements have emerged, however, over whether developing countries would be legally bound to make these reductions after receiving assistance for NAMAs and hence whether the MRV provisions on the NAMAs would hold developing countries to a rigorous form of accountability in exchange for assistance.

6. Although I realize that the polluter-pays principle is not usually understood as being bound temporally one way or another, for much of the history of these negotiations many parties have asserted in different contexts that emissions factor into CBDR only with respect to historical emissions. The realization that developing countries will eclipse developed countries with respect to historical emissions has tempered this somewhat and has changed the views of some parties. If the polluter-pays principle should not be temporally understood, then in some sense the US Senate was offering a correction to a misunderstanding of it here, which is slowly catching on.

7. A good example is the reference to a right to sustainable development in article 3.4 of the Convention. While it is referenced by many parties, it isn't easily operationalized and instead has been used by some parties to assert the right to even more controversial moral claims that would probably never find their way into an agreement, such as the assertion by the Indian government of a right to "equitable access to atmospheric space." See United Nations (2011b).

8. The last few years have also seen entirely new moral arguments appearing in the climate negotiations, which I do not have room to discuss here. In particular, as was mentioned in chapter 42, is the idea of "loss and damage" growing out of the negotiations on the adaptation pillar in the run up to the creation of the Paris Agreement in 2015. Although implications of loss and damage are unsettled, it raises interesting questions such as whether a

system of compensation could ever be created for poor countries that will suffer some of the more catastrophic impacts of climate change, and to what extent we can measure non-economic losses due to climate change (see the text of the 2013 "Warsaw International Mechanism on Loss and Damage" for the beginning of the UNFCCC's response to this issue and the Paris Agreement (United Nations 2015) for the current status of this issue).

9. This fund has now been created and reached its first goal in 2014 of amassing over $10 billion in commitments for its initial capitalization (Ogden and Taraska, 2015).

10. Of particular note, the aim was to create either a "protocol, another legal instrument or an agreed outcome with legal force under the Convention applicable to all Parties" (United Nations, 2011a: para. 2). In stipulating that the outcome would be "applicable to all Parties," the agreement presupposes that, whatever cuts in emissions the parties agreed to, the same legal requirements should be common for all.

11. Some limitations on this restriction were proposed for Paris, such as the no-backsliding provision and the idea that parties that do not submit a pledge that contains at least some non-contingent elements (such as elements not dependent on external support) cannot be part of the agreement.

12. Indeed, as Robert Stavins has argued (2010), this array of other forums for climate diplomacy was deployed effectively in 2010 to get an expanded version of the agreement that was blocked in Copenhagen, agreed to a year later in Cancún.

13. There have been many discussions in various literatures of how different trade regimes could be used to enhance or enforce a global climate agreement, or alternatively be used to punish non-participatory parties without invoking WTO violations. For a variety of perspectives see Barrett (2005), Frankel (2010), and Gardiner (2004).

14. For example, when Canada announced that it would not meet its commitments under the first commitment period of the Kyoto Protocol in 2006, it suffered no penalties because the provisions for failure to meet a commitment under Kyoto only impacted a party's obligations in successive commitment periods of the protocol (see Grubb, 1999—any amount of reduction not achieved in the first commitment period was tied to a party's required reductions in the next period plus a penalty). As Canada was effectively pulling out of the Protocol (though they would not make this official until 2011 when they were expected to join a second commitment period), it suffered no direct consequences in the Convention.

15. There are other notable examples as well where we don't know but can suspect that non-climate carrots and sticks were used to achieve climate outcomes. For example, while there has been plenty of praise for how then Mexican Foreign Minister Patricia Espinoza handled the negotiations to produce the Cancún Agreements after the failure at Copenhagen, little has been written (because little is known) about the back-door regional diplomacy that the Mexicans engaged in to achieve the success that they did in 2010 (see Stavins, 2010). The hold-out countries in Copenhagen blocking consensus were Sudan and four member of the left-leaning "ALBA" alliance: Bolivia, Cuba, Nicaragua, and Venezuela. Reigning in the ALBA block to essentially agree to the same structure that it had opposed at Copenhagen required diplomatic efforts focusing on regional cooperation—which Mexico could provide and Denmark could not—that probably went beyond narrow considerations of the climate agreement.

REFERENCES

Aldy, J., and Stavins, R. (2008). "Climate Policy Architectures for the Post-Kyoto World." *Environment* 50(3): 6–17.

Barrett, S. (2005). *Environment and Statecraft*. Oxford: Oxford University Press.

den Elzen, M. G. J., Olivier, J. G. J., Höhne, N., and Janssens-Maenhout, G. (2013). "Countries' Contributions to Climate Change: Effect of Accounting for All Greenhouse Gases, Recent Trends, Basic Needs and Technological Processes." *Climatic Change* 121(2): 397–412.

EU Climate Change Expert Group. (2008). *The 2°C Target*. Brussels: The European Commission.

Frankel, J. (2010). "Global Environment and Trade Policy." In *Post-Kyoto International Climate Policy*, edited by J. Aldy and R. Stavins, 493–529. Cambridge: Cambridge University Press).

G8. (2009). *Responsible Leadership for a Sustainable Future*. L'Aquila, Italy: G8.

Gardiner, S. (2004). "The Global Warming Tragedy and the Dangerous Illusion of the Kyoto Protocol." *Ethics and International Affairs* 18: 23–39.

Grubb, M. (1999). *The Kyoto Protocol: A Guide and Assessment*. London: The Royal Institute of International Affairs.

Intergovernmental Panel on Climate Change. (IPCC). (2014). *Climate Change 2014, Mitigation of Climate Change. Contribution of Working Group III to the Fifth Assessment Report of the Intergovernmental Panel on Climate Change*, edited by O. Edenhofer, R. Pichs-Madruga, Y. Sokona, E. Farahani, S. Kadner, K. Seyboth, A. Adler, . . . J. C. Minx. Cambridge, England: Cambridge University Press.

Leong, A. (2014). "The Principle of Common but Differentiated Responsibilities and the SDGs." *Post 2015.org*. May 27. http://post2015.org/2014/05/27/the-principle-of-common-but-differentiated-responsibilities-and-the-sdgs/

Light, A. (2011). "Why Durban Matters." Washington, D.C.: Center for American Progress. http://www.americanprogress.org/issues/2011/12/why_durban_matters.html

Light, A. (2013). "Beyond Durban: A New Agenda for Climate Ethics." In *Justice, Sustainability, and Security: Global Ethics for the 21st Century*, edited by E. Heinze. New York: Palgrave Macmillan.

Ogden, P., and Taraska, G. (2015). *"Don't Rob Peter to Pay Paul: The Importance of International Climate Finance in the President's FY16 Budget."* Washington, D.C.: Center for American Progress. February 5.

Podesta, J., and Light, A. (2010). "Key Pact in Global Warming Fight." *Politico*. December 17. http://www.politico.com/story/2010/12/key-pact-in-global-warming-fight-046487

Shue, H. (1993). "Subsistence Emissions and Luxury Emissions." *Law and Policy* 15: 39–59.

Stavins, R. (2010). "What Happened (and Why): An Assessment of the Cancun Agreements." *An Economic View of the Environment*. December 13. http://www.robertstavinsblog.org/2010/12/13/successful-outcome-of-climate-negotiations-in-cancun/

Stern, T. (2014). "Seizing the Opportunity for Progress on Climate." Washington, D.C.: US Department of State. October 14. http://www.state.gov/s/climate/releases/2014/232962.htm

Taraska, G. (2014). "Climate Change: How to Make Sense of the Lima Talks." *Newsweek*, December 5.

United Nations. (1992). *United Nations Framework Convention on Climate Change*. New York: United Nations.

United Nations. (1998). *Kyoto Protocol to the United Nations Framework Convention on Climate Change*. New York: United Nations.

United Nations. (2009). *The Conference of the Parties Takes Note of the Copenhagen Accord.* New York: United Nations.

United Nations. (2011a). *Establishment of an Ad Hoc Working Group on the Durban Platform for Enhanced Action.* New York: United Nations.

United Nations. (2011b). *Proposals by India for Inclusion of Additional Agenda Items in the Provisional Agenda of the Seventeenth Session of the Conference of the Parties.* New York: The United Nations.

United Nations. (2013). *Submission by the Like-Minded Developing Countries on Climate Change Implementation of All the Elements of Decision 1/CP.17,* (b) Matters related to paragraphs 7 and 8. Ad-Hoc Working Group on the Durban Platform for Enhanced Action (ADP). New York: United Nations.

United Nations. (2015). *Adoption of the Paris Agreement.* New York: United Nations.

United States Senate. (1997). *Senate Resolution 98 (The Byrd-Hagel Resolution).* 105th Congress, First Session. Washington, D.C.

U.S.-China Joint Announcement on Climate Change. (2014). November 12. Washington, D.C.: The White House. https://www.whitehouse.gov/the-press-office/2014/11/11/us-china-joint-announcement-climate-change

U.S.-China Joint Presidential Statement on Climate Change. (2015). September 25. Washington, D.C.: The White House. https://www.whitehouse.gov/the-press-office/2015/09/25/us-china-joint-presidential-statement-climate-change

CHAPTER 42

GEOENGINEERING

Ethical Questions for Deliberate
Climate Manipulators

STEPHEN M. GARDINER

Star Trek's Montgomery Scott ("Scotty") is the patron saint of engineers. Whatever fix the Starship *Enterprise* and her illustrious crew get into, however severe the damage to the ship and the superiority of their opponents, Scotty always seems able to work a technological miracle to bail them out. In our time, we face a threat potentially as daunting as the Klingons, Romulans, or Borg. The threat is global environmental change—as manifested in problems such as climate change, ocean acidification, mass extinction, and so on—and it is of our own making. In the case of climate, we have been trying to address the threat for more than twenty years, but to little avail, and the situation is deteriorating. Some say that the time when conventional strategies alone (including conventional engineering) might be able to cope is fast receding. Perhaps "desperate times call for desperate measures." Should we call for Scotty?[1]

Many august writers and institutions seem to think so, and are now calling for serious research on grand technological interventions. Over the last few years, supportive statements and reports have been issued by the President of the National Academy of Sciences, the American Meteorological Association, the Royal Society, and the UK House of Commons, to name but a few. Some scientists have even begun to call for deployment in the near future. As the environmental situation worsens, this clamor is likely to intensify.

Many acknowledge that a drive toward grand technological interventions would have social implications. Indeed, the Royal Society's influential early report (Royal Society 2009) goes so far as to declare that acceptability "will be determined by social, legal, and political factors as much as by scientific and technical factors" (ix), and "ethical considerations are central to decision-making in this field" (39). Moreover, the Society insists that "the *greatest challenges* to . . . successful deployment . . . may be . . . social, ethical, legal and political . . ., rather than scientific and technical" (xi; emphasis added), since deployment "before appropriate governance mechanisms are in place" would be "highly undesirable" (ix). Consequently, it recommends that "analysis of ethical and social issues associated with research and deployment" should be a central research priority (53).

In the spirit of aiding the emerging conversation, this chapter asks two basic questions: What are the central ethical issues? How do they affect how responsible policy should be conducted?

1 GEOENGINEERING

Early discussions of grand technological interventions occur under the heading "geoengineering." Etymologically, the term marries "geo" and "engineering," and so means simply "earth engineering." Beyond this, however, the terminology quickly becomes more difficult.

1.1 Defining Features

To begin with, there is disagreement about the more specific defining features of geoengineering. For instance, Thomas Schelling suggests that the word implies "something global, intentional, and unnatural" (Schelling, 1996), but others further restrict the term to include (for example) only interventions that combat anthropogenic climate change, are for the sake of human interests (Broad, 2006; Fogg, 1995), or involve "a countervailing measure" (Keith, 2000a).[2]

Such additional criteria bring on understandable disagreement. For instance, the "for the sake of human interests" requirement implies that intervention motivated by concern for other species (e.g., the polar bear or other charismatic megafauna), specific places (e.g., the Everglades), or nature as a whole would not count as geoengineering. Similarly, the combating and countervailing measure conditions suggests "grand projects" such as "removing the arctic sea ice to warm Russia" (thereby *enhancing* climate change) would also not qualify (Keith, 2000a: 251). Yet such claims seem unduly restrictive.

Related concerns beset the definition's more central components. For instance, must intervention be unnatural to count as geoengineering? But what about a policy of "planting vast areas of Earth's surface with trees selected and managed for their carbon sequestering properties" (Jamieson, 1996: 325)? In one sense, this seems very "natural," yet it does seem to be some kind of "engineering." More generally, the terms "natural" and "unnatural" are often thought to be philosophically puzzling. The usual contrast is between the natural and the artificial. Yet humans are also part of nature (Vogel 2011); hence, it is unclear why what humans make does not also count as natural (especially since birds' nests and beavers' dams usually do).

It is also unclear what role intention should play. On the one hand, many insist that it is irrelevant. We are already "engineering" the planet (they say), through such actions as emissions of greenhouse gases and ozone-depleting chemicals. The fact we did not intend the consequences is neither here nor there.[3]

On the other hand, intentionality seems to play an important role in many people's thinking. For instance, even those who reject making intentionality part of the definition of geoengineering often have strong (and conflicting) intuitions about the implications. For example, some imply that what we have already done gives us reason to regard intentional interventions more kindly. (Since the milk is already spilled, does it really matter if we spill a bit more in order to clean up the mess?) However, others resist this, saying "two wrongs do not make a right." Some even suggest that further intervention would be worse than the initial wrong.

It is also unclear what is at stake in insisting that geoengineering must be genuinely global. For instance, large-scale regional engineering projects, such as damming the Strait of Gibraltar and Bering Strait to control climate effects in the North Atlantic and Arctic[4] seem to bear the hallmarks of global engineering projects and bring on similar concerns.[5]

On the other hand, many actions have consequences that are in some sense global, but some of these senses seem trivial. For example, suppose I intentionally kill a hundred birds migrating through Seattle to prevent them reaching their winter feeding grounds. If something else takes up their ecological niche in South America, transforming the local habitat, have I engaged in geoengineering? Intuitively, I have not: the sense in which this effect is "global" seems neither extensive nor fundamental enough to qualify as the kind of intervention we are interested in when we use the term. Still, if this is right, what are we really gesturing toward? For instance, just how extensive or fundamental does the influence need to be, and why (Keith, 2000b)?

1.2 Intervention

Questions about how to understand geoengineering go beyond issues of definition to the basic idea of intervening in nature.

To begin with, it is unclear what counts as an appropriate benchmark against which to understand something as an intervention. One obvious answer would be the natural background. However, this idea is more difficult than it initially seems. For instance, is the natural background the state that would obtain were there no humans? Initially, this seems tempting. However, humans have already had significant effects on most ecological and many other earth systems (Ruddiman, 2003). What is to be said about these effects? Moreover, why consider the *nonhuman* background the relevant benchmark? Isn't the effect of the system on humanity important? Surely it is. However, how should humanity be included? Ought we take the benchmark to be some prehistoric, hunter-gatherer situation, or a (clearly counterfactual) ideal circumstance in which more technologically advanced humans live in a (yet-to-be-specified) state of "harmony" with nature?

Related issues surround how one understands a particular intervention. Pre-theoretically, people are inclined to see interventions that aim to "remove" some existing problem already caused by human activity differently from those that try to "compensate for" such a problem, or "improve" the natural situation. For instance, it seems likely that interventions aimed at countering threats to human and nonhuman life posed by "natural" processes (such as shifts in the Earth's orbit or super volcanoes) would be seen more kindly than those aimed at engineering our way into a utopia. Current proponents of geoengineering, for instance, typically seek to limit overall human impact on the climate system by aiming at targets such as restricting global temperature rise to 2 degrees Celsius or restoring the atmospheric concentration of carbon dioxide to preindustrial levels. Thus, their proposals seem more palatable to many people than proposals that aim at optimizing climate to suit wider human goals (e.g., food production).

Still, the intuitions surrounding terms like "removal," "compensation," and "improvement" seem to require philosophical clarification, especially with respect to their moral implications (see Hourdequin, "Ecosystem Managment," this volume). Arguably, they are drawn from ordinary, everyday experience. However, the context of geoengineering may make such intuitions inappropriate. One reason would be if everyday causal intuitions are not a good guide in complex systems such as global climate. Another would be if such intuitions inform a morality that is itself not well adapted to large-scale contexts. So, for example, some philosophers argue that our present moral intuitions and principles evolved relatively recently in "low-population-density and low-technology societies, with seemingly unlimited access to land and other resources," and so are ill-suited to genuinely global, intergenerational, and interspecies problems (Jamieson, 1992: 148).

1.3 Implications

These various difficulties make discussion of geoengineering more challenging than it might otherwise be. For instance, many proposals for climate intervention have been made, and it is not clear which count as geoengineering and which do not. This makes it hard to make general remarks about geoengineering, considered as such. In addition, disagreement about what counts complicates arguments over competing technologies. For instance, sometimes people respond to arguments for or against one candidate (e.g., marine cloud brightening) by invoking some other candidate (e.g., carbon capture) as a counterexample. Yet such counterexamples are slippery when what counts as geoengineering can be contested in myriad ways.[6] Finally, such issues are exacerbated by the fact that various, and sometimes competing, rationales are offered for geoengineering (even of ostensibly the same kind). For instance, occasionally proposals are made to "improve" the climate (e.g., Soviet "weather modification" efforts); sometimes geoengineering is seen as a cheap remediation option; sometimes it is advocated as a way of "buying time" for more desirable policies; and often it is seen as a "last resort," only to be deployed to forestall or mitigate some impending disaster when all other options have failed.

For these (and other) reasons, some doubt that "geoengineering" is a useful term and advocate jettisoning it altogether. Nevertheless, this conclusion seems premature. For one thing, it seems clear that important and interesting issues are at stake, and that some kind of terminology with which to discuss them would be useful. For another, on reflection, the conceptual difficulties are neither surprising nor unusual.

They are not surprising because a good part of developing a taxonomy in this area will (surely) involve identifying which features of various proposals are relevant to policy and which are not. However, this enterprise raises important moral and political questions—that are unlikely to be solved merely by definitional fiat. In other words, if we do not have a firm grip on what concerns us about various proposals and what does not, then advance classification is likely to be difficult, especially if we are trying to employ narrowly descriptive terms to craft the definitions. Indeed, under such conditions, it may be unreasonable to expect clear and precise definitions to emerge prior to detailed theoretical work. In particular, if our concerns are primarily normative, and if a good part of what we are trying to do is to articulate to ourselves and to others what those concerns are, ethics will play an important role in classification, so that the task cannot simply be farmed out to descriptive science. Consequently, on this understanding of what is going on, settling on a definition of geoengineering (or whatever set of terms is needed) is not a preliminary to serious discussion, but the substance and (perhaps) conclusion of it. In short, until we know the point of inquiring into geoengineering, we should not expect a robust taxonomy; hence, demanding one in advance is a mistake, especially if it leads one to abandon the whole topic.

It is also worth emphasizing that such conceptual difficulties are hardly unusual. Similar problems arise in other realms of practical ethics. Consider, for example, debates about how to define "torture," "terrorism," or (closer to hand) "humanitarian intervention." In those contexts, ethically loaded discussion of the meaning of the key terms is regarded a part and parcel of the work to be done, not an insurmountable obstacle to it.

In the absence of a clear definition, how might we proceed? My approach is to begin with the working assumption that we have at least one clear paradigm case. Recent discussion of climate engineering has centered around stratospheric sulfate injection (SSI): proposals to insert sulfur into the stratosphere to deflect a small portion of incoming sunlight, cool down the surface, and so offset much of the temperature rise expected from climate change. Such proposals are a good starting point both because no one doubts that they count as geoengineering, and because they dominate much of the early policy discussion.[7]

2 ETHICS

What ethical issues does SSI raise? I propose beginning with a broad understanding of ethics as including the domains of moral and political philosophy, legal theory, and the normative foundations of economics. As with geoengineering science, geoengineering ethics is in its early days. In particular, though existing theories are relevant, these were not developed with this problem (or, arguably, anything much like it) in mind. In addition, as with climate itself, geoengineering involves a complex convergence of topics where contemporary theories face major challenges (e.g., intergenerational ethics, international justice, humanity's relationship with nonhuman nature, scientific uncertainty, etc.). Given this, rather than simple applications of existing ethical theories, we might expect some evolution, and perhaps even transformation, of them over time (cf. Gardiner, 2011a).

That being said, mainstream ethical concepts pick out a range of salient considerations, many of which are at risk of neglect in the initial policy debate. Let me begin by identifying a few and then turn to the risk of neglect.

At least ten ethical values emerge as relevant to geoengineering from the early literature:

1. Welfare (e.g., benefits/harms) (Jamieson, 1996)
2. Justice (e.g., procedural, distributive, gender; international, intergenerational, across species; Buck et al., 2013; Gardiner, 2010, 2011b; Preston, 2012; Svoboda et al., 2012)
3. Rights (e.g., national self-defense; sovereignty; individual protections) (Gardiner, 2013a; Whyte, 2012)
4. Relationship with nature (e.g., less intrusive interventions; Buck et al., 2013; Gardiner, 2011c; Jamieson, 1996)
5. Intention (e.g., doing vs. allowing; foreseen vs. unintended consequences; Morrow, 2014a)
6. Responsibility (e.g., compensation; rectifying injustice; Gardiner, 2010, 2011c, 2013a)
7. Precaution (e.g., catastrophe avoidance; Elliot, 2010; Hartzell-Nichols, 2012)

8. Virtue and vice (e.g., hubris, recklessness, inflicting tragic choices; Gardiner, 2010, 2012, 2013b; Hamilton, 2013)
9. Political legitimacy (Gardiner, 2010; Morrow et al., 2013)
10. Control and domination (Sandler, 2012; Smith, 2012)

This list is presumably incomplete, and we should expect future additions; nevertheless, it illustrates the richness of geoengineering, ethically speaking. We can illustrate this by high-lighting a few of these values. (We return to several in subsequent sections.)

The first—welfare—is the most familiar. Some argue that geoengineering will promote global welfare, even to the extent of benefiting everyone (e.g., because SSI prevents global catastrophe); while others claim that it presents a grave risk to welfare (e.g., because of effects on precipitation, the Indian monsoon, etc.; cf. Ricke et al., 2010; Robock, et al. 2008). Consequently, disputes about welfare are right at the heart of current policy discussion.

Second, and also somewhat familiar, are issues of justice. These include concerns about the distribution of positive and negative effects of geoengineering (winners and losers), and questions of procedural justice (e.g., "Whose hand is on the thermostat?"). However, there are also foundational questions about how to include concern for those affected by geoen-gineering, given that the effects of SSI are likely to be felt not only globally but across many generations and all species. Given that the most vulnerable (the global poor, future gener-ations, and nonhuman nature) are unable to represent themselves, there are threats of an undue emphasis (or indeed profound bias) in geoengineering policy toward the richer and more powerful populations, the current generation, and narrowly human interests.

Third, rights come into play. For instance, at the national level, there is a real question about whether nations have the right to geoengineer in their own self-defense, either against severe climate impacts or perhaps against the rival geoengineering interventions of others (Gardiner, 2013a). Similarly, at the individual level, there are serious questions about whether other agents have the right to attempt to take control of the climate, either on my behalf or with indifference to my interests. For instance, perhaps individuals have rights against such intervention. Moreover, even if such rights can be overridden (e.g., because of the threat of catastrophe), further questions arise about whether they can only on the condition that those doing the overriding supply those affected with some form of protection, consultation, compensation, and rights of redress.

Fourth, such issues connect with concerns about control and domination. One major worry about SSI and similar techniques is that would-be climate controllers attempt to exert control over the basic physical structure of the planet. If they succeed, their choices affect very many people around the world, and especially future generations, deeply and perva-sively, to the extent of becoming at least a major determinant of the basic life prospects of others, and perhaps the dominant factor. What would such climate controllers owe those put under their yoke? Chances are, it would be extensive. Consider an (admittedly imper-fect) analogy. One of John Rawls' most influential ideas is that questions of justice arise in contemporary societies in part because social life shapes the basic life prospects of citizens through its creation of a set of institutions backed by coercive power (the "basic structure" of society). Rawlsians tend to think that what is owed to those subject to such power is exten-sive. (For instance, Rawls' infamous Difference Principle demands that social and economic inequalities should be arranged so as to maximally benefit the least well-off.) By contrast, the early debate about geoengineering contains almost no discussion of strong norms being adopted. Indeed, the contrary assumption is common: some assert that sulfate injection is politically easier than reducing emissions because in principle one country (or even a rich individual) could practice it without the cooperation of others. This appears to be a serious mistake. It is difficult to see how those who would take control of the *basic physical structure* of the planet could possibly be morally justified in doing so without accepting that "with great power comes great responsibility."

Fifth, this leads us to the human relationship to nature. For one thing, there are concerns about the interests of, and our responsibilities to, the nonhuman world and whether these can be adequately or appropriately captured through familiar ethical concepts such as welfare, justice and rights. For another thing, many would rebel against the profound politicization of nature suggested by SSI and related interventions. They would resist turning global climate (say) into a political domain where justice and legitimacy are the salient values. To motivate this concern, consider another analogy. Suppose a device is invented that allows someone to insert thoughts inside another person's brain. Few would argue that the main concern of public policy should be to facilitate the most *efficient* methods of thought control, or that the most important questions concern what thought controllers owe their victims in terms of *procedural justice* and the *distribution of burdens* (however demanding). Instead, thought control ought simply to be off limits, and governments should prevent such power being exerted.

Many have the same instincts when it comes to climate. They are appalled to have reached the point where sulfate injection schemes are even on the table. In response, they do not crave a grand ethics that tells us how to do "just" or "efficient" geoengineering. Instead, they favor *withdrawing* interference with the climate (e.g., mitigation) over "managing" it. In short, other things being equal, they seek an ethics that forecloses some options, as incompatible with who we are and aspire to be. Even if we get to the point where some geoengineering seems the "lesser evil," this saddens them and comes at some moral cost. They may even feel that it mars humanity from an ethical point of view (Gardiner, 2011b, ch. 10). We were given a serviceable planet, but have messed it up. Geoengineering to combat climate change is a sign of a deep moral failure.

As with thought control, the central issues involve (first) concerns about extending the powers of humans over one another, and (second) a broader vision of how we want to live. In the climate case, "how we want to live" includes not just our relationship with each other, here and now, but also with future generations and nature. In part, it involves taking seriously the question of what limits we want to set in order to respect such relationships.

In my view, discussion of such ethical concerns (e.g., welfare, justice, rights, the human relationship to nature) and the philosophical theories associated with them is urgent if geoengineering is to be seriously considered. However, in practice, and apart from some initial lip service, they are often neglected in the early debate. In what follows, I suggest some reasons for this.

3 MISLEADING FRAMINGS

The first set of reasons concerns ways in which geoengineering is introduced which tend to marginalize ethical concerns. Consider three examples.

3.1 "For or Against"?

The first is the common: "Geoengineering: are you for it, or against it?"[8] In my view, this is a poor question. On the one hand, no one favors geoengineering under just any circumstances, for just any reason. For example, a program aimed at making sure the Sun always shone on the reigning British monarch would be morally absurd. More realistically, most proponents of SSI believe deployment right now would be too risky given our ignorance about the consequences. On the other hand, it seems likely that most people would accept geoengineering under *some* circumstances, if (for example) the only alternative were truly dire enough, sufficiently legitimate and morally just governance mechanisms were in place, and the consequences of the intervention were reasonably benign and understood with *very* high confidence. What matters, then, is what these conditions are and whether they are likely to be satisfied (especially on a timescale relevant to our current predicament).

Given this, a better question would be: "Under what conditions do you think pursuit of geoengineering (whether through research, deployment, or much else in between and beyond) might become justified?" Such conditions may include the threat to be confronted, the background circumstances, the governance mechanisms needed, the individual protections to be provided, the compensation provisions to be made, and so on. Call this, "the justificatory question."

3.2 Emergency

A second problematic framing is provided by the ubiquitous emergency arguments. For example, people regularly say such things as "like it or not, a climate emergency is a possibility, and geoengineering could be the only affordable and fast-acting option to avoid a global catastrophe" (Caldeira and Keith, 2010: 57), or "[faced with catastrophic climate impacts] we would *simply have to* practice geoengineering as the "least evil" (cf. Schneider, 1996).[9]

I have written extensively about such arguments elsewhere (Gardiner, 2010, 2013b). Here all I will say is that one troubling feature of emergency arguments is that they often seem to *dodge* the justificatory question. For instance, they are stated in a very general form, with the key terms—"catastrophe," "lesser evil"—left undefined; they do not address any of the other potential conditions just mentioned (such as compensation); and they appear simply to assume (without argument) either that such conditions are met, or else that their relevance is overwhelmed by whatever "catastrophe" lurks in the background, so that anything else is a side issue at best.

This dodging is worrying in itself. It implies that, as stated, the emergency arguments are *opaque*: it is not clear what they actually claim. In addition, the dodging suggests that the initial consensus on the emergency framing may be *shallow*: on closer inspection, the emergency arguments mean very different things to different people. For example, whereas an ecologist might think that a catastrophe is a loss of 60% of existing species, an economist might think that it is merely a 2% drop in the rate of economic growth sustained for 2 years. With such diverse interpretations, the surface agreement between the many proponents of emergency arguments for geoengineering may disguise much deeper disagreements, and in ways that seriously affect policy.

3.3 Universal Benefit

A third problematic framing comes from the common assumption that geoengineering will benefit everyone (e.g., as is sometimes implied when SSI is said to be a "global public good"; Gardiner, 2013c, 2014; Morrow, 2014b).[10] As a descriptive statement about geoengineering as such, this assumption is clearly false. As we have seen, though "geoengineering" lacks a widely accepted definition, it is generally thought to mean something like "intentional, large-scale manipulation of the environment" (Keith, 2000a) or "deliberate large-scale intervention in the Earth's climate system, in order to moderate global warming" (Royal Society, 2009: ix). Yet nothing in these definitions guarantees that geoengineering will benefit everyone. Some interventions would harm at least some people; others would harm everyone (e.g., massive SSI that results in a "nuclear winter"-type scenario).

Perhaps the universal benefit claim can be interpreted in a different way, as the normative (and overtly ethical) requirement that any *ethically acceptable* geoengineering must benefit everyone (cf. perhaps the influential Oxford Principles for geoengineering (Rayner et al., 2013)). Still, this version of the view is also not compelling. For one thing, SSI would affect an enormous number of people, globally and intergenerationally, not to mention (many more) nonhumans; hence, the requirement that absolutely everyone affected benefit sees extremely demanding and perhaps empirically unsatisfiable. More important, from an ethical point of view, the universal benefit standard looks both too demanding and too lax. It seems too demanding because many lesser standards seem acceptable. (For example, consider an intervention that protected the basic interests of the most vulnerable at a modest cost to the very rich.) However, the requirement also seems too lax because it ignores considerations other than welfare, such as rights and justice. To illustrate the point, consider an everyday example. Perhaps it would benefit me if you were to break into my house and clean it for me. However, that is not sufficient to justify your actions. You violate my rights. The fact that you also benefit me does not automatically justify what you have done.

This kind of case seems relevant to SSI. Intentionally intervening in the atmosphere so as to influence my climate situation may benefit me (if we are lucky), but that fact by itself is not enough to justify it. Instead, we need to identify a more sophisticated and appropriate standard, and this is work for ethics. Indeed, it may be that a range of standards would be helpful: for example, of good, minimally decent, or even tolerably indecent forms of geoengineering. To see why, let us turn to another pressing issue.

4 THE CONTEXTUAL QUESTION

All three examples of common misframings of geoengineering—"for or against," emergency, universal benefit—obscure the task of developing sophisticated ethical standards for geoengineering. In my view, this task requires more attention. Still, we should recognize a further issue. When offering answers to the justificatory question, we must also consider: "Are the standards we have identified relevant to the world we live in or one that may plausibly emerge in the foreseeable future?"

To illustrate this concern, consider how much of the literature—including the most influential—explains why geoengineering is now on the table. The Royal Society states that "decarbonisation at the magnitude and rate required [to avoid global average temperatures exceeding 2 degrees C above pre-industrial levels this century] *remains technically possible,*" and "global failure to make sufficient progress on mitigation of climate change is *largely due to social and political inertia*" (Royal Society, 2009; cf. National Research Council, 2015). Similarly, the Nobel Laureate Paul Crutzen, in his seminal piece, states bluntly: "Finally, I repeat: the very best would be if emissions of the greenhouse gases could be reduced so much that the stratospheric sulfur release experiment would not need to take place. Currently, this looks like a *pious wish*" (Crutzen, 2006).

Such claims suggest that the decision to pursue geoengineering is being made under ethically compromised circumstances. It is mainly because we have failed—and continue to fail—to do what we should have done, ethically speaking (e.g., seriously decrease emissions), that geoengineering is being considered at all. Hence, in pondering the ethics of geoengineering, it is as if we are asking a paradoxical (though not necessarily incoherent) question: "What should we do, ethically speaking, given that we have not done, and will continue not to do, what we should be doing?"

The paradoxical question illuminates many ethical misgivings about the pursuit of geoengineering. For instance, it fuels standard worries, such as about moral hazards, slippery slopes, moral schizophrenia, techno-fixes that do not respond to the real roots of the problems, and so on. Still, in my opinion, its real import lies in raising fundamental questions about what drives political inertia on mainstream climate action, and whether geoengineering policy is likely to be compromised by the same forces, perhaps severely.

My own view has been that a central source of political inertia is that climate change involves a difficult collective action problem that I call a "perfect moral storm." I will not revisit that argument here; but I will say that it has implications for how we understand the challenge of ethical geoengineering. In a perfect moral storm, we (the current generation, especially in the more powerful nations) face strong temptations to behave badly toward people in other parts of the world, nonhuman nature, and especially future generations (e.g., by violating reasonable ethical standards). We also lack adequate institutions and theories to defend against these temptations (e.g., effective intergenerational institutions). Consequently, the situation is ripe for corruption, where this includes distortion of the way we think and talk about the problem.

The perfect storm analysis suggests several major threats to the prospects for an ethically geoengineering policy, including competitive geoengineering (e.g., different countries engaging in rival SSI schemes), predatory geoengineering (e.g., interventions aimed at damaging one's geopolitical rivals), and parochial geoengineering (e.g., short-term geoengineering "fixes" on behalf of the current generation, without regard to the long-term consequences for future people). In my view, geoengineering policy must take such threats seriously and employ explicit steps to confront them (e.g., in institutional design). I am especially concerned about parochial geoengineering. A real danger exists that, even if ethically enlightened forms of geoengineering are available in principle, the geoengineering policy that ultimately emerges will be one that aims to benefit the current generation (e.g., by holding off some of the worse climate impacts for the next 50 years or so), at the cost of making things even worse for future generations than allowing climate change to unfold. Worryingly, such threats are obscured by the most common (emergency, universal benefit, global public good) framings of geoengineering; yet such distortion is just what the perfect moral storm analysis would predict.

5 Conclusion

This chapter explored the relevance of ethics (moral, political, legal, economic philosophy) to geoengineering.

First, it identified a large number of highly salient concerns (including welfare, rights, justice, political legitimacy, etc.).

Second, it argued that early policy framings (e.g., "for or against," emergency, global public good) tend to marginalize these concerns, avoiding important questions of justification and making the quest for a good set of ethical standards for geoengineering especially urgent.

Third, the chapter suggested that, in the climate case, where it is widely held that geoengineering has become a serious option mainly because of political inertia, there are important contextual issues, especially around the paradoxical question ("What should we do, ethically speaking, given that we have not done, and will continue not to do, what we should be doing?"), and the live risk of moral corruption. Taking such issues seriously helps to explain why some regard geoengineering as so ethically troubling and also underlines several central ethical concerns, including the largely neglected threat of parochial geoengineering. In my view, this threat and those like it highlight the risk that, far from being a welcome new tool for climate action, geoengineering policy may become *another manifestation of the underlying problem.*

While none of this entails that the idea of ethical geoengineering is either incoherent or unachievable in the real world, such challenges should not be blithely assumed away. Most notably, one disconcerting thing about the early debate is the numerous ways in which it tends to obscure the contextual question and its central threats, and how predictable this is in a perfect moral storm. If we call on Scotty, we need to know more about who he will be working for and what constraints he faces. (So does Scotty.) If, instead of the heroic Captain Kirk, these are the same forces that produced the mess in the first place, complacency about ethics may be one of most dangerous aspects of the pursuit of geoengineering.

Notes

1. Versions of this chapter were presented to the National Research Council's Committee on Geoengineering (September 2013) and the American Association for the Advancement of Science (February 2015). I thank both audiences for their comments and also Dustin Schmidt and Allen Thompson.
2. Keith initially states "geoengineering is defined as intentional large-scale manipulation of the environment"; however, when he discusses climatic engineering more specifically he speaks of it having three "defining attributes," "scale, intent, and the degree to which the action is a countervailing measure" (pp. 247–250).
3. For discussion, see Morrow 2014a.

4. Cf. McCracken 2006. McCracken intends these as examples of alternatives to geoengineering, since they deal with climate effects rather than climate change itself or its causes.
5. This is presumably why Keith refers to "large-scale," rather than global projects.
6. For many, the term necessarily has negative connotations: the very idea of "engineering" the Earth is abhorrent to them. This complicates debates about terminology in at least two ways. First, it seems likely to make even enthusiasts reluctant to label their proposals "geoengineering." Second, as David Keith has pointed out, it makes it probable that society will shift in its usage of the term over time—as a given technology comes to be seen in a more favorable light, "geoengineering" will be withdrawn from it.
7. Iron fertilization of the ocean, global afforestation projects, and large-scale diversions of major bodies of water I regard as interesting intermediate, or borderline cases. Geological carbon capture (GCC) I view as an unclear case. On the one hand, if we assume that the capture is *prior* to any release to the biosphere and the storage *perfect*, then GCC does not seem to be geoengineering; on the other hand, if we think of the storage as potentially very leaky and capture as imperfect, then it may well be at least an intermediate case. Of course, how GCC is correctly understood is partly an empirical matter, uncertainty about which itself has implications for policy.
8. The next two sections draw from Gardiner (2013b).
9. Reporting remarks of Robert Frosh to National Academy of Science report of 1992; emphasis added.
10. This section is drawn from Gardiner 2013c.

References

Broad, W. (2006). "How to Cool a Planet (Maybe)." *New York Times*: June 27, 2006.
Buck, H. J. et al. (2013). "Gender and Geoengineering." *Hypatia* 10(10): 1–19.
Caldeira, K. and Keith, D. (2010). "The Need for Climate Engineering Research." *Issues in Science and Technology* 57: 57–62.
Crutzen, P. (2006). "Albedo Enhancement by Stratospheric Sulphur Injections: a Contribution to Resolve a Policy Dilemma?" *Climatic Change* 77: 211–219.
Elliot, K. (2010). "Geoengineering and the Precautionary Principle." *International Journal of Applied Philosophy* 24(2): 237–253.
Fogg, M. J. (1995). *Terraforming: Engineering Planetary Environments*. Warrendale, PA: SAE International.
Gardiner, S. M. (2010). "Is 'Arming the Future' with Geoengineering Really the Lesser Evil?" In *Climate Ethics: Essential Readings*, edited by S. M. Gardiner et al., 284–312. Oxford: Oxford University Press.
Gardiner, S. M. (2011a). "Rawls and Climate Change: Does Rawlsian Political Philosophy Pass the Global Test?" *Critical Review of International Social and Political Philosophy* 14(2): 125–151.
Gardiner, S. M. (2011b). *A Perfect Moral Storm*. Oxford: Oxford University Press.
Gardiner, S. M. (2011c). "Some Early Ethics of Geoengineering: A Commentary on the Values of the Royal Society Report." *Environmental Values* 20: 163–188.
Gardiner, S. M. (2012). "Are We the Scum of the Earth? Climate Change, Geoengineering, and Humanity's Challenge." In *Ethical Adaptation to Climate Change: Human Virtues of the Future*, edited by A. Thompson and J. Bendik-Keymer, 241–260. Boston: The MIT Press.

Gardiner, S. M. (2013a). "The Desperation Argument for Geoengineering." *Political Science and Politics* 46(1): 28–33.

Gardiner, S. M. (2013b). "Geoengineering and Moral Schizophrenia: What Is the Question?" In *Climate Change Geoengineering: Philosophical Perspectives, Legal Issues, and Governance Frameworks*, edited by W. Burns and A. Strauss, 11–38. New York: Cambridge University Press.

Gardiner, S. M. (2013c). "Why Geoengineering Is Not a 'Global Public Good', and Why It Is Ethically Misleading to Frame It as One." *Climatic Change* 121: 513–525.

Gardiner, S. M. 2014. "Why 'Global Public Good' is a Treacherous Term, Especially for Geoengineering." *Climatic Change* 123: 101–106.

Hamilton, C. (2013). *Earthmasters: The Dawn of the Age of Climate Engineering*. New Haven: Yale University Press.

Hartzell-Nichols, L. (2012). "Precaution and Solar Radiation Management." *Ethics, Policy, and Environment* 15(2): 158–171.

Jamieson, D. (1992). "Ethics, Public Policy, and Global Warming." *Science, Technology, and Human Values* 17(2): 139–153.

Jamieson, D. (1996). "Ethics and Intentional Climate Change." *Climatic Change* 33: 323–336.

Keith, D. (2000a). "Geoengineering the Climate: History and Prospect." *Annual Review of Energy and Environ* 25: 245–284.

Keith, D. (2000b). "Geoengineering." *Encyclopedia of Global Change*. Oxford: Oxford University Press.

McCracken, M. C. (2006). "Geoengineering: Worthy a Cautious Evaluation?" *Climatic Change* 77: 235–243.

Morrow, D. R. et al. (2013). "Political Legitimacy in Decisions about Experiments in Solar Radiation Management." In *Climate Change Geoengineering: Philosophical Perspectives, Legal Issues, and Governance Frameworks*, edited by W. Burns and A. Strauss, 146–167. New York: Cambridge University Press.

Morrow, D. R. (2014a). "Starting a Flood to Stop a Fire? Some Moral Constraints on Solar Radiation Management." *Ethics, Policy and Environment* 17(2): 123–128.

Morrow, David R. (2014b). "Why Geoengineering Is a Public Good, Even If Its Bad." *Climatic Change* 123: 95–100.

National Research Council (2015). *Climate intervention: Reflecting Sunlight to Cool Earth*. Washington DC: The National Academies Press.

Preston, C. J. (2012). "Solar Radiation Management and Vulnerable Populations." In *Engineering the Climate*, edited by C. Preston, 77–94. UK: Lexington Books.

Rayner, S. et al. (2013). "The Oxford Principles." *Climatic Change* 121: 499–512.

Ricke, K. L. et al. (2010). "Regional Climate Response to Solar Radiation Management." *Nature Geoscience* 3: 537–541.

Robock, A. et al. (2008). "Regional Climate Responses to Geoengineering with Tropical and Arctic SO2 Injections." *Journal of Geophysical Research* 113: D16101.

Royal Society (2009). *Geoengineering the Climate: Science, Governance and Uncertainty*. London: Royal Society.

Ruddiman, W. F. (2003). "The Anthropogenic Greenhouse Era Began Thousands of Years Ago." *Climatic Change* 61(3): 261–293.

Sandler, R. L. (2012). "Solar Radiation Management and Nonhuman Species." In *Engineering the Climate*, edited by C. Preston, 95–110. UK: Lexington Books.

Schelling, T. (1996). "The Economic Diplomacy of Geoengineering." *Climatic Change* 33: 303–307.

Schneider, S. H. (1996). "Geoengineering: Could—or Should—We Do It?" *Climatic Change* 33: 291–302.

Smith, P. T. (2012). "Domination and the Ethics of Solar Radiation Management." In *Engineering the Climate*, edited by C. Preston, 43–62. UK: Lexington Books.

Svoboda, T. et al. (2012). "Sulfate Aerosol Geoengineering: The Question of Justice." *Public Affairs Quarterly* 25(3): 157–180.

Vogel, S. (2011). "Why 'Nature' Has No Place in Environmental Philosophy." In *The Ideal of Nature: Debates about Biotechnology and the Environment*, edited by G. Kaebnick, 84–97. Maryland: Johns Hopkins University Press.

Whyte, K. P. (2012). "Now This! Indigenous Sovereignty, Political Obliviousness and Governance Models for SRM Research." *Ethics, Policy, and Environment* 15(2): 172–187.

PART VIII

SOCIAL CHANGE

Doing What We Ought to Do

CHAPTER 43

··

ENVIRONMENTAL CONFLICT

··

DAVID SCHMIDTZ

THE fundamental question with which moral philosophy begins is the question of how to live. It is obvious how discussion of justice—the question of how to live in a *community*—could and should connect, but also painfully obvious that much of our theorizing about justice no longer does connect. In scholarly circles, talk of justice can have an abstract quality, strangely devoid of implications for what individuals should do. One hears talk of principles of distribution and of classes to which primary goods are to be distributed. To recover a measure of relevance to the fundamental question, theorizing about principles of justice would have to orient itself around questions about which principles have a history of being demonstrably the organizing principles of flourishing communities.

Habitable principles—principles that real people can live with—are first of all principles by which we avoid and resolve conflict. A philosopher might presume that principles of justice somehow are more fundamental than principles of conflict resolution. But moral philosophy done well is neither as autonomous as that, nor as naïve. Moral philosophy done well tracks truth about the human condition, which means it tracks truth about what it actually takes in the real world for people to live in peace. Therefore, the relationship between justice and conflict resolution is not one-way. It is instead an evolving process of mutual specification, anchored to facts about what helps people get along and make progress. If we want to understand what people have reason to expect from each other and what they have reason to regard as their due, we would do well to start by learning how people avoid and resolve conflict and thereby build lives such that people can know that their neighbors are better off with them than without.

This essay describes three varieties of environmental conflict, with a particular focus on a contrast between conflict of values and conflict of priorities.[1] I reflect on how people cope with these kinds of environmental conflict and on how our ways of coping implicitly distinguish environmental conflict resolution from environmental justice. I close by noting ways in which economic analysis can help us understand environmental conflict and what might help us resolve it. While reducing all values to economic values is uncalled for, the fact remains that economies exhibit a certain logic. To ignore the logic of human economy is to ignore the logic of human ecology and thus to ignore the logic of ecologies where humans are a keystone species. It would be a shame to be led by environmental values to such a damaging isolation from ecological reality.

1 VARIETIES OF ENVIRONMENTAL CONFLICT

1.1 Conflicting Use

The simplest kind of conflict occurs when people get in each other's way. Call this *conflict in use*. Conflict in use comprises literal and figurative traffic jams. In particular, when the uses to which different parties would put common resources or common spaces leads to congestion, the effect is that people aiming to use said resources find themselves in each other's way.[2] Societies cope with conflicting use by developing institutions that in effect manage traffic. The tools of literal traffic management—stop lights, speed limits, and such—are primary examples of such institutions. At any given moment, a snapshot of a framework of green and red lights looks like a zero-sum game—facilitating the movement of some at the expense of others. But the static perspective is a fool's perspective, because over time the game reveals itself to be good for everyone. So long as the system is responding well to the volume of traffic, all (including even pedestrians) reach their destinations safer, faster, and more predictably.

Among the primary tools of traffic management considered more figuratively, a system of property establishes common and known expectations establishing rights of way, whereas people's preferences regarding the use of a given resource put them on course for potential collision.[3] Allocating rights to post and enforce a rule of "no trespassing" or "no hunting" is a way of managing access to and thus traffic on a given parcel of land.

1.2 Conflicting Values

Settling on a system of property is one way of settling environmental conflicts. It does not always work. Why not? For one thing, not all conflicts concern who has the right of way. Some conflicts concern whether *anyone* should have the right of way. Some conflicts are about what rightly can be treated as property in the first place. This second kind of conflict is a conflict of *values*.

What if Kenya's Masai claim a right to treat lions and elephants as pieces of property? Doing so gives the Masai an incentive to protect lions and elephants from poachers, which has to count for something. Granting a property right creates both latitude and motive to erect a fence and a "no trespassing" sign, thereby protecting an owner's right to what lies inside. However, critics of this way of protecting wildlife sometimes say, in effect, that to establish property rights in elephants is to commodify them. It is degrading, just another way of destroying them. At very least it destroys what these charismatic animals stand for in the hearts of people who cherish a vision of nature wild and free.

Similar issues arise regarding the conservation of sub-Saharan rhinos. A portion of a rhino horn can be removed without hurting the animal. The removable portion is today worth a quarter of a million dollars.[4] There are perhaps 20,000 rhinos left in the African wild, not nearly enough to meet exploding Asian demand. Market forces under current Prohibition-style laws encourage organized crime. Federal helicopter gunships and drones accompany wild rhinos, but soldiers manning the helicopters are themselves, often enough, in the employ of organized crime, and their actual function is to warn poachers when uncorrupted rangers are near.

One alternative is to allow the ranching of captive-bred rhinos. Captive rhinos would be no more in danger of extinction than any other form of cattle. In that sense, the problem would be solved. The downside is that, although captive rhinos would survive, they would after all be surviving as a form of cattle.[5]

To some people, saving rhinos in this way is abhorrent. In their eyes, it would be better for rhinos to go extinct. Consider a somewhat related view of Cynthia Moss's. Moss writes about her life among elephants, sharing their hopes and dreams even while acknowledging what makes them wild and alien. She says she would prefer elephants going extinct to seeing them murdered as a means of managing herd size in places where elephant overpopulation is devastating the landscape and driving other animals, especially rhinos, to extinction (Moss, 1988: 226). Moss may not feel the same way about raising captive-bred rhinos in order to meet the demand for rhino horn in a way that prevents rhinos from going extinct, but her intransigent opposition both to hunting and to culling is easy to understand.

There are places where "canned" lions, raised in captivity, are released into game parks on demand, as orders for trophy lions are placed by customers willing to pay tens of thousands of dollars to be made to feel like a lion hunter. Immediately before the hunt begins, a lion is released into an unfamiliar and disorienting habitat where it is a reliably easy kill.[6] Needless to say, some people oppose this practice. The conflict that results, however, is not a conflict in use. There is no dispute about who owns "canned" animals. Farms indisputably are licensing the hunting of their own livestock, not someone else's. This quarrel is not over who has the right of way—how to manage traffic in these lions—but whether traffic in trophy lions should exist at all.

Clearly, then, we have here a kind of conflict not resolved or even acknowledged merely by settling who owns the resource. The dispute concerns whether anyone has any right to treat rhinos, lions, or elephants as resources at all rather than as beings with independent moral standing.[7]

Anthropocentric (i.e., human-centered) orientations toward nature are contrasted with biocentric (i.e., nature-centered) orientations. Where a *conservationist's* concern is anthropocentric (saying nature should be used wisely), a *preservationist's* concern is biocentric (saying nature's moral standing does not depend on its being of use to humans.) To preservationists, there are species and ecosystems that should be free from human management (Norton, 1991: 12–13).[8] This kind of clash is an important example of the second variety of conflict: conflicting values.

1.3 Conflicting Priorities

A final category of conflict is a matter of conflicting *priorities*. What distinguishes conflict of priorities from conflict of values? The crucial point: goals can come into conflict *even when values are relevantly similar*. For example, a group might pledge allegiance to preservationism's "no use at all" policies. Will local people be eager to join this fight on the side of the international conservation lobby? Perhaps. Yet all too often local people denounce international lobbyists as hypocrites, ignorant meddlers, or outright criminals. Why? Is it because local farmers, their local experience notwithstanding, are too ignorant and too uneducated to understand what they should care about? Sometimes, at least, farmers decline to participate in the cause of cosmopolitan environmentalism because they cannot *afford* it.

The issue, conceptually and practically, is that priorities can conflict even when values do not. For example, suppose our children matter even more to us than elephants do but elephants matter far more to us than do ivory chess sets. Could *agreeing* on this ranking lead to conflict? Absolutely. Conflicts arise when Americans reject hunting elephants, since ivory chess sets are not worth enough to justify killing elephants, while Africans accept elephant hunting, since feeding their children *is* worth enough to justify killing elephants. Americans and Africans differ, but not because they embrace different values. Indeed, they embrace the same values but pay different prices for what they value. To the American, the price of no elephant hunting is no ivory chess sets; to the African, the price of no elephant hunting is no children.

When getting enough to eat is a daily challenge for subsistence farmers, they can have priorities unlike ours. Underlying the differing priorities is a fact about values—not that our values are so different but that our values are so similar. Some conflicts have roots not in differing values so much as in differences in what we can afford under differing circumstances.

Consider the implications. Africa's subsistence farmers need to put land to productive use. Unless coexisting with elephants is a way of putting land to productive use (that is, unless they can sell photo safaris, ivory, or hunting licenses), they will need some other way of putting their land to productive use: that is, cattle or crops. If the idea of rural Africans exploiting elephants seems obviously wrong, then consider that, for them, their next best option involves *converting elephant habitat into farmland.*

Elephants today live on land that they share with people. Whether they can survive is a question of whether people can afford to share (Kreuter et al., 2010: 161).[9] The difference between conflicts like this and conflicting values is philosophically interesting and practically momentous.

2 IDEALS AND COMPROMISE

Philosophers, one could argue, earn a living by envisioning a more perfect world. But although there may be some point in an environmental ethic that is mainly an exercise in envisioning ideals, environmental conflict resolution is an exercise in the art of compromise. Successful conflict mediation typically involves negotiating win-win solutions. Does that presuppose that both parties would win in a morally ideal world? Not at all. We need to be able to coexist with all of our neighbors, not only the ideal ones. Conflicting priorities, however, can be a problem even among ideal neighbors who embrace each other's values and thus have no grounds for treating such conflicts as clashes between good and evil. When we hear about waves of settlers burning the Amazon and wonder whether we can stop it, we may have a conflict of *values* with two-dimensional villains borrowed from a low-budget movie: condominium developers wanting to burn forests for no apparent reason other than to get the thrill that vandals get from destroying things. More realistically, we might be looking instead at *priorities* that conflict with farmers wanting to feed their children. We might find their values unobjectionable. We might well share their values. It may even be the rule rather than the exception that there is no point in trying to win by making our imagined enemies lose.

Further, there are times for attending not only to our values but to other people's too, even if we do not share their values and indeed find them alien. Why? Because other people's values are integral parts of ecosystems about which we claim to care. We do not decide how other people will act any more than we decide how elephants or viruses will act. People decide for themselves. If we aim to respond to them in an environmentally sound way, then our question should be, under what conditions do people with *their* values and *their* priorities act in environmentally sound ways?

To mediators, the first principle of conflict resolution is to focus on interests, not positions (Fisher and Ury, 1991). (*Positions* are conceptions of how things ought to be. Positions need not have anything to do with here and now. To stand on the rightness of one's vision is to take a position. An *interest* by contrast is grounded in an evaluation of where we are, where such evaluation naturally requires updating along with changing circumstances, or changing information about those circumstances. There is an interest where something is at stake—where things can go better or worse starting from here.) Successful mediation avoids letting negotiation turn into a contest of wills where the point is to make the other side lose. It leads people to focus on the actual problem, that is, on the task of finding a negotiated agreement that parties will regard as "win-win" (Klick and Wright, 2012).[10]

Acting on behalf of genuine interests can require negotiation. Negotiation tends to require compromise on positions. So-called values sometimes are glorified positions with little connection to real interests. Climate change may be the most uncomfortable example. I know someone who was censured by his department *explicitly* because he edited a volume wherein a contributing author wrote that an effective response to climate change would start by acknowledging an ongoing controversy over what is changing, what is causing the change, how such change poses a problem, and what if anything would mitigate the problem. The worry: people are being ostracized for taking a scientific *interest* as opposed to a political position. We have evidence of a major problem, we have made little progress toward identifying an effective response, yet we bully colleagues into behaving as if the time for scientific inquiry as over. This seems a hysterical rather than a rational reaction to the possibility that our interest in mitigating climate change is altogether real.

Let us concede to Mark Sagoff that at its best, government "regulation expresses what we believe, what we are, what we stand for as a nation" (Sagoff, 1988: 16). Yet however true and important Sagoff's point may be, we never want to find ourselves endorsing regulations only because of what they symbolize. Before endorsing regulations, we should want to be sure they do not *undermine* a value in the course of *symbolizing* it.[11]

To do that, we must anticipate how a regulation will work, what it will induce people to do, in practice. Otherwise, if we let ourselves be swayed by symbolic value unreflectively, we are in effect taking an environmentalist *position* at the expense of an environmental *interest*. In the process, we do precisely what the theory and practice of conflict resolution teaches us to avoid.[12]

3 A Lesson for Environmental Ethics

We environmental philosophers spend a lot of time discussing what we call environmental justice, but we never (to my knowledge) discuss environmental conflict resolution. A general unease on the part of consumers of this literature—a feeling that there is something "ivory tower" about the whole idea of environmental justice—is not misleading. Some purported ideals have a tangible reality. They are worthy of aspiration in the real world. These include ideals of environmental conflict resolution. The rhetoric of environmental justice too often is something else, a form of posturing not even intended to inspire conflicting or potentially conflicting parties to work toward building better lives together.

From a mediator's perspective, the test of theory is how it works in practice, and in practice there is no progress without negotiation and compromise, aiming for a solution that everyone can live with. It is one thing to triumph by the lights of a particular ideology. It is another thing to get a result with which no one is delighted but to which parties can adjust without feeling as if they are being sacrificed on the altar of a vision that they do not (and are not expected to) share.

In our theorizing about justice, we want to imagine morally pristine original positions from which bargaining can proceed untainted by contingent historical circumstance. That is the wrong thing to imagine. In the real world, we start from here. If we want to make progress start-ing from here, then we have to theorize about what can be built on a foundation of here and now: what is feasible and what people with different histories and incompatible expectations can count as progress starting from here. Actual progress starting from here, needing the coop-eration of other stakeholders who have no reason to regard our claims as trumping theirs, and who may or may not share our values, will be unlike what we imagine justice to be.[13] So much the worse for what we imagine justice to be. A mediator deals with actual situations.

Whether our theorizing matters will depend on whether we can do likewise. Environmental ethicists need to start with conflict on the ground rather than with visions. If humanity were a decision-making entity whose components had no hopes and dreams of their own, we could imagine this "whole" rationally pruning itself back, amputating over-grown parts, thus making room for wildlife. But consider how unconscionable it would be to apply this superficially biocentric ideal to the people of Africa. In Africa, if people succeed in protecting their habitat, it will be because protecting their habitat is in their interest, not because doing so is in the interest of "the whole."

As Ben Minteer notes in his entry on Pragmatism for this volume, "environmental ethics would benefit from a significant collaboration with sustainability science. And this argu-ment can similarly be pushed harder: the field of environmental ethics *ought to* adopt a more praxis-oriented approach, that is, it should engage actual and pressing sustainability prob-lems at the intersection of science, value, and society." Minteer is thinking specifically about the biological sciences, but presumably he would agree that transdisciplinary sustainability science needs to encompass social science too.[14] In any case, consider that when we philoso-phers say our principles should be put into practice, we imply that our principles are con-sistent with sound practice. But that implies that we have done our homework. So never actually doing the hard work of grounding our theories in requirements of sound practice, but nevertheless going ahead and recommending our theory to practitioners, would be dis-honest. When practitioners ignore such theorizing, they manifestly do the right thing.

4 Ecology as Economics

Conflicting priorities tend to be economic as well as environmental conflicts. The conflicts have their roots in circumstances where decision makers face different trade-offs. Such con-flicts will not be resolved as environmental conflicts unless treated as economic conflicts.

People first absorbing the basic tenets of ecological reasoning can wave the flag for such reasoning within narrow confines but then overlook the need to apply ecological reasoning to human ecology. Environmentalists often view the field of economics with suspicion, regarding it as enemy territory. Even mainstream philosophers like Eugene Hargrove sometimes flatly dismiss "the economic approach to nature preservation" (1989: 210). Hargrove's attitude makes sense in context. I, too, reject any "economic approach" that consists of aiming to treat all values as nothing more than prices (Sagoff, 1981).

However, seeing the limits of economic value-reductionism is one thing; ignoring the logic of economic systems is another. When priorities conflict, ignoring the economic logic of human interaction is environmentally unsound. In that sense, failing to take an economic approach is failing to take an ecological approach.

Economic and ecological reasoning alike are ways of reasoning about competition, scarcity, unintended consequences, and the general principles that describe the logic of how systems respond to attempts to manipulate them. Because systems have a logic, we can never take for granted that an intervention will work as intended. Having one's heart in the right place is not enough. Progress requires a willingness to work with a system's logic rather than against it. We may be able to predict how people or elephants will respond, but we are never in a position simply to decide how they will respond. Even dictators cannot *decide* how things are going to go, any more than exterminators can decide whether insects will evolve resistance to a pesticide.

Preservationist ideals express reverence for nature and respect for animals. They are a way of taking ourselves seriously as moral agents. However, preservationism often and predictably fails in contexts where people who do not (and perhaps cannot afford to) embrace a preservationist ideal are expected to take responsibility for realizing it. Our frustration may tempt us to see their recalcitrant behavior as ignorant, but the truth in that case is that we are the ones who are refusing to track reality.

Within the environmental community, we all see the attraction of Aldo Leopold's view of humans as plain citizens of the biotic community (Leopold, 1966: 240). But Leopold was calling not only for realistic humility but for realistic logic. He aspired to a unified view of the logic of ecosystems in which human action is a key part. He would agree with Bryan Norton and with Gary Varner that the theoretical separation of anthropocentrism from biocentrism obscures a more fundamental fact that now, more than ever, even from an *anthropocentric* perspective, we have compelling reason for learning to think biocentrically (Varner, 1998: 129).

Varner is right, as is Norton. I wish only to add that the point works both ways: we have biocentric reasons for thinking anthropocentrically. If we do not tend to people, we will not be tending to ecosystems to which people belong either. When we ignore anthropocentric perspectives, we fall into assessing options as though priorities unlike our own (and possibly values very much like our own!) do not count: a disastrous oversight even from a biocentric perspective.

To ignore priorities unlike our own is to commit ourselves to mismanaging ecologies in which those ignored priorities are a driving force.[15] Africans often seem to understand: policies that work take humanity into account. Consider Zimbabwe's CAMPFIRE program. In its heyday, under the auspices of CAMPFIRE, village headmen in local districts were authorizing hunting permits, tourist ventures, and so on. Local communities were keeping 80% of the revenue. The World Wildlife Fund (WWF) opposed such programs initially but did a 180-degree turn as key decision makers within that organization came to grasp that in Africa, we are not an invasive species. Human beings and their ancestors have been keystone species within African ecosystems for millions of years, and their presence needs to be factored into ecological models accordingly. WWF came to champion CAMPFIRE's Rhodesian precursors in the mid-1970s and actively worked to persuade village headmen of the economic benefits of, for example, using a bidding process to allocate hunting permits.[16] Within a generation, hunting was generating so much money that villagers were taking down fences and letting rangeland revert to wildlife habitat (Matzke and Nabane, 1996: 80).[17]

This is not to ignore the fact that preservationists tend to find the whole idea of sport hunting appalling. But we naturally assume what is in fact untrue: namely that regular tourism is benign whereas hunting by comparison is relatively destructive. In truth, tourism tends to do more environmental damage than hunting relative to the money it brings in; dollar for dollar, hunting requires less infrastructure. Hunters demand relatively less than do tourist resorts by way of swimming pools and wilderness-fragmenting highways.

The sad end to this encouraging tale is that within a year of my visit, Zimbabwe became one of the world's most brutal dictatorships, its economy shattered. So-called war veterans were authorized first to resettle the lands of evicted white farmers. Having eaten all they could find on once-productive farms, these people are now settling in the national parks and poaching the wildlife.

Bans on hunting and on trade in wildlife products sometimes are vehicles for making a statement and proving that one's heart is in the right place. This aim is not illegitimate on its face, but neither does it have an obvious connection to the further aim of actually saving a species. The first aim is a position, the second is a genuine interest, and connecting the two is an achievement. To keep one's interests and positions together, one has to understand cause and effect in markets for hunting and wildlife products. And one has to anticipate that markets will take different shapes and will have different effects in different countries and as applied to different species. CAMPFIRE was a unique, home-grown market in rural Zimbabwe that achieved real success for a time, but the planet on which CAMPFIRE evolved is long on possibilities and short on guarantees, and the program may not outlive an increasingly corrupt and senile dictator.

There are examples of people and wildlife flourishing together, but those circumstances are not easily replicated, and they can be ephemeral. The truth seems to be that there is no settled answer, and perhaps never will be a "one size fits all" answer, to the question of what sort of response to the problem of conflicting priorities would give us the best chance of saving charismatic species. It is one thing to theorize about the effects of well-enforced property rights, or well-enforced bans, but (to put it mildly) effective enforcement in sub-Saharan Africa cannot be taken for granted. We understand that effective enforcement is a function of whether local people have the ability and the incentive to protect wildlife. In turn, whether they have ability or incentive depends greatly in whether wildlife is help or hindrance when it comes to feeding their children.

5 NATURAL ENEMIES

Some of us endorse economic values. Some endorse preservationist values. This does not make us enemies. Indeed, some of us embrace both, without being conflicted. If we want the actions of others—if indeed we want *our own* actions—to be environmentally sound, we must work to understand human ecology. We should resist the temptation to see economics as the enemy, if for no other reason than that such antipathy is environmentally unsound. It distracts us from thinking about human beings in realistically ecological terms, thus distracting us from resolving conflicts of priorities in environmentally benign ways.

Where there is conflict, especially where conflict is more specifically a conflict of priorities, we must put people first, if we care about people, or even if we do not. Suppose we care only about wildlife but that our concern is not merely to prove that our hearts are in the right place but to make room for wildlife. In that case, we would start by acknowledging that whether there will be room for wildlife is a question to be decided mainly by the people who live with it, and they will decide for reasons of their own.

It is within our power to make sacrifices for the sake of wildlife preservation and ecological sustainability. It is in some sense in our power to sacrifice other people to our cause if and when we judge our cause to be that important. As a matter of fact, however, it is not in our power to choose that *other people* sacrifice themselves, and this fact—about what is within our power and what is not—is central to the ecological and wildlife issues we now face. (See John Meyer on SACRIFICE in this volume.) Other people's choices are theirs to make, and they will choose by the lights of their own values and priorities.

Expecting African farmers to regard their family's health and safety as a lower priority than African wildlife is not a winning strategy. We might want to do that—take a hard-line position—to prove that our hearts are in the right place but not if our hearts genuinely are in the right place, because we would be proving that our hearts are in the right place by sacrificing the wildlife. If we care about wildlife, we will focus on giving locals reasons to cooperate. Successful terms of cooperation will place our interest in preserving wildlife alongside local interest in being able to live with it.

ACKNOWLEDGEMENT

My work on this essay was supported by a grant from the John Templeton Foundation. The opinions expressed here are those of the author and do not necessarily reflect the views of the John Templeton Foundation. I thank the Property and Environment Research Center in Bozeman, Montana for providing a superb work environment in the summers of 2012 and 2013. I also thank the Earhart Foundation for support in the fall of 2013. In particular, I thank Dan Benjamin, Terry Anderson, Dean Lueck, Michael t'Sas-Rolfes, and P. J. Hill for suggestions and collegial support. I remain responsible for errors. This entry is a descendant, thoroughly rewritten, of "Natural Enemies," originally published in *Environmental Ethics*, 22 (2000) 397–408. © David Schmidtz.

NOTES

1. I use the term "environmental conflict" to refer to conflict where one party voices concerns about the environmental impact of another party's projects.
2. Two definitions: First, a *commons tragedy* is the result of individually rational use of a common resource culminating in a pattern of collective overuse that exceeds the resource's

carrying capacity. Second, *carrying capacity* is a core concept of the field of ecology, referring to the level of use or traffic that a resource can sustain indefinitely without degradation.

3. Property institutions help people avoid, manage, and resolve conflict insofar as they (1) facilitate orderly use of a common resource; (2) facilitate orderly removal of resources from the commons; and (3) help people cope with *externalities*, including new externalities that emerge as property regimes evolve. Property regimes can be a kind of public good if and when they solve commons problems and induce overall patterns of sustainable use.

4. Quoting from National Public Radio's "Can Economics Save the African Rhino?" by Gregory Warner, *Planet Money,* May 13, 2013. Archived at http://www.npr.org/blogs/money/2013/05/15/184135826/can-economics-save-the-african-rhino. See also Michael t'Sas-Rolfes, "The Rhino Poaching Crisis: A Market Analysis," (February 2012). Archived at http://davidschmidtz.com/sites/default/files/files/tSas-Rolfes.pdf

5. Current efforts to save wild rhino populations would presumably continue. Farmed rhinos would be a genomic insurance policy.

6. See "What Will It Take to Save the East African Lion from Extinction? Hunting or Herding?" *Africa Geo* editorial (May 31, 2013). Accessed at http://blog.africageographic.com/africa-geographic-blog/wildlife/what-will-it-take-to-save-the-east- african-lion-from-extinction-hunting-or-herding/

    For some indication of the contrast between Tanzania and Kenya, see also http://blog.sun-safaris.com/2013/06/21/this-is-why-trophy-hunting-will-not-save-our-lions/

7. See John O'Neill's essay on Economic Systems and Valuation in this volume. I thank Allen Thompson for observing that many people also feel queasy about formalizing rights to pollute in the form of marketable property rights in emissions permits. This uneasiness is about propertization independently of any concerns about moral standing.

8. Quite properly, however, Bryan Norton (1991: 12–13) cautions against exaggerating the practical importance of the divide between conservation and preservation. Indeed, most of us have both conservationist and preservationist sympathies. Norton argues for a consensus-building approach in the policy arena.

9. Kreuter and Simmons (1995: 161) conclude that, because elephants "compete directly with humans for use of fertile land, we believe elephants will continue to be eliminated unless they provide . . . direct personal benefits to the people who incur the cost of coexisting with them."

10. For a prosaic example of the hazards of letting factual questions be deemed "politically incorrect," see Klick and Wright (2012).

11. My father was a farmer. When I was eight years old, a pair of red foxes built a den and raised a litter in our wheat field. I can remember watching Dad on his tractor in the late afternoon, giving the foxes a wide berth and leaving that part of our field uncultivated that year. He protected the den because he could afford to (and even then, I admired him for it). If there had been a law prohibiting farming on land inhabited by foxes, analogous to laws that prohibit logging in forests inhabited by spotted owls, then Dad would have had to make sure his land was not inhabited by foxes. Which is to say, Dad probably would have killed them. Although he loved them, he would not have been able to afford to let them live.

    A "No Surprises" regulation was incorporated into the Endangered Species Act in 1998, offering some protection from such possibilities to landowners who enter into a long-term agreement on a Habitat Conservation Plan. The regulation is controversial and survived a serious legal challenge in 2007. I thank Lynn Scarlett, former Deputy Secretary of the Interior, for helpful conversation.

12. We also need to accept that what we stand for as a nation differs from what we *want* to stand for. Things for which nations stand are products of ongoing, piecemeal political compromise. We do well not to glorify the expressive value of such compromised ideals.

13. When justice is treated as dictating destinations rather than as managing traffic, it fails to coordinate. It fails to be a solution to a problem. Progress comes to a halt. Traffic management is a literal issue, but also a metaphor for something more general, namely transaction cost. In all kinds of ways, when we reduce transaction cost, we spur progress.

14. Minteer speaks of the unresponsiveness of environmental ethics and sustainability science as having to do with "the stubborn methodological and cultural divide between ethics and the natural sciences. Despite its normative character and ubiquitous 'transdisciplinary' rhetoric, sustainability science still aspires to be a 'Science' committed to naturalistic methods and empirical metrics."

15. We could put this point in the language of ecosystem management by saying that effective adaptive management and comprehensive ecological systems thinking must also be an exercise in collaborative management. See the entry by Marion Hourdequin on Ecosystem Management in this volume.

16. I thank Urs Kreuter for sharing his personal experience of CAMPFIRE's early history in Rhodesia.

17. Matzke and Nabane (1996: 80). Note that this is crucial; the bigger threat to wildlife tends to be cattle, not hunting. Cattle crowds out wildlife. Pastoral herds are one problem; farms and ranches are another. Nomadic Maasai herdsmen compete with wildlife for space and water but do not cut off migration routes by erecting fences or otherwise defending their turf. See Moss (1988: 209, 301).

REFERENCES

Fisher, R., and Ury, W. (1991). *Getting to Yes,* 2nd ed. New York: Penguin Books.

Hargrove, E. C. (1989). *Foundations of Environmental Ethics.* Englewood Cliffs, NJ: Prentice-Hall.

Klick, J., and Wright, J. (2012). "Grocery Bag Bans and Foodborne Illness." Philadelphia, PA: University of Pennsylvania Institute for Law and Economic Research.

Kreuter, U., Peel, M., and Warner, E. (2010). "Wildlife Conservation and Community-Based Natural Resource Management in Southern Africa's Private Nature Reserves." *Society and Natural Resources* 23: 507–524.

Kreuter, U., and Simmons, R. T. (1995). "Who Owns the Elephants?" *Wildlife in the Marketplace,* edited by T. Anderson and P. J. Hill, 147–165. Lanham, MD: Rowman and Littlefield.

Leopold, A. ([1949], 1966). *Sand County Almanac.* New York: Oxford Press.

Matzke, G. E., and Nabane, N. (1996). "Outcomes of a Community Controlled Wildlife Utilization Program in a Zambezi Valley Community." *Human Ecology* 24: 65–85.

Moss, C. (1988). *Elephant Memories.* New York: William Morrow.

Norton, B. (1991). *Toward Unity Among Environmentalists.* New York: Oxford University Press.

Sagoff, M. (1981). "At the Shrine of Our Lady of Fatima, or Why Political Questions Are Not All Economic." *Arizona Law Review* 23: 1283–1298.

Sagoff, M. (1988). *The Economy of the Earth.* Cambridge, England: Cambridge University Press, 1988.

Varner, G. (1998). *In Nature's Interests?* New York: Oxford University Press.

CHAPTER 44

....

ENVIRONMENTAL ETHICS, SUSTAINABILITY SCIENCE, AND THE RECOVERY OF PRAGMATISM

....

BEN A. MINTEER

1 THE CHALLENGE OF SUSTAINABILITY SCIENCE

....

SUSTAINABILITY science has emerged over the past two decades as a "transdisciplinary" field devoted to studying and steering the interactions between social and natural systems into more "sustainable trajectories" (see, e.g., NRC, 1999; Clark and Dickson, 2003; Kates, 2012). As a mission-oriented science focused on both understanding and shaping human-nature relationships, sustainability science would seem to benefit from a close collaboration with environmental ethics. After all (and as this volume illustrates), environmental ethics is the field devoted to understanding the character and structure of environmental values and clarifying the responsibilities these create for moral agents and for society as a whole. This project would appear to be quite relevant to a new science tasked with supporting the maintenance of social-environmental systems for the long run.

The argument for such an alliance could be pushed even harder. One of the distinctive aspects of sustainability science is its embrace of interventions into ecological systems to design solutions for an increasingly human-dominated planet. A strong argument could be made that it therefore *should* be informed by the sense of ethical restraint and concern for nature preservation articulated by environmental ethics to help it set appropriate standards for such interventions. The converse is also true: environmental ethics would benefit from a significant collaboration with sustainability science. And this argument can also be pushed harder: the field of environmental ethics *ought to* adopt a more praxis-oriented approach, that is, it should engage actual and pressing sustainability problems at the intersection of science, value, and society. As sustainability scientists pursue lines of research that may reduce human pressure on biodiversity and ecosystems, environmental ethics can help clarify and justify such efforts, while also proposing moral limits for scientific and technological interventions in nature in the era of planetary stewardship.

Yet this collaboration, as important as it may be for both fields, does not appear to be happening. No doubt one reason is the stubborn methodological and cultural divide between ethics and the natural sciences. Despite its normative character and ubiquitous "transdisciplinary" rhetoric, sustainability science still aspires to be a "Science," committed to naturalistic methods and empirical metrics. Environmental ethics, on the other hand, has privileged itself as primarily a prescriptive field, typically one with only a broadly metaphysical connection to ecological science and with little historical interest in issues emerging in applied ecological problem solving (Minteer and Collins, 2008).

Yet I think there is also a more particular philosophical incompatibility between environmental ethics and sustainability science, one that merits further attention. Specifically, there appears to be a significant ethical disparity between these two fields that share the aim of improving our environmental condition but that approach this goal from very different moral vantage points. This division, I believe, needs to be examined and rethought if we wish to see the development of a more ethically inclusive sustainability science *and* a more pragmatic and cooperative environmental ethics that can contribute to sustainability practice moving forward.

2 Pragmatism and Environmental Ethics

But what exactly does it mean for environmental ethics to be more "pragmatic"? Philosophical pragmatism is a heterogeneous tradition, with distinct and not always compatible "paleo" and "neo" varieties. In its classical mode, that is, the tradition represented by the work of American philosophers Charles Sanders Peirce, William James, and John Dewey, pragmatism may be characterized as a loosely organized collection of theories about truth, meaning, inquiry, and value. Chief among the original pragmatist commitments is the rejection of foundationalism, that is, the denial of the idea that knowledge and belief must be grounded in a class of certain, fixed, and basic beliefs. Pragmatism thus challenges the traditional epistemological commitments of both rationalism and empiricism, rejecting, in Dewey's phrase, philosophy's "quest for certainty" and adopting a more experimental and fallibilistic view of knowledge (Minteer, 2012).

This prominence of inquiry is another distinctive feature of the tradition. For classical pragmatists philosophical inquiry is a process or method modeled after the sciences, but it is a generic method that they believed could fruitfully be applied across all realms of experience, including to aesthetic and ethical questions. As naturalists, pragmatists stress the basic continuity of human experience, an insight that leads them to reject any sharp ontological division between fact and value. This in turn has a special bearing on discussion of ethics: facts about human experience ultimately provide evidence for moral judgments. Inquiry and experience, however, are ongoing, so this evidence is always capable of being overturned in light of successive experience (Anderson, 1998).

Classical pragmatists such as Peirce and Dewey privileged the epistemic qualities of what they saw as the self-correcting nature of the community (Bernstein, 1997). For Peirce, who was more wedded to a metaphysical view of science than Dewey, truth would emerge from the well-run, collective experimental process over the long run. For Dewey, this was the more democratic method of "social intelligence," a method that would allow the community of citizens (not just scientific and technical experts) to solve public problems more effectively and develop more secure and widely shared values in the process.

The rejection of foundationalism and the emphasis on the method of inquiry and experience lead pragmatists to support a strongly pluralistic view of value and the good. James described a "multiverse," a pluralistic universe in which we continually experience variety and difference so that any singular or reductionist view of the good can only ever be partial and contingent (James, 1909). Dewey would build his model of moral philosophy upon this insight by suggesting that since experience teaches us that new ethical situations and novel problem contexts are always present, rigid adherence to any single moral principle trades adaptability for an illusory sense of security.

The pragmatic turn in environmental ethics that began in the 1990s (see, e.g., Norton, 1991; Light and Katz, 1996) largely followed the path set down by the early American pragmatists. "Environmental pragmatists" were motivated to reconstruct environmental ethics as a more engaged, experimental, and adaptive form of inquiry, one that embraces the value pluralism of society and argues for accommodating this variety in environmental decision-making and practice. Although the classical pragmatists did not write much about conservation or environmental protection, the human—environment continuity reinforced by their naturalism provides what might be considered an "ecological" view of the human self in which the individual is seen as thoroughly enmeshed in larger natural and cultural—historic systems.

As environmental pragmatism evolved its proponents also defended their work as offering a more methodologically naturalistic and interdisciplinary approach to environmental ethics (Minteer and Manning, 1999, Norton, 2003). Some writers also tapped into the tradition's political and epistemological commitments, suggesting that a pragmatic environmental ethics was more compatible with democratic norms and processes—and that it offered as well an effective means for bridging the chasm between ethical theorizing and environmental decision-making (e.g., Norton, 2005; Minteer, 2012). Others expanded environmental pragmatism's methodological and axiological dimensions, potentially widening the constituency for the new approach beyond devotees of the classical model (e.g., Light, 2000, 2002; Weston, 2009).

Despite the growth and diversification of the approach, the response to environmental pragmatism by nonanthropocentric theorists has mostly been negative. Pragmatism has been conflated with all manner of vices in environmental ethics, including economism, utilitarianism, and political expediency (see, e.g., Rolston, 1998; Callicott, 1999, 2002; Eckersley, 2002). It has been branded as an arrogant humanism that can offer only an exploitative instrumentalism toward nature. Pragmatism, of course, has a long history of being misunderstood by critics (see, e.g., Mumford, 1926). But the reception of pragmatism in environmental ethics is clearly a result of the field's idiosyncratic historical development. Since the early 1970s, many environmental ethicists, including those closely linked with the field's academic founding, have searched for a radically different ethic for the human-nature relationship, one that would be marked not by the humanism of the conventional Western philosophical worldview (such as pragmatism), but by a nature-centered worldview privileging nonhuman organisms, populations, and ecosystems (see, e.g., Routley, 1973; Rolston, 1975). As the field developed in the 1980s and 1990s, the nonanthropocentric argument frequently took on an exclusivist character: the nonanthropocentric ethic *had* to be adopted to guarantee good environmental policy (see, e.g., Rolston, 1994; Katz, 1997; Callicott, 1999).

3 THE ASCENT OF SUSTAINABILITY SCIENCE

Although environmental ethics is still a comparatively young field, sustainability science is even younger. Like conservation biology (which organized in the mid-1980s), sustainability science emerged as a fundamentally normative science intended to help steer society toward a desired end, that is, an ecologically supportable, just, and prosperous human future. It remains a rather diffuse science, however, with a fuzzy historical lineage and unclear disciplinary margins. Indeed, it is not always clear today who should be counted as a "sustainability scientist" (including, perhaps, to the scientists themselves). All of this makes pinning down an "environmental ethic" for sustainability science difficult. Still, we can make progress on this question by looking at some of the key policy documents and statements that have informed this new field since the 1980s.

There is, for example, the well-known formulation found in the United Nations World Commission on Environmental and Development report, *Our Common Future* (aka the Brundtland report) in 1987, which defined sustainable development as "Development that meets the needs of the present without compromising the ability of future generations to meet their own needs" (WCED, 1987: 43). This attention to human needs would be repeated a dozen years later in the similarly named, *Our Common Journey* (1999), an influential US National Research Council report that in hindsight set the agenda for sustainability science. The report directed that a "sustainability transition" should "be able to meet the needs of a much larger but stabilizing human population, to sustain the life support systems of the planet, and to substantially reduce hunger and poverty" (NRC, 1999: 31). Although the "life support systems" language incorporates an acknowledgment of nonhuman species and ecosystems, the context makes it clear that these are primarily important for their ability to sustain human life rather than for their own sake.

As sustainability science developed out of this larger policy discourse in sustainable development beginning the late 1990s, it retained the focus on human welfare while introducing the scientific model of coupled human and natural systems, a framework that would become associated with the new field. It proved to be a powerful formulation. Defining sustainability science in an important 2001 article in *Science* magazine, Kates et al. described the field as an attempt "to understand the fundamental character of interactions between nature and society" in a way that would also allow society to guide these interactions toward paths that were more socially desirable and enduring (Kates et al., 2001: 641). Others quickly followed suit, including Harvard University's William Clark, one of sustainability science's most prominent intellectual architects. Writing in the *Proceedings of the National Academy of Science* (*PNAS*) in 2007, Clark described how the coupled systems approach would provide the scientific foundations for the field's engagement with human needs and environmental problem solving (Clark, 2007).

PNAS would become one of the leading scientific outlets for work in the new field, with the journal's website describing sustainability science as: "an emerging field of research dealing with the interactions between natural and social systems, and with how those interactions affect the challenge of sustainability: meeting the needs of the present and future generations while substantially reducing poverty and conserving the planet's life support systems" (http://sustainability.pnas.org/). In 2006, a special sustainability science section was added to the publication; that same year the journal *Sustainability Science* was launched. Both events suggested a growing disciplinary and institutional organization for the new field.

The novelty of sustainability science appears to reside in its specific problem focus rather than in any bold new disciplinary content (Clark, 2007). It is envisioned as an attempt to use the coupled-systems understanding of nature-society interrelationships in order to chart a more productive, durable, and equitable developmental pathway. In doing so, it draws from other natural and social scientific and technical fields, including most prominently ecology, engineering, economics, and, to a lesser but perhaps increasing degree, science and technology studies (Miller, 2013).

Furthermore, the anthropocentrism of this new field is clear: ecological systems (and the nonhuman-populations and processes they contain) are viewed as essential life support systems for society, with their management fueled by a concern for maintaining a range of human benefits within and between generations. And unlike the vision of strong nonanthropocentric preservationists in environmental ethics that have at times turned away from development concerns when nature is significantly threatened (e.g., Rolston, 1996; Katz, 1997), the discussion of "well-being" in sustainability science discussions frequently emphasizes poverty alleviation and hunger eradication, thus carrying forth the original values and wider policy mission of sustainable development as the framework emerged in the early 1980s.

This does not mean that the ethical foundations of this new science are not valid commitments. The forward-looking anthropocentrism and social equity concerns motivating sustainability science comprise a legitimate and important value system, and in many respects are a corrective to the historical emphasis on a narrower form of nature preservationism and the study of more pristine landscapes in ecology. Still, it is true that a deeper concern with conservation values, with wildness, and so on—that is, a concern for nature protection for its own sake—is not really a part of sustainability science discourse.

4 STRATEGIES FOR RECONCILIATION

If nonanthropocentrism is the position most closely identified with environmental ethics historically (and the moral outlook that typically defines the field to many non-philosophers, including environmental scientists), and if a liberal anthropocentrism has emerged as the dominant value system supporting sustainability science, we might have a problem. That is, we might have a problem if we wish to encourage a more significant collaboration between environmental ethics and sustainability science. These rival ethical foundations certainly would appear to frustrate any effort to form useful alliances between the two fields.

Which way forward? One option would be to simply embrace the prevailing nonanthropocentric model of environmental ethics and reject sustainability and sustainability science as too anthropocentric (e.g., Newton and Freyfogle, 2005). The problem with this strategy, however, is that it is not very realistic: the sustainability agenda is not going away. It is also not a politically attractive option for environmental ethics given the field's flirtations with misanthropy over the years. Doubling down on a strong nonanthropocentrism will not only subvert collaborative efforts, it will weaken the influence of environmental ethics in sustainability science programs and practices.

A second option would be to attempt to achieve greater compatibility within a "conver-gence" model. That is, we could try to make the empirical claim that both normative-ethical systems ultimately lead to the same policy agenda. This is the argument of the environmen-tal pragmatist Bryan Norton, who has long defended a "convergence hypothesis" suggesting that the philosophical differences between nonanthropocentrism and a pluralistic anthro-pocentrism do not preclude practical agreement on policies to protect wild species and eco-systems (thus making nonanthropocentric claims unnecessary). Although there appears to be strong support for Norton's theory, including empirical work, many nonanthropocen-tric environmental ethicists have and continue to reject his thesis (see, e.g., Callicott, 2009; Katz, 2009).

If the convergence argument remains a nonstarter for philosophers who want to defend the necessity of the nonanthropocentric position, we might consider a third strategy. This tack might not make the two fields more collaborative but it would at least not put them into open conflict. We could settle on a disciplinary "zoning": environmental ethics and sustain-ability science could be viewed as separate domains of research and practice, with orthogo-nal environmental value frameworks. Sustainability scientists would continue to focus on those environmental dynamics and problems concerning present and future human well-being (e.g., the study and enhancement of urban ecosystems, ecosystem services), while environmental ethicists would continue to emphasize the preservation of wildlands and natural areas, endangered species, and so on—for their own sake. Environmental ethicists would thus continue to commit their collaborative energy to other fields, such as conserva-tion biology, which has long been identified with nonanthropocentric arguments for biodi-versity preservation (e.g., Soulé, 1985).

The problem with this tactic, however, is that the field of conservation biology is changing. It is being pushed into a more anthropocentric model of "conservation science" less cen-tered on wilderness and endangered species conservation and more oriented toward ecosys-tem services, resource management, and the agenda of sustainable development (see, e.g., Kareiva and Marvier, 2012). Although this effort is encountering serious resistance in the conservation community (see, e.g., Foreman, 2012; Soulé, 2013), consigning nature-centered environmental ethics to conservation biology nevertheless promises to become more com-plicated by the gravitational pull of the sustainability worldview.

Finally, and mirroring the first strategy, we could simply dismiss environmental ethics as too nonanthropocentric and as irrelevant to sustainability science. As with the first path, this is not an attractive option if we wish to encourage fruitful collaboration between the fields. Unfortunately, however, it may be the current de facto "strategy" in sustainability science. A revealing analysis published in *PNAS* of scientific paper titles containing the terms "sustain-able development" and/or "sustainability" over the past three decades produced an interesting "word cloud" graphic that, among other things, was noticeable for the absence of terms evok-ing explicit ethical regard for nature (Bettencourt and Kaur, 2011; see also Kates, 2011).

5 RECONSTRUCTING THE NARRATIVE

Obviously, none of these options are satisfying if we desire a closer collaboration between environmental ethics and sustainability science. But if the fast developing and increasingly influential field of sustainability science is to enrich and expand its ethical vision beyond a fairly traditional anthropocentrism, and if environmental ethics is in turn to achieve more significant societal and policy impact by influencing the agendas and practices of this new science, then I believe that we need to find ways to close the philosophical gap that exists between them. One way this can be done, I would suggest, is by rethinking the established narrative of environmental ethics.

As we have seen, the traditional account promulgated by environmental ethicists suggests that there is a stark contrast between anthropocentric and nonanthropocentric ethics. This judgment is often supported by a narrative reinforcing the dualism of environmental ethics, a historical account that draws from the pioneering work of first generation environmental historians such as Roderick Nash (1967) and Donald Worster (1977), among others. The bifurcated structure of the narrative, for example, conservation versus preservation, anthropocentrism versus biocentrism, and so on, also assumes a moral directionality: the emergence of nonanthropocentric ethics in the 1970s becomes for many philosophers the fullest and mature expression of the moral tradition of Thoreau, John Muir, Aldo Leopold, and Rachel Carson.

This account has been enormously influential in the development of American environmental ethics. But it greatly simplifies the intellectual and ethical diversity and richness of environment thought. In particular, it reduces the complex pluralism and pragmatism of the tradition into a polarized clash of ideologies that bears little resemblance to the more nuanced projects those environmental writers who laid the moral groundwork for the rise of environmental ethics in the 1970s.

Indeed, a more careful reading reveals that in fact pragmatism has always coursed through the American environmental tradition. Although the classical pragmatists did not devote much attention to environmental questions of their day, a broadly pragmatist sensibility runs through the work of key early twentieth-century progressive conservationists and planners, including both well-known and lesser-known thinkers such as Liberty Hyde Bailey, Lewis Mumford, Benton MacKaye, and Aldo Leopold (Minteer, 2006). Despite their differences, this diverse group of influential environmental writers emphasized (as did the philosophical pragmatists) the significance of human experience in the environment and its role in shaping and transforming belief and value. And, in sympathy with classical pragmatists such as Dewey, a clear democratic and civic impulse animated their environmental projects: natural values and civic ideals about the good community were mutually reinforcing, each seen as necessary for the promotion of the other.

Most intriguingly for current environmental ethics, these early environmental pragmatists accepted the pluralism of environmental values, implicitly denying through their own work any necessary schism between nature-centered and humanistic moral outlooks. Furthermore, theirs was a vision that supported an understanding of responsible human agency in nature: human environmental action was not to be disparaged a priori. Instead, it was to be judged by its ability to successfully adjust and adapt human affairs to a changing landscape. As Leopold wrote in the Foreword to his 1949 classic, *A Sand County Almanac*:

> We abuse land because we regard it as a commodity belonging to us. When we see land as a community to which we belong, we may begin to use it with love and respect. There is no other way for land to survive the impact of mechanized man, nor for us to reap from it the esthetic harvest it is capable, under science, of contributing to culture (Leopold, 1949, p. viii).

These words remind us just how sophisticated and layered Leopold's environmental ethic was. It deftly combined a quasi-nonanthropocentric regard for the biotic community with a frank realism about the task of ecological sustainability ("There is no other way for land to survive . . ."). In Leopold's moral system we are to venerate the land (ecosystem), but we are also expected to use it wisely and to benefit from this use. Leopold thus was neither a narrow biocentrist nor a conventional (i.e., managerial) anthropocentrist; rather, he embraced elements of a respect for nature ethic within a greater concern for the cultural, aesthetic, and economic sustainability of the community.

As mentioned previously, Leopold's assimilation of a respect for nature ethic within a broader and non-exploitative instrumentalist vision is shared by many of the most prominent voices in the American environmental tradition that similarly avoided creating any sort of ontological division between natural and human values. Environmental pragmatism is thus not a development of philosophers in the 1990s: it is a significant part of the intellectual heritage of environmental ethics. Dismissing it therefore undercuts the field's own philosophical foundations. The recovery of pragmatism as a "third way" tradition, one running between dogmatic preservationism and utilitarianism, reveals what has been lost in narrowing the pluralism and complexity of this tradition to a simplified nonanthropocentrism (Minteer, 2006).

6 ENVIRONMENTAL PRAGMATISM VERSUS PROMETHEANISM

This pragmatist counter-narrative in environmental ethics provides the anchor point for building a more significant collaboration with sustainability science. It advances an understanding of environmental ethics that does not place the traditional nature-centered moral project at odds with the more anthropocentric or prudential concern with human well-being and flourishing. Rather, it knits them together, linking human aesthetic, cultural, and economic interests—and an acceptance of responsible human agency—with the holding of a proper attitude toward nonhuman nature, that is, a moral outlook toward other species and the environment as a whole.

A pragmatist environmental ethics that acknowledges the interplay of intrinsic and instrumental values of nature in human experience is better suited to influencing the values and goals of a developing sustainability science. It offers a moral grounding that can help widen the vision of the latter so that sustainability becomes more than a question of maintaining a desirable level of human welfare and development: it becomes as well a question of our obligation to protect biodiversity and promote ecological integrity. The pragmatist tradition accommodates this preservationist insight while recognizing the strong societal and scientific interest in establishing and stewarding a healthy human-environment relationship.

Interestingly, many of those who profess to be environmental pragmatists today seem to miss these nuances. Consider, for example, the argument of environmentalists Michael Shellenberger and Ted Nordhaus, authors of the controversial "death of environmentalism" thesis and founders of the Breakthrough Institute, a progressive environmental think tank. Self-described "pragmatists," they reject the essentialism driving nature preservationism and the "politics of limits" that they argue is curtailing human ambition and innovation in the environmental movement. For them, environmentalism remains stuck in the muck of preservationism. In their provocative book, *Break Through* (2009), Shellenberger and Nordhaus single out Rachel Carson for special criticism, suggesting that her negative remarks in *Silent Spring* about the "arrogance" driving the human desire to control nature have had disastrous consequences for human-environment relations. As they put it, "It is this reality—human agency—that most bothers environmentalists like Carson. For her, human attempts to control Nature inevitably end in tragedy" (Nordhaus and Shellenberger, 2009: 134).

Although they are right to take environmentalism to task for some of its ideological excesses, Nordhaus and Shellenberger misread Carson—and misconstrue pragmatism. They are correct that Carson condemned the attitude of human arrogance toward nature as manifest in the use of "biocides" like DDT. But her environmentalism was far from an assault on human agency in nature. For example, just a few lines before the "control of nature" remark in *Silent Spring* highlighted by Nordhaus and Shellenberger, Carson wrote the following:

> Through all these new, imaginative, and creative approaches to the problems of sharing our earth with other creatures there runs a constant theme, the awareness that we are dealing with life—with living populations and all their pressures and counter-pressures, their surges and recessions. Only by taking account of such life forces and by *cautiously seeking to guide them into channels favorable to ourselves* can we hope to achieve a reasonable accommodation between the insect hordes and ourselves (Carson, 2002 (orig. 1962): 296; emphasis added).

Carson (like Leopold) did not condemn significant human activity in nature. Rather, she argued that such manipulations should be much more intelligent and more careful, and they should be informed by a deeper ecological understanding. This more enlarged ecological sensibility, she wrote, offered the only hope for reconciling human will and environmental health over the long run.

The danger in some of the current appropriations of pragmatism in environmentalism is that the humility, caution, and contingency of the tradition is disregarded in the desire to be fresh, innovative, and different, that is, to "break through" the historical logjams of environmental politics and policy that have stifled progress and hamstrung environmental ethics. But pragmatism, we should remember, is not Prometheanism. It is more accurately viewed as a midpoint on a continuum between strongly nonanthropocentric and anthropocentric poles in environmental thought (Figure 44.1).

So, for example, when "pragmatists" like Nordhaus and Shellenberger (2009) write that, "Whether we like it or not, humans have become the meaning of the earth" (p. 272), they are expressing a Promethean view that is actually quite foreign to the pragmatism of philosophers such as John Dewey. Although Dewey's humanism and perspectival anthropocentrism is well known, it falls well short of the kind of full-blown ontological anthropocentrism embraced by Nordhaus and Shellenberger. "Humanity is not, as was once thought, the end for which all things were formed," Dewey wrote in *The Public and its Problems* (1927). "It is but a slight and feeble thing, perhaps an episodic one, in the vast stretch of the universe" (p. 345).

I have mentioned that the classical pragmatists did not say much about what we would today consider environmental concerns. That is certainly true. But if we take a wider view about what counts as an "environmental ethic," we find in many places an articulate expression of respect and humility toward nature. For example, in Dewey's major statement on

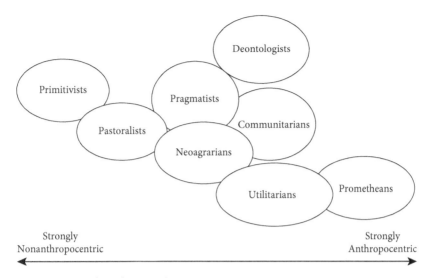

FIGURE 44.1 Expanding the Moral Vision.

religious experience, *A Common Faith* (1934), he writes of the attitude of "natural piety," which suggested a veneration of the enabling conditions of lived experience; that is, the natural and social processes that support and help to shape human life. We are parts of a larger whole, Dewey reminds us, and we forget this profound social and environmental embeddedness at our peril. But for Dewey (as with Leopold and Carson), we are also parts of nature with a difference: we possess "intelligence and purpose," and so we have the ability—and, importantly, the responsibility—to carefully adapt both nature *and* ourselves to achieve a more harmonious and sustainable state (Dewey, 1934: 18).

7 CONCLUSION: MEETING IN THE MIDDLE

In order to build a stronger collaboration between sustainability science and environmental ethics, both fields will need to expand their moral vision. Environmental ethics must take responsibility for the intelligent shaping of a more sustainable future in a manner that does not dismiss legitimate human values and interests. The pragmatist environmental tradition offers a way to rethink some of the calcified assumptions and arguments of the field and come to an understanding that retains a respect for nature while recognizing that this attitude should not trump wise interventions in nature to promote valued human *and* natural goods.

For its part, sustainability science must adopt a *genuinely* pragmatic attitude of restraint and precaution when considering interventions in environmental systems. This posture is all the more essential as we puzzle through the implications of life in the Anthropocene, which requires a sense of humility in the face of proposed large-scale interventions in earth systems (e.g., geoengineering) as part of a broader shift toward a "planetary manager" worldview (see Rolston, this volume). An ethically broadened sustainability science can help provoke an explicit and authoritative public discussion about which human-environment trade-offs should simply not be made given our powerful commitments to nature preservation, even as we confront the realities of a rapidly changing world. And it should encourage the protection and provision of societal pathways to promote respect for nature as constitutive of human well-being in addition to its more traditional managerial and development aims.

In his stimulating account of sustainability, cultural historian Ulrich Gruber arrives at a basic moral truth about the idea that has provoked so much international discussion and debate in policy and scientific circles. "Let it be—to forego something that is within one's power—that wisdom is inscribed in the concept of sustainability. That is its great strength" (Grober, 2012: 190). An authentically pragmatic environmental ethics in the "age of humans," rather than justifying our more Promethean impulses, can help a young sustainability science acknowledge the full extent of natural and human values at stake in the daunting but vital search for a more sustainable future.

References

Anderson, E. (1998). "Pragmatism, Science, and Moral Inquiry." In *In Face of the Facts: Moral Inquiry in American Scholarship*, edited by R. W. Fox and R. B. Westbrook, 10–39. Washington, DC: Woodrow Wilson Center and Cambridge University Press.

Bernstein, R. (1997). "Pragmatism, Pluralism, and the Healing of Wounds." In *Pragmatism: A Reader*, edited by L. Menand, 382–401. New York: Vintage Books.

Bettencourt, L. M. A., and Kaur, J. (2011). "The Evolution and Structure of Sustainability Science." *Proceedings of the National Academy of Sciences* 108: 19540–19545.

Callicott, J. B. (1999). *Beyond the Land Ethic: More Essays in Environmental Philosophy*. Albany, NY: SUNY Press.

Callicott, J. B. (2002). "The Power and Promise of Theoretical Environmental Ethics: Forging a New Discourse." *Environmental Values* 11: 3–25.

Callicott, J. B. (2009). "The Convergence Hypothesis Falsified: Implicit Intrinsic Value, Operational Rights, and De Facto Standing in the Endangered Species Act." In *Nature in Common? Environmental Ethics and the Contested Foundations of Environmental Policy*, edited by B. A. Minteer, 142–166. Philadelphia: Temple University Press.

Carson, R. (2002). *Silent Spring*. Boston: Mariner Books.

Clark, W. C. (2007). "Sustainability Science: A Room of its Own." *Proceedings of the National Academy of Sciences* 104: 1737–1738.

Clark, W. C., and Dickson, N. (2003). "Sustainability Science: The Emerging Research Program." *Proceedings of the National Academy of Sciences* 100: 8059–8061.

Dewey, J. (1927). *The Public and Its Problems. In Volume 2 of The Later Works of John Dewey, 1925–1953*, edited by J. A. Boydston. Carbondale, IL: Southern Illinois University Press, 1984.

Dewey, J. (1934). *A Common Faith. In Volume 9 of The Later Works of John Dewey, 1925–1953*, edited by J. A. Boydston. Carbondale, IL: Southern Illinois University Press, 1986.

Eckersley, R. (2002). "Environmental Pragmatism, Ecocentrism, and Deliberative Democracy: Between Problem-Solving and Fundamental Critique." In *Democracy and the Claims of Nature: Critical Perspectives for a New Century*, edited by B. A. Minteer and B. Pepperman Taylor, 49–69. Lanham, MD: Rowman & Littlefield.

Foreman, D. (2012). *Take Back Conservation*. Raven's Eye Press.

Grober, U. (2012). *Sustainability: A Cultural History*. Devon, UK: Green Books.

James, W. (1909). *A Pluralistic Universe*. New York: Longmans, Green, and Co.

Kareiva, P., and Marvier, M. (2012). "What Is Conservation Science?" *BioScience* 62: 962–969.

Kates, R. W., Clark, W. C., Corell, R., Hall, J. M., Jaeger, C. C., Lowe, I., McCarthy, J. J., et al. (2001). "Sustainability Science." *Science* 292: 641–642.

Kates, R. W., Clark, W. C., Corell, R., Hall, J. M., Jaeger, C. C., Lowe, I., McCarthy, J. J., et al. (2011). "What Kind of a Science Is Sustainability Science?" *Proceedings of the National Academy of Sciences* 108: 19449–19450.

Kates, R. W., Clark, W. C., Corell, R., Hall, J. M., Jaeger, C. C., Lowe, I., McCarthy, J. J., et al. (2012). "From the Unity of Nature to Sustainability Science: Ideas and Practice." In *Sustainability Science: The Emerging Paradigm and the Urban Environment*, edited by M. P. Weinstein and R. E. Turner, 3–20. New York: Springer.

Katz, E. (1997). *Nature as Subject: Human Obligation and Natural Community.* Lanham, MD: Rowman & Littlefield.

Katz, E. (2009). "Convergence and Ecological Restoration: A Counterexample." In *Nature in Common?: Environmental Ethics and the Contested Foundations of Environmental Policy*, edited by B. A. Minteer, 185–195. Philadelphia: Temple University Press.

Leopold, A. (1949). *A Sand County Almanac.* Oxford, England: Oxford University Press.

Light, A. (2000). "Ecological Restoration and the Culture of Nature: A Pragmatic Perspective." In *Restoring Nature: Perspectives from the Social Sciences and Humanities*, edited by P. Gobster and B. Hull, 49–70. Washington, D.C.: Island Press.

Light, A. (2002). "Methodological Pragmatism, Pluralism, and Environmental Ethics." In *Environmental Ethics: The Big Questions*, edited by D. Keller, 318–326. Cambridge, MA: Blackwell Publishers.

Light, A., and Katz, E., eds. (1996). *Environmental Pragmatism.* London: Routledge.

Miller, T. R. (2013). "Constructing Sustainability Science: Emerging Perspectives and Research Trajectories." *Sustainability Science* 8: 279–293.

Minteer, B. A. (2006). *The Landscape of Reform: Civic Pragmatism and Environmental Thought in America.* Cambridge, MA: MIT Press.

Minteer, B. A. (2012). *Refounding Environmental Ethics: Pragmatism, Principle, and Practice.* Philadelphia: Temple University Press.

Minteer, B. A., and Collins, J. P. (2008). "From Environmental to Ecological Ethics: Toward a Practical Ethics for Ecologists and Conservationists." *Science and Engineering Ethics* 14: 483–501.

Minteer, B. A., and Manning, R. E. (1999). "Pragmatism in Environmental Ethics: Democracy, Pluralism, and the Management of Nature." *Environmental Ethics* 21: 193–209.

Mumford, L. (1926). *The Golden Day.* New York: Boni and Liveright.

Nash, R. (1967). *Wilderness and the American Mind.* New Haven, CT: Yale University Press.

National Research Council (NRC). (1999). *Our Common Journey: A Transition Toward Sustainability.* Washington, D.C.: National Academies Press.

Newton, J. L., and Freyfogle, E. T. (2005). "Sustainability: A Dissent." *Conservation Biology* 19: 23–32.

Nordhaus, T., and Shellenberger, M. (2009). *Break Through: Why We Can't Leave Saving the Planet to Environmentalists.* New York: Mariner Books.

Norton, B. G. (1991). *Toward Unity Among Environmentalists.* Oxford, UK: Oxford University Press.

Norton, B. G. (2003). *Searching for Sustainability: Interdisciplinary Essays in the Philosophy of Conservation Biology.* Cambridge, UK: Cambridge University Press.

Norton, B. G. (2005). *Sustainability: A Philosophy of Adaptive Ecosystem Management.* Chicago: University of Chicago Press.

Rolston, H. III. (1975). "Is There an Ecological Ethic?" *Ethics* 85: 93–109.

Rolston, H. III. (1994). *Conserving Natural Value*. New York: Columbia University Press.

Rolston, H. III. (1996). "Feeding People versus Saving Nature?" In *World Hunger and Morality*, 2nd ed., edited by W. Aiken and H. LaFollette, 244–263. Upper Saddle River, NJ: Prentice-Hall.

Rolston, H. III. (1998). "Saving Nature, Feeding People, and the Foundations of Ethics." *Environmental Values* 7: 349–357.

Routley, R. (1973). "Is There a Need for a New, an Environmental Ethic?" *Proceedings of the 15th World Congress of Philosophy* 1(6): 205–210.

Soulé, M. (1985). What Is Conservation Biology? *BioScience* 35: 727–734.

Soulé, M. (2013). "The 'New Conservation.'" *Conservation Biology* 27: 895–897.

Weston, A. (2009). *The Incompleat Eco-Philosopher: Essays from the Edges of Environmental Ethics*. Albany: SUNY Press.

World Commission on Environment and Development (WCED). (1987). *Our Common Future*. New York: Oxford University Press.

Worster, D. (1977). *Nature's Economy: The Roots of Ecology*. San Francisco: Sierra Club Books.

CHAPTER 45

SACRIFICE AND THE POSSIBILITIES FOR ENVIRONMENTAL ACTION

JOHN M. MEYER

THIS chapter's title, as well as its placement within a book on environmental ethics, would seem to suggest that it is an ethical appeal for individuals to begin sacrificing to address pressing environmental concerns. It is not. Instead, it is intended as an exploration of one aspect of a key political-strategic question for environmental action: *When and how do environmental concerns resonate widely with citizens?* This question invites reflection upon how the rhetoric of "sacrifice," especially as often used within wealthy consumer societies, shapes and constrains the political imaginary and discourse surrounding environmental concerns. We might then use this insight to reorient talk about sacrifice in a manner that expands our imaginary and opens up broader possibilities for action.

1 SACRIFICE IN CONTEMPORARY ENVIRONMENTAL DISCOURSE

The rhetoric of sacrifice has become a political sticking point that often entangles environmental discussions in a false dichotomy between sacrifice and self-interest. Here, sacrifice is misleadingly identified as self-abnegation; performed by heroes or saints, but not willingly by ordinary people. Google "sacrifice" and "the environment" and one finds pages of full-throated oppositional views asserting that the contemporary environmental movement expresses a death-wish for humanity, that it privileges small insignificant species at the expense of humans, and that it demands the rejection of human civilization itself. For example, in an essay titled "Environmentalism and Human Sacrifice" from the *National Review Online* and widely republished, Denis Prager attacks environmentalist opposition to genetically modified rice, DDT, and the Keystone XL pipeline, concluding "the movement known as environmentalism is not only a false religion, it is one that allows human sacrifice" (Prager 2013). In another article, Michael Berliner, former director of the Ayn Rand Institute writes,

> The guiding principle of environmentalism is self-sacrifice, the sacrifice of longer lives, healthier lives, more prosperous lives, more enjoyable lives, i.e., the sacrifice of human lives. But an individual is not born in servitude. He has a moral right to live his own life for his own sake. He has no duty to sacrifice it to the needs of others and certainly not to the "needs" of the nonhuman. (Berliner, 2014)

Although not all critics are so strident, this identification of sacrifice with self-abnegation is widespread. It has led environmental activists and thinkers of many stripes to go to great lengths to distance environmentalism from any hint of an association with sacrifice. Andrew McLaughlin set the tone years ago when he argued:

> As long as environmentalism seems to require only denial and sacrifice, its political effectiveness will be limited. Emphasis needs to be placed on the fact that changes sought are intended to increase quality of life. (McLaughlin, 1993: 184).

In the words of Thomas Princen, the aim is to convince potential supporters that environmentally sound choices do not involve "abstinence" or "hardship;" are "not second best, not a concession, not a sacrifice" (Princen, 2005: 2).[1] "The problem," as activists Ted Nordhaus and Michael Shellenberger describe it, "is that none of us, whether we are wealthy environmental leaders or average Americans, are willing to significantly sacrifice our standard of living" (Nordhaus and Shellenberger, 2007: 125). Notice that all these arguments identify self-abnegation with sacrifice, in the course of advancing an argument for an alternate vision of environmentalism said to be associated with neither.

A recent book edited by this author and Michael Maniates collected essays on a variety of intersections between the rhetoric of sacrifice and environmental politics. In diverse ways, the authors of these essays argue, and present cases to suggest, that sacrifice need not be contrary to self-interest or human flourishing, nor synonymous with the denial of freedom (Maniates and Meyer, 2010). Yet the association between sacrifice and self-abnegation is deeply rooted enough that some have misread the book as expressing precisely the opposite claim. For example, arguing against "the prospect of global degrowth," Rasmus Karlsson references the book to support the claim that such an agenda would require "sacrifices in terms of individual freedom" (Karlsson, 2013: 6).

The premise of such assertions—by both environmentalists and their critics—seems to be that we know both what sacrifice is, and that it is not a significant part of our present-day social existence. Sacrifice thus becomes a placeholder for forms of action that one assumes are both beyond the ken of contemporary experience and politically unpalatable to propose. Associating environmentalism with sacrifice become a political "third rail" to be avoided lest one get burned. The consequence is to narrow the range of environmental discourse, privileging either those that make confident assertions that their approach does not involve sacrifice or conversely those that argue that catastrophic conditions will ultimately override a posited popular sensitivity to sacrifice, forcing its imposition.

2 TECHNOLOGICAL OPTIMISM VERSUS
PESSIMISTIC CATASTROPHISM

Perhaps the most alluring alternative to a discussion of sacrifice emerges from the optimistic discourse of those suggesting the feasibility of a purely technocratic way out of our ecological challenges. Often discussed under the rubric of "ecological modernization" in Europe, this view has been captured in US works including Paul Hawken, Amory Lovins, and Hunter Lovins' *Natural Capitalism* (1999), and William McDonough and Michael Braungart's *Cradle to Cradle* (2002).[2] According to this view, the same technological changes needed to avert crisis will also, happily, make all our lives uniformly more comfortable and enjoyable. The opening pages of *Natural Capitalism* make this claim vividly:

> Imagine... a world where cities have become peaceful and serene because cars and buses are whisper quiet, vehicles exhaust only water vapor, and parks and greenways have replaced unneeded urban freeways... Industrialized countries have reduced resource use by 80% while improving the quality of life... Is this the vision of a utopia? *In fact, the changes described here could come about in the decades to come as the result of economic and technological trends already in place.* (Hawken et al. 1999: 1–2, emphasis added)

The key point that I have highlighted in this quotation is that such change is characterized as entirely dependent upon "economic and technological trends already in place." It is because the authors are convinced of the extant power of these currents that they can assert that their imagined world is neither naïve nor utopian, but likely. This view of economy and technology as autonomous displaces both the need and the value of a more vigorous conception of democratic citizenship or social movements for change, since the task at hand is avowedly instrumental: "It is neither conservative nor liberal in its ideology ... [s]ince it is a means, and not an end" (Hawken et al., 1999: 20).[3] "Sacrifice"—or loss of any kind—is uncalled for; their vision is presented as merely an improved means of achieving already established and desirable ends (Wapner, 2010: 37–40).

Much of the contemporary advocacy of geoengineering can also be viewed as fitting this optimistic narrative. As Simon Nicholson observes, "... geoengineering seems, to many ... a *sacrifice-free* form of action. The thinking goes that if the development of new technologies can allow the earth's living and life-supporting systems to be manipulated at will, then climate change ... can be readily managed as discrete, solely technical problems" (Nicholson, 2010: 272). Nicholson argues convincingly that there are material, political, and existential sacrifices embedded, yet typically unrecognized, in proposals for geoengineering the climate, making them far less promising than they might otherwise appear.

It is important to note that the narrative sketched here goes beyond a conviction that technological innovation and change is an important *component* of any meaningful strategy for addressing environmental challenges. Instead, this depoliticized narrative posits seamless technological adoption as the strategy in and of itself. Its optimism is a reflection of how little it seems to require of us to achieve the changes deemed necessary. Anthony Weston captures this minimalism in his account of a Toyota Prius salesperson who enthuses about the hybrid vehicle that "The only real change is under the hood!" (Weston, 2012: 47). Yet if changes limited to what is "under the hood" are deemed insufficient or inappropriate to the nature of contemporary environmental challenges, then what's the alternative? Again, the inability or unwillingness to confront the ambiguities surrounding sacrifice narrows the available options. Catastrophism—in the sense of a pessimistic conviction that only whole-sale collapse or (perhaps) its imminent reckoning will be sufficient to instigate environmental action—appears as the primary alternative (e.g., Lovelock, 2009; cf., Bruckner, 2013).

For some, apocalyptic visions are regarded as an autonomous trigger for necessary action taken in the absence of choice or freedom. For others, the *threat* of catastrophe might become so real and imminent that people will "see the light" and be convinced to do what experts deem to be necessary. But by presuming an enlightened "we" who are apart from those who behave in environmentally destructive ways, such tactics come across as pater-nalistic—more likely to alienate than to motivate change. In other contexts (e.g., the "war on terror"), flaunting "expert" knowledge or warning about catastrophe has been a reli-able basis for top-down, coercive political action; there has been a powerful strand in the history of environmental discourse that makes precisely this association as well (Ophuls, 1973; Heilbroner, 1980; Flannery, 2006: 290–295; see discussion in Yuen, 2012). The point, in raising critical questions about catastrophism, is emphatically not to call into question scientific knowledge of environmental problems. It is to challenge those who presume, con-sciously or otherwise, that this knowledge leads directly to a specific strategy for change that can effectively address these problems.[4] Despair and pessimism feeds this sort of stra-tegic response.

In all of this, however, the concept of sacrifice itself—in its multifaceted and sometimes contradictory connotations—remains curiously unexamined. For techno-optimists and apocalyptic pessimists alike, confronting sacrifice appears as an unnecessary distraction. By contrast, those who aim to address environmental challenges while strengthening demo-cratic impulses and institutions require hope. This hope is something altogether different than optimism.[5] Unlike optimism, hope offers no assurances of easy adoption, nor confi-dence of likely outcomes.[6] What it does offer is the possibility that with struggle and hard work, a better world just might be achieved. Surprisingly, perhaps, hope can be fortified by a closer examination of the concept of sacrifice.

3 RETHINKING THE CONCEPT OF SACRIFICE

The dichotomy between self-interest and sacrifice is rooted in a narrowly individualistic conception of self-interest that is relatively commonplace, particularly among economists, rational choice theorists, and at least some other liberal theorists.[7] Randians like Berliner (above) embrace it as "egoism"; Charles Taylor critiques it as "atomism" (Taylor, 1992); C.B. Macpherson as "possessive individualism" (MacPherson, 1962). Danielle Allen characterizes it as a "rivalrous" conception of self-interest, which she—like other critics—attributes largely to western culture's patrimony from Hobbes (Allen, 2004: 137–138). When self-interest is tightly circumscribed like this, there is less room for envisioning sacrifice as anything other than self-abnegation—a giving up "to the needs of others," as Berliner asserts above, whether these others are human or nonhuman. The narrow construction of individual self-interest can be contrasted, then, to a more expansive and relational understanding—one that Tocqueville described as the doctrine of "self-interest properly understood" and which is integral to many contemporary feminist analyses (Tocqueville, 1969: 525; Plumwood, 1991).

Closer attention to the meaning of "sacrifice" makes it clear that a complementary relationship with this more expansive sense of self-interest is well-established. The most prominent context for speaking of sacrifice has long been religious, where the *Oxford English Dictionary* (*OED*) defines it as "an offering to God or a deity" (defn. 1.a.). A seminal work by Hubert and Mauss describes sacrifice as *"communication between sacred and profane worlds, through the mediation of a victim, that is, of a thing that in the course of the ceremony is destroyed"* (Hubert and Mauss, 1964: 97–98; cf., Bourdillon and Fortes, 1980: 10–12). This communication with the sacred, then, is the goal of the sacrifice. We, the profane, elevate ourselves to something holy—at least enough to be able to communicate with the sacred. This elevation is a consequence of our sacrifice. There is an offering, but also a return. "Thus sacrifice shows itself in a dual light; it is a useful act and it is an obligation. *Disinterestedness is mingled with self-interest*" (Hubert and Mauss, 1964: 100; emphasis added). The "victim" here is understood to be in the possession of the sacrificer, yet the role of the agent and the victim of sacrifice are distinct, in this description, even in those cases where their identity is the same (i.e., "self-sacrifice").

When the term is used in a secular context, there is often a similar mingling with self-interest. The *OED* definition is "[t]he destruction or surrender of something valued or desired for the sake of something having, or regarded as having, a higher or more pressing claim" (defn. 4.a.). Rather than the negation of interest, here it is "regarded as" the pursuit of a higher interest, albeit at a recognizable cost. It is in this sense, for example, that we often speak of parents making a "sacrifice" to create opportunities for their children. Yet some, perhaps many, parents— gaining satisfaction from the flourishing of their children—deny that they have "sacrificed" at all. Of course, the sacrifice that such parents deny is one conceptualized as the negation of their self-interest (understood in a narrowly individualistic sense). It is, instead, an act rooted in a relational sense of self. A consequence of this sense is to view their hopes and aspirations for their children, and hence for the future, as in their own interest. When sacrifice is viewed as consistent with this definition, such a parent would be less likely to deny having made a sacrifice while simultaneously more likely to be comfortable describing their children's flourishing as a manifestation of their own interest (Peterson, 2010).

Environmentally sound policies and choices can—in many contexts and for many people—improve quality of life and hence facilitate changes consistent with one's self-interest broadly construed. Where others assert that such changes make sacrifice unnecessary, however, we might now recognize the opposite: sacrifice is, in fact, enabled by a more expansive sense of self-interest. As Tocqueville puts it, this understanding of self-interest, "does not inspire great sacrifices, but every day it prompts some small ones" (Tocqueville, 1969: 527). By highlighting rather than marginalizing sacrifice, we become more likely to recognize ourselves in a relational web that weakens an atomistic sense of self and self-interest. As Jane Mansbridge has argued, this sort of recognition can also be an important facilitator of action:

> . . . because thinking that another has acted unselfishly often leads people to behave unselfishly themselves, underestimating the frequency of altruism can itself undermine unselfish behavior. (Mansbridge. 1990: 141)

In sum, sacrifice and human flourishing need not be mutually exclusive and *can* be mutually reinforcing.

And yet a reader has good reason to remain wary of, if not resistant to, the possibilities for an environmental politics of sacrifice at this point. Even if we are persuaded that sacrifice *can* be consistent with self-interest, after all, this is not sufficient to give us confidence that any sacrifice we make actually *will* promote human flourishing. The worry—and the danger— here is that sacrifice will be imposed from the top rather than initiated from the bottom; that it will do more to protect the interests of the powerful than of those sacrificing. To address this, we must recognize the ubiquity of sacrifice to everyday life and society, in contrast to its frequent presentation as something extraordinary to be newly introduced.

4 SACRIFICE AS UBIQUITOUS

Contrary to its colloquial association with narrow self-interest and so individualism, a critical investigation of sacrifice becomes a vehicle for discerning the structural in the everyday. The question is not merely about individual attitudes and behaviors, with the attendant focus upon guilt or responsibility. It is also upon everyday practices, social rules, norms, and relationships that facilitate some forms of action while discouraging others. Recognizing the role of these practices and structures is vital to imagining new possibilities for action.

The presumption that citizens are unwilling to forego aspects of our current social or economic condition for future gain rests on the rather implausible belief that most of us are wholly content with our lives and the society within which we live now—that we regard this as the best of all possible worlds. Only in this circumstance would we (across lines of gender, class, and race) experience any change in our consumption or our behavior on behalf of addressing environmental challenges as a net and intolerable loss. By contrast, any interrogation of sacrifice must *uncover* some of the many and varied forms of sacrifice that always, already permeate daily life. These sacrifices are often gendered and frequently fall disproportionately—and in distinctive ways—on the poor and disadvantaged. They must be understood not just as a response to environmental issues but driven by livelihood, family, opportunity, and social expectations. Understood broadly in this manner, society itself—to say nothing of environmental commitment—could not be sustained in the absence of regular acts of sacrifice, both great and small. Whether or not to sacrifice is simply not the issue at stake. Instead, the vital question becomes: who sacrifices, and on behalf of what—or whom—do we sacrifice? When we come to appreciate the ubiquity of sacrifice, our attention can be more readily drawn to the many ways that it is structured by social and political institutions. If environmental debate illuminates the ubiquity of sacrifice in everyday life, a politics can emerge to temper or redress some of these existing patterns of sacrifice.

Take, for example, private cars. Given that automobile usage accounts for a sizeable percentage of fossil fuel consumption and greenhouse gas emissions, no serious effort to curb climate change can ignore it. Yet simply raising the issue is easily characterized as a call to sacrifice personal mobility. It must be understood, however, within the social and political system that has been termed "automobility"—often facilitated by the tax code, enabled by massive investments of public and private infrastructure, broad cultural associations, and mitigation of public safety and health effects through wide-ranging regulation (Paterson, 2007; Rajan, 1996; Urry, 2004). In this context, we can recognize that driving is not always a choice but is often a structural necessity due to the geographic distribution of residential and commercial spaces, the absence of convenient public transportation, and growing impediments to walking and bicycling as auto traffic increases. For many—the young, elderly, poor, and disabled—access and mobility is therefore already sacrificed. One study, for example, found that elderly nondrivers become increasingly isolated, making 15% fewer trips to the doctor and 65% fewer trips for social, family, and religious activities than those who drive (Palmquist, 2008: 18).

As for those of us who do own a vehicle and drive, studies correlate living in more car-dependent communities with poorer health and greater weight gain (Zhao and Kaestner, 2010: 779). Moreover, when we are stuck in rush-hour traffic, when we have to take time off of work to transport an elderly parent to the doctor, when we shuttle our children to-and-from school, friends, or sports, it should become clear that while many may feel that they make such everyday sacrifices willingly, they are sacrifices nonetheless. In places where political choices lead to a different communal structure—one that makes it convenient to walk, bike, and use public transportation—then these particular sacrifices can become both more visible and less necessary (cf. Williams, 2010; Cannavò, 2010). The gendered, raced, and classed character of such shuttling also means that an alternate structure will alleviate sacrifices differentially among the members of a given community.

An environmentalist appeal is comprehensible only in this broader context of sacrifice: to call for reduced auto usage without simultaneously addressing this broader context is to be aloof from the lived experience of those whose driving one hopes to reduce. To *call for* "sacrifice" suggests a belief that sacrifice is only now being introduced; that in the absence of such a call, most would regard this as a world in which their interests are being realized and in which change would be regarded as a loss. But we do not live in the best of all possible worlds; sacrifice exists all around us. A failure to recognize sacrifice thus becomes a basis for misrecognizing the obstacles to reduced auto use. By clearly recognizing the sacrifices many people already make, we can open a discussion about social and political change that might lessen or redistribute its burden, thereby enabling more effective environmental action. It is when extant sacrifice is recognized that it also becomes possible to imagine it treated in a more democratic manner.

Danielle Allen has argued:

> Of all the rituals relevant to democracy, sacrifice is preeminent. No democratic citizen, adult or child, escapes the necessity of losing out at some point in a public decision. "It is our fate as human beings," Ellison writes, "always to give up some good things for other good things, to throw off certain bad circumstances only to create others." . . . Only vigorous forms of citizenship can give a polity the resources to deal with the inevitable problem of sacrifice. (Allen, 2004: 28–29).

To see sacrifice as commensurate with self-interest is to provide a basis for recognizing it in a broad variety of acts, including the sort of democratic decision making described by Allen. While such acts are sometimes extraordinary, they might also be much more familiar and ordinary ones (Peterson, 2010: 103–112). Here, individuals appear in relation to others, and sacrifice is understood in a way that navigates between the poles of egoism and altruism, ultimately denying conceptual power to both extremes. What makes sacrifice necessary, as

Cheryl Hall argues compellingly, is "a situation where values are competing, either through inherent incompatibility or through external limits on satisfying them all" (2010: 69).

5 AGENTS VERSUS VICTIMS

The grammar of sacrifice itself is revealing. As a verb, I can actively and willingly sacrifice; as a noun, I can also be sacrificed. In the first case, I am an agent; in the second case, I am a victim. This distinction is often elided, yet it is vital—and at least partly a matter of perception and judgment.

For example, in the context of organized religion, where sacrifice is a frequent theme, how do we distinguish between making a willing sacrifice because we believe that a just god commanded it and being victimized by the directive of religious authorities? Similarly, in the fog of war, does a soldier sacrifice life and limb willingly, out of loyalty to nation and comrades, or does he feel like cannon-fodder, beholden to the ambitions of a tyrannical ruler? Does a mother sacrifice her time and opportunities willingly for her children or is she constrained by unjust gender roles?

Answers in such cases depend in large part upon the judgments of the actors themselves, and those judgments are formed through their perceptions of both justice and efficacy. When I perceive the distribution of burden to be unfair; when those calling for change don't also appear to be participating or leading the way, I'm more likely to view myself as a sacrificial victim and be more likely to resist such a call as hypocritical. When the United States urges emissions reductions in China and India—where per capita emission rates remain radically lower—it has this character. When social critics clearly recognize and acknowledge that people are already giving up something of value, taking the lead in meaningful action themselves, it can go a long way to countering this perceived hypocrisy and patronizing tone. As a consequence it can also affect our individual perceptions and collective judgments about whether we are agents or victims.

Sacrifice often begets anxiety because we are afraid that our sacrifices will be for naught. To make a willing sacrifice, this anxiety must be tempered with the hope that what we give up now will, in fact, lead to some future good. A willing sacrifice must be motivated by the conviction—or at least the hope—that our actions can matter and that they might succeed in bringing us closer to that which we value. But this hope can rarely be sustained through individual action alone, because the likelihood of success is diminished by the familiar conundrum of collective action—if I act when others don't, I'll incur personal costs without social benefit; if I don't act when others do, I'll share in the benefit without cost. By contrast, when action is coordinated communally and politically, a variety of options become feasible: for example, large-scale investment in infrastructure and renewable energy, land-use and urban planning policy to reduce dependence on cars and foster more walkable communities, and incentives to promote green jobs.

It would be illusory to suggest that such action is painless: public investment requires tax dollars, land-use policy generates winners and losers, green jobs may be at the expense of brown ones. What distinguishes such measures is their potential for both improving lives through the reduction of coerced and inequitable sacrifice now and for tempering the coerced and inequitable impact of climate change and other environmental harms in the future. If the genuine promise of sacrifice is, as the *OED* would have it, "The destruction or surrender of something valued or desired for the sake of something having, or regarded as having, a higher or more pressing claim," then it could really only be fulfilled in this manner.

In sum, attending to the rhetoric of sacrifice in environmentalist discourse does not commit one to a specific set of policies or campaign talking points. Yet it does allow us to sketch some characteristics of a different way of thinking and talking about environmental challenges. In the end, engaged and salient social criticism must build upon the radical hope that our future can be a better one for which it is worth taking action. In a world with no guarantees, it is this hope that might motivate change—in a way that neither despair nor optimism can.

Notes

1. In more recent writing, Princen rethinks this negative characterization of sacrifice in a manner more consistent with the analysis in this chapter. See, "Consumer Sovereignty, Heroic Sacrifice: Two Insidious Concepts in an Endlessly Expansionist Economy," in *The Environmental Politics of Sacrifice* (MIT Press, 2010), 153–162.

2. Cf., Fred Pearce, "New Green Vision: Technology As Our Planet's Last Best Hope," *Yale Environment 360*, accessed July 29, 2013, http://e360.yale.edu/feature/new_green_vision_technology_as_our_planets_last_best_hope/2671/.

3. The classic source for a discussion of "autonomous" technological development as the displacement of politics is Langdon Winner, *Autonomous Technology: Technics-out-of-Control as a Theme in Political Thought* (Cambridge, MA: MIT Press, 1977).

4. Science studies scholars have termed this a "linear model:" Roger A Pielke, *The Honest Broker: Making Sense of Science in Policy and Politics* (Cambridge: Cambridge Univ. Press, 2011), 12–14.

5. For more on the distinction between hope and optimism, see: Rebecca Solnit, "Hope: The Care and Feeding of," *Grist*, accessed January 27, 2014, http://grist.org/living/2011-08-02-hope-the-care-and-feeding-of/.

6. Jonathan Lear's book *Radical Hope: Ethics in the Face of Cultural Devastation* (Cambridge, Mass.: Harvard University Press, 2006) offers an especially provocative and insightful meditation on hope. For two valuable efforts to connect Lear's notion of radical hope to environmental challenges, see: Allen Thompson, "Radical Hope for Living Well in a Warmer World," *Journal of Agricultural and Environmental Ethics* 23, no. 1–2 (June 17, 2009): 43–59, doi:10.1007/s10806-009-9185-2 and John Barry, *The Politics of Actually Existing Unsustainability* (Oxford University Press, 2012), 54–61.

7. On rational choice in particular, see Michael Taylor, *Rationality and the Ideology of Disconnection* (Cambridge: Cambridge University Press, 2006).

References

Allen, D. (2004). *Talking to Strangers: Anxieties of Citizenship after Brown v. Board of Education.* Chicago: University of Chicago Press.

Berliner, M. (2014). "The Danger of Environmentalism." *Capitalism Magazine*, April 22, 2014, http://capitalismmagazine.com/2014/04/the-danger-of-environmentalism/.

Bourdillon, M. F. C., and Fortes, M., eds. (1980). *Sacrifice*. London: Academic Press.

Bruckner, P. (2013). *The Fanaticism of the Apocalypse: Save the Earth, Punish Human Beings* (Cambridge, UK: Polity Press).

Cannavò, P. (2010). "Civic Virtue and Sacrifice in a Suburban Nation." In *The Environmental Politics of Sacrifice*, edited by M. Maniates and J. M. Meyer, 217–246. Cambridge, MA: MIT Press.

Flannery, T. F. (2006). *The Weather Makers: How Man Is Changing the Climate and What It Means for Life on Earth*. Grove Press.

Hall, C. (2010). "Freedom, Values, and Sacrifice: Overcoming Obstacles to Environmentally Sustainable Behavior." In *The Environmental Politics of Sacrifice*, edited by M. Maniates and J. M. Meyer, 61–86. Cambridge, MA: MIT Press.

Hawken, P., Lovins, A., and Lovins, H. (1999). *Natural Capitalism: Creating the Next Industrial Revolution*. Boston: Little, Brown, and Co.

Heilbroner, R. (1980). *An Inquiry into the Human Prospect: Updated and Reconsidered for the 1980s*. New York: Norton.

Hubert, H., and Mauss, M. (1964). *Sacrifice: Its Nature and Function*. Chicago: University of Chicago Press.

Karlsson, R. (2013). "Ambivalence, Irony, and Democracy in the Anthropocene." *Futures* 46(February): 6, doi:10.1016/j.futures.2012.12.002.

Lovelock, J. E. (2009). *The Vanishing Face of Gaia: The Final Warning*. New York: Basic Books.

MacPherson, C. B. (1962). *The Political Theory of Possessive Individualism: Hobbes to Locke*. Oxford: Oxford University Press.

Maniates, M., and Meyer, J. M., eds. (2010). *The Environmental Politics of Sacrifice*. Cambridge, MA: MIT Press.

Mansbridge, J. J. (1990). "On the Relation of Altruism and Self-Interest." *Beyond Self-Interest*, 133–145. Chicago: University of Chicago Press.

McDonough, W., and Braungart, M. (2002). *Cradle to Cradle: Remaking the Way We Make Things*. New York: North Point Press.

McLaughlin, A. (1993). *Regarding Nature: Industrialism and Deep Ecology*. Albany, NY: SUNY Press.

Nicholson, S. (2010). "Intelligent Design? Unpacking Geoengineering's Hidden Sacrifices." In *The Environmental Politics of Sacrifice*, edited by M. Maniates and J. M. Meyer, 271–292. Cambridge, MA: MIT Press.

Nordhaus, T., and Shellenberger, M. (2007). *Break Through: From the Death of Environmentalism to the Politics of Possibility*. Boston: Houghton Mifflin.

Ophuls, W. (1973). "Leviathan or Oblivion?" In *Toward A Steady State Economy*, edited by H. E. Daly, 215–230. San Francisco: W. H. Freeman.

Palmquist, M. (2008). "Old Without Wheels." *Pacific Standard*, July, accessed November 16, 2015, (http://www.psmag.com/books-and-culture/old-without-wheels-4419).

Paterson, M. (2007). *Automobile Politics: Ecology and Cultural Political Economy*. Cambridge, England: Cambridge University Press.

Pearce, F. (2013). "New Green Vision: Technology as Our Planet's Last Best Hope." *Yale Environment 360*, accessed July 29, 2013, (http://e360.yale.edu/feature/new_green_vision_technology_as_our_planets_last_best_hope/2671/).

Peterson, A. (2010). "Ordinary and Extraordinary Sacrifices: Religion, Everyday Life, and Environmental Practice." In *The Environmental Politics of Sacrifice*, 91–115. Cambridge, MA: MIT Press.

Pielke, R. A. (2011). *The Honest Broker: Making Sense of Science in Policy and Politics.* Cambridge, England: Cambridge University Press.

Plumwood, V. (1991). "Nature, Self, and Gender: Feminism, Environmental Philosophy, and the Critique of Rationalism." *Hypatia* 6(1, Spring): 3–27.

Prager, D. (2013). "Environmentalism and Human Sacrifice." *National Review Online*, accessed July 1, 2013 (http://www.nationalreview.com/article/341519/environmentalism-and-human-sacrifice-dennis-prager).

Princen, T. (2005). *The Logic of Sufficiency.* Cambridge, MA: MIT Press.

Princen, T. (2010). "Consumer Sovereignty, Heroic Sacrifice: Two Insidious Concepts in an Endlessly Expansionist Economy." In *The Environmental Politics of Sacrifice*, 145–164. Cambridge, MA: MIT Press.

Rajan, S. C. (1996). *The Enigma of Automobility: Democratic Politics and Pollution Control.* Pittsburgh: University of Pittsburgh Press.

Solnit, R. (2011). "Hope: The Care and Feeding of." *Grist*, accessed January 27, 2014, http://grist.org/living/2011-08-02-hope-the-care-and-feeding-of/.

Taylor, C. (1992). "Atomism." In *Communitarianism and Individualism*, edited by S. Avineri and A. de-Shalit, 29–50. New York: Oxford University Press.

Taylor, M. (2006). *Rationality and the Ideology of Disconnection.* Cambridge: Cambridge University Press.

Tocqueville, A. de (1969). *Democracy in America*, translated by George Lawrence and J. P. Mayer. Garden City, NY: Anchor Books.

Urry, J. (2004). "The "System" of Automobility." *Theory, Culture, and Society* 21(4/5): 25–39.

Wapner, P. (2010). "Sacrifice in an Age of Comfort." In *The Environmental Politics of Sacrifice*, edited by M. Maniates and J. M. Meyer, 33–60. Cambridge, MA: MIT Press.

Weston, A. (2012). *Mobilizing the Green Imagination: An Exuberant Manifesto.* Gabriola Island, BC: New Society Publishers.

Williams, J. (2010). "Bikes, Sticks, Carrots." In *The Environmental Politics of Sacrifice*, edited by M. Maniates and J. M. Meyer, 247–269. Cambridge, MA: MIT Press.

Winner, L. (1977). *Autonomous Technology: Technics-out-of-Control as a Theme in Political Thought.* Cambridge, MA: MIT Press.

Yuen, E. (2012). "The Politics of Failure Have Failed: The Environmental Movement and Catastrophism." In *Catastrophism: The Apocalyptic Politics of Collapse and Rebirth*, edited by S. Lilley et al., 15–43. Oakland, CA: PM Press.

Zhao, Z., and Kaestner, R. (2010). "Effects of Urban Sprawl on Obesity." *Journal of Health Economics* 29(6): 779–787.

CHAPTER 46

....

FROM ENVIRONMENTAL ETHICS TO ENVIRONMENTAL ACTION

....

AVNER DE SHALIT

MANY philosophers might find the question of how to move from theory to action an improper one. The well-known British political philosopher Michael Oakeshott opened his book *Experience and its Modes* with a personal comment in which he asserted that philosophy relating to practice ceased to be philosophy; the philosopher had to be neutral, otherwise he would abuse his profession; it would be what Oakeshott termed a "holiday excursion." Philosophy was to be "independent of the futile attempt to persuade." I mention this particular book and this particular declaration because it was published in 1933, the very year Hitler rose to power and the world entered one of its most horrific times. Obviously, in retrospect declaring that philosophers should not get their hands dirty by trying to persuade at such horrific times sounds a bit out of touch.

Unfortunately, in many ways the world is now facing a huge challenge as well, even if of a very different kind. I refer the deterioration of the environment in general and unprecedented climate change in particular. Thankfully, though, most *environmental* philosophers distance themselves from a purist position such as Oakeshott's. They do acknowledge the linkage between theory in environmental ethics and taking action. They argue that environmental philosophy's uniqueness is not only its subject matter but also the way it is practiced: it bridges the gap between philosophy and action because its motivation is not only to find metaphysical truth but also to keep the flag flying, contributing toward resolution of environmental issues (Light and de Shalit, 2003: 9). And so environmental philosophers at the very least promote private action and changes in lifestyle (a vegan diet, use of public transportation), but more and more often they recommend also public and political action. Thus my question in this chapter is how to move from environmental ethics—discussing reasons for action—to environmental action: doing, being engaged. The question is what this move should imply. My argument is pluralistic, in the sense that I believe that different modes of action are worthy of pursuing and are of equal moral weight, and they are equally inspired by environmental ethics.

Perhaps I should add a word of clarification. I am not asking whether we have a duty to act. I assume we do (Cripps, 2013; Gardiner, 2011b; Nihle´n Fahlquist, 2008).[1] Instead I am asking: Suppose that one is persuaded—what should one do? The problem is not only theo-retical but also urgently practical because in environmental issues often action has to oppose dominant political powers. Consider climate change: on the one hand, and arguably follow-ing the successful campaign led by Al Gore, new policies are gradually being introduced. In 2009, Lester Brown, president of Earth Policy Institute, wrote: "Wind, solar and geothermal energy are replacing oil, coal and natural gas, at a pace and on a scale we could not have imagined even a year ago" (Brown, 2009). On the other hand, as Gardiner (2011) argues, rich countries can get away with some of the bad consequences of climate change because the cost can be passed on to poorer nations; and other costs can be passed on to the not yet born. These possibilities allow the anti-environmentalist lobby to put forward many arguments as to why, even if there is a problem, it is not that urgent and need not cause contemporaries to change their lifestyle dramatically (the "non-problematicity" claim); not to mention those who deny any problem of global warming and rely on "research" conducted in conservative think-tanks to "prove" this (Jacques et al., 2008; McRight and Dunlap, 2003). So how should one act?

The first question is whether to focus on moral awareness or political consciousness. Let me explain. As in many spheres of contemporary democratic politics, there is often a huge gap between the way we discuss politics and what we can actually do. We can think of this gap as a gap between vision and practice. The vision consists of both a widespread understanding of "what's the problem" and a prevalent belief about how to fix it. With regard to the environ-ment two main problems have been discussed. One has to do with moral awareness and one with political consciousness. By moral awareness I mean a state of mind that acknowl-edges that environmental matters affect our life to such a degree that they pose certain moral dilemmas, such as animal rights, intrinsic value in nature, or humans' responsibility for the non-human world. By political consciousness I mean holding a belief that environmental matters constitute a political issue that should be treated not merely as a technological case, but rather as a political one, if it is to be resolved. The two definitions for what the problem is—moral awareness and political consciousness—are rival in their demands for action (as we shall soon see), nevertheless they do not necessarily contradict each other; in other words the two definitions can both be true.

So let me elaborate about the two definitions for the problem. The problem as a moral awareness problem has to do with how people think about the environment and what their perception of the environment is. Often the claim is that humans have been too chauvin-istic toward other species, in the sense that they hold a misguided belief about some kind of superiority vis-à-vis the non-human world. Sometimes the claim is that most humans have a binary idea of the environment: humans are conceived of as external to nature. Some philosophers argue that the problem is our scientific mode of reasoning about everything, including the environment. Others argue that it is our economic mode of reasoning about everything, including the environment.

Those who define the problem in the realm of political consciousness offer a variety of arguments, and while I cannot do justice here to the various theories, arguably one of the most commonly held view is that our political institutions are constructed in a way that does not give enough weight to the demands of the environment. Often it is because of political interests of certain classes or corporations when states (governments, parliaments, cities) end up ignoring the rights of the disadvantaged populations to clean and healthy environ-ment. The latter includes issues of climate change that affect mainly developing countries (e.g., Bangladesh's delta and the issue of rising water), remote islands, desert areas, the rising tide of environmental refugees, where the figures projected are between 50 to 60 million refugees by 2020.

Now, why is it important to begin with how the problem is defined in a chapter that deals with action? The reason is that often in politics the way the problem is defined determines the language, the sphere, and tools for fixing it. For example, if the problem in a state's education system is defined as "children at schools do not try hard enough," then the solution might be to think of ways of persuading, or even tempting, the children to try harder. But if the problem is defined as "children at schools find studying boring," the solution might be to supervise teachers in new ways of teaching.

What would be the implications of defining the environmental problem in terms of moral awareness or political consciousness? It seems to me clear that when the problem is defined as a matter of moral awareness—reasons precede politics and policy (Callicott, 1999: 43)—the solution and action are in the sphere of education. This, for environmental philosophers, is a trivial task, as the traditional role of philosophy has been to help us rethink our worldviews. Thus, for example, a new journal was issued recently called *Environmental Humanities,* aiming "to provide a significant new forum for the sharing and cross fertilization of important ideas and approaches between the diverse environmental scholars working in the humanities." Philosophy is in fact action. Warwick Fox therefore argues that the best way to persuade people for action without leaving the realm of philosophy is establish philosophically the idea of intrinsic value in nature, because the moment we are persuaded that non-human entities possess intrinsic value, the burden of proof, so to speak, is on the developer; in other words the default would be to preserve, as any other policy would harm the intrinsic value of these entities (Fox, 2006). Other environmental philosophers thought that science would soon teach us to respect nature, and therefore they promoted scientific teaching of ecology, again, as action. Recently Mark Sagoff (2013) argued that science is a bit confusing in what it teaches us about what the environment is, and that at the end of the day people are moved to protect the environment because of their "cultural, aesthetic and moral ties" to the places they love and cherish. Well, one could argue that Sagoff's prescription leaves us with a question: If it is all about places we cherish, how do we shift people to start thinking in broader terms, e.g. about places they do not know, let alone cherish? Whatever the answer is, we can see that if the problem is defined as one of moral awareness, the sought action is usually within the realm of education.

If, on the other hand, the problem is and ought to be defined as one of political consciousness, namely that our political institutions are constructed in a way that does not give enough weight to the demands of the environment, then action should be focused on modifying our political institutions. Perhaps we ought to revise our constitution, strengthen participatory elements in our democracy, or maybe elect trustees (Thompson, 2010) or members of parliament (Dobson, 1996) whose role will be to represent the interests of future generations.

From this we learn that whether the problem is defined as a question of moral awareness or as a matter of political consciousness, the relevant solutions and actions will involve gaining popular support and legitimacy for radical changes (either changes of mind or institutional changes) and this might take time. Obviously, educating people takes time. But also when policies and institutions have to be designed, and then debated, and people should raise doubts and challenge the policies, this is time consuming. In fact, with many policies, but certainly with environmental ones, that involve people's everyday behavior, if a policy does not enjoy wide popular support it is not likely to be implemented.

However, many environmentalists argue, there is no time. We must consider a solution that is here and now, and for this a different type of action is needed, one that is not searching for legitimacy and support. Therefore the second question is whether action should be within or external to democracy. Indeed, some activists consider getting rid of democracy. They claim that when it comes to environmental issues, democracy is nothing but an obstacle. These people assume that democracy, like all politics, is set against a background of cleavages, interests, hostilities, and conditions of scarcity. Perhaps democracy is a regime that might suit conditions of affluence and minimal competition, but it does not suit the conditions in which we operate nowadays. Under these conditions cooperation is unlikely to occur, as people will protect their interests, they will be free riders, and they will cynically exploit democratic institutions to protect their self-regarding interest. The more powerful and rich they are, the more they will do so (Ophuls, 1997, 2013).

The argument according to which democracy is less relevant under circumstances of scarcity sounds to many activists reasonable; alas, it is empirically false, and activists should be well aware of the empirical data when they come to construct policies for action. Circumstances of scarcity cause people to betray each other and to become selfish only when the cause for scarcity is human-caused disasters or failures or when it is a nation's own government that is responsible for this situation. The reason is that indeed in such cases citizens lose trust: they lose trust in the government, they lose trust in politics as a mechanism of problem solving, and they lose trust in each other. But in cases of natural disasters or crises due to outside agencies (e.g., foreign attacks like the 9/11), people tend to find comfort in each other's presence, and they seek to cooperate to overcome the crisis. Thus in such circumstances belief in democracy as a way of cooperating is likely to intensify. Moreover, sociological studies (Cohen, 1996; see also Gilbert, 2010) show that most environmental events are not automatically interpreted as disasters, but rather it all depends on the circumstances. Therefore it is not necessarily the case that because of the current circumstances people will tend to prefer non-democratic to democratic institutions.

Moreover, these theorists err in that they fail to distinguish between the problem and the solution. The problem according to these scholars is that corporations rely on polluting technology to make their revenues and manage to influence policy so that we end up with policies that contradict the public's interest. Thus this is deviation from democracy. The solution, therefore, is not to remain outside the realm of democracy but rather to neutralize the influence of these corporates by fostering and revising democracy's institutions so that they are not subject to the influence of these corporates in that way.

Consider, for example, one reason that corporates with invested interests manage to make such an impact on policymakers. It is their ability to make use of general ignorance and confusion about what they do. They first try to hide information of what they manufacture and trade with, and then, if and when this information is leaked and revealed, the corporates rush to blur the discourse by applying confusing language and terminology. As Jacques, Dunlap, and Freeman argue (2008), often this is supported by conservative think tanks and an elite-driven counter movement. Recently Christopher Wright and Daniel Nyberg (2014) analyzed how these corporates create and apply myths so that, while pretending as though they internalize and adopt the critique of corporate capitalism, enable ever more imaginative ways of exploiting nature.

Consider, for example, the case of Trafigura Oil Company and the dumping of toxic waste in Abidjan, Ivory Coast, a case that the *Guardian* described as "massive cover up in one of the worst pollution disasters in recent history"(Leigh, 2009).[2] Trafigura tried first (July 2006) to get rid of several hundred tons of toxic waste by unloading it in the port in Amsterdam; but since it was so toxic, treating it in Holland would have been very expensive. So Trafigura decided to ship the material to an African country. Ivory Coast accepted the material, after receiving deceptive information from the company about what it was. In September–October 2006, around 100,000 Abidjani people got ill and ten died after being exposed to the material that was dumped without being treated first (*New York Times,* October 3, 2006). The company's reply to complaints by the government of Ivory Coast was to deny that the material was so toxic, but later the *Guardian* found out that the company was fully aware of how toxic the material was. The company did all it could to cover up and to prevent the public from knowing the facts. It launched a libel case against the BBC Newsnight, where it was argued that the company had known the material was "highly toxic, potentially lethal and posed a serious risk to public health," and demanded that the *Guardian* delete articles, saying it was "gravely defamatory" to describe the material as toxic, and even threatened journalists in Norway and Holland with legal threats. However, emails that were leaked to the *Guardian* revealed that the company did know that their planned chemical operation generated dangerous waste, which was widely outlawed in the West. Still, the company publicly announced that reports about the correlation between the dumping and the deaths and illnesses were "premature," "inaccurate," "potentially damaging," "poorly researched," and "deeply flawed." The company used such terminology often, even after losing their case in court, when its lawyer sent the message that the general public could not understand the case: "I think it's important to notice that the convictions relate to highly technical, complex legal matters and we will carefully study the judgment to look at the possibility of an appeal."

What we see in this event is that the corporate first deceives and hides information; then it tries to deny and threaten; and finally it sends the message that the case is not that bad and that the public is not competent enough to judge the case for itself, as it lacks the knowledge to really grasp what is at stake. Eventually, Trafigura paid a $50 million out-of-court settlement to individuals in Ivory Coast, as well as compensation to the government.

The company was chased and the truth revealed by NGOs like Greenpeace, individual experts and activists, and mainly the media (the *Guardian*, the *BBC*). They could all do this freely and with no fear because they operated within a democracy. The crucial role of democracy is precisely to protect the rights of those who try to expose all this—media, NGOs, individual experts and activists—and to guarantee that they can openly chase pollution and risks and criticize those causing it. Democracy is all about free competition of opinions and free speech, and in that sense keeping the discourse open, not allowing such interested corporations to hide information and to deceive the public.

So if moving from environmental ethics to action should be within the democratic route, in which sphere or arena should one act? The third question, then, relates to different arenas of action: action at home; action within one's community; action within the workplace; and finally action within the public sphere—city, state, or the cyber sphere. These kinds of action demand different degrees of professionalism and different sacrifices on behalf of the activist.

They are all meant to help humanity in its goal to limit the impact of humans on the environment and reduce the risk of environmental catastrophe. In what follows I argue that these kinds of action are of equal weight and are all worthy of pursuing.

Activists often tend to attach more value to action in the public arena (Stern et al., 1999). They are right to argue that any act in the public sphere makes a large impact, especially compared to acts at home. But they tend to overlook a simple fact: that we cannot expect, nor do we need, everybody to be politically active. This is because in order to act politically one needs to have the skills of how to survive in the political realm. In other words, while the public arena has the advantage of making a large impact when one acts, acting is much more difficult and demands certain skills, which very few possess. Moreover, because action in the political arena involves overcoming opposition on behalf of the polluters, who are often equipped with their lawyers and huge campaign budgets, success in environmental campaigns is rather rare. So when one argues that action in the public realm implies greater impact, one has to take into account that often these actions end up in failures. Thus when considering whether to take action in the private sphere, for example at home, or in the public sphere, in politics one should take into account not only the impact of any act should it succeed but also the chances of success. The latter works in favor of taking action at home as well.

Consider, for example, changing all your inefficient light bulbs at home to more environment-friendly and economic bulbs. This is easy to do and it does not require any skill and not even a large budget. Perhaps a little bit more difficult in terms of self-discipline is changing your diet by not eating food that is imported from far away or that is based on genetic engineering or perhaps by becoming vegan. All these actions "translate" environmental ethics theory to action. Admittedly, their impact is relatively low if done only by one person; however, the aggregation of many people acting this way is impressive. Now, of course, reaching a situation whereby many people act this way is a political act, so ideally speaking we will want to have some people active in the political realm as well. I elaborate about this later, but first let me elaborate about the two additional arenas, community and workplace.

Action within a community (e.g., neighborhood or children's school) or workplace involves more than just doing the thing oneself, as one needs to communicate, promote, and persuade. Still, assuming that the relevant relationships (e.g., with teachers or with one's employer) are not too complicated, the chances of success are high and the amount of time and the skills needed are not very high. One could ask one's employer to shut down all electricity when everybody is gone, to see that recyclable and reusable garbage is separated from organic and other waste at the workplace's or school's kitchen, and so on. These actions at a workplace or in one's community are much easier than, say, initiating a national campaign to boycott genetically engineered food or to promote certain legislation.

Some public and political acts are not that difficult, though. Lester Brown (2009: 263) calculates that the additional annual expenditures needed to meet social goals and to restore the Earth (these include providing universal primary education, school lunches, and universal basic health care; planting trees to reduce flooding and conserve soil; protecting topsoil on cropland; restoring fisheries; protecting biological biodiversity; and so on) is a grand total of $187 billion (in 2009 terms), whereas the amount the world is spending on military budgets is $1,464 billion. If each person writes to his or her representative in the legislature or the city mayor or a prominent bureaucrat, saying that it is a disgrace that a world that spends so much on wars and security cannot spend 12.7% of this amount on solving all environmental issues, this won't consume more than an hour of this person's time and yet would make an incredible impact, provided that others do so as well.

This brings me to *the* difficulty in acting in the political arena. Even such an easy act, sitting down and sending an email or a letter, is pointless if others do not do the same. And it might be the case that many others out there are ready to do the same, but they do not know that you are doing this. In other words, politics needs coordination. By the latter I do not mean any managerial top-down process; instead, coordination can be bottom-up, initiated by individuals, who regard their own actions as not detached from others' actions. Moreover, they believe that only if their actions are adjusted to and interlinked with others' actions will their own actions become meaningful. They therefore aim at coordination. And as said, it does not have to be dictated by some managerial agency. With today's new media, coordination can be done by individuals who act on the ground.

Remember, that with regard to action at home we also argued that some coordination is needed because it is pointless if only one person acts. Notice, though, that with regard to action at home, acting alone is pointless because the issues at stake—what Judith Lichtenberg calls "new harms" (Lichtenberg, 2010)—are such that if I act alone I am still pretty much part of the problem. Every bite we take, every purchase we make, Lichtenberg rightly writes, is part of what creates global warming and climate change, and if only I change the bulb at home I shall make no impact at all. In other words, I cannot avoid being part of the grand picture simply by changing all electric bulbs in my home or by using only public transportation, because even if, for example, I personally don't drive a car, I am still part of a system that relies heavily on and produces oil and greenhouse gases and so on. Let me stress that the point is not only that if I personally become vegan or stop using cars the impact on climate change is so marginal that it is pointless; the point is that in many other ways I continue to be part of *a system* that is committing all the harms and wrongs as usual. In that sense, even if I change the electronic bulb to a more environment friendly one, I shall remain guilty just the same. I shall not be guilty just the same for the actual consumption of electricity because I did try my best to reduce my own share; but I shall remain guilty just the same of, for example, the fact that the world is relying heavily on the idea of profit as a driving force for human economic activity, because, at the end of the day, the efficient light bulb was manufactured in order to make a profit, and as long as this is the main driving force in economics, the environment will suffer more and more.

Now, one could answer that the individual who changes the bulb can count on many others to do the same, and therefore in a way it is enough to act at home, with no need to coordinate with others. Acting at home, for example by becoming vegan or changing the electric bulb, is enough because what counts is the aggregation of such individuals' actions. To this we need to answer that coordination brings about a change not in volume (as others will have acted anyway) but in category. Perhaps if you consider only the ecological impact of many people acting, the aggregation of their non-coordinated acts would be just the same as the impact of their actions if were they coordinated. But culturally, politically, and socially speaking, there is a difference in the meaning of an action that is a collective action, a coordinated action of many individuals, as opposed to an aggregation of many individuals' actions. Politically it makes such an action a different category of actions. It is, for example, much more of a threat to the system than a mere aggregation of actions.

What about action within politics? Prima facie the case differs from acting at home because if I act (in particular, if I also succeed) I cannot be held responsible for the general system and its harms. If I do my best it can be said that I have done what morality demands from me (Pogge, 2008). Yet the question that interests activists is not only whether they comply with certain moral principles but also whether they can make an impact, namely, if they succeed. And in order to succeed in politics one needs legitimacy (in the form of popular support). So when it comes to action in politics, acting alone is pointless not because unless others join one will remain guilty just the same (as was the case with action at home); rather, it is because unless one has others' help or at least moral support (legitimacy), one is likely to fail. So it is in order to be *politically effective* that one needs coordination.

There is yet another and equally important reason that we need coordination when it comes to action in politics. In most environmental campaigns there are various bodies involved, each with its good will and energy, but unfortunately often they all push in different directions: the ministry of the environment, the Green parties, scientists, activists, different (and often competing) NGOs, and so on. Often coordinating among them would make a huge difference. Consider road accidents. When people are asked why there are road accidents, often their first answers are bad infrastructure, cars that are too old or not well maintained, or careless driving culture. But when people study the issue, their answer is that the reason for accidents is first and foremost lack of coordination between the various bodies that try to reduce road accidents. The same is often true for environmental issues. Scientists hold the knowledge, activists the good will and time for action, governmental bodies have the budget, and NGOs the networking and skills, but knowledge does not reach the right persons, good will is wasted on bizarre projects, and so on. Coordination is therefore the key factor. In fact Russel Hardin (1999) argues that one of the main reasons democracies have been so much better than autocratic states in coping with environmental matters and have managed to improve the environmental situation while continuing to flourish is that, relatively speaking, there is much more coordination in democracies. And the larger and more complicated the body politic is, the more important it is to see that there is coordination (Olson, 1965). The reason is that in relatively small populations somebody is going to take it upon themselves to do the necessary job because it is very likely that at least one of the members will find that her personal gain from having the collective good (e.g., a clean stream or river) is greater than the cost she has to pay to ensure it. This is because in small groups it is often the case that each member gets a substantial enough proportion of the total gain simply because there are only a few others in the group.

To conclude, whether the problem is defined in terms of environmental awareness (in which case the solution and action are in the realm of education) or of environmental consciousness (in which case action should be about modifying our political institutions), environmental action should be pursued within a framework democracy. It can then take many forms, all of which are more or less equally worthy. It can be either at home, in one's community, workplace, or in the public sphere. All these are equally worthy because while some actions are more likely to have a large impact, others are more likely to succeed. The big question, though, is how to achieve effective coordination, because whatever the activists want to achieve they will need others to cooperate (also see Cripps, 2013).

NOTES

1. For a rigorous argument as to why we are under a duty to act and to whom this duty is owed see Cripps (2013: 27–85), as well as Gardiner (2011b). For an interesting distinction between backward looking and forward looking such obligations see Nihle'n Fahlquist(2008). See also the chapters in Section 2 in this volume.
2. David Leigh, *The Guardian* (September 19, 2009).

REFERENCES

Brown, L. (2009). *Plan 4.0: Mobilizing to Save Civilization*. New York: Norton.
Callicott, B. (1999). *Beyond the Land Ethic: More Essays in Environmental Philosophy*. Albany, NY: SUNY Press.
Cohen, M. (1996). "Economic Dimensions of Environmental and Technological Risks Events." *Industrial and Environmental Crisis* 9 (4): 448–481.
Cripps, E. (2013). *Climate Change and the Moral Agent*. Oxford: Oxford University Press.
Dobson, A. (1996). "Representative Democracy and the Environment." In *Democracy and the Environment*, edited by W. M. Lafferty and J. Meadowcroft, 124–139. Cheltenham, UK: Edward Elgar.
Fox, W. (2006). *A Theory of General Ethics; Human Relationship, Nature and the Built Environment*. London: Routledge.
Gardiner, S. (2011). *A Perfect Moral Storm: The Ethical Tragedy of Climate Change*. Oxford: Oxford University Press.
Gardiner, S. (2011 b). "Is No One Responsible for Global Environmental Tragedy? Climate Change as a challenge to our Ethical Concepts." In *The Ethics of Global Climate Change*, edited by D. G. Arnold, 38–59. Cambridge: Cambridge University Press.
Gilbert, C. (2010). "Top 10 Environmental Disasters." *Time* (May 3, 2010).
Jacques, P. J., Dunlap, R. E., and Freeman, M. (2008). "The Organisation of Denial: Conservative Think Tanks and Environmental Skepticism." *Environmental Politics* 17 (3): 349–385.
Leigh, D. "How UK Oil Company Trafigura Tried to Cover Up African Pollution Disaster." *The Guardian* (September 16, 2009).
Lichtenberg, J. (2010). "Negative Duties, Positive Duties, and the New Harms." *Ethics* 120 (3): 557–577.
Light, A., and de Shalit, A., eds. (2003). *Moral and Political Reasoning in Environmental Practice*. Cambridge, Mass: MIT Press.
McRight, A. M., and Dunlap, R. E. (2003). "Defeating Kyoto: The Conservative Movement's Impact on U.S. Climate Change Policy." *Social Problems* 50 (3): 348–373.
Nihle'n Fahlquist, J. (2008). "Moral Responsibility for Environmental Problems—Individual or Institutional?" *Journal of Agricultural and Environmental Ethics* 22: 109–124.
Olson, M., Jr. (1965). *The Logic of Collective Action*. Cambridge, MA: Harvard University Press.
Ophuls, W. (1997). *Requiem for Modern Politics*. Boulder, CO.: Westview Press.
Ophuls, W. (2013). *Plato's Revenge: Politics in the Age of Ecology*. Cambridge, Mass: MIT Press.
Pogge, T. (2008). *World Poverty and Human Rights*. Cambridge: Polity.
Russell, H. (1999). "Democracy and Collective Bads." In *Democracy's Edges*, edited by I. Shapiro and C. Hacker-Cordón, 63–83. Cambridge: Cambridge University Press.

Sagoff, M. (2013). "What Does Environmental Protection Protect?" *Ethics, Policy and Environment* 16: 239–257.

Stern, P. C., Dietz, T., Abel, T., Guagnano, G., and Kalof, L. (1999). "A Value-Belief-Norm Theory of Support for Social Movements: The Case of Environmentalism." *Human Ecology Review* 6 (2): 81–97.

Thompson, D. F. (2010). "Representing Future Generations: Political Presentism and Democratic Trusteeship." *Critical Review of International and Political Philosophy* 13 (1): 17–37.

Wright, C., and Nyberg, D. (2014). "Creative Self-Destruction: Corporate Responses to Climate Change as Political Myths." *Environmental Politics* 23: 205–223.

INDEX

ability-to-pay principle (APP), in mitigation, 469, 475

abrupt change, 467

accidents, 114, 116, 392. *See also* essence-accident ethics

acidification, of oceans, 2, 465, 469–70, 474, 484n7

acid rain, 267–68, 279, 369, 370

adaptation, 465. *See also* climate adaptation

  CBA and, 466–67

  climate change and, 108–9, 466

  humanist view of, 63

  incremental, 477

  IPCC definition of, 484n8

  justice in, 7

  low-income countries and, 7, 467–69

  of nature, by humans, 63–65

  transformational, 477, 478

adaptive management, 452–53

Ad-hoc Working Group, on Durban Platform for Enhanced Action, 492, 498n10

Adorno, Theodor, 293, 439

aesthetic experience, 5, 187, 193–94, 194n3

aesthetic judgments, 187, 192

  noncognitivism, 188–89, 194n2

  scientific cognitivism and, 188

aesthetic sensibility, of Sandler, 191

aesthetic theory, of Kant, 188, 189, 190

aesthetic values, 5, 186–87, 194

  appreciation, 188

  environmental ethics and, 192–93

  integrated, 189

  natural beauty, 191

  of natural world, 15, 404

  pluralism and, 188–92

  ugliness, 191–92

agent-centered deontology, 216–20

agents *versus* victims, in sacrifice, 548–49

aggregationism, 212–13

agrarianism, 410

The Agrarian Vision (Thompson), 442

agriculture, 6, 409–13

  animals suffering in production of, 93, 99n4

  public interest in, 404–5

  stories on, 406–8

air pollution, 51, 369, 494

  human health harms from, 27

  WHO on, 391

Alley, Richard, 65

altruistic behavior, of animals, 120–21

American Wind Energy Association, 395

Animal Liberation (Singer), 15, 201

animals, 80. *See also* conscious animals; non-human entities

  altruistic behavior, 120–21

  existence struggles, 118

  as experiment subjects, 31, 115

  Leopold on, 119

  medical research, 228, 372

  moral status of, 23n6

  rational, 114

  rights of, 16, 115, 201, 215, 227–28

  utilitarianism liberation of, 115

  welfare, 16, 227–29

animal suffering, 92, 95–96, 99n2

  in agriculture production, 93, 99n4

  biocentric egalitarianism on, 103

  climate change and, 108

animism, 257n1, 257n2

Annex 1 parties, of Kyoto Protocol, 489–90

Anscombe, G. E. M., 200–201

Anthropic climate, 68–69

Anthropocene Epoch, 4, 128

  attitudes toward, 62–63

  Bendik-Keymer and, 63

  biosphere and technosphere, 64–65

  ethics and respect for nature, 69–71

  future of, 71, 85–87

Anthropocene Epoch (*Cont.*)
  geoengineering, 66–67
  Leopold and, 63
  Millennium Ecosystem Assessment, 63–64
  perspective on, 1–2
  planetary management, 65–66
  sustainability focus, 62
  Thompson and, 63
anthropocentric instrumental value, 82
anthropocentric intrinsic value, 81–83
anthropocentric theories, 15, 22n2
  weak intrinsic value, 20, 79, 82, 83, 87n4,
    87n6, 88n8, 88n11
anthropocentrism, 3, 4, 15, 77–88, 199, 519.
    See also ethical anthropocentrism
  conceptual, 78, 79, 82, 86
  in environmental law, 55
  EVE and, 226–27
  forms of, 81–83
  hermeneutics and, 166–67
  human-centered, 77–79, 84, 143
  of human rights, 301
  moral ontology, 114
  moral status and, 277
  Norton and, 20, 88n8, 523
  ontological, 78–79
  policy perspectives, 19–20
  pragmatism and, 19–20
  strong, 79, 87n6
  of sustainability science, 532
  Varner and, 523
anthropogenic climate change, 54
  biocentric ethics and, 106–10
  from GHGs and carbon dioxide, 474
  moral responsibility in, 107
  Nolt on, 107
anthropogenic mass extinction, 6
anthroponomy, 433–34
anti-consequentialism, 212–15
antirealism, 141, 148n7
APP. *See* ability-to-pay principle
applied philosophy of science, 439, 443–44
appreciative virtues, 188–91
appropriation, 164–66
Aristotelian, 49, 86, 219, 291
Aristotle, 232n1
  on character traits, 228

on rationality, 114, 160n8
  on responsibility, 266, 399
assessment. *See also* risk assessment
  EPA on science evidence, 29, 36n5
  of ethical anthropocentrism
    alternatives, 83–85
  tools, in science, 29
Assessment Report, of IPCC, 477
Attfield, Robin, 86, 87
  deontological ethics, 105
  on flourishing, 105, 106
  inegalitarianism of, 201
autodestruction
  cultural value, 431
  environmental justice, 431
  mass extinction and, 430–31
  moral corruption of techno-optimism, 431

Bachelard, Gaston, 174, 175
back-to-the-land movement, 252
Bacon, Francis, 438, 439
Bali Action Plan, 490
banality of evil, 432–33
Barndt, Deborah, 297
BAT. *See* best available technology
Bayesian response, to utility theory, 322, 323
Bayes' Theorem, 28, 33, 36n1, 36n2
deBeauvoir, Simone, 174, 294
being-in-the-world, of Heiddeger, 174,
    176, 181
Bendik-Keymer, Jeremy, 63, 67, 69
beneficiary-pays principle (BPP), in
    mitigation, 469, 475
Bentham, Jeremy, 80
  nonanthropocentric ethic precedent, 115
  as utilitarian founder, 115, 201
Berliner, Michael, 542, 544
best available technology (BAT), for pollution
    elimination, 375
Betz, G.
  on contextual values, 34, 36n6
  on inductive risk, 34
"Beyond Intrinsic Value: Pragmatism in
    Environmental Ethics" (Weston), 19
biocentric consequentialism, 5, 202
  on animal suffering and climate change, 108
  on basic needs, 105

climate change and, 107–9, 305
on flourishing reduction from climate
change, 108
states of affairs valued by, 105
wildness and, 108
biocentric egalitarianism, 4, 81, 102
on animal suffering, 103
on organisms complexity, 108
biocentric ethics, 106–10
biocentric individualists
on moral status of all living things,
16, 80, 84
Schweitzer as, 201
Sterba as, 102, 104
Taylor as, 16–17, 102, 106, 201
biocentric inegalitarianism, 102
moral significance of organisms, 103
organism complexity in, 108
value pluralism of, 103–4
biocentrism, 3, 101, 107–10, 254. *See also*
deontological biocentrism
egalitarian, 4, 81, 102–3, 108
ethical theory and, 104–6
holistic form of, 81
inegalitarian, 4, 201
kinship ethics, 253
life and other values, 103–4
monistic, 4
moral value in all living things, 16, 80, 84
Norton and Varner on, 523
pluralistic, 4, 81
sentiocentrism objections to, 82
value of living individuals, 101–2
virtue, 104–5
biochemical nitrogen and phosphorus cycle, 2
biodiversity
intrinsic value of, 69–70
in low-income countries, 383
Worldwide Fund for Nature on, 383–84
biodiversity markets, 4, 46–47
biodiversity offsets, 2, 69, 133, 350
habitat corridors for, 27
markets for, 4, 46–47
biological tradition, of ethical theory, 120, 121
biophilia hypothesis, 252
biosphere
in Anthropocene Epoch, 64–65

degradation of, 128
Ecological Society of America focus, 64
ethical concern about climate change, 113
Royal Swedish Academy of Sciences
focus, 64
biotic communities, 1, 119, 122
Birnie, P., 51, 52, 55
Blackstone, William T., 14
body self-sensing, Husserl on, 181–82
Boldt Decision, 237
Bookchin, Murray, 440, 441
bottom-up climate architecture, 491–95
Boyle, A., 51, 52, 55
BPP. *See* beneficiary-pays principle
Braungart, Michael, 543
BTM Consultants, on wind energy, 395
burden of proof, in pollution risk
assessment, 375
Burke, Edmund, 338, 362, 364
Byrd-Hagel Resolution, 490, 495

Callicott, J. Baird, 17–18, 81, 86, 207n5
ecocentrism, 83, 202
on ecological illiteracy, 412
non-anthropocentric intrinsic value
theory, 82
on values as human valuing product,
88n10, 148n9
CAMPFIRE program, in Zimbabwe,
523–24, 527n16
Cancún Adaptation Framework, 484n9
Cancún Agreement, 492, 495,
498n12, 498n15
Caney, S., 304, 306–7
cap and trade schemes, 41, 44, 46
carbon, 392, 395, 396, 397, 400
offsets, in emissions trading, 45
carbon dioxide emissions, 7, 472
CBDR on, 489
climate change from, 466, 469–70, 489
cumulative carbon metric for, 471
IPCC on ocean as sink for, 465–66
ocean acidification from, 2, 465, 469–70,
474, 484n7
UNFCCC pledges to reduce, 493
carbon dioxide removal (CDR)
technologies, 476

carcinogenicity
  EPA risk assessment, 29, 36n5
  scientific models on, 31
caring, 234
  feminist care ethics and, 241–43
  in indigenous environmental ethics,
    5, 236–38
  Leopold and Naess on, 235
  meaningful relationships, 157–59
Carroll, Ronald, 189, 451
Carson, Rachel, 13, 223, 292, 371, 440, 536
  natural environmental model of, 188
  on sacred in nature, 252
Cartagena Dialogue, 494
Carter, Alan, 204, 207n7
The Case for Animal Rights (Regan), 16
causal responsibility, 266, 270
CBA. *See* cost-benefit analysis
CBDR. *See* common but differentiated
    responsibilities
CDR. *See* carbon dioxide removal
Character and Environment (Sandler), 205
character ethics, 232
  flourishing and, 226–27
  virtue ethics compared to, 223
character traits, Aristotle on, 228
China
  climate change global action, 495, 496
  emission reductions agreement, 490
Chipko Andolan movement, 234, 235, 243
Christian theology
  anthropocentrism and, 77, 78
  human being's moral significance, 77
  on male domination, 13, 21
circumstances of justice, 385
circumstances of moderate scarcity, 282–83
citizenship
  green republicanism on, 6, 334–38, 341
  resistance activism, 338, 340–41
  sustainable economic, 338–40
civic sustainability service, 336–38
civil disobedience, 238
Clean Air Act, of 1956, in Britain, 51, 391
Clean Development Mechanism, 490
Clean Energy Ministerial, 494
clean power sources, 7
clientelism

democracy corruption from, 335
  economic security and, 335
  International Labor Organization on, 335
  liberal democracy feature of
    dependent, 334–35
  market-based solutions to
    unsustainability, 336
climate adaptation, 108–9, 466
  APP, BPP, and CPP in, 475
  CDR technologies and, 476
  cultural identity in, 479–84
  injustice and, 479–80, 483
  material interests and, 478–79, 480
  re-imagining, 480–83
  resilience increase by, 477, 478
  responses to, 476–79
  Thompson on, 483n2
  UNFCCC on, 474–75
  vulnerability, 477
Climate and Clean Air Coalition on Short-
    Lived Climate Pollutants, 494
climate change, 2
  abrupt change in, 467
  adaptation and, 108–9, 466
  anthropogenic, 54, 68–69, 106–10, 474
  biocentric consequentialism and,
    107–9, 305
  biocentric perspectives on, 106–7
  biosphere and, 113
  carbon dioxide as factor in, 466,
    469–70, 489
  as collective action problem, 269
  deontological biocentrism and,
    109–10, 305
  emissions reduction for, 476, 483
  environmental harms from, 265,
    269–72, 304
  environmental law and, 55–56, 58, 59
  ethical concern about, 113
  flourishing and, 107, 108
  fossil fuels and, 392
  Gardiner on, 269, 383
  global, 7, 20, 68, 113, 122, 495, 496, 498n13
  global policy concern of, 308
  human impact on, 128
  human rights-based approach to, 304–5
  Jamieson on responsibility for, 272, 273

justice and, 27
market knowledge and, 47–48
mitigation for, 465, 474–75, 492, 510
population reduction from, 350
Preamble to the Paris Agreement, 293
rectification for, 476, 477, 483
sink enhancement for, 465–66, 476, 483
SRM for, 476, 483, 484n7
sustainable development and, 468–69
US-China Joint Presidential Statement
    on, 496
climate diplomacy, 7, 497–98
Cartagena Dialogue, 494
Clean Energy Ministerial, 494
Climate and Clean Air Coalition on Short-
    Lived Climate Pollutants, 494
climate-related initiatives, 494–96
individual agreements on, 494
beyond Kyoto Protocol, 491–94
Major Economies Forum, 494
UN climate negotiations, 487–91
climate emergency, 508
climate engineering, 7, 510
climate governance, 508
climate justice, 475, 506, 508
climate negotiations, bottom-up architecture
    for, 491–95
climate scientific models, 31
coal, 391, 392, 395, 396
cognitivism
in metaethics, 140, 143, 145, 148n8
scientific, 5, 188, 189
collaboration, 453
collective action problems, 14, 268
climate change as, 269
collectives formed for, 271
collective harms, 5–6, 271–72
collective responsibility, 274n1
collective rights, human rights and, 304–5
collectives. See ecological collectives
collectivist system, 53–54
command-and-control legal mechanisms, 4,
    52–54, 56, 58, 451, 453
command of ecological space, 6, 315–17,
    318n9, 319n6
common but differentiated responsibilities
    (CBDR), 488–89

distributive justice in, 493–94
Kyoto Protocol and, 490
A Common Faith (Dewey), 536–37
common-goods approach to water, 416,
    422, 423n8
common-pool resources, 357–59
communal goods, 365n11, 365n12
communitarianism, of sustainability, 6, 348
community harm and, 363
intergenerational ethics and, 362
communities
caring relations within, 5
environmental conflict and, 517
harm, 362–63
justice, 280–81
Leopold on motivational repertoire
    and, 155
participation in adaptive
    management, 453
complexity theory, 322, 324
computation science models, 31
conceptual anthropocentrism, 78, 79, 82, 86
Conference on Environment and
    Development, UN. See Rio Earth Summit
Conference on the Human Environment,
    UN, 305
Conferences of the Parties (COPs), of
    UNFCCC, 488, 492, 493, 496
conflict, environmental, 526–27
community and, 517
conflicting priorities and values, 128,
    518–20, 525
ecology as economics, 522–24
ethics and, 521–22
habitable principles, 517
ideals and compromise, 520–21
interests in, 521
markets and, 522–24, 526n7
natural enemies, 524–25
preservationism, 522–23, 526n8
conflict resolution, justice relationship with, 7,
    517, 521–22, 526n13
conscious animals
characteristics of, 96–98
interests of, 91–93, 96–97, 99n2
objective list of, 95
predation problem, 1, 93–95

conscious animals (*Cont.*)
  respect of other animals, 98–99
  subjective theories of well-being, 95–96
  beyond suffering, 95–96
  unnecessary suffering, 92–93, 99n2
consciousness
  historically affected, 163–64
  political, 7, 553–54, 558–59
  sentience and, 84
consensus, hard won, 30, 36n8
consensus, in science, 30
consequentialism, 207–8. *See also* biocentric
    consequentialism; non-consequentialism
  aggregationism and, 212–13
  Anscombe on, 200–201
  anthropocentric view of value, 199
  anti-, 212–15
  consequences of, 212–15
  demandingness objections, 214
  ecocentric, 5, 202
  Elliot on, 203, 207n4
  holism, 199
  human action's disruption of natural
      system, 203
  multidimensional, 204
  on non-human entities intrinsic value,
      199, 204–6
  objections to, 211
  rule-, 205
  sentient, 201, 202
  system, 202–4, 206
  utilitarian, 5, 199
  welfarism and, 212
consequentialist ethical theory, 4, 5
conservation, 125, 128, 518–19
  biology, 531, 533
  economically based, 458
  as human expression of values, 69–70
  large-unit/deep branching, 434
  Norton on, 526n8
  Pinchot on benefit of, 200
conservative non-anthropocentric moral
    ontology, 114–16
conservers society, in Parfit's Paradox, 361
constitutive goods, for flourishing, 156
constructionist approach, to religion, 249
contestatory politics, 340–41

contextualist view, on moral status of
    nature, 168
contextual values, in science, 32–35,
    36n6, 36n7
contractarians, on intergenerational
    ethics, 348
contrast value, for wild, 130
contributor-pays principle (CPP), in
    mitigation, 469, 475
contributory responsibility, 266–67,
    272–73, 274n1
convergence hypothesis, 20, 533
cooperatives
  Gardiner on, 364n6
  worker, 339–40
Copenhagen Accord, 488, 492, 495, 498n12
COPs. *See* Conferences of the Parties
corporate capitalism, 555–56
cost-benefit analysis (CBA), 6, 215, 307
  adaptation and, 466–67
  in environmental policy formation, 4
  incommensurability and, 330n4
  natural world and, 21
  on pollution, 375
  PP and, 376
  RCPP objections compared to, 326–27
  for risk assessment, 321–24
  of shadow prices, 41
  water and, 423n6
CPP. *See* contributor-pays principle
Cradle to Cradle (McDonough and
    Braungart), 543
cradle-to-cradle industrial design, for
    pollution, 372, 377
Cranor, Carl, 375, 444
The Crisis of European Sciences (Husserl), 177
critical environmental hermeneutics, of van
    Buren, 169
critical pluralism, 189–91, 193
critical theory of technology, 439–41
cross-habitat diversity, 360
Crow members, cultural identity of, 481
Crutzen, Paul, 68, 510
cultural identity, 7, 484n15
  in climate adaptation, 479–84
  of Crow members, 481
  of Inuit people, 479–81

cultural value, autodestruction and, 431
cumulative carbon, for carbon dioxide
    metric, 471
Curse of Cain, 115

Dancy, Jonathan, 155–56, 158
dark green religion, 254–56
Darwin, Charles, 250, 253
    ethics evolution, 117–19
    on group selection in environmental
        theory, 120
death of environmentalism thesis, 535
*The Death of Nature: Women, Ecology and the
    Scientific Revolution* (Merchant), 295
d'Eaubonne, Françoise, 20
debt-based consumer capitalism, 334
decision making
    Bayesian response, 322, 323
    CBA in, 321–24
    ecological ethos facilitation of, 58
    ex ante, 321, 325
    PP, 321, 324–30, 375–77, 443
    risk in, 321
    uncertainty in, 29, 321–25, 327
    unknown unknowns and, 330n1
    utility theory, 322, 323
Declaration of the Rights of Indigenous
    Peoples, UN, 237
deep ecology, 3, 23n4, 23n6
    holism, 18–19
    intrinsic value to all living things, 19
    Naess on, 217, 371
Deep Ecology movement, 18, 106
deep uncertainty, 29
deforestation, 296, 466, 476
demandingness objections, of
    consequentialism, 214
democracy, 6, 335
    for change, 7, 547, 555–56
    technology and environment, 444–46
deontological biocentrism
    climate change and, 109–10, 305
    Deep Ecology movement and, 18, 106
    human duties toward rights of living things
        focus, 106
    moral relevance of climate change, 109
deontological ethical theory, 4, 5

sentiocentrism and, 80
    Taylor and, 16, 105, 106
deontology, 204
    agent-centered, 216–20
    non-consequentialism and, 215–17
    patient-centered, 216–17
    ratiocentric, 224–26
Department of Energy (DOE), US, 395, 396
dependent clientelism, 334–35
depleters society, in Parfit's Paradox, 361
desires, reasons and, 152
developing world narrative, 411
Dewey, John, 529, 534, 536–37
Dialectic of Sex (Firestone), 290
Difference Principle, of Rawls, 506–7
dirty energy, 393
    intention excuse for, 399
    readiness excuse for, 394–95
    Sunstein on, 398
*Dirty Virtues: The Emergence of Ecological
    Virtue Ethics* (van Wensveen), 21
disciplinary zoning, 533
discounting, of costs and benefits,
    346–47, 364n4
discount rates, 365n6
dissimilar groups criterion, in mass
    extinction, 428
distantiation, 164–66
distributive justice, 280, 282, 303
    in CBDR, 493–94
    climate change and, 305
    Rawls on, 56–57, 279
    water justice and, 419–20
DOE. *See* Department of Energy
domestic justice, 279
domination, 293
    Christian theology on male, 13, 21
    geoengineering concerns, 506–7
    nature by humans, 62, 63, 65
Durban Platform for Enhanced Action,
    492, 498n10
duty not to deprive ecological space, 317
dwelling, poetic, 175, 183–84

earth, 180–81, 253
Earth Day, 439
    dark green spirituality after, 254–55

Earth Policy Institute, 533
Earth: The Operator's Manual (Alley), 65
ecocentric consequentialism, 5, 202
ecocentrism, 80, 254, 318n3
    of Callicott, 83, 202
    holistic view of, 81
    of Rolston, 83
ecofascism, 17–18, 412. *See also*
        environmental fascism
ecofeminism, 3, 19–21, 23n6, 252, 289, 295.
        See also women
ecoholism, 3
ecological collectives, 4, 271
    conservative non-anthropocentric moral
        ontology, 114–16
    environmental fascism, 119–20, 202–4
    essence-accident ethical theory, 114, 116,
        117, 121–23
    ethical theory and, 113–14
    land ethic, 118–19
    new moral ontology, 122–23
    non-anthropocentric ethical theory, 116–17
ecological cooperation, 420–22, 423n7
ecological ethos
    decision making facilitated by, 58
    governance and, 4, 56–59
    non-state actors and, 52, 58–59
    participatory approach in, 58
    rejectionist approach in, 58
    state interventionist role, 58–59
ecological footprint, 314, 315, 318n9, 319n12,
        383, 385
ecological illiteracy, Callicott on, 412
ecological integrity, 360, 450–51, 454, 455
ecological modernization, 441
ecological niche, 312, 318n6, 318n7
ecological restoration, 20, 23n5, 193, 456–57
Ecological Society of America, 64
ecological space, 279, 318n4
    command of, 6, 319n16
    descriptive meaning of, 311–14
    duty not to deprive, 317
    ecological footprint, 314, 315, 318n9,
        319n12, 383, 385
    ecological niche, 312, 318n6, 318n7
    endosomatic use of, 317
    environmental harm and, 311, 318n3

    ethical implications of, 311, 318n1
    exosomatic use of, 317, 318n10
    as human rights concern, 316–17,
        319n17, 319n18
    natural relations, 311, 318n2
    normative significance of, 314–16
    occupation of, 6, 315, 319n14, 319n15
    radical inequalities, 317, 319n20
    realized niche of, 312–13, 318n7, 318n11
    resources and, 311, 313–14, 316, 319n16
    use of, 6, 314–15, 318n10, 318n11, 319n12
ecological systems thinking, 452
ecology. *See also* deep ecology
    defined, 312
    as economics, 522–24
    of land, 119
    shallow, 18
    sustainability defined by, 355
economic growth, 41
    environmental and social limits to, 48–49
    sustainability defined by, 355
    technologically oriented, 336
economic narrative, 411
economic over-exploitation, 357–59,
        361–62, 363
economic regulation, of pollution, 374
economics, ecology and, 522–24
economic security, clientelism and, 335
economists, weak sustainability advocated by,
        356, 359
The Economy of the Earth (Sagoff), 274n4
ecophenomenology, 174
    chiasm, 181–83
    earth, 180–81
    elements, 180–81
    lifeworld, 178, 179–80
    poetic dwelling, 175, 183–84
ecosystem health, 455
ecosystem management, 7, 459, 527n15
    adaptive management, 452–53
    collaboration, 453
    conceptual challenges, 454–55
    directional change, 455–57
    dynamism challenge, 455–57
    ecological integrity, 360, 450–51, 454, 455
    ecological restoration, 20, 23n5,
        193, 456–57

ecological systems thinking, 452
ecosystem health, 455
ecosystem services, 63–64, 155, 457–58
evolution of, 449–51
key ideas in contemporary, 451–53
resilience, 457–58
stability, 454–55
sustainability, 450–51
ecosystems, 449
environmental change and, 1–2
intrinsic value and, 19, 81
Leopold on value of, 203, 360
Millennium Ecosystem Assessment
on, 65–66
properties of, 454
Rolston on systemic value to, 18
sentient beings and, 19
Thompson and Bendik-Keymer on, 67
value of, 203, 360
values as integral parts of, 520–21
ecosystem services, 63–64, 155, 457–58
effective history, 163–64
electricity, 394–98, 400
elements, 180–81
Elliot, Robert, 20
on consequentialism, 203, 207n4
on EVE, 205
on nature's intrinsic value, 131
Ellis, Erle, 64
Emerson, Ralph Waldo, 250
emissions. See also carbon dioxide;
greenhouse gases
reduction for climate change, 476, 483
US per-capita, 497n3
emissions trading, 31
cap and trade schemes, 41, 44, 46
carbon offsets, 45
ethical defensibility arguments, 45
grandfathering, 44
quotas in, 53
rights for, 4
solidarity arguments, 45
empathy, 4, 98–99
emplacement, 170
emplotment, 166, 170
empowerment
human rights and, 307

of women, 292–93, 295
Endangered Species Act, No Surprises
regulation in, 526n11
endosomatic use, of ecological
space, 317
energy choice, ethical, 391
energy ethics and future, 400–401
environmental ethics issues, 393
expense excuse, 394, 396–97
fossil fuels harms, 6, 392–94
intention excuse, 394, 399–400
intermittency excuse, 394–96
nuclear energy, 392–93
readiness excuse, 394–95
regulations excuse, 394, 398–99
third-order analysis in, 393–94
entangled empathy, 98–99
environment
ecophysical features of, 6
food narratives on, 405–12
history on food, agriculture and, 407
legal rights of natural objects in, 14
liberal conception of, 281–84
as private property, 283
public interest in agriculture
and, 404–5
stories on food, agriculture and, 406–8
technology on, 409–10, 444–46
environmental action, 552–60
democracy for change, 7, 555–56
global climate change, 495, 496
legitimacy of, 554–55, 559
environmental aesthetics, 187
environmental commitment, practical
reasons, 151–60
environmental degradation
of biosphere, 128
from human arrogance, 143
humans responsibility for, 65–66
impact of, 21
of wildness, 125
environmental discourse, sacrifice
in, 541–42
environmental ethics, 229
in landscapes, 66
meaning and, 167
pollution significance to, 371–72

environmental ethics history, 2, 23
    Blackstone's environmental ethics
        conference, 14
    Carson's *Silent Spring* impact, 13
    ecological feminism, 20–21
    EVE, 21–22
    Hardin's "The Tragedy of the Commons"
        impact, 13–14
    holistic theories, 17–19
    individualistic theories, 15–17
    1970s emergence of, 14–15
    pragmatism and anthropocentrism, 19–20
    Rolston's "Is There an Ecological Ethic?," 14
    Routley's "Is There a Need for a New, an
        Ecological Ethic?," 14
    Stone's "Should Trees Have Standing," 14
    White, Jr.'s "The Historical Roots of Our
        Ecological Crisis" impact, 13
environmental fascism, 118–20, 202–4
environmental goods
    cap and trade schemes, 41, 44, 46
    preferences and, 43–44
    property rights and, 41, 42
    shadow prices over, 40–41, 47
    social relations and ethical commitments
        for, 43, 48
environmental harms. *See also* responsibility,
        for environmental harms
    acid rain, 267–68, 279, 369, 370
    from air pollution to human health, 27
    from climate change, 265, 269–72, 304
    collective, 5–6, 271–72
    communities, 361–63
    contributory responsibility, 266–67, 272–
        73, 274n1, 303
    ecological space and, 311, 318n3
    from fossil fuels energy, 6, 392–94
    human rights and, 6, 303, 307
    individual contribution to, 271–72
    individual responsibilities and, 266–67
    from nuclear power, 6, 392–93
environmental hermeneutics, 172
    approaches compared to, 168–70
    critical, of van Buren, 169
    environmental philosophy and, 166–71
    interpretation role, 162–63
    meaning and, 167, 169

        place and, 167–68
        recent contributions to, 170–71
environmental history, 249–54, 538
environmentalism
    deontic perspective, 5
    Leopold on, 151
    pragmatic approach to, 5, 206
    spirituality, 5, 248, 254–55
    thesis on death of, 535
    virtue perspective, 5
    Williams on wild nature basis for, 131
"Environmentalism and Human Sacrifice"
        (Prager), 541–42
environmental justice, 6, 176, 444
    autodestruction and, 431
    command-and-control legal mechanisms,
        4, 52–54, 56, 58, 451, 453
    environmental law and, 52, 54
    liberalism conception of, 281–84
    market-based protection mechanisms,
        4, 52, 53
    movement, 276, 280, 281
    resistance to, 278
environmental law. *See also* state
        environmental law
    anthropocentrism in, 55
    challenges of, 52
    climate change and, 55–56, 58, 59
    environmental justice and, 52, 54
    intergenerational justice, 55
    international, 51, 54–55, 302, 307
    markets and, 4, 52, 53–54
environmental philosophy, 2–3, 552
    environmental hermeneutics and, 166–71
    social constructivist view, 169, 255, 257
environmental policy, 6, 62, 349, 445
    anthropocentric perspectives on, 19–20
    CBA formation of, 4
    global justice and, 6
    in landscapes, 66
environmental protection, 7, 192–93, 255
    human rights link to, 306–7
    market-based mechanisms, 4, 52, 53
    strong sustainability and, 361
Environmental Protection Agency (EPA), US,
        29, 36n5, 51, 243
environmental rights, 306

environmental virtue ethics (EVE), 21–22, 86, 87, 205
  animal rights, 227–28
  anthropocentrism and, 226–27
  characterization of, 224–26
  right action and, 230–31
environment-economy relations, 282
EPA. *See* Environmental Protection Agency
error-statistical account of evidence, 29
essence, moral, 114–16
essence-accident ethics, 114, 116, 117, 121–23
ethical anthropocentrism, 79
  alternatives to, 80–81
  assessment of alternatives to, 83–85
  Christianity and, 77, 78
  Hargrove on, 82
  Norton on, 82
ethical commitments, environmental goods and, 43, 48
ethical defensibility arguments, 45
ethical nonanthropocentrism, 87n6
  biocentrism, 80
  ecocentrism, 80
  on nature's intrinsic value, 79, 87n3
  Rolston's view of, 81
  sentiocentrism, 80
ethical theory
  biocentrism and, 104–6
  biological tradition of, 120, 121
  consequentialist, 4, 5
  ecological collectives and, 113–14
  essence-accident, 114, 116, 117, 121–23
  moral intuition and, 114
  moral philosophy and, 113–14
  non-anthropocentric, 116–17
  value and normativity in, 223
ethical values, 5, 505
ethics. *See also* intergenerational ethics;
    metaethics; nonanthropocentric ethic;
    virtue ethics; water ethics
  alterity, 175
  biocentric, 106–10
  environmental conflict and, 521–22
  eudaimonistic virtue, 227
  evolution, 117–21
  feminist care, 5, 241–43
  intergenerational obligations and, 360–63

intertemporal, 361
  of place, 167
  of reciprocity, 347–48
  on SSI, 505–7
  temporal scope of, 352–53
ethos, water, 421–22. *See also*
    ecological ethos
eudaimonistic virtue ethics, 227
European Environment Agency, 325
European settlers, 250
EVE. *See* environmental virtue ethics
evidence, in science, 27, 36n4
  assessment tools, 29
  Bayes' Theorem, 28, 33, 36n1, 36n2
  defined, 28
  EPA assessment of, 29, 36n5
  error-statistical account of, 29
  IPCC on, 29
ex ante, 321, 325
excellence concept of virtue, 227
exosomatic ecological space, 317, 318n10
expanding circle of moral considerability
    framework, 4
expense excuse, for energy choice,
    394, 396–97
experience, revindication of, 177
  Merleau-Ponty on intentional
    relatedness, 176
  natural attitude of, 175, 176
  naturalism and, 176
Experience and its Modes (Oakeshott), 552
experientialism, 91, 99n1
externalism, 152, 153–54, 159n5, 160n6
  intrinsic value appeal, 156

"Faking Nature" (Elliot), 20
family resemblances approach, to religion, 248
Feenberg, Andrew, 440, 442, 445
feminism. *See also* ecofeminism
  cultural and symbolic associations between
    nature and, 290, 291
  nature and, 289–92
  transformative power of, 290
  water justice approach, 423n3
Le Feminisme ou la Mort (Feminism or Death)
    (d'Eaubonne), 20
feminist care ethics, 5, 241–43

Fifth Assessment Report, of IPCC, 483n1

Firestone, Shulamith, 290

First Agricultural (Neolithic) Revolution, 1

First Stewards Symposium: Coastal Peoples Address Climate Change, 238

flesh ontology, of Merleau-Ponty, 175, 182

flexible labor, of women, 297

flourishing, 202. *See also* human flourishing
  Attfield on, 105, 106
  character ethics and, 226–27
  climate change and, 107, 108
  constitutive goods for, 156
  of global poor, 430
  wild rarity of, 158

food, 6, 404, 413
  history on agriculture and environment, 407
  narratives on, 405–12
  stories on agriculture, environment and, 406–8
  technology on, 409–10

food scares, 404–5

Forest Service, US, 200, 450–51, 453

Formula of Humanity, of Kant, 219

fossil fuels energy
  climate change and, 392
  environmental harms from, 6, 392–94
  evidence suppressed on, 373
  generated electricity, 400
  population reduction from, 351
  Sunstein against regulation of, 398
  vehicles health risks, 400

Foundations of Environmental Ethics (Hargrove), 15

Frasz, Geoffrey, 21

freedom as nondomination, 337

free-market environmentalists, 398

fusion of horizons, Gadamer on, 164, 171n2

future generation rights. *See* intergenerational justice

future generations
  fossil fuels and, 351
  future people, 344–47
  intergenerational ethics, 347–48
  nonhumans future generations, 351–52
  non-identity problem, 109–10, 348–49
  population reduction, 350–51
  Repugnant Conclusion, 350

  temporal scope of ethics, 352–53

future people
  economic approaches for, 345
  existence of, 344
  risks and, 345
  spatiotemporal separation of, 345–47, 364n4
  utilitarianism responsibilities to, 347
  welfare of, 345

G8 parties, UNFCCC and, 488

Gadamer, Hans-Georg, 162, 171n1
  on effective history, 164
  on fusion of horizons, 164, 171n2
  on historically effected consciousness, 164
  romantic hermeneutic criticism, 163

GAO. *See* Government Accountability Office

Gardiner, Stephen, 430, 553
  on climate change, 269, 383
  on cooperatives, 364n6
  on geoengineering, 7, 20, 501–12, 512n7
  on intertemporal relationships, 364n4
  on PP, 325–26, 329
  on RCPP, 326, 329–30

GCC. *See* geological carbon capture

gender. *See* women

gender, environmental ethics and, 6, 289, 291–92, 298
  global injustice and, 293
  naturalizing of, 296

gendered work, 296–97

genetically modified organisms (GMOs), 52, 370, 409

genetic pollution, 369
  from GMOs, 52, 370, 409

Geneva Convention on Long-range Transboundary Air Pollution, 308

geoengineering, 7, 512n4, 543
  climate case example, 509–11
  climate emergency, 508
  climate governance, 508
  control and domination concerns, 506–7
  Crutzen on, 68
  defining features, 502–5, 511n2
  ethics, 505–7
  Gardiner on, 7, 20, 501–12, 512n7
  global climate change, 68
  human relationship to nature, 507

implications, 504–5
intervention, 503–4
Jamieson on, 272–73, 502, 504
justificatory question for, 508
perfect moral storm analysis, 510
policy framings for, 507–9
procedural justice, 507
Rolson on, 65–68
social contexts of, 67
universal benefit claim, 509
welfare, 506
geological carbon capture (GCC), 512n7
GHGs. *See* greenhouse gases
global action, for climate change, 495, 496
*The Global Climate 2001-2010, A Decade of
    Extremes*, UN report, 68
global climate change, 7, 20, 68, 113, 122, 495,
    496, 498n13
global commons, in water justice, 419
global economy, 283
global injustice, 293
global justice, 316, 317, 419, 431
    policy formation of, 6
    population and, 383, 386–88
global warming potential (GWP), 470–72
GMOs. *See* genetically modified organisms
goal- or end-directed living individuals,
    101, 102
Godlovitch, Rosalind, 15
Goodpaster, Kenneth, 102, 217
governance, 4, 51
    ecological ethos and, 4, 56–59
    environmental law and state, 52–56, 58
Government Accountability Office
    (GAO), 396
grandfathering of emissions markets, 44
Great Acceleration, after World War II, 1–2
Great Britain
    Clean Air Act, of 1956, 51, 391
    Great Smog of 1952, 51
    London's Great Smog, of 1952, 51
    Public Health Act of 1848 on industrial
        emissions, 51
Great Chain of Being, 78
Great Smog of 1952, in Britain, 51
Green Belt Movement, 244
green chemistry, for pollution, 372, 377
green citizenship, 6, 334–36

civic sustainability service by, 337
contestatory politics and, 340–41
Green Climate Fund, 492, 496
greenhouse development rights, 388n2
greenhouse gases (GHGs) emissions, 27,
    269, 270, 308. *See also* carbon dioxide
    emissions
    Kyoto Protocol on, 489–90
    mitigation for, 474–75
    UNFCCC pledges to reduce, 492–93
green political theory, 336
green republicanism, 6, 335
    for civic sustainability service, 336–38
    debt-based consumer capitalism, 334
    dependent clientelism antipathy, 334
    instrumental and intrinsic value of
        citizenship, 337
    unsustainability and, 341
green technology, 387
group agency, in water ecological cooperation,
    421, 423n7
GWP. *See* global warming potential

Habermas, Jürgen, 5, 219
habitable principles, in environmental
    conflict, 517
habitat corridors, for biodiversity offsets, 27
Hardin, Garrett, 364n3
    environmental ethics and population, 382
    tragedy of the commons, 13–14, 268–69,
        355, 357, 421
hard won consensus, 30, 36n8
Hargrove, Eugene, 15, 22n2, 86
    on conceptual anthropocentrism, 82
    on ethical anthropocentrism, 82
    nonanthropocentric intrinsic value theory
        of, 82, 83, 87n4, 88n11
Harsanyi, J., 326
hedonistic utilitarianism, 224, 225
Heidegger, Martin, 441, 442
    being-in-the-world of, 174, 176, 181
    on earth, 180
    hermeneutics development by, 162
    on metaphysics, 178
    on modernist assumptions, 178
    phenomenology and, 174
    on poetic dwelling, 175, 183–84
    on technological rationality, 439

hermeneutics. *See also* environmental
    hermeneutics
  anthropocentrism and, 166–67
  Heidegger development of, 162
  interpretation, 5, 162–64, 171n2, 171n4
  phenomenology and, 168–70
  philosophical, 162–66, 170, 172n7
  place and, 166, 167–68, 171
  social constructivist environmental
    philosophy and, 169
Hetch Hetchy Valley dam, 200, 251–52
historically affected consciousness, 163–64
historical or process-based approaches to
  values, 132–33
"The Historical Roots of Our Ecological
  Crisis" (White, Jr.), 13, 77
history, on food, agriculture and
  environment, 407
holism, 17, 84, 217
  biocentrism as form of, 81
  Callicott on, 17–18
  consequentialism, 199
  deep ecology, 18–19
  ecocentrism view, 81
  on individual living things intrinsic
    value, 156
  Rolston on, 18
Holland, Alan, 168
  on environmental responsibility, 267
  on natural, 127
  pragmatism of, 191
Horkheimer, Max, 293, 439
human-centered anthropocentrism, 77–79,
  84, 143
human chauvinism, 84, 85, 168
human flourishing, 19, 69, 158
  climate change and, 109
  EVE and, 22
human identity, place and, 175
humanist view of adaptation, 63
human marginal cases, for rationality, 115
human rights, 308–9
  anthropocentrism of, 301
  challenges for approaches of, 303–6
  climate change and, 304–5
  collective rights and, 304–5
  defense of approaches of, 306–7

ecological space concern, 316–17,
  319n17, 319n18
  empowerment and, 307
  environmental harms and, 6, 303, 307
  environmental protection link to, 306–7
  international law and, 302, 307
  justice and, 303
  moral foundations of, 302–3
  moral responsibility and, 301
  to water, 6, 417–18
humans
  air pollution harms to health of, 27
  arrogance, environmental degradation
    from, 143
  biosphere and technosphere, 64–65
  as caretakers of values, 66
  Christian theology on morally
    significant, 77
  environmental degradation
    responsibility, 65–66
  Kant on special status of, 156
  as moral agents, 86
  natural system disruption by, 203
  nature adaptation by, 63–65
  nature dominated by, 62, 63, 65
  nature relationship with, 507
  planetary management by, 65–67
  realized niche of, 312–13, 318n7, 318n11
  as value source, 141–42
Hume, David, 117, 121, 148n9
hunting, 524, 527n17
Husserl, Edmund, 439, 441
  on body self-sensing, 181–82
  on intentionality, 174, 176, 181
  on natural attitude, 176
  on nature, 177–78
  phenomenology and, 174

IACHR. *See* Inter-American Commission on
  Human Rights
ICC. *See* Inuit Circumpolar Conference
Idle No More movement, 238
Ihde, Don, 441, 442
The Imperative of Responsibility (Jonas), 443
incommensurability, 329–30
  in CBA, 330n4
  of RCPP, 326

uncertainty and, 327
incremental adaptation, 477
indigenous environmental movements, 281
   Boldt Decision, 237
   caring in, 5, 236–38
   civil disobedience, 238
   Declaration of the Rights of Indigenous
      Peoples, 237
   Idle No More, 238
   Inter-American Court, 237
   Kari-Oca 2 declaration, 237
   knowledge, responsibility, reciprocity and
      moral repair in, 238–41
   philosophy articles of, 237
indigenous people
   adaptation initiatives for, 482
   communities, 281
   illness decimation of, 250
Indigenous Peoples Kyoto Water
    Declaration, 239
Indigenous Peoples Parallel Forum of the
    Fourth World Water Forum, 239
indirect responsibility, 266–67
individualism, 15–17, 23n3, 81, 84, 144
individual moral responsibility, 273, 274
individual responsibility, 266–67,
    271–74, 274n1
inductive risk, 33, 34
industrialism, mass extinction and, 429–30
industrialization, 438–39
inegalitarian biocentrism, 4, 201
inherent value
   of sentient beings, 16, 80
   Taylor on all living things, 16, 88n11, 201
injustice
   in climate adaptation, 479–80, 483
   fight against, 340
   global, 293
instrumentalist framing, 5
instrumental value, 77, 87n2, 207n1
   green republicanism on citizenship, 337
   of wild, 129–30
integrated aesthetic values, 189
Intended Nationally Determined
    Contributions, 493
intensive farming, 15
intentionality, Husserl on, 174, 176, 181

intention excuse, for energy choice, 394,
   399–400
Interagency Ecosystem Management Task
    Force, 450
Inter-American Commission on Human
    Rights (IACHR), Inuit people and, 307
Inter-American Court of Human Rights,
   237, 479
interdependence, 234, 236, 238, 241, 252
interests, in environmental conflicts, 521
interests, of conscious animals, 15, 91
   avoiding suffering, 92–93, 99n2
   Mill on satisfaction of, 96–97
interference guidelines, in risk assessment, 373
intergenerational ethics, 6, 352–53
   communitarianism and, 362
   contractarians and, 348
   ethics of reciprocity, 347–48
   obligations, 360–63
intergenerational justice, 279–80, 431
   environmental law limitations, 55
   Oposa v. Factorian on, 55–56
   water justice and, 419–20
Intergovernmental Panel on Climate Change
    (IPCC), 29, 32, 350, 476
   adaptation definition, 484n8
   on carbon dioxide, 471–72
   Fifth Assessment Report, 483n1
   on mitigation, 465
   on ocean as sink for carbon dioxide, 465–66
   on transformation, 477
   uncertainty in forecasts, 29, 323
intermittency excuse, for energy
    choice, 394–96
internalism, 152–54, 160n6
International Commission on Stratigraphy, 2
international cooperation, 487, 490, 496
International Covenant on Civil and Political
    Rights, 308
International Energy Agency, 395
International Labor Organization, on
    clientelism, 335
international law, 51, 54–55
   human rights and, 302, 307
   IACHR and Inuit people, 307
interpretation, 5, 162–64, 165, 169,
    171n2, 171n4

intertemporal ethics, 361
intertemporal relationships, 364n4
interventionist role, of state, 58–59
intrinsic values, 5, 87n2, 207n1. *See also* weak
    anthropocentric intrinsic value theory
    of all living things, 18, 19, 87n3
    anthropocentric, 81–83
    of biodiversity, 69–70
    consequentialism on non-human entities,
        199, 204–6
    Dancy on appeal to, 155–56, 158
    dark green religion on, 254
    ecosystems and, 19, 81
    ethical nonanthropocentrism on nature's,
        79, 87n3
    green republicanism on citizenship, 337
    Hargrove's nonanthropocentric theory of,
        82, 83, 87n4, 88n11
    holism on individual living things', 156
    of humans, 77
    kinship ethics and, 250
    metaethics and, 142–43, 148n10
    naturalism on pleasure identified
        with, 142
    of nature, 131, 207n9
    of non-human entities, 78, 80, 86, 142,
        199–206
    practical reasons appeal to, 155–56
    responsibility and, 267, 274n2
    Rolston on, 14, 18, 87n3, 131, 142
    of species, 14, 22n2, 81, 83–84, 142
    of wild nature, 69, 70, 130–32, 168
Inuit Circumpolar Conference (ICC),
    479, 494n12
Inuit people, 484n11
    climate adaptation and, 479–84
    cultural identify of, 479–81
    IACHR and, 307
IPAT equation, 383, 386, 387, 388n1
IPCC. *See* Intergovernmental Panel on
    Climate Change
irreversible damage, in PP, 326
"Is There an Ecological Ethic?" (Rolston), 14
"Is There a Need for a New, an Ecological
    Ethic?" (Routley), 14
itemizing approach to environmental
    values, 168

Jamieson, D.
    on climate change responsibility, 272, 273
    on geoengineering, 272–73, 502, 504
    on moral responsibility, 266
Johnson, Baylor, 20, 104
Joint Implementation program, 490
Jonas, Hans, 439, 442–43, 445
*Journal for the Study of Religion, Nature and
    Culture*, 257n5
*Journal of Agricultural and Environmental
    Ethics*, 404
justice, 6, 276, 285. *See also* distributive justice;
    environmental justice; global justice;
    intergenerational justice; water justice
    adaptation and, 7
    circumstances of, 385
    climate, 475, 506, 508
    climate change and, 27
    community, 280–81
    conflict resolution and, 7, 517,
        521–22, 526n13
    environmental ethics and, 277–78
    fight against injustice, 340
    human rights and, 303
    liberal conception of environment, 281–84
    liberal theories of, 278–81
    natural resources and, 420
    procedural, 507
    Rawls' principles of, 56–57, 506
    as remedial virtue, 278
    as social practice, 278

Kant, Immanuel
    aesthetic theory of, 188, 189, 190
    Formula of Humanity, 219
    on humans special status, 156
    intergenerational ethics and, 347
    on rationality, 114
Keith, David, 511n2, 512n5, 512n6
kinship ethics, of Leopold, 250, 253
knowledge
    in indigenous environmental
        movements, 238–41
    markets and climate change, 47–48
Kolers, Avery, 318n11, 319n16
Korsgaard, Christine, 97, 219
Kyoto Protocol, of 1997, 308, 470, 495, 498n14

Annex 1 parties of, 489–90
climate diplomacy beyond, 491–94
on GHGs, 489–90
US and, 490, 497n4
Kyoto Treaty, of 2002, 54

Land Ethic, of Leopold, 5, 81, 88n9, 154,
217, 256
all living things and, 17
Callicott's proponent of, 17–18
on ethics evolution, 118–19 120–121
on land community regard, 5, 155, 156, 223,
253, 362–63, 454
"The Land Ethic" (Leopold), 118, 122,
202, 454
landscapes, 1, 5
management, 65–67
naturalness in, 64–65
rewilding, 170, 193
land system use, 2
large-unit/deep branching conservation, 434
Last Man (Routley), 77–78
Late Pleistocene Extinction Event, 1
Lear, Jonathan, 481, 484n16
legal rights, of environment's natural
objects, 14
legitimacy, of environmental action,
554–55, 559
Leopold, Aldo, 17, 63, 87n5, 154, 431, 534–35.
See also Land Ethic, of Leopold
on biotic communities, 119, 122
on caring for nature, 235
on collective action, 269
ecocentric consequentialism of, 202
on ecological integrity, 360
on economically based conservation, 458
on economically motivated actions, 155
on ecosystem value, 203, 360
on environmentalism, 151
kinship ethics, 250, 253
on logic of ecosystem, 523
on wilderness, 130
Levinas, Emmanuel, 175, 180
liberal democracy, 333–34
liberal individualism, 281
liberalism, 276, 281–84, 439
liberal theories of justice

on circumstances of moderate
scarcity, 282–83
community justice, 280–81
distributive justice, 56–57, 279, 280, 282,
303, 305, 419–20, 493–94
domestic justice, 279
environment as private property, 283
environment-economy relationship, 282
intergenerational justice, 55–56,
279–80, 419–20
participatory or political justice, 280
lifeworld, 178–80
Light, Andrew, 168
on environmental responsibility, 267
on natural, 127
pragmatism of, 82, 191
light pollution, 369
limits to growth, 48–49
living individuals
biocentrism on value of, 101–2
goal- or end-directed, 101, 102
moral significance of, 103
Taylor on, 101–2, 104
value of, 101–2
Living Planet Index (LPI), 383, 386
living things, all
Attfield, Schweitzer on value of, 201
biocentric individualists on moral status of,
16, 80, 84
biocentrism on moral value in, 16, 80, 84
deep ecology on intrinsic value of, 19
identification with, 18–19
land community and, 17
Rolston on intrinsic value of, 18, 87n3
Taylor on inherent value of, 16, 88n11, 201
Lotka-Volterra equations, in scientific models, 31
Love Canal, 438
Lovins, Hunter, 543
low-income countries
adaptation and, 7, 467–69
biodiversity, 383
ecological footprint in, 383
flourishing of, 430
pollution threat to, 6
population policies and, 383
LPI. *See* Living Planet Index
luxury emissions, 45

magnitude criterion, in mass extinction, 428

Major Economies Forum, 494

male domination, Christian theology
    on, 13, 21

Mandaluyong Declaration, 240

Man's Responsibility for Nature (Passmore),
    15, 87n3

market-based
    protection mechanisms, 4, 52, 53
    unsustainability solutions, 336

market boundaries, 42

market norms, 4, 41

markets
    biodiversity, 4, 46–47
    cap and trade schemes, 41, 44, 46
    for emission rights, 4
    emissions, 44–46
    environmental conflict and, 522–24, 526n7
    environmental goods, 41
    environmental growth limits, 48–49
    environmental law and, 4, 52, 53–54
    instruments used by, 44–47
    knowledge and climate change, 47–48
    market economies, 48–49
    monetary values extension, 42–44
    shadow prices, 40
    skepticism of, 41–42
    state environmental law and, 53
    willingness-to-pay measures, 43–44

market-skeptical positions, 41–42, 48

Marx, Karl, 318n8, 337, 439

Massachusetts Toxic Use Reduction Act, 377

mass extinction, 6, 435–36
    anthroponomy, 433–34
    autodestruction, 430–31
    banality of evil, 432–33
    Big Five events, 427–29
    dissimilar groups criterion, 428
    future, 352
    industrialism and, 429–30
    large-unit/deep branching
        conservation, 434
    magnitude criterion, 428

material interests, climate adaptation and,
    478–79, 480

maximin decision rule, in PP
    defense of, 327–28

examples of, 328–29
    Harsanyi's objection to, 326
    RCPP for, 325

McDonough, William, 543

McShane, Katie, 86, 87, 455

meaningful relationships, 157–59

meanings
    critical environmental hermeneutics and,
        167, 169
    of hermeneutics text, 163, 164, 167, 171n2
    human understanding of, 171n5
    nature interpretation, 5, 162–64,
        171n2, 171n4

measurement, reporting, and verification
    (MRV), 490–92, 497n5

Merchant, Carolyn, 250, 295

Merleau-Ponty, Maurice, 439
    on chiasm, 181–82
    on flesh ontology, 175, 182
    on naturalism, 176
    phenomenology and, 174

metaethics, 4, 139, 147n1, 148
    Callicott and Hume on, 148n9
    cognitivism in, 140, 143, 145, 148n8
    intrinsic value and, 142–43, 148n10
    moral facts and, 140, 147n4
    naturalism in, 5, 144, 145, 147n4, 148n5
    noncognitivism in, 5, 140, 141, 143, 145,
        148n7, 148n8
    normativity of, 144, 145–47

metaphysical approach, to religion, 249

metaphysical assumptions, 175, 177–78

metaphysical naturalism, 176

Mill, John Stuart, 96, 126, 206

Millennium Ecosystem Assessment, 63–66

Minteer, Ben, 79, 205, 522, 526n14

mitigation, 466–72
    APP, BPP and CPP principles in, 469
    for climate change, 465, 474–75, 492, 510
    for GHGs emissions, 474–75
    IPCC on, 465
    social and political inertia, 510
    sustainable development and, 468–69
    UNFCCC and, 474–75, 492

models. *See* scientific models

modernist assumptions, 175, 177–78

monistic biocentrism, 4

monoculture, 296–97
Monocultures of the Mind (Shiva), 296
Moore, G. E., 146, 207n8
moral awareness, 553–54
moral facts
    metaethics and, 140, 147n4
    normativity and, 146
    objectivity and, 140, 148n5
    realism and antirealism, 141
moral foundations, of human rights, 302–3
moral ontology
    anthropocentric, 114
    essence-accident terms for, 114, 116,
        117, 121–23
    ethical theory and, 113–14
    moral sentiments and, 117–19, 121–22
    non-anthropocentric, 114
    on rationality, 115
moral patients
    Curse of Cain and, 115
    human marginal cases, 115
    rationality and, 115
moral philosophy
    ethical theory and, 113–14
    on rationality, 115
moral relevance
    climate change and, 109
    Goodpaster on, 102, 217
moral repair, in indigenous environmental
        movements, 238–41
moral responsibility, 5–6, 15, 17, 266, 346
    in anthropogenic climate change, 107
    for future, 352
    human rights and, 301
    of individual, 273, 274
    inductive risk and, 33
    spatiotemporal separation and, 346
moral rights, 240
    of sentient beings, 16, 84
    of water, 417–18
moral sentiments, 117–19, 121–22
moral status, 280–81
    of all living things, 16, 80, 84
    of animals, 23n6
    anthropocentrism and, 277
    contextualist view on nature, 168
    pluralism approach to, 224, 229–30, 232

right action and, 224, 230–31
moral strength and concern, virtue
        biocentrism on, 104–5
Mother Earth Water Walk, 234, 235,
        239, 244
motivational repertoire, 154, 159n2
    Leopold on community and, 155
    meaningful relationships and, 158
    Williams on, 153
MRV. *See* measurement, reporting, and
        verification
Muir, John, 200, 251, 252
multidimensional consequentialism, 204
multigenerational community, 356,
        358, 363–64

Naess, Arne, 18, 23n4
    on caring for nature, 235
    on deep ecology, 217, 371
    on equal rights of living things, 106
NAMAs. *See* nationally appropriate mitigation
        actions
nanotechnology, 370, 377, 445
narrative identity, 164–66, 170, 172n7
narratives
    agrarian, 410
    developing world, 411
    economic, 411
    on food and environment, 405–12
    on GMOs, 409
    non-fictional stories functions, 406–8
    reconstruction of environmental
        ethics, 533–35
    religious, 412
    on respect for water, 418
    Romantic, 410
    scientific, 408–9
    technophobic, 409–10
    techno-utopian, 409
    travelogue, 411–12
Nash, Roderick, 250, 534
National Academy of Sciences, US, 392
National Environmental Policy Act, in
        1969, 51
nationally appropriate mitigation actions
        (NAMAs), 490–91, 494, 497n5
National Park Service, US, 128

National Research Council (NRC), US,
    372–73, 531
natural, 127
    attitude of experience, 175, 176, 179
    capital, 356, 364n2
    dimensions of, 64–65
    landscapes and, 64–65
    legal rights of objects, 14
    valuing of, 63–64
natural beauty, 191
Natural Capitalism (Lovins), 543
natural environmental model, of Carson, 188
naturalism
    Heidegger, Husserl, Merleau-Ponty on, 176
    Husserl on, 177
    intrinsic value identification with
        pleasure, 142
    metaethics and, 5, 144, 145, 147n4, 148n5
natural piety, 537
natural resources
    Anthropocene proponents on, 70–71
    common ownership of, 55
    justice and, 420
    Pinchot on conversation of, 200
    vulnerability of water, 421
natural world, 203
    aesthetic values of, 15, 404
    CBA and, 21
    Christian theology and exploitation of, 13
    Hargrove on aesthetic value of, 15
    humans, morality and, 144–45
    meaningful relationships within, 159
    value of, 404
    women attunement with, 21
nature
    aesthetic values for, 186–87
    contextualist view on moral status of, 168
    economic approach to, 5
    ethical nonanthropocentrism on intrinsic
        value of, 79, 87n3
    feminism and, 289–92
    future of, 71
    humans relationship with, 507
    Husserl on, 177–78
    intrinsic value of, 131, 207n9
    managerial approach to, 5
    Mill on meanings of, 126

    race and, 289
    respect for, 69–71, 215, 216
    rights, rules, and respect for, 211–20
    technocratic approach to, 5
    Thoreau on sacredness of, 250–51
    ugliness of, 191–92
Neolithic Revolution. *See* First Agricultural
    Revolution
New Woman/New Earth (Ruether), 20
noise pollution, 369
Nolt, John, 107, 361, 362
non-anthropocentric ethic
    Bentham's precedent for, 115
    on future non-human entities, 351–52
    on pollution, 371
non-anthropocentric instrumental value, 82
non-anthropocentric moral ontology, 114–16
non-anthropocentric theories, 22n2, 88n10
    Callicott's intrinsic value, 82
    on ecological collectives, 116–17
    Hargrove's intrinsic value, 82, 83,
        87n4, 88n11
    on non-human entities value, 15
    of Repugnant Conclusion, 350–52
nonanthropocentrism, 532–33. *See also*
    ethical nonanthropocentrism
noncognitivism
    in aesthetic judgments, 188–89, 194n2
    in metaethics, 5, 140, 141, 143, 145,
        148n7, 148n8
non-consequentialism
    deontology and, 215–17
    normative theory, 5
non-human entities. *See also* animals
    Bentham on, 80
    consequentialism and intrinsic value of,
        199, 204–6
    expression of interests by, 92
    future generations of, 351–52
    instrumental value of, 77
    intrinsic value of, 78, 80, 86, 142, 199,
        201, 204–6
    sentiocentrism and, 4, 80, 82, 103
    value of, 15, 83–84
non-identity problem, 109–10, 348–49
non-instrumental value, 205–6, 229
non-state actors, environmental law and, 58

non-violent direct action (NVDA), 340–41
Nordhaus, Ted, 535, 536, 542
normativity, 5, 202, 223
    metaethics and, 144, 145–47
    Moore on, 146
    moral facts and, 146
    values and, 147
    virtue ethics and, 224–26, 232, 232n1
North American environmental history,
        249, 254
    back-to-the-land movement, 252
    Carson on sacred in nature, 252
    Emerson's Transcendentalism, 250
    European settlers, 250
    Hetch Hetchy Valley dam, 251–52
    Leopold reverence for earth, 253
    Muir anthropocentric theism criticism, 251
    Muir on interdependence, 252
    Schweitzer on sacred, 252–53
Norton, Bryan, 83
    on adaptive management, 452–53
    on anthropocentrism and biocentrism, 20,
        88n8, 523
    on communal goods, 365n11
    on conservation, 526n8
    convergence hypothesis, 533
    on ethical anthropocentrism, 82
    on pragmatism, 82
    weak anthropocentrism, 20, 82, 88n8
No Surprises regulation, in Endangered
        Species Act, 526n11
NRC. See National Research Council, US;
        Nuclear Regulatory Commission
nuclear energy, 6, 392–93, 395–97
Nuclear Regulatory Commission (NRC),
        US, 396
NVDA. See non-violent direct action

Oakeshott, Michael, 552
objective final values, 226
objective probabilities, 322
objective theories, of welfare, 212
objectivity
    moral facts and, 140, 148n5
    in science, 32–35, 178
obligation, 270, 271
ocean

acidification, 2, 465, 469–70, 474, 484n7
    as sink for carbon dioxide, 465–66
Ogus, Anthony, 53
Omnivore's Dilemma (Pollan), 411–12
O'Neill, John, 83, 86, 132–33, 156, 168
    on environmental responsibility, 267
    on human flourishing, 158
    on living individuals values, 102
    on natural, 127
    pragmatism of, 191
On the Origin of the Species (Darwin), 250, 253
ontological anthropocentrism, 78, 85
operative reasons, 151, 153
Oposa v. Factorian, 55
opportunity freedom, of Sen, 362
organisms, 103, 108. See also genetically
        modified organisms
ought-implies-can principle, 394
overconsumption, human, 4, 125
overdevelopment, human, 4, 125
overpopulation, human
    tragedy of the commons on, 357
    wildness and, 4, 125

pain
    of animals in agricultural production,
        93, 99n4
    avoidance of, 80, 92–93
    capacity, in sentience, 115, 224
    Varner on conditions for, 93
pantheism, 257n1, 257n2
Parfit, Derek, 109–10, 350–52
Parfit's Paradox, 356, 361
Paris Agreement, 293, 488, 492–95
participatory approach, in ecological ethos,
        52, 58–59
participatory justice, 280
particular threats concern, of PP, 326
Passmore, John, 15, 89n3
patient-centered deontology, 216–17
perfect moral storm analysis, on
        geoengineering, 510
person-affecting principles, 349
person-regarding principle, 361, 362
pessimistic catastrophism, technological
        optimism versus, 543–44
pesticides, 371, 375

phenomenology, 5, 168, 174, 179–84, 439. *See also* ecophenomenology
  experience revindication, 175–77
  hermeneutics and, 168–70
  metaphysical and modernist critiques of, 177–78
  of technology, 441–42
philosophical hermeneutics, 162
  appropriation and, 164–66
  distantiation, 164–66
  effective history and historically affected consciousness, 163–64
  narrative identity, 164–66, 170, 172n7
Philosophy and Environmental Crisis (Blackstone), 14
Philosophy of Civilization (Schweitzer), 101
philosophy of technology, 438–40, 441–43
Pinchot, Gifford, 200, 202, 251
place
  hermeneutics and, 166, 167–68, 171
  human identity and, 175
Planetary Boundaries Analysis
  biochemical nitrogen and phosphorus cycle, 2
  biodiversity loss, 2
  climate change, 2
  land system use, 2
  ocean acidification, 2
  stratospheric ozone, 2
planetary management, 65–67, 278
"Planet of No Return: Human Resilience on an Artificial Earth" (Ellis), 64
pluralism
  aesthetic values of nature and, 188–92
  critical, 189–91, 193
  moral status approach, 224, 229–30, 232
  Parsons on, 190
  value, 19, 103–5, 534
pluralistic biocentrism, 4, 81
PNAS. See Proceedings of the National Academy of Science
political consciousness, 7, 553–54, 558–59
political inertia in climate change mitigation, 510
political justice, 280
Pollan, Michael, 410, 411–12
polluter-pays principle, 469, 491, 497n6

pollution
  air, 27, 51, 369, 391, 494
  BAT use for elimination of, 375
  CBA on, 375
  challenges to definition of, 369–70
  cradle-to-cradle industrial design for, 372, 377
  economic regulation of, 374
  environmental ethics significance, 371–72
  genetic, 52, 369, 370, 409
  green chemistry for, 372, 377
  low-income countries threat from, 6
  ongoing issues, 377
  pesticides, 371
  PP, 375–77
  regulation of, 6, 374–75
  risk identification and assessment, 372–74, 377
  safety by design for, 377
  social costs of, 374–75
  soil contamination, 369
  sources of, 369–71
population. *See also* overpopulation
  climate change reduction of, 350
  ecological footprint, 383
  environmental ethics and, 382
  global justice and, 383, 386–88
  growth, 6, 13, 350, 380, 420
  narrow view cost, 382–84
  policies and permissibility, 381–82
population-tied policies, 384–86
  choice-providing, 382
  ecological footprints and, 385
  procreation rights, 381–82
  soft incentive-changing policies, 382, 383, 388
PP. See precautionary principle
practical identities, 219
practical reasons
  desires and, 152
  distinctions, 151–52
  environmental commitment and, 151–60
  functions of, 151
  internalism and externalism, 152–54
  intrinsic value appeal, 155–56
  Leopold's Land Ethic, 154–55
  meaningful relationships, 157–59

nature of, 151–54
operative reasons, of Scanlon, 151
Prager, Denis, 541–42
pragmatism, 3, 82, 191, 204, 522, 529–30, 534
anthropocentrism and, 19–20
convergence hypothesis in, 20
environmentalism and, 5, 206
plurality of values, 19
prometheanism *versus*, 535–37
Preamble to the Paris Agreement on climate
change, 293
precautionary principle (PP), 321, 330, 443
criticism of, 376
decision rule of, 329
Gardiner on, 325–26, 329
incommensurability of, 326
irreversible damage, 326
maximin decision rule in, 325–29
particular threats concern, 326
political articulations of, 324
pollution and, 375–77
risk assessment and, 324, 329
strengths of, 376
Sunstein on, 324–25
uncertainty and, 325
Wingspread Declaration, 375–76
predation, 1, 94–95
preservation, of wild, 125, 129–30, 132, 134,
519, 525
preservationism, 192–93, 522–24, 526n8
prima facie duties, 277, 302, 400–401
Princen, Thomas, 66, 441, 542, 549n1
Principia Ethica (Moore), 146
priorities, conflicting, 519–20, 525
private law, regulation compared to, 53
private ownership, 283, 357–59
privatization, of resources, 357–59
procedural justice, 507
*Proceedings of the National Academy of Science
(PNAS)*, 531, 533
procreative rights, 381–82
property rights, 319n21
environmental goods and, 41, 42
Shue on, 317
state environmental law and, 53
The Public and its Problems (Dewey), 536
Public Health Act, of 1848, 51

public interest
in agriculture and environment, 404–5
in sustainable communities, 356, 363–64
public policy decisions, as non-identity cases, 349

R₂P. *See* Responsibility to Protect
race, 289, 298
Radical Hope (Lear), 481
radical inequalities, 317, 319n20
rainforest, *Oposa v. Factorian* on, 55
ratiocentric deontology, 224–26
rationality
Aristotle on, 114, 160n8
human marginal cases for, 115
Kant on, 114
moral philosophy on, 115
Regan on, 114–15
speciesist, 168
of technology, 439
Rawls, John, 213
Difference Principle of, 506–7
on distributive justice, 56–57, 279
intergenerational ethics and, 347
on intergenerational reciprocity, 348
on principles of justice, 56–57, 506
on utilitarianism, 305
Rawlsian Core Precautionary Principle
(RCPP), 325
CBA objections compared to, 326–27
Gardiner on, 326, 329–30
REACH. *See* Registration, Evaluation,
Authorisation, and Restriction of Chemicals
readiness excuse, for energy choice, 394–95
realism, 18, 141
realized niche, of humans, 312–13,
318n7, 318n11
reasonable of actions, 219–20
reciprocity, in indigenous environmental
movements, 238–41
rectification, for climate change, 476, 477, 483
Redgwell, C., 51, 52, 55
Regan, Tom, 16, 99n1, 412
on animal rights, 16, 115, 201, 215
on environmental fascism, 202
on rationality, 114–15
on subjects-of-a-life moral rights,
80, 115–16

Registration, Evaluation, Authorisation, and Restriction of Chemicals (REACH) legislation, of European Union, 375
regulation, 398
    command and control, 53–54, 58
    of GMOs, 52
    of pollution, 6, 374–75
    private law compared to, 53
    of property ownership, 52
    pursuit of justice relation to state, 56–57
    state on environmental impact, 51–53, 56–57
Regulation: Legal Form and Economic Theory (Ogus), 53
regulations excuse, for energy choice, 394, 398–99
rejectionist approach, in ecological ethos, 58
religion
    constructionist approach to, 249
    defined, 248
    family resemblances approach, 248
    metaphysical approach to, 249
    sacred and, 248–49
religious narratives, 412
remedial virtues, 278
remediation, 302, 303
renewable energy, 386–87
Repugnant Conclusion, 350–52
research. See scientific research
resilience
    climate adaptation increase of, 477, 478
    in ecosystem management, 457–58
    of resource systems, 360
    sustainability and, 355, 359
resistance citizenship activism, 338, 340–41
resources. See also natural resources
    common-pool, 357–59
    depletion, 371
    ecological space and, 311, 313–14, 316, 319n16
    open access to, 357, 358
    privatization, 357–58, 359
respect
    by conscious animals of other animals, 98–99
    for nature, 69–71, 215, 216
    for water, 418–19, 421, 422

Respect for Nature (Taylor), 101–2
responsibility. See also moral responsibility
    Aristotle on, 266, 399
    for energy-related harms, 399–400
    in indigenous environmental movements, 238–41
    institutions, social practices, individual, 266–67, 271–74, 274n1
    intrinsic values and, 267, 274n2
    for nature, 215, 218–20
    of utilitarianism to future people, 347
responsibility, for environmental harms, 267, 274
    Caney on, 304, 306–7
    climate change and, 265, 269–71
    contributory, 266–67, 272–73, 274n1, 303
    Gardiner on, 505, 507
    individual contribution to collective harms, 271–72
    Jamieson on climate change, 272
    Shue on, 468–69, 475
    Sinnott-Armstrong on, 265, 269–70
    tragedy of the commons, 268–69
Responsibility to Protect (R_2P) doctrine, 306
revealed preference methods, of shadow price construction, 40
Reverence for Life, 80, 101
rewilding, in cultural landscapes, 170, 193
Ricoeur, Paul, 162, 170, 171n3
    on appropriation, 165
    on interpretation in hermeneutics, 165, 169
    on narrative identity, 165–66
right action, 5, 219, 232
    EVE and, 230–31
    moral status and, 224, 230–31
rights. See also human rights; moral rights; property rights; water rights
    of animals, 16, 115, 201, 215, 227–28
    greenhouse development, 388n2
    natural objects' legal, 14
    for nature, 215–16
    procreative, 381–82
    of sentience, 99n1
Rio Declarations, 1990, 308, 443
Rio Declarations, 1992, 55
Rio Earth Summit, 487
risk and precaution, 6, 321–30

risk assessment, 444
  burden of proof, 375
  CBA for, 321–24
  interference guidelines, 373
  on pollution, 372–74, 377
  PP and, 324, 329
  risk management compared to, 373
  science narrative for, 409
  technical analyses and deliberation, 373
  weight of evidence in, 372
Risk Assessment in the Federal Government, of
    National Research Council, 372
risk management, risk assessment compared
    to, 373
Rolston, Holmes, III, 87, 134, 205
  ecocentrism of, 83
  on ecosystem's systemic value, 18
  ethical nonanthropocentrism view, 81
  on geoengineering, 65–68
  on intrinsic value, 14, 18, 87n3, 131, 142
  realism of, 18
  on wildness, 130
romantic hermeneutics, 163
Romantic narrative, 410
Routley, Richard, 14, 77–78
Royal Society, 501, 510
Royal Swedish Academy of Sciences, 64
Ruether, Rosemary Radford, 20
rule-consequentialism, 205
rules, for nature, 219

sacred in nature perception, 5
  North American environmental history
      and, 249–54
  persistence of, 256–57
  religion and, 248–49
  wilderness as, 251
sacrifice, 7
  agents *versus* victims, 548–49
  in environmental discourse, 541–42
  rethinking concept of, 544–46
  self-interest and, 542
  technological optimism *versus* pessimistic
      catastrophism, 542–44
  as ubiquitous, 546–48
safety by design, for pollution, 377
Sagoff, Mark, 43–44, 215, 274n4, 521, 554

A Sand County Almanac (Leopold), 17,
    154, 534
Sandler, Ronald, 105, 191, 205
Scanlon, Tim M., 151, 219
Schweitzer, Albert
  on all living things value, 201
  Reverence for Life principle, 80, 101
  on sacred, 252–53
science, 3–4, 37. *See also* sustainability
    science
  applied philosophy of, 439, 443–44
  consensus in, 30
  contextual values in, 32–35, 36n6, 36n7
  energy-ethics, 401
  evidence in, 27–29, 33, 35, 36n1, 36n2,
      36n4, 36n5
  human impact on revolution of, 1
  narrative, utilitarianism and, 409
  objectivity, 28
  scientific models, 30–32, 35–36
  uncertainty, 29–30, 32, 34, 36n7, 321–23
  value-free ideal for, 33, 34, 36n6
  values and objectivity, 32–36
Science, 531
  on climate change, 395
  on fossil fuels, 393
scientific cognitivism, 5, 188, 189
scientific models, 35–36
  on carcinogenicity, 31
  on climate, 31
  construction of, 32
  dismissal of, 31
  Lotka-Volterra equations, 31
  target system and, 30
  on weather forecasting, 31
scientific narrative, 408–9
scientific research, 6
  animals' medical, 228, 372
  funding influence on, 373–74
  polluters' manipulation of, 373
The Second Sex (Beauvoir), 294
self-interest, 7, 542, 544–45
Sen, Amartya, 362
sentience
  consciousness and, 84
  pleasure and pain capacity, 115, 224
  rights of, 99n1

sentient beings
    individualistic theories and, 16–17
    inherent value of, 16, 80
    moral rights of, 16, 84
    Regan on value of, 16
    Singer on interests of, 16
    Weston on intrinsic value of, 19
sentient consequentialism, 201, 202
sentiocentrism
    biocentrism objections to, 82
    deontological approach to, 80
    empathy and respect, 4
    moral significance in, 103
Sequoia National Forest, 14
sexism, 290, 291–92
sexual politics, 288, 298
    feminist solidarity with nature, 289–92
    gendered work, 296–97
    linked harms and proximity
        association, 292–93
    monoculture, 296–97
    women and nature, 293–96
shadow prices, over environmental goods,
    40–41, 47
"The Shallow and the Deep, Long-Range
    Ecology Movement: A Summary"
    (Naess), 18
shallow ecology, 18
Shellenberger, Michael, 535, 536, 542
Shiva, Vandana, 296
"Should Trees Have Standing" (Stone), 14
Shue, Henry, 386
    on basic rights, 317, 417
    on property rights duties, 317
Sierra Club, 200
Silent Spring (Carson), 13, 252, 371, 440, 536
Singer, Peter, 15–16, 99n1
    on pain avoidance, 80, 92
    on suffering, 102
    on utilitarianism, 201
single-species management, 450, 451
sink enhancement, for climate change, 465–
    66, 476, 483
Sinnott-Armstrong, Walter
    on climate change harms, 272
    on environmental harm responsibility,
        265, 269–70

on individual responsibilities, 271
    on obligation, 270, 271
social and political inertia in climate change
    mitigation, 510
social constructivist environmental
    philosophy, 169, 255, 257
social context, of geoengineering, 67
social costs, of pollution, 374–75
social economy, sustainable economic
    citizenship and, 338–40
social intelligence, of Dewey, 529–30
social limits, to economic growth, 48–49
social relations, environmental goods
    and, 43, 48
Society for Ecological Restoration, 456
soft incentive-changing population policies,
    382, 383, 388
soil contamination, 369
solar energy, 394–97
solar radiation management (SRM), for
    climate change, 476, 483, 484n7
sound deliberative route, 153–54
spatiotemporal separation, 345–47, 364n4
species, 88n12
    identification of, 85
    intrinsic value of, 14, 22n2, 81, 83–84, 142
    single-species management, 450, 451
    -typical behaviors, 97
speciesism, 84, 85
speciesist rationality, 168
spirituality, 5, 248, 254–55
SRM. See solar radiation management
SSI. See stratospheric sulfate injection
stability, in ecosystem management, 454–55
stated preference methods, of shadow price
    construction, 40–41
state environmental law, 51–58
    collectivist system, 53–54
    command and control regulation, 53–54, 58
    market system, 53
    sustainable energy and, 54
states of affairs, consequentialist biocentrism
    value of, 105
Sterba, James P., 102, 104
Stern, Nicholas, 346–47, 400
stewardship, by planetary management, 66
Stockholm Declaration, of 1972, 55, 305–6

Stone, Christopher, 14
stories, on food, agriculture and
    environment, 406–8
stratospheric ozone, 2
stratospheric sulfate injection (SSI), 505–7
"A Stroll Through the Worlds of Animals and
    Men: A Picture Book of Invisible Worlds"
    (von Uexküll), 99n6
strong anthropocentrism, 79, 87n6
strong sustainability, 355, 356f
    community values emphasis, 363
    cross-habitat diversity, 360
    ecologists advocating, 356
    environmental protection and, 361
    natural capital, 356, 364n2
    within-habitat-diversity, 360
subjective probabilities, 322
subjective theories, 95–96, 212
subjectivity, 140, 142, 148n6
subjects-of-a-life, 80, 84, 115–16
subordination, of women, 294
suffering, 225. See also animal suffering
    predation problem, 1, 94–95
    Singer on, 102
    virtue ethics and, 228
Sunstein, Cass, 324–25, 398
sustainability, 364–65, 525, 526n14. See also
    strong sustainability
    Anthropocene focus on, 62
    civic service for, 336–38
    communitarianism of, 6, 348, 362, 363
    as contested concept, 355–56
    economic growth definition of, 355
    in ecosystem management, 450–51
    ethics and intergenerational
        obligations, 360–63
    LPI on, 386
    Nolt on, 361, 362
    nonanthropocentrism and, 364n1
    PP and, 330
    private owners for, 357–58
    resilience and, 355, 359
    weak, 355, 356, 359, 356f
sustainability science, 7, 537–38
    anthropocentrism of, 532
    ascent of, 530–32
    challenge of, 528–29

convergence model, 533
    disciplinary zoning, 533
    well-being in, 532
Sustainability Science journal, 532
sustainable communities, 356, 363–64
sustainable development, 497n7, 531, 532
    climate change and, 468–69
    mitigation and, 468–69
sustainable economic citizenship
    social economy and, 338–39
    worker cooperatives, 339–40
sustainable energy, 54, 394
system consequentialism, 202–4, 206

"Taking Empirical Data Seriously"
    (Warren), 292
Tangled Routes: Women, Work and
    Globalization on the Tomato Trail
    (Barndt), 297
target system, scientific model and, 30
Taylor, Paul
    on all living things value, 16, 88n11, 201
    as biocentric individualists, 16–17, 102,
        106, 201
    deontological approach to respect, 215
    deontological ethical theory and, 16,
        105, 106
    on living individuals, 101–2, 104
    on restitution from climate change, 109
    as virtue theorist, 104–5
    on wildness, 103, 106
technological optimism, 549n3
    moral corruption of, 431
    pessimistic catastrophism versus, 543–44
technology, 6–7, 375, 438
    applied philosophy of science, 439, 443–44
    critical theory of, 439–41
    economic growth and, 336
    empirical turn in philosophy of, 442–43
    environment, 409–10, 444–46
    on food, 409–10
    green, population and, 387
    phenomenology of, 441–42
    philosophy of, 438–43
    rationality of, 439
    Royal Society on interventions
        acceptability, 501

technophobic narrative, 409–10
technosphere, 64–65
techno-utopian narrative, 409
teleological center-of-a-life, 80, 116
temporal scope, of ethics, 352–53
thermal pollution, 369
Thompson, Allen, 63, 67, 442, 483n2, 484n16
Thoreau, Henry, 223, 440
    on nature as sacred, 250–51
    on wildness, 126–27, 134
Tlatokan Atlahuak Declaration, 239
Toxic Substances Control Act (TSCA), 375
Trafigura Oil Company, 556
tragedy of the commons, 13–14, 268–69, 355
    assumptions of, 357
    on environmental problems, 357
    on overpopulation, 357
    water resources vulnerability to, 421
"The Tragedy of the Commons"
    (Hardin), 13–14
Transcendentalism, of Emerson, 250
transcendent focus, 5, 179–80
transformation, IPCC on, 477
transformational adaptation, 477, 478
travelogue, 411–12
Treading Softly: Paths to Ecological Order
    (Princen), 66
Truth and Method (Gadamer), 171n1
TSCA. *See* Toxic Substances Control Act

UDHR. *See* Universal Declaration of
    Human Rights
ugliness, of nature, 191–92
umwelt, 97, 99n6, 166–67
UN. *See* United Nations
uncertainty, in decision making
    CBA and, 321–23
    complexity theory and, 322, 324
    incommensurability and, 327
    in IPCC forecasts, 29, 323
    objective probabilities and, 322
    PP and, 325
uncertainty, in science, 30, 32, 34, 36n3, 36n7
    deep, 29
    IPCC on, 29, 323
Understanding Risk, of National Research
    Council, 373

UNFCCC. *See* United Nations Framework
    Convention on Climate Change
United Nations (UN)
    Conference on the Human
        Environment, 305
    Declaration of the Rights of Indigenous
        Peoples, 237
    *The Global Climate 2001-2010, A Decade of
        Extremes* report, 68
    Green Climate Fund, 492, 496
    World Commission on Environmental and
        Development report, 531
United Nations climate negotiations
    COPs, of UNFCCC, 488, 492, 493, 496
    Rio Earth Summit, 487
United Nations Framework Convention on
    Climate Change (UNFCCC), 7, 469,
    487, 494
    Cancún Agreements, 492, 495,
        498n12, 498n15
    CBDR of, 488–89
    on climate adaptation and, 474–75
    Copenhagen Accord, 488, 492, 495, 498n12
    COPs of, 488, 492, 493, 496
    G8 parties and, 488
    GHGs emissions reduction pledges, 492–93
    Intended Nationally Determined
        Contributions, 493
    mitigation and, 474–75, 492
    Paris Agreement, 293, 488, 492–95
United States (US). *See also specific agencies*
    climate change global action, 495, 496
    Kyoto Protocol and, 490, 497n4
    per-capita emissions, 497n3
universal benefit, geoengineering claim of, 509
Universal Declaration of Human Rights
    (UDHR), 302, 306, 308
unknown unknowns, in decision
    making, 330n1
unsustainability, 334
    green republicanism and, 341
    market-based solutions to, 336
US. *See* United States
US-China Joint Presidential Statement, on
    climate change, 496
utilitarian consequentialism, 5, 199
utilitarianism, 20, 199, 206, 305

animal liberation in, 115
Bentham as founder of, 115, 201
hedonistic, 224, 225
person-affecting principles rejected by, 349
responsibilities to future people, 347
science narrative and, 409
utility theory, Bayesian response to, 322, 323

value-free ideal for science, 33, 34, 36n6
value judgments, cognitivism and
    noncognitivism, 140
value pluralism, 19, 105
being alive and, 104
of biocentric inegalitarianism, 103–4
environmental, 534
values. *See also* aesthetic values;
    inherent value; instrumental value;
    intrinsic values
anthropocentric instrumental, 82
anthropocentric view of, 199
conceptual anthropocentrism and, 79
conflicting, 128, 518–19
conservation as human expression
    of, 69–70
contextual, 32–35, 36n6, 36n7
ecosystem integral, 520–21
environmental policy and, 62
ethical, 5, 505
humans as caretakers of, 66
humans as source of, 141–42
as human valuing product, 88n10
inductive risk, 33
itemizing approach to environmental, 168
of living individuals, 101–2
loss of, 6
metaethics on, 139, 147n1
of natural world, 404
nonanthropocentric instrumental, 82
of non-human entities, 15
non-instrumental, 205–6, 229
normativity and, 147
objective final, 226
plurality of, 19
Regan on sentient beings, 16
in science, 32–36
Warren on dualism of, 21
wildness and, 128

value theory, 232n1
Callicott's non-anthropocentric
    intrinsic, 82
Hargrove's non-anthropocentric intrinsic,
    82, 83, 87n4, 88n11
van Buren, John, 169, 172n8
van Wensveen, Louke, 21–22
Varner, Gary
on anthropocentrism and
    biocentrism, 523
on climate change, 109
on pain-related conditions, 93
virtue biocentrism, 104–5
virtue ethics, 4, 5, 21–22, 229
    character ethics compared to, 223
    criticism of, 224, 226–27
    eudaimonistic, 227
    normativity and, 224–26, 232, 232n1
    suffering and, 228
virtues
    appreciative, 188–91
    excellence concept, 227
    justice as remedial, 278
    of moral strength and concern, 104–5
    Thompson on adapting, 484n16
virtue theory, 3, 204, 223
von Uexküll, Jakob, 99n6
vulnerability
    in climate change adaptation, 477
    water resources, 421

Warren, Karen J., 21, 292, 295
Warsaw International Mechanism, 484n9
water, 6
    CBA and, 423n6
    common-goods approach to, 416,
        422, 423n9
    ethos, 421–22, 423n10
    human rights to, 6, 417–18
    pollution, 369
    vulnerability to tragedy of the
        commons, 421
*Water Declaration of the Anishinaabek,
    Mushkegowuk, and Onkwehonwe*, 238–39
water ethics, 416–17
    ecological cooperation, 420–22, 423n8
    respect for water, 418–19, 421, 422

water justice, 6, 422
   distributive justice, 419–20
   feminist approach to, 423n3
   global commons, 419
water rights, 417–18, 423n1
weak anthropocentric intrinsic value theory,
   79, 87n6
   of Hargrove, 82, 83, 87n4, 88n11
   of Norton, 20, 82, 88n8
weak sustainability, 355, 356, 359, 356f
weather forecasting scientific models, 31
weight of evidence, in risk assessment, 372
welfare, 531
   animals, 16, 227–29
   of future people, 345
   geoengineering and, 506
   objective theories of, 212
   Repugnant Conclusion on, 350
   subjective theories of, 212
well-being
   subjective theories of, 95–96
   in sustainability science, 532
Weston, Anthony, 19, 82, 543–44
White, Lynn, Jr., 13, 77, 250, 253
WHO. See World Health Organization
Whyte, Kyle Powys, 240, 418
wild
   contrast value for, 130
   flourishing rarity in, 158
   instrumental value of, 129–30
   preservation of, 125, 129–30, 132, 134,
     519, 525
wilderness, 70
   European settlers lack of experience
     with, 250
   Leopold on, 130
   percentages of, 64
   as sacred place, 251
   social construction of, 255
wild nature
   decreasing human influence on, 128
   diminishing of, 70, 125
   end-state or outcome-based value
     approaches, 132
   historical or process-based value
     approaches, 132–33
   instrumental value of, 129–30

   intrinsic value of, 69, 70, 130–32, 168
   management arguments, 132
   minimal human influence in, 64
   myth of, 70
   valuing of, 125–34
   wildness defined, 126–29
wildness, 70, 71
   biocentric consequentialism and, 108
   defined, 126
   degradation of, 125
   human overconsumption and, 4, 125
   human overpopulation and, 4, 125
   Rolston on, 130
   Taylor on living things, 103, 106
   Thoreau on, 126–27, 134
   values conflicting in, 128
Williams, Bernard
   on human values, 79
   internalism and, 160n6
   on limited control of nature, 418
   on motivational repertoire, 153
   on wild nature basis for
     environmentalism, 131
willingness-to-pay measures, in
   markets, 43–44
wind energy, 395, 397
Wingspread Declaration, 375–76
Winner, Langdon, 442, 445
within-habitat-diversity, 360
women. See also ecofeminism; feminism
   care ethics and, 241–43
   Carson on, 252
   cultural and symbolic connections between
     nature and, 290, 291
   ecofeminism, 3, 19–21, 23n6, 252,
     289, 295
   empowerment, 292–93, 295
   environmental degradation impact on, 21
   environmental ethics perspective, 6
   flexible labor of, 297
   natural world attunement, 21
   sexual double-standards, 292
   sexual politics, nature and, 293–96
   subordination of, 294
women/nature association theory, 294
worker cooperatives, 339–40
workplace democracy, 339–40

World Commission on Environmental and Development report, UN, 531

World Health Organization (WHO), on air pollution, 391

World War II, Great Acceleration after, 1–2

Worldwide Fund for Nature (WWF), 383–84

World Wildlife Fund (WWF), 523–24

Worster, Donald, 250, 534

WWF. *See* Worldwide Fund for Nature; World Wildlife Fund

Zimbabwe, CAMPFIRE program in, 523–24

zoocentric, 204